Th

Varieties of English 3
The Pacific and Australasia

Edited by
Kate Burridge and Bernd Kortmann

Mouton de Gruyter · Berlin · New York

Mouton de Gruyter (formerly Mouton, The Hague)
is a Division of Walter de Gruyter GmbH & Co. KG, Berlin.

♾ Printed on acid-free paper which falls within the guidelines of the
ANSI to ensure permanence and durability.

Library of Congress Cataloging-in-Publication Data

The Pacific and Australasia / edited by Kate Burridge, Bernd Kortmann.
  p. cm. — (Varieties of English ; 3)
  Includes bibliographical references and indexes.
  ISBN 978-3-11-019637-5 (pbk. : alk. paper)   1. English language —
Dialects — Pacific Area.   2. English language — Variation — Pacific
Area.   3. English language — Dialects — Australasia.   4. English lan-
guage — Variation — Australasia.   5. Pidgin English.   6. Creole dia-
lects, English.   I. Burridge, Kate.   II. Kortmann, Bernd, 1960—
  PE3600.P33   2008
  427'.99—dc22

2007045288

Bibliographic information published by the Deutsche Nationalbibliothek

The Deutsche Nationalbibliothek lists this publication in the Deutsche Nationalbibliografie;
detailed bibliographic data are available in the Internet at http://dnb.d-nb.de.

ISBN 978-3-11-019637-5

Cover design: Martin Zech, Bremen.
        Imagery provided by Google Earth/TerraMetrics, NASA.
Typesetting: Dörlemann Satz GmbH & Co. KG, Lemförde.
Printing and binding: AZ Druck und Datentechnik GmbH, Kempten (Allgäu).
Printed in Germany.

In memory of Terry Crowley

Tribute

Professor Terry Crowley (1 April 1953–16 January 2005) of the University of Waikato was a prolific documenter of indigenous languages of Australia and Vanuatu. He wrote grammars and dictionaries of a number of languages and more than 20 books and 70 scientific papers – a prodigious achievement. He made distinguished contributions to several different branches of linguistics. His untimely death at 51 has cut a short lifetime of engagement with the speaker of these languages, not just an analyst (a task at which he excelled) but as a friend. He will be remembered by many villagers in Vanuatu as one of the few white people to learn some of their language, and byIndigenous people in Australia for his work in NSW (Bandjalang and Yaygir), Cape York (on Uradhi, Mpak-withi/Anguthimiri, and Cape York Creole) and for his analysing early sources of Tasmanian languages. He wrote a grammar and dictionary of Bislama, the national language of Vanuatu, and his Beach-la-mer to Bislama: The emergence of a national language in Vanuatu (OUP 1990) is a standard reference work.

Born in England, but a Shepparton boy from an early age, he trained as a linguist at ANU where his Honours work involves fieldwork with Bandjalang speakers from north-eastern NSW, and a description of that language. His PhD research was on Paama in Vanuatu and was immediately followed by a post in the Department of Language and Literature at the University of Papua New Guinea from 1979 to 1983. He was the founding Director at the Pacific Languages Unit at USP in Port Vila from 1983 to 1990 and then he took up a position at the University of Waikato in New Zealand

Just as many Aboriginal languages have disappeared, many of the 1300 or so languages indigenous to the Pacific Islands are in danger of extinction, and Terry was on of a small band of linguists fighting a race against time to record as many of them as possible. He clearly relished his time in Vanuatu villages, whether on the Islands of Paama, Erromango or, more recently, Malakula, ar-ranging his teaching load so as to be able to be there for a part of each year. Students from Vanuatu regularly boarded with him while in Maikato and his return visits to their communities soon established new field locations. Terry loved fieldwork and had a great sense of humour as seen by this comment from his draft work 'Street smarts for field linguists': "for your grammar to be truly worthy, you must have suffered at least one bout of malaria – or at least some other impressive-sounding tropical ailment – in its writing, or you should have had at least one toenail ripped off by your hiking boots, or you should have developed a nasty boil on a unmentionable part of your body", all of which, he went on to assure the reader, he had endured.

While the description of language structure and use may be considered a fai-
ly esoteric pursuit with not much practical outcome, this was not the case with
Terry's work. He was concerned to produce material for use by the speakers
of the language he work with and was also involved with policy issues around
the use of vernacular languages in education. Terry was a remarkable scholar
and a generous and much-loved teacher and colleague. His contribution to this
particular volume went far beyond his two chapters on Bislama.

Nick Thieberger (University of Melbourne)
Andy Pawley (Australian National University)
Kate Burridge (Monash Univesity)

Contents

Tribute   vii

Contents of companion volumes   xii

Abbreviations   xx

List of features: Phonology and phonetics   xxiii
Edgar W. Schneider

List of features: Morphology and syntax   xxix
Bernd Kortmann

General introduction   1
Bernd Kortmann and Edgar W. Schneider

General references   8

Introduction: varieties of English in the Pacific and Australasia   23
Kate Burridge and Bernd Kortmann

Phonology

New Zealand English: phonology   39
Laurie Bauer and Paul Warren

Regional and social differences in New Zealand: phonology   64
Elizabeth Gordon and Margaret Maclagan

Maori English: phonology   77
Paul Warren and Laurie Bauer

Australian English: phonology   89
Barbara M. Horvath

Regional characteristics of Australian English: phonology   111
David Bradley

Australian creoles and Aboriginal English: phonetics and phonology . . .   124
Ian G. Malcolm

Bislama: phonetics and phonology   142
Terry Crowley

Solomon Islands Pijin: phonetics and phonology   164
Christine Jourdan and Rachel Selbach

Tok Pisin in Papua New Guinea: phonology 188
Geoff P. Smith

Hawai'i Creole: phonology 210
Kent Sakoda and Jeff Siegel

Fiji English: phonology 234
Jan Tent and France Mugler

Norfolk Island-Pitcairn English: phonetics and phonology 267
John Ingram and Peter Mühlhäusler

Synopsis: phonetics and phonology of English spoken in the Pacific
and Australasian region 292
Kate Burridge

Morphology and Syntax

New Zealand English: morphosyntax 305
Marianne Hundt, Jennifer Hay and Elizabeth Gordon

Australian English: morphology and syntax 341
Peter Collins and Pam Peters

Australian Vernacular English: some grammatical characteristics 362
Andrew Pawley

Hypocoristics in Australian English 398
Jane Simpson

Australian creoles and Aboriginal English: morphology and syntax 415
Ian G. Malcolm

Bislama: morphology and syntax 444
Terry Crowley

Solomon Islands Pijin: morphology and syntax 467
Christine Jourdan

Tok Pisin: morphology and syntax 488
Geoff Smith

Hawai'i Creole: morphology and syntax 514
Kent Sakoda and Jeff Siegel

Fiji English: morphology and syntax 546
France Mugler and Jan Tent

Norfolk Island-Pitcairn English (Pitkern Norfolk): morphology and
syntax 568
Peter Mühlhäusler

Synopsis: morphological and syntactic variation in the Pacific
and Australasia 583
Kate Burridge

Index of subjects 601
Index of varieties and languages 616

Contents of volume 1

Contents of companion volumes vii

Abbreviations xvi

List of features: Phonology and phonetics xix
Edgar W. Schneider

List of features: Morphology and syntax xxv
Bernd Kortmann

General introduction 1
Bernd Kortmann and Edgar W. Schneider

General references 8

Introduction: varieties of English in the British Isles 23
Bernd Kortmann and Clive Upton

Phonology

English spoken in Orkney and Shetland: phonology 35
Gunnel Melchers

Scottish English: phonology 48
Jane Stuart-Smith

Irish English: phonology 71
Raymond Hickey

Welsh English: phonology 105
Robert Penhallurick

English dialects in the North of England: phonology 122
Joan Beal

The English West Midlands: phonology 145
Urszula Clark

The dialect of East Anglia 178
Peter Trudgill

The dialects in the South of England: phonology 194
Ulrike Altendorf and Dominic Watt

Channel Island English: phonology 223
Heinrich Ramisch

Received Pronunciation   237
Clive Upton

British Creole: phonology   253
Peter L. Patrick

Synopsis: phonological variation in the British Isles   269
Clive Upton

Morphology and Syntax

English spoken in Orkney and Shetland: morphology, syntax and
lexicon   285
Gunnel Melchers

Scottish English: morphology and syntax   299
Jim Miller

Irish English: morphology and syntax   328
Markku Filppula

Welsh English: morphology and syntax   360
Robert Penhallurick

English dialects in the North of England: morphology and syntax   373
Joan Beal

The dialect of East Anglia: morphology and syntax   404
Peter Trudgill

English dialects in the Southwest: morphology and syntax   417
Susanne Wagner

The varieties of English spoken in the Southeast of England:
morphology and syntax   440
Lieselotte Anderwald

British Creole: morphology and syntax   463
Mark Sebba

Synopsis: morphological and syntactic variation in the British Isles   478
Bernd Kortmann

Index of subjects   497
Index of varieties and languages   510

Contents of volume 2

Contents of companion volumes viii

Abbreviations xvi

List of features: Phonology and phonetics xix
Edgar W. Schneider

List of features: Morphology and syntax xxv
Bernd Kortmann

General introduction 1
Bernd Kortmann and Edgar W. Schneider

General references 8

Introduction: varieties of English in the Americas and the Caribbean . . . 23
Edgar W. Schneider

Phonology

Standard American English pronunciation 37
William A. Kretzschmar, Jr.

New England: phonology 52
Naomi Nagy and Julie Roberts

New York, Philadelphia, and other northern cities: phonology 67
Matthew J. Gordon

Rural Southern white accents 87
Erik R. Thomas

The urban South: phonology 115
Jan Tillery and Guy Bailey

The West and Midwest: phonology 129
Matthew J. Gordon

English in Canada: phonology 144
Charles Boberg

Newfoundland English: phonology 161
Sandra Clarke

African American Vernacular English: phonology 181
Walter F. Edwards

Gullah: phonology 192
Tracey L. Weldon

Cajun Vernacular English: phonology 208
Sylvie Dubois and Barbara M. Horvath

Chicano English: phonology 219
Otto Santa Ana and Robert Bayley

Bahamian English: phonology 239
Becky Childs and Walt Wolfram

Jamaican Creole and Jamaican English: phonology 256
Hubert Devonish and Otelemate G. Harry

Eastern Caribbean English-derived language varieties: phonology 290
Michael Aceto

Bajan: phonology 312
Renée Blake

The creoles of Trinidad and Tobago: phonology 320
Valerie Youssef and Winford James

Suriname creoles: phonology 339
Norval Smith and Vinije Haabo

Synopsis: phonological variation in the Americas and the Caribbean . . . 383
Edgar W. Schneider

Morphology and Syntax

Colloquial American English: grammatical features 401
Thomas E. Murray and Beth Lee Simon

Appalachian English: morphology and syntax 428
Michael B. Montgomery

Rural and ethnic varieties in the Southeast: morphology and syntax 468
Walt Wolfram

Newfoundland English: morphology and syntax 492
Sandra Clarke

Urban African American Vernacular English: morphology and syntax . . 510
Walt Wolfram

Earlier African American English: morphology and syntax 534
Alexander Kautzsch

Gullah: morphology and syntax 551
Salikoko S. Mufwene

Chicano English: morphology and syntax 572
Robert Bayley and Otto Santa Ana

Bahamian English: morphology and syntax 591
Jeffrey Reaser and Benjamin Torbert

Jamaican Creole: morphology and syntax 609
Peter L. Patrick

Eastern Caribbean English-derived language varieties: morphology and
syntax 645
Michael Aceto

The creoles of Trinidad and Tobago: morphology and syntax 661
Winford James and Valerie Youssef

Surinamese creoles: morphology and syntax 693
Donald Winford and Bettina Migge

Belize and other central American varieties: morphology and syntax . . . 732
Geneviève Escure

Synopsis: morphological and syntactic variation in the Americas
and the Caribbean 763
Edgar W. Schneider

Index of subjects 777
Index of varieties and languages 796

Contents of volume 4

Contents of companion volumes viii

Abbreviations xvi

List of features: Phonology and phonetics xix
Edgar W. Schneider

List of features: Morphology and syntax xxv
Bernd Kortmann

General introduction 1
Bernd Kortmann and Edgar W. Schneider

General references 8

Introduction: varieties of English in Africa and South and Southeast
Asia 23
Rajend Mesthrie

Phonology

Nigerian English: phonology 35
Ulrike B. Gut

Nigerian Pidgin English: phonology 55
Ben Elugbe

Ghanaian English: phonology 67
Magnus Huber

Ghanaian Pidgin English: phonology 93
Magnus Huber

Liberian Settler English: phonology 102
John Victor Singler

Cameroon English: phonology 115
Augustin Simo Bobda

Cameroon Pidgin English (Kamtok): phonology
Thaddeus Menang 133

East African English (Kenya, Uganda, Tanzania): phonology 150
Josef Schmied

White South African English: phonology 164
Sean Bowerman

Black South African English: phonology 177
Bertus van Rooy

Indian South African English: phonology 188
Rajend Mesthrie

Cape Flats English: phonology 200
Peter Finn

St. Helena English: phonology 223
Sheila Wilson

Indian English: phonology 231
Ravinder Gargesh

Pakistani English: phonology 244
Ahmar Mahboob and Nadra Huma Ahmar

Singapore English: phonology 259
Lionel Wee

Malaysian English: phonology 278
Loga Baskaran

Philippine English: phonology 292
Ma. Lourdes G. Tayao

Synopsis: the phonology of English in Africa and South and Southeast
Asia 307
Rajend Mesthrie

Morphology and Syntax

Nigerian English: morphology and syntax 323
M.A. Alo and Rajend Mesthrie

Nigerian Pidgin English: morphology and syntax 340
Nicholas Faraclas

Ghanaian English: morphology and syntax 368
Magnus Huber and Kari Dako

Ghanaian Pidgin English: morphology and syntax 381
Magnus Huber

Liberian Settler English: morphology and syntax 385
John Victor Singler

Cameroon English: morphology and syntax 416
Paul Mbangwana

Cameroon Pidgin English (Kamtok): morphology and syntax 428
Miriam Ayafor

East African English (Kenya, Uganda, Tanzania): morphology and
syntax 451
Josef Schmied

White South African English: morphology and syntax 472
Sean Bowerman

Black South African English: morphology and syntax 488
Rajend Mesthrie

Indian South African English: morphology and syntax 501
Rajend Mesthrie

Cape Flats English: morphology and syntax 521
Kay McCormick

St. Helena English: morphology and syntax 535
Sheila Wilson and Rajend Mesthrie

Indian English: syntax 546
Rakesh M. Bhatt

Butler English: morphology and syntax 563
Priya Hosali

Pakistani English: morphology and syntax 578
Ahmar Mahboob

Singapore English: morphology and syntax 593
Lionel Wee

Malaysian English: morphology and syntax 610
Loga Baskaran

Synopsis: morphological and syntactic variation in Africa and South
and Southeast Asia 624
Rajend Mesthrie

Index of subjects 636
Index of varieties and languages 652

Abbreviations

AAVE	African American Vernacular English
AbE/C/P	(Australian) Aboriginal English / Creole / Pidgin
AfBahE	Afro-Bahamian English
AfkE	Afrikaans English
AmE	American English
AnBahE	Anglo-Bahamian English
AppE	Appalachian English
AusE/VE/C	Australian English/Vernacular English/Creoles
BahE	Bahamian English
Baj	Bajan (Barbadian Creole)
BelC	Belizean Creole
BIE	Bay Islands English (Honduras)
BrC	British Creole
BrE	British English (= EngE + ScE + WelE)
ButlE	Butler English (India)
CajE	Cajun English
CAmC	Central American Creoles (Belize, Miskito, Limón, etc.)
CamP/E	Cameroon Pidgin/English
CanE	Canadian English
CarE	Caribbean English
Car(E)C	Caribbean (English-lexicon) Creoles
CFE	Cape Flats English
ChcE	Chicano English
ChnP	Chinese Pidgin English
CollAmE	Colloquial American English
CollSgE	Colloquial Singapore English
EAfE	East African English
EMarC	Eastern Maroon Creole
EngE	English English
EModE	Early Modern English
ME	Middle English
OE	Old English
ESM	English in Singapore and Malaysia
FijE	Fiji English
GhE/P	Ghanaian English/Pidgin
GuyC	Guyanese Creole
HawC	Hawaii Creole

HKE	Hong Kong English
IndE	Indian English, Anglo-Indian
InlNE	Inland Northern (American) English
IrE	Irish English
JamC/E	Jamaican Creole / English
KenE	Kenyan English
KPE	Kru Pidgin English
LibC/E	Liberian Creole/English
LibSE	Liberian Settler English
LibVE	Liberian Vernacular English
LimC	Limonese Creole (Costa Rica)
LonVE	London Vernacular English
LnkE	Lankan English
MalE	Malaysian English
NEngE	New England English
NfldE	Newfoundland English
NigP/E	Nigerian Pidgin / English
NZE	New Zealand English
NYCE	New York City English
OzE	Ozarks English
PakE	Pakistani English
PanC	Panamanian Creole
PhilE	Philadelphia English
PhlE	Philippines English
RP	Received Pronunciation
SAfE	South African English
BlSAfE	Black South African English
CoSAfE	Coloured South African English
InSAfE	Indian South African English
WhSAfE	White South African English
SAmE	Southern American English
SAsE	South Asian English
SEAmE	South Eastern American English enclave dialects
ScE	Scottish English, Scots
ScStE	Scottish Standard English
SgE	Singapore English
SLVE	St. Lucian Vernacular English
SolP	Solomon Islands Pidgin
StAmE	Standard American English
StAusCE	Standard Australian Colloquial English

StAusFE	Standard Australian Formal English
StBrE	Standard British English
StE	Standard English
StGhE	Standard Ghanaian English
StHE	St. Helena English
StIndE	Standard Indian English
StJamE	Standard Jamaican English
SurC	Suriname Creoles
TanE	Tanzanian English
TobC	Tobagonian Creole
Trad-RP	Traditional Received Pronunciation
TrnC	Trinidadian Creole
T & TC	Trinidadian & mesolectal Tobagonian Creoles
TP	Tok Pisin, New Guinea Pidgin, Neomelanesian
WAfE/P	West African English/Pidgin
WelE	Welsh English
WMwE	Western and Midwestern American English
ZamE	Zambian English

More abbreviations

ESL	English as Second Language
EFL	English as Foreign Language
EIL	English as International Language
ENL	English as Native Language
L1	First Language
L2	Second Language
P/C	Pidgins and Creoles

List of features: Phonology and phonetics

Edgar W. Schneider

Please indicate whether or to what extent the following features / variants occur in the variety that you have discussed by inserting A, B or C in the left-most column as follows:

A   occurs normally / is widespread
B   occurs sometimes / occasionally, with some speakers / groups, in some environments
C   does not normally occur.

If you have covered more than one variety, please give your set of responses for each of them, or give a summary assessment for a group of related varieties as specified.

Elements in parentheses (../..) are optional; ">" suggests a direction of movement.

Please note that the variants suggested for a single item (e.g. lexical set) are meant to be relatively exhaustive but not necessarily mutually exclusive.

Phonetic realization: vowels (lexical sets)

1. KIT [ɪ]
2. KIT raised / fronted, > [i]
3. KIT centralized, > [ə]
4. KIT with offglide, e.g. [ɪə/iə]
5. DRESS half-close [e]
6. DRESS raised, > [i]
7. DRESS half-open [ɛ]
8. DRESS backed, > [ʌ/ɐ]
9. DRESS with centralizing offglide, e.g. [eə]
10. DRESS with rising offglide, e.g. [eɪ]
11. TRAP [æ]
12. TRAP raised, > [ɛ/e]
13. TRAP lowered, > [a]
14. TRAP with offglide, e.g. [æə/æɛ/æɪ/ɛə]
15. LOT rounded, e.g. [ɒ]
16. LOT back unrounded, e.g. [ɑ]

17. LOT front unrounded, e.g. [a]
18. LOT with offglide, e.g. [ɒə]
19. STRUT [ʌ]
20. STRUT high back, > [ʊ]
21. STRUT central [ə/ɐ]
22. STRUT backed, > [ɔ]
23. FOOT [ʊ]
24. FOOT tensed [u]
25. FOOT back, lower, e.g. [ʌ]
26. BATH half-open front [æ]
27. BATH low front [a]
28. BATH low back [ɑ]
29. BATH long
30. BATH with offglide, e.g. [æə/æɪ/ɛə]
31. CLOTH rounded [ɔ/ɒ]
32. CLOTH back unrounded [ɑ]
33. CLOTH front unrounded [a]
34. NURSE central [ɜ:/ɚ]
35. NURSE raised / fronted / rounded, e.g. [ø]
36. NURSE mid front [ɛ/e(r)]
37. NURSE [ʌ(r)] (possibly lexically conditioned, e.g. WORD)
38. NURSE backed, e.g. [o/ɔ]
39. NURSE diphthongal, e.g. [əɪ/ɔɪ]
40. FLEECE [i:]
41. FLEECE with centralizing offglide, e.g. [iə]
42. FLEECE with mid/central onset and upglide, e.g. [əɪ/ei]
43. FLEECE with high onset and upglide, e.g. [ɪi]
44. FLEECE shortened, e.g. [i/ɪ]
45. FACE upgliding diphthong with half-close onset, e.g. [eɪ]
46. FACE upgliding diphthong with half-open or lower onset, e.g. [ɛɪ/æɪ]
47. FACE upgliding diphthong with low / backed onset, e.g. [a(:)ɪ/ʌɪ]
48. FACE upgliding diphthong with central onset, e.g. [əɪ]
49. FACE monophthong, e.g. [e:]
50. FACE ingliding diphthong, e.g. [ɪə/ɪɛ]
51. PALM low back [ɑ(:)]
52. PALM low front [a(:)]
53. PALM with offglide, e.g. [ɑə/ɒə]
54. THOUGHT [ɔ(:)]
55. THOUGHT low [a:/ɑ:]
56. THOUGHT with offglide, e.g. [ɔə/ʊə]

57.   GOAT with central onset, e.g. [əʊ/əʉ]
58.   GOAT with back rounded onset, e.g. [oʊ/ou]
59.   GOAT with low or back unrounded onset, e.g. [a(:)u/aʉ/ʌʊ/ʌʉ]
60.   GOAT with relatively high back onset [ʊu]
61.   GOAT ingliding, e.g. [ʊə/uɔ/ua]
62.   GOAT monophthongal, e.g. [o(:)]
63.   GOOSE [u:]
64.   GOOSE fronted, > [ʉ(:)]
65.   GOOSE gliding, e.g. [ʊu/ɪu/ə(:)ʉ]
66.   PRICE upgliding diphthong, e.g. [aɪ/ɑɪ/ʌɪ]
67.   PRICE monophthong [a:] before voiced C
68.   PRICE monophthong [a:] in all environments
69.   PRICE with raised / central onset, e.g. [əɪ/ɜɪ]
70.   PRICE with backed onset, e.g. [ɔ(:)ɪ/ɒɪ]
71.   PRICE with mid-front offglide, e.g. [ae/aɛ]
72.   CHOICE [ɔɪ]
73.   CHOICE with low onset [ɒɪ]
74.   CHOICE with central onset [əɪ/əi]
75.   MOUTH [aʊ/ɑʊ]
76.   MOUTH with raised and backed onset, e.g. [ʌu/ɔʊ]
77.   MOUTH with raised onset [əʊ] only before voiceless C
78.   MOUTH with raised onset [əʊ] in all environments
79.   MOUTH with fronted onset, e.g. [æʉ/æʊ/æo/ɛo]
80.   MOUTH low monophthong, e.g. [a:]
81.   MOUTH mid/high back monophthong, e.g. [o:]
82.   NEAR [ɪə(r)]
83.   NEAR without offglide, e.g. [ɪr]
84.   NEAR with tensed / raised onset, e.g. [i(:)ə]
85.   NEAR with half-closed onset [e(:/ə/r)/ea]
86.   NEAR with half-open onset [ɛ(:/ə/r)]
87.   NEAR high-front to low glide, e.g. [ia]
88.   SQUARE with half-open onset [ɛə]
89.   SQUARE with half-closed onset [eə/ea]
90.   SQUARE with high front onset [ɪə]
91.   SQUARE with relatively open onset, possibly rising [æə/æɪ]
92.   SQUARE half-closed monophthong, [e(:/r)]
93.   SQUARE half-open monophthong, [ɛ(:/r)]
94.   START low back unrounded, e.g. [ɑ(:/r)]
95.   START central, e.g. [ɐ(:/r)]
96.   START low front, e.g. [a(:/r)]

97.   START front, raised, e.g. [æ(:/r)]
98.   START with offglide, e.g. [ɑə/ɒə)]
99.   NORTH half-open monophthong [ɔ(:/r)]
100. NORTH half-closed monophthong [o(:/r)]
101. NORTH [ɒ]
102. NORTH with offglide, e.g. [ɒə/oa]
103. FORCE half-open monophthong [ɔ(:/r)]
104. FORCE half-closed monophthong [o(:/r)]
105. FORCE ingliding, e.g. [ɔə(r)/oə(r)/oa]
106. FORCE with upglide, e.g.[oʊ(r)]
107. CURE [ʊə/ʊr]
108. CURE with tensed / raised onset, e.g. [u(:)ə/ur]
109. CURE lowered monophthong, e.g. [o:/ɔ:]
110. CURE with upglide, e.g. [oʊ(r)]
111. CURE low offglide, e.g. [ua/oa(r)]
112. happY relatively centralized, e.g. [ɪ]
113. happY central, e.g. [ə]
114. happY tensed / relatively high front, e.g. [i(:)]
115. happY mid front, e.g. [e/ɛ]
116. lettER [ə]
117. lettER (relatively) open, e.g. [a/ʌ]
118. horsES central [ə]
119. horsES high front [ɪ]
120. commA [ə]
121. commA (relatively) open, e.g. [a/ʌ]

Distribution: vowels

122. homophony of KIT and FLEECE
123. homophony of TRAP and BATH
124. homophony of *Mary* and *merry*
125. homophony of *Mary*, *merry* and *marry*
126. homophony of TRAP and DRESS before /l/
127. merger of KIT and DRESS before nasals (*pin = pen*)
128. homophony of DRESS and FACE
129. homophony of FOOT and GOOSE
130. homophony of LOT and THOUGHT
131. homophony of LOT and STRUT
132. homophony of NEAR and SQUARE

133. vowels nasalized before nasal consonants
134. vowel harmony / cross-syllable assimilation phenomena in some words
135. vowels short unless before /r/, voiced fricative, or in open syllable (SVLR)
136. commA/lettER (etc.): [ɑ/ɛ/i/ɔ/u], reflecting spelling

Phonetic realization and distribution: consonants

137. P/T/K-: weak or no aspiration of word-initial stops
138. -T-: lenisation / flapping / voicing of intervocalic /t/ (*writer* = *rider*)
139. -T: realization of word-final or intervocalic /t/ as glottal stop
140. K-: palatalization of velar stop word-initially: e.g. kj-/gj-in *can 't/ garden*
141. B-: word-initial *bw*- for b-: e.g. *bw*- in *boy*
142. S-/F-: voiceless initial fricatives voiced: [z-/v-]
143. TH-: realization of word-initial voiced TH as stop, e.g. *dis*, 'this'
144. TH-: realization of word-initial voiceless TH as stop, e.g. *ting, 'thing'*
145. TH-: realization of word-initial voiced TH as affricate [dð]
146. TH-: realization of word-initial voiceless TH as affricate [tθ]
147. WH-: velar fricative onset retained, i.e. *which* is not homophonous with *witch*
148. CH: voiceless velar fricative [χ/x] exists
149. h-deletion (word-initial), e.g., *'eart* 'heart'
150. h-insertion (word-initial), e.g. *haxe* 'axe'
151. L-: palatal (clear) variant in syllable onsets
152. L-: velar variant in syllable onsets
153. –L: palatal variant in syllable codas
154. "jod"-dropping: no /j/ after alveolars before /u:/, e.g. in *news, tune*
155. deletion of word-initial /h/ in /hj-/ clusters, e.g. in *human, huge*
156. labialization of word-central voiced -TH-, e.g. [-v-] in *brother*
157. labialization of word-final / word-central voiceless –TH, e.g. [-f] in *mouth, nothing*
158. intervocalic /-v-/ > [b], e.g. in *river*
159. W: substitution of labiodental fricative /v/ for semi-vowel /w/
160. word-final consonant cluster deletion, monomorphemic
161. word-final consonant cluster deletion, bimorphemic
162. deletion of word-final single consonants
163. simplification of word-initial consonant clusters, e.g. in *splash, square*
164. non-rhotic (no postvocalic –r)

165. rhotic (postvocalic –r realized)
166. phonetic realization of /r/ as velar retroflex constriction
167. phonetic realization of /r/ as alveolar flap
168. phonetic realization of /r/ as apical trill
169. /r/ uvular
170. intrusive –r–, e.g. *idea-r-is*
171. post-vocalic –l vocalized
172. neutralization / confusion of liquids /l/ and /r/ in some words
173. realization of velar nasals with stop: -NG > [-ŋg]
174. velarization of some word-final nasals, e.g. /-ŋ/ in *down*

Prosodic features and intonation

175. deletion of word-initial unstressed syllables, e.g. 'bout, 'cept
176. stress not infrequently shifted from first to later syllable, e.g. *indi'cate,
      holi'day*
177. (relatively) syllable-timed rather than stress-timed
178. HRT (High-Rising Terminal) contour: rise at end of statement
179. tone distinctions exist

List of features: Morphology and Syntax

Bernd Kortmann

The features in the catalogue are numbered from 1 to 76 (for easy reference in later parts of the chapter) and provided with the short definitions and illustrations. They include all usual suspects known from survey articles on grammatical properties of (individual groups of) non-standard varieties of English, with a slight bias towards features observed in L1 varieties. The 76 features fall into 11 groups corresponding to the following broad areas of morphosyntax: pronouns, noun phrase, tense and aspect, modal verbs, verb morphology, adverbs, negation, agreement, relativization, complementation, discourse organization and word order.

Pronouns, pronoun exchange, pronominal gender

1. *them* instead of demonstrative *those* (e.g. *in them days, one of them things*)
2. *me* instead of possessive *my* (e.g. *He's me brother, I've lost me bike*)
3. special forms or phrases for the second person plural pronoun (e.g. *youse, y'all, aay', yufela, you ... together, all of you, you ones/'uns, you guys, you people*)
4. regularized reflexives-paradigm (e.g. *hisself, theirselves/theirself*)
5. object pronoun forms serving as base for reflexives (e.g. *meself*)
6. lack of number distinction in reflexives (e.g. plural *-self*)
7. *she/her* used for inanimate referents (e.g. *She was burning good* [about a house])
8. generic *he/his* for all genders (e.g. *My car, he's broken*)
9. *myself/meself* in a non-reflexive function (e.g. *my/me husband and my-self*)
10. *me* instead of *I* in coordinate subjects (e.g. *Me and my brother/My brother and me were late for school*)
11. non-standard use of *us* (e.g. *Us George was a nice one, We like us town, Show us 'me' them boots, Us kids used to pinch the sweets like hell, Us'll do it*)
12. non-coordinated subject pronoun forms in object function (e.g. *You did get he out of bed in the middle of the night*)
13. non-coordinated object pronoun forms in subject function (e.g. *Us say 'er's dry*)

Noun phrase

14.   absence of plural marking after measure nouns (e.g. *four pound, five year*)
15.   group plurals (e.g. *That President has two Secretary of States*)
16.   group genitives (e.g. *The man I met's girlfriend is a real beauty*)
17.   irregular use of articles (e.g. *Take them to market, I had nice garden, about a three fields, I had the toothache*)
18.   postnominal *for*-phrases to express possession (e.g. *The house for me*)
19.   double comparatives and superlatives (e.g. *That is so much more easier to follow*)
20.   regularized comparison strategies (e.g. in *He is the regularest kind a guy I know, in one of the most pretty sunsets*)

Verb phrase: Tense & aspect

21.   wider range of uses of the Progressive (e.g. *I'm liking this, What are you wanting?*)
22.   habitual *be* (e.g. *He be sick*)
23.   habitual *do* (e.g. *He does catch fish pretty*)
24.   non-standard habitual markers other than *be* and *do*
25.   levelling of difference between Present Perfect and Simple Past (e.g. *Were you ever in London?, Some of us have been to New York years ago*)
26.   *be* as perfect auxiliary (e.g. *They're not left school yet*)
27.   *do* as a tense and aspect marker (e.g. *This man what do own this*)
28.   completive/perfect *done* (e.g. *He done go fishing, You don ate what I has sent you?*)
29.   past tense/anterior marker *been* (e.g. *I been cut the bread*)
30.   loosening of sequence of tense rule (e.g. *I noticed the van I came in*)
31.   *would* in if-clauses (e.g. *If I'd be you, ...*)
32.   *was sat/stood* with progressive meaning (e.g. *when you're stood* 'are standing' *there you can see the flames*)
33.   *after*-Perfect (e.g. *She's after selling the boat*)

Verb phrase: Modal verbs

34.   double modals (e.g. *I tell you what we might should do*)
35.   epistemic *mustn't* ('can't, it is concluded that… not'; e.g. *This mustn't be true*)

Verb phrase: Verb morphology

36.   levelling of preterite and past participle verb forms: regularization of irregular verb paradigms (e.g. *catch-catched-catched*)
37.   levelling of preterite and past participle verb forms: unmarked forms (frequent with e.g. *give* and *run*)
38.   levelling of preterite and past partiple verb forms: past form replacing the participle (e.g. *He had went*)
39.   levelling of preterite and past partiple verb forms: participle replacing the past form (e.g. *He gone to Mary*)
40.   zero past tense forms of regular verbs (e.g. *I walk* for *I walked*)
41.   *a*-prefixing on *ing*-forms (e.g. *They wasn't a-doin' nothin' wrong*)

Adverbs

42.   adverbs (other than degree modifiers) have same form as adjectives (e.g. *Come quick!*)
43.   degree modifier adverbs lack *-ly* (e.g. *That's real good*)

Negation

44.   multiple negation / negative concord (e.g. *He won't do no harm*)
45.   *ain't* as the negated form of *be* (e.g. *They're all in there, ain't they?*)
46.   *ain't* as the negated form of *have* (e.g. *I ain't had a look at them yet*)
47.   *ain't* as generic negator before a main verb (e.g. *Something I ain't know about*)
48.   invariant *don't* for all persons in the present tense (e.g. *He don't like me*)
49.   *never* as preverbal past tense negator (e.g. *He never came* [= he didn't come])
50.   *no* as preverbal negator (e.g. *me no iit brekfus*)
51.   *was–weren't* split (e.g. *The boys was interested, but Mary weren't*)
52.   invariant non-concord tags, (e.g. *innit/in't it/isn't* in *They had them in their hair, innit?*)

Agreement

53. invariantpresenttenseformsduetozeromarkingforthethirdpersonsingular (e.g. *So he show up and say, What's up?*)
54. invariant present tense forms due to generalization of third person *-s* to all persons (e.g. *I sees the house*)
55. existential/presentational *there's, there is, there was* with plural subjects (e.g. *There's two men waiting in the hall*)
56. variant forms of dummy subjects in existential clauses (e.g. *they, it,* or zero for *there*)
57. deletion of *be* (e.g. *She ___ smart*)
58. deletion of auxiliary *have* (e.g. *I ___ eaten my lunch*)
59. *was/were* generalization (e.g. *You were hungry but he were thirsty*, or: *You was hungry but he was thirsty*)
60. Northern Subject Rule (e.g. *I sing* [vs. **I sings*], *Birds sings, I sing and dances*)

Relativization

61. relative particle *what* (e.g. *This is the man what painted my house*)
62. relative particle *that* or *what* in non-restrictive contexts (e.g. *My daughter, that/what lives in London, …*)
63. relative particle *as* (e.g. *He was a chap as got a living anyhow*)
64. relative particle *at* (e.g. *This is the man at painted my house*)
65. use of analytic *that his/that's, what his/what's, at's, as'* instead of *whose* (e.g. *The man what's wife has died*)
66. gapping or zero-relativization in subject position (e.g. *The man ___ lives there is a nice chap*)
67. resumptive / shadow pronouns (e.g. *This is the house which I painted it yesterday*)

Complementation

68. *say*-based complementizers
69. inverted word order in indirect questions (e.g. *I'm wondering what are you gonna do*)
70. unsplit *for to* in infinitival purpose clauses (e.g. *We always had gutters in the winter time for to drain the water away*)

71. *as what / than what* in comparative clauses (e.g. *It's harder than what you think it is*)
72. serial verbs (e.g. *give* meaning 'to, for', as in *Karibuk giv mi*, 'Give the book to me')

Discourse organization and word order

73. lack of inversion / lack of auxiliaries in *wh*-questions (e.g. *What you doing?*)
74. lack of inversion in main clause *yes/no* questions (e.g. *You get the point?*)
75. *like* as a focussing device (e.g. *How did you get away with that like? Like for one round five quid, that was like three quid, like two-fifty each*)
76. *like* as a quotative particle (e.g. *And she was like "What do you mean?"*)

General introduction

Bernd Kortmann and Edgar W. Schneider

This book, together with its three companion volumes on other world regions, derives from the *Handbook of Varieties of English*, edited by Kortmann, Schneider et al. (2004). To make the material compiled in the *Handbook* more easily accessible and affordable, especially to student pockets, it has been decided to regroup the articles in such a way that all descriptive papers on any of the seven major anglophone world regions distinguished there are put together in a set of four paperback volumes, and accompanied by the CD-ROM which covers data and sources from all around the world. In this brief introduction we are briefly revisiting and summarizing the major design features of the *Handbook* and its contributions, i.e. information which, by implication, also characterizes the articles in the present volume.

The all-important design feature of the *Handbook* and of these offspring paperbacks is its focus on structure and on the solid description and documentation of data. The volumes, together with the CD-ROM, provide comprehensive up-to-date accounts of the salient phonological and grammatical properties of the varieties of English around the world. Reliable structural information in a somewhat standardized format and presented in an accessible way is a necessary prerequisite for any kind of study of language varieties, independent of the theoretical framework used for analysis. It is especially important for comparative studies of the phonological and morphosyntactic patterns across varieties of English, and the inclusion of this kind of data in typological studies (e.g. in the spirit of Kortmann 2004).

Of course, all of this structural information can be and has to be put in perspective by the conditions of uses of these varieties, i.e. their sociohistorical backgrounds, their current sociolinguistic settings (not infrequently in multilingual societies), and their associated political dimensions (like issues of norm-setting, language policies, and pedagogical applications). Ultimately, all of the varieties under discussion here, certainly so the ones spoken outside of England but in a sense, looking way back in time, even the English dialects themselves, are products of colonization processes, predominantly the European colonial expansion in the modern age. A number of highly interesting questions, linguistically and culturally, might be asked in this context, including the central issue of why all of this has happened, whether there is an underlying scheme that has continued to drive and motivate the evolution of new varieties of English (Schneider 2003, 2007). These linguistic and sociohistorical background issues will be briefly addressed in the regional introductions and in some of the individual chapters, but it should be made clear that it is the issue of structural description and comparison which is at the heart of this project.

The chapters in the four paperbacks are geared towards documenting and mapping the structural variation among (spontaneously spoken) non-standard varieties of English. Standard English is of course that variety, or set of closely related varieties, which enjoys the highest social prestige. It serves as a reference system and target norm in formal situations, in the language used by people taking on a public persona (including, for example, anchorpersons in the news media), and as a model in the teaching of English worldwide. Here, however, it is treated as is commonplace in modern descriptive linguistics, i.e. as a variety on a par with all other (regional, social, ethnic, or contact) varieties of English. Clearly, in terms of its structural properties it is not inherently superior to any of the non-standard varieties. Besides, the very notion of "Standard English" itself obviously refers to an abstraction. On the written level, it is under discussion to what extent a "common core" or a putatively homogeneous variety called "International English" actually exists: there is some degree of uniformity across the major national varieties, but once one looks into details of expression and preferences, there are also considerable differences. On the spoken level, there are reference accents like, for example, Received Pronunciation for British English, but their definition also builds upon abstractions from real individuals' performance. Thus, in the present context especially the grammar of (written) Standard English figures as no more than an implicit standard of comparison, in the sense that all chapters focus upon those phenomena in a given variety which are (more or less strikingly) different from this standard (these being perceived as not, note again, in any sense deficient or inferior to it).

The articles in this collection cover all main national standard varieties, distinctive regional, ethnic, and social varieties, major contact varieties (pidgins and creoles), as well as major varieties of English as a Second Language. The inclusion of second-language varieties and, especially, English-based pidgins and creoles may come as a surprise to some readers. Normally these varieties are addressed from different perspectives (such as, for example, language policy, language pedagogy, linguistic attitudes, language and identity (construction), substrate vs. superstrate influence), each standing in its own research tradition. Here they are primarily discussed from the point of view of their structural properties.

This will make possible comparisons with structural properties of, for example, other varieties of English spoken in the same region, or second-language or contact varieties in other parts of the English-speaking world. At the same time the availability of solid structural descriptions may open new perspectives for a fruitful interaction between the different research traditions within which second-language and contact varieties are studied. The boundaries of what is considered and accepted as "varieties of English" has thus been drawn fairly widely. In accepting English-oriented pidgins and creoles in the present context, we adopt a trend of recent research to consider them as contact varieties closely related to, possibly to be categorized as varieties of, their respective superstrate languages (e.g. Mufwene 2001). Creoles, and also some pidgins, in many regions vary along a continuum from acrolectal forms, relatively close to English and used by the higher sociolinguistic strata in formal contexts, to basilects, "deep" varieties maximally different from English. Most of our contributions focus upon the mesolects, the middle ranges which in most creole-speaking societies are used most widely.

For other varieties, too, it may be asked why or why not they have been selected for inclusion in this collection. Among the considerations that led to the present selection, the following figured most prominently: amount and quality of existing data and research documentation for the individual varieties, intensity of ongoing research activities, availability of authors, and space constraints (leading, for example, to the exclusion of strictly local accents and dialects). More information on the selection of varieties will be given in the regional introductions.

While in the *Handbook* there is one volume each for phonology and grammar (i.e. morphology and syntax), this set of paperbacks has been arranged by the major world regions relevant for the discussion of varieties of English: the British Isles; the Americas and the Caribbean; Africa, South and Southeast Asia; and the Pacific and Australasia. Each of the volumes comprises all articles on the respective regions, both on phonology and on grammar, together with the regional introductions, which include accounts of the histories, the cultural and sociolinguistic situations, and the most important data sources for the relevant locations, ethnic groups and varieties, and the regional synopses, in which the editors summarize the most striking properties of the varieties of English spoken in the respective world regions. Global synopses offering the most noteworthy findings and tendencies on phonological and morphosyntactic variation in English from a global perspective are available in the two hardcover Handbooks and in the electronic online version. In addition, there is a list of "General references", all of them exclusively book publications, which are either globally relevant or central for for individual world regions.

What emerges from the synopses is that many of the features described for individual varieties or sets of varieties in this Handbook are not unique to these (sets of) varieties. This is true both for morphology and syntax and for phonology.

As a matter of fact, quite a number of morphosyntactic features described as salient properties of individual varieties may strike the reader as typical of other varieties, too, possibly even of the grammar of spoken English, in general. In a similar vein, it turns out that certain phonological processes (like the monophthongization of certain diphthongs, the fronting, backing or merging of some vowels, and some consonantal substitutions or suprasegmental processes) can be documented in quite a number of fairly disparate language varieties – not surprisingly, perhaps, given shared underlying principles like constraints of articulatory space or tendencies towards simplification and the reduction of contrasts.

The distributions of selected individual features, both morphosyntactic and phonological, across varieties world-wide is visualized by the interactive world maps on the accompanying CD-ROM. The lists of these features, which are also referred to in some contributions, especially the regional synopses, are appended to this introduction. On these maps, each of a set of selected features, for almost all of the varieties under discussion, is categorized as occurring regularly (marked as "A" and colour-coded in red), occasionally or only in certain specified environments (marked as "B" and represented by a yellow circle) or practically not at all ("C", black). These innovative maps, which are accompanied by statistical distribution data on the spread of selected variants, provide the reader with an immediate visual representation of regional distribution and diffusion patterns. Further information on the nature of the multimedia material accompanying these books is available on the CD itself. It includes audio samples of free conversations (some of them transcribed), a standard reading passage, and recordings of the spoken "lexical sets" which define and illustrate vocalic variation (Wells 1982).

The chapters are descriptive survey articles providing state-of-the-art reports on major issues in current research, with a common core in order to make the collection an interesting and useful tool especially from a comparative, i.e. cross-dialectal and cross-linguistic, point of view. All chapters aim primarily at a qualitative rather than quantitative perspective, i.e. whether or not a given feature occurs is more important than its frequency. Of course, for varieties where research has focused upon documenting frequency relationships between variants of variables, some information on relevant quantitative tendencies has been provided. Depending upon the research coverage in a given world region (which varies widely from one continent to another), some contributions build upon existing sociolinguistic, dialectological, or structural research; a small number of other chapters make systematic use of available computerized corpora; and in some cases and for some regions the chapters in this compilation provide the first-ever systematic qualitative survey of the phonological and grammatical properties of English as spoken there.

For almost all varieties of English covered there are companion chapters in the phonology and morphosyntax parts of each paperback volume. In these cases it is in the phonology chapter that the reader will find a concise introductory section on the historical and cultural background as well as the current sociolinguistic situation of the relevant variety or set of varieties spoken at this location.

In order to ensure a certain degree of comparability, the authors were given a set of core issues that they were asked to address (provided something interesting can be said about them in the respective variety). For the phonology chapters, this set included the following items:

- phonological systems
- phonetic realization(s) and (phonotactic) distributions of a selection of phonemes (to be selected according to salience in the variety in question)
- specific phonological processes at work in the relevant variety
- lexical distribution
- prosodic features (stress, rhythm)
- intonation patterns
- observations/generalizations on the basis of lexical sets à la Wells (1982) and Foulkes/Docherty (1999), a standard reading passage and/or samples of free conversation.

It is worth noting that for some of the contributions, notably the chapters on pidgins and creoles, the lexical sets were not sufficient or suitable to describe the variability found. In such cases authors were encouraged to expand the set of target words, or replace one of the items. The reading passage was also adjusted or substituted by some authors, for instance because it was felt to be culturally inappropriate.

This is the corresponding set for the morphology and syntax chapters:

- tense – aspect – modality systems
- auxiliaries
- negation
- relativization
- complementation
- other subordination phenomena (notably adverbial subordination)
- agreement
- noun phrase structure
- pronominal systems
- word order (and information structure: especially focus/topicalizing constructions)

– selected salient features of the morphological paradigms of, for example, auxiliaries and pronouns

Lexical variation was not our primary concern, given that it fails to lend itself to the systematic generalization and comparability that we are interested in in this project. However, authors were offered the opportunity to comment on highly salient features of the vocabulary of any given variety (briefly and within the overall space constraints) if this was considered rewarding. The reader may find such information on distinctive properties of the respective vocabularies in the morphology and syntax chapters. Especially for a student readership, short sets of exercises and study questions have been added at the end of all chapters in the four paperback volumes.

In the interest of combining guidance for readers, efficiency, and space constraints, but also the goal of comprehensiveness, bibliographic references are systematically divided between three different types of reference lists. As was stated above, in each paperback a "General references" list can be found which compiles a relatively large number of books which, taken together, are central to the field of world-wide varieties of English – "classic" publications, collective volumes, particularly important publications, and so on. It is understood that in the individual contributions all authors may refer to titles from this list without these being repeated in their respective source lists. Each of the individual chapters ends with a list of "Selected references" comprising, on average, only 15–20 references – including the most pertinent ones on the respective variety (or closely related varieties) beyond any others possibly included in the General references list, and possibly others cited in the respective article. In other words, the Selected references do not repeat any of the titles cited in the list of General references. Thirdly, a "Comprehensive bibliography", with further publications specifically on the phonology and morphosyntax of each of the varieties covered, for which no space limitations were imposed, is available on the CD-ROM. The idea behind this limitation of the number of references allowed to go with each article was to free the texts of too much technical apparatus and thus to increase their reader-friendliness for a target audience of non-specialists while at the same time combining basic guidance to the most important literature (in the General References list) with the possibility of providing comprehensive coverage of the writings available on any given region (in the Bibliographies on the CD-ROM). It must be noted, however, that at times this rule imposed limitations upon possible source credits allowed in the discussions, because to make the books self-contained authors were allowed to refer to titles from the General and the Select References lists only. In other words, it is possible that articles touch upon material drawn from publications listed in the CD-ROM bibliographies without explicit credit, although every effort has been made to avoid this.

A publication project as huge as this one would have been impossible, indeed impossible even to think of, without the support of a great number of people devoted to their profession and to the subject of this Handbook. The editors would like thank the members of their editorial teams in Freiburg, Regensburg, and Cape Town. We are also much indebted to Elizabeth Traugott, for all the thought, support and feedback she gave to this project right from the very beginning of the planning stage, and to Jürgen Handke, who produced the rich audio-visual multimedia support on the CD. Furthermore, we have always benefitted from the support and interest invested into this project by Anke Beck and the people at Mouton de Gruyter. Finally, and most importantly, of course, the editors would like to thank the contributors and informants for having conformed to the rigid guidelines, deadlines and time frames that we set them for the various stages of (re)writing their chapters and providing the input material for the CD-ROM.

This collection truly represents an impressive product of scholarly collaboration of people from all around the globe. Right until the end it has been an exciting and wonderful experience for the editors (as well as, we would like to think, for the authors) to bring all these scholars and their work together, and we believe that this shows in the quality of the chapters and the material presented on the CD-ROM. We hope that, like the *Handbook*, it will be enjoyed, appreciated and esteemed by its readers, and treasured as the reference work and research tool it was designed as for anyone interested in and fascinated by variation in English!

References

Kortmann, Bernd (ed.)
   2004   *Dialectology meets Typology: Dialect Grammar from a Cross-Linguistic Perspective*. Berlin/New York: Mouton de Gruyter.
Kortmann, Bernd, and Edgar W. Schneider, with Kate Burridge, Rajend Mesthrie, and Clive Upton (eds.)
   2004   *A Handbook of Varieties of English*. Vol. 1: *Phonology*. Vol. 2: *Morphology and Syntax*. Berlin/New York: Mouton de Gruyter.
Schneider, Edgar W.
   2003   "The dynamics of New Englishes: From identity construction to dialect birth." *Language* 79: 233-281.
Schneider, Edgar W.
   2007   *Postcolonial English: Varieties Around the World*. Cambridge: Cambridge University Press.

General references

The following is a list of general reference works relevant across the world regions covered in the Handbook and for individual of these world regions. The list consists exclusively of book publications. Those monographs, dictionaries and collective volumes in the list which are referred to in the chapters of the four paperbacks will not be separately listed in the selected references at the end of the individual chapters.

Aceto, Michael and Jeffrey Williams (eds.)
  2003   *Contact Englishes of the Eastern Caribbean.* (Varieties of English around the World, General Series 30.) Amsterdam/Philadelphia: Benjamins.
Aitken, Jack and Tom McArthur (eds.)
  1979   *The Languages of Scotland.* Edinburgh: Chambers.
Algeo, John
  2006   *British or American English? A Handbook of Word and Grammar Patterns.* Cambridge: Cambridge University Press.
Algeo, John (ed.)
  2001   *The Cambridge History of the English Language, Volume VI: English in North America.* Cambridge: Cambridge University Press.
Allen, Harold B.
  1973
  –1976   *Linguistic Atlas of the Upper Midwest.* 3 Volumes. Minneapolis: University of Minnesota Press.
Allen, Harold B. and Gary Underwood (eds.)
  1971   *Readings in American Dialectology.* New York: Appleton-Century Crofts.
Allen, Harold B. and Michael D. Linn (eds.)
  1997   *Dialects and Language Variation.* New York: Academic Press.
Alleyne, Mervyn C.
  1980   *Comparative Afro-American: An Historical-Comparative Study of English-Based Afro-American Dialects of the New World.* (Linguistica Extranea 11.) Ann Arbor: Karoma.
Allsopp, Richard (ed.)
  1996   *Dictionary of Caribbean English Usage.* Oxford: Oxford University Press.
Anderson, Peter M.
  1987   *A Structural Atlas of the English Dialects.* London: Croom Helm.
Anderwald, Lieselotte
  2002   *Negation in Non-standard British English: Gaps, Regularizations, Asymmetries.* (Routledge Studies in Germanic Linguistics 8.) London/New York: Routledge.
Atwood, E. Bagby
  1953   *A Survey of Verb Forms in the Eastern United States.* (Studies in American English 2.) Ann Arbor: University of Michigan Press.

Avis, Walter S., Charles Crate, Patrick Drysdale, Douglas Leechman and Matthew H. Scargill
  1967   *A Dictionary of Canadianisms on Historical Principles.* Toronto: Gage.
Bailey, Beryl Loftman
  1966   *Jamaican Creole Syntax.* Cambridge: Cambridge University Press.
Bailey, Richard W. and Jay L. Robinson
  1973   *Varieties of Present-Day English.* New York: Macmillan.
Bailey, Richard W. and Manfred Görlach (eds.)
  1982   *English as a World Language.* Ann Arbor: University of Michigan Press.
Bailey, Guy, Natalie Maynor and Patricia Cukor-Avila (eds.)
  1991   *The Emergence of Black English: Text and Commentary.* (Creole Language Library 8.) Amsterdam/Philadelphia: Benjamins.
Baker, Philip and Adrienne Bruyn (eds.)
  1998   *St. Kitts and the Atlantic Creoles: The Texts of Samuel Augustus Mathews in Perspective.* (Westminster Creolistics Series 4). London: University of Westminster Press.
Bamgbose, Ayo, Ayo Banjo and Andrew Thomas (eds.)
  1997   *New Englishes – A West African Perspective.* Trenton, NJ: Africa World Press.
Baugh, John
  1983   *Black Street Speech: Its History, Structure, and Survival.* Austin: University of Texas Press.
Baumgardner, Robert J.
  1996   *South Asian English: Structure, Use, and Users.* Urbana, IL: University of Illinois Press.
Bell, Allan and Koenrad Kuiper (eds.)
  2000   *New Zealand English.* (Varieties of English around the World, General Series 25.) Amsterdam/Philadelphia: Benjamins and Wellington: Victoria University Press.
Bernstein, Cynthia, Thomas Nunnally and Robin Sabino (eds.)
  1997   *Language Variety in the South Revisited.* Tuscaloosa: University of Alabama Press.
Bickerton, Derek
  1975   *Dynamics of a Creole System.* Cambridge: Cambridge University Press.
  1981   *Roots of Language.* Ann Arbor: Karoma.
Blair, David and Peter Collins (eds.)
  2001   *English in Australia.* (Varieties of English around the World, General Series 26.) Amsterdam/Philadelphia: Benjamins.
Bliss, Alan J.
  1979   *Spoken English in Ireland 1600–1740.* Dublin: Dolmen Press.
Bolton, Kingsley
  2003   *Chinese Englishes. A Sociolinguistic History.* Cambridge: Cambridge Univeristy Press.
Bolton, Kinglsey and Braj B. Kachru (eds.)
  2006   *World Englishes: critical concept in linguistics.* 6 vols. London: Routledge.

Bolton, Kingsley (ed.)
  2002   *Hong Kong English: Autonomy and Creativity.* Hong Kong: Hong Kong
          University Press.
Britain, David (ed.)
  2007   *Language in the British Isles.* Cambridge: Cambridge University Press.
Burchfield, Robert (ed.)
  1994   *The Cambridge History of the English Language, Volume V: English in
          Britain and Overseas: Origins and Development.* Cambridge: Cambridge
          University Press.
Carrington, Lawrence D., Dennis Craig and Ramon Todd Dandare (eds.)
  1983   *Studies in Caribbean Language. Papers Presented at the 3ʳᵈ Biennial
          Conference of the Society for Caribbean Linguistics Held in Aruba,
          Netherlands Antilles from 16–20 Sept 1980.* St. Augustine, Trinidad:
          Society for Caribbean Linguistics.
Carver, Craig M.
  1987   *American Regional Dialects: A Word Geography.* Ann Arbor: University
          of Michigan Press.
Cassidy, Frederic G.
  1961   *Jamaica Talk: 300 Years of the English Language in Jamaica.* London:
          Macmillan.
Cassidy, Frederic G. (ed.)
  1985
  –2002   *Dictionary of American Regional English.* 4 Volumes to date. Cambridge,
          MA/London: The Belknap Press of Harvard University Press.
Cassidy, Frederic G. and Robert B. LePage (eds.)
  1967   *Dictionary of Jamaican English.* Cambridge: Cambridge University
          Press.
Chambers, J.K.
  2003   *Sociolinguistic Theory: Linguistic Variation and its Social Significance.*
          2nd edition. (Language in Society 22.) Oxford: Blackwell.
Chambers, J.K. and Peter Trudgill
  1998   *Dialectology.* 2nd edition. (Cambridge Textbooks in Linguistics.)
          Cambridge: Cambridge University Press.
Chambers, J.K. (ed.)
  1975   *Canadian English: Origins and Structures.* Toronto: Methuen.
Chambers, J.K., Peter Trudgill and Natalie Schilling-Estes (eds.)
  2002   *The Handbook of Language Variation and Change.* (Blackwell Handbooks
          in Linguistics.) Malden, MA: Blackwell.
Cheshire, Jenny L. (ed.)
  1991   *English Around the World: Sociolinguistic Perspectives.* Cambridge:
          Cambridge University Press.
Cheshire, Jenny L. and Dieter Stein (eds.)
  1997   *Taming the Vernacular: From Dialect to Written Standard Language.*
          Harlow: Longman.

Christian, Donna, Nanjo Dube and Walt Wolfram
  1988   *Variation and Change in Geographically Isolated Communities: Appalachian English and Ozark English.* (American Dialect Society 74.) Tuscaloosa: University of Alabama Press.
Christie, Pauline, Lawrence Carrington, Barbara Lalla and Velma Pollard (eds.)
  1998   *Studies in Caribbean Language II. Papers from the Ninth Biennial Conference of the SCL, 1992.* St. Augustine, Trinidad: Society for Caribbean Linguistics.
Clarke, Sandra (ed.)
  1993   *Focus on Canada.* (Varieties of English around the World, General Series 11.) Amsterdam/Philadelphia: Benjamins.
Collins, Peter and David Blair (eds.)
  1989   *Australian English: the Language of a New Society.* St. Lucia: University of Queensland Press.
Corbett, John, J. Derrick McClure and Jane Stuart-Smith (eds.)
  2003   *The Edinburgh Companion to Scots.* Edinburgh: Edinburgh University Press.
Crystal, David
  2003   *The Cambridge Encyclopedia of the English Language.* 2nd edition. Cambridge: Cambridge University Press.
D'Costa, Jean and Barbara Lalla
  1989   *Voices in Exile: Jamaican Texts of the 18th and 19th Centuries.* Tuscaloosa/ London: University of Alabama Press.
Davis, Lawrence M.
  1983   *English Dialectology: An Introduction.* University, Alabama: University of Alabama Press.
Day, Richard R. (ed.)
  1980   *Issues in English Creoles: Papers from the 1975 Hawaii Conference.* (Varieties of English around the World, General Series 2.) Heidelberg: Groos.
De Klerk, Vivian (ed.)
  1996   *Focus on South Africa.* (Varieties of English around the World, General Series 15.) Amsterdam/Philadelphia: Benjamins.
De Wolf, Gaelan Dodds
  1992   *Social and Regional Factors in Canadian English. Study of Phonological Variables and Grammatical Items in Ottawa and Vancouver.* Toronto: Canadian Scholar's Press.
DeCamp, David and Ian F. Hancock (eds.)
  1974   *Pidgins and Creoles: Current Trends and Prospects.* Washington, D.C.: Georgetown University Press.
Devonish, Hubert
  1989   *Talking in Tones: A Study of Tone in Afro-European Creole Languages.* London/Barbados: Karia Press and Caribbean Academic Publications.
Eckert, Penelope (ed.)
  1991   *New Ways of Analyzing Sound Change.* (Qualitative Analyses of Linguistic Structure 5.) New York/San Diego: Academic Press.

Edwards, Viv
  1986   *Language in a Black Community.* (Multilingual Matters 24.) Clevedon:
          Multilingual Matters.
Edwards, Walter F. and Donald Winford (ed.)
  1991   *Verb Phrase Patterns in Black English and Creole.* Detroit: Wayne State
          University.
Ellis, Alexander J.
  1869
  –1889   *On Early English Pronunciation.* 5 Volumes. London: Trübner.
Fasold, Ralph W.
  1972   *Tense Marking in Black English: A Linguistic and Social Analysis.* (Urban
          Language Series 8.) Arlington, VA: Center for Applied Linguistics.
Fasold, Ralph W. and Roger W. Shuy (eds.)
  1970   *Teaching Standard English in the Inner City.* (Urban Language Series 6.)
          Washington, D.C.: Center for Applied Linguistics.
  1975   *Analyzing Variation in Language. Papers from the Second Colloquium
          on New Ways of Analyzing Variation.* Washington, D.C.: Georgetown
          University Press.
Ferguson, Charles and Shirley Brice Heat (eds.)
  1981   *Language in the USA.* Cambridge: Cambridge University Press.
Filppula, Markku
  1999   *The Grammar of Irish English: Language in Hibernian Style.* (Routledge
          Studies in Germanic Linguistics 5.) London/New York: Routledge.
Foley, Joseph A. (ed.)
  1988   *New Englishes – The Case of Singapore.* Singapore: Singapore University
          Press.
Foley, Joseph A., Thiru Kandiah, Bao Zhiming, Anthea F. Gupta, Lubna Alasgoff, Ho
          Chee Lick, Lionel Wee, Ismail S. Talib and Wendy Bokhurst-Heng
  1998   *English in New Cultural Contexts: Reflections from Singapore.* Singapore:
          Oxford University Press.
Foulkes, Paul and Gerard Docherty (eds.)
  1999   *Urban Voices: Accent Studies in the British Isles.* London: Arnold.
Francis, W. Nelson
  1958   *The Structure of American English.* New York: Ronald Press.
Frazer, Timothy C. (ed.)
  1993   *'Heartland' English: Variation and Transition in the American Midwest.*
          Tuscaloosa: University of Alabama Press.
García, Ofelia and Ricardo Otheguy (eds.)
  1989   *English across Cultures, Cultures across English: A Reader in Cross-
          Cultural Communication.* (Contributions to the Sociology of Language 53.)
          Berlin/New York: Mouton de Gruyter.
Gilbert, Glenn (ed.)
  1987   *Pidgin and Creole Languages: Essays in Memory of John E. Reinecke.*
          Honolulu: University of Hawaii Press.

Gordon, Elizabeth and Tony Deverson
1998   *New Zealand English and English in New Zealand.* Auckland: New House
        Publishers.
Gordon, Matthew J.
2001   *Small-Town Values and Big-City Vowels: A Study of the Northern Cities
        Shift in Michigan.* (Publication of the American Dialect Society 84.)
        Durham: Duke University Press.
Görlach, Manfred (ed.)
1985   *Focus on Scotland.* (Varieties of English around the World, General
        Series 5.) Amsterdam/Philadelphia: Benjamins.
Görlach, Manfred and John A. Holm (eds.)
1986   *Focus on the Caribbean.* (Varieties of English around the World, General
        Series 8.) Amsterdam/Philadelphia: Benjamins.
Green, Lisa
2002   *African American English: A Linguistic Introduction.* Cambridge: Cam-
        bridge University Press.
Guy, Gregory, John Baugh, Crawford Feagin and Deborah Schiffrin (eds.)
1996   *Towards a Social Science of Language, Volume 1: Variation and Change
        in Language and Society.* Amsterdam/Philadelphia: Benjamins.
1997   *Towards a Social Science of Language, Volume 2: Social Interaction and
        Discourse Structures.* Amsterdam/Philadelphia: Benjamins.
Hackert, Stephanie
2004   *Urban Bahamian Creole. System and Variation.* Amsterdam/Philadelphia:
        Benjamins.
Hancock, Ian F., Morris Goodman, Bernd Heine and Edgar Polomé (eds.)
1979   *Readings in Creole Studies.* Ghent: Story-Scientia.
Hewitt, Roger
1986   *White Talk, Black Talk: Inter-Racial Friendship and Communication
        amongst Adolescents.* Cambridge: Cambridge University Press.
Hickey, Raymond
2004   *The Legacy of Colonial English: Transported Dialects.* Cambridge:
        Cambridge University Press.
2005   *The Sound Atlas of Irish English.* Berlin/New York: Mouton de Gruyter.
Holm, John A.
1988
–1989   *Pidgins and Creoles.* 2 Volumes. Cambridge: Cambridge University
        Press.
2000   *An Introduction to Pidgins and Creoles.* Cambridge: Cambridge University
        Press.
Holm, John A. and Peter Patrick
forthcoming   *Comparative Creole Syntax: Parallel Outlines of 18 Creole
        Grammars.* London: Battlebridge.
Holm, John A. (ed.)
1983   *Central American English.* (Varieties of English around the World, Text
        Series 2.) Heidelberg: Groos.

Huber, Magnus and Mikael Parkvall (eds.)
  1999   *Spreading the Word: The Issue of Diffusion among the Atlantic Creoles.*
          London: University of Westminster Press.
Hughes, Arthur and Peter Trudgill
  1996   *English Accents and Dialects: An Introduction to Social and Regional
          Varieties of English in the British Isles.* 3rd edition. London: Arnold.
Hymes, Dell H. (ed.)
  1971   *Pidginization and Creolization of Languages: Proceedings of a Conference,
          Held at the University of the West Indies Mona, Jamaica, April 1968.*
          Cambridge: Cambridge University Press.
James, Winford and Valerie Youssef
  2002   *The Languages of Tobago. Genesis, Structure and Perspectives.* St. Au-
          gustine, Trinidad: University of the West Indies.
Jones, Charles (ed.)
  1997   *The Edinburgh History of the Scots Language.* Edinburgh: Edinburgh
          University Press.
Kachru, Braj B.
  1983   *The Indianization of English: The English Language in India.* Delhi:
          Oxford University Press.
Kachru, Braj B. (ed.)
  1982   *The Other Tongue: English Across Cultures.* Urbana: University of Illinois
          Press.
Kachru, Braj B. (ed.)
  2005   *Asian Englishes. Beyond the Canon:* Hong Kong: Hong Kong University
          Press.
Kachru, Braj B., Yamuna Kachru and Cecil L. Nelson (eds.)
  2006   *The Handbook of World Englishes.* Oxford: Blackwell.
Kachru, Yamuna and Cecil L. Nelson
  2006   *World Englishes in Asian Contexts.* Hong Kong: Hong Kong University
          Press.
Kautzsch, Alexander
  2002   *The Historical Evolution of Earlier African American English. An Em-
          pirical Comparison of Early Sources.* (Topics in English Linguistics 38.)
          Berlin/New York: Mouton de Gruyter.
Keesing, Roger M.
  1988   *Melanesian Pidgin and the Oceanic Substrate.* Stanford: Stanford
          University Press.
Kirk, John M. and Dónall P. Ó Baoill
  2001   *Language Links: The Languages of Scotland and Ireland.* Belfast: Cló
          Olscoill na Banríona [Queen's University Press].
Kirk, John M., Stewart Sanderson and John D.A. Widdowson (eds.)
  1985   *Studies in Linguistic Geography: The Dialects of English in Britain and
          Ireland.* London et al.: Croom Helm.
Kortmann, Bernd, Tanja Herrmann, Lukas Pietsch and Susanne Wagner
  2005   *A Comparative Grammar of British English Dialects: Agreement, Gender,
          Relative Clauses.* Berlin/New York: Mouton de Gruyter.

Kortmann, Bernd (ed.)
2004 *Dialectology Meets Typology: Dialect Grammar from a Cross-Linguistic Perspective*. Berlin/New York: Mouton de Gruyter.
Krapp, George P.
1925 *The English Language in America*. 2 Volumes. New York: Century.
Kretzschmar, William A. and Edgar W. Schneider
1996 *Introduction to Quantitative Analysis of Linguistic Survey Data: An Atlas by the Numbers*. (Empirical Linguistics Series.) Thousand Oaks, CA: Sage.
Kretzschmar, William A., Virginia G. McDavid, Theodore K. Lerud and Ellen Johnson (eds.)
1993 *Handbook of the Linguistic Atlas of the Middle and South Atlantic States*. Chicago: University of Chicago Press.
Kurath, Hans
1949 *A Word Geography of the Eastern United States*. Ann Arbor: University of Michigan Press.
Kurath, Hans and Raven I. McDavid, Jr.
1961 *The Pronunciation of English in the Atlantic States. Based upon the Collections of the Linguistic Atlas*. (Studies in American English 3.) Ann Arbor: University of Michigan Press.
Kurath, Hans (ed.)
1939
–1943 *Linguistic Atlas of New England*. Providence: Brown University Press.
Labov, William
1966 *The Social Stratification of English in New York City*. (Urban Language Series 1.) Washington, D.C.: Center for Applied Linguistics.
1972a *Language in the Inner City: Studies in the Black English Vernacular*. (Conduct and Communication 3.) Philadelphia: University of Pennsylvania Press.
1972b *Sociolinguistic Patterns*. (Conduct and Communication 4.) Philadelphia: University of Pennsylvania Press.
1980 *Locating Language in Time and Space*. (Quantitative Analyses of Linguistic Structure.) New York: Academic Press.
1994 *Principles of Linguistic Change, Volume 1: Internal Factors*. (Language in Society 20.) Oxford/Malden, MA: Blackwell.
2001 *Principles of Linguistic Change, Volume 2: Social Factors*. (Language in Society 29.) Oxford/Malden, MA: Blackwell.
Labov, William, Richard Steiner and Malcah Yaeger
1972 *A Quantitative Study of Sound Change in Progress: Report on National Science Foundation Contract NSF-GS-3278 University of Pennsylvania*. Philadelphia: University of Pennsylvania Regional Survey.
Labov, William, Sharon Ash and Charles Boberg
2006 *Atlas of North American English: Phonetics, Phonology and Sound Change*. (Topics in English Linguistics 41.) Berlin/New York: Mouton de Gruyter.

Lalla, Barbara and Jean D'Costa
  1990   *Language in Exile: Three Hundred Years of Jamaican Creole.* Tuscaloosa:
          University of Alabama Press.
Lanehart, Sonja L. (ed.)
  2001   *Sociocultural and Historical Contexts of African American English.*
          (Varieties of English around the World, General Series 27.) Amsterdam/
          Philadelphia: Benjamins.
Leitner, Gerhard
  2004a   *Australia's Many Voices. Australian English – The National Language.*
          Berlin/New York: Mouton de Gruyter.
  2004b   *Australia's Many Voices. Ethnic Englishes, Indigenous and Migrant
          Languages. Policy and Education.* Berlin/New York: Mouton de Gruyter.
LePage, Robert B. and Andrée Tabouret-Keller
  1985   *Acts of Identity: Creole-based Approaches to Language and Ethnicity.*
          Cambridge: Cambridge University Press.
Lim, Lisa (ed.)
  2004   *Singapore English. A Grammatical Description.* Amsterdam/Philadelphia:
          Benjamins.
Lindquist, Hans, Maria Estling, Staffan Klintborg and Magnus Levin (eds.)
  1998   *The Major Varieties of English: Papers from MAVEN 97, Växjö 20–22
          November 1997.* (Acta Wexionensia: Humaniora; 1.) Växjö: Växjo
          University.
Matthews, William
  1938   *Cockney Past and Present: A Short History of the Dialect of London.*
          London: Routledge.
McArthur, Tom
  1992   *The Oxford Companion to the English Language.* Oxford: Oxford
          University Press.
  2002   *Oxford Guide to World English.* Oxford: Oxford University Press.
McMillan, James B. and Michel B. Montgomery
  1989   *Annotated Bibliography of Southern American English.* Tuscaloosa/
          London: University of Alabama Press.
McWhorter, John H. (ed.)
  2000   *Language Change and Language Contact in Pidgins and Creoles.* (Creole
          Language Library 21.) Amsterdam/Philadelphia: Benjamins.
Mehrotra, Raja Ram
  1998   *Indian English – Text and Interpretation.* (Varieties of English around the
          World, Text Series 7.) Amsterdam/Philadelphia: Benjamins.
Melchers, Gunnel and Philip Shaw
  2003   *World Englishes.* London: Arnold.
Mencken, Henry
  1963   *The American Language: An Inquiry into the Development of English in
          the United States. With the Assistance of David W. Maurer.* New York:
          Knopf.

Mesthrie, Rajend (ed.)
  1995   *Language and Social History: Studies in South African Sociolinguistics.*
          Cape Town: David Philip.
  2002   *Language in South Africa.* Cambridge: Cambridge University Press.
Milroy, James
  1981   *Regional Accents of English: Belfast.* Belfast: Blackstaff.
Milroy, James and Lesley Milroy (eds.)
  1993   *Real English: The Grammar of English Dialects in the British Isles.* (Real
          Language Series.) London: Longman.
Montgomery, Michael B. and Guy Bailey (eds.)
  1986   *Language Variety in the South: Perspectives in Black and White.* University,
          AL: University of Alabama Press.
Montgomery, Michael B. and Thomas Nunnally (eds.)
  1998   *From the Gulf States and Beyond. The Legacy of Lee Pederson and LAGS.*
          Tuscaloosa, AL/London: University of Alabama Press.
Mufwene, Salikoko S.
  2001   *The Ecology of Language Evolution.* (Cambridge Approaches to Language
          Contact.) Cambridge: Cambridge University Press.
Mufwene, Salikoko S., Guy Bailey, John Baugh and John R. Rickford (eds.)
  1998   *African-American English. Structure, History and Use.* London:
          Routledge.
Mufwene, Salikoko S. (ed.)
  1993   *Africanisms in Afro-American Language Varieties.* Athens: University of
          Georgia Press.
Mühleisen, Susanne
  2002   *Creole Discourse: Exploring Prestige Formation and Change across
          Caribbean English-Lexicon Creoles.* (Creole Language Library 24.)
          Amsterdam/Philadelphia: Benjamins.
Mühlhäusler, Peter
  1997   *Pidgin and Creole Linguistics.* (Westminster Creolistic Series 3.) London:
          University of Westminster Press.
Murray, Thomas and Beth Lee Simon (eds.)
  2006   *Language Variation and Change in the American Midland: A New Look at
          "Heartland" English.* Amsterdam/Philadelphia: Benjamins.
Muysken, Pieter and Norval Smith (eds.)
  1986   *Substrata versus Universals in Creole Genesis. Papers from the Amsterdam
          Creole Workshop, April 1985.* (Creole Language Library 1.) Amsterdam/
          Philadelphia: Benjamins.
Myers-Scotton, Carol
  2002   *Contact Linguistics: Bilingual Encounters and Grammatical Outcomes.*
          (Oxford Linguistics.) Oxford: Oxford University Press.
Nagle, Stephen J. and Sara L. Sanders (eds.)
  2003   *English in the Southern United States.* (Studies in English Language.)
          Cambridge: Cambridge University Press.

Neumann-Holzschuh, Ingrid and Edgar W. Schneider (eds.)
  2000   *Degrees of Restructuring in Creole Languages.* (Creole Language Library 22.) Amsterdam/Philadelphia: Benjamins.
Nihalani, Paroo, Priya Hosali and Ray K. Tongue
  1989   *Indian and British English: A Handbook of Usage and Pronunciation.* (Oxford India Paperbacks.) Delhi: Oxford University Press.
Noss, Richard B. (ed.)
  1984   *An Overview of Language Issues in South-East Asia: 1950–1980.* Singapore: Oxford University Press.
Orton, Harold (ed.)
  1962
  –1971   *Survey of English Dialects: The Basic Material.* 4 Volumes. Leeds: Arnold.
Orton, Harold, Stewart Sanderson and John Widdowson (eds.)
  1978   *The Linguistic Atlas of England.* London: Croom Helm.
Parasher, S.V.
  1991   *Indian English: Functions and Form.* (Sell-series in English Language and Literature 19.) New Delhi: Bahri.
Parkvall, Mikael
  2000   *Out of Africa: African Influences in Atlantic Creoles.* London: Battlebridge.
Patrick, Peter L.
  1999   *Urban Jamaican Creole: Variation in the Mesolect.* (Varieties of English around the World, General Series 17.) Amsterdam/Philadelphia: Benjamins.
Pederson, Lee (ed.)
  1986
  –1992   *The Linguistic Atlas of the Gulf States.* 7 Volumes. Athens, GA: University of Georgia Press.
Plag, Ingo (ed.)
  2003   *Phonology and Morphology of Creole Languages.* (Linguistische Arbeiten 478.) Tübingen: Niemeyer.
Platt, John, Mian Lian Ho and Heidi Weber
  1983   *Singapore and Malaysia.* (Varieties of English around the World, Text Series 4.) Amsterdam/Philadelphia: Benjamins.
  1984   *The New Englishes.* London: Routledge and Kegan Paul.
Poplack, Shana and Sali Tagliamonte
  2001   *African American English in the Diaspora.* (Language in Society 30.) Oxford/Malden, MA: Blackwell.
Poplack, Shana (ed.)
  2000   *The English History of African American English.* (Language in Society 28.) Oxford/Malden, MA: Blackwell.
Preston, Dennis R. (ed.)
  1993   *American Dialect Research: An Anthology Celebrating the 100th Anniversary of the American Dialect Society.* (Centennial Series of the American Dialect Society.) Amsterdam/Philadelphia: Benjamins.

Rampton, Ben
1995   *Crossing: Language and Ethnicity among Adolescents.* (Real Language Series.) London: Longman.
Rickford, John R.
1987   *Dimensions of a Creole Continuum: History, Texts, and Linguistics Analysis of Guyanese Creole.* Stanford: Stanford University Press.
1999   *African American Vernacular English: Features, Evolution, Educational Implications.* (Language in Society 26.) Oxford/Malden, MA: Blackwell.
Rickford, John R. and Suzanne Romaine (eds.)
1999   *Creole Genesis, Attitudes and Discourse: Studies Celebrating Charlene J. Sato.* (Creole Language Library 20.) Amsterdam/Philadelphia: Benjamins.
Roberts, Peter A.
1988   *West Indians and their Language.* Cambridge: Cambridge University Press.
Romaine, Suzanne
1988   *Pidgin and Creole Languages.* (Longman Linguistics Library.) London/ New York: Longman.
Schmied, Josef J.
1991   *English in Africa: An Introduction.* (Longman Linguistics Library.) London: Longman.
Schneider, Edgar W.
1989   *American Earlier Black English. Morphological and Syntactical Variables.* Tuscaloosa, AL/London: University of Alabama Press.
Schneider, Edgar W. (ed.)
1996   *Focus on the USA.* (Varieties of English around the World, General Series 16.) Amsterdam/Philadelphia: Benjamins.
1997a   *Englishes Around the World, Volume 1: General Studies, British Isles, North America: Studies in Honour of Manfred Görlach.* (Varieties of English around the World, General Series 18.) Amsterdam/Philadelphia: Benjamins.
1997b   *Englishes Around the World, Volume 2: Caribbean, Africa, Asia, Australasia. Studies in Honour of Manfred Görlach.* (Varieties of English around the World, General Series 19.) Amsterdam/Philadelphia: Benjamins.
2007   *Postcolonial English.* Cambridge: Cambridge University Press.
Sebba, Mark
1993   *London Jamaican: Language Systems in Interaction.* (Real Language Series.) London: Longman.
1997   *Contact Languages – Pidgins and Creoles.* (Modern Linguistics Series.) London: Macmillan.
Singh, Ishtla
2000   *Pidgins and Creoles – An Introduction.* London: Arnold.
Singler, John V. (ed.)
1990   *Pidgin and Creole Tense-Mood-Aspect Systems.* (Creole Language Library 6.) Amsterdam/Philadelphia: Benjamins.

Spears, Arthur K. and Donald Winford (eds.)
1997   *The Structure and Status of Pidgins and Creoles. Including Selected Papers from the Meetings of the Society for Pidgin and Creole Linguistics.* (Creole Language Library 19.) Amsterdam/Philadelphia: Benjamins.

Spencer, John (ed.)
1971   *The English Language in West Africa.* (English Language Series.) London: Longman.

Thomas, Erik R.
2001   *An Acoustic Analysis of Vowel Variation in New World English.* (Publication of the American Dialect Society 85.) Durham: Duke University Press.

Thomason, Sarah G.
2001   *Contact Languages.* Edinburgh: University of Edinburgh Press.

Thomason, Sarah G. and Terrence Kaufman
1988   *Language Contact, Creolization and Genetic Linguistics.* Berkeley: University of California Press.

Tristram, Hildegard, L.C. (ed.)
1998   *The Celtic Englishes.* (Anglistische Forschungen 247.) Heidelberg: Winter.
2000   *The Celtic Englishes II.* (Anglistische Forschungen 286.) Heidelberg: Winter.
2003   *The Celtic Englishes III.* (Anglistische Forschungen 324.) Heidelberg: Winter.

Trudgill, Peter
1974   *The Social Differentiation of English in Norwich.* (Cambridge Studies in Linguistics 13.) Cambridge: Cambridge University Press.
1986   *Dialects in Contact.* (Language in Society 10.) Oxford: Blackwell.
1999   *The Dialects of England.* 2nd edition. Oxford: Blackwell. also: *The Dialects of England.* 2nd edition. Oxford: Blackwell.

Trudgill, Peter and Jean Hannah
2002   *International English: A Guide to Varieties of Standard English.* 4th edition. London: Arnold.
1994   *International English: A Guide to Varieties of Standard English.* 3rd edition. London: Arnold.
1985   *International English: A Guide to Varieties of Standard English.* 2nd edition. London: Arnold.
1982   *International English: A Guide to Varieties of Standard English.* London: Arnold.

Trudgill, Peter (ed.)
1978   *Sociolinguistic Patterns in British English.* London: Arnold.
1984   *Language in the British Isles.* Cambridge: Cambridge University Press.

Trudgill, Peter and J.K. Chambers (eds.)
1991   *Dialects of English: Studies in Grammatical Variation.* (Longman Linguistics Library.) London/New York: Longman.

Upton, Clive, David Parry and John D.A. Widdowson
1994   *Survey of English Dialects: The Dictionary and Grammar.* London: Routledge.

Viereck, Wolfgang (ed.)
1985   *Focus on England and Wales.* (Varieties of English around the World, General Series 4.) Amsterdam/Philadelphia: Benjamins.
Wakelin, Martyn
1981   *English Dialects: An Introduction.* London: Athlone Press.
Wakelin, Martyn F. (ed.)
1972   *Patterns in the Folk Speech of the British Isles. With a Foreword by Harold Orton.* London: Athlone Press.
Watts, Richard and Peter Trudgill (eds.)
2002   *Alternative Histories of English.* London: Routledge.
Wells, John C.
1982   *Accents of English.* 3 Volumes. Cambridge: Cambridge University Press.
Williamson, Juanita and Virginia M. Burke (eds.)
1971   *A Various Language. Perspectives on American Dialects.* New York: Holt, Rinehart and Winston.
Winer, Lise
1993   *Trinidad and Tobago.* (Varieties of English around the World, Text Series 6.) Amsterdam/Philadelphia: Benjamins.
Winford, Donald
1993   *Predication in Carribean English Creoles.* (Creole Language Library 10.) Amsterdam/Philadelphia: Benjamins.
2003   *An Introduction to Contact Linguistics.* (Language in Society 33.) Malden/Oxford/Melbourne: Blackwell.
Wolfram, Walt
1969   *A Sociolinguistic Description of Detroit Negro Speech.* (Urban Language Series 5.) Washington, D.C.: Center for Applied Linguistics.
Wolfram, Walt and Ralph W. Fasold
1974   *The Study of Social Dialects in American English.* Englewood Cliffs, NJ: Prentice Hall.
Wolfram, Walt and Donna Christian
1976   *Appalachian Speech.* Arlington, VA: Center for Applied Linguistics.
Wolfram, Walt and Natalie Schilling-Estes
2005   *American English: Dialects and Variation.* (Language in Society 25.) 2nd ed. Malden, MA/Oxford: Blackwell.
Wolfram, Walt, Kirk Hazen and Natalie Schilling-Estes
1999   *Dialect Change and Maintenance on the Outer Banks.* (Publication of the American Dialect Society 81.) Tuscaloosa, AL/London: University of Alabama Press.
Wolfram, Walt and Erik R. Thomas
2002   *The Development of African American English.* (Language in Society 31.) Oxford/Malden, MA: Blackwell.
Wolfram, Walt and Ben Wards (eds.)
2006   *American Voices: How Dialects Differ from Coast to Coast.* Oxford: Blackwell

Wright, Joseph
  1898
 –1905   *The English Dialect Dictionary*. Oxford: Clarendon Press.
  1905   *The English Dialect Grammar*. Oxford: Frowde.

Introduction: varieties of English in the Pacific and Australasia*

Kate Burridge and Bernd Kortmann

1. A note on geographical coverage

This volume provides linguistic sketches of the most significant Englishes currently spoken in the Pacific (on islands between the American continents, Asia and Australia) and Australasia (in Australia and New Zealand and on neighbouring islands of the South Pacific Ocean). These sketches cover a range of the different variety types (including both native and contact varieties) that have evolved as a consequence of the spread of English into these regions. Even though the Hawaiian Islands are politically part of the United States, and have been since 1958, they are included in this volume on account of their geographical location in the northern Pacific, and the special linguistic relationship with other Pacific rather than North American varieties.

2. Australian and New Zealand English

Both Australia and New Zealand have in common a relatively recent history of European settlement and both share transplanted Englishes. Towards the end of the 18th century, the population of the British Isles was only about 15 million. A considerable number of these people spoke their own Celtic languages and little or no English. Moreover, a good many of the English speakers spoke only their regional dialects and dialect differences could be striking – we are after all talking of a time when horses and sailing vessels were the most efficient means of travel and communication. This then was roughly the state of the language when exploration southwards established the first English-speaking settlements in the Antipodes.

For Australia, the first appearance of English coincides with the arrival of Captain Cook in 1770. However, it wasn't until later in 1788 that we can really talk about a European settlement there. Over the course of the next 20 years or so Britain established its first penal colony in Sydney in order to alleviate the problem of its overcrowded prisons. The early arrivals were therefore largely prisoners, prison officers and their families. Non-convicts, or free settlers as they were known, did not really reach significant numbers until the middle of the 19th century.

On the other side of the Tasman, English got off to a later and somewhat slower start. Cook had charted the islands around the same time he visited Australia, and although there was unofficial settlement in New Zealand as early as the late 1700s (involving small numbers of people often from Australia), the official colony was not established until 1840. After this time immigration from both Australia and Britain increased dramatically.

The different mixes of original dialects, the different dates of settlement, the different settlement patterns and the contact with the different indigenous languages have meant that varieties growing up in Australia and New Zealand are already quite distinct. The physical separation from other English-speaking regions has allowed this distinctiveness to flourish. Regional variation within Australian and New Zealand English, however, is minor compared to other varieties. The blending of the original British dialects (the so-called "melting pot" effect) has left behind remarkable regional homogeneity – even within Australia, a continent some thirty times the size of Britain. Notwithstanding stylistically and socially marked variation, there is very little in the way of clearly identifiable regional variation. There is one notable exception; namely, those speakers from the Southern part of the South Island of New Zealand. This group have a striking semi-rhotic variety of English; in other words, /r/ is (variably) pronounced in postvocalic positions, especially after the NURSE vowel (cf. the chapters by Gordon and Maclagan and also Bauer and Warren).

However, lay perceptions are quite different. Speakers are often puzzled by linguists' claims of regional homogeneity, pointing to obvious vocabulary differences they have encountered in their travels. A type of large, smooth sausage in Auckland is *polony*, in Christchurch *saveloy* and in Southland *Belgium* or *Belgium roll/sausage*. Both *polony* and *saveloy* are familiar terms for some Australians, although people in Adelaide (South Australia) are more comfortable with *fritz*, Brisbanites (Queensland) and Sydney-siders (New South Wales) with *devon*. Lexical variation of this kind will always exist of course and is certainly fascinating to speakers, but it does not make for distinct dialects. Moreover, popular claims that people can identify someone's place of origin purely on the basis of how s/he speaks are exaggerated. With the exception of the so-called Southland "burr" just mentioned, accent and dialect differences are more likely to be a matter of statistical tendency, with certain differences occurring more or less frequently in one place than another. Some of these differences have existed from the beginning of settlement. They evolved because of the different dialect mixes in each region. The Southland "burr", for example, can be explained by the significant number of Scots who settled in these southern regions.

Although there is limited regional diversity now, we might expect that over time both physical and social distance will have the effect of increasing regional differences in Australia and New Zealand. Also the fact that there is no single prestige regional variety of the language in either country means that varieties will be freer to go their separate ways. In other words, speakers will not want to shift towards a distinctively Canberra or Wellington usage because it has more status. Certainly the separation of urban and rural communities looks currently to be inspiring the richest regional diversity in these places. In Australia, for example, we already find significant differences, particularly with respect to speed and also broadness of accent. For example, people in the city of Melbourne (Victoria) tend to speak faster than those in rural Victoria of the same socio-economic background. There is also a greater proportion of broad speakers in the rural regions. This is one popular stereotype that does appear to have some basis in reality (although cf. Bradley, this volume). Rural speakers of vernacular varieties are not only showing distinctness of accent and vocabulary, there are also signs of significant grammatical differences emerging (cf. Pawley's chapter). But social factors are crucial here as well. It is difficult to talk about regionally defined variation without appealing to social aspects of the area. Non-standard vernacular varieties are also typical of the lower socio-economic classes in a speech community – basically, the higher up the social scale you go, the closer the speakers tend to be to the standard language and therefore the less remarkable the regional differences are. Moreover these grammatical features are by no means confined to the vernacular Englishes of Australia and New Zealand. Features such as irregular verb forms, special pronouns for plural "you", and *never* as a general negator crop up in non-standard varieties all over the English-speaking world.

Effects of globalization are also contributing to this increasing diversity by fostering new socially-defined ethnic variation in these countries. Massive flows of people, including tourists, refugees and migrants, have produced an intermixing of people and cultures which is unprecedented. Clearly culture and language at the local level have been changed irrevocably by this "international" movement of people. And as each individual group seeks to assert its own identity, different ethnic varieties of English can become an important means of signalling the group boundaries. Italian or Greek features in a group's English, for example, can be potent markers of that group's ethnicity. To give some idea of the potential for diversity here, consider that over the last 30 years or so, speakers from well over 40 different ethnic groups have migrated to Australia. These different ethnic mixes are now adding a vibrant new socially relevant aspect to Australian English. In cities such as Melbourne and Sydney, for example, the Italian and Greek communities are of particular interest because of their size and also because they have been in these places long enough now to have teenagers who were born in the country.

Ethnicity is clearly a crucial part of social identity and is something that people want to demonstrate through their use of language. Even though New Zealand English and Australian English have incorporated very little from Maori or Aboriginal languages respectively, varieties of Maori English and Aboriginal English are providing an interesting new dimension to the "Extra-territorial Englishes" in the Antipodes (cf. section 3 below on contact varieties). In the face of the disappearance of local indigenous languages in these two countries, such distinct Englishes have become an important means of signalling these speakers' cultural and social identity. Of the 200–250 Aboriginal languages that existed in Australia at the time of earliest European contact, only around 90 have survived and of these as few as 20 can be described as robust; e.g. Warlpiri, Arrente and Western Desert, each with about 3,000 speakers (see Schmidt 1990). In New Zealand, by the 1980s the number of Maori speakers was already as low as 12% of the total Maori population. Few contexts remain where Maori is the natural means of communication (cf. Benton 1991). In both Australia and New Zealand vigorous efforts are now being made to maintain, even revive, these languages, and time will tell how successful they are in reversing the overall trend toward language death.

Another consequence of the rise of the global village is that native Englishes such as New Zealand English and Australian English are now much more open than ever before to global influence. There is of course a pervasive American dimension to much of what is global – a clear distinction between globalization and American cultural imperialism is at times difficult to maintain. It would be surprising therefore, given the global presence of the United States and the inevitable loosening of ties between Britain and its former Antipodean colonies, if there were not some sort of linguistic steamrolling going on. Certainly, the "Americanization" of Australian and New Zealand English is currently a hot topic within these speech communities – and reactions are generally hostile. Newspaper headlines like "Facing an American Invasion" go on to "condemn this insidious, but apparently virile, infection from the USA". In letters to the editor and talkback calls on the radio, speakers rail against "ugly Americanisms" (many of which, it turns out, are not Americanisms at all; cf. the discussion in Burridge and Mulder 1998: ch. 12). Lay concerns about language usage are not based on genuine linguistic matters, but reflect deeper and more general social judgements. In this case, the current hostility towards American usage is undoubtedly born of the linguistic insecurity that comes from the dominance of America as a cultural, political, military and economic superpower.

In fact, the actual impact of American English on Antipodean Englishes is difficult to determine. Most of the complaints centre around vocabulary. Lexical influences are the most obvious to speakers and intensify the wide-spread perception of American influence. This is undoubtedly fuelled by the high visibility of spelling – although Australian and New Zealand spelling conventions derive traditionally from the British, the technological presence of America means this is an area of rapidly growing American influence. Certainly there are areas, such as fast food industry and technology, where American influence on the lexicon is evident. There is also a strong American aspect to teenage slang. Elsewhere, however, influence remains slight. Phonological and grammatical transfers are also not much in evidence. Apparent American imports in the area of phonology include features of stress (such as *pri'marily* in place of *'primarily*), affrication of /tr/ and /str/ (where *tree* sounds much like "chree") and flapping or tapping of inter-vocalic /t/ (where *latter* and *ladder* become similar in pronunciation). Since examples like these illustrate natural phonological changes, however, it is difficult to establish the exact role of American influence here. Contact with American English could simply be accelerating trends already underway. Apparent grammatical imports such as an increase in the use of the subjunctive could also represent independently motivated change rather than direct borrowing. And while the resurgence of conservative features like *gotten* may well be due to American English influence too, it is also possible that these come from the vestiges of dialectal users downunder (cf. further discussion in the chapter by Hundt et al.).

As a final note, we use linguistic labels such as Australian English or New Zealand English, as if each were a single immutable language variety. Clearly, this is not the reality. The reality is that speakers from different regions, from different social classes, of different ages, of different occupations, of different gender identification, of different sexual orientation will all talk differently. People talk differently in different contexts too – an informal chat, an interview, a lecture and so on. It must always be remembered that labels like Australian English or New Zealand English are convenient cover terms for what are really clumps or clusters of mutually intelligible speech varieties.

2.1.   A note on source material

For both New Zealand and Australian English there are several notable corpora that the authors here have drawn from: the Canterbury Corpus (containing recordings since the mid 1990s made by students enrolled in the New Zealand English Course at the University of Canterbury), the Wellington Corpus of Written New Zealand English (comprising texts from 1986), the Australian

Corpus of English held at Macquarie University (one million words of published material from 1986). Descriptions in the morphosyntax chapters also derive from elicitation tests and popular surveys (local or national-wide), as well as secondary references (such as usage guides and grammatical handbooks).

3.   Contact varieties

A number of the contributions in this volume focus on the English-based pidgin and creole languages in the Pacific and Australasia. Generally speaking, pidgins are a type of makeshift language that springs up when speakers of different linguistic backgrounds come into contact and need to talk. In the formation of a pidgin, there are always two (or more) languages that are involved, although the pidgin takes one language, usually the socially dominant one, as its point of origin for the lexicon. It is this language that contributes most of the vocabulary, though significant features of the grammar are likely to derive from other sources. At one time there were many more pidgin varieties in these regions. In the pearling fisheries around Broome in Western Australia, for example, pidginized forms of Malay were used during the early part of the last century. But pidgins such as this one are typically as short-lived as the social circumstances that spawned them and Broom Pearling Pidgin is now extinct. If the contact ceases or the different groups end up learning each other's language, the pidgin will then drop by the wayside.

If the situation stabilizes, however, and the contact continues, there can be a very different outcome as the language expands beyond its original very limited context of use. Change is then typically rapid, especially in vocabulary and grammar, as the makeshift pidgin metamorphoses into a fully-fledged and dynamic language, able to serve its speakers in all kinds of settings and circumstances. In theory it is straight-forward to say when a pidgin ends and a creole begins, at least according to those definitions that see pidgins and creoles as separate stages in a single process of development – as soon as children in a community are brought up speaking the pidgin as their first language, it becomes a creole. Accordingly, a creole is simply a nativized pidgin. The linguistic reality, however, is another matter – linguistically it is impossible to say where the boundary lies. Even before a pidgin becomes somebody's first language, it can develop a highly elaborated structure (close to that of a so-called creole), if it is used for a number of different purposes. For this reason some linguists avoid the labels "pidgin" and "creole" and refer to these varieties straightforwardly as "contact languages" (cf. the chapter by Crowley).

Clearly, both Australia and New Zealand offer situations where English comes into close contact with other languages. Since European contact, Aboriginal Australia and Maori New Zealand have seen members of several language groups living in the same community and engaging in daily interaction. In Australia, pidgins based on English appeared not long after the arrival of the Europeans. The pidgin varieties became increasingly important for contact, not only between Aboriginal speakers and English speakers, but also as a *lingua franca* between speakers of different Aboriginal languages.

It has long been observed that linguistic change follows closely on the heels of drastic social upheaval. We see striking illustration of this in the evolution of the creoles in these regions. After the arrival of Europeans in Australia, for example, there came extreme social disruption with the movement of Aboriginal people to mission stations, pastoral properties and towns. More than ever before Aboriginal people from different linguistic groups found themselves together and needing to communicate. Although there had always been widespread bilingualism among adults, this was not adequate to cover communicative needs in these new settlements, where children of different linguistic backgrounds were thrown together and where there was continued uneven interaction between Aboriginal and English speakers. Pidgins therefore fulfilled the communicative needs of these speakers. Out of these, creoles evolved in the Kimberley Region, the Roper River area and parts of North Queensland. These various English-based creoles have much in common, but they also show some regional differences too. These depend on the Aboriginal languages represented in the community where the pidgin originated and also influences from other pidgins and creoles brought into Australia from the outside (cf. Malcolm, this volume).

In New Zealand the situation was somewhat different. As Ross Clark (1979) documents, in the early 1880s a "foreigner-talk" system known as South Seas Jargon was used in various parts of the Pacific primarily between European whalers and indigenous crew members, some of whom were Maori. In New Zealand this jargon developed into Maori Pidgin English which was used for early contact between Maori and Pakeha (or European New Zealanders). However, this pidgin never stabilized enough to evolve further. For one, in New Zealand there was only ever a single indigenous language, so there was never a need for a *lingua franca* between indigenous groups as there was in Australia. The historical records also suggest that the most common pattern was for English speakers to learn enough Maori to communicate. As a result the New Zealand pidgin was short-lived. However, Maori continue to be recognizable linguistically when speaking English through their preferential use of a wide range of linguistic forms, especially with respect to pronunciation (cf. Warren and Bauer, this volume).

This volume contains descriptions of six other contact languages: Bislama (as spoken in Vanuatu), Solomon Islands Pijin, Tok Pisin (as spoken in Papua New Guinea), Hawai'i Creole, Fiji English and Norfolk Island-Pitcairn English. The first three creoles all have their roots in earlier Melanesian Pidgin and share lexical patterning and a number of structural characteristics. However, different external influences (for example, contact with French for Bislama and with German for Tok Pisin) and interaction with different local languages have given rise to distinct developments within these varieties. Hawai'i Creole is another English-lexifier contact language, but also draws vocabulary from Hawaiian and Japanese. Although its story is very different, it does have episodes in common with the creoles from the southwestern Pacific: (1) early links with South Seas Jargon (as mentioned above, a jargon variety used for short-term communication by crews on ships and by individuals on shore in various locations around the Pacific Islands) and (2) input from Melanesian Pidgin spoken by labourers recruited for the sugarcane plantations in the early 1800s. These four Pacific contact varieties have, since the beginning of the 20th century, undergone substantial functional and structural expansion.

Fiji English shows many characteristically creole features although it is technically not a creole. For one, there is the absence of a stable pidgin at an earlier stage. Descriptions such as "creoloid" and "semi-creole" for this variety attest to the blurred nature of the category creole (cf. discussion earlier). Fiji English also has historical links with the previous creoles and these links are still evident in lexical and grammatical relics of Melanesian Pidgin (originally introduced by plantation labourers during the 19th century).

Norfolk Island-Pitcairn English represents the linguistic outcome of contact between the British English of the *Bounty* mutineers and Tahitian. It is a remarkable example of a contact language since we know precisely the number of speakers who originally settled on Pitcairn in 1790, the places of origin of these speakers and even their names. However, its subsequent development has not yet been fully established and although there are clear early influences from the Pacific Pidgin English of the Melanesian islanders on Norfolk, the exact relationship of Norfolk Island-Pitcairn English to the contact varieties just described is problematic.

Variation within these speech communities is considerable. Speakers of Melanesian Pidgin, for example, frequently switch between, say, Bislama or Tok Pisin and their local variety of Standard English. The situation can become even more complicated because of the so-called "creole continuum". Take the example of the interaction of Kriol with Aboriginal English and Australian English. As previously discussed, linguistic labels such as these give the impression of easily identifiable and neatly compartmentalized entities, but such tidy classifications are not reality. The many different varieties of English and creole that Aboriginal people speak range from something which is virtually identical to Standard Australian English in everything but accent (dubbed the "acrolect") through to pure creole which is so remote from Standard Australian English as to be mutually unintelligible (dubbed the "basilect"). In between these two polar extremes you find a whole range of varieties (or "mesolects"). Generally, speakers have command of a number of these varieties and they move along the continuum according to the situation and the audience.

The label "variety of English" might at first seem problematic when dealing with these creole varieties, especially at the basilectal end of the continuum. These are very different Englishes in all respects – vocabulary, grammar and phonology. The very "unEnglish-looking" structures that characterize creoles, as well as their unique development (as contact languages resulting from pidgins), set them apart. There is also the question of the lack of mutual comprehension. Moreover, these languages have distinct names of course – Bislama, Tok Pisin, Kriol. The speakers themselves would never call their language a kind of English. Nonetheless, these contact languages share vocabulary and grammatical features that align them with the English of the international community. All have links of some sort with the group of continental Germanic dialects that ended up in the British Isles sometime in the 5th century AD. These off-springs of English are clearly an important dimension to the diversification of English world-wide (cf. also the discussion in the General Introduction).

4. A note on the order of chapters

The chapters are arranged (partly on linguistic and partly on geographical grounds) in the following order: New Zealand English, Maori English, Australian English, Aboriginal English together with Kriol and Torres Strait Creole (Australia), Bislama (Vanuatu), Solomon Islands Pijin, Tok Pisin (Papua New Guinea), Hawai'i Creole, Fiji English and Norfolk Island-Pitcairn English.

Clearly, all the chapters are self-contained entities and are not intended to be read left to right, chapter by chapter – although of course readers can do that if they wish. Nonetheless, the reader's attention is drawn to certain contributions in this volume that complement each other and are best read as companion chapters. The shared linguistic features and trends between Australia and New Zealand and the question of an Antipodean standard (as distinct from the supervarieties of the northern hemisphere) make these chapters obvious ones for comparison. Similarly, since Maori English and Australian Aboriginal English show some of the same characteristics as their respective standard languages, the readers should also think of these chapters collectively. A tangled linguistic history unites the various contact varieties that follow. The Australian creoles that feature earlier also share in this tangled history. The similar socio-historical conditions that gave rise to these off-springs of English, coupled with common input early on from nautical jargon, have given rise to obvious similarities between these varieties (similarities also due in part to linguistic universals). Particularly striking are the linguistic resemblances between the contact varieties of Vanuatu, Solomon Islands and Papua New Guinea. Their common origin in earlier Melanesian Pidgin naturally unites the three relevant chapters here, and readers will find Crowley's sociohistorical backdrop for Bislama a useful backdrop also for Solomon Islands Pijin and Tok Pisin. The account of Norfolk Island-Pitcairn English is placed last in this group of Pacific contact varieties on account of the fact that the diffusion of creole features from St Kitts now places this variety linguistically closer to Atlantic creoles.

All varieties have counterpart chapters in both the phonology and morphosyntax parts. There is not complete parallelism, however. Variation in New Zealand English phonology has two special chapters devoted to it – one on general social and regional differences, especially those that relate to on-going changes, and another that looks specifically at Maori English. Morphosyntactic variation in New Zealand English, on the other hand, is included within only the one general chapter. The reader's attention is also drawn to an additional contribution in the morphosyntax part. This is a chapter that deals specifically with features of lexical morphology in Australian English.

4.1.   The chapters on phonology

In the opening chapter, Bauer and Warren provide an account of the consonant and vowel systems, as well as the prosodic features, of New Zealand English. Attention is also paid to contact with Maori, in particular the pronunciation of words of Maori origin. The next two chapters are natural companion chapters. Gordon and Maclagan focus on the social and regional variation in New Zealand English phonology. Although, as they point out, regional variation is slight compared to other varieties, there are notable differences to be heard in the Southern part of the South Island (the variable rhoticity of Southland-Otago is something Bauer and Warren also take up in their chapter). These two authors highlight in particular those aspects of variation that are indicative of vowel and consonant changes in progress (e.g. NEAR-SQUARE merger, vocalization of /l/ and affrication of /tr/ and /str/). In a separate chapter, Warren and Bauer go on to focus on the characteristics of Maori English phonology. They emphasize that although many of these consonant and vowel features appear in

Pakeha English (spoken by European New Zealanders), they are nonetheless more prevalent and more consistently maintained in Maori English and therefore go to make this a distinct variety. Strikingly different features also obtain within Maori English prosody, most notably with respect to voice quality and rhythm.

The next three chapters move to Australia. Horvath examines the features of Australian English phonology, the most significant being the vowels. She also picks up on social dimensions, focusing on those sounds that are indicative of change in progress. Bradley takes up the issue of change but looks at regional characteristics. As alluded to earlier in this Introduction, these regional differences are not striking but they do exist and they are on the increase, especially within the system of vowels. Of particular interest with respect to variation elsewhere in the English-speaking world are the regional differences in the BATH vowel class. In the next chapter, Malcolm examines the complex variation that exists within the Aboriginal and Torres Strait Islander speech communities. This includes the phonological systems of two creole varieties, Kriol and Cape York Creole (with focus on the basilectal varieties), and also Aboriginal English. Malcolm concludes by examining some of the serious educational implications, especially the question of better integration of these Englishes into the school system.

The next chapters present sketches of the other contact varieties. Crowley begins with a description of the phonological features of Bislama. This is followed by Jourdan and Selbach on Solomon Islands Pijin and Smith on Tok Pisin. Sakoda and Siegel's account focuses on the variety of Hawai'i English that differs most strikingly from mainstream varieties of English (namely, the basilectal or "heavy" varieties) and compares these to the mesolectal varieties placed closer to English. The descriptions in all four chapters attest to the rich diversity that exists in the Englishes of these regions. This is diversity involving an array of different factors such as education, bilingualism and location (in particular, urban versus rural).

Tent and Mugler go on to examine the extraordinary variation that exists within the phonological systems of the different varieties that are included under the broad umbrella of Fiji English. The authors point out that variation here depends largely on two factors: (1) education of the speaker and (2) first language of the speaker (principally Fijian and Fiji Hindi). Accordingly, these authors divide their discussion into "Pure Fiji English" (spoken by indigenous Fijians and part-Europeans) and "Indo-Fijian Fiji English" (spoken by Indo-Fijians or "Fiji Indians") – readers are also provided with a brief phonological sketch of Fiji Hindi for comparison. Mühlhäusler and Ingram conclude this part of the volume with a description of the most salient aspects of the phonological system of Norfolk Island-Pitcairn English, specifically that variety spoken on Norfolk Island (Norfuk). They base their analysis initially on recordings made in 1957 (the Flint dialogues), which they then compare with recordings made in 2002 of seven Norfuk speakers.

4.2.   The chapters on morphosyntax

The first two papers in this part of the volume are heavily corpus-based. Hundt, Gordon and Hay present their analysis of the standard and non-standard features of New Zealand English morphosyntax as they stand in relation to British English, American English and also Australian English. The authors identify those features that are genuinely New Zealand English and those that are used either more or less frequently in New Zealand English as against other varieties. Their chapter highlights the problem of identifying the shared morphosyntactic features that are the result of external influences (principally in this case American English influence) and those that represent parallel but independent developments. Collins and Peters' analysis of Australian English is a useful companion chapter. In particular, these authors examine the case for endonormativity; in other words, the extent to which Australian English is "consolidating its own norms as an independent national standard". Comparisons are made with New Zealand English and the two northern hemisphere standards.

Pawley's contribution looks at regional variation within Australia, with a focus on Tasmania. In particular, he examines the "Australianness" of what he calls Australian Vernacular English, an informal spoken English, largely working class, male and rural. This variety has a number of non-standard grammatical features that can be found in many places where English is spoken, including other parts of Australia. However, Pawley also identifies some distinctive features, most notably the system of gender assignment (where animate pronouns *he/she* are used in reference to inanimate objects). The next paper by Simpson shows the interface between lexicon and grammar. One earmark of Australian English has become the rich system of nominal derivation that produces forms like *Chrissie* (< *Christmas*) and *rellie* or *rello* (< *relative*), *journo* (< *journalist*) and *arvo* (< *afternoon*), or what Simpson calls "hypocoristics". Here she examines the meanings and uses of these forms and also the linguistic processes that produce them. In the next chapter, Malcolm compares the morphology and syntax of Aboriginal English and Kriol and Torres Strait Creole (in particular how these last two differ from Atlantic creoles).

The following four chapters are also concerned with contact varieties and complement each other and Malcolm's contribution nicely. Crowley presents the morphosyntactic features of Bislama, Jourdan the features of Solomon Islands Pijin, Smith those of Tok Pisin and Sakoda and Siegel those of Hawai'i Creole (with focus on the basilectal varieties). The grammatical structures examined in these four chapters are strikingly different from mainstream Englishes. They include, for example, extensive patterns of verb serialization, lack of inflectional morphology, elaborate pronoun systems, distinguishing, for example, dual, sometimes even trial, and plural as well as inclusive and exclusive first person.

In the chapter that follows, Mugler and Tent focus on those features that are distinctively Fijian English and those shared by other varieties of English. Many of these features are creole-like. The descriptions here are based on 80 hours of recordings, television news and advertisements and also written sources (principally newspapers). Once again, variation is rife within this speech community (again depending largely on education and different first languages).

Finally, Mühlhäusler's contribution highlights the creole features of Norfuk that are shared with other Pacific contact varieties, and also those features that place this variety typologically closer to the creoles of the Atlantic. The reader's attention is also drawn here (as it is in many of the previous chapters) to the increasing influence of English on the morphosyntax of this variety.

Readers of this part of the volume will be struck by the grammatical similarities that obtain not only between the contact varieties in Vanuatu, Solomon Islands and Papua New Guinea (i.e. derived from earlier Melanesian Pidgin), but also between the English-based contact languages in the Pacific and Australasian regions generally. Indeed contact varieties globally share striking resemblances, and most dramatically in their grammars (cf. the creoles described in the Americas and Caribbean volume). Moreover, many of the features are also prevalent in colloquial non-standard varieties of English spoken in places where English is the first language of the majority; cf. for instance Pawley's chapter on Australian Vernacular English. Discussion of these shared features can be found in the synopses.

*   We are very grateful to the late Terry Crowley for his comments on an early version of this introduction

References

Benton, Richard A.
   1991   Maori English: A New Zealand Myth? In: Jenny Cheshire (ed.), *English Around the World: Sociolinguistic Perspectives*, 187–199. Cambridge: Cambridge University Press.

Burridge, Kate and Jean Mulder
   1998   *English in Australia and New Zealand: An Introduction to its Structure, History and Use.* Melbourne: Oxford University Press.
Clark, Ross
   1979   In Search of Beach-La-Mar: Towards a History of Pacific Pidgin English. *Te Reo* 22: 3–64.
   1991   Pidgin English and Pidgin Maori in New Zealand. In: Jenny Cheshire (ed.), *English Around the World: Sociolinguistic* Perspectives, 187–113. Cambridge: Cambridge University Press.
Schmidt, Annette
   1990   *The Loss of Australia's Aboriginal Heritage.* Canberra: Aboriginal Studies Press.

Phonology

New Zealand English: phonology

Laurie Bauer and Paul Warren

1.   Introduction

1.1.   The historical background

The first discoverers of New Zealand were Polynesian explorers around AD 925, and settlement by Polynesians was well established by 1150. Europeans arrived in the form of the Dutchman Abel Tasman in 1642. A result of Tasman's visit is the name New Zealand, given to the islands by Dutch cartographers later in the seventeenth century. The first contact of New Zealand with the English language can be dated to Captain Cook's arrival on the *Endeavour* in 1769. It was Cook who claimed New Zealand for the British Crown. Until the arrival of Europeans, the only language spoken in New Zealand had been Maori, the language of the Polynesian settlers. English-speakers were not the only European settlers, but clearly made up a large proportion of the early missionaries and traders to come to New Zealand. Many of these early English-speaking settlers came not from Britain, but from Australia, where there were strong trading links. Indeed, until 1841 New Zealand was officially a dependency of New South Wales. Although it had been established as the language of the colonial administration by the early nineteenth century, English was still not widespread amongst the Maori population. The Treaty of Waitangi, signed in 1840 by Maori chiefs and representatives of the British Government, established British colonial rule in New Zealand, and opened the way for more systematic migration from Britain and Australia. Large-scale organized settlement now began in earnest, for instance, the Europeans in New Zealand numbered some 2,000 in 1838 but nearer 10,000 by 1842. This increase in settlement meant that by the middle of the nineteenth century the English-speaking population outnumbered Maori-speakers.

We can distinguish different waves of settlement which may have had influence on the development of New Zealand English. The first covers the period 1840–1860, and involved planned settlement by a number of organizations. The New Zealand Company established settlements in Wellington and Nelson, with populations originating from London and the south-east of England. The Plymouth Company placed settlers from Devon and Cornwall in the Taranaki region, founding the city of New Plymouth. In the South Island, Otago in the deep south was settled by the Scottish free-church, while Canterbury's early settlers were Anglo-Catholic. Other historically interesting pockets of settlement include Waipu in Northland, which was settled by Scottish highlanders who had become dissatisfied with their earlier attempts to establish a community in Nova Scotia.

The second wave of settlement followed the discovery of gold, and resulted in a dramatic increase in the population of gold-field areas in the period 1860–1870. The areas most affected were Otago and the West Coast of the South Island, which gained a large number of settlers from Australia.

Planned immigration from the 1870s onwards forms the third wave of settlement. The majority of the early settlers in this period originated from southern England, and as many as 10 per cent from Cornwall alone.

By 1890 the population growth from New Zealand-born Europeans exceeded that from new settlement and it is probably from this point that the influence on New Zealand English from native New Zealanders begins to outweigh that of British or Australian varieties.

It is interesting to note that despite the pattern of rather focused early settlement from certain areas of Britain into certain areas of New Zealand, the forms of English that have evolved in New Zealand are remarkably homogeneous, with very little dialectal variation throughout New Zealand (cf. the chapter by Gordon and Maclagan, this volume). It is also noteworthy that the early influence of Australia was strong. Not only was Australia an early trading partner and provider of continuing settlement, but also many of the trading and communication links between parts of New Zealand occurred via Australia. For instance, the sea-link from Auckland across the Tasman and back to Wellington was for a long time easier than the land route through the New Zealand bush.

1.2.   Contact with Maori

The major contact language which might be expected to have had some influence on New Zealand English is of course Maori. The phonology of Maori (cf. the chapter by Warren and Bauer, this volume) is considerably simpler than that of English, with five vowels /i, ɛ, a, ɔ, u/ and ten consonants /p, t, k, m, n, ŋ, f, h, r, w/ in a (C)V(V) syllable structure. The vowels in a VV sequence can be identical (i.e. a long vowel) or different (when the result may be either a sequence of vowels or a diphthong depending on the vowels concerned). Voiceless stops were originally unaspirated, but have increasingly become aspirated under the influence of English. /t, n/ can be alveolar or dental, /r/ is a voiced alveolar tap. The nature of /f/ varies between dialects of Maori – it was written *wh* by the early missionaries suggesting that it was heard as [ʍ], though [ɸ] is also heard. A further significant feature of Maori concerns its rhythm, which is mora-timed. Where Maori is concerned, a mora is a unit of length such that a short vowel constitutes a single mora and a long vowel or diphthong constitutes two. In mora-timing, a sequence of two syllables each containing one short vowel is rhythmically equivalent to a single syllable containing a long vowel.

2. Phonological systems

2.1. Stressed vowel system

New Zealand English has, with very minor exceptions, a standard non-rhotic stressed vowel system. The lexical sets are assigned to phonemes as below, with the first symbol in the set of illustrative qualities being the one we select for a phonemic transcription.

FLEECE	iː, ɪi
BATH, START, PALM	ɐː
NURSE	ɵː, œː, øː
THOUGHT, NORTH, FORCE	oː, oə, o.ɐ
GOOSE	ʉː, ʏː, ɪʉ, ɐʉ
KIT	ɘ, ə, ə̣, ɪ
DRESS	e, ȩ, e̩
TRAP	ɛ
STRUT	ɐ , ɐ̣
LOT	ɒ , ɡ̣
FOOT	ʊ , ị
FACE	æe, ɐe, ɐi
PRICE	ɑe, ɒe, ɑi
CHOICE	oe, oi
GOAT	ɐʉ , ɐi
MOUTH	æʉ, ɛʉ
NEAR	iə, iː.ɐ, e.ɐ, eə
SQUARE	eə, iː.ɐ, e.ɐ, iə
CURE	ʉə, ʉ.ɐ

Some of these will be discussed in more detail below, in particular the NEAR
–SQUARE merger is a process of great interest in the phonology of current New
Zealand English.

Lip-rounding and spreading is never strong in New Zealand English. There
is some as-yet unexplained articulatory compensation for lip-rounding which
can give the auditory impression of lip-rounding without any difference in
the actual lip-position. Talk of lip-rounding in the descriptions below must
be understood in terms of this mechanism rather than in terms of the expected pouting gesture. A video of one female speaker pronouncing a number
of New Zealand English vowels is provided on the accompanying CD-ROM
and in the online version. Her lip movement seems to us to be greater than is
found with many speakers – perhaps because of the formal environment of
the recording and the fact that she was reading isolated words. An interesting
comparison can be made to illustrate this, using the recordings for *herd* and
word. The former is taken from the word-list and the latter from an impromptu
remark by the speaker, albeit produced with accompanying laughter, which
contributed to the different lip shape. The comparison is interesting not just as
an illustration of the different lip shape in formal and informal contexts, but
also because auditory and acoustic comparison of the two /ɵː/ vowels shows
that they are remarkably similar, despite the different lip configuration. As
observed above, there would appear to be some other compensatory articulatory configuration that results in the rounded quality in the absence of rounded
lip shape.

The fundamental system given above is subject to considerable neutralization before /r/ and /l/. Much of the neutralization is variable, particularly that
before /l/, so that no simple statement of the system in neutralized positions
can be given. Furthermore, the context of neutralization does not seem to be
consistent for all vowels. In some cases there is neutralization before any /l/,
in others the position of neutralization appears to be restricted to where /l/ is
in a syllable coda (i.e. after the vowel but in the same syllable), in others to
environments where the /l/ is not only in a coda but followed by an obstruent
(perhaps particularly voiceless obstruents).

The phonemes instantiated in the following lexical sets are generally neutralized before /r/:

FLEECE, NEAR	iː
DRESS, SQUARE	e
GOOSE, CURE	ʉː

Note that this pattern is complicated by the NEAR-SQUARE merger where that occurs.

The phonemes instantiated in the following lexical sets are frequently neutralized before /l/:

FLEECE, NEAR

There is only one potential minimal pair here, *reel* vs. *real*, and these are homophones for all New Zealand English speakers.

DRESS, TRAP

This neutralization is a sociolinguistic variable, but the neutralization is heard from the majority of younger speakers before any /l/. Such speakers may therefore not distinguish *Alan* and *Ellen*, or *salary* and *celery*. In Wellington data we have analyzed, the neutralized vowel is realized as a vowel which is opener and more retracted than either of DRESS or TRAP, although it appears that values intermediate between DRESS and TRAP are also found.

FOOT, GOOSE

These are commonly neutralized before coda-/l/, making *pull* and *pool* homophonous.

KIT, FOOT

These are often neutralized before a coda-/l/, e.g. in *pill* and *pull*.

KIT, GOOSE

This follows from the last two examples: *pill* and *pool*, or *skills* and *schools* may be indistinguishable.

KIT, STRUT

These may be neutralized, but are most usually kept distinct before /l/, even in a pair like *cult* and *kilt*.

LOT, GOAT

These are regularly neutralized before coda-/l/. The vowel in *troll* may not clearly belong to either phoneme, and is perhaps an instance of a new GOLD vowel (see further below).

THOUGHT, GOAT

These may be neutralized before coda-/l/.

FOOT, THOUGHT
These may be neutralized before coda-/l/.

These last three can lead to homophony among *poll, pole, pull, Paul*.
This leads to a minimum of a six-vowel monophthongal system before /l/:
three long and three short vowels (ignoring the diphthongs). Individual speakers may, of course, have more contrasts than this, depending on their age, gender, ethnicity and so on, but none will have the full set of contrasts found in
Received Pronunciation (RP).

2.2.   Unstressed vowel system

The unstressed vowel system is made up of three contrasting units, one of
which has two major allophones. The first of the units is the *happ*Y vowel,
which naïve speakers relate to the FLEECE vowel rather than to the KIT vowel
in phonemic terms. The patterns of diphthongization for FLEECE and *happ*Y are
probably not identical, although both can be diphthongized. The second unit
is made up of vocalized realizations of /l/. The phonetics of this vowel vary in
ways which have not been fully described. The actual vowel may be more or
less rounded and more or less back or open, rarely more open than cardinal [o]
and generally more back than central. Phonemically, it may be transcribed as
/ɯ/, but this is no more than a viable symbol. The third member of the system
is rather more problematic. Introductory students identify it as the STRUT vowel
when it is in final position (and especially when it is in utterance-final position), and occasionally also in word-initial position, and with the KIT vowel
when it is in other positions. This corresponds to the *comm*A vowel in RP, but
also to the *hors*ES vowel, since *chatted* and *chattered*, *villages* and *villagers*
are homophones for nearly all New Zealand English speakers.

*comm*A, *hors*ES	ɘ, ə, ɜ, ɐ
*happ*Y	i, ə̣i, iˑ
*treac*LE	ɯ, ɔ̣, o, ʊ, u, ɤ

In phonemic transcriptions we use the first symbols in all of these sets.

2.3.   The consonant system

The consonant system of New Zealand English is set out in the table. There
is nothing unexpected in this system except possibly the lack of /ʍ/, which is
discussed below.

	Bilabial	Labio-dental	Dental	Alveolar	Post-alveolar	Palatal	Velar	Glottal
Plosive	p b			t d			k g	
Affricate					tʃ dʒ			
Fricative		f v	θ ð	s z	ʃ ʒ			h
Nasal	m			n			ŋ	
Lateral approximant				l				
Approximant	w				r	j		

Some conservative speakers still maintain a voiceless labial-velar fricative [ʍ] in words like *when* and *whimper*, but this may be represented as /hw/ when it occurs. It seems likely that where this feature is retained it now serves to mark regionalism or social status.

The glottal plosive [ʔ] may be argued to be gaining phonemic status in word-final position in utterances such as [ʃʌʔ ʌʔ] *shut up*, though for many speakers it occurs only as an allophone of /t/ except where it is reinforcing one of [p, t, k, tʃ].

3. The vowels

3.1. The acoustic structure of the vowels

Published values for formants 1 and 2 in the more monophthongal of New Zealand English vowels are presented in the table below. In the table headings, M means 'male' and F means 'female'. A represents speakers from Auckland, analyzed by Hall (1976), C represents speakers from Christchurch analyzed by Maclagan (1982), and G represents speakers recorded in Dunedin but coming from throughout New Zealand and analyzed by Watson, Harrington, and Evans (1998). It is thus possible that there are diachronic and regional differences between the speakers sampled. See also Easton and Bauer (2000).

Table 1.   Published values for New Zealand English vowel formants

Vowel	Formant	AM	CF	CM	GF	GM
FLEECE	F1	378	370	350	349	273
	F2	2300	2750	2400	2022	2325
KIT	F1	489	500	460	598	487
	F2	1922	2200	1800	2022	1710
DRESS	F1	467	420	410	455	365
	F2	2144	2600	2200	2662	2248
TRAP	F1	631	680	580	701	579
	F2	1939	2460	2000	2278	1951
STRUT	F1	747	920	800	952	759
	F2	1525	1600	1500	1577	1303
START	F1	783	920	800	985	789
	F2	1478	1520	1480	1583	1315
LOT	F1	677	780	620	739	615
	F2	1119	1200	1080	1132	964
FORCE	F1	444	430	410	438	384
	F2	800	900	700	769	713
FOOT	F1	431	550	490	562	472
	F2	1111	1140	1100	1223	1044
GOOSE	F1	339	420	410	365	287
	F2	1778	1600	1600	1926	1605
NURSE	F1	450	430	440	492	430
	F2	1721	1900	1750	1954	1630

3.2.   The short vowels

The short front vowels are the site of the vowel shift which is so characteristic of New Zealand English (as of other varieties, especially southern-hemisphere varieties). Fundamentally, this means that KIT, DRESS and TRAP are phonetically displaced one slot clockwise from their equivalent vowels in conservative RP. This will be seen in the descriptions of the individual vowels below.

KIT

The KIT vowel in New Zealand English is notoriously centralized, to such an extent that it is parodied by Australians using their STRUT vowel. While KIT is rarely as open as this suggests in New Zealand English, it is very centralized, probably varying between [ə] and [ə] or [ə̈]. The KIT vowel provides one of the shibboleths for distinguishing between Australian and New Zealand speakers, the phrase *fish and chips* being one which causes hilarity on both sides of the Tasman when spoken by people from the other side of the sea.

Because of the very central quality of this vowel, there is no phonetic distinction between the KIT vowel and the *comm*A vowel where that occurs in non-final position. In other words, *comm*A and *hors*ES do not contrast phonemically, leading to homophony between *boarded* and *bordered*, and also between *effect* and *affect*. The first type of homophony is occasionally overcome by the use of the NURSE vowel in *bordered*, especially in slow speech or if a distinction is to be drawn. The second type may be overcome by the use of full vowels [iː] and [æ] respectively, even in less careful speech.

The vowel before [ŋ] in words like *sing* and *coming* requires some comment. It is much closer than other variants of the KIT vowel, and is regularly associated with the FLEECE vowel by students. Theoretically, there are at least three possibilities here: (i) it is a close allophone of the same vowel as in KIT; (ii) it is an allophone of the vowel in FLEECE, and the only tense vowel permitted before [ŋ]; (iii) it is a stressed variant of the *happ*Y vowel. It is not clear how these possibilities are to be distinguished from each other. For some speakers, but not all, the same variant is found before [g] in words like *big*, *wriggle* (the latter forming a minimal pair with *regal*). Close variants before other consonants are sporadic.

If vowels are to be paired in terms of length/tension, then in New Zealand English the KIT vowel should be paired with the NURSE vowel, as being the closest long vowel in terms of quality. Thus, *bid* and *bird* may for some speakers be distinguished primarily by vowel length.

DRESS

The DRESS vowel is close in New Zealand, even by Australian standards, and may overlap with the FLEECE vowel in terms of its formant structure, although more central variants are also common.

There is neutralization with SQUARE before /r/ (making *ferry* and *fairy* homophonous) and neutralization with TRAP before /l/ (as in *Ellen* and *Alan*).

If vowels are to be paired in terms of length/tension, then in New Zealand English the DRESS vowel should be paired with the FLEECE vowel, as being the closest long vowel in terms of quality.

TRAP

The New Zealand English TRAP vowel is close even by Australian standards, and unlike the corresponding vowel in RP and some varieties of Australian English, shows no signs of becoming opener as yet. As in many other varieties of English, there is some evidence of a TRAP-split, with longer and shorter versions potentially contrasting in pairs such as *banned* and *band*. There is neutralization with DRESS before /l/, whether or not the /l/ is in a coda. TRAP cannot be easily paired with any long vowel in New Zealand English.

STRUT

STRUT is a near-open central-to-front vowel [ɐ] or [ɐ̝]. The STRUT vowel may occur syllable-finally in expressions like *See ya!*, or the word *the* used as a citation form, though even here it may be followed by [ʔ]. Word or phrase-final vowels in words like *colour, data, koala, structure, tuatara* may be open enough to fall into the same area of the vowel chart as the STRUT vowel.

If vowels are to be paired in terms of length/tension, then in New Zealand English the STRUT vowel should be paired with the START vowel, with which it is virtually identical in terms of formant structure, resulting in a distinction primarily of length between *cut* and *cart*.

LOT

The LOT vowel is slightly more centralized than its RP congener, and could be transcribed as [ɒ̈]. There is neutralization with GOAT before coda-/l/, whether or not the /l/ is vocalized. Thus *doll* and *dole* are not distinguishable as they are in RP. For some speakers, the vowel here may be phonemically distinct from both LOT and GOAT. We refer to this above as the GOLD vowel. Note though that none of the speakers in our sample data appear to have this as a distinct vowel.

LOT cannot be easily paired with any long vowel in New Zealand English.

FOOT

The FOOT vowel appears to be undergoing a dramatic diachronic change which leaves it with two very different variants, distinguished at the moment in terms of their lexical occurrence. The conservative value is a centralized back slightly rounded vowel, [ʊ], while the innovative value is much more a central vowel and unrounded. The innovative value is particularly common in the word *good*. It is long established in the greeting *good day* (frequently written as <gidday>), but has spread into other uses of the word *good*. Although there is danger of overlap with the KIT vowel, this does not appear to be happening, and accordingly we choose to transcribe this variant as [ɨ].

The FOOT vowel is neutralized with several other vowels before /l/. FOOT and GOOSE are neutralized before /l/ in words like *full* and *fool*. Here the vocalization of the /l/ makes it disappear entirely, and we are left with a long back rounded vowel, [uː]. There is also neutralization with KIT before /l/ in pairs like *fill* and *full*. If all three are not neutralized together, the outcome here may be a back rounded vowel, not as long as that for *fool*. This neutralization does not occur before onset-/l/.

If vowels are to be paired in terms of length/tension, then in New Zealand English the FOOT vowel should be paired with the THOUGHT vowel, with which it is sometimes virtually identical in terms of formant structure, so that *put* and *port* may differ only in vowel length.

3.3.   The long vowels

FLEECE

The FLEECE vowel is usually slightly diphthongized. It is a rising diphthong (Catford 1977: 216) with a very brief first element, which may nevertheless be quite open.

FLEECE and NEAR are neutralized before an /l/, so that *reel* and *real* are never distinct. They are also neutralized before an /r/, so that *searing* rhymes with *key-ring* (and *caring* and *key-ring* may be homophonous where the NEAR-SQUARE merger applies). In both these cases the vowel heard is monophthongal rather than diphthongal.

BATH, PALM, START

The phonetic quality of this vowel overlaps with the quality for STRUT. The difference between the two is purely length for many speakers, as in the *cut*, *cart* example cited earlier.

Modern New Zealanders use this same vowel in words like *dance* and *example*. Although there are New Zealanders (particularly conservative South Island speakers) who use the TRAP vowel in this environment, and although there are Australian speakers who use the same vowel in *dance* and *palm*, this is perceived as a shibboleth distinguishing Australian and New Zealand varieties of English.

THOUGHT, NORTH, FORCE

This vowel is pronounced very close, near to Cardinal 7 position. This also makes it the backest vowel in New Zealand English. For some speakers, there is overlap in quality between FOOT and THOUGHT, the two being distinguished by length.

This vowel is frequently diphthongized in long positions, and may become disyllabic in free position, especially when utterance-final, e.g. [foˑɐ] *four*.

GOOSE

The GOOSE vowel is very front, and should probably be considered a front rather than a central vowel. It is, for example, much fronter than the RP GOOSE vowel, and comparable to the Australian and South African qualities. When it is followed by /l/ as in *school*, the /l/ vanishes and the quality of the vowel becomes genuinely back. Consequently, *spoon* and *spool* sound extremely different. This contrasts with the situation in, say, New South Wales or Victoria, and acts as a shibboleth in distinguishing Australian and New Zealand varieties of English.

The GOOSE vowel may be diphthongized. When it is, it is a rising diphthong, with a very short first element, which may nevertheless be quite open, starting from near [ə]. However, this is changing. In the phrase *thank you*, shop assistants regularly use an extremely wide diphthong, which almost sounds like the GOAT vowel. This may be a sign of an impending change in New Zealand English: not long ago it was a pronunciation heard only in the speech of children.

NURSE

Acoustic studies of the NURSE vowel show it overlapping with the GOOSE vowel. This implies a very close pronunciation of NURSE, perhaps [ø]. Impressionistically, this seems like quite a broad pronunciation, with more open variants being more prestigious. Given this overlap, it becomes an open question as to how GOOSE and NURSE are distinguished; there does not appear to be any merger, and yet the difference in diphthongization is not necessarily present. There may be a potential or incipient merger here: personalized car number plates show re-spellings such as *2MIN8OR* for 'terminator' suggesting that a NURSE-GOOSE merger is on the cards.

Particularly in formal or slow speech, NURSE is used in many positions where RP would have /ə/, notably where it corresponds to an <er> orthography.

3.4. The diphthongs

Diphthong shift applies to FACE, PRICE and CHOICE in New Zealand English, moving them one slot anti-clockwise from their position in RP. NEAR and SQUARE are variably merged, with many young speakers unable to distinguish them now.

FACE

The starting point for the FACE diphthong is considerably opener in New Zealand English than for its RP equivalent, to the extent that it may be perceived as PRICE by British speakers.

PRICE

The starting point for the PRICE diphthong is considerably further back in New Zealand English than in RP, to the extent that it may be perceived as CHOICE by British speakers. This confusion is understandable when speakers of a broad variety are heard, since they may also round the first element of the diphthong, giving something like [ɒe]. Many speakers retain an unrounded first element, [ɑe]. PRICE + /ə/ in words like *fire* either results in a disyllabic sequence or may result in a monophthong, probably the same phoneme as in BATH/PALM/START.

CHOICE

The first element of the CHOICE diphthong is raised, approximately to the position of the THOUGHT vowel.

GOAT

The GOAT diphthong has a very open and central starting position. The second element usually corresponds to a pronunciation of the GOOSE vowel. However, for some speakers, especially in the word *no* or where the vowel falls under the tonic syllable, the final element is becoming unrounded, giving a pronunciation like [ɐɪ] or [ɐi].

MOUTH

MOUTH has a relatively close starting position, with closer variants belonging to broader variants of the New Zealand accent. New tokens of MOUTH are arising from DRESS or TRAP plus vocalized /l/, so that words like *twelve*, *self* and *health* often contain a vowel which, if it is not identical with MOUTH, is extremely close phonetically. Not only is this creating new tokens of MOUTH, it is widening the distribution of MOUTH, which can occur before labials (*help*) and velars (*talc*).

MOUTH + unstressed /ə/ in words like *tower* either results in a disyllabic sequence or results in a monophthong, probably to be associated with the BATH/PALM/START phoneme, although closer values than for BATH/PALM/START can be heard.

NEAR, SQUARE

The NEAR and SQUARE diphthongs are undergoing merger in New Zealand English, and many young speakers not only fail to distinguish the two in production but also have difficulty perceiving the distinction. There is some debate as to the direction of the merger (see Gordon and Maclagan, this volume), but the consensus appears to be that it is towards a close variant, [iə]. Monophthongal vowels are produced by some speakers, especially before /l/ and /r/, resulting in the neutralization of FLEECE and NEAR in this position, and also therefore of FLEECE and SQUARE for speakers who merge NEAR and SQUARE. Word pairs like *merry* and *Mary* are as a result distinguished largely by vowel length.

CURE

The CURE diphthong has a starting point comparable to that of GOOSE, and an open central end-point. When the vowel occurs in open position, it may become disyllabic.

GOOSE and CURE are neutralized before /r/, where the vowel heard is monophthongal rather than diphthongal. There is no contrast before /l/ either.

The CURE vowel is heard in New Zealand English only following /j/. In words like *poor*, *moor*, *tour* it has been largely replaced by FORCE. The overall result is that the CURE vowel has very little functional load in New Zealand English.

4. The consonants

4.1. The plosives

The voiceless velar plosive is usually affricated (released with audible friction at the point of articulation) in all positions. Alveolar [t] is affricated initially in stressed syllables, but usually voiced and tapped between sonorants in words such as *getting*, *butter*, *bottle*. The tapping may occur over word-boundaries as well as within words, both within a foot and over foot-boundaries. (A foot here is a sequence of a stressed syllable and any following unstressed syllables up to but not including the next stressed syllable.) It occurs over word-boundaries only where the /t/ is word-final, e.g. in *get eggs*. In *a tall person*, aspiration/affrication of /t/ blocks the tapping. There are some slight indications that a glottal plosive may be starting to replace this tap, but it is too soon to say whether this feature will spread. A glottal plosive [ʔ] is in free variation with an affricated plosive in final position. The bilabial [p] can be heard aspirated in all positions. Both [p] and [k] and also [tʃ] may get glottal reinforcement in word-final position, and this variant seems to be gaining ground rapidly, having been virtually unknown in the 1970s. After syllable-initial [s], [p, t, k] are unaspirated.

The so-called voiced plosives have very little voicing, and are distinguished from their voiceless counterparts mainly by their lack of aspiration/affrication. There may be no phonetic difference between an intervocalic /t/ and an intervocalic /d/, but this has not been carefully analyzed.

4.2. The fricatives

The most important feature of the fricatives is the devoicing of the so-called voiced fricatives. It is not always clear whether the devoicing is phonemic or just phonetic, nor whether the same cause underlies all instances of fricative-devoicing. For example the pronunciation of *thither* with an initial [θ] is probably a lexical difference, parallel with the pronunciation found in Scottish English and some American varieties. The pronunciation of *president* as though homophonous with *precedent* seems more like a process of devoicing, which is currently variable in New Zealand English. There may nevertheless be a lexical dimension to this devoicing: *president, positive* seem particularly susceptible to it. So far, studies of the phenomenon have not distinguished between phonetic devoicing and vowel-shortening, so that it is not always clear whether a phonemic distinction is being lost or not. Certainly, it seems to be true that there is more sibilant-devoicing than there is corresponding vowel-shortening.

In /stj/ and /str/ clusters we find complex assimilation taking place. In /stj/ clusters there is coalescent assimilation of the /tj/ to [tʃ], and the post-alveolar quality is then passed on to the /s/ to give [ʃtʃ], frequently heard in words like *student*. In /str/ clusters, the very slight retroflection of the /r/ was originally passed to the whole of the cluster, giving something that we might transcribe as [ʂʈɭ] (although this seems to imply greater retroflexion than is actually found), but this has been reinterpreted by younger speakers as [ʃtɹ], as in words like *strange*.

/θ/ and /ð/ in New Zealand are usually interdental fricatives rather than post-dental fricatives. An apparently innovative dental variant of /s/ has been described in studies carried out in Auckland, but it is not yet clear whether this is a regionalism or how widespread it is. There is some loss of /θ/ in favour of /f/, but this is not yet a major tendency.

4.3.   /r/ and /l/

4.3.1.   Variable rhoticity

New Zealand English is usually described as being non-rhotic except for the Southland-Otago area where non-pre-vocalic /r/ is pronounced. Both characterizations leave something to be desired.

First, although it is true that standard New Zealand English is generally non-rhotic, there are two words which are frequently heard with a non-prevocalic /r/. The first of these is the name of the consonant 'R', and the second is the name of the country *Ireland*. These are both heard with [ɹ] across social classes and across regions.

Other words or phrases are heard with sporadic non-prevocalic /r/. Expressions and catchwords borrowed from American TV programmes or movies are frequently pronounced with a pseudo-American /r/. Such expressions include *whatever, wiener* (as a term of abuse among children). This type of /r/-usage is clearly lexically driven.

Some types of popular music appear to use non-prevocalic /r/ more systematically. A recent study of New Zealand hip-hop music by one of our students found that non-prevocalic /r/ was used systematically after the NURSE vowel (*bird, heard*), but nowhere else. This is despite the fact that this type of music is usually produced by people of Maori or Pacific Island ethnicities, who have no obvious reason to be more rhotic than anyone else.

Finally, although it is true that the Southland-Otago region is more rhotic than other parts of New Zealand, the rhoticity is variable. It is particularly prevalent following the NURSE vowel, much rarer elsewhere (despite the fact that one of the words in which this type of pronunciation is most aped by the general populace is the word *Gore*, the name of the town perceived as being central to the area of rhoticity).

4.3.2. Consonant quality and vocalization

Both /r/ and /l/ are devoiced in stressed onset position when preceded by a voiceless plosive. In this position, /l/ is usually pronounced [ɬ], though /r/ is not consistently fricated. Devoicing following voiceless fricatives (in words like *free*, *flea*, *slide*, *shrimp*) is much less marked, and may be absent. We find fricative /r/ after both /t/ and /d/, voiceless in the first case, voiced in the second, e.g. in *train* and *drain*.

Like RP, New Zealand English has clearly different allophones of /l/ in onset and in coda position. In onset position we usually find a slightly velarized lateral, [lˠ]. In coda position there is variation between a 'darker' lateral, perhaps [lˀ], and a vowel of variable quality. This vocalized /l/ may merge with the preceding vowel (and recall that the number of contrasts before /l/ is diminished) to form a diphthong, or it may form a disyllabic sequence. Some typical outcomes are transcribed below.

milk   mɤk, mɪɯk, hypercorrect mɪlʲk

smile   smɑo, smɑe.ʉ, smɐe.ɯ

bottle   bɒtɯ, bɒtʉ, bɒto, bɒtə̈lˤ

help   hæʉp, hɐ̈ʉp (NB: there is potential clash with MOUTH here)

feels   fiː.ʉz, fiː.ʊz, fiː.oz

One of the results of this is that most New Zealand speakers do not have a dental allophone of /l/, since the places where dental allophones arise in other varieties are precisely those where there is a vowel in New Zealand English.

Following /θ/, /r/ is variably realized as [ɾ] in words like *through*, *three*.

4.3.3. Linking /r/ and linking /l/ (or [w]) in New Zealand

Like other non-rhotic varieties of English, New Zealand English has both linking and intrusive /r/, and in precisely the same environments for which these are described in RP, for example. The interesting thing is that both appear to be variable, although really thorough studies of these phenomena are just beginning. A phrase such as *far off* may be pronounced as any of [fɐːɹɒf], [fɐːɒf], [fɐːəɒf], [fɐːʔɒf]. Self-conscious speech appears to prefer the version with [ʔ]. At the same time, however, the use of intrusive /r/ is being extended to an environment following MOUTH. A common word in which this is heard is *how*[ɹ]*ever*. It is not entirely clear why only MOUTH is affected. It might be assumed that such intrusion would take place only when MOUTH was monophthongized (and thus phonetically similar to START), but that does not seem to hold true.

Just as linking /r/ developed with the vocalization of /r/, so a linking /l/ is developing with the vocalization of /l/. A word-final /l/ followed by a word-initial vowel in the same breath-group is resyllabified, and the onset-allophone is realized. This (along with speaker intuition – probably strongly influenced by orthography) is the strongest argument for seeing the vocalized version as still being an allophone of /l/. However, there is an alternative to a linking /l/, though it is not as common: it is linking /w/. Occasional pronunciations such as [fiːwət] for *feel it* are heard alongside the expected [fiːlʲət]. Such pronunciations suggest that the vocalization is starting to be reinterpreted as a new series of vowels. So far, linking [w] does not appear to be found word-internally.

4.4.   Glides

A distinction between /w/ and /hw/ was robust in New Zealand into the 1960s, distinguishing *Wales* from *whales* and *witch* from *which*, but now seems to be receding quickly. It has gone from the North Island except in a few conservative individuals and is in retreat in the South Island. It may end up being retained as a regional marker, though this currently seems unlikely.

/w/ and /j/ are strongly devoiced following stressed-syllable-initial [p, t, k], and we could transcribe [tʍiːk], [cçʉː], [pçʉːtə] for *tweak, queue, pewter*. Similar devoicing of /j/ is found in words like *huge, hue* [çʉːdʒ, çʉː].

There is often a rather strong palatal or labial-velar glide following respectively a front or back vowel in hiatus with another vowel. So in examples such as *see it, allowing, doing, happiest* there may be a stronger glide element than would be expected in RP, although there is still a distinction to be drawn between the glides in, for example, *do one* and *do unlikely things*.

Yod-dropping is variable in New Zealand English. After /r/ in words like *rule*, /j/ has vanished, as elsewhere in English. After /l/, in words like *lewd*, *illuminate*, it is extremely rare, though it is retained where the relevant syllable does not carry primary stress in words like *prelude*. After /θ/ in words like *enthuse*, yod is very rare. After /s, z/ the presence or absence of yod is to some extent determined by the environment. In *Zurich*, which provides the only potential case of /zjʉ/ the /j/ is variable (possibly reflecting the German [y] pronunciation of the vowel, see below). After most /s/ types it has virtually vanished: for example *Susan* would never have a /j/ and *super(intendent)*, *superstitious* etc. have /j/ only extremely rarely from very conservative speakers (these were still occasionally heard fifteen years ago, but have become much rarer). In the set of words including *assume, consume, presume, resume* there are many competing pronunciations. If we take *assume* as a model, we can find any of /əsjuːm/, /əʃuːm/, /əsuːm/, /əʃjuːm/, and the same variants arise for the other words in this set. The first of these is perceived as being the most standard, but the others are common. These words are the only place where /ʃj/ clusters can arise. The clusters /tj/ and /dj/ usually coalesce to affricates, but there are a few exceptional words: *tuna* is usually /tuːnə/ whether the large salt-water fish or the eel (from Maori *tuna*) is intended. The orthography <tu> never gives rise to /tjuː/ pronunciations in Maori words. Yod-dropping is variable after /n/, especially in a few lexemes including *new* (particularly in *New Zealand, Air New Zealand* and similar high frequency collocations), *nude* and *nuisance*. The orthography <nu> in Maori words is nevertheless sometimes pronounced as /njuː/.

The glide /w/ is also regularly dropped in the words *quart* and *quarter*, with the result that *quart* and *court/caught* become homophonous. It is not clear whether this is lexical or due to the phonological environment, since there are so few words which fit this pattern.

5.　The pronunciation of Maori words in New Zealand English

A political language issue in New Zealand is the pronunciation of Maori words when they are used in English. Broadly, we can sketch two extreme positions: (i) an assimilationist position, according to which all Maori words are pronounced as English, and (ii) a nativist position, according to which all Maori words are pronounced as near to the original Maori pronunciation as possible. There are, of course, intermediate positions in actual usage. Some of the variation is caused by the fact that the original Maori pronunciation may not be easily determinable. Not only is vowel length sometimes variable even in traditional Maori, in some cases the etymology of place names may be in dispute within the Maori community (*Paraparaumu* provides an instance of this, where it is not clear whether the final *umu* is to be interpreted as 'earth oven' or not).

Where vowels are concerned, the major difficulty in pronouncing Maori words with their original values is that vowel length (usually marked by macrons in Maori orthography, as in *Māori*) is rarely marked on public notices. Not only can this affect the way in which the particular vowel is pronounced, it can affect stress placement as well, since stress in Maori words is derivable from moraic structure. The reluctance to use macrons in public documents may simply be a typographical problem (even today with computer fonts easily available, very few newspapers or journals appear to have fonts with macrons available to them), but in the past has also been supported by the sentiments of Maori speakers who have found the macron unaesthetic. There may be good linguistic reasons for this, though they remain largely unexplored. The point is that although all vowels show contrastive length in Maori, long may be pronounced as short and short may be pronounced as long in English. Since Maori has no reduced vowels while English tends to reduce vowels in unstressed syllables (though this is less true of New Zealand English than it is of RP), almost any Maori vowel may be reduced under appropriate prosodic conditions. Where toponyms are concerned, there has also been a very strong Pakeha tradition towards abbreviating the longer names (a tradition which does not appear to spread to English names). For example, Paraparaumu is frequently called *Paraparam*, the Waimakariri river is called the *Waimak*, Wainuiomata is frequently called *Wainui*. While there is also a tradition for the abbreviation of names within Maori itself, and the two traditions may support each other to some extent, they appear to be largely distinct traditions with different outcomes. Pakeha abbreviations of toponyms are frowned upon within the nativist position on the pronunciation of Maori.

Table 2 shows a range of possible pronunciations of the individual vowels of Maori, assuming that length has been correctly transferred to English. Table 3 provides some typical examples with a range of possible pronunciations, going from most nativist to most assimilationist. Maori pronunciations are also heard, and these may be considered to provide instances of code-shifting.

Table 2. Typical values for vowels in Maori loan words used in English

Maori vowel	Short		Long	
	Nativist	**Assimilationist**	**Nativist**	**Assimilationist**
i	ə	ə	iː	iː
ɛ	e, æe / __ #	e, i / __ #	æe	æe
a	ɐ	ɛ	ɐː	ɐː
ɔ	ɒ	ɒ	oː	ɐʉ
u	ʊ	ʊ, ɐ	ʉː	ʉː , jʉː

Table 3. Some examples of Maori loan words in New Zealand English

Word	Maori value	English values
Aotearoa 'New Zealand'	aɔˈtɛarɔa	ˌ̞ɐːɔtæeɔˈɹ̞oːə, ˌæeɔtiːəˈɹ̞ɐɐ
katipo 'poisonous spider'	katiˈpɔː	ˈkɐtɔpɐɐ, ˈkɛtipɐɐ
manuka 'tree species'	ˈmaːnɐka	ˈmɐːnəkə, məˈnɐːkə
pohutukawa 'tree species'	pɔːˈhɐtɐkawa	pəˌhɐːtəˈkɐːwə
taonga 'property, treasure'	ˈtaɔŋa	ˈtæɐŋə, tæeˈɒŋɡə
Wanganui toponym	waŋaˈnɐi	wɒŋəˈnɐi, wɒŋəˈnjɐi, wɒŋɡəˈnjɐi

The assimilation of /a/ to /ɔ/ after /w/ appears also to be a feature of Maori, at last in some varieties.

Maori diphthongs and vowel sequences do not transfer well to English. Maori /aɛ/ and /ɔɛ/ are merged with Maori /ai/ and /ɔi/ respectively as English /ɑe/ and /oe/. Similarly Maori /aɔ/ and /au/ may not be distinguished in English. Maori /au/, which in modern Maori is pronounced with a very central and raised allophone of /a/, is replaced by /ɐɐ/ in nativist pronunciations (where it may merge with Maori /ɔu/), but by /æɐ/ in assimilationist pronunciations. Because of the NEAR-SQUARE merger in New Zealand English, Maori /ia/ and /ɛa/ are not distinguished in English. Maori /ɛu/ is often transferred into English as /jɐː/ (presumably on the basis of the orthography). Vowel sequences are transferred to English as sequences of the nearest appropriate vowel, but often involve vowel reduction in English which would not be used in Maori.

Most Maori consonants have obvious and fixed correspondents in English, although this has not always been so. Some early borrowings show English /b, d, ɡ/ for Maori (unaspirated) /p, t, k/ and occasionally English /d/ for Maori tapped /r/: for example English *biddybid* is from Maori *piripiri*. The phonetic qualities of the voiceless plosives and /r/ are now modified to fit with English habits. However, Maori /ŋ/ is variably reproduced in English as /ŋ/ or as /ŋɡ/, especially when morpheme internal. (See the pronunciations of *Wanganui* given in Table 3.) Word-initial /ŋ/ is always replaced in English by /n/. The Maori /f/, written as <wh>, has variable realizations in English. This is partly due to the orthography, partly due to variation in the relevant sounds in both English and Maori: [ʍ] is now rare as a rendering of graphic <wh> in English, and the /f/ pronunciation is an attempt at standardising variants as disparate as [f], [ʍ], [ɸ], [ʔw]. The toponym *Whangarei* may be pronounced /fæŋɐræe, fɐŋəræe, wɒŋəræe, wɒŋɡəræe/.

6.   Lexical distribution

There are not many differences in lexical distribution of vowels between New Zealand English and RP. The most obvious differences are listed below.

basic	in old-fashioned pronunciation had TRAP in the first syllable, particularly in the combination *basic slag*; now FACE is usual
because	variation between LOT, THOUGHT and STRUT
geyser	always has stressed PRICE in the first syllable
gross	pronounced with GOAT when a children's term meaning 'disgusting', often pronounced with LOT by adults in other meanings
maroon	sometimes heard with GOAT in the second syllable
off	a rare THOUGHT is still heard alongside the usual LOT
project	variably pronounced with LOT or GOAT in the first syllable
pronunciation	non-standardly but frequently pronounced with MOUTH in the second syllable
proven	often pronounced with GOAT in the stressed syllable as an alternative to GOOSE
tuna	frequently has no yod
vitamin	always has stressed PRICE in the first syllable
women	pronounced as homophonous with *woman*, with FOOT in the first syllable
worry	increasingly with LOT
yoghurt	has GOAT in the first syllable

When French loan-words which have /y/ in French are pronounced in New Zealand English, the /y/ is replaced with GOOSE rather than with a /j/ and then GOOSE. So we find things like *debut* /dæebʉː/.

There is a marked tendency to spelling-pronunciation in New Zealand English. *Trentham* is pronounced with /θ/ (although *Thames*, *Thomas* and *Thompson* are not); *Davis* will be pronounced differently from *Davies*; *Catriona* is frequently pronounced /kætriˈʉnə/; *occurrence*, *deterrent* with NURSE as the stressed vowel are not infrequent; *Wednesday* may still be heard pronounced with two /d/s. Many other examples are heard sporadically.

7. Prosodic features

7.1. Lexical stress placement

Lexical stress in New Zealand English largely conforms to the pattern of RP. A few differences have been noted, such as *spectator*, *dictator* and *frustrate* stressed on the first syllable, and *agriculture* variably on first or third, as well as a tendency towards strong secondary stress in words ending in *-ary/-ory*. Some of these patterns may be attributable to the influence of other Englishes on New Zealand English such as Scottish English, or possibly American English in the case of *spectator*, *dictator* and *frustrate*.

Unpublished studies of bisyllabic verb/noun pairs such as *import* and *survey* show that these also largely conform to the pattern of second syllable stress for verbs and first syllable stress for the noun, with the qualification that stress placement for the verb forms appears to be more variable.

7.2. Rhythm

The use of full vowels in unstressed syllables in New Zealand English has been noted for some time. It affects both weak monosyllabic words – mainly function words – and weak syllables in polysyllabic words. A number of reasons can be conjectured for some of these full vowel forms. One is the unclear distinction between *comm*A and *hors*ES, meaning that contrasts which in other varieties may be dependent on this (e.g. *affect* vs. *effect*) are realized differently – if at all – in New Zealand English. Another is spelling pronunciation, possibly accounting for a full vowel in the first syllable of *botanical* and *placate*, for instance. A third factor involves the rhythm of New Zealand English, which has been claimed to be more syllable-timed than in other varieties. This tendency towards syllable-timing (which is not nearly as marked as for some varieties such as Singapore English) is reflected in the equalization of stressed and unstressed syllables (full vowels for reduced, long vowels for short), as well as in overall timing structures. Contact with the Maori language, with its mora-based timing, could have contributed to the rhythmic pattern of New Zealand English (see the chapter on Maori English).

7.3. Intonation

The most widely noted intonational feature of New Zealand English is the High Rising Terminal, a rising nucleus high in the speaker's pitch range that is found on declaratives. This feature is not unique to New Zealand English. Sociolinguistic studies have shown that this feature is a positive politeness marker, and functions to include the hearer in the discourse. Other aspects of New Zealand English intonation that have been commented on include a relatively 'flat' but high intonation pattern through most of the tone unit, with extreme and quite sudden nuclear pitch movements.

Exercises and study questions

1. Many listeners not familiar with Antipodean varieties of English find it difficult to distinguish between New Zealand English and Australian English. Some of the characteristic distinguishing features have been commented on in our discussion of the vowels of New Zealand English. Listen to the vowels in the word list of New Zealand English on the CD-ROM. Which vowel sounds appear to be most reliable in identifying this variety?

2. The pattern of realization of the short front vowels in New Zealand English has been described in terms of a "second Great Vowel Shift" (Bauer 1979). On the basis of evidence from the audio samples and comparison with the corresponding vowels in Received Pronunciation, what is the nature of this vowel shift?

3. What evidence is there of /l/-vocalization in the conversation sample of two 20-year-old females (cf. free passage on CD-ROM)? How variable is /l/-vocalization in the speech of these young speakers?

4. To what extent is the realization of the MOUTH and FACE diphthongs determined by stylistic differences between the word list and conversational data of the 20-year-old females (cf. free passage)?

5. Comment on the pattern of glottal articulation of voiceless plosives (including glottalization and/or glottal replacement) in the audio sample of conversational speech of the two 20-year-old females (cf. free passage).

Selected references

Please consult the General references for titles mentioned in the text but not included in the references below. For a full bibliography see the accompanying CD-ROM.

Catford, John C.
   1977   *Fundamental Problems in Phonetics*. Edinburgh: Edinburgh University Press.
Easton, Anita and Laurie Bauer
   2000   An acoustic study of the vowels of New Zealand English. *Australian Journal of Linguistics* 20: 93–117.
Hall, Moira
   1976   An acoustic analysis of New Zealand vowels. M.A. thesis, University of Auckland.
Maclagan, Margaret A.
   1982   An acoustic study of New Zealand vowels. *The New Zealand Speech Therapists' Journal* 37: 20–26.
Watson, Catherine I., Jonathan Harrington and Zoe Evans
   1998   An acoustic comparison between New Zealand and Australian English vowels. *Australian Journal of Linguistics* 18: 185–207.

Regional and social differences in New Zealand: phonology

Elizabeth Gordon and Margaret Maclagan

1. Historical background

The beginning of the main European settlement of New Zealand is usually dated from 1840, when representatives of the British government signed the Treaty of Waitangi with about 430 Maori chiefs. From 1840 to 1880 the European population of New Zealand grew from about 2,000 people to half a million and by the 1880s the number of New-Zealand-born in the non-Maori population had exceeded the number of immigrants. In this period between 1840 and 1880 the immigrants came mainly from the British Isles; 49% came from England, 22% from Scotland, 20% from Ireland and 7% from Australia (McKinnon 1997). The first immigrants came to planned settlements, established by the New Zealand Company, where there was some attempt to control the mix and the nature of the colonists. This soon proved to be ineffectual, and in 1861 with the discovery of gold thousands of immigrants arrived in an unplanned way, including considerable numbers of Irish Catholics, a group the original planners had tried to exclude. In the 1860s, there was a period of conflict, now known as the New Zealand Wars, between Europeans and certain North Island Maori tribes, which saw large numbers of soldiers brought into New Zealand. They were given land when they were eventually discharged and they also became settlers. In the 1870s, large numbers of immigrants arrived, recruited and paid for by the New Zealand government. In 1874 alone, 32,000 assisted immigrants arrived in New Zealand.

The early settlers were a diverse collection of people who had come to New Zealand for a better life. We know that in spite of different circumstances, historical events and social situations, in a relatively short period of time very different individuals in all parts of the country were beginning to develop a common language, so that by the end of the 19th century complaints were being heard all over New Zealand of a "colonial twang", something akin to "Austral English" (though not quite so bad) the product of "the home and the street". Throughout the early part of the 20th century the complaints grew in number and ferocity. The new New Zealand accent was said to be an abomination, so bad that it could even cause "minor throat and chest disorders" (quoted in

Gordon and Deverson 1998: 162). At the same time there were consistent complaints about New Zealanders who tried to emulate Received Pronunciation (RP). A member of a Commission on Education in 1912 complained: "What hope is there for change when we find two of the Principals of the largest secondary schools in New Zealand in giving evidence, using these expressions: 'taim-table' for 'time-table'; 'Ai' for 'I'; 'may own' for 'my own'; 'faive' for 'five'; 'gairls' for 'girls'." (*Appendices to the Journal of the House of Representatives*, E-12: 624)

Recent research at the University of Canterbury has shown that the earliest manifestations of the New Zealand accent probably occurred much earlier than the appearance of written complaints. The analysis of a 1940s archive of recordings of old New Zealanders, some born as early as the 1850s (the Mobile Unit archive), shows that the rate of development of the NZ accent depended very much on social factors. Speakers from homogeneous towns, like Milton or Kaitangata in Otago for example, where the majority of the settlers came from Scotland, were more likely to retain features of Scottish pronunciation and syntax. Speakers from towns with a very mixed population, like the Otago gold-mining town of Arrowtown, for example, were more likely to develop early manifestations of New Zealand English.

2. Regional variation in New Zealand English

The early immigrants to New Zealand came from all parts of the British Isles and Australia. Of those who came from England (who made up 49% of the total – see above), by far the largest number of immigrants came from the South of England, and this was the trend at every stage of New Zealand's development. People from the south, and in particular the southeast, made up a majority of the earliest settlers in the planned settlements (1840–1852); they made up the majority in later government-assisted immigration schemes (1871–1880). The Southern English influence could also have been reinforced by any Australian influence (seen especially at the time of the gold rush and the New Zealand Wars), as Australia was also settled predominantly from the South of England. So although over 20% of the early immigrants to New Zealand were Scottish and a similar percentage were Irish, in the end their phonological influence was overwhelmed by Southern English; the influence of other areas of the British Isles can be seen only in a few lexical and morphological examples.

Table 1. New Zealand locations of UK immigrants (1871)
(taken from http://www.nzhistory.net.nz/gallery/brit-nz/)

	English	**Scottish**	**Irish**
Auckland	54.9	17.0	27.2
Taranaki	69.6	9.5	20.5
Hawke's Bay	55.2	20.9	23.2
Wellington	63.5	20.0	15.4
Nelson	56.4	15.9	25.9
Marlborough	62.1	20.4	16.4
Canterbury	62.7	16.9	19.4
Westland	40.1	19.9	37.9
Otago	31.0	51.5	16.9
Southland	24.4	61.4	13.9
New Zealand	49.7	27.3	22.0

There is one exception to this general rule, and that is in the Southern part of the South Island of New Zealand – Southland and parts of Otago – where many of the early settlements were predominantly Scottish as shown in Table 1. This influence can still be heard in what is known locally as "the Southland burr", a semi-rhotic variant of New Zealand English (NZE).

Although the Southland variety of NZE is the only regional variety attested by linguists, there are strongly held lay views that there are other dialects of NZE. A recent broadcast series on "Coastal Dialects of NZE", for example, claimed that there were strong regional differences in New Zealand. These programmes based this assertion on recordings of single speakers from different parts of New Zealand, without any linguistic comment or discussion. Work by Pamela Gordon (1997) on attitudes towards varieties of NZE demonstrated strongly held local beliefs about the "pseudo-English" of Christchurch and Canterbury, the slowness of West Coast speech, and so on. The view of linguists is that regional phonological variation in New Zealand (apart from Southland) has so far not been demonstrated. However, new evidence is currently emerging that there are intonational differences in Taranaki in the North Island. Folk linguistic knowledge has described Taranaki intonation as "sing song", and analysis is demonstrating that there are, indeed, more pitch shifts per intonation unit than in other areas of New Zealand. Results like this indicate that detailed analysis may reveal some differences in other regions around the country. Nevertheless such regional differences are minor when compared with those that characterise dialects in other varieties of English, or the Southland variety of NZE to which we now turn.

2.1.   The Southland variety of NZE

The Southland variety of NZE has been commented on for many years but has only recently been the subject of systematic research. In the 1990s Chris Bartlett carried out interviews in Invercargill and rural districts of eastern and central Southland with speakers from three age groups: 15–19 years, 40–49 years and 65 years and over (see Bartlett 1992). He found that while the majority of the phonological features of Southland English (SldE) appear to fall within the normal range of variation for NZE there were also some distinctive features. The primary consonantal feature of SldE is the presence of rhotic forms, which has always been the salient diagnostic feature of the variety. Bartlett indicates that the realisation of postvocalic /r/ in SldE is approximal rather than rolled or flapped. He found considerable variation in the degrees of rhoticity ranging from nearly fully-rhotic speakers (especially older males from rural areas) to non-rhotic speakers. However, partially rhotic speakers were in the majority with extremes being rare. Bartlett's research has shown that phonological context is highly significant in the mechanism of /r/ maintenance (or loss). In words like *first term* (the standard lexical set NURSE) the /r/ is more consistently maintained than in any other context, though in this context it is realised as an r-coloured vowel. Younger speakers produce more tokens of /r/ in this context than do older speakers. The /r/ in word final position (e.g. in *car*) or a syllabic /r/ (e.g. in *letter*) is maintained to widely varying degrees. Preconsonantal /r/ (e.g. *card*, *fort*) is less likely to be maintained by a partially rhotic speaker. Bartlett's research found that rural speakers over the age of 65 were more likely to be rhotic; those aged 40–49 were variably rhotic and those 20–29 were likely to maintain the /r/ only on the NURSE vowel. Examples of speakers from these three age groups are given on the accompanying audio clip.

Bartlett found two other less marked phonological characteristics in his study of Southland. It is often noted that Southland speakers use the TRAP vowel in the BATH lexical set. This usage is declining rapidly, though older Southland speakers still use TRAP in the word *castle* and also in *dance* and *chance*. In younger speakers, TRAP is being replaced by the standard NZE BATH.

He also found that older speakers retained a contrast between /ʍ/ and /w/ as in *which* and *witch*. There was a correlation between the age of the speaker and the extent of /ʍ/ retention, with older speakers retaining /ʍ/ in a greater variety of words. All speakers were more likely to retain it in lexical words than in grammatical words. Bauer and Warren (this volume) note that the /ʍ/ ~ /w/

distinction is disappearing in NZE. It appears to be being retained for a slightly longer time in Southland.

The three Southland speakers in the attached audio clip illustrate the gradual loss of rhoticity in Southland speakers over time. Arthur, aged 77 (the oldest speaker), is rhotic on almost every opportunity. He is rhotic on THOUGHT, START, MOUTH and NEAR as well as NURSE and *lett*ER. The only potential site for rhoticity that is not realised is in *board*. Paul, aged 44 (the middle aged speaker), is considerably more variable. *Never* and *farm* are sometimes pronounced with rhotic vowels and sometimes without. He has two examples of rhotic START (*farm* and *car*), but most of the rhotic vowels are NURSE and *letter*. Jim, aged 16 (the youngest speaker), uses a rhotic vowel for all the tokens of NURSE, but not for *lett*ER or for any other vowels. There are no examples of possible voiceless /ʍ/ in content words for any of the speakers. Arthur, however, uses a voiceless /ʍ/ for *whether*, but not on any other function word. Neither Paul nor Jim use /ʍ/ on function words. There are no examples of *chance* words in these recordings.

3.   Social class variation in New Zealand

The earliest settlements in New Zealand planned by the New Zealand Company aimed to replicate a vertical slice of British society with the top and the bottom levels removed so that there were not large numbers of people from the highest class in Britain or the very lowest class:

> The pioneers of New Zealand were not from the highest, nor were they usually from the most down-trodden sections of British society. They were people who while poor, while usually from the upper working class or lower middle class – 'the anxious classes' Wakefield called them – had lost neither enterprise nor ambition. (Sinclair 1991: 101)

Social class stratification in early New Zealand settlements differed from Britain. The historian James Belich (1996: 321) remarks: "Colonial life blurred class boundaries and mixed together all elements of society. Jack considered himself in many respects as good as his master. But there were still boundaries to blur and elements to mix. Master was still master, and Jack was still Jack". Evidence from the Mobile Unit archive shows that some of those who would have been considered upper class in New Zealand maintained strong ties with Britain and their speech shows little or no evidence of a New Zealand accent. Miss Brenda Bell, for example, a third generation New Zealander born in 1880 in Otago who talks at length about her titled ancestors, and who was educated by an imported English governess, speaks old-fashioned RP. Mrs Catherine Dudley, born six years later also in Otago, who was married to a road mender, is always identified by New Zealand university students as "sounding like a New Zealander".

Although New Zealanders like to portray themselves as a "classless society" it is widely recognised that social class differences exist in present-day New Zealand. Social scientists, however, are very wary of using imported standards of classification. The standard New Zealand index used by social scientists to assign social class (Elley and Irving 1985) is based on occupation, and needs to be used with some caution. The Elley-Irving scale gives a numerical category of 6 to those in the lowest social class (e.g. unskilled labourers and supermarket checkout assistants) and 1 to professional workers (e.g. lawyers, doctors and university lecturers). For recordings in the Canterbury Corpus archive at the University of Canterbury (see Maclagan, Gordon and Lewis 1999), a revised version of the Elley-Irving scale prepared by the New Zealand Ministry of Education (1990) is used for occupations. A 6-point education scale is also used where a rating of 6 is given to those who have no secondary school education and 1 to those with a Ph.D. or higher tertiary degree. The two ratings are combined so that the final social class categorisation is based on both occupation and education.

However, the conventional method of classification used to define social class variation within NZE is the system devised for Australian English by Mitchell and Delbridge (1965) of Cultivated NZE, General NZE and Broad NZE. On a continuum, Cultivated NZE is nearer to RP, and Broad NZE is farthest from RP. These are not discrete categories but rather points on a continuum.

3.1. Cultivated, General and Broad NZE

Differences because of social class are clearly identifiable in present-day NZE. The three young women in the accompanying audio clip were selected in terms of social class. Karen is from a middle social class, Christine from a lower social class and Wendy from a higher social class. However, the recordings can be clearly differentiated linguistically as can be heard in the accompanying audio clip. Wendy speaks Cultivated NZE, Karen General NZE and Christine Broad NZE. The letter they are reading is widely used in investigations of NZE. It contains most of the key vowels in stressed position. The text is given in Table 2.

Table 2.   Text of letter containing features characteristic of NZE

Dear Mum and Dad,

Hi, How are you? Well here I am in the big city. Although the weather is nice at the moment the forecast is for hail, but that should soon clear. I bought a new coat because they say it gets really cold. I have to stay at Auntie Deb's house for now but I'm hoping to get a flat soon.
The trip up was great even though it took about ten hours.
Well I must go. You know how rarely I write, but I'll try to do better this year.
Love,
Claire.

Social class is marked most clearly by the pronunciation of the closing diphthongs, FACE, PRICE, GOAT and MOUTH, with women from higher social classes in particular avoiding pronunciations associated with lower social classes. The front vowels, KIT, DRESS and TRAP and the centring diphthongs NEAR and SQUARE also receive different pronunciations from different social groups. The consonant that shows social class differentiation most clearly is /θ/, which is fronted, so that *think* is pronounced /fɪŋk/ by many speakers from lower social classes. TH-fronting is overtly stigmatised by those who speak Cultivated NZE, and speakers from the higher social classes avoid it. Another consonant which shows social class differentiation is /l/, which is vocalised less by speakers of Cultivated NZE. Cultivated NZE speakers are also less likely to use flaps in words like *city* or to affricate /tr/ and /str/ so that they sound like [tʃɹ̥] and [ʃtɹ̥]. In the previous section, we noted that the /ʍ/ ~ /w/ contrast is still maintained by some speakers in Southland. Some older women from the higher social classes from other parts of the country also maintain this distinction, but more often in reading than in speech. Table 3 compares the pronunciation of Cultivated and Broad speakers of NZE. Most of these features are illustrated in the recordings.

Table 3.   The main differences between Cultivated and Broad NZE

Variable	Cultivated NZE speaker	Broad NZE speaker
kit	ɪ̯	ə
DRESS	e̞	e̞
TRAP	ɛ̞	ɛ̞
FACE	æe̞	ɐe
PRICE	ɑe	ɒ˔e or ɔe

Table 3. (continued)   The main differences between Cultivated and Broad NZE

MOUTH	aʊ	e̞ə
GOAT	ɵʊ	ɐʉ
NEAR/SQUARE	i̯ə (e̞ə) / e̞ə	i̯ə FOR BOTH
Dark /l/	often [ɫ]	usually [ʊ]
Intervocalic /t/	usually [tʰ]	usually [ɾ]
/tr/ and /str/	usually [t̠ɹ̝̊] and [st̠ɹ̝̊]	usually [tʃɹ̝̊] and [ʃt̠ɹ̝̊] or [ʃtʃɹ̝̊]
/θ/	θ	f, especially in *with*
/ʍ/	[w] or [ʍ]	[w]

The consequences of using a Broad NZE accent can be particularly marked for women. In 1993 Elizabeth Gordon carried out a study (Gordon 1997) where subjects listened to recordings of the three young women chosen to represent Cultivated, General and Broad NZE in the audio clip described above. They were then asked to match the individual recordings to three different photos of the same model wearing clothes chosen to represent three social classes – higher to lower. Subjects were then given subjective tests in which they answered questions about each person represented by the voice/photo pairings. The results showed very clearly that the clothes and speech variety associated with a young lower class New Zealand woman produced a depressing stereotype, in which she was said to have the lowest intelligence, lowest family income, and be most likely to smoke and to be promiscuous. When asked for a possible occupation, the most frequent responses given by the subjects were "unemployed," "single parent" or "prostitute".

4.   Sound change in progress

Many of the phonemes mentioned in the previous sections are currently undergoing change in NZE. The post-vocalic /r/ that is still heard in Southland, for example, is decreasing markedly in frequency. Some older rural males, for example, still use it over 80% of the time, but most younger urban speakers use it only after the NURSE vowel and no more than 20% of the time. As post-vocalic /r/ has decreased in most contexts in Southland, urban speakers have increased their use of a rhotic NURSE vowel, so that it may be becoming a mark of Southland identity. These patterns are demonstrated in the audio clips from the three Southland speakers, described above. The /ʍ/ ~ /w/ distinction that is still maintained by some speakers in Southland has almost disappeared elsewhere. Older women from higher social classes now use it less than 50% of the time in reading tasks and less still in conversation. The most salient class markers, the closing diphthongs FACE, PRICE, MOUTH and GOAT, have changed slightly over time, but the relative differences between Cultivated and Broad pronunciations have been maintained. Younger speakers, however, both male and female, are leading in the move to pronounce the second element of MOUTH as [ə] rather than a [ʊ] or [ʉ].

We will consider the vowel changes that are currently taking place in NZE followed by the consonantal changes. Most of the information in this section comes from analyses of the Canterbury Corpus, an archive held at the University of Canterbury which consists of over 350 recordings of speakers chosen so that there are approximately equal numbers of younger (20–30 years) and older (45–60 years) speakers, of upper and lower social class speakers and of men and women (see Maclagan and Gordon 1999). Each speaker reads a word list designed to emphasise features of NZE and engages in 30 minutes of casual conversation with a student interviewer.

4.1.   Vowel changes

The most obvious vowel change taking place in NZE is the merger between the vowels of NEAR and SQUARE, so that *ear* and *air* or *cheer* and *chair* can no longer be distinguished. Because these two vowels are relatively rare, it is usually only the word pair *really* and *rarely* that causes comprehension problems – did they *really* do something, or was it only *rarely*? Gordon and Maclagan have followed the progress of this merger for twenty years, and it has now worked its way through most of the social and age groups studied. Most New Zealand speakers pronounce all NEAR and SQUARE words with a close onset [iə], but some older women of the higher social classes use a more open onset for some NEAR words, as Wendy did for *really* on the audio clip.

Over the twentieth century the front vowels DRESS and TRAP raised (to [e̝] and [ɛ̝] for the most advanced speakers), and KIT centralised and lowered so that the most advanced NZE speakers now use a vowel more open than schwa [ɜ]. Australian English KIT raised over the same period so that the pronunciation of KIT is one of the most striking differences between the two varieties of English, and one that is commented on by speakers in both countries. New Zealanders accuse Australians of saying *feesh and cheeps* and Australians accuse New Zealanders of saying *fush and chups*. Very few New Zealand speakers now use a vowel that is as front as [ɪ] for KIT, though some older Maori or higher social class Pakeha women, i.e. women of European descent, still may. Within New Zealand the changes to the front vowels are not stigmatised, and young women who would not dream of using Broad NZE variants of the closing diphthongs use the most advanced variants of KIT, DRESS and TRAP, leading to what we have called "the white rabbit [ʌaet ɹɛbɐt] phenomenon", where the stigmatised PRICE diphthong in *white* receives a conservative pronunciation but the non-stigmatised TRAP vowel in *rabbit* receives an advanced pronunciation.

A different sort of change that is increasingly common in NZE is the pronunciation of *-own* past participles like *grown, known* and *thrown* as disyllables /ɡrouən/, /nouən/ and /θrouən/, presumably on the model of words like *take, taken.* There are very few such participles, but the disyllabic pronunciation produces the new minimal pairs of *grown, groan, mown, moan* and *thrown, throne.* The disyllabic pronunciation is now used by approximately 50% of all speakers middle-aged and younger, regardless of social class, so that it seems that both the monosyllable *grown* pronunciations and the disyllable *growen* pronunciations are now regarded as equally correct within New Zealand.

4.2.   Consonantal changes

The vocalisation of /l/ mentioned under social class is a consonantal change that is very advanced in New Zealand. In this change, post-vocalic /l/ (also called 'dark' /l/) which is articulated with the back of the tongue raised, loses its tongue tip contact so that it is articulated as the vowel [u] or [ɣ̈]. Women from the higher social class in the Canterbury Corpus still use an alveolar lateral when this sound occurs in a word list just over 60% of the time, but the younger, lower social class speakers, both male and female, now vocalise /l/ almost 70% of the time even in this most formal of contexts. The rate of /l/-vocalisation is higher still in casual speech. /l/-vocalisation has reached the level of consciousness within New Zealand, and people write letters of complaint to the paper about it (one writer complained about seeing a sign advertising *warnuts* for sale). /l/ has not yet been lost in most words, so that *child* and *chide* are still distinct. Vocalisation of post-vocalic /l/ is parallel to the loss of post-vocalic /r/, and eventually the /l/ in *child* may be completely lost so that *child* and *chide* become homophonous as *father* and *farther* are in NZE.

Another consonantal change that is moving quickly in NZE is the affrication of /tr/ and /str/. The /t/ in /tr/ has always partially devoiced the following /r/ so that the cluster has been pronounced with friction in NZE. Now, however, the lips are being rounded, and the cluster is pronounced as though it were spelt *chr*, so that *tree* is now pronounced [tʃɹi]. /str/ is also affected so that *street* may be pronounced [ʃtɹit] or even [ʃtʃɹit]. People are not yet aware of this sound change, so we have not yet found letters complaining about it. The younger lower class males are in the lead with affrication for more than 60% of word list tokens. The other younger speakers and the older lower class males affricate approximately 40% of tokens, while the older female professional speakers affricate less than 20%.

TH-fronting, where *mother* is pronounced as /mʌvə/, is still avoided in formal contexts by people from the higher social classes. Its use is spreading rapidly among younger speakers from the lower social classes, women as well as men. It now reaches just over the 5% level for young, lower class males in the Canterbury Corpus reading tasks, but is considerably more common in the casual conversation. The first word to be pronounced with /f/ for most speakers is *with*. If a speaker does not say /wɪf/, they will probably not use /f/ for /θ/ in other words either. There are already two possible pronunciations for *with* in NZE, /wɪθ/ and /wɪð/. It has been suggested that the variability in the pronunciation of this word created the conditions for the development of the new pronunciation, /wɪf/ or /wɪv/. Informal observation indicates that words like *the* and *them* are often spelt *ve* and *vem* by young children who are just learning to read and spell.

Another consonantal change that is also still not common in formal speech is flapping or tapping of /t/ in intervocalic position in words like *city* or *letter*. Although it is very common in the conversations, only 11% of the Canterbury Corpus speakers use flaps in the word lists. However, each set of words in these word lists is preceded by a number which the speakers read out. Although only 11% of speakers use flaps on the words in the list, 55% use flaps in some of the numbers, especially *thirteen, fourteen* and *thirty*. Speakers do not consider that the numbers are part of the word list, and use a more casual style in reading them thus demonstrating that /t/ flaps are used much more often in more casual speech. As expected, older, higher social class women seldom use them. In the Canterbury Corpus, the lower social class men, older as well as younger, are leading this change, though the younger, lower class women are close behind them. There is little indication yet that the younger higher class women are involved, though other research has shown them using a high percentage of /t/ flaps in casual speech.

Exercises and study questions

1. Using the material in Table 3 and the sound files on the CD-ROM, analyse the three speakers, Karen (letter 1 on the CD-ROM, General NZE), Christine (letter 2 on the CD-ROM, Broad NZE), and Wendy (letter 3 on the CD-ROM, Cultivated NZE), to determine whether they consistently use the vowel and consonantal variants that are typical of General, Broad and Cultivated NZE respectively.

2. Wendy pronounces *really* with a more open starting position. This is contrary to the current movement of the merger between NEAR and SQUARE in NZE. More typical pronunciations of *really* can be heard from Karen and Christine. How do you explain Wendy's pronunciation?

3. Listen to the three Southland speakers, Arthur (farmer, 77, in free passages section), Paul (farmer, 44, in free passages section) and Jim (student, 16, in free passages section), and determine the extent to which their pronunciation of post-vocalic /r/ is consistent. Do you notice any changes in the pronunciation of post-vocalic /r/ over time for these speakers? Can you see any reasons for the inconsistencies in Arthur and Jim's pronunciations?

4. Listen to the three Southland speakers, Arthur, Paul and Jim, and determine the extent to which their vowels are consistent with the standard pronunciations given for NZE. You will need to compare them with the examples for the New Zealand lexical set. See also Warren and Bauer, this volume.

5. Read the chapters on Australian English by Horvath and Bradley in this volume and listen to the vowels in the standard lexical set. Compare the monophthongs and the diphthongs between Australian and New Zealand English. Where do you see the main similarities and differences?

6. What sound changes seem to be taking place currently in Australian English? What similarities and differences do you see between the current sound changes in Australian and New Zealand varieties of English?

Selected references

Please consult the General references for titles mentioned in the text but not included in the references below. For a full bibliography see the accompanying CD-ROM.

Bartlett, Christopher
    1992   Regional variation in New Zealand English: the case of Southland. *New Zealand English Newsletter* 6: 5–15.
Belich, James
    1996   *Making Peoples*. Harmondsworth: Allen Lane.
Elley, Warwick B. and James C. Irving
    1985   The Elley-Irving socio-economic index: 1981 census revision. *New Zealand Journal of Educational Studies* 20: 115–128.
Gordon, Elizabeth M.
    1997   Sex, speech and stereotypes: why women use prestige forms more than men. *Language in Society* 26: 47–63.
Gordon, Pamela
    1997   What New Zealanders believe about regional variation in New Zealand English: a folklinguistic investigation. *New Zealand English Journal* 11: 14–25.
Gordon, Elizabeth and Tony Deverson
    1998   *New Zealand English and English in New Zealand*. Auckland: New House Publishers.
Maclagan, Margaret A. and Elizabeth Gordon
    1999   Data for New Zealand social dialectology: the Canterbury Corpus. *New Zealand English Journal* 13: 50–58.
Maclagan, Margaret A., Elizabeth Gordon and Gillian Lewis
    1999   Women and sound change: conservative and innovative behaviour by the same speakers. *Language Variation and Change* 11: 19–41.
McKinnon, Malcolm (ed.)
    1997   *New Zealand Historical Atlas*. Auckland: Bateman.
Mitchell, Alex G. and Arthur Delbridge
    1965   *The Speech of Australian Adolescents*. Sydney: Angus and Robertson.
Sinclair, Keith
    1991   *A History of New Zealand*. Auckland: Penguin.

Maori English: phonology

Paul Warren and Laurie Bauer

1.   Introduction

1.1.   Background

The existence of a particular variety of New Zealand English referred to as 'Maori English' has been indicated for some time, yet many commentators have noted that the variety continues to be rather elusive. Nevertheless, there are several distinguishing features that are generally agreed on, and these will be outlined later in this chapter. An important fact to note at the outset is that these features are largely also features that can characterize 'Pakeha' New Zealand English ('Pakeha' is a term widespread amongst both Maori and European New Zealanders that is used to refer to the latter). The difference is that these features are more clearly evident (in terms of degree, consistency and their co-occurrence) in Maori English than in Pakeha English, and it is this that makes it a distinct variety. It is a variety that is used by its speakers as an expression of ethnic and cultural identity, regrettably replacing the Maori language in that function for many speakers. It has also been suggested (e.g. Richards 1970) that there are two types of Maori English, one possibly 'broader' than the other. The existence and use of a Maori English variety has not always been welcomed, notably in official education documentation in the 1970s.

The ancestors of the present Maori people were Polynesian explorers who first arrived in New Zealand around AD 925. They came into increasing contact with English from the time of early European settlement, and were quick to adopt English as a language of trade and negotiation. From the middle of the nineteenth century, scarcely more than a century after European settlement began in earnest, English speakers outnumbered Maori speakers. Unsurprisingly English had a marked impact on the Maori language, not only in terms of the ensuing threat to its very existence, but also on aspects of its pronunciation (such as the aspiration of previously largely unaspirated voiceless plosives). Maori, as a contact language, has in turn had an influence on the English of New Zealanders and can be implicated in a number of features identified in the chapter on New Zealand English phonology, as well as on the lexis of New Zealand English. It is in this last characteristic that Maori English is possibly also most distinguishable from Pakeha New Zealand English, i.e. in the level of incidence of terms (largely but not exclusively relating to features of Maori culture) from the Maori language.

The phonology of Maori is considerably simpler than that of English, with five vowels /i, ɛ, a, ɔ, u/ and ten consonants /p, t, k, m, n, ŋ, f, h, r, w/ in a (C)V(V) syllable structure. The vowels in a VV sequence can be identical (i.e. a long vowel) or different. If different, they may yield a diphthong or a disyllabic sequence, depending on the vowels concerned, but also on the context: in situations requiring greater clarity disyllabic sequences become more common. Voiceless stops were originally unaspirated, but have increasingly become aspirated under the influence of English. /t, n/ can be alveolar or dental, /r/ is a voiced alveolar tap. The nature of /f/ varies between dialects of Maori: it was written *wh* by the early missionaries, suggesting that it was heard as [ʍ], though [ɸ] is also heard. A further significant feature of Maori concerns its rhythm, which is mora-timed. Where Maori is concerned, a mora is a unit of length such that a short vowel constitutes a single mora and a long vowel or diphthong constitutes two. In mora-timing, a sequence of two syllables each containing one short vowel is rhythmically equivalent to a single syllable containing a long vowel.

The following sections highlight some of the distinctive features observed for Maori English. In other respects, Maori English shows the same characteristics as New Zealand English, and so the reader is referred also to the chapter on New Zealand English phonology (Bauer and Warren, this volume).

1.2.   'Maori English'

It should be noted at the outset that Maori English is not a homogeneous variety, and that there may be several distinguishable Maori Englishes. It should also be noted that there is a great deal of research which indicates clearly that Maori English cannot simply be equated with 'the English spoken by people of Maori ethnicity'. There are Pakehas who speak Maori English, and Maori people who speak Pakeha English. Experiments in which New Zealanders are asked to judge the ethnicity of other New Zealanders on the basis of their accent typically find low rates of accuracy. What we are dealing with is, thus, to some extent a stereotype of a variety, a stereotype which is nevertheless well recognized in New Zealand. Bell (2000) terms it 'Maori Vernacular English' or 'MVE'. Because this stereotype is most often met among young men of relatively low socio-economic status, the variety has low overt prestige in New Zealand. Speakers of high socio-economic status or speakers who aspire to high socio-economic status may use a very modified version of Maori English, although they may also be bi-dialectal. Most of the speakers in the sound recordings deviate from the most stereotypical forms of Maori English in this way, although they do have audible 'Maori' features in their speech. As noted above, for many Maori people, Maori English appears to provide an expression of identity, and as such has its own set of values attached to it, separate from the low overt prestige it bears within the Pakeha community.

2. Phonological systems

The systems of Maori English are fundamentally those of New Zealand English, and usually relatable to the variants that are found in the broader realizations of that variety. We continue to use the same notation as is used in the chapter on the phonology of New Zealand English (Bauer and Warren, this volume).

Alongside the English system, speakers of Maori English frequently have a Maori system which they use when code-switching into Maori (or, an alternative interpretation, when using Maori loan words in their English). This is a marked contrast to the way in which most Pakeha speakers of English in New Zealand operate, where Maori loan words are assimilated to the English sound system to a much greater extent. This shift to a Maori system can be heard on personal names and toponyms as well as on Maori terms used in the middle of English sentences. This relatively dense use of Maori vocabulary is a marker of one particular type of Maori English, and the Maori terms which will be used are not (from a Pakeha point of view) entirely predictable – although words for Maori cultural institutions are clearly among them.

3. The vowels

3.1. The acoustic structure of the vowels

The values for formants 1 and 2 of the more monophthongal of the Maori English vowels are presented in the table below. These figures are for male Maori speakers from Kaikohe, analysed by Hall (1976). They may represent old fashioned values, and they may also represent regionally specific values, but we have no other comparable figures.

Table 1.   Vowel formant figures for Maori male speakers (Hall 1976)

Vowel	F1	F2
FLEECE	383	2387
KIT	447	2277
DRESS	461	2236
TRAP	593	2010
STRUT	773	1480
START	830	1443
LOT	687	1057
FORCE	479	807
FOOT	457	1285
GOOSE	417	1389
NURSE	480	1767

Patterns of neutralization appear to be similar to those for general New Zealand English, with a similar range of variation.

There is in Maori a general rule of phrase-final vowel devoicing, especially for close vowels. Although there are some reports of this phenomenon being transferred to Maori English, we have not heard it.

3.2.   The short vowels

The KIT vowel is considerably less centralized in Maori English than in Pakeha English, possibly as a result of the Maori substrate short /i/, which has the same quality as Maori long /iː/. The LOT vowel is rather more peripheral than in Pakeha English, with a quality like [ɔ].

3.3.   The long vowels

The FLEECE vowel is probably rather less diphthongized than in Pakeha English, and possibly a little closer, reflecting the quality of Maori /iː/.

The BATH/START vowel is backer than in Pakeha English, while still not clearly a back vowel.

The THOUGHT/FORCE vowel is slightly less close than the corresponding vowel in Pakeha English, perhaps [o].

The GOOSE vowel is even more fronted in Maori English than in Pakeha English: Bell (2000) suggests a quality such as [y] in many cases. The fronting of Maori /u/ is usually attributed to the influence of English. Perhaps the perception of English GOOSE as fronter than Maori /u/ has led to the very front GOOSE vowel in Maori English.

3.4.   The diphthongs

The diphthongs do not differ in terms of variants heard from those which occur in other varieties of New Zealand English, although claims have been made that the NEAR-SQUARE merger is on a more open variant in Maori English than in Pakeha English.

4.   The consonants

4.1.   The plosives

Despite the fact that Maori plosives have generally become aspirated (presumably, though not necessarily, because of contact with English), there is variable loss of aspiration on voiceless plosives in Maori English. Figures of around 20% deaspiration are frequently cited, although this may include instances where the stop is aspirated, but not as strongly as would be the norm in other varieties of English. The discussion is sometimes focussed on /t/, where the frequent affrication in general New Zealand English may provide a confusing factor. Intervocalic /t/ is tapped as in other varieties of New Zealand English.

4.2.   The fricatives

Devoicing of voiced fricatives was commented on as being a feature of general New Zealand English, but it is an even stronger feature of Maori English. Again figures of around 20% total devoicing are cited. The discussion in the literature centers on /z/ devoicing, but the other voiced fricatives are also devoiced, though we have no quantitative studies of the extent of such devoicing.

The dental fricatives are sometimes replaced, not by labio-dentals (as might be expected given both English variation and the structure of Maori) but by affricates, [tθ] and [dð].

4.3.   /r/ and /l/

The fact that Maori has only one liquid, usually pronounced as an alveolar tap [ɾ], but occasionally heard as a lateral, might lead to the expectation that /r/ and /l/ would be confused in Maori English or that /r/ would be tapped. There is no such evidence, except for the usual possible tapping after /θ/ in words like *thread*. The lack of tapped /ɾ/ may be the result of the fact that intervocalic /t/ is tapped.

5.   Lexical distribution

There is little difference between the lexical distribution of sounds in New Zealand English and in Maori English. The use of the LOT vowel in the first syllable of *worry* is perhaps more frequent in Maori English, and some spelling pronunciations may also be more frequent in Maori English.

6.   Prosodic features

Studies of the rhythm of New Zealand English have observed that Maori English in particular strongly reflects a tendency towards syllable-based timing found more generally in New Zealand varieties. Syllable-based timing is where there is a near-equal interval between the beginnings of adjacent syllables, regardless of the type of syllable. This contrasts with stress-based timing, typically attested for most main varieties of English, where the unit of rhythm is the stress foot. In stress-based timing the intervals between the beginnings of stressed syllables are near-equal, regardless of the number of unstressed syllables between the stressed syllables. The tendency towards syllable-based timing has been demonstrated both in acoustic comparison of the timing patterns with those of Received Pronunciation, and in the greater incidence of full vowels for weak vowels in unstressed syllables (Warren 1999). As with other varieties, such as Singapore English, differences in timing patterns may be the influence of contact, in this case with Maori. Maori itself is mora-timed, as mentioned above, but it has been observed that the influence of mora-based timing on a stress-timed language such as English is comparable to that of syllable-based timing (Grabe and Low 2002).

It seems likely that the most distinctive feature of stereotypical Maori English is the voice quality, with, however, men's and women's voice qualities being different. For male speech some of the following features seem to characterize Maori English: lowered larynx, greater lingual tension, a degree of pharyngealization (constriction of the pharynx during speaking, resulting in a "dark" voice quality), possibly greater nasalization than is used in Pakeha English (for further descriptions of voice qualities, see Laver 1994, chapter 13).

According to Robertson (1994) speech rate may correlate with Maori English, speakers who are identified as Maori speaking rather more slowly in reading and rather faster in conversation than speakers who are identified as Pakeha. This has not been confirmed on a wider sample of speakers.

7.   Intonation patterns

The high rate of use of High Rising Terminals (HRTs) was noted in the chapter on New Zealand English. This intonation pattern is prevalent also in Maori English, and may indeed be in more general use than in Pakeha English, where HRT use is more typical of female speakers than male speakers (Bell and Johnson 1997). It has also been commented that Maori speakers maintain a relatively high level of pitch overall, which may also be an influence from Maori.

8.   The sound recordings

Because of the very nature of Maori English, getting good recordings of this variety in formal settings, in a Pakeha institution (a university) and with Pakeha researchers is difficult. None of the recordings provided here is completely prototypical, even when we have Maori people speaking to each other without Pakeha people present. Nevertheless, some of the typical features of Maori English can be heard in these recordings.

The sound files provided include a short conversation about a recent graphic series of drink-driving ads on New Zealand television, the 'South Wind' passage, and the extended word list. The passage and word list are read by one of the two speakers in the conversation (speaker C, who is on the left channel of the stereo file). The speaker is a young female from the Wellington region, and who identifies as Maori. In addition, the words from the word list have also been made available in separate speech files, in which each word is paired with the version produced by speaker F, the young female speaker of Pakeha New Zealand English (see the chapter on New Zealand English phonology by Bauer and Warren, this volume).

Many of the features that might be commented on in the Maori English samples can be characterized as features of a broad New Zealand English pronunciation. As noted above, it is a high level of co-occurrence of such features that may contribute to the character of Maori English. Nevertheless, some of the characteristics of the read speech in these Maori English samples are ambiguous in their interpretation, since they could reflect a careful speech style rather than being features of Maori English. For instance, the more peripheral vowels found in weak syllables might reflect the tendency in Maori English towards syllable-based rhythm (and a consequential lessening of the contrast between full and reduced vowels), but they might also be a result of a more deliberate reading style. Similarly, the two-vowel like nature of some of the diphthongs might result from careful reading. However, some of these features can also be identified in the conversation recording, and so may be more broadly charac-teristic of this Maori English speaker.

The second conversation is an interview between a male Maori interviewer and a female Maori interviewee, originally broadcast by Radio New Zealand. The male interviewer sounds rather more obviously Maori than the female speakers in the first conversation. For the interviewee, code-switching on Maori words is very obvious, although the Maori words do not always get the value that they would have in monolingual Maori.

Finally, there is a comment by a mature, male Maori speaker. This is a read passage, written by the speaker, The Right Reverend Muru Walters, MA, Dip Ed, LTh (Aot), Adv Dip Tchg, PGD (Arts) who is the Maori Anglican Bishop of Aotearoa (New Zealand) for the district ki te Upoko o te Ika (the Wellington region). The passage was first broadcast on Radio New Zealand. This speaker illustrates the use of English by someone who is a fluent Maori speaker, older than the other speakers illustrated here, and also highly educated. The voice quality is typical of a speaker of his generation, and the code-switching into Maori is obvious. Because the passage is read for broadcast, it is very clearly enunciated, and in that respect is not typical of conversational Maori English.

8.1.   Conversation sample 1

8.1.1.   The short vowels

The KIT vowel is less centralized than in Pakeha New Zealand English, in both *kit* and *sing* from the word list.

The TRAP and DRESS vowels are very similar to those of the Pakeha New Zealand English speaker, but the merger before /l/, exemplified in *malady* and *melody*, appears to be towards a more open variant (see also *belt* in the conver-sation at around 75 seconds).

The short vowels in the read material appear somewhat longer than in the Pakeha New Zealand English sample, but this may be due to the more deliber-ate reading style. A consequence of this additional length is that the /ɐ/ vowel in *us* is almost /ɐː/-like.

8.1.2.   The long vowels

The FLEECE vowel is somewhat closer than that of the Pakeha New Zealand English speaker.

BATH/START – The words *bath* and *palm* have very similar vowels for the two speakers. In the word *start*, the Maori English vowel is somewhat fronter, despite our general observation that BATH/START is backer than in Pakeha New Zealand English.

The GOOSE vowel is clearly fronter than Pakeha New Zealand English.

The NURSE vowel seems much more rounded and fronter than Pakeha New Zealand English, both in *nurse* and in *girl*, which has a very broad pronunciation in this set. This quality for NURSE is also noticeable in the conversation, in the words *work* (around 23 seconds) and *first* (around 161 seconds).

8.1.3.   The diphthongs

The merger of NEAR and SQUARE is more noticeable for this Maori English speaker than for the Pakeha English speaker. Contrary to Bell and Johnson's (1997) observations, the merger is to a closer onset. A close onset to the diphthong is also found in occurrences of the word *where* in the conversation (57 and 72 seconds).

The FACE vowel in the word list has a more distinctly two-part diphthong, but it is not clear if this is a result of a deliberate reading style.

The second part of the GOAT vowel is quite front (matching the GOOSE vowel), especially noticeable in a number of words in the conversation (e.g. *home* at 54 seconds, *road* at 62 and 96 seconds).

It is not clear that these realizations of diphthongs are characteristically Maori English, or just more generally broad New Zealand English.

8.1.4.   The reduced vowels

In each of the words *comma, horses, nothing, happy* and *letter*, the reduced vowel is more peripheral than in the Pakeha New Zealand English recordings. The second syllable of *letter* may be the result of spelling pronunciation. A peripheral pronunciation is also found in the conversation, in words such as *lady* (a clear FLEECE vowel at 58 and 72 seconds) and *pushing* (60 seconds). In *disgusting* (110 seconds) and *driving* (123 seconds) the final vowel is FLEECE-like in its quality and also has a brief /ə/ onglide. In all of these cases, the vowel is a more extreme version of the Pakeha New Zealand English one, and may well result from the lessening of the distinction between full and reduced vowels that arises as a consequence of syllable-based timing.

8.1.5. Vowels before /l/

The forms *pool* and *pull* overlap in the Maori English word list, but were distinct in the Pakeha New Zealand English.

8.1.6. /l/-vocalization

Vocalization of /l/ is more widespread than in the Pakeha New Zealand English word list, again probably reflecting a generally more broad pronunciation. Where there is no vocalization, there is a tendency towards a clear /l/ postvocalically.

8.1.7. The plosives

The conversation contains many examples of the tapping of /t/ and /d/ as in other varieties of New Zealand English. This speaker also frequently replaces final /k/ with a glottal stop or glottalization.

8.1.8. Prosodic features

Although there is little clear evidence of consistent syllable-based timing, the more peripheral realizations of many of the weak vowels supports the tendency towards this type of rhythm, and there are some short stretches of the conversation that appear more syllable timed (notable around 114–117 seconds and 125–129 seconds).

8.2.   Conversation sample 2

Although we have marked instances which appear to show code-switching to Maori (indicated by, for example the use of a tap [ɾ]), vowel qualities are variable across these, and while they sometimes show pronunciations modified in the direction of Maori, they do not do so consistently or in the same way. Some of the Maori phrases used are translated below:

kapa haka	Maori cultural performance
kete	basket of woven flax
korero	speak, talk
mana wahine	woman power, feminism
Ngati Palangi	*Ngati* means 'people' or 'tribe' and is the usual word for one of the Maori tribes; *palangi* is a Pacific word for Maori *pakeha* 'person of European descent'; the entire phrase means 'white people'.

pakeha	person of European descent, white
te ara reo	the language path
te reo Maori	the Maori language
tikanga Maori	Maori custom
waiata	song
whare wananga	house of instruction, university

Note the unexpectedly back vowel in the second syllable of *demand*, the variable pronunciation of coda-/l/ (especially after back vowels), the use of full vowels in a number of unstressed or unaccented words, variable NEAR-SQUARE merger, the quality of the vowel in what might be thought of as GOAT + /l/ contexts (but which should probably be reanalyzed as GOLD contexts), the pronunciation of *pronunciation* showing its derivation from *pronounce* (though the two nuclei are far from identical phonetically), the quality of STRUT when followed by coda-/l/, tapped /n/ in *ninety*. Plosives appear to have standard English values throughout, even in Maori words, and devoicing, while marked on occasions, is not pervasive. High Rising Terminals are found, but are not as common as one might expect from a young female relating a narrative.

Exercises and study questions

1. Using the the word list in the vowel comparison section of the CD-ROM, comment on any differences between Māori English and New Zealand English vowels.

2. Comment on the pattern of glottal articulation of voiceless plosives (including glottalization and/or glottal replacement) in the Māori English audio sample of conversational speech (free passage). Is there more or less evidence of glottalization in this sample than in the New Zealand English conversational sample (4 free passages)? Do different speakers show different patterns or not?

3. What evidence is there from vowel qualities (e.g. full for reduced) in the conversational sample (free passage) for a more syllable-based timing in Māori English?

4. Comment on the extent of /l/-vocalization in the audio samples.

5. What is the typical realization of intervocalic /t/ in the reading passage and the free passage? Does it vary between the Māori English speakers, and does it vary with stylistic differences between the samples?

6. Using the speech files for the words *happy*, *horses* and *comma* in the lexical sets on the CD-ROM, comment on the differences between Māori English and New Zealand English (Pākehā) unstressed vowels.

Selected references

Please consult the General references for titles mentioned in the text but not included in the references below. For a full bibliography see the accompanying CD-ROM.

Bell, Allan
   2000   Maori and Pakeha English: a case study. In: Bell and Kuiper (eds.), 221–248.
Bell, Allan and Gary Johnson
   1997   Towards a sociolinguistics of style. University of Pennsylvania Working Papers in Linguistics 4: 1–21.
Grabe, Esther and Low, Ee Ling
   2002   Durational variability in speech and the rhythm class hypothesis. In: Carlos Gussenhoven and Natasha Warner (eds.), Papers in Laboratory Phonology 7, 515–546. Berlin/New York: Mouton de Gruyter.
Hall, Moira
   1976   An acoustic analysis of New Zealand vowels. M.A. thesis, University of Auckland.
Laver, John
   1994   Principles of Phonetics. Cambridge: Cambridge University Press.
Richards, Jack
   1970   The language factor in Maori schooling. In: John L. Ewing and Jack Shallcrass (eds.), Introduction to Maori Education, 122–132. Wellington: New Zealand Universities Press.
Robertson, Shelley A.
   1994   Identifying Maori English: a study of ethnic identification, attitudes and phonetic features. M.A. thesis, Victoria University, Wellington.
Warren, Paul
   1999   Timing properties of New Zealand English rhythm. Proceedings of the 14th International Congress of Phonetic Sciences, 1843–1848. San Francisco.

Australian English: phonology

Barbara M. Horvath

1. Introduction

English was brought to Australia in 1788 and the people who provided the original linguistic input to what was to become a distinctive national variety of English came from all over England, Scotland, Wales and Ireland. People from the whole social spectrum were represented but the colony began with its own built-in social division based on whether a person was a freeman or a convict, and this social division was passed on to the children of these original settlers as well. In the early days, men far outnumbered women. We know very little about how this diversity of input dialects was distributed across that social spectrum nor how that social spectrum helped to structure the ways of speaking of the first generations of native born speakers of Australian English (AusE). We do know that migration from England, Scotland, Wales and Ireland has continued from the earliest days and that these migrants have been joined by others, initially from northern Europe, and since the 1950s from southern Europe and the Middle East and in more recent times from Asia. Although the varieties of AusE are many, only some have been described in any detail. The English spoken by some Aborigines, for instance, is only just being examined as are the ethnolects, the particular contributions to AusE by the many migrants who learned English as a second language.

There is only the beginning of a discussion about how all of these diverse dialects of English came together to form AusE, but in the earliest descriptions of the phonology of AusE in the 1940s, Alexander G. Mitchell recognized a spectrum of pronunciations which were spread over the whole of the Australian continent. He believed, as did many others following his lead, that there were no social dialects (i.e. dialects associated with social class) nor any regional dialects. He later recognized three points on the pronunciation spectrum which he labelled Broad, General and Cultivated Australian English and these three have remained to this day as descriptors of the range of variation in pronunciation. On the prestige scale, Cultivated is the highest and is estimated to be spoken by only about 10% of Australians. Broad, spoken by about a third of the people, has the most marked AusE characteristics and has the least prestige. General falls in between these two varieties, is spoken by a majority of the people, and may well be increasing in strength as speakers move away from the more stigmatized Broad variety.

In the early 1960s Mitchell and Delbridge (1965) surveyed a large sample of high school students from across Australia and provided a detailed account of the phonological system of AusE. Later acoustic analysis by Bernard (1970) provided the basis for the pronunciations given in the *Macquarie Dictionary* published in 1981, the first dictionary of AusE. Mitchell and Delbridge found little to differentiate Australians either among themselves or other English speakers in the pronunciation of the consonants, but found the greatest source of variety in the FLEECE, GOAT, GOOSE, FACE, PRICE and MOUTH vowels. They took the position that Australian English was a single dialect with three varieties because they found no firm regional or cultural boundaries (Mitchell and Delbridge 1965: 87). More recent studies have shown that, although it is certainly the case that regional and social variation exists, the differences in pronunciation are often quantitative rather than qualitative. The consonants, too, have now been more widely studied and have also been found to represent sociolinguistic and/or geolinguistic variables. The vocalization of /l/, for instance, is widespread in Adelaide, not so prevalent in Sydney, and hardly ever heard in Brisbane. We will begin with a description of the vowel system for AusE and then proceed to discuss just those consonants which either have some particular significance or which have been the topic of research.

2.   The vowel system of AusE

As in most varieties of English, the most distinctive characteristic of the phonological system of AusE are the vowels. In this section we will approach the description of the AusE vowels from three perspectives. First of all, an auditory description of the phonetic variants following Clark (1989: 209–212) will be presented. An acoustic description taken from the work of Harrington, Cox and Evans (1997) will demonstrate how the variants are distributed across the three major varieties of AusE, Broad, General and Cultivated. Finally, the sociolinguistic description of a selection of vowels will show how the Broad, General and Cultivated vowels are distributed across social dialects.

2.1.   An auditory description of AusE vowels

Clark (1989) divides the vowels into four groups: simple target long vowels, simple target short vowels, complex target long vowels and complex target short vowels.

Table 1.   An auditory description of AusE vowels (Clark 1989: 209–212)

Vowel Type	Keyword	Phonetic Symbol	Phonetic Description
Simple target long vowels	START	[ɐː]	A long low central vowel; very stable; may be marked retraction in extreme cases of speakers aspiring towards an RP model. Some instances of a central offglide may occur.
Simple target long vowels	START	[ɐː]	A long low central vowel; very stable; may be marked retraction in extreme cases of speakers aspiring towards an RP model. Some instances of a central offglide may occur.
	NURSE	[ɜː]	A long mid-high central vowel; some variability but central form is most common.
Simple target short vowels	KIT	[ɪ], [ə]	A short high front vowel; first variant may be more fronted than its RP counterpart. The second variant is commonly heard as a reduced form in AusE.
	DRESS	[e], [ɛ]	A short mid-high front vowel; second variant may occur with very open front vowels but not common.
	STRUT	[ɐ]	A short low central vowel; very stable and has a true length contrast with the START vowel.
	FOOT	[ʊ]	A short mid-high back vowel.
Complex target long vowels	FLEECE	[iː], [ᵊi], [əi]	A long high front vowel with an onglide. The latter two are very commonly heard in AusE with a continuum of realisations varying from slight onglide to full diphthongization.
	CLOTH	[oː], [oᵊː], [oə]	A long mid-high back vowel with an offglide. All are common and in some cases the degree of inglide may warrant treating this sound as a true diphthong.

Table 1. (continued)   An auditory description of AusE vowels (Clark 1989: 209–212)

Vowel Type	Keyword	Phonetic Symbol	Phonetic Description
	GOOSE	[ʉː], [ᵊʉː], [ʉᵊː]	A long high central vowel with an onglide; an unstable target as evidenced by onglide or offglide due to its unpressured position in the phonological vowel space. In some extreme cases the target realization may approach [yː]. The phonetic properties of this sound in AusE are problematic.
	FACE	[ɛe], [æe]	A mid-low front vowel with a closing glide.
	PRICE	[ɑe], [ɔe]	A low central vowel with a closing glide.
	GOAT	[əʉ]	A mid-low central vowel with a closing glide.
	MOUTH	[æɔ], [ɐɔ]	A mid-low front vowel with a retracting glide.
	CHOICE	[oɪ]	A mid-high back vowel with a fronting glide.
	NEAR	[ɪə], [ɪᵊ], [ɪː]	A high front vowel with an offglide; a dominant first target, and marginal diphthongal status with a weak centralised second target. In some speakers this becomes either a weak central offglide gesture or a simple target long vowel. The general tendency seems to be to trade the second target for length.
	SQUARE	[eə],[eᵊ], [eː]	A mid-high front vowel with an offglide. The variant forms parallel those found in the NEAR vowel. The tendency to replace the central second target or offglide with length is probably even more common.

Table 1. (continued) An auditory description of AusE vowels (Clark 1989: 209–212)

Vowel Type	Keyword	Phonetic Symbol	Phonetic Description
	CURE	[ʊə], [ʉə], [oː]	A mid-high back vowel with an off-glide; may have diphthongal status or may be a two vowel sequence; auditorily very difficult to distinguish from [ʊə] in some instances. The third and commonly heard variant parallels the sound change occurring in the two preceding vowels in which the central second target is replaced by length, with the additional consequence of losing contrast with the CLOTH vowel.
Complex target short vowels	TRAP	[æ], [æᵊ], [æː]	Varying degrees of offglide occur and some instances of lengthening.
	LOT	[ɔ], [ɔᵊ], [ɔə]	The first and second forms are most common but the diphthongal form is possible in extreme cases of central offglide.
The indeterminate vowel	commA lettER horsES	[ə]	Realised in a wide range of auditory qualities around the vowel space; strongly influenced by phonetic context.

Although Clark does not include it in his description, the happY vowel is realized as [i].

2.2.   An acoustic description of AusE vowels

The acoustic description of AusE vowels by Harrington, Cox and Evans (1997) involved a sample of 119 men and women who had been identified as speakers of Broad, General and Cultivated AusE; the goal was to describe the characteristics of the vowels that differentiate the three varieties. Table 2 shows the phonetic symbol or symbols that, according to Harrington, Cox and Evans (1997) best describe the vowel in AusE; however, much of the variability associated with one or the other of the varieties is lost in the choice of a single symbol. The comments on the table indicate the variability associated with each vowel. Harrington, Cox and Evans (1997) divide the vowels into four types: tense and lax monophthongs and rising and falling diphthongs.

Table 2.   A comparison of Broad, General and Cultivated vowels in AusE (Harrington, Cox and Evans 1997)

KEY WORDS	Proposed Transcription	COMMENTS (B - Broad; G - General; C- Cultivated)
	TENSE MONOPHTHONGS	
FLEECE	iː	Long onglide from a central vowel at onset; B considerably longer onglide than either G or C; clear B/G/C differentiation for males for onglide.
GOOSE	ʉː	Fronted for B; shorter onglide than FLEECE; not clear that onglide starts at a central vowel.
CLOTH	oː	
BATH	ɐː or æ	lexical/social/regional variation
NURSE	ɜː	Fronted for B.
	LAX MONOPHTHONGS	
KIT	ɪ	Fronted for B.
FOOT	ʊ	
LOT	ɔ	
STRUT	ɐ	
DRESS	e	Fronted for B.
TRAP	æ	
	RISING DIPHTHONGS	
FACE	æe	Low first target; more fronted for C than G or B.
GOAT	əʉ or əʊ	Ends between /ʊ/ and /u/; more fronted for B; more raised in G than C.

Table 2. (continued)   A comparison of Broad, General and Cultivated vowels in AusE (Harrington, Cox and Evans 1997)

KEY WORDS	Proposed Transcription	COMMENTS (B - Broad; G - General; C- Cultivated)
RISING DIPHTHONGS		
CHOICE	oɪ	
PRICE	ɑe	Raised and backed first target for B (extends into boundary between /a/ and /ɒ/ vowel space.
MOUTH	æɔ	First target fronted; raised for B; ends at /ɒ/ more than /ɔ/ or /u/.
FALLING DIPHTHONGS		
NEAR	ɪə; ɪː	Long monophthong and bisyllabic variants; second target ends in /æ/ or /a/ vowel space.
SQUARE	eə; eː	Long monophthong and bisyllabic variant; second target ends in /æ/ or /a/ vowel space.
CURE	ʊə and ɔ	Long monophthong and bisyllabic variant; first target more open and fronted than /ʊ/; second target ends in /æ/ or /a/ vowel space.

2.2.1.   Monophthongs

The ellipse plots of the vowel targets for male and female tense and lax monophthongs are given in Figure 1. Each ellipse includes at least 95% of the tokens. The labels *b*, *g*, and *c* represent the mean F1 and F2 values for Broad, General and Cultivated speakers (Harrington, Cox and Evans 1997: 164).

There is not much variation across the three varieties in the targets for the monophthongs. No significant differences were found between General and Cultivated, but there were some for Broad, particularly for the GOOSE vowel for both men and women and the NURSE vowel for women. The GOOSE vowel was fronted for men and women and the NURSE, KIT and DRESS vowels were fronted for Broad speaking women. Ongliding for both FLEECE and GOOSE have often been noted as characteristic of AusE. In this study FLEECE was

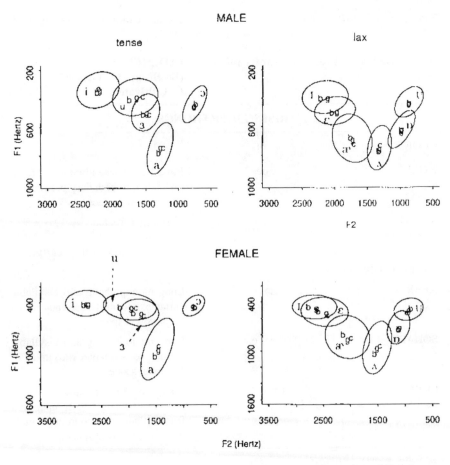

Figure 1.   Ellipse plots of vowel targets in the formant plane for male and female
monophthongs (Harrington, Cox and Evans 1997: 164)

found to have an onglide from a more central vowel but there was much less
evidence for ongliding of the GOOSE vowel. The longest onglide was found
for Broad speakers for the FLEECE vowel; the oldest Broad speakers exhibited
the most extensive onglides and young Cultivated speakers the least marked
onglide.

2.2.2.   Rising diphthongs

The rising diphthongs are often cited as a feature of AusE that distinguishes it
from many other dialects of English. FACE has a low first target; MOUTH has a

fronted first target which is also raised for Broad speakers; and the first target of the PRICE vowel for Broad speakers is raised and backed, extending into the boundary between the /a/ and /æ/ vowel spaces. The second target for the front-rising diphthongs FACE and CHOICE point toward the /ɪ/ vowel space but is much lower for PRICE. The two back-rising diphthongs, GOAT and MOUTH, point toward the /ʊ/ space but fall well short of it.

When Harrington, Cox and Evans (1997) compared the rising diphthongs across the three varieties of AusE, they found that the first targets of these vowels, unlike the monophthongs, were important differentiators within AusE, particularly so for the PRICE and MOUTH vowels. The first target for PRICE is higher and more retracted for Broad speakers than for either General or Cultivated speakers and for MOUTH, the Broad speakers' first target is considerably fronted and raised compared to the others. For both PRICE and MOUTH, the Cultivated speakers have the lowest first target and General falls between the two. The GOAT vowel indicates that women classified as Broad speakers have a more fronted first target. The CHOICE vowel shows the least amount of differentiation.

2.2.3. Falling diphthongs

What is most characteristic of AusE with respect to the falling diphthongs is the [ɔ] pronunciation of the CURE vowel. This is especially so for the lexical item *sure* but is frequent for all words containing the CURE vowel. There is very little differentiation in the articulation of the falling diphthongs among the three varieties. The first target is close to the corresponding lax monophthongs /ɪ ɛ ʊ/ and the offset ends near the /æ a/ vowel space. The pronunciation actually varies from a fully two-targeted variant, to a diphthongal variant (having an offglide), to a long monophthongal variant. Although Harrington, Cox and Evans (1997) found only a small number of monophthongal variants in their study, they suggest that this may be an artefact of the corpus.

3.   The social distribution of Broad, General and Cultivated varieties of AusE

The earliest work on AusE by Mitchell and Delbridge and the acoustic studies of Bernard presented the phonological continuum as one with little association with social or geographical boundaries. Much work since the 1960s has been done to investigate whether such is the case (Horvath 1985; Bradley 1989; Cox and Palethorpe 2001). Certainly regional variation is being found

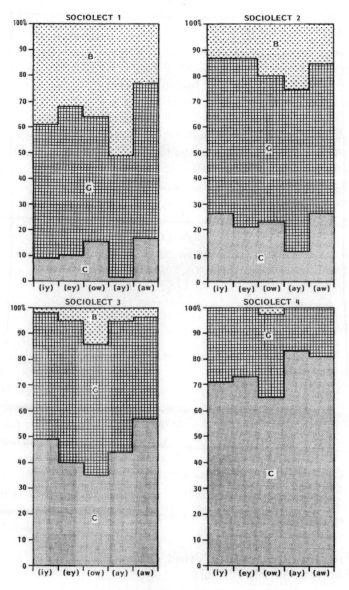

Figure 2.   The social distribution of Broad, General and Cultivated vowels (Horvath 1985: 77)

for a number of phonological features (see the chapter on regional variation in AusE by Bradley in this volume) and Horvath's study of Sydney English drew attention to the social class, gender and ethnic correlates of the Broad, General and Cultivated continuum.

3.1.   The social dimensions of the phonological continuum – vowels

Whereas most other researchers have classified speakers as belonging to one of the three varieties, Horvath approached the description of the vowel system from a different perspective. Using a statistical procedure called principal components analysis, she was able to group the speakers from her sociolinguistic study who were similar in their overall linguistic behavior on five vowels (FLEECE, FACE, GOAT, PRICE and MOUTH). In place of a three-way division of the AusE spectrum, she argued for a four way division and simply named them Sociolects 1–4, with Broad corresponding most closely to Sociolect 1, Cultivated to Sociolect 4 and General to Sociolects 2 and 3. As Figure 2 shows, no speaker used only Broad, General or Cultivated vowels but each variety consisted of a mix of all of the vowel pronunciations; the Broad variety used more 'broad' vowels and the Cultivated used more 'cultivated' vowels, but all speakers often used 'general' vowels. No variety existed in a 'pure' form. Furthermore, the varieties correlated with social class and gender. At the Broad end of the continuum men and the working class predominated while women and the middle class were associated with the Cultivated end. In fact, at the most Cultivated end of the continuum, there were only women.

The falling diphthongs also show an interesting social and linguistic distribution. Horvath (1985) found that the NEAR vowel was more than twice as often pronounced with the two targeted variant [iə] than it was for the SQUARE vowel. The reverse was true for the monophthongal variant: speakers are more than twice as often heard pronouncing *hair* as [he:] than they are heard saying [bi:] for *beer*. The social distribution indicates that the middle class favours some kind of diphthongal realization, either an offglide or a two-targeted variant. The monophthongal variant was associated with working class speakers, older speakers, and men.

3.2.   The social dimensions of the phonological continuum – consonants

Little attention until recently has been paid to the consonants in AusE since it is the vowels that most dramatically differentiate the speakers of AusE and it is the vowels that have been the focus of attention. Although the consonant system of AusE does not differ to any great extent from other dialects of English, there are a number of consonants that vary among its speakers, but even these are also characteristic of various other dialects of English. The consonants that have been studied are the plosive, flapping, frication, and glottalization of /t/; the palatalization of /t, d, s, z/; h-deletion; [n] substituted for [ŋ] for the -*ing* morpheme; 'thing' words such as *nothing* and *anything* pronounced with [ŋk] substituted for [ŋ]; and the substitution of [f] and [v] for /θ/ and /ð/, respectively. The vocalization of /l/ is one of the sounds of AusE that is currently a change in progress and it will be discussed at some length because of its interest both historically and phonologically.

3.2.1. Flapping, frication and glottalization of /t/

There are two pronunciations of /t/ that are particularly associated with AusE. One is strongly fricated [tˢ] and most noticed in prepausal position, for instance in an expression such as 'And that's as far as it went.' [wentˢ]. The other is a flap or tap [ɾ] and is heard widely in the pronunciation of the numbers *thirteen* [θɜˈɾin] or *eighteen* [eiˈɾin]. It is interesting to note that the first, [tˢ], is not widely distributed over the speech community and is more likely to be heard by speakers of Cultivated AusE. Although the [ɾ] is often thought to be a feature of Broad AusE, it is actually widely used by Australians.

A recent study of AusE (Tollfree 2001) gives a detailed account of the four variants of /t/. The first of these, plosive [t], has the usual English allophonic distribution for the aspirated and unaspirated variants but in addition it also has a voiced tap [ɾ], a glottalized variant [ʔ], and a fricated variant [tˢ]. The voiced tap [ɾ] occurs in intervocalic final contexts, e.g. *lot of, get up*, and in medial contexts, e.g. *bitter, mutter*. For some words, such as *attitude, beauty, data* or *city*, Tollfree found that [ɾ] was almost categorical while in words followed by a syllabic /l/ like *bottle* or *subtle* or by a syllabic /n/ like *mutton* or *baton* both plosive [t] and [ɾ] were found. The glottalized variant was also found in medial positions such as *cutlass* or *hitman*, occasionally in intervocalic medial contexts like *lot of* or *get out*, but they were not found in intervocalic medial contexts like *bitter*. The fricated [tˢ] was found in intervocalic and prepausal contexts. As mentioned earlier, the [tˢ] variant was associated with women and the middle class, along with Cultivated vowel usage, in Horvath (1985). Tollfree (2001) also notes its occurrence in prepausal position in the formal style of young lower socioeconomic speakers but it occurred more often in both the prepausal and intervocalic medial contexts in both formal and informal styles in the speech of middle socioeconomic speakers. In comparing the three variants quantitatively, Tollfree found a small number of the fricated variant [tˢ] and she believes that it is receding in AusE; tapping and glottalized /t/ were more prolific but in those contexts where both could be used, tapping was strongly favored over glottalization.

3.2.2. Palatalization of /t, d, s, z/

AusE shares with a number of other English dialects a possible realization of /t, d, s, z/ preceding the GOOSE vowel [u] either as the as [tʲ, dʲ, sʲ, zʲ] or the corresponding palatals /tʃ, dʒ, ʃ, ʒ/. Thus the following variants regularly occur:

tune	[ˈtʲun] [ˈtʃun]
due	[ˈdʲu] [ˈdʒu]
assume	[əˈsʲum] [əˈʃum]
presume	[prəˈzʲum] [prəˈʒum]

Horvath (1985) found that the palatalized consonants occurred more frequently when the following [u] was in an unstressed syllable (*attitude, fortune, educate, insulate*) than when it was stressed, as in the preceding list of words. In examining the lexicon, a great deal of variability is found: in some cases, e.g., *fortune* and *educate*, the Macquarie Dictionary lists only the [tʃ] and [dʒ], respectively, and these are certainly not only the standard AusE pronunciations but also the most usual. However, for *attitude* the dictionary shows only [tʲ] and for *insulate* only the palatal [ʃ] and these do tend to vary across the speech community, although [ˈætətʃud] may well be heard more often than [ˈɪnsʲleɪt]. The makers of the Macquarie Dictionary recognized the high degree of variability in the pronunciations of /tj/ and /dj/ and chose to record the way the words would most likely be pronounced by speakers of Cultivated Australian. The results of Horvath's study suggested that men, young people, and the speakers from the working class were most likely to use the palatals.

3.2.3. /h/ deletion

The deletion of /h/ in initial position is frequent in all English dialects, especially in normal conversational speech in words that receive little or no stress. For the pronouns *his, her, him,* or *hers,* for instance, the deletion of /h/ is commonplace. However, when /h/ is deleted in initial position in stressed words, it is frequently remarked upon. There are two indications that the widespread deletion of /h/ is probably linked to a former period in AusE. The first is an indication that /h/ deletion and /h/ insertion at one time worked hand-in-hand; a number of people remember that it used to be true that someone riding on a train might "drop their aitch in 'aberfield and pick it up again in Hashfield". The saying is no longer so well known nor is the linguistic practice. The other bit of nostalgia is an advertisement that was popular on television until the company disappeared; a variety of scenarios were shown, all of which concluded with an old man, obviously working class, recommending that the listeners go for their building requirements to "'udson's, 'udson's with a haitch".

Horvath's study of /h/ found no /h/ insertion and the rate of /h/ deletion was low. However, the distribution of /h/ deletion was clearly at the Broad AusE end of the dialect continuum and occurred infrequently in Cultivated AusE. It was also more likely to be heard by men than women.

3.2.4. [f, v] substitution for /θ, ð/

The substitution of [f] for /θ/ and [v] for /ð/ are rarely recognized variants in AusE but they are nonetheless widespread. Horvath's study of [f] for /θ/ found a very low frequency (less than 5%) but the social distribution was unusual in that it was one of the consonant variables that never occurred in Cultivated AusE. It is, in fact, a pronunciation that many speakers are certainly aware of and which is generally avoided by many and in times past has been cause for referral to the speech therapist by teachers.

3.2.5. The -ing variable

Shnukal's (1988) study of the -*ing* variable has shown that the common substitution of [n] for [ŋ] is also prevalent in AusE but not with the high frequencies that have been found for British and American varieties of English. In general most studies of AusE have found that [n] is substituted in only about a quarter of the potential occurrences. It will not be surprising either to learn that men use the [n] substitution more often than women or that speakers at the Broad AusE end of the spectrum are more likely to use the variant and Cultivated AusE speakers almost never use it.

3.2.6. The -thing words

Words such as *nothing, something, anything, everything* share with a number of British English dialects the substitution of [ŋk] for [ŋ]. This substitution is more clearly associated with the Broad end of the spectrum and is never found in the Cultivated variety.

3.2.7. The social distribution of the consonantal variants

It is beneficial to look at these four consonantal variants in terms of their spread across the AusE spectrum as shown in Figure 3 because it gives a clearer picture of the clusters of phonological variables that go together to make up the social dialects of AusE.

4.   Intonation: High Rising Tone

AusE has a distinctive intonation pattern which has been the subject of a number of studies (Guy and Vonwiller 1984; Horvath 1985 and Guy et al. 1986). The pattern is variously referred to as High Rising Tone (HRT) or Australian Questioning Intonation and is defined as a rising contour on a declarative clause. This intonation pattern receives a good deal of media attention and is widely believed to be used excessively by teenage girls and to be a sign of insecurity. Below is an example of a description of a primary school by an AusE speaker. The arrow indicates where the rising tone occurred.

> All right, um, there were two sections really. Uh, there was the juniors and the seniors. The juniors was composed of the old Marrickville High building ↗, and a few portables ↗, old fashioned portables, not the modern ones, the, you know, not the uh, aluminium ones, just the wooden ones ↗, and it had a big, big area for playground, it's all green grass ↗, two areas really, big. Uh, um, had an asphalt centre ↗.

In order to study the distribution of this intonation pattern, a large number of interviews with AusE speakers was subdivided into the following text types: descriptions, opinions, explanations, factual texts, and narratives. Statistical analysis showed that HRTs were most likely to be found in descriptions and narratives and least likely in opinions and factual texts. Explanations neither favour nor disfavour the use of HRTs. The length of the turn at talk was also investigated and it was found that multi-clause turns were most likely to include an HRT. The social distribution matches somewhat the public perception: it is indeed teenage working class girls who are most likely to use HRTs but it certainly is the case that HRTs are used by speakers of all ages and from both working and middle class backgrounds. In fact, the case has been made that the HRT is a language change that is currently going on in AusE and is one that is being led by women. A number of potential interpretations of the function of HRTs has been offered including seeking verification of the listener's comprehension or as requesting the heightened participation of the listener – both of which are plausible when extended turns at talk are taken, e.g. in narratives. It certainly does not seem to

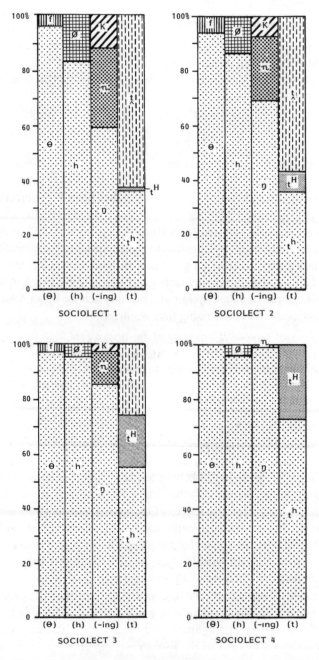

Figure 3.   The social distribution of some consonant variants in AusE
(Horvath 1985: 99)

be an indicator of insecurity since it is not found as often in factual texts or opinions, texts in which the speaker might have some concern about the correctness of their facts or the acceptability of their opinions to the listener.

5.   Phonological change in AusE

5.1.   Changes in vowels

A number of phonological changes have been studied since the descriptions of AusE by Mitchell and Delbridge and Bernard first appeared. Cox and Palethorpe (2001: 25–29) compared their acoustic study of vowels collected from a group of men during the 1990s with a similar acoustic study reported by Bernard (1970) who collected his data in the 1960s, also from males. The summary of the changes are shown in Table 3. They note that these changes follow patterned relationships. The raised second target of the MOUTH vowel follows the raised LOT vowel and the fronted second target of the GOAT vowel follows the fronted GOOSE vowel. The fronted GOOSE and NURSE vowels represent a parallel shift and raised LOT and FOOT provide an example of a change shift.

Table 3.   Changes in AusE vowels between 1960s and 1990s

KEYWORD	TRANSCRIPTION	CHANGE
KIT	/ɪ/	Raised
TRAP	/æ/	Lowered and Retracted
LOT	/ɒ/	Raised
FOOT	/ʊ/	Raised
GOOSE	/u/	Raised and Fronted
NURSE	/ɜ/	Fronted
FACE	/eɪ/	Fronted Target 1
PRICE	/aɪ/	Retracted Target 1 and Lowered Target 2
MOUTH	/aʊ/	Lowered Target 1 and Raised Target 2
GOAT	/oʊ/	Fronted Target 2

The variation in the pronunciation of the GOAT vowel is of particular interest. Mitchell and Delbridge were the first to comment on the unusual behaviour of this vowel in their survey of adolescents in the 1960s. "A curiously variable glide is heard in the South Australian recordings. It ranges from [ɛʊ] to [ɛy] and from [ɔʊ] to [ɒy]. This group of sounds is the only one that emerged from our survey which seemed to be regionally distinctive" (Mitchell and Delbridge 1965: 84). Cox and Palethorpe (2001: 40) indicate that for their Sydney speakers, the first target has shifted toward [ɔ] and the upward glide is quite fronted, approaching [y] before /d/.

5.2.   The vocalization of /l/

Among consonant changes perhaps one of the most interesting is the vocalization of /l/ (e.g. Borowsky 2001; Horvath and Horvath 2001, 2002). The vocalized variant of /l/ has the sound of a back vowel [u] and may or may not be rounded or labialized. Although /l/ vocalization occurs in many dialects of English, the reported occurrence of a vocalized /l/ in intervocalic position found in some American dialects is not found in AusE; however, /l/ vocalization in London English does appear to be comparable to AusE. Borowsky (2001) gives an account of the phonological processes involved in vocalization. She begins with an articulatory description of English /l/ as given by Sproat and Fujimura (1993). According to their account, /l/ is bigestural since it has both a tongue tip (coronal) gesture and a tongue body gesture (dorsal). It is the timing of the dorsal gesture in relation to the apical gesture that accounts for the allophonic distribution of dark *l* and light *l* in English and that timing depends on where in the syllable the /l/ occurs. Each gesture has a strong affinity for different parts of the syllable (Sproat and Fujimura 1993: 291). The tongue body gesture is inherently vocalic and has an affinity for the syllable nucleus and the tongue tip gesture is inherently consonantal and has an affinity for the syllable onset. Dark *l* is produced when the /l/ is in the nucleus or near the nucleus because the tongue body gesture precedes the tongue tip gesture; light *l* is produced when /l/ is the onset of a syllable since the tongue tip gesture precedes. A quantitative study of AusE speakers indicated that syllable type was indeed important to the understanding of the vocalization of /l/. An important finding was that vocalized /l/ never occurred in onset position, whether initially in a word, intervocalically or pre-vocalically. Three syllable types were found to promote vocalization of /l/: coda cluster (*milk*), syllabic (*pickle*) and coda (*fool/fill*). Coda /l/ was further analysed into those syllables containing a long vowel (*fool*), in which the /l/ tends to be syllabic, and those containing a short vowel, where the /l/ is just a coda consonant and does not get the extra promotion effect of being in a nuclear position. The comparison of the occurrence of a vocalized /l/ in the four environments is given in Table 4.

Table 4. The comparison of vocalized /l/ for syllable type (Borowsky 2001: 74)

Syllable Type	KEYWORD	Vocalized /l/ (Percentage)
Coda Cluster	MILK	28
Coda (Long Vowel)	FOOL	19
Syllabic	PICKLE	15
Coda (Short Vowel)	FULL	11

Three other conditioning factors have an effect on the occurrence of a vocalized /l/: (i) the place of articulation of a preceding or following consonant, (ii) whether the following environment is a consonant, a vowel or a pause, and (iii) the backness of the preceding vowel. For both coda clusters and syllabic /l/, the preceding or following segment is a primary factor in vocalization. The vocalization of /l/ is most likely when a dorsal consonant follows, next most likely when a labial consonant follows and least likely when a coronal consonant follows the /l/. It is interesting to note that this process is paralleled in the history of English. In the early Modern English period [l] was lost between some vowels and a following labial or dorsal: *talk, half, balm,* and *folk,* and [lt] and [ld] are the only clusters that still occur after these vowels: *halt, bolt, fold* (Borowsky 2001: 75). When the effect of the place of articulation of a preceding consonant is considered, dorsals clearly enhance the likelihood of vocalization.

A following word beginning with a consonant has the strongest effect in promoting vocalization for all coda /l/ syllables, and a following pause weakly promotes vocalization. A following vowel, however, strongly inhibits vocalization because the /l/ becomes a syllable onset, where, as we have seen, the consonantal gesture is most likely. The effect of a following vowel for syllabic /l/ on the vocalization process is interesting because it does not have the strong effect that a following vowel has for coda /l/. Borowsky (2001: 82–83) explains that the differences occur because when an /l/ is followed by a vowel-initial word, a final /l/ becomes ambisyllabic and provides an onset for the following vowel. A syllabic /l/, however, functions as the nucleus of its own syllable as well as as the onset of the following one. Thus a conflict arises for syllabic /l/ in prevocalic environments that does not occur for coda /l/.

The place of the preceding vowel for clustered /l/ and coda /l/ also affects the occurrence of vocalization. In both syllable types, vocalization is more likely following a central or back vowel and is inhibited following a front vowel. Vowel height also plays an important role in the vocalization of /l/. A preceding high vowel promotes vocalization for both syllable types and while mid vowels disfavour vocalization, low vowels strongly inhibit the process. In fact for clustered /l/, as noted above, the process of /l/ vocalization which began in Early Modern English after low back vowels in such words as *palm* and *calm* has resulted in the loss of /l/ in those contexts.

The study of AusE vocalization of /l/ has shown that the process is promoted by backness – adjacent backness of both consonants and vowels in combination with syllable position.

6.   Outstanding issues

The study of AusE has a firm foundation in the numerous studies that have been done since the 1940s. The research questions that are currently being addressed have to do with regional descriptions of AusE, as well as the description of ethnolects. The contributions that migrants from non-English speaking backgrounds have made to AusE are only beginning to be understood, not only in adding to the lexicon or the pronunciation of AusE but also to the process of language change. The origins of AusE and the relationship of AusE to New Zealand English, and for that matter other Southern Hemisphere Englishes, can now be addressed because of the advances made so far in dialect description. The further study of Aboriginal and Torres Straits Island English is a neglected area that is also beginning to attract the attention of linguists (see Malcolm, this volume).

Exercises and study questions

1. Each of the three descriptions of the AusE vowel system gives a picture of the phonological system. What are the separate contributions of the auditory, the acoustic and the sociolinguistic accounts of AusE vowels?

2. A good deal of discussion goes on in AusE studies about selecting a transcription system that best describes the vowels. Based on the three descriptions, which one would you choose? Why?

3. The two other regional variants of English that AusE is thought to be close to are Cockney English and New Zealand English. Compare these varieties and describe the similarities and differences in both vowels and consonants. Does Cultivated AusE resemble Received Pronunciation?

4. The vocalization of /l/ is a sound change that occurs widely in English accents. Besides AusE, the change has been noted in both London English and New Zealand English. What reasons can be given for such a change occurring in such widely separated accents?

5. Describe the variability in AusE vowels given the sociolinguistic distribution of the Broad, General and Cultivated vowels shown in Figure 2.

6. Describe the cluster of vowel and consonant pronunciations that form the Broad, General and Cultivated varieties of AusE.

Selected references

Please consult the General references for titles mentioned in the text but not included in the references below. For a full bibliography see the accompanying CD-ROM.

Bernard, John
    1970   Towards the acoustic specification of Australian English. *Zeitschrift für Phonetik* 2/3: 113–128.
Borowsky, Toni
    2001   The vocalization of dark /l/ in Australian English. In: Blair and Collins (eds.), 69–87.
Bradley, David
    1989   Regional dialects in Australian English phonology. In: Collins and Blair (eds.), 260–270.
Clark, John
    1989   Some proposals for a revised phonetic transcription of Australian English. In: Collins and Blair (eds.), 205–213.
Cox, Felicity and Sallyanne Palethorpe
    2001   The changing face of Australian English vowels. In: Blair and Collins (eds.), 17–44.
Delbridge, Arthur John R.L. Bernard, David Blair, Pam Peters and Sue Butler (eds.)
    1981   *The Macquarie Dictionary*. North Ryde: Macquarie Library.
Guy, Gregory, Barbara Horvath, Julia Vonwiller, Elaine Daisley and Inge Rogers
    1986   An intonational change in progress in Australian English. *Language in Society* 15: 23–51.
Guy, Gregory and Julia Vonwiller
    1989   The high rising tone in Australian English. In: Collins and Blair (eds.), 21–34.
Harrington, Jonathan, Felicity Cox and Zoe Evans
    1997   An acoustic phonetic study of broad, general, and cultivated Australian English vowels. *Australian Journal of Linguistics* 17: 155–184.

Horvath, Barbara M.
  1985   *Variation in Australian English: The Sociolects of Sydney.* Cambridge: Cambridge University Press.
Horvath, Barbara M. and Ronald J. Horvath
  2001   A multilocality study of a sound change in progress: the case of /l/ vocalization in New Zealand and Australian English. *Language Variation and Change* 13: 37–57.
  2002   The geolinguistics of /l/ vocalization in Australia and New Zealand. *Journal of Sociolinguistics* 6: 319–346.
Mitchell, Alexander G. and Arthur Delbridge
  1965   *The Speech of Australian Adolescents.* Sydney: Angus and Robertson.
Shnukal, Anna
  1988   *You're gettin' somethink for nothing*: two phonological variables of Australian English. *Australian Journal of Linguistics* 2: 197–212.
Sproat, Richard and Osamu Fujimura
  1993   Allophonic variation in English /l/ and its implications for phonetic implementation. *Journal of Phonetics* 21: 291–311.
Tollfree, Laura
  2001   Variation and change in Australian consonants: reduction of /t/. In: Blair and Collins (eds.), 45–67.

Regional characteristics of Australian English: phonology

David Bradley

1. Introduction

The regional phonological characteristics of Australian English are much more subtle than those in the British Isles or North America, but they exist and are continuing to develop. As the contribution to this volume by Horvath indicates, these regional differences are much less substantial than the pervasive socio-lectal differences. The regional differences are especially in vowel realisations, as is usual throughout English, but also in a few areas of consonant realisations. Australian speakers are much less aware of most of them than they are of the substantial sociolectal differences, though some speakers are aware of some of the most salient regional differences.

Most older scholarly sources, following Mitchell and Delbridge (1965), state that there are no such differences. This is increasingly the subject of derisive comment by popular commentators on language, for example Buzo (2002).

2. Vowel characteristics

2.1. Variation between [æ] and [aː]

The clearest example of a regional difference which is stereotyped (known to many non-linguists) is in the BATH vowel class. For most lexical items in Australian English of all regional and social varieties, the distribution of the earlier TRAP vowel between the modern PALM and TRAP vowels generally follows the southeastern British pattern: mainly PALM before /f, s, θ/, variable before nasal plus obstruent – more so in Australia than in England – and mainly TRAP elsewhere. As is well-known, there are exceptions both ways in southeastern British English and in Australian English, such as *gas* with TRAP and the second syllable of *banana* with PALM, and some forms such as *plastic* and the prefix *trans-* still vary in Britain.

However, for about sixty morphemes which are now mainly invariant PALM in southeastern British English, especially preceding a nasal + obstruent, but also a smaller number of prefricative words such as *castle*, *graph*, and so on, there is regional and social variation in Australia between TRAP and PALM vowels. This clearly distinguishes Australian English from New Zealand English, which has a much stronger tendency to follow the more recent British distribution maximising the number of former TRAP words now pronounced with PALM.

The current Australian regional distribution appears to reflect the historical and social characteristics of settlement, and allows the chronology of this change within southeastern British English to be traced indirectly, as suggested in Bradley (1991): places settled by the early nineteenth century, and primarily by people of lower socio-economic status, use more PALM as in Sydney, Hobart and Brisbane. Melbourne, settled in the mid-nineteenth century, with a more mixed population, shows a higher proportion of TRAP. Adelaide, settled later in the nineteenth century primarily by people of middle or higher socio-economic status, uses the highest proportion of PALM, and shows a more advanced stage of the shift before nasal + obstruent than elsewhere in Australia, though not quite as far advanced as New Zealand or modern southeastern British English. This implies that the change in southeastern England was underway during the settlement of Australia, and that PALM was a lower-status form in the late eighteenth and early nineteenth century, but had reversed its social value and become a high status form by the late nineteenth century. Furthermore, the change in the nasal + obstruent environment must have followed the prefricative environment by quite some time.

Tables 1 and 2 (from Bradley 1991: 229–230) show the overall regional distribution of words which vary across four major cities, and the difference between the two phonological environments: the earlier environment, before anterior fricatives, and the later environment, before nasal + obstruent.

Table 1.   Per cent [æ] by socioeconomic status: middle class (MC) versus working class (WC)

	Adelaide	Melbourne	Brisbane	Hobart
MC	6	27	45	54
WC	29	60	48	65

Table 2.   Per cent [æ] by phonological environment

	Before Nasal + Obstruent	Before Fricative
Adelaide	9	30
Melbourne	42	11
Brisbane	42	31
Hobart	93	38

Table 1 shows a status difference which is substantial everywhere except Brisbane: the PALM form is used more by those of higher status. There is also a parallel stylistic difference, not shown in the tables: the proportion of PALM increases as style becomes more formal. Table 2 shows how the more recent environment is less likely to have the PALM form, except in Adelaide where the pattern shows an interesting reversal. Table 3 (from Bradley 1991: 230, with supplementary information on Sydney from Horvath and Horvath 2001a: 350) shows the distribution of the alternatives in seven frequent words. The striking differences show that the lexical diffusion of PALM in this word class is proceeding differently in each part of Australia.

Table 3. Per cent [æ] by lexical item

Hobart	Melbourne	Brisbane	Sydney	Adelaide
graph (100)	graph (70)	dance (89)	chance (100)	contrast (29)
chance (100)	castle (70)	castle (67)	dance (93)	castle (14)
demand (90)	dance (65)	graph (44)	demand (50)	dance(14)
dance (90)	chance (40)	demand (22)	grasp (30)	chance (14)
castle (40)	demand (22)	chance (15)	graph (30)	graph (14)
grasp (10)	grasp (11)	grasp (11)	contrast (9)	demand (0)
contrast (0)	contrast (0)	contrast (0)	castle (0)	grasp (0)

Many Australian non-linguists can cite regional differences in place names containing *castle*, such as *Newcastle* or *Castlereagh Street* in New South Wales (with the PALM vowel) and *Castlemaine* in Victoria (with the TRAP vowel), or other words which vary, such as *dance*. Apart from the regional pattern, there is an overlying social pattern in which the PALM vowel is the more formal or high sociolect form, especially for words with nasal + obstruent. So, for example, the first word in the title and last line of the chorus of the national anthem, *Advance Australia Fair*, is variable but much more likely to have the PALM vowel than the word *advance* in other contexts, and may do so even in places or sociolects which do not normally have PALM in this or similar words.

In areas where the TRAP vowel is usual for a word, its pronunciation with the PALM vowel is regarded as an affectation; so in Sydney *dance* is usually as in TRAP, and with the PALM vowel it is regarded there as a British form, or an affected pronunciation. Sometimes this is attributed, inaccurately, to the "other" – by Sydney speakers, who actually use the TRAP vowel more frequently in most words, to "posh" Melburnians, who actually use less PALM than Sydney speakers, and so on. Of the people interviewed in our regional sociolinguistic survey, some in every state and nine per cent overall were aware of this variation, and in all cases they attributed the PALM form to somewhere else. Many Australians have quite strong negative feelings about PALM in these words, which also reflects an increasing departure from the former RP-as-superposed-prestige-norm situation. Conversely, there is also some style shift towards PALM: when something happens in *Castlemaine* in central Victoria, locally always TRAP, and is mentioned by a Melbourne newsreader of the Australian Broadcasting Corporation, the mainly high-sociolect national government network, it can then have the PALM vowel.

Also involved in the action here is the FACE vowel, a third alternative for many variable words as in other varieties of English as well. While *tomato* has the PALM and not the FACE vowel and *potato* is always FACE and never PALM in Australian English, there are many words such as *basic* which vary between FACE (in most places) and TRAP (mainly in Queensland). Others vary between FACE and PALM, and there are even a few words such as *data* and *lambaste* which can have FACE, TRAP or PALM. Again, quite a few of these are regionally distributed, like *cicada* which has PALM in Sydney and FACE in Melbourne.

2.2.   Varieties of /u/ and /oʊ/

Another particularly obvious and consistent regional difference, this one even noted by Mitchell and Delbridge (1965: 84), is the front-of-central rounded onset of the GOAT vowel, with a parallel in the GOOSE vowel, in Adelaide and elsewhere in South Australia. As they say, this is especially noticeable in the speech of higher socioeconomic status females, but is also used by males and lower-status females there. Again, some nonlinguists are aware of this feature. These realisations contrast greatly with the "cultivated" high sociolectal forms elsewhere which are much further back, though still not as far back as in many other varieties of English, and also with the "broad" forms elsewhere, which show some centralisation and more diphthongisation but much less rounding and fronting.

There is a particularly stark contrast in Adelaide between the realisations of GOOSE and GOAT words before a lateral as opposed to elsewhere. In most regional varieties, similar vowel qualities occur for these vowels with or without a following lateral: vowels between back and central, with more or less rounding and diphthongisation according to sociolectal form and region. But in South Australia the vowels of words such as *school* and *goal* are fully back, and so differ very markedly from the central-to-front vowels of Adelaide words such as *coo* or *go*, and from the more or less central vowels heard elsewhere in Australia.

A difference first noted in Oasa (1979, cited in Bradley 1980) is that the trajectory offglide in the GOOSE vowel differs somewhat between regions of Australia. It starts well front of central and remains there in South Australia (other than before a lateral), starts slightly back of central and moves slightly further back in Victoria, and starts further back from central and moves slightly further front in Sydney and much further front in Brisbane. There is also a tendency to palatalise the consonant preceding GOOSE + lateral, as in *cool*, *school* or *pool*; this is both youthspeak for *cool*, and a Queensland tendency. This is also the second-most-frequently cited regional stereotype: nearly eight per cent of our regional sample cited differences in *school* or *pool*, correctly attributing a palatalised form to Queensland. Surprisingly, this is more salient than the more extreme differences involving a postvocalic lateral.

2.3.   Vowels before postvocalic /l/

In many varieties of English, there are interesting vowel changes in progress in prelateral environment; see Ash (1982) for the case of Philadelphia, with some remarks on other related phenomena in North America. In addition, the /l/ itself is often vocalised. Both are also happening in Australian English.

In Australian English, there are various regionally-differentiated vowel mergers underway before postvocalic /l/. These include a nearly-completed merger of DRESS into TRAP in Melbourne, which is shared with New Zealand (Buchanan 2001) and Brisbane, but not with Sydney, Hobart, Adelaide or Perth. Thus *Ellen* and *Allen*, *pellet* and *pallet*, *telly* and *tally* and so on become homophonous. Melbourne speakers learning phonetics have no hesitation in transcribing words which are unambiguously DRESS + lateral elsewhere, such as *Melbourne*, with [æ]; but there is also limited variation and hypercorrection in the other direction, with prelateral DRESS and even some TRAP words occasionally pronounced with the DRESS vowel.

There is also regionally and socially distributed variation between [æ] ~ [ɔ] before a lateral in *mall*, *Albany*, *Malvern* etc. In Melbourne there is variation in *Bourke Street Mall*, which is usually [æ] but occasionally [ɔ]; in Perth there is *Hay Street Mall*, which is usually [ɔ] but sometimes [æ]. All other cities in Australia have [ɔ] in their pedestrian malls: Adelaide's *Rundle Mall*, Sydney's *Pitt Street Mall*, Brisbane's *Queen Street Mall*, Hobart's *Elizabeth Street Mall* and Launceston's *Brisbane Street Mall*. The [æ] pronunciation in Melbourne and Perth is perhaps influenced by spelling, or may reflect a more archaic form; the brand name of the former *Malvern Star* bicycle was usually pronounced with [æ], but the suburb of Melbourne where its factory was located is now mainly pronounced with [ɔ], which is also the more prestige form, and more like modern RP. In another small word class there is variation between [ɔ] ~ [ɒ] as in *off* or *Launceston*, but this reflects mainly age and social differences rather than region.

There are two mergers in progress which tend to collapse prelateral high tense vowels into the corresponding high lax vowel: FLEECE becomes KIT, and GOOSE and CURE become FOOT; for example, *deal* merges on *dill*, *fool* merges on *full*, and *fuel* also merges on the FOOT vowel, but keeps its medial [j] glide. This merger is furthest advanced in Adelaide and Hobart, somewhat less so in Sydney and Brisbane, and least so in Melbourne; note also the differences between front and back vowel patterns. Table 4 shows the regional distribution for four cities; comparable Sydney data is not available. Table 5 shows the social and stylistic stratification of these variables in Melbourne.

Table 4.   Shortened prelateral high vowels (interview style, per cent)

	Melbourne	Brisbane	Adelaide	Hobart
/il/ to /ɪl/	8	10	34	37
/ul/ to /ʊl/	25	20	41	40

Table 5.   Social and gender differences in Melbourne shortened prelateral high vowels (interview style, per cent)

	MC female	MC Male	WC female	WC male
/il/ to /ɪl/	0	5	12	16
/ul to /ʊl/	3	10	50	35

A parallel phenomenon also variably merges GOAT into GOT before /l/, especially in words of more than one syllable, so that *poll* usually has the GOAT vowel, but *polling* very often has the GOT vowel.

2.4.   Offglides

There is considerable variation in the presence and prominence of offglides in the formerly mainly rhotic word classes NEAR, CURE, SQUARE, CLOTH. The main regional characteristic here is the very frequent presence of long monophthongal forms for NEAR and CURE vowels in Sydney. Monophthongs are very much less frequent elsewhere other than preconsonantally within a word as in *years* or *toured.* In addition, they are prevalent when prelateral in certain frequently-occurring polysyllabic words such as *really*. Monophthongs for NEAR in Melbourne range from three to 18 per cent of tokens overall, showing strong social and smaller gender and stylistic differences: working class speakers, males and casual style use more monophthongisation. Monophthongs represent 0 to 17 per cent of final and 10 to 35 per cent of preconsonantal NEAR tokens, again with a strong social difference, but also a substantial gender and style difference.

Monophthongal forms of SQUARE and CLOTH words are by contrast extremely frequent throughout Australia, with environmental constraints; a following consonant within the word favours a monophthong, parallel to NEAR and CURE. Conversely, strong stress and final position permit a virtually disyllabic realisation, [ɪjɜ] for NEAR, [(j)ʊwɜ] for CURE, [ɛjɜ] for SQUARE, and [ɔwɜ] for CLOTH words without final consonant such as *paw* or *pore* (or for that matter *poor*; in Australian English many CURE words without a preceding /j/ glide have merged into the CLOTH class, and even those with the glide also vary between [jʊwɜ] and [jɔ] realisations). Table 6 (Bradley and Bradley 1979: 78) shows the pattern of monophthongisation for the NEAR vowel in Melbourne among tertiary-age students, favouring the offglide in isolation and also showing differences between speakers based on the type of secondary school attended, reflecting social differences. In the sample, there were no female students who had attended technical secondary schools.

Table 6. Monophthong pronunciation of /ɛə/ by Melbourne tertiary students (gender, style, type of secondary school, per cent)

	Male		Female	
	interview	wordlist	interview	wordlist
Technical	92	62		
Catholic	37	23	86	48
Private	57	27	59	14
Prestige Private	75	13	81	19

2.5.   Lax vowels

The regional differences in front lax vowels are clear: Sydney and Newcastle, just to its north in New South Wales, have substantial centralisation of the KIT vowel, though less extreme than in most sociolects of New Zealand English.

Melbourne has this vowel raised nearly to cardinal [i], and also has raised both DRESS and TRAP vowels consistently more than other areas of Australia, as first noted in Bradley and Bradley (1979). This occasionally leads to misunderstanding° between Melbournians and other Australians. The New Zealand centralisation or KIT and raising of DRESS and TRAP are carried much further, but represent a continuation of this unusual pattern of raising of lax vowels (Labov 1994: 138) already incipient in Australian English before its transfer to New Zealand, and extended further in Melbourne.

3.   Regional consonant characteristics

In Australia there is a clear regional difference in postvocalic /l/ vocalisation to [ɤ], which is quite frequent in South Australia and considerably less frequent elsewhere in Australia, as in words such as *fill, fell, feel, fail, fool, full, fuel* and so on. The result is a half-open nearly-back unrounded offglide following the vowel. D'Onghia (1995) found an overall frequency of 40.8 per cent vocalization, both in the capital, Adelaide, and in Millicent, a rural town. It is slightly more frequent in more casual speech and in the speech of those who are younger, higher-status, and male. For full quantified details see D'Onghia (1995).

Horvath and Horvath (2001b) give further details on the regional pattern: New Zealand has much more vocalisation, nearly half overall; in Australia, vocalization is least frequent in Brisbane and Melbourne, intermediate in Hobart and Sydney, and greatest in South Australia (both Adelaide and Mount Gambier, a large town in the southeast of the state). Vocalisation is increasing; it is more frequent among younger speakers. The preconsonantal environment shows under ten per cent vocalisation in Brisbane and Melbourne and roughly similar proportions of around 20 per cent elsewhere, but the major regional difference resides in vocalisation of final /l/ which ranges from under ten per cent in Brisbane to over 40 per cent in South Australia (Horvath and Horvath 2001b: 40–42).

Vocalisation of syllabic /l/ as in *pickle* again differs within Australia; least (three per cent) in Brisbane, nine to 15 per cent in Melbourne, Hobart and Sydney, and 26 and 28 per cent in Adelaide and Mount Gambier in South Australia. In New Zealand, syllabic /l/ vocalizes much more frequently (about 60 per cent); furthermore, the conditioning environment also differs: a preceding velar consonant favours vocalisation most in Australia, but a preceding labial favours it most in New Zealand (Horvath and Horvath 2001b: 42–45).

The pronunciation of *-thing* in *something/nothing/everything/anything* with [ɪŋk] is socially and regionally variable in Australia, as in southeastern England. The London-like [ɪŋk] is more frequent in informal speech and the speech of those of lower social status across Australia, but is particularly frequent in some mining towns in the Hunter Valley north of Sydney in New South Wales, as documented by Shnukal (1982: 204) for Cessnock, where the overall frequency of [ɪŋk] is nearly 60 per cent, and much lower elsewhere, as for example in Melbourne where we found 33 per cent for males and 15 per cent for females (Bradley and Bradley 1979: 81).

There are various forms, such as the [f] and [v] realisations of /θ/ and /ð/, which are found throughout Australia but are somewhat more often used in Sydney (overall frequency of 4.4 per cent) than in Melbourne and elsewhere. Horvath shows that this is more frequent among those of Italian background, males and those of lower socioeconomic status; but it is by no means restricted to these groups (Horvath 1985: 98–102). In addition to the usual pattern of sociostylistic variation in which the [f] and [v] are the informal and low-status forms, there are numerous individuals in all parts of Australia, not all male or of low status, who use a very high proportion of [f] and [v]. Certain very frequent words such as *with* also favour the [f] or [v] alternative.

4.   Regional lexicon

The examples of regional differences in Australian English most often given by non-linguists are lexical. One well-known instance is a kind of processed cooked meat in a tube, called *German sausage* up to 1914. With anti-German feeling due to World War I, all manufacturers around Australia changed the name: in Melbourne, to *Stras(s)burg* (usually shortened to *Stras(s)*), in Adelaide to *Fritz*, in Sydney to *Devon*, in Brisbane to *Windsor*, in Tasmania to *Belgium* and in Perth to *Polony*. Other examples abound, in names of plants and animals, childhood and school activities, household items, and so on. Some are more subtle: the Tasmanian predilection to specify types of potatoes (*pinkeye*, *sebago* and so on) while most other regions do so much less. For a very large number of further examples, see Bryant (1985, 1989).

Indeed, one of the popular criticisms of the first edition of the otherwise excellent *Macquarie Dictionary* (Delbridge et al. 1981) is that it gives mainly or only the Sydney or New South Wales forms. Most of these gaps are lexical, but some, including words showing TRAP/PALM/FACE differences, are in regional pronunciation; note, for example, *cicada* – the first edition gives only the Sydney PALM alternative (1981: 346). Later editions have attempted to correct this bias; see (Delbridge et al. 1987: 326) and the Federation edition (Delbridge et al. 2001: 353), which give both PALM and FACE for this word, but with the Sydney form first and without attempting to localise the alternatives. Other minor errors in this area include *basic* with TRAP cited as American; this is actually an older, especially Queensland alternative to the more usual FACE pronunciation, and is not American. Here we have another example of stereotyping: attributing sociolectally low-status things to American influence, a long-standing Australian tendency.

5.   Rural versus urban

One popular stereotype about regional differences is that rural speech is more broad (see the chapter by Horvath, this volume; briefly, the low-status socio-lect) and urban speech is more cultivated; or that the entire rural hinterland speaks much the same – more slowly, more nasally, and more broadly. This is a part of the national reverence for the bush (rural Australia) and the idea that it is more typically Australian. It is clear that a higher proportion of rural Australians use a greater frequency of broad vowels than urban Australians. The first to quantify this were Mitchell and Delbridge (1965: 39), who found that 43 per cent of adolescents outside capital cities used broad vowels, while only 23 per cent of urban youth did so; and conversely, 19 per cent of urban adolescents but only four per cent of others used cultivated (high-status so-ciolect) vowels.

However, the rural hinterland of each capital city shows much the same regional (as opposed to social) characteristics as that city. Examples include the treatment of postvocalic laterals in Millicent and Mount Gambier in South Australia, the distribution of TRAP and PALM, and so on. The regional phono-logical boundaries do not correspond exactly to state boundaries; from a lin-guistic point of view, part of northern New South Wales is a part of Queensland, part of southwestern New South Wales around Broken Hill is similar in some ways to South Australia, and the Riverina region of southern New South Wales forms part of Victoria.

6.   Conclusion

On the whole, the regional differences in Australian English phonology are small, but growing. Some have started to come to the notice of more language-aware members of the speech community, but curiously continue to be denied by most Australian linguists. As is usual in many varieties of English, these differences reside mainly in the vowel system. Like many other non-rhotic varieties of English, some changes involve the vowels affected by that de-constriction and the rearrangements of the system which result, as in the case of TRAP/PALM and so on. Some current changes in progress revolve around the next wave of vowel shifts found in many varieties of English, those associated with postvocalic laterals: vocalisation and/or changes in preceding vowels.

Exercises and study questions

All of the following exercises can be attempted with any speaker who is believed to be Australian. The first two exercises will distinguish New Zealand and other speakers from Australians. Exercises 2 to 7 should enable the regional origin of the Australian speaker to be identified. Exercises 6 and 7 also illustrate some of the changes in progress within Australian English.

1. Listen to the vowels of the following words: *bid, bed, bad, beard, bared.*
   What is the phonetic value of these vowels, and does this suggest whether the speaker is from Australia or from New Zealand? Hint: New Zealand English has a systematic shift in the short front vowels, which centralises the high vowel of KIT and raises the vowels of DRESS and TRAP, an irregular NEAR vowel instead of the DRESS vowel in the word *bed*, and frequently merges the SQUARE vowel into the NEAR vowel. Australian English does not have these changes.

2. Check the pronunciation of the following words which may vary between long /aː/ as in PALM and short /æ/ as in TRAP: *castle, graph, chance, demand, dance, contrast, grasp.*
   Looking at Table 3, where is it likely that the speaker comes from Melbourne, Sydney, Adelaide, Hobart or Brisbane? Note that if the speaker is from New Zealand, all these words will have the PALM vowel.

3. Compare the vowel in the following words as said by an Australian speaker: *coo, cool, go, goal.*
   How great is the difference between the prelateral and non-prelateral allophones of the GOOSE and GOAT vowels? Is your speaker likely to come from Adelaide?

4. In words such as *here* and *tour, beard* and *toured,* with the NEAR and CURE vowels, is the vowel a diphthong, a long monophthong (without a schwa offglide), or a triphthong with a medial glide? What does this suggest about where in Australia the speaker is from?

5. Listen to words which usually have the DRESS vowel before a lateral, such as *bell, fellow, Ellen, pellet, Melbourne* and words which have the TRAP vowel before a lateral, such as *fallow, Allen, pallet* and so on.

   Are they distinct? If not, where is the speaker from? Note that this merger is also characteristic of New Zealand English, but is not found in most of Australia.

6. Listen to the vowel in the second last syllable of words such as *really, ideally* and similar vowels with the NEAR vowel before a lateral.

   Is this vowel a diphthong or is it a short monophthong like the KIT vowel as in *fill* or *dill*? Where could the speaker be from?

7. Listen carefully to the L sound after the vowel in words such as: *feel, fail, file, foil, fill, fell, full, fool, foal, fuel* and so on.

   Are the laterals vocalised (without tongue tip contact)? Of course, this is also characteristic of many other regional varieties of English, such as London. If the speaker is Australian and there is frequent vocalisation, where are they likely to be from?

Selected references

Please consult the General references for titles mentioned in the text but not included in the references below. For a full bibliography see the accompanying CD-ROM.

Ash, Sharon
   1982   The vocalization of /l/ in Philadelphia. Ph.D. dissertation, University of Pennsylvania, Philadelphia.
Bradley, David
   1980   Regional differences in Australian English. *University of Melbourne Working Papers in Linguistics* 6: 73–93.
   1991   /æ/ and /aː/ in Australian English. In: Cheshire (ed.), 227–234.
Bradley, David and Maya Bradley
   1979   Melbourne vowels. *University of Melbourne Working Papers in Linguistics* 5: 64–84.
Bryant, Pauline
   1985   Regional variation in the Australian English lexicon. *Australian Journal of Linguistics* 4: 55–66.
Bryant, Pauline
   1989   The South-East lexical usage region of Australian English. *Australian Journal of Linguistics* 9: 85–134.

Buchanan, Hannah
    2001   Neutralisation of DRESS and TRAP before /l/ in New Zealand English. *Wellington Working Papers in Linguistics* 13: 15–29.
Buzo, Alec
    2002   Reggie Vee is alive: regional variation in Australasian English. *Quadrant* 35: 68–71.
Delbridge, Arthur, John R.L. Bernard, David Blair, Pam Peters and Sue Butler (eds.)
    1981   *The Macquarie Dictionary.* North Ryde: Macquarie Library.
    1987   *The Macquarie Dictionary.* 2nd edition. North Ryde: Macquarie Library.
    2001   *The Macquarie Dictionary.* Federation edition (2 Volumes). North Ryde: Macquarie Library.
D'Onghia, Peter
    1995   Adelaide English: the right way to order a Cooper's peɪl eɪɤ. B.A. Honours thesis, La Trobe University, Melbourne.
Horvath, Barbara
    1985   *Variation in Australian English: The Sociolects of Sydney.* Cambridge: Cambridge University Press.
Horvath, Barbara and Ronald J. Horvath
    2001a   Short A in Australian English: a geolinguistic study. In: Blair and Collins (eds.), 341–355.
    2001b   A multilocality study of a sound change in progress: the case of /l/ vocalization in New Zealand and Australian English. *Language Variation and Change* 13: 37–56.
Mitchell, Alexander G. and Arthur Delbridge
    1965   *The English of Australian Adolescents.* Sydney: Angus and Robertson.
Oasa, Hiroaki
    1979   Is regional dialectology possible in Australia? A quantitative study of systematic regional variations in the pronunciation of Australian university students. Unpublished manuscript, Australian National University, Canberra.
Shnukal, Anna
    1982   *You're getting somethink for nothing*: two phonological variables in Australian English. *Australian Journal of Linguistics* 2: 197–212.

Australian creoles and Aboriginal English: phonetics and phonology

Ian G. Malcolm

1. Introduction

English speakers began to occupy Australia on a permanent basis in 1788. The Aboriginal and Torres Strait Islander encounter with English led to the development of "restructured English" varieties which Holm (1988–1989: 538) sums up as "ranging from contact jargon, pidgin, and creole to post-creole Aboriginal English." Aboriginal and Torres Strait Islander influence has not been the only factor leading to the development of contact varieties in Australia. As Mühlhäusler (1991: 160) has pointed out, there have been three major pidgin traditions in Australia: Aboriginal, Chinese and Melanesian. However, the most widespread and enduring contact varieties have been those associated with Aboriginal and Torres Strait Islander speakers and it is with these that this chapter will be concerned.

There are two major creole varieties currently spoken in Australia: Kriol, spoken mainly in the Northern Territory and extending into North West Queensland and the Kimberley region of Western Australia, and Cape York Creole, or Broken, spoken in the Torres Strait Islands and neighbouring parts of the Cape York Peninsula. There is one major variety of Aboriginal English, which embraces a number of regional varieties. It is spoken within the context of Aboriginal and Torres Strait Islander communities in all parts of Australia. It is arguable that the creole varieties, although English-derived, are not, like Aboriginal English, varieties of English. The treatment of the creoles and Aboriginal English here will therefore be separate, with the creoles being discussed first.

2. Historical and cultural background

Prior to 1788, an Indigenous population of some 300,000 people distributed across what is now Australia spoke an estimated 250 languages and perhaps again as many distinctive dialects. The speech communities were relatively self-contained (though not necessarily monolingual), typically comprising 500 to 600 people united with a common inheritance of language, land and world-view. There had, indeed, been some foreign contact prior to the coming of Captain Cook in 1770, including visits in the early 17th century from Spanish and Dutch navigators (see Dutton 1970: 140–142) and contacts in northern regions with Portuguese and Malay traders (Harris 1991: 196). There is, however, little or no linguistic legacy from these contacts.

The British occupation of the area around Port Jackson in New South Wales (NSW) from 1788 brought Aboriginal people for the first time into more or less intensive contact with English speakers. From the first, the local people preferred to keep with their own kind and entered into communication with the English speakers only on an intermittent basis. However, as the number of colonists increased and Indigenous society became increasingly devastated and depleted through the effects of the colonial experience, cross-cultural communication increased, drawing on the resources of both the local Indigenous varieties and the various dialectal and sociolectal varieties of English brought by the newcomers.

It has been demonstrated by Troy (1990) that between 1788 and 1845 the interaction between the Aboriginal people and the English-speaking colonists led to the development of a jargon, incorporating elements of the Sydney language and of English, which progressively stabilized into a variety, or varieties, of pidgin, referred to as NSW Pidgin. Although the jargon served the purposes of communication between Aboriginal people and colonists, its use soon extended beyond this. The process by which it expanded in structure and function to become NSW Pidgin was favoured by a number of factors. These included the contribution of existing contact varieties developing in the Pacific (Mühlhäusler 1991: 169), the disruption of pre-contact social and territorial patterns, the bringing-together of Indigenous people requiring a lingua franca, and the Indigenous people's need for a linguistic variety in which they "could rationalise the radical social changes they experienced as a result of contact with the colonists" (Troy 1990: 7).

NSW Pidgin, then, became a highly significant medium of communication in colonial Australia, and it developed two major varieties, one, more influenced by the English superstrate, serving the needs of cross-cultural communication and the other, more influenced by the Aboriginal substrate languages, serving the needs of communication among Aboriginal people (Troy 1990). As it was used for Indigenous-based communication along traditional trade routes (Troy 1990: 2; Harris 1991: 199) and in the colonial explorations and expansion of pastoral properties (Harris 1991: 198; Sandefur 1979: 12) taking place to the north, west and south of the original settlement, as well as on ocean navigation routes (Malcolm 2001: 213), it provided the framework for the development of associated pidgins, creoles and non-StE varieties in many parts of Australia.

It is likely that the circumstances of contact in New South Wales (and in the other southern states) did not lead towards the development of creole varieties. The Pidgin performed the useful function of a lingua franca among Aboriginal people and, where it was supplanted under the ongoing and growing influence of English, it gave way to a non-StE ethnolect (Aboriginal English) rather than developing into an independent language. The creoles which developed in the Northern Territory and the Torres Strait Islands came about relatively more recently, favoured by significantly different sociolinguistic circumstances.

By the late 19th century, the pastoral industry, which had expanded progressively from its origins in New South Wales, had enabled the influence of NSW Pidgin to extend through Queensland into the Northern Territory. It seems likely, according to Harris (1991), that other pidgins developed in various locations where Aboriginal people settled down on stations or settlements, but that, under the influence of the Pidgin which had come from New South Wales, these had, by the beginning of the 20th century, converged towards one widely-understood standard, which he calls Northern Territory Pidgin English. The creolization of this Pidgin began to occur in the context of an Anglican Church mission at Roper River which had been established in 1908. This mission, according to Harris (1991: 201), provided a refuge for Aboriginal people from eight different groups who had been facing "near annihilation" from hunting gangs. The creole began to form when the Pidgin was adopted by a generation of children at the mission as their language. The Roper River Creole (incorporating at least one other variety which developed later elsewhere) came to be spoken widely across the north of the continent, and by the mid-20th century had come to displace an increasing number of Indigenous languages (Hudson 1981: 1). In 1976 this creole came to be referred to by the name Kriol, following the orthography which had been developed for the language (Hudson 1981: 169). It has at least 20,000 speakers.

The second major creole variety in Australia arose in the Torres Strait Islands where, according to Shnukal (1988: 5), following the discovery of commercial quantities of various products of the sea, large numbers of Europeans, South Sea Islanders, Papua New Guineans and others came to exploit these resources. A common language was required and an existing variety, Pacific Pidgin English, came to be used. Torres Strait Islanders who worked in the marine industries came to use this Pidgin, and by the 1890s it was being used by children of Torres Strait Islander and immigrant origin on one of the islands. Some years later the Pidgin creolized independently on another island. The use of the creoles spread throughout the islands, because they were not only found to be useful but also assumed by many to be English (Shnukal 1991: 183). Torres Strait Creole (or "Broken", as it is called locally) has around 3,000 native speakers and up to 12,000 second language speakers (Shnukal 1991: 180).

The origins of Aboriginal English varieties are diverse. Mühlhäusler (1991: 170) has pointed out that there is evidence for the independent development of pidgins in a number of parts of Australia, and there is thus the possibility that independent Aboriginal English varieties arose in association with these. However, there is also significant evidence of the widespread influence on Aboriginal English in many parts of the country of NSW Pidgin (Malcolm 2001: 212–213). In places where creoles developed, the Aboriginal English varieties show some evidence of having undergone processes of decreolization. They have also been shown to bear clear resemblances to local Aboriginal languages and to non-standard Australian English (Eagleson, Kaldor and Malcolm 1982: 134). Evidence from cognitive linguistic research (Sharifian 2002) supports the view that even varieties which are formally close to Australian English maintain a significantly different conceptual basis. The strong resemblances between Aboriginal English varieties Australia-wide, and their maintenance as distinct from Australian English, suggest that to a large extent convergence has taken place upon an agreed ethnolect.

3.   The phonology of Australian creoles

As Mühlhäusler (1991: 165) has indicated, the scholarly study of Australian pidgins and creoles is both scarce and recent in origin. There has been no extended study of the phonology of an Australian creole, although phonological features have been included in a number of descriptions, and what follows here will be drawn from these, with the focus being particularly on Kriol (as spoken in Bamyili [Barunga], Roper River and Fitzroy Valley) and Torres Strait Creole (Broken) and will focus particularly on their more basilectal or "heavy" varieties. The voices in the accompanying audio-material are those of Kriol speakers from the Kimberley Region of Western Australia.

3.1.   Vowels

Both Kriol and Cape York Creole, have reduced the number of vowel phonemes of English to five: /i/, /e/, /a/, /o/ and /u/, allowing for some further differentiation on the basis of lengthening. Table 1 (below) shows the effects of this on the pronunciation of the 28 words in Wells' (1982) list.

Table 1.   Vowels in Australian creoles

KIT	i > ɪ	FLEECE	ɪ	*NEAR	ija
DRESS	e ~ a	FACE	e ~ eɪ	SQUARE	eja
TRAP	e ~ a	PALM	a	START	a
LOT	a	*THOUGHT	o	NORTH	o
STRUT	a	*GOAT	o ~ oʊ	FORCE	o
FOOT	u	GOAL	o	*CURE	jʊa
*BATH	a	GOOSE	u	HappY	i
CLOTH	a	PRICE	a ~ aj ~ aɪ	lettER	a
NURSE	oː ~ aː ~ eː	CHOICE	oj ~ aj ~ oɪ	horsES	idj
		MOUTH	a ~ aʊ	commA	a

This table needs to be read with caution, since some of the words on it (those in-dicated with an asterisk) were identified by Kriol informants as not occurring in their language. Generally, the same trends are apparent in Kriol and Torres Strait Creole, though the monophthongization of diphthongs and the phonemically distinctive use of vowel length have been reported only with respect to the former. The open-close contrast among vowels is less significant than in StE. It has been suggested with respect to Fitzroy Valley Kriol (Fraser 1977) that – under the influence of the local language Walmajarri – the open-close con-trast is less salient than the short-long contrast. This may well apply more widely. It is noteworthy that most Aboriginal languages have only three vow-els, /i/, /a/ and /u/, though sometimes distinguishing long and short forms of these (Eagleson, Kaldor and Malcolm 1982: 41). The creole systems are closer to such a pattern than to the pattern of StE with the 28 discriminations represented in Wells' (1982) table.

3.2.   Consonants

Australian creoles do not always recognize the voiced-voiceless consonant distinction, nor do they reliably discriminate most fricatives. Kriol varieties may incorporate a number of retroflexed and lamino-palatal consonants not found in StE. The consonants of basilectal Fitzroy Valley Kriol have been represented (using Kriol orthography) by Hudson (1981: 28) in the follow-ing table:

Table 2. Consonants of basilectal Kriol (Hudson 1981)

	Bilabial	Inter-dental	Alveolar	Retro-flexed	Lamino-palatal	Velar
Stop	p	th	t	rt	tj	k
Nasal	m		n	rn	ny	ng
Fricative			s			
Lateral			l	rl		
Rhotic			rr			
Semi-consonant	w			r	y	

Torres Strait Creole (Broken) has 15 consonant phonemes, represented in Broken orthography by Shnukal as follows:

Table 3. Consonants of Torres Strait Creole (Broken) (Shnukal 1991: 186)

	Bilabial	Dental	Palatal	Velar
Stops	p, b	t, d		k, g
Nasals	m	n		ng
Fricatives		s, z		
Liquids		l, r		
Semi-consonants	w		y	

It is common for stops to substitute for fricatives and affricates. Fraser (1977) reports that in Fitzroy Crossing Children's Pidgin the bilabial stop /p/ substitutes for /b/, /v/ and /f/ and that a dental /t/ substitutes for /tʃ/, /dʒ/ and non-final /s/, /z/ and /ʒ/. Similar substitutions occur in Ngukurr-Bamyili Kriol (Sandefur 1979: 37).

Although voiced and unvoiced stops both occur in Torres Strait Creole, their distribution may not be the same as in StE. Crowley and Rigsby (1979) note the replacement of a voiceless stop with a voiced one when it occurs between two vowels, as in /peba/ for 'paper'. There is no phonemic opposition in Torres Strait Creole between [p] and [f], between [t] and [θ], between [d] and [ð] or between [b] and [v].

In Fitzroy Crossing Kriol, /d/ may alternate with /t/. Also, Sandefur (1979: 37) observes that in Kriol, /d/ may be replaced by a flapped rhotic [ř] when it occurs in a word between two vowels.

It will be observed from Table 2 that the sound represented in Kriol orthography as <th> is not the interdental fricative of StE but an interdental stop. Similarly, the retroflexed <rt> and the lamino-palatal <tj> function as stops (Hudson 1981: 28).

All the nasal consonants of StE, /m/, /n/ and /ŋ/ also occur in Australian creoles. There are, however, in basilectal Kriol additional retroflexed and palatalized nasals.

Fricatives are generally absent from basilectal Kriol though in basilectal Fitzroy valley Kriol, there is one fricative, /s/. Fricatives are reduced in occurrence in Torres Strait Creole. There is no phonemic opposition in Torres Strait Creole between [s] and [ʃ] (Crowley and Rigsby 1979; Dutton 1970). In Kriol, sibilants tend to be deleted to avoid consonant clusters (Sharpe and Sandefur 1976); in Bamyili (Barunga) the affricates /tʃ/ and /dʒ/ are replaced by a lamino-palatal stop /dj/ (Sandefur 1979: 37). The glottal fricative /h/ is generally absent from the creoles.

The lateral /l/ is common to English and most Aboriginal languages and is retained in the creoles. Basilectal Kriol also has retroflexed and palatalized laterals.

The rhotic /r/ is trilled in basilectal Kriol and Torres Strait Creole. It may also be flapped when it occurs between two vowels (Sandefur 1979: 37).

3.3.   Supra-segmental features

In Kriol, the primary stress is usually on the first syllable. Hence /ˈdilib/ 'tea', /ˈginu/ 'canoe'. In Torres Strait Creole words derived from English normally retain their original stress (Shnukal 1991: 185).

The intonation patterns of Kriol and Torres Strait Creole are comparable to those of English except for a distinctive pattern associated with ongoing action, in which the pitch of the verb rises and is maintained over the verb's successive repetitions, accompanied by vowel lengthening before a final fall or rise. Such a pattern would accompany a sentence such as: "*ay bin wed wed wed wed wed wed najing,* 'I waited for ages but nothing (came)'" (Sharpe and Sandefur 1977: 53). Fraser (1977) observes that in Fitzroy Crossing Children's Pidgin there are three contours: a "sequence contour" in which the primary stress is on the first syllable and the secondary stress on the final, with higher pitch; an "emphatic contour" in which the final syllable receives primary stress, length and higher pitch; and a "question contour" where the primary stress and pitch rise are on the final syllable.

Sharpe and Sandefur (1977) and Fraser (1977) have observed among Kriol speakers a characteristic laryngealisation accompanying high-pitched segments. This may be especially in evidence in certain speech acts with a scolding or correcting function.

3.4.   Phonotactic rules

In Kriol, and to a lesser extent in Torres Strait Creole, there is a resistance to consonant clusters in initial or final position. Many of the phonotactic processes observed by Holm (1988–1989) in Atlantic creoles are also in evidence in Australian creoles. For example the omission of one or more sounds at the beginning of a word ("aphesis"), as in /ton/ 'stone', /piya/ 'spear' (Sandefur 1979: 39); the omission of one or more sounds from the middle of a word ("syncope"), as in Torres Strait Creole, where the middle consonant of three is often dropped word-medially (Crowley and Rigsby 1979); the omission of one or more sounds from the end of a word ("apocope"), as in /ek/ 'axe', /fren/ 'friend' (Sandefur 1979: 40); the addition of a sound at the beginning of a word ("prothesis"), as in *njusimpat* 'to use' (Fraser 1977: 152) and *nother* 'other' (Dutton 1970: 151); the insertion of a sound in the middle of a word ("epenthesis"), as in *jineg* 'snake', *jilib* 'sleep' (Sharpe and Sandefur 1977: 52), *burrum* 'from' (Sharpe and Sandefur 1977: 58) and *anis* 'ants' (Shnukal 1991); the addition of a sound to the end of a word ("paragogue"), as in *wandi* 'want' (Sharpe and Sandefur 1977: 56) and *aksi* 'ask' (Dutton 1970); and the changing of the order in which two sounds occur in a word ("metathesis"), as in *aksi* 'ask' (Dutton 1970: 144).

Vowel harmony may be observed between affix and stem, as in the case of the transitive verb suffix allomorphs, e.g. *tjak-am* 'throw', *kuk-um* 'cook' (Hudson 1981: 37).

4.   The phonology of Aboriginal English

Like Australian English, Aboriginal English is characterised by a recognizably similar pronunciation across the continent. Unlike Australian English, it may bear interlanguage features in some areas associated with Indigenous languages or creoles.

The treatment here will be inclusive, providing information on the main areas where, at least in some places, Aboriginal English shows most contrast with StE. There has been no focused study on the phonology of Aboriginal English, but descriptions have been provided (often for the assistance of school teachers) in the context of descriptions of the dialect as a whole. The description here will draw principally on work carried out in Queensland (e.g. Readdy 1961; Alexander 1968; Flint 1968), the Northern Territory (e.g. Sharpe 1976) and Western Australia (Eagleson, Kaldor and Malcolm 1982; Malcolm 2001).

4.1.   Vowels

Speakers in many areas distinguish fewer vowels and diphthongs than in StE. At the more extreme end of the continuum of varieties, Aboriginal English would show little difference from Australian creoles with respect to its repertoire of vowels. Thus, for example, in a description of Aboriginal English as spoken in Queensland, Flint (1968: 12) identifies the dialect as having five vowels, /i/, /e/, /a/, /o/ and /u/, with phonemic length on /i/, /a/, /o/ and /u/. The dialect is, however, much more inherently variable than this would suggest, and some of the variability is suggested in the following table based on Wells' (1982) word list:

Table 4.   Vowels in Aboriginal English

KIT	ɪ ~ i > ɛ	FLEECE	ɪ ~ i	NEAR	i
DRESS	ɛ > æ	FACE	eɪ ~ e > ʌɪ	SQUARE	ɛ
TRAP	æ > ɛ	PALM	a	START	a
LOT	ɒ ~ ɔ	THOUGHT	ɔ > ɒ	NORTH	ɔ
STRUT	ʌ ~ æ ~ ɒ ~ ɪ	GOAT	oʊ ~ o(ʊ) ~ ɔ ~ ʌʊ	FORCE	ɔ
FOOT	ʊ	GOAL	ɒ	CURE	jʊə
BATH	a	GOOSE	u	happY	i
CLOTH	ɒ	PRICE	aɪ ~ a > ɒɪ	lettER	a ~ ʌ > ə
NURSE	ɜ ~ e > ɜə	CHOICE	ɔɪ	horsES	əz
		MOUTH	aʊ ~ æ > a(ʊ)	commA	a

It will be observed with respect to high front vowels that (as in the case of the varieties reported on by Holm 1988–1989), Aboriginal English may sometimes not observe the opposition between /i/ and /ɪ/ or may simply observe long and short forms of /i/. In addition, there may be no discrimination between the mid front vowels /ɛ/ and /æ/, or between these and the high front vowels.

The mid central vowel /ɜ/ is not consistently present. It may alternate with, or be supplanted by, the mid front vowels /ɛ/ or /e/, or by the diphthong /ɛə/

(Alexander 1965: 57). The neutral short vowel /ə/ tends to be replaced by the mid central vowel /ʌ/, as in /jʌsɛlf/ 'yourself' or by the low central vowel /a/. The StE vowel /ʌ/, for its part, may not always occur in contexts where it would be expected, but may alternate with either front or back vowel alternatives. In Woorabinda, Queensland, the following alternations have been noted: [ʌ ~ ɪ ~ æ ~ ɒ] (Alexander 1968).

The low central vowel /a/, which is the most commonly-occurring in Aboriginal languages Readdy (1961: 60), is widely distributed in Aboriginal English and often occurs in contexts where StE would use /ə/.

The mid back vowels /ɒ/ and /ɔ/ are often used interchangeably, thus /dɔg/ 'dog', and, under influence from creole, they may also alternate with /o/ (Alexander 1968).

The high back vowel /u/, which is widespread in Aboriginal languages and creoles, is also widespread in Aboriginal English.

There is a strong tendency in Aboriginal English (shared to some extent by Australian English, as well as by creoles) for diphthongs to be monophthongized (Readdy 1961: 64; Alexander 1968; Eagleson, Kaldor and Malcolm 1982). Only /ɔɪ/ and /ʊə/ seem unaffected by this. With respect to the other diphthongs, /eɪ/ may become /e/ or /ɛː/, /oʊ/ may become /o/, /aɪ/ may become /aː/; /aʊ/ may become /a(ʊ)/ or, under the influence of Australian English, /æ/, /ɪə/ may become /i/ and /ɛə/, /ɛː/.

Although Australian English is well known for its diaphonic variation which distinguishes cultivated from broad and general speech, the influence on Aboriginal English of the broad variants is not as pervasive as might be expected, and some of the Aboriginal English vowels have been compared to American rather than broad Australian variants (Sharpe 1976: 15–16). Broad Australian variants are, however, not entirely absent from Aboriginal English.

4.2.   Consonants

The inventory of consonants in Aboriginal English, and their distribution, show the influence of the pidgin/creole history of the dialect, although historic records show that many of the phonetic modifications which took place in the early stages of pidginization are no longer operating (Malcolm and Koscielecki 1997: 59). Table 5 represents the consonants of Aboriginal English, showing some of the common substitutions which take place:

Table 5.   Consonants of Aboriginal English

	Bi-labial	Inter-dental	Labio-dental	Alveolar	Retro-flexed	Lamino-palatal	Velar	Glottal
Stop vl	p			t			k	
v	b			d			g	
Nasal	m			n			ŋ	
Fricative vl		θ	f	s		ʃ		(h)
v		ð	v	z		3		
Affricate vl				tʃ				
v				dʒ				
Lateral				l				
Rhotic				rr ← r				
Semi-consonant	w					y		

Most of the consonants of Australian English, with the exception of /h/ in some cases, may be heard in Aboriginal English, but the phonemic boundaries of the latter are much more porous, with respect to voicing versus non-voicing, stop versus fricative articulation and alveolar versus lamino-palatal place of articulation.

There is clearly a preference for stop over fricative articulations. Bilabial, alveolar and velar stops are strongly in evidence, and often substitute for other sounds. The distinction between voiced and voiceless stops is not strongly maintained, with the general exception of when they are in the initial position (Flint 1968: 12; Alexander 1968; Sharpe 1976). There is a preference for voiceless stops except before nasals (Sharpe 1976: 13). Although the /t/ is represented on the chart as alveolar, in some communities it is dental (Flint 1968).

The labio-dental fricatives /f/ and /v/ are often replaced by stops, as in /pɔl/ 'fall' and /hæp/ 'have', though the substitution of the fricatives may be selective, as in /faɪp/ 'five' (Eagleson, Kaldor and Malcolm 1982: 82). The interdental fricatives /θ/ and /ð/ are highly vulnerable to substitution by alveolar plosives /t/ and /d/, as in most contact and non-standard forms of English. /θ/ may also become /s/, as in /nasɪŋ/ 'nothing'. Sibilants are not always clearly distinguished and may be substituted for one another. This also affects the affricates /tʃ/ and /dʒ/ which may become /ʃ/. The status of the glottal fricative /h/ is unresolved in Aboriginal English. The tendency to remove it initially and medially is balanced by an equally strong tendency, at least in some areas, to add it initially where it does not occur in StE (see 4.4. below).

The nasals, which have counterparts in Aboriginal languages and creoles, generally occur as in StE, except for the common substitution of the allomorph /-an/ for /-ɪŋ/, as in /sɪŋan/ 'singing'.

The Aboriginal English consonant inventory, in places where there is influence from Aboriginal languages and creole, includes a trilled variant of /r/, which may occur where /t/ comes between vowels, as in *gorrit* 'got it' and *purrit* 'put it' (Sharpe 1976: 15). In some places the variant is flapped rather than trilled, as in /hɪɾɪm/ 'hit him' or /ʃʌɾʌp/ 'shut up' (Eagleson, Kaldor and Malcolm 1982: 81).

4.3.   Suprasegmentals

Generally, the stress patterns of Aboriginal English are comparable to those of Australian English, except for the tendency (observed also in Kriol) to stress initial syllables, resulting in pronunciations like /ˈkæŋgru/ 'kangaroo' and /ˈtibi/ 'TV'. Some Western Desert languages tend towards syllable timing, which reflects on the stress patterns of Aboriginal English speakers in these areas.

As in Australian creoles, the intonation patterns are generally compatible with those of Australian English, but the expression of prolonged or repeated action (as in Kriol) is accompanied by a rise in pitch and the repetition or lengthening of the vowel in the relevant word, as in

	go go go			*g-o-o-o-o-o*	
We bin		or	*We bin*		(Sharpe 1976: 6).

A rise of pitch and a slowing down of pace may occur wherever emphasis is being sought, as in, as in *bi-i-iggest shark* 'very big shark' (Eagleson, Kaldor and Malcolm 1982: 88) or *We bin go wi-i-i-ight aroun ebrywhere* 'We went all around'. The high final level intonation of Aboriginal English, as in

	long way	
Me and Patrick wen		(Eagleson, Kaldor and Malcolm 1982: 84)

enhances narrative effect. Unlike the high rise terminal of Australian English, it is level, not rising, and does not function as an attention holding device.

A number of scholars (Sharpe 1976: 5; Alexander 1968) have commented on the relatively high speed of Queensland Aboriginal English, particularly among children. Sharpe (1976: 5) suggests that, in this regard, Queensland Aboriginal children's speech may contrast with that of their Alice Springs counterparts.

Aboriginal English vocal quality can vary distinctly from that of Australian English. Sharpe (1976: 4) has observed the huskiness of the pronunciation of Aboriginal children in Alice Springs at low volume, which contrasts with its penetrating quality at high volume and has attributed this to "faucalisation, or tightening of the faucal pillars at the back of the mouth."

4.4.   Phonotactic rules

Like Australian creoles, Aboriginal English tends to reduce consonant clusters in ways common to Atlantic creoles, as described by Holm (1988–1989).

Aphesis is common, as in *bout* 'about', *roun* 'around', *cos* 'because' (Sharpe 1976), *leven* 'eleven', *long* 'along', *way* 'away', *I'z* 'I was', *we'z walking* 'we was walking', *onna table* 'on the table', *alla people* 'all the people' (Sharpe 1977), *we'ent* 'we went'. There are also frequent cases of the omission of initial /h/. Syncope occurs occasionally, as in *akn* 'acting'. Apocope often occurs, especially involving the loss of final stops after nasals, as in /hɛn/ 'hand', /hævn/ 'haven't' and /wɛn/ 'went'. The cases of prothesis noted in Kriol are carried over into Aboriginal English, with *nused to* 'used to' and *nother* 'other'. In addition, /h/ is frequently added to words where it does not occur in StE, as in *hant* 'aunt', *happle* 'apple' (Alexander 1968), *hoval* 'oval' and *huncle* 'uncle'. Epenthesis occurs in /imiju/ 'emu' (Sharpe 1976). The common case of paragogue from non-standard Australian English, *anythingk* 'anything', occurs at least in Sydney Aboriginal English (Eagleson, Kaldor and Malcolm 1982: 135).

4.5.   Morphophonemics

The forms of liaison which apply in StE are not always carried over into Aboriginal English. Thus /ðə/ 'the' does not become /ði/ before a vowel. Nor does /ə/ 'a' become /æn/ 'an'. The contractions which are common in StE, such as *I'll*, *we're*, are not as common in Aboriginal English, partly because of the less frequent use of auxiliaries. However, the /ð/ of *the* may be assimilated to the preceding consonant (Sharpe 1977) and the preverbal tense marker *bin* may be contracted to *'n*, as in *They'n see it* (Dwyer 1974: 19). Initial /w/ may be lost in words in both stressed and unstressed positions, as in /aɪʌs/ 'I was' (Readdy 1961: 94) and *I na wear it on* 'I want to wear it' (Dwyer 1974: 19). Aboriginal English speakers, unlike Australian English speakers, do not always neutralize the vowels in function words such as *at*, *from* and *to* when they are unstressed.

5. Practical and research issues

The existence and the importance of Australian creoles and Aboriginal English have long been disputed in public discourse in Australia. Although school systems are beginning to recognize the fact that creoles and Aboriginal English may be coherent linguistic systems, there is still a reluctance to allow them any significant place in the development of school literacy. It is assumed that literacy skills in StE will be best acquired by concentrating only on that variety, despite research evidence of the relevance of home language to effective learning of standard varieties. The better integration of creoles and Aboriginal English into school learning depends on continued research to produce fuller descriptions of these varieties and the development of a greater range of quality learning resources in them.

In parts of Australia where creoles are spoken one practical problem is the differentiation between creole and Aboriginal English. In some cases, the creole speakers have long believed that in speaking creole they have been speaking English. As Aboriginal English in such areas may be (at least in part) describable as a post-creole continuum, there are practical problems in deciding, for educational purposes, where to draw the line between the creole and the English, although the line has been drawn in written language with the development of an alternative orthography for Kriol. The problem of differentiating Kriol from Aboriginal English has implications for the development of learning materials and for pedagogical approaches.

There have been some attempts to describe the patterning of variation between Aboriginal English and creole by employing the concept of the implicational scale. An implicational scale is a continuum of features which form a hierarchy, where each feature can be assumed to apply the existence of features above it. As Blumer (1987: 1) who has been working on such a project puts it, "[o]ne example of implication is the observation that if an Aboriginal creole speaker can pronounce the fricative [th], he/she can and will also pronounce [t]. That is, the presence of the phonetic feature [th] implies the presence of the phonetic feature [t], but not vice versa." On the basis of implicational analysis of data from over 900 children living in regions close to where Kriol was spoken, Blumer (1987: 14) found that the data fitted "a model implicational scale extremely well", suggesting that a geographical continuum existed in the area studied. It remains to be seen from further research whether other continua (e.g. socio-economic) can also be traced.

Exercises and study questions

1. Records made by early settlers in Australia (reported in Malcolm and Koscielecki 1977: 22–23) include representations of Aboriginal speakers' pronunciation of English as follows: *midger* 'mister', *nuffer* 'snuffers', *massa* 'master', *gemmen* 'gentlemen', *top* 'stop', *tausan* 'thousand' and *pose* 'suppose'. Express the implied variations from StE pronunciation in terms of rules. To what extent do these rules still apply to Australian creoles and Aboriginal English?

2. Australian Aboriginal languages commonly exhibit the following phonological features (Eagleson, Kaldor and Malcolm 1982: 37–41):

   a) three main vowels, /i/, /a/ and /u/
   b) no fricative consonants
   c) non-recognition of the voiced/voiceless distinction in consonants
   d) phonemic recognition of palatal articulations of nasals and laterals
   e) phonemic recognition of retroflex articulations of nasals and laterals
   f) trilled or flapped variants of rhotics
   g) unaspirated initial stops.

   To what extent can evidence of these features be seen in Australian creoles and Aboriginal English?

3. The following variant forms have been recorded in Roper Creole (Kriol) (Sharpe and Sandefur 1977: 52):

biya, spiya	'spear'
jabi, sabi, savi	'know (savvy)'
sap, shop	'shop'
emini, hemeni	'how many'
thrribala, thribala	'three'
jarre, tharre	'there (that way)'
jineg, sineg, snek	'snake'

   Sort the examples into acrolectal, mesolectal and basilectal variants as appropriate and explain the processes which underlie the variation.

4. In the following extract from a reading lesson in a Year 4 (primary) class, a teacher is trying to bring an Aboriginal student's pronunciation into line with StE. What is the feature involved? Does it appear to impair the child's comprehension or comprehensibility? What is the effect of the teacher's efforts to change it? Why? (Malcolm 1979: 47–48).

Kevin: (reading) ... *and she would shake er dark air and run like a wind with the children chasing and calling the and and laughing be'ind er-*

Teacher: *Kevin, what do we say about the "ers"? What were we going to try and do? Sound the?*

Student: *Aitch.*

Teacher: *Sound the?*

Kevin: *Dunno.*

Teacher: *Aitches. Keep going.*

Kevin: (reading) *She had lived for ten years in a village at the foot of um of the mountain all that time no-one ad ever seen er angry and bad tempered. Everyone loved er an everyone wondered about her.*

5. Both Kriol and Torres Strait Creole (Broken) are written in a phonemic orthography rather than the orthography used for *StE*. This, of course, reduces the intelligibility of the written form of the creoles to English speakers who do not know creole. What might be some of the advantages to creole speakers of using a phonemic orthography?

6. Listen to the speech samples for Australian Creoles and Aboriginal English on the CD-Rom and, on the basis of selected variables, take note of:

   a) variation between the Australian Creoles and Aboriginal English;
   b) variation within Australian Creoles and Aboriginal English;
   c) variants which are common to other creoles or non-standard varieties of English.

   Consider how each of these kinds of variation may be accounted for.

7. a) Listen to the following utterances extracted from the Free Passage for Aboriginal English on the CD-Rom and show with a line above them their distinctive intonation patterns:

   Line 18   Not worth! [= "It wouldn't be worth it"] (0:38 m)
   Lines 33–34 Dey can see us comin for miles in dem white ones. (1:05 m)
   Lines 35–36 You know what for? They can blend in with the bush, al. (1:07 m)

   b) Listen to the Lexical Set for Aboriginal English and for Australian Creoles. What phonetic processes are observable in the Aboriginal English speaker's pronunciation of SQUARE and LETTER? What modifications has the Kriol speaker made to the word list, and what do these show about the lexicon and the phonology of Kriol?

Selected references

Please consult the General references for titles mentioned in the text but not included in the references below. For a full bibliography see the accompanying CD-ROM.

Alexander, Diane H.
 1965   Yarrabah Aboriginal English. B.A. Honours thesis, Department of English, University of Queensland, Brisbane.
Alexander, Diane H.
 1968   Woorabinda Australian Aboriginal English. M.A. thesis, Department of English, University of Queensland, Brisbane.
Blumer, Caroline
 1987   Linguistic variation in the Kimberley region. Unpublished paper.
Crowley, Terry and Bruce Rigsby
 1979   Cape York Creole. In: Timothy Shopen (ed.), *Languages and Their Status*, 153–207. Cambridge, MA: Winthrop.
Dutton, Thomas E.
 1970   Informal English in the Torres Straits. In: William S. Ramson (ed.), *English Transported: Essays on Australasian English*, 137–160. Canberra: Australian National University Press.
Dwyer, John
 1974   The school and the Aboriginal child. *The Aboriginal Child at School* 2: 3–19.
Eagleson, Robert D., Susan Kaldor and Ian G. Malcolm
 1982   *English and the Aboriginal Child*. Canberra: Curriculum Development Centre.
Flint, Elwyn
 1968   Aboriginal English: linguistic description as an aid to teaching. *English in Australia* 6: 3–22.
Fraser, Jill
 1977   A phonological analysis of Fitzroy Crossing Children's Pidgin. *Work Papers of SIL-AAB* A 1: 145–204.
Harris, John W.
 1991   Kriol – the creation of a new language. In: Suzanne Romaine (ed.), *Language in Australia*, 195–203. Cambridge: Cambridge University Press.
Hudson, Joyce
 1981   Grammatical and semantic aspects of Fitzroy Valley Kriol. M.A. thesis, Australian National University, Canberra.
Malcolm, Ian G.
 2001   Aboriginal English: adopted code of a surviving culture. In: Blair and Collins (eds.), 201–222.

Malcolm, Ian G. and Marek M. Koscielecki
  1997   *Aboriginality and English*. Mount Lawley, Western Australia: Centre for
          Applied Language and Literacy Research, Edith Cowan University.
Mühlhäusler, Peter
  1991   Overview of pidgins and creole languages of Australia. In: Suzanne
          Romaine (ed.), *Language in Australia*, 159–173. Cambridge: Cambridge
          University Press.
Readdy, Coral
  1961   South Queensland Aboriginal English. B.A. Honours thesis, Department
          of English, University of Queensland, Brisbane.
Sandefur, John R.
  1979   *An Australian Creole in the Northern Territory: A Description of Ngukurr-
          Bamyili Dialects* (Part 1). Work Papers of SIL-AAB, Series B, Volume 3.
          Darwin: Summer Institute of Linguistics.
Sharifian, Farzad
  2002   Conceptual-Associative System in Aboriginal English: Evidence from
          Western Australian Urban Aboriginal Primary-School Children. Ph.D.
          dissertation, School of International, Cultural and Community Studies,
          Edith Cowan University, Mount Lawley.
Sharpe, Margaret C.
  1976   *The English of Alice Springs Aboriginal Children: Report to Teachers*,
          Part 1. Alice Springs: Traeger Park Primary School.
  1977   Alice Springs Aboriginal English. In: Ed Brumby and Eric Vaszolyi (eds.),
          Language Problems and Aboriginal Education, 45–50. Mount Lawley,
          Western Australia: Aboriginal Teacher Education Program, Mount Lawley
          College of Advanced Education.
Sharpe, Margaret C. and John Sandefur
  1976   The creole language of the Katherine and Roper River areas, Northern
          Territory. In: Michael Clyne (ed.), *Australia Talks: Essays on the Sociology
          of Australian Immigrant and Aboriginal Languages*, 63–77. Canberra:
          Research School of Pacific Studies, Australian National University.
  1977   A brief description of Roper Creole. In: Ed Brumby and Eric Vaszolyi
          (eds.), *Language Problems and Aboriginal Education*, 51–60. Mount
          Lawley, Western Australia: Aboriginal Teacher Education Program,
          Mount Lawley College of Advanced Education.
Shnukal, Anna
  1988   *Broken: An Introduction to the Creole Language of Torres Strait*. (Pacific
          Linguistics Series C 107.) Canberra: Australian National University.
  1991   Torres Strait Creole. In: Suzanne Romaine (ed.), *Language in Australia*,
          180–194. Cambridge: Cambridge University Press.
Troy, Jakelin
  1990   *Australian Aboriginal Contact with the English Language in New South
          Wales: 1788 to 1845*. Canberra: Department of Linguistics, Research
          School of Pacific Studies, Australian National University.

Bislama: phonetics and phonology[*]

Terry Crowley

1. Historical and cultural background

Bislama is an English-lexifier contact language spoken in Vanuatu in the southwest Pacific which initially developed as a distinct variety over about half a century between the mid-1800s and the end of the nineteenth century. The earliest developments in the history of Bislama took place outside of Vanuatu, which was then known as the New Hebrides. Soon after the establishment of the British colony of New South Wales in 1788, a pidgin developed which was used between settlers and Aboriginal peoples along the ever-expanding frontier (Baker 1993). Features of this pidgin made their way into what has often been referred to as South Seas Jargon, which was spoken by ships' crews and individuals on shore in a wide variety of locations around the Pacific islands in the early 1800s (Clark 1979–1980; Keesing 1988).

Bislama first became established in southern Melanesia on trading stations established by Europeans in the southern islands of Vanuatu and the Loyalty Islands of New Caledonia from around the mid-1800s (Crowley 1990: 60–65). Europeans were engaged in a three-way trade which involved sandalwood and sea slugs (or *beche de mer*) that were sold in China, tea from China that was sold in the Australian colonies, and iron, cloth and other trade goods from the colonies of eastern Australia that were traded for sandalwood and sea slugs in southern Melanesia. The European traders employed substantial numbers of people from a variety of different islands on their shore stations with the result that these stations were linguistically very mixed. The fairly unstable pre-existing South Seas Jargon, based largely on an English lexicon, quickly became the basis for a new variety of contact language used in association with these stations. This variety began to stabilize during the 1850s–1860s and acquired a number of local characteristics. Given its association with the sandalwood and beche de mer trades, it came to be known alternatively as Sandalwood English or Beche de Mer English. The name Sandalwood English was soon replaced completely by Beche de Mer English, which eventually became Bislama, the name by which the language is generally known in Vanuatu today.

These developments were further promoted by the widespread use of the contact language throughout the 1870s–1890s by Melanesian labourers on the sugar plantations of Queensland. The subsequent repatriation of most Vanuatu labourers after Queensland entered the new Commonwealth of Australia in 1901 ensured that knowledge of Bislama had become fairly widespread not only in the south but also in the central and northern islands of Vanuatu. However, while Bislama spread throughout Vanuatu during this era, it underwent contraction in the Loyalty Islands of New Caledonia, and it was gradually replaced there as the lingua franca by French in the decades after France established itself as the colonial power in 1853 (Crowley 1990: 65–70).

It was not until 1906 that colonial government was established in Vanuatu, making the islands probably the last part of the world to be placed under colonial control. The system of government that was established was also unique in that the New Hebrides were jointly administered by Britain and France as a "condominium". A local plantation economy was established during this period which further encouraged the spread of Bislama throughout the entire archipelago, as this promoted internal population movement. The language underwent a variety of lexical and structural developments, to the point where it had come to acquire the basic features that we find in Bislama today by the second quarter of the twentieth century. Contact with both English and French on these plantations – as many of the plantations were in fact French-owned – provided a point of contrast in the development of Bislama with the mutually intelligible varieties of Melanesian Pidgin spoken in Solomon Islands (where it is known as Pijin) and Papua New Guinea (where it is known as Tok Pisin).

The traditional animist religions of Vanuatu have for the most part been replaced by, or perhaps merged with, introduced Christianity. However, people continue to live for the most part in small rural villages and are dependent on subsistence agriculture for their livelihoods. The Melanesian speakers of Bislama are culturally and physically quite different from the indigenous people of Australia to the west, as well as being quite different from their Polynesian neighbours to the east. However, the Melanesian people of Vanuatu exhibit many cultural and physical similarities with their Melanesian neighbours in Solomon Islands and Papua New Guinea to the north and northwest, as well as with the indigenous people of New Caledonia to the south.

One major point of linguistic similarity between Vanuatu, the Solomon Islands and Papua New Guinea relates to the continued use of different varieties of Melanesian Pidgin in the three countries. Intensive contact between people from the three countries ceased with the end of recruiting to the sugar plantations of Queensland after the federation of the Australian colonies in 1901. With more than a century of independent development since then each variety has acquired a number of distinctive features. For part of this period, speakers of Tok Pisin in German New Guinea were exposed to German and there has been some lexical influence from this language which is absent in both Bislama and Solomons Pijin. Mention has already been made of contact with French in Vanuatu which has resulted in a significant input of French vocabulary that we do not find in the other two national varieties. Finally, of course, the different vernaculars in the three countries have each contributed a certain amount of vocabulary from local sources.

2.   Sociolinguistic situation

The New Hebrides became politically independent from Britain and France in 1980. The nation renamed itself at that time as Vanuatu, a word which derives from widely distributed indigenous words of the shape *vanua* 'land' and *tu* 'stand', which was intended to symbolize the independent status of the new republic. Vanuatu is a highly multilingual nation boasting at least 80 actively spoken languages (and up to a couple of dozen other languages that have either become extinct or which have become moribund since initial contact with Europeans) distributed across a population of about 200,000 (Crowley 2000). It has the most complex linguistic demography of any country in the world in terms of the number of languages per head of population.

At independence, Bislama was declared by the constitution to be the national language, largely in order to avoid the need to make what would have been a politically divisive choice between English and French. This declaration makes Vanuatu unique among the countries of the world in that it has a former pidgin language that has higher constitutional status than a former colonial language. English and French are recognized alongside Bislama as co-equal "official languages", and they (but not Bislama) are also declared to be "languages of education". However, Bislama is effectively the default language throughout the country when people with different vernacular backgrounds come together, with English and French seldom being used informally or conversationally.

Bislama began its life as a plantation pidgin performing a fairly restricted range of functions and having, therefore, a relatively restricted vocabulary. However, over the last few decades it has dramatically expanded in the range of contexts in which it is used. It is now widely used as a language, particularly in urban areas, of religious worship, national and local politics (including parliamentary debate), the bureaucracy, the legal system, shopping, work, sport, the radio, friendship and romance, and even family life. As a result, the lexicon of Bislama has expanded dramatically to allow its speakers to meet a wide variety of new needs. Much of this expansion has been met by borrowing from English (e.g. *palemen* 'parliament') or, to a lesser extent, French (e.g. *lepap* 'pope' < *le pape*), though a fair amount of new vocabulary has also developed spontaneously on the basis of original Bislama roots (e.g. *mama loa* 'constitution' < *mama* 'mother' + *loa* 'law').

A national identity for the new Republic of Vanuatu is currently being forged, but this identity is largely expressed through the medium of Bislama rather than any of the local vernaculars, or through English or French. Accompanying this sense of national identity expressed through Bislama, associated to a significant extent with the relatively young urban population in the main centres of Port Vila and Luganville, is a very rapid stylistic expansion of the language into areas of youthful enthusiasm and adventure. Since independence, there has been a dramatic resurgence of traditional kava drinking, which is largely carried out through the medium of Bislama. Patterns of youthful indulgence in alcohol, partying and dancing, along with urban issues such as unemployment and inter-communal disputes have also brought Bislama into new social domains for which its speakers have needed to acquire new vocabulary and stylistic variation (Crowley 1989).

Although nearly all children these days attend English- or French-medium primary schools for six years where metropolitan languages represent the dominant (or only) medium of instruction – and smaller numbers proceed to secondary and even tertiary education –, neither English nor French has any significant use informally among Ni-Vanuatu (as citizens of Vanuatu are called). These formerly colonial languages function as "high" languages in a kind of diglossic relationship with Bislama at the national level, being reserved largely for written or official purposes, with Bislama being the language of choice even for most tertiary-educated Ni-Vanuatu in informal and spoken contexts.

Despite the fact that Bislama began its history as nobody's first language, thereby qualifying unambiguously as a pidgin language, it has gradually been acquiring small numbers of first-language speakers. Possibly as much as ten percent of the population today grows up speaking Bislama and no local vernacular, largely as a result of marriages between people from different language groups living in urban centres or on plantations. Because of this, some writers insist on referring to Bislama as a "creole" rather than as a "pidgin", though in reality there are no clearly recognizable features by which Bislama acquired as a second language and Bislama acquired as a first language can be differentiated, with the distinction therefore being essentially meaningless in the local context. My own preference is to avoid such a pointless distinction by referring to Bislama generically as a "contact language".

3.   Lexicon

Although the lexicon of Bislama is predominantly English in origin, there is nevertheless a substantial minority of words which derive from other sources (compare Crowley 1995 for a fairly comprehensive and up-to-date dictionary of Bislama). About 3.75% of the total number of entries in the Bislama lexicon derive from local vernacular sources (e.g. /nakamal/ 'meeting house', /nawita/ 'octopus', /nawimba/ 'Pacific pigeon'), while between 6% and 12% derive from French (e.g. /masut/ 'diesel' < *mazout*, /pamplimus/ 'grapefruit' < *pamplemousse*), and about 0.25% of the lexicon derives from a variety of other sources (e.g. /pikinini/ 'child' < Portuguese *pequenho* 'small' via South Seas Jargon, /burau/ '*Hibiscus tiliaceus*' < Tahitian *pūrau*, /nalnal/ 'club' < Early Australian Aboriginal Pidgin *nalanala*). The range 6–12% for words of French origin rather than a fixed figure is because the forms of a substantial number of words are ambiguous betweeen an English and a French origin, e.g. /sigaret/ < *cigarette*, /plastik/ < English *plastic* or French *plastique*, /letrik/ < English *electric* or French *électrique*.

Melanesian etyma are most widely encountered in semantic fields for which neither English nor French provided terms which were readily accessible to Europeans in the early contact situation (or since). We therefore find a substantial number of names for local flora and fauna being expressed by means of words of local origin, e.g. /nakavika/ 'Malay apple', /nakatambol/ 'dragon plum', /nanai/ 'native almond', /natora/ 'island teak', /nasiviru/ 'coconut lory', /natamap/ 'castrated boar'. Terminology relating to Melanesian cultural practices and artefacts is also often expressed by words of local origin, e.g. /nakaimas/ 'sorcerer', /nakamal/ 'meeting house', /nimangi/ 'grade-taking ceremony', /nasama/ 'outrigger (of canoe)', /laplap/ 'type of food'. It should be noted that nouns of Melanesian origin are often, though by no means always, incorporated into Bislama with the widely distributed noun phrase marker proclitic (or prefix) /na-/ reanalyzed as an invariant part of the noun.

French etyma are distributed across a wider range of semantic fields, making it more difficult to predict what meanings are likely to be expressed by means of words of English origin and which will be expressed by words of French origin. Some words of French origin clearly relate in a variety of ways to the French colonial presence, either through administrative terminology such as /delege/ 'French district agent' < *délégué*, /lameri/ 'town hall' < *la mairie*, terminology associated with catholicism such as /lames/ 'mass' < *la messe*, /per/ 'priest' < *père*, or terminology associated with fine cuisine and restaurant dining such as /lai/ 'garlic' < *l'ail*, /pima/ 'chilli' < *piment*, /susut/ 'choko' < *chouchoutte*, /gato/ 'cake' < *gateau*. It will be noted once again that nouns from French are often incorporated into Bislama with the preposed definite article *le* or *la* attached as an inseparable part of the noun itself as /le-/ or /la-/.

However, other meanings seem to be fairly unpredictably expressed by means of words of French or English origin. It is difficult, for example, to see why the children's game of tag should be referred to in Bislama as /lelu/ (< French *le loup*) rather than by a word of English origin, or why some playing cards are referred to by words of French origin (e.g. /las/ 'ace' < *l'ace*, /pik/ 'spades' < *pique*) while others are referred to by means of English etyma (e.g. /daiman/ 'diamonds', /hat/ 'hearts'). It should also be noted that there is a substantial number of synonymous pairs involving words of both English and French origin, e.g. /ariko/ (< French *haricot*) and /bin/ 'bean', /pistas/ (< French *pistache*) and /pinat/ 'peanut', /lapul/ (< French *l'ampoule*) and /glop/ 'light globe'.

The bulk of the Bislama lexicon, however, is clearly of English origin. In some cases, either the form or the meaning of an English word, or both, has been substantially changed in Bislama (or the English form from which a Bislama word has been derived is now seldom used in modern English). We therefore find examples such as /purumbut/ 'step on' (< *put 'im foot*), /kolta/ 'bitumen' (< *coal tar*), /giaman/ 'tell lies' (< nineteenth-century Australian English *gammon*), /solmit/ 'promiscuous' (< *salt-meat*).

In yet other cases, the English source of a Bislama form is immediately obvious, though the meaning may have been substantially modified, often under the direct influence of vernacular semantic patterns. Thus, Bislama /han/ comes from English *hand*, but it translates as both 'arm' and 'hand', following the widespread lack of separate terms for these meanings in vernaculars. In the same way, Bislama /lek/ (from English *leg*) covers the meaning of both 'leg' and 'foot' in English.

There is a substantial component of the lexicon involving words that are ultimately based on English lexical sources yet which have been compounded creatively by speakers of Bislama to express meanings without having to resort to direct lexical copying from English. During the Second World War, for example, when Ni-Vanuatu were first exposed to grenades through their association with American troups, they coined their own term for this, i.e. /hanbom/ < /han/ 'hand/arm' + /bom/ 'bomb'. The same pattern has been used for the more recent coinage /roketbom/ 'missile' < /roket/ 'rocket' + /bom/ 'bomb'. Local flora and fauna also often came to be referred to by means of such compound terms, e.g. /blufis/ 'parrotfish' < /blu/ 'blue' + /fis/ 'fish', /retwut/ 'Java cedar' < /ret/ 'red' + /wut/ 'wood'.

4.   Phonemic contrasts and phonetic realizations

4.1.   Vowels

Table 1.   Bislama vowels – summary

Orthographic form	Phonetic form	English source
FIT	[fit]	fit
DRES	[dres]	dress
TRAK	[trak]	truck
HOT	[hot]	hot
GAT	[gat]	gut
PUTUM	[putum]	put him
PAS	[pas]	pass
KOF	[kof]	cough
NES	[nes]	nurse
PIS	[pis]	piece
FES	[fes]	face
PAMA	[pama]	Paama (island)
DOTA	[dota]	daughter
KOT	[kot]	coat
JUS	[tʃus]	juice
PRAES	[prais]	price
JOES	[tʃois]	choice
MAOT	[maut]	mouth
BIA	[bia]	beer
SKWEA	[skwea]	square
STAT	[stat]	start
NOT	[not]	north
FOS	[fos]	force
SUA	[sua]	sure
HAPI	[hapi]	happy
LETA	[leta]	letter
MASIS	[masis]	matches
BARAKUTA	[barakuta]	barracouda

Bislama is usually described as having the following five-way vowel contrast (with no phonemically contrastive length):

i   u
e   o
      a

These segments have phonetic values that correspond closely to the cardinal IPA values, with little observable allophonic variation. There is a tendency for rural or lesser educated speakers from the island of Tanna to phonetically lengthen a stressed vowel in a disyllabic word, and to reduce an unstressed vowel in a closed final syllable to a high central vowel, resulting in alternations for a form such as /apol/ 'apple' as [ápol] and [áːpɨl]. Such pronunciations, however, are strongly stigmatized, and their appearance seems to be exaggerated as a result of stereotyping.

As with the consonants, there are some fairly regular correspondences between the shapes of Bislama words and their corresponding English or French etyma, with substantial reduction in the number of contrasts between English and Bislama. English /aː/, /æ/ and /ʌ/, for example, regularly correspond to Bislama /a/, e.g. /mak/ 'mark', /man/ 'man', /taŋ/ 'tongue'. New words are constantly being incorporated into the language from English and French by generalizing on these correspondences. This is not to say, however, that the forms of Bislama words can be unfailingly predicted from the shape of an English word. There are substantial numbers of unpredictable shifts such as /talem/ 'tell' (rather than /telem/), /rusum/ 'roast' (rather than /rosem/) and /flaik/ 'flag' (rather than /flak/). The most regular patterns of correspondence between English and French vowels on the one hand and Bislama vowels on the other are set out in Table 2.

Table 2.   Bislama vowels from English and French sources

Eng.	Fr.	Bis.	Source word	Bislama word	
i	i	i	*leak*	lik	'leak'
			pique	pik	'spades (in cards)'
ɪ	ɪ	i	*lick + him*	likim	'lick'
			quitte-à-quitte	kitkit	'draw (in sport)'
–	e	e	*pétanque*	petoŋ	'French bowls'
ɛ	ɛ	e	*leg*	lek	'foot, leg'
			arrière	arier	'reverse'

Table 2. (continued)   Bislama vowels from English and French sources

Eng.	Fr.	Bis.	Source word	Bislama word	
æ	–	a	*man*	man	'man'
a	a	a	*mark*	mak	'mark'
			mazout	masut	'diesel'
ʌ	–	a	*tongue*	taŋ	'tongue'
-ə	—	-a	*together*	tugeta	'together'
o	o	o	*sauce*	sos	'sauce'
			gateau	gato	'cake'
ɔ	ɔ	o	*salt*	sol	'salt'
			pilote	pilot	'tug boat'
u	u	u	*boot*	but	'boot'
			bouton	butoŋ	'button'
ʊ	ʊ	u	*cook*	kuk	'cook'
			gourmand	gurmoŋ	'sucker (of plant)'
–	y	i	*putain*	piteŋ	'whore'
–	ʏ	i	*butteur*	biter	'shooting marble'
–	ø	e	*monsieur*	misie	'sir'
–	œ	e	*butteur*	biter	'shooting marble'
–	ɛ̃	eŋ	*putain*	piteŋ	'whore'
–	ɔ̃	oŋ	*bouchon*	busoŋ	'cork, stopper'
—	ã	oŋ	*croissant*	kwasoŋ	'croissant'

It should be noted that non-final central vowels tend to be fairly unpredictably reflected in Bislama as /o/, /e/, /i/ or /a/. We therefore find English etyma such as the following where /ɜː/ is reflected invariably as /o/: /bon/ 'burnt', /wok/ 'work'. In /tanem/ 'turn' it is reflected invariably as /a/, in /gel/ 'girl' it is reflected as /e/, while in the word for 'shirt' it is reflected variably as /set ~ sot/. Non-final schwa also often varies between /o/, /e/ or /a/, as in /ofisol ~ ofisel ~ ofisal/ 'official'.

Words in English containing diphthongs beginning with mid vowels and ending in a high vowel of the same value for frontness and roundedness tend to be somewhat variable in their Bislama reflexes. Word-medially, such diphthongs are generally reflected simply as mid vowels with no off-glide, e.g.

Eng.	*Bis.*	*Source word*	*Bislama word*	
oʊ	o	*post*	pos	'post'
eɪ	e	*cake*	kek	'cake'

Word-finally, there is rather more variation between monophthongal and diphthongal reflexes in Bislama, e.g.

Eng.	*Bis.*	*Source word*	*Bislama word*	
-oʊ	-o(u)	*blow*	blo ~ blou	'blow'
-eɪ	-e(i)	*day*	de ~ dei	'day'

Word-final diphthongs beginning with a mid vowel and having a schwa off-glide – corresponding to post-vocalic /r/ in rhotic dialects of English – also vary in their Bislama reflexes between a simply mid vowel and sequences of /ea/ and /oa/, e.g.

Eng.	*Bis.*	*Source word*	*Bislama word*	
-oə	-o(a)	*more*	mo ~ moa	'more'
-eə	-e(a)	*where*	we ~ wea	'where'

4.2.   Consonants

Table 3 sets out the consonants which can be shown to contrast in Bislama.

Table 3.   Bislama consonants

p	t	c	k	
b	d		g	
m	n		ŋ	
v				
f		s		h
	r			
	l			
w		j		

This inventory represents something of a mesolectal variety which is quite widely distributed among speakers of Bislama throughout Vanuatu. As will be demonstrated in section 4.3., there are some variations to this phoneme inventory.

These segments once again have phonetic realizations by and large that are suggested by the IPA values. The liquid represented as /r/ is phonetically normally an alveolar flap, though an occasional trilled articulation can be heard as a free variant. Some speakers produce instead a retroflex flap for this sound, though this is a strongly stigmatized pronunciation associated with speakers of particular local languages. The symbol /j/ represents a palatal semi-vowel. Particular note should be made of the fact that /c/ is generally realized as a voiceless post-alveolar grooved affricate, i.e. [tʃ], though there is often a slightly fronted realization, i.e. [ts].

Words of vernacular origin tend to be adopted into Bislama with minimal change in shape, as the Bislama consonant inventory very closely resembles that of widely distributed vernacular patterns. With a consonant inventory that is substantially reduced vis-à-vis those of English and French, however, we find that a number of contrasts are systematically merged in Bislama. In particular, the English contrasts between /s/, /z/, /ʃ/ and /ʒ/ are merged as /s/, e.g. /sain/ 'sign', 'shine', /resa/ 'razor'. The contrasts between /t/ and /θ/ on the one hand and /d/ and /ð/ on the other are merged as /t/ and /d/ respectively, e.g. /tin/ 'tin' and /tiŋtiŋ/ 'think', /dis/ 'dish' and /disfala/ 'this (< *this* + *fellow*)'. The contrast between voiced and voiceless segments is lost word-finally in Bislama, with only voiceless segments being found. Thus, the contrast between English *dog* and *dock* results in the homophonous form /dok/ meaning 'dog' and 'warehouse (< *dock*)' in Bislama.

The main patterns of correspondence between consonantal contrasts in standard English and French on the one hand and Bislama on the other are set in Table 4, along with illustrations of each pattern (with an English etymon presented first and a French etymon presented second).

Table 4.   Bislama consonants from English and French sources

Eng.	Fr.	Bis.	Source word	Bislama word	
p	p	p	*place*	ples	'place'
			pistolet	pistole	'pistol'
t	t	t	*tongue*	taŋ	'tongue'
			tricot	triko	'sweater'
k	k	k	*kitchen*	kicin	'cook-house'
			claquettes	klaket	'flip-flops'

Table 4. (*continued*)   Bislama consonants from English and French sources

Eng.	Fr.	Bis.	Source word	Bislama word	
b	b	b	*book*	buk	'book'
			barre à mine	baramin	'crowbar'
d	d	d	*dog*	dok	'dog'
			dame-jeanne	damsen	'flagon (of wine)'
g	g	g	*girl*	gel	'girl'
			délégué	delege	'district agent'
m	m	m	*man*	man	'man'
			manivelle	manivel	'starting handle'
n	n	n	*knife*	naif	'knife'
			cochonet	kosone	'jack (in bowls)'
–	-ɲ	-in	*champagne*	sompain	'champagne'
ŋ	–	ŋ	*tongue*	taŋ	'tongue'
l	l	l	*light*	lait	'light'
			le loup	lelu	'tag (game)'
rV	rV	rV	*right*	rait	'right'
			robinet	robine	'tap'
–	Vr	Vr	*arrière*	arier	'reverse'
h	–	h	*house*	haus	'house'
f	f	f	*friend*	fren	'friend'
			profiter	profite	'take advantage'
v	v	v	*vinegar*	viniga	'vinegar'
			avocat	avoka	'lawyer'
θ	–	t	*think + think*	tiŋtiŋ	'think'
ð-	–	d-	*this + fellow*	disfala	'this'
-ð-	–	-r-	*an + other + fellow*	narafala	'other'
s	s	s	*saucepan*	sospen	'saucepan'
			lycée	lise	'secondary school'
z	z	s	*razor*	resa	'razor'
			mazout	masut	'diesel'
ʃ	ʃ	s	*ship*	sip	'ship
			bouchon	busoŋ	'cork, stopper'

Table 4. (*continued*)   Bislama consonants from English and French sources

Eng.	Fr.	Bis.	Source word	Bislama word	
3	3	s	*decision*	disisen	'decision'
			gendarme	sondam	'French police'
tʃ	tʃ	c	*church*	cec	'church'
			caoutchouc	kaucuk	'rubber'
dʒ	–	c	*judge*	cac	'judge'
w	w	w	*west*	wes	'west'
			oui + oui	wiwi	'French (arch.)'
j-	–	j-	*you*	ju	'you (sg.)'
–	-j	-i	*l'ail*	lai	'garlic'

Note that with respect to French words containing /ɲ/, forms have only been attested as being incorporated into Bislama in which this segment appears word-finally, e.g. *champagne*. Note also that the correspondences presented above for /r/ hold up despite the substantial phonetic difference between this liquid in the three languages. Finally, words beginning with /j-/ are extremely rare in French and none of these have been incorporated into Bislama, hence the lack of examples above.

While it is often possible to predict by these fairly regular correspondence statements what form a word of English origin will take in Bislama, there is by no means a completely regular set of correspondences. Thus, while English /tʃ/ generally corresponds to Bislama /c/ as in /cec/ 'church', the form /sakem/ 'throw (< *chuck*)' is idiosyncratically reflected as /s/. Also, while English /r/ is the primary source of /r/ in Bislama, there are some forms in which Bislama intervocalic /r/ unexpectedly derives from a number of other sounds, as in /griri/ 'greedy' (where /-d-/ is reflected as /-r-/ rather than /-d-/) and /wora/ 'water' (where /-t-/ is reflected as /-r-/ rather than /-t-/). However, it is certainly not the case that all instances of intervocalic /-d-/ and /-t-/ in English can be reflected with /-r-/ in Bislama, as evidenced by invariant forms such as /hotel/ 'hotel' and /lada/ 'ladder'.

4.3.   Phonemic variation

Although many speakers operate with the consonant inventory just presented, there is considerable individual (and regional) variation in the maintenance of this set of contrasts with particular words. No comprehensive regional study of phonological diversity has ever been carried out on Bislama, nor has there been any empirically-based quantitative study of phonological variation. Phonological variation is also often related in informal comment locally to an individual's language of education – whether one is considered to be 'anglophone' or 'francophone' – though such comments have once again not been subjected to detailed empirical scrutiny.

It is difficult to present statements which cover all possibilities regarding variation from this basic pattern of consonantal contrasts given that there is a fairly extensive range of possibilities. The following general observations can be made about the loss of phonemic contrasts vis-à-vis the basic consonant inventory, though it should be recognized that some additional phonemic mergers may be encountered among small groups of speakers, or in particular lexical sets with some speakers:

(i)   The contrast between voiced and voiceless stops is not consistently made. For some speakers, there appears to be little contrast at all, with only voiceless unaspirated stops found in all environments. It is far more common, however, for a contrast to be made, but for the contrast to be lost with some words. That is, while some speakers may contrast /dok/ 'dog' and /tok/ 'talk' on the one hand and /draim/ 'dry (something)' and /traim/ 'try' on the other, other speakers may merge /dok/ and /tok/ as /tok/ while maintaining a contrast between /draim/ and /traim/, and yet other speakers may merge /draim/ and /traim/ as /traim/ while maintaining a contrast between /dok/ and /tok/. If any merger takes place, it is most likely to be in the direction of the voiceless stops rather than the voiced stops.

(ii)   The contrast between /v/ and /f/ is also not very stable. The /v/ segment is not nearly as widely distributed as /f/ in any case, and some speakers lose the contrast entirely, having only /f/. This results in alternations such as /vanuatu/ and /fanuatu/ 'Vanuatu' within the speech community.

(iii) For many, perhaps even most, speakers, the contrast between voiced and voiceless stops is lost in homorganic nasal-stop clusters, this time in the direction of phonetically voiced segments. Thus, while for some speakers there may be a voicing difference in pairs such as /stampa/ 'base (< from English *stump*)' and /namba/ 'number', most people pronounce /stamba/ and /namba/ respectively.

(iv)   A small minority of speakers may go further than this in tending to lose the contrast between voiced and voiceless stops *and* homorganic nasal-stop clusters, pronouncing all as voiced prenasalized stops, particularly in word-initial position. Thus, a word that will be pronounced by many as /pik/ 'pig' may occasionally be encountered as /mbik/.

(v)   There also is a substantial amount of unpredictable alternation between voiceless stops and the corresponding voiceless fricatives, with /pik/ 'pig' and /faia/ 'fire' occasionally being heard as /fik/ and /paia/ respectively. This kind of alternation is strongly stigmatized with some words, but quite widespread with others.

(vi)   There is a tendency for the distinction between /c/ and /s/ to be lost among some speakers, or with some words, resulting in alternations such as /calus ~ salus/ 'jealous' and /cenis ~ senis/ 'change'.

(vii) The glottal fricative /h/ is often lost. This is especially frequent intervocalically with pronunciations such as /biain/ 'behind' being far more common than /bihain/, though it can also be lost word-initially, resulting in not-infrequent alternations such as /harem ~ arem/ 'hear'. (Note that /h/ is never found word-finally in Bislama.)

Given that for the vast majority of speakers, Bislama is acquired after the acquisition of one of 80 or so local vernaculars in childhood, these kinds of phonological mergers, as might be expected, correspond to some extent to the distribution of particular features in the substrate languages. It has been noted, for example, that in a number of languages from the island of Malakula, while there is a prenasalized /ᵐb/ phoneme, there is no correponding plain voiceless /p/, and it is precisely with speakers of such languages that more widely distributed pronunciations such as /pik/ 'pig' are encountered as /mbik/. The stigmatized retroflex flap articulation of /r/ that was mentioned earlier also appears to correspond closely to the distribution of retroflex rather than alveolar flap realizations of /r/ in local vernaculars, particularly those of northern Efate and parts of Pentecost island.

However, having pointed to a correlation between such variations from the basic phonological pattern described above and differences between local vernacular phonologies, we should exercise some caution in assuming that *all* regional phonological variation shares the same explanation. Not only do we have an inadequate knowledge of the distribution of variants to this basic phonological system of Bislama, but we have a detailed knowledge of the phonologies of only a small number of vernaculars (Lynch and Crowley 2001: 14–19). Even with the limited knowledge that we do have, it is not difficult to point to features of vernacular phonologies which are *not* carried over into Bislama. In the Paamese language, for instance, there is word-final neutralization of the contrast between /p/ and /v/ with phonetic free variation between stop and fricative realizations, though this does not seem to correspond to any tendency among speakers of Paamese to loose their contrast between the stop and fricative word-finally when they are speaking Bislama.

In addition to the kinds of phonological mergers just described, there are speakers who operate with somewhat expanded consonant and vowel inventories, at least for some words. This seems to correspond to a considerable extent to a higher command of English or French. With such speakers, we tend to find that not only is the contrast between /s/ and /c/ maintained, but there is also a tendency to distinguish between /s/ and /ʃ/ in words of English or French origin. Thus, in contrast to the majority pronunciations of /sup/ 'soup' and /sus/ 'shoe' we may encounter /sup/ and /ʃus/ respectively.

There also appears to be a tendency among better-educated speakers for the contrast between long (or diphthongized) and short (monophthongal) vowels in English – which is ordinarily completely lost in Bislama – to be maintained in the form of a tense-lax distinction. Thus, while /set/ for many speakers is the pronunciation for 'shirt' and 'agreed' (< *set*), some speakers may make a contrast between /sɛt/ 'agreed' and /set/ 'shirt'. It should be pointed out, however, that as far as I am aware, such an observation has not been offered in any previously published account of the language and study needs to be carried out by a well-trained phonetician to verify (or disconfirm) this.

Another area of phonemic uncertainty involves the relationship between vowel quality and phonemically contrastive voicing with stops in word-final position in words of English origin. It was indicated above that there is no contrast in Bislama word-finally between /p, t, k/ on the one hand and /b, d, g/ on the other, with minimally contrasting pairs in English ending up as homophones in Bislama. Although I am fairly confident that there is indeed no final voicing contrast in Bislama, it may be worth investigating the possibility that there may be some kind of surviving contrast in nature of the preceding vowel. My suspicion is that there may be some kind of acoustically detectable laxness in the vowel of forms such as /pik/ 'pig' in contrast to a more tense vowel in /pik/ 'plectrum (< *pick*)'. Such a test would need to be carefully constructed so that it is based on natural pronunciations without any possibility of contamination from spelling pronunciations.

4.4. Orthography

Bislama is a written language with a spelling system that has been developing for several decades. The development of the written form of the language coincided initially with the greater use of the language for religious purposes with the first translations of the gospels being produced in the 1970s, leading up to a translation of the entire Old and New Testaments by 1997. The 1970s also saw a rise of political consciousness associated with a sense of nationalism. The struggle for independence, along with political debates and campaigns since then, have largely been conducted through the medium of both spoken and written Bislama.

The spelling system largely reflects the set of phonemic contrasts presented at the beginning of this chapter, with orthographic *ng* representing /ŋ/, *j* representing /c/, *y* representing the glide /j/, and *ae* and *ao* representing the diphthongs /ai/ and /au/ respectively. Some etymologically – rather than phonemically – based spellings have become more or less universally accepted. In particular, the word-final voicing contrast in English is typically maintained in the Bislama spelling system for words of English origin, even though the voicing contrast is not made by most speakers. We therefore find an orthographic contrast in Bislama between *dok* 'warehouse (< *dock*)' and *dog* 'dog', even though phonemically both can be represented as /dok/.

5.　　Phonotactics

Bislama phonotactics can be described in general as being somewhat simplified with respect to the consonant-cluster possibilities that we find in English. Word-final clusters which undergo sporadic reduction word-finally in English are systematically simplified in Bislama, e.g. /distrik/ 'district', /han/ 'hand, arm'. Other final clusters which do not undergo simplification in English are also regularly reduced in Bislama, e.g. /stam/ 'stamp', /stiŋ/ 'stink'. Some word-final clusters involving a consonant followed by a sibilant are optionally separated by an epenthetic front vowel, e.g. /bokis ~ boks/ 'box', /sikis ~ siks/ 'six', /canis ~ cans/ 'chance'. Other consonant sequences are also sporadically affected by vowel epenthesis, e.g. /melek/ 'milk', /lasitern ~ lasiterin/ 'in-ground water reservoir (< French *la citerne*)', /film ~ filem/ 'film'.

Initial and medial consonant clusters are much less likely to undergo reduction, though changes are nonetheless encountered. Three-member intervocalic clusters may be simplified by deleting one of the consonants, e.g. /letrik/ 'electricity (< *electric*)', while initial two-member clusters may be simplified by the optional insertion of an epenthetic vowel, e.g. /bulu ~ blu/ 'blue'. Sometimes, consonant cluster simplification may not involve a reduction in the number of consonants involved but involve instead assimilation of one consonant to another, e.g. /fraimpan/ 'frying pan'.

Despite the general tendency for the simplification of consonant clusters in Bislama, a substantial number of relatively complex consonant sequences are retained, e.g. /faktri/ 'factory', /distrik/ 'district'. Many of the kinds of consonant clusters that are retained directly reflect permissible sequences in English. Thus, just as we encounter three-member word-initial sequences of /str-/ in English but no instances of /stl-/, so too do we find words in Bislama such as /strap/ 'belt (< *strap*)' but no instances of Bislama words beginning with /stl-/.

It should be pointed out that statements about phonotactic changes between English and Bislama do not invariably involve either retention of original clusters or the simplification of original clusters. There is plentiful evidence also for the development of new clusters in Bislama from English-derived forms where there were no clusters to begin with. We therefore find instances of vowel loss between English and Bislama which result in consonant clusters such as /wokbaut/ 'walk (about)'. In some cases, we find competing forms involving the presence or absence of a vowel between consonants, e.g. /sidaun ~ staun/ 'sit (down)', /sigaret ~ skaret/ 'cigarette', /basikel ~ baskel/ 'bike (< *bicycle*)', /finisim ~ finsim/ 'finish'.

Apart from these observations about consonant clusters, Bislama phonotactics is for the most part covered by the same kinds of observations that hold for English. There are, of course, subcomponents of the lexicon which do not derive from English for which other kinds of phonotactic statements can be made. In particular, those words which have local vernacular sources are based by and large on syllable structures of the type CV(C), which allows for word-initial single consonants, word-final single consonants or vowels, and two-member medial clusters, in words such as /nakatambol/ 'dragon plum'.

6.   Phonological processes

There are very few general morphophonemic processes in Bislama. One of the characteristic features of pidgin and creole languages is the tendency to avoid derivational complexity in phonology and morphology. However, attention is drawn to variation in the form of the transitive suffix canonically represented as /-Vm/. The functions of this suffix will be dealt with in the chapter on Bislama morphosyntax (see Crowley, this volume), and I will concentrate here only on the forms of the suffix.

With verbs ending in consonants preceded by either a diphthong or by a non-high single vowel, the transitive suffix appears as /-em/, e.g. /tan-em/ 'turn', /bon-em/ 'burn', /let-em/ 'permit, let', /boil-em/ 'boil', /fain-em/ 'find'. Following a consonant-final root preceded by a high vowel, the vowel of the suffix harmonizes with the final vowel of the root, e.g. /kil-im/ 'kill', /pul-um/ 'pull'. With vowel-final roots, the transitive suffix appears as /-m/ after front vowels, e.g. /ciki-m/ 'be cheeky to', /pe-m/ 'pay', as /-em/ after /o/, e.g. /boro-em/ 'borrow', as /-im/ after /u/, e.g. /blu-im/ 'blow' and as /-rem/ after /a/, e.g. /hama-rem/ 'hammer'.

7.   Prosodic features and intonation patterns

Stress in Bislama is not predictable. Although this means that stress is phonemically contrastive, I am not aware of any pair of lexical items which differ in meaning solely by the position of stress. However, there are words in Bislama in which stress appears on the initial syllable in words of very similar phonotactic shape, e.g. /nákamal/ 'meeting house', /kálabus/ 'prison', /píkinini/ 'child', the second syllable, e.g. /novémba/ 'November', /nabáŋga/ 'banyan', the third syllable, e.g. /demonstrésen/ 'demonstration', /nakatámbol/ 'dragon plum', and even words in which stress appears on the final syllable, e.g. /lakaskát/ 'waterfall'.

It probably makes more sense to subdivide the vocabulary of Bislama into its etymological source languages, treating English, French and Melanesian etyma separately. Words originating from local vernaculars behave overwhelmingly according to the pattern that we find in Oceanic languages whereby stress is systematically applied to the penultimate syllable. This would therefore account for the position of stress in words such as /nabáŋga/ 'banyan' and /nakatámbol/ 'dragon plum' presented above. Following widespread vernacular patterns, a diphthong in a final closed syllable is also stressed in Bislama, e.g. /namaláus/ '*Garuga floribunda*'. Where two syllables have been historically reduplicated, the second element does not count for syllable-counting purposes, meaning that stress is found on the penultimate syllable of the unreduplicated root, e.g. /napíripiri/ 'sea hearse tree', /nadúledule/ 'red silkwood'.

However, the generalizations just presented represent strong tendencies in Bislama rather than exceptionless rules, and some forms of vernacular origin exhibit stress patterns which vary from these. In some cases, we find that the initial syllable is stressed, e.g. /námarai/ 'eel', /nákamal/ 'meeting house', while in other cases the second syllable is stressed, e.g. /namáriu/ 'acacia tree'. These irregularities are unlikely to derive from divergent patterns in the substrate language, so there seems to have been a genuine unpredictable shift of stress in these cases.

Forms of French origin are often found with stress on the final syllable, which is what we would expect given the ultimate-syllable stress pattern of the source language. Thus: /glasóŋ/ 'ice block', /restoróŋ/ 'restaurant', /limonát/ 'soft drink (< *limonade*)', /maratóŋ/ 'running shoes (< *marathon*)'. However, final stress in words of French origin is again not universal, and we do find forms in which stress has shifted, e.g. /kálsoŋ/ '(men's) underpants', /pétoŋ/ 'French bowls (< *pétanque*)', /bóndi/ 'criminal (< *bandit*)'.

Finally, we have the English-derived bulk of the lexicon. Unlike French and the Melanesian languages, stress is not predictable in English, and this unpredictability is mirrored in words of English origin in Bislama. For the most part, the position of stress in Bislama can be deduced from the position of stress in English, e.g. /pálamen/ 'parliament', /haibískis/ 'hibiscus', /demonstrésen/ 'demonstration'.

One feature of Bislama that is immediately obvious to even a new learner of the language is its intonation pattern. Not only is the primary intonation pattern of Bislama clearly different from that of English and the various vernacular languages, but it is also quite distinct from what we find in mutually intelligible Solomons Pijin and Papua New Guinea Tok Pisin. In talking about Bislama intonation, it is difficult (for the present writer at least) to go beyond vague impressions, but there does seem to be a substantially greater rise towards the end of a statement, followed by a much more noticeable drop immediately afterwards at the end of the statement than we find in any of the other languages (or varieties of Melanesian Pidgin) to which I have just referred. This gives the impression that Bislama has something of a "sing-song" intonation. My only suggestion for a possible source for this intonation is that it may reflect a French source, though this is little more than an impression which would need to be verified by checking against a detailed empirical comparison of the intonation patterns of both languages.

The amount of descriptive material relating to Bislama has increased substantially since the 1970s, and we now have a fairly comprehensive published dictionary (Crowley 1995), as well as quite detailed discussions of particular aspects of the grammar, but there is still no publicly available grammar of the language. Matters of phonology have typically also been covered briefly (or not at all) in published material relating to Bislama. As far as I know, this chapter contains the only published statement of any kind relating to stress in Bislama, brief as this may be. There has also been no acoustic verification of the set of phonemic contrasts postulated for Bislama, and this chapter has – albeit somewhat tentatively – presented a number of specific suggestions regarding areas that might be worthy of investigation. Finally, of course, there is a real need to follow up the suggestion in the preceding paragraph regarding the need for a comparative study of Bislama intonation patterns.

* Many thanks to John Lynch for comments to an earlier version of this paper. Final responsibility for all claims, however, remains with the author.

Exercises and study questions

1. Look at the following words and say what you think the corresponding
   Bislama words should be:
   corner
   Monday
   name
   rabbit
   meat

2. Look at the following words in French and say what you think the corresponding Bislama words should be:
   légume 'vegetable'
   cérise 'cherry'
   chouchoutte 'choko'
   bonbon 'sweets'
   bougie 'spark plug'

3. Examine the following words and say what you think the English origin of
   each is:
   /nanigot/ 'goat'
   /bolpik/ 'uncastrated boar'
   /klosap/ 'near'
   /sotwin/ 'puff'
   /kaufis/ 'dugong'

4. Add the correct form of the transitive suffix to the following roots to make a
   transitive verb:
   /rit/ 'read'
   /kuk/ 'cook'
   /dro/ 'draw'
   /melek/ 'milk'
   /smok/ 'smoke'
   /draun/ 'sink'
   /tait/ 'tight'
   /pam/ 'pump'

5. Each of the following words exhibits some kind of irregular change from
   its English source. What do you think the English sources are and what is
   irregular about these forms in Bislama?
   /punpun/ 'skinny'
   /merikanrop/ 'kind of vine'

/solap/ 'swollen'
/kapa/ 'roofing iron'
/kapsait/ 'tip over'

6. Compare the following Bislama words with their English sources, and say what sorts of phonotactic changes appear to have taken place in Bislama:
/distrik/ 'district'
/brodkas/ 'broadcast'
/simen/ 'cement'
/silik/ 'silk'
/bokis/ 'box'
/turu/ 'true'
/steret/ 'straight'

Selected references

Please consult the General references for titles mentioned in the text but not included in the references below. For a full bibliography see the accompanying CD-ROM.

Baker, Philip
    1993   Australian influence on Melanesian Pidgin English. *Te Reo* 36: 3–67.
Clark, Ross
    1979–1980
            In search of Beach-la-mar: towards a history of Pacific pidgin English. *Te Reo* 22/23: 3–63.
Crowley, Terry
    1989   Referential and expressive expansion in Bislama. *English World-Wide* 16: 85–118.
    1990   *Beach-la-mar to Bislama: The Emergence of a National Language in Vanuatu.* (Oxford Studies in Language Contact.) Oxford: Clarendon.
    1995   *A New Bislama Dictionary.* Suva: Institute of Pacific Studies and Pacific Languages Unit, University of the South Pacific.
    2000   The language situation in Vanuatu. *Current Issues in Language Planning* 1: 47–132.
Lynch, John and Terry Crowley
    2001   *Languages of Vanuatu: A New Survey and Bibliography.* Canberra: Pacific Linguistics.

Solomon Islands Pijin: phonetics and phonology[*]

Christine Jourdan and Rachel Selbach

1. Sociohistorical background

1.1. A brief history of Solomon Islands Pijin

Solomon Islands Pijin is one of the three Melanesian pidgins (along with Tok Pisin spoken in Papua New Guinea, and Bislama spoken in Vanuatu) that are, more or less directly, the offshoots of the Pacific trade jargon of the early 19th century, known as Beach-la-Mar (Clark 1979; Keesing 1988). This early jargon is probably based on a pidgin that developed in Australia between the British settlers in New South Wales and the aboriginal population at the end of the 18th century (Troy 1985; Baker 1993). It further expanded and stabilized during the plantation period of the second part of the 19th century that linked the Melanesian archipelagos of Vanuatu and the Solomons to Australia. The labour trade to Queensland lasted for roughly 40 years, from 1863 to 1906. At the beginning of the trade period, the Australian planters started to recruit in New Caledonia, the New Hebrides, the Melanesian archipelago closest to Australia; when recruiting in the southern islands became difficult, they moved north towards the Banks Islands, the Santa Cruz archipelago and later, around 1874, toward the Solomon Islands. Around 13,000 Solomon Islanders were taken to Queensland during the forty-year period. The pidgin language (called Kanaka Pidgin English) that was used on the plantations became the lingua franca spoken among Melanesian workers (the Kanakas, as they were called) who did not share the same language, and between Melanesians and European overseers. When Solomon Islanders went back to the Solomons at the end of their contract, or when they were forcefully repatriated at the end of the labour trade period (1904), they brought Melanesian pidgin to the Solomon Islands. The result was that the pidgin became quite spread-out throughout the eastern part of the archipelago, but, not having a social *raison d'être*, it remained largely unused, except for affect. Back in the 1980s, old people could still remember the stories that were told by the old former Queensland hands many years after their return.

Following the annexation of the Solomon Islands by the British (1893), the pidgin became the medium by which Solomon Islanders interacted with British colonial officers and with other Solomon Islanders from different ethnic groups. Some employees of the early colonial administration, such as the constabulary, were recruited among pidgin speakers because their knowledge of the language meant that they had had previous contact with Europeans.

One of the first outcomes of the Pax Britannica in the Solomon Islands (1920) had been the expansion of a small local plantation economy that had appeared as early as 1910. The plantations required many labourers, and they were recruited from different islands. Solomon Islanders began to migrate within the archipelago, between the areas supplying the labour force (typically Malaita island) and the plantation areas (Guadalcanal and Russell islands). Not surprisingly, the first labourers to be recruited to work on the Solomon Islands plantations were men who had been to Queensland before and who knew pidgin. Thus, the Kanaka Pidgin English of Queensland was reactivated on a larger scale by people building on their previous knowledge of it. In those days, young men did not learn to speak that language until they went to work on the plantations. Over the years, circular migration allowed one or two generations of young men to be in contact with the pidgin, particularly in work-related activities. As a result, the pool of pidgin speakers progressively enlarged, and the language proved so successful as a lingua franca that it expanded very quickly within the population. On plantations, workers and overseers alike learnt the pidgin by listening to other people talk; workers learnt it from their fellow workers. The unspoken sociolinguistic rule was that people spoke their vernacular language with people belonging to their language group and used the pidgin with everybody else, the overseers included. Some old-timers acted as interpreters for the newcomers (*niusam*). Progressively the pidgin acquired local characteristics (phonetic and lexical particularly) and speakers came to refer to it as Pisin. It is now called Pijin and referred to as such hereafter.

Another important event in the history of Pijin is World War II and the presence of the American army in the archipelago in 1942. Even though most plantation labourers were repatriated during that time, many Solomon Islands men (around 2,000) were enrolled in the Solomon Islands Labour Corps and in the British Solomon Islands Protectorate Defence Force, in which 680 Islanders enlisted (Laracy 1983). Solomon Islanders who witnessed that period say that they spoke to the American soldiers in pidgin and sometimes in English when it was known to them. Many of the American soldiers had some very rudimentary knowledge of the Pidgin English spoken then in New Guinea. This pidgin, now called Tok Pisin, then called Melanesian pidgin, was one of the forty Pacific languages that the American army deemed potentially useful to their soldiers fighting in the Pacific. They taught it to the troops through the medium of a small handbook that had some phrases in Tok Pisin. Even though it is difficult to assess the degree of the transformation that Pijin underwent during that period, it is obvious that the more intensive the contact with English, the more the presence of English was going to be felt in Solomons Pijin.

It is during the time of Maasina Rulu 'the rule of brotherhood' (*maasina* 'brotherhood' 'Are'Are, a language spoken in Papua New Guinea, and *rulu* 'rule' English), the politico-religious movement that swept the island of Malaita after World War II (1944–1952) that Pijin became a political tool. The lingua franca became crucial to the movement very early on, as it was the only language that could be understood by all ethnic groups alike. It is through Pijin that the political ideology of the movement was disseminated in the Protectorate. Pijin assisted in the communication of the ideas of Maasina Rule (Bennett 1979), but also in forging the unity of the movement: linguistic barriers were broken down, and the notion of group identity gradually incorporated the wider notion of brotherhood. Through Pijin, the movement mobilized the Malaitan population and spread through traditional exchange networks, through mission links and through very large political meetings where people from different language groups came together.

1.2.   Contemporary Pijin

Solomon Islands Pijin is now spoken throughout the Solomons archipelago. It is, by far, the primary lingua franca of the island group, superseding missionary lingua francas. In view of its social history, Pijin from the start was used predominantly by adult males, most women and children simply having no access to it. It is still quite common nowadays to come across mature women in remote areas of the Solomon Islands who do not know Pijin at all. People, and women in particular, who were not incorporated into the traditional settings or contexts of Pijin usage and transmission (plantations, mission stations or schooling) had never had any need for Pijin, and/or any opportunities or incentive to learn it. The situation is being modified nowadays with increasing urbanization, widespread primary schooling, encroachment of a cash economy everywhere in the country, and growing transport links that make it possible for people to move back and forth between the villages and Honiara, the main Pijin-speaking area of the country. All these activities provide all members of the society, and not only men as had been the case before, with opportunities (and sometimes money) for travel within the island group. With increasing mobility, people of different linguistic traditions come in contact in a way and on a scale that differs drastically from traditional inter-group and/or inter-islands contacts. This has opened the way for Pijin to establish itself as the main language of the country.

1.3.   Sociolinguistic situation of contemporary Pijin

Since the 1960s, Pijin has become the main language of the capital city of Honiara and the mother tongue of many young urban adults and of a new generation of young urban children who know no other language but Pijin. Pijin is not only the medium of communication of urban life, it is the medium of a type of culture that is different in many respects from the cultural world of the plantations and villages. In Honiara, the strong position of Pijin is reinforced by the very high degree of language diversity we find in town (most of the 64 vernaculars of the country are represented in Honiara). People migrating to town had to learn Pijin quickly if they wanted to create a social life for themselves outside of the limits of the *wantok* system (*wantok* 'friend'). Due to the high number of inter-ethnic marriages in town, Pijin progressively found its way within the family circle, whereas it used to be used almost exclusively with non-family members, and particularly, with non-*wantok* people. The contexts of Pijin usage in town are far more diverse than they were when the language served as a plantation pidgin: Pijin is used for church services and church-related activities, in the public service, on the radio, in political circles and in parliament, in family life and other domains of urban social life. Over the years, Pijin has acquired some cultural depth that is expressed lexically through the borrowing of new words from English (e.g. *kompiuta* 'computer') or through expansion of the lexicon from Pijin roots (e.g. *masta liu* 'unemployed' *masta* 'master' + *liu* 'hang around'). The opposite result is that the lexicon, and the phonology, are changing quickly. A sociolinguistic norm essentially based on urban Pijin is appearing and is becoming the measure by which young urban people evaluate Pijin competence in others: they are quick to denigrate and make fun of non-urban ways of speaking the language, and to associate 'old' words with provincial ways of speaking and with lack of social sophistication. In the process, old words such as *panikini* 'cup', *furumbutu* 'step on', *gras* 'hair' are progressively being lost from the vocabulary of young urban people and are replaced by *kap* 'cup', *stepem* 'step on' and *hea* 'hair'. This meets with much resistance from provincial and older speakers, who are quick to qualify urban Pijin as *rabis* ('bad') and overly anglicized. In the provincial areas of the country, people tend to have access to Pijin at a much earlier age and in wider contexts of communication than before.

Despite not having the official status of a national language, Pijin has become the true national language of the Solomon Islands, the only linguistic mortar that has the potential of binding this new country together. Papua New Guinea and Vanuatu have recognized the major roles played by Tok Pisin and Bislama respectively in these countries by giving them national language status. One hopes that the Solomon Islands will soon do the same for Pijin.

But although Pijin is widely spoken, it is not widely written. Despite the efforts made by the Literacy Association of the Solomon Islands (LASI) and the Solomon Islands Christian Association (SICA) through the works of Solomon Islands Translation Advisory Group (SITAG), the language is not a popular medium of written communication. There are many reasons for this situation: Pijin lacks institutional support from government agencies, and it lacks cultural legitimacy. In addition, schooling at advanced levels is done in English, the official language of the country, and this puts pressure on the children to learn English at an early age. Over the years, new tools such as word lists (Beimer 1995) and dictionaries (Simons and Young 1978; Jourdan 2002) have been produced. No comprehensive grammar is publicly available yet.

Along with the lack of official legitimacy of the language comes a lack of a bona fide standard variety of Pijin. Variation therefore can and does flourish, both within and across sociolinguistic boundaries. This poses some difficulties for the unitary description of Pijin, including the level of phonology and phonetics. We have attempted to provide a conservative description of the phoneme inventory of Pijin below, followed by an introduction to the range and types of variation that may be displayed by different speakers. It should be kept in mind that even such basic description will be unavoidably tinged by analysis, and that what we provide here is a preliminary sketch of a complex situation.

2.   Phoneme inventory

Solomon Islands Pijin has a basic phoneme inventory that accommodates the sounds of the lexifier language English, but is simpler than that of English in having fewer phonemes. This also makes the phonology of Solomon Islands Pijin more like that of the substrate languages (all except for eight of the languages spoken on the Solomon Islands are Austronesian languages) whose presence in the archipelago antedates that of English and of Pijin, and on which the sound system can be said to be mapped. Very clear influence from the various Austronesian vernaculars is found in the phonetics of Pijin, where there is a great deal of both regional and idiolectal variation that can often be linked to the speakers' prior or other linguistic knowledge. There is also phonetic influence from English that is becoming apparent in some speakers of Taon Pijin (Pijin spoken in Honiara). We first describe the basic phoneme inventory, noting that it eschews uniform, unambiguous description. We then discuss further the range and type of variation that is actually found in the pronunciation of Pijin.

Orthographic form	Phonological form	English source
FIT	/fit/	*fit*
DRES	/dres/	*dress*
MAP	/map/	*map*
HOT	/hot/	*hot*
NAT	/nat/	*nut*
PUT	/put/	*put*
PAS	/pas/	*pass*
KOF	/kof/	*cough*
NES	/nes/	*nurse*
PIS	/pis/	*piece*
FES	/fes/	*face*
PAM	/pam/	*palm (tree)*
DOTA	/dota/	*daughter*
NANIGOT	/nanigot/	*goat*
LUS	/lus/	*loose*
PRAES	/prais/	*price*
CHOISEUL	/soisol/	*Choiseul (Island)*
MAOT	/maut/	*mouth*
BIA	/bia/	*beer*
SKWEA	/skwea/	*square*
STAT	/stat/	*start*
NOT	/not/	*north*
FOS	/fos/	*force*
KIUREM	/kyurem/	*cure*
HAPI	/hapi/	*happy*
LETA	/leta/	*letter*
MASIS	/masis/	*matches*
KOMMA	/koma/	*comma*

2.1.   Vowels

	Front	**Central**	**Back**
High	i		u
Mid	e		o
Low		a	

The phonetic realizations of the vowels depend on whether they occur in open or closed syllables. Vowels may be laxed and slightly lowered in closed syllables, such that /e/ will be realized as [ɜ] and /o/ as [ɔ] in such environments; cf. [drɛs] 'dress' and [hɔt] 'hot'.

Many speakers also make a phonetic distinction between long and short vowels, such as between the short [a] of *puskat* 'cat' and the long [aː] of *baa* 'bar', and between the [u] of *tufala* 'two' and the [uː] of *tuu* 'also'. Vowel length and syllable structure will be discussed in section 4 below.

Finally, there are speakers who use more than the three main diphthongs [ae], [ao] and [oe]. In these more anglicized varieties, they will thus also make a distinction between [ao] and [au], in such pairs as *haos* [haos] 'house' and *maut* [maut] 'mouth'. Other speakers use tense [ai] rather than [ae], distinguishing between the diphthongs in *baitim* [baitim] 'bite', and *bae* [bae] (future/Tense-Mood-Aspect [TMA] marker).

Some examples of the vowels are given in the following set of Pijin words:

/a/	*mama*	'mother'	/ae/	*faet*	'fight'
/e/	*save*	'know'	/ao/	*taon*	'town'
/i/	*pikinini*	'child'	/oe/	*boe*	'boy'
/o/	*orens*	'orange'	/au/	*maut*	'mouth'
/u/	*sukul*	'school'	/ai/	*baitim*	'bite'

2.1.   Consonants

		Labial	Alveolar	Palatal	Velar
Stops		p	t		k
		b	d		g
Fricatives		f	s		h
		v			
Affricate				č	
Nasals		m	n		ŋ
Approximants					
	Lateral		l		
	Central			y	w
Tap			ɾ		

In general, Pijin consonants are rather similar to the corresponding consonants of English, except that English /r/ is typically replaced by an alveolar flap /ɾ/. A more thorough comparison of Pijin words and their English cognates follows in section 5 below.

There is a good deal of variation across individual speakers' phoneme inventories, and as a result the decisions on inclusion and exclusion of phonemes in the above inventory are to some degree arbitrary. Not all speakers make use of the same set of distinctive features in their phoneme inventories, so that certain consonants will be conflated along different lines for different speakers. The voicing distinction is not always clear-cut, but both voiced and voiceless stops are included in the inventory as proposed above. For the alveolar fricative and the palatal affricate, however, we do not consider this distinction to be a phonemic one for most speakers. In reality, [č] alternates with [ǰ], which in turn alternate with [dy] and [d] in speakers who do not have palatal affricates. The palatal affricate may also be replaced with a fricative. The place of articulation of the fricative varies between alveolar [s] and palatal [ʃ].

č ~ ǰ ~ dy ~ d
č ~ ǰ ~ s ~ ʃ

[ǰ] and [ʃ] are not included in the inventory above, but are here considered phonetic variants of /č/ and /s/ respectively. Similarly, we will subsume [z] and [ʃ] under the voiceless /s/ as free variants, though clearly, some speakers apply a voicing distinction here. Slight feature differences in voicing, manner and place of articulation may therefore alter the individual speakers' distribution of sounds in their phonemic and phonetic systems.

Other salient variants in the system proposed here resulting from such minimal differences occur with speakers who replace [p] with [f], or others who replace [f] with [p]. Also, voiced stops are often prenasalized, a feature that is also present in the vernaculars. Consonants /b/, /d/, /g/ are then realized as [mb], [nd], and [ŋg]. In some cases, written forms include the homorganic nasal, but in others, they do not, the spellings selectively reflecting the variation, e.g. *sindaon* or *sidaon* 'sit down' and *babu* or *bambu* 'bamboo'. The influence of the vernaculars on these variants will be sketched below; see also Table 1 for examples of frequently heard alternate pronunciations.

3.   Analysis of variation

Pijin phonetics and phonology are highly variable and change from region to region. Three predominant factors create this variability:

1. the presence of vernaculars;
2. the presence of English; and
3. urbanization.

3.1.   The vernaculars

Vernacular refers to the languages that were present in the Solomon Islands before the arrival of the Europeans. Vernacular languages continue to be spoken in rural areas as well as in the capital Honiara, there often as a first but not as a main language. They were thus present before, during and after the formation of Pijin, and their influence on the new language continues to be felt. The pronunciation of Pijin is remarkable in that it resembles very much the pronunciation of these vernacular languages. This indicates that speakers tend to apply to Pijin the phonological rules that govern their own vernaculars. While keeping to vernacular sound patterns, lexemes derived from English must be reshaped in order to be accommodated, often in different ways by speakers of different vernaculars. This pattern explains in part the differences that exist between speakers, according to their islands of origin, or according to the vernacular they speak.

The variable influence of the vernaculars takes at least three different forms:

a. phonological substitution;
b. insertion of epenthetic vowels;
c. addition of final vowels

3.1.1.   *Phonological substitutions*

As not all the languages of the Solomon Islands have all the consonantal phonemes of 'standard' Pijin as it is coming to be codified, they will characteristically replace some Pijin consonants with the closest equivalents available in their vernaculars. They contrast, where possible, with the more canonical ones in no more than a single distinctive feature. Below are some examples of frequent substitutions.

(1)   voiced consonants > devoiced consonants

/b/ >   [p]
/g/ >   [k]
e.g. *big*   >   [pik]   'big'

(2)   fricatives > stops; stops > fricatives

       /f/ >   [p]   (e.g. speakers of Tolo)

       e.g. *finis* >   [pinis]   'finish'; TMA marker

       sif   >   [sip]   'chief'

       tufala   >   [tupala]   'two'

       /p/ >   [f]   (e.g. speakers of Kwaio)

       e.g. *Pijin* >   [fisin]   'Pijin'

(3)   (palatal) affricate >

       a.   alveolar fricative

       /č/ >   [s]

       e.g. *jej*   >   [ses]   'church'

          jifkuk >   [sifkuk]   'chef'

       b.   alveolar stop

       /č/ >   [d]

       e.g. *Japan* >   [dyapan]   'Japan'

          jes   >   [des]   'just'

(4)   voiced stops > nasalized voiced stops

       /b/ >   [mb]

       /g/ >   [ŋg]

       e.g. *tabu*   >   [tambu]   'taboo'

          sigaret >   [siŋgaret]   'cigarette'

For example, if one's mother tongue includes /p/ and not /f/, as in Tolo (an Austronesian language spoken on the island of Guadalcanal), the Pijin spoken by Tolo speakers will likely use [p] whenever [f] is standard. Children growing up in town and using Pijin as their main language, and sometimes as their mother tongue, will tend not to make this substitution, as their phoneme inventory will be likely to include both sounds.

Table 1 provides more examples of the possible substitutions most likely to take place motivated by the phonological system of the speaker's vernacular.

Table 1.   Sound variations due to the vernaculars

Substitution		Pijin		English gloss
/b/	[p]	*blong*	[plong]	belong
/b/	[v]	*kabis*	[kavis]	edible greens
/b/	[mb]	*baebae*	[baembae]	shall, will
/d/	[t]	*nogud*	[nogut]	bad
/d/	[nd]	*oda*	[onda]	order
/f/	[b]	*fis*	[bis]	fish
/f/	[p]	*wanfala*	[wanpala]	one, a, an
/g/	[k]	*pig*	[pik]	pig
/g/	[ŋg]	*sigaret*	[siŋgaret]	cigarette
/j/	[s]	*jamp*	[samp]	jump
/j/	[di]	*jamp*	[diamp]	jump
/l/	[r]	*liu*	[riu]	to wander aimlessly
/p/	[b]	*pensol*	[bensol]	pencil
/p/	[f]	*pijin*	[fisin]	pidgin
/r/	[l]	*riva*	[liva]	river
/r/	[d]	*rabis*	[dabis]	rubbish
/v/	[f]	*riva*	[rifa]	river
/v/	[b]	*muv*	[mub]	move
/v/	[w]	*hevinat*	[hewinat]	sago palm and nut
/w/	[ŋw]	*wesis*	[ŋwesis]	wages

3.1.2. Epenthesis

In addition, as consonant clusters do not occur in most of the languages of the Solomon Islands, speakers will tend to insert epenthetic vowels in Pijin words in order to avoid such clusters. The choice of the vowel is directed by rules of vowel harmony.

skul	>	[sukul]	'school'
olketa	>	[oloketa]	'they'; plural marker
spun	>	[supun]	'spoon'
trae	>	[tarae]	'try'
bisnis	>	[bisinis]	'business'
klaem	>	[kalaem]	'climb'

In town, and under the influence of English, this epenthetic vowel, more typical of rural Pijin, tends to disappear from the speech of many speakers, young
ones especially.

3.1.3. Paragogue

Just as vernaculars permit fewer consonant clusters, very seldom do they have
words ending with consonants. And just as epenthesis can break up unwanted
consonant clusters, paragogue is used in avoidance of word-final consonants.
Most rural speakers, and older speakers for whom vernaculars are the overwhelming medium of communication will tend to add a final vowel to Pijin
words derived from English words ending in a consonant, again according to
the same principle of vowel harmony. Hence, several of the words listed above
may be further expanded as follows, in order to arrive at preferred CV(CV)
syllable structures:

sukul	>	[sukulu]
supun	>	[supuni]
bisinis	>	[bisinisi]
kabis	>	[kabisi]	'leafy greens'

In sum, it should be stressed that (a) there are regional differences in the phonology of Pijin and that (b) even in the capital city Honiara, there is no uniform,
homogenized variety. However, as explained in the introduction, sociolinguistic norms are developing. People can often tell where someone comes from by
their accent; age, education and other sociolinguistic variables play an important role in determining how people will speak.

3.2.   English

Another cause of variation in Pijin is the speakers' contact with English, made
particularly important through schooling carried out in that language. Since the
majority of the Pijin lexicon is essentially derived from English, one's knowledge of English can more easily influence one's Pijin. Pijin /t/ or /d/ will then
become [ð]; /s/ will become [č]. This pattern is more predominant in town than
in the villages, according to the different roles that English plays in these two
areas. Under the guise of hypercorrection, Anglicization as a social marker is
also present in the speech of some speakers, exemplified by an overuse of [č],
[ð] etc. Below are examples of the adoption of non-Pijin phonemes (into long-
established core Pijin lexemes):

brata	>	[braða]	'brother'
diswan	>	[ðiswan]	'this'
vilis	>	[vilič]	'village'
sios	>	[čoč]	'church'
siusim	>	[čusim]	'choose'

Similarly to the continued effects of the local vernaculars on Pijin, the creole is therefore in a special situation regarding Anglicization. The recent phonological effects of English are superimposed on the Pijin system, which, while accommodating English-derived lexemes, is strongly influenced by Austronesian phonemic systems.

3.3.   Urbanization

Among most rural speakers and many older urban speakers, the phonetic interferences from the vernaculars are obvious. In the urban Pijin of the younger generation, particularly of the children, these variations tend to be neutralized. This phenomenon is associated with the children's loss of contact with vernaculars. It seems obvious from research that the less the children are exposed to vernaculars and their phonology, the less their Pijin retains the phonological features of these languages. The phonetic system is regularized, often moving it away from that of the vernacular, and for some speakers, clearly in the direction of English. The epenthetic vowels are disappearing, along with some etymological ones; the result is that consonant clusters are more common in urban Pijin than they are in rural Pijin (although here, too, many ensuing clusters are rapidly eliminated by further reduction). Paragogic and other final vowels are also disappearing. This leads to the overall effects of regularization and, inevitably, shortening. For example:

['olketa]	> ['oketa]	> ['okta] > ['ota] > ['ot]	'they'; plural marker
['mifala]	> ['mifaa]	> ['mifa] > ['mia]	'we'
[sa'pos]	> ['spos]	> ['pos]	'if'
	> [sa'os]	> ['sos]	
[bi'kos]	> [bi'os]	> ['bis]	'because'
['wanfala]	> ['wanfaa]	> ['wafa]	'one'
[bi'long]	> ['blong]	> ['blo]	'of'
[baem'bae]	> [ba'bae]	> ['bae]	TMA marker

Notice that the words most prone to such reduction are pronouns, conjunctions, prepositions and other grammatical markers. Function words are, perhaps in part due to their high frequency and their unstressed position in the sentence, most prone to be affected by the tendency to shorten and reduce phonological material.

4.   Phonotactics

As described in section 3.1., Solomons Pijin, like other Austronesian languages, generally disfavors most consonant clusters. When English cognate forms from which the Pijin word is derived have such unwanted clusters, Pijin can resolve the conflict in one of three ways: by epenthesis, paragogue, or elision. Epenthesis and paragogue have been discussed in 3.1.2. and 3.1.3.

A final strategy open for dissolution of clusters is elision, specifically apocope. Pijin has used this strategy as well in order to derive canonical Pijin words from English source lexemes, as in *suam* 'swamp', *kol* 'cold', and *klos* 'closed'.

Presumably, all these strategies are guided by the aim to achieve a more optimal syllable structure. The constraints imposed by various vernacular languages certainly play a role in determining the shape of the Pijin form, as do for example principles of sonority hierarchies. Systematic study is needed in order to pinpoint more precisely what rules which speakers use. In general, it can be said that the preferred syllable structure for Pijin lexical words is CV(CV). In monosyllabic words, there is a requirement for the syllable to be heavy, which means that the syllable must either be closed (CVC, e.g. *kam*) or that the vowel is a long one (CVV, e.g. *baa*, *kaa*, *saa*, *tuu*). In the first cases, the vowel could alternatively be described as being the result of compensatory lengthening for an etymological final-r deletion; however, this is not true for words like *tuu*. Minimal word weight requirements therefore account for why long vowels are found primarily in monosyllabic words.

The trochee is the preferred foot structure, but again, as seen in several of the examples of reduction above, successive stages of reduction produce new sequences that may not conform to this pattern. Such forms may be more or less stable, but are all present in the speech of urbanites. Hence, changes in phonotactics through reduction and Anglicization are also occurring.

In the urban center, the effects of the loss of vernaculars and the influence of English are compounded. Further, as it is a locus for new settings of standards, speakers are learning and creating new systems of consensus. Very few rules in Pijin are not open to negotiation, and most are tendencies rather than absolutes. The most general rule is that in the process of reduction, the stressed parts of the source word are retained longest.

Phonological reduction can also have consequences for other parts of the grammar, and an interplay between phonology and syntax and semantics can then be observed. For instance, heavy reduction may allow different forms of the word to precipitate, which in turn are available to take on new meanings. Functions that were formerly taken on by the same word can now be distributed across separate words. For instance, the gradual reduction of *olketa* (the third person plural pronoun 'they', and also the nominal plural marker) has produced a range of phonological forms, from *oloketa* to *ot*. The short form *ota* now is used mostly as a plural marker, while the longest forms such as *olketa* are reserved for expressing third person plural pronoun in object position (cf. Selbach 2000). The range of phonological variation permissible and usual in Pijin thus appears to make generous room for grammaticalization to occur.

5.   Historical derivation from English: comparison to source language

In the preceding section, we showed how final consonant deletion and vowel lengthening are processes employed for attaining more optimal Pijin syllable structure. The examples of *suam* and *baa* so derived by constraints on Pijin syllable structure are standard Pijin forms and do not illustrate synchronic dialectal or idiolectal variation, such as that exemplified in Table 1.

Given the amount of variation so characteristic of Solomons Pijin, it is nevertheless often quite difficult or impossible to assess which rules are active phonological processes and which ones represent historical change, which are due to Anglicization or the ongoing influence of the vernaculars. In section 5.1., we focus on the historical relationship of Pijin and English. We provide a comparison of the creole and its lexifier and sketch the rules historically deriving Pijin lexemes from English lexemes. The following sections 5.1 and 5.2 owe a great deal to a 1998 manuscript by Marc Picard, *The Naturalization of English loandwords in Pijin*. We are extremely grateful for his generosity in liberally sharing it with us.

5.1.   Vowels

The vowels of the various English dialects which supplied the lexical material to Pijin were reduced to a basic 5-cardinal-vowel system. Without study of the precise dialects of English that played a decisive role in the formation of Pijin, it is not possible to provide more than a few of the basic brushstrokes that determined adaptations to Solomon Islands Pijin phonology. The table of vowels below (Table 2) is meant as such a broad indication of some of the mergers and correspondences. Bold face vowels are those of both Pijin and English; this means that the normal font vowels had to merge with the bold face ones. These correspondences are set out below.

Table 2.   Vowels of English and Pijin

	Front	Central	Back
High	**i**		**u**
	↑		↑
Semi-high	ɪ		ʊ
Mid	**e** ← — ə — →		**o**
Mid-low	ε	ʌ	ɔ
Low	æ — →	a	

5.1.1.   Raising of front and back vowels

For front and back vowels, the problem was solved by raising: Front and back semi-high vowels merged with their mid-high counterparts:

		English	Pijin	
ʊ	> u	[kʊk]	[kuki]	'cook'
ɪ	> i	[aksɪdent]	[aksiden]	'accident'

Mid-low vowels merged with their mid-high counterparts:

		English	Pijin	
ɔ	> o	[pɔ]	[popo]	'paw'
ε	> e	[əgεn]	[agen]	'again'

5.1.2.   Fronting, backing, lowering of central vowels

The central vowels [ə] and [ʌ] merge with [e], [o] or [a] by fronting, backing or lowering. This is partly determined by context:

Fronting to [e] (a context-free change, but applies especially to long and syllable-final central vowels):

[profet]	'prophet'
[meresin]	'medicine'
[deleget]	'delegate'

Backing to [o] before [l] (a context-sensitive change: [əl] > [ol]):

[pensol]	'pencil'
[handol]	'handle'
[pipol]	'people'

Lowering to [a] before etymological [r] (often context-sensitive: [er] > [a]):

[aftanun]	'afternoon'
[namba]	'number'
[taepraeta]	'typewriter'

While backing before [l] and lowering before [r] is largely predictable, some contexts are not. For instance, there are several changes possible before [n]:

[neson]	'nation'
[leman]	'lemon'
[poesen], [poisin]	'poison'

The remaining short vowels become low central.

5.1.3. *Processes affecting long mid vowels and diphthongs*

Long mid vowels and diphthongs ([ey], [eː], [ou], [oː]) of English were reduced to [e], [o], while other diphthongs are retained

[eː], [ey]	
[pe]	'pay'
[ples]	'place'
[fevarit]	'favourite'
[seksek]	'shiver', 'shake'

[oː], [ou]	
[kol]	'cold'
[holem]	'hold'

[ao], [oe], [ae] remain unchanged:

[kaontem]	'count'
[boe]	'boy'
[karae]	'cry'

5.2. Consonants

Pijin mostly retains the consonants of the English source, but again, those consonants not found in Pijin merged with similar ones. As described in section 2.2., there is much variation in how the sounds of English were reanalyzed as phonemes of Pijin, and there is much variation across individual speaker's consonantal inventories. Generally, the choices made for distributing the consonants missing from the Pijin inventory across the new system were the following:

5.2.1. Dental fricatives became stops

a) Voiceless dental fricative becomes voiceless apical stop ([θ] > [t]):

[tanda]	'thunder'
[tosde]	'Thursday'
[trifala]	'three'
[tingting]	'think'

b)   Voiced dental fricative becomes voiced apical stop ([ð] > [d])

[disfala]	'this'
[wedekos]	'Weather Coast'

5.2.2. Changes affecting affricates and palatals:

Voiceless affricates (often) became fricatives:
[sest]   'chest'

Voiced affricates (often) became stops:
[des]   'just'

Palatals became alveolars (ʃ > s):
[susut]   'shoot'

5.2.3. Stop deletion

As described in section 4, final stops of English were deleted following sonorant consonants (e.g. *suam* 'swamp', *govamen* 'government'), and as indicated in 5.1.2. above, English syllable-final *-er* was generally replaced by Pijin /a/ (e.g. *pepa* 'pepper', *snapa* 'snapper').

6.   Productive morphophonological processes

Certain aspects of Pijin phonology are clearly productive, and thus not easily traced to the direct influence of the substrate or the superstrate. There are several actively productive morphophonological processes specific to Pijin, such as the vowel harmony displayed by the transitivizing suffix, and the morphophonetic rules of reduplication.

6.1.   Transitive suffix -Vm: vowel harmony

As described in the chapter on the morphology and syntax of Solomon Islands Pijin (see Jourdan, this volume), Pijin transitive verbs are marked with a suffix -Vm, variously -*em*, -*im* or -*um*. As with insertion of paragogic vowels, the vowel in -Vm is selected with respect to rules of vowel harmony. The specific rules of harmony can again vary from one speaker to the next. One possible system is the one illustrated below, where roots containing mid and low vowels take -*em* as a suffix, but roots with high vowels will take the identical high vowel in the suffix,-*im* or -*um*.

Verb stem vowel	Suffix	Example
/a/	-*em*	*katem*
/e/	-*em*	*tekem*
/o/	-*em*	*kolem*
/i/	-*im*	*hitim*
/u/	-*um*	*hukum*

Thus, while *kat-*, *tek-* and *kol-* become *katem, tekem* and *kolem*, /huk/ 'to hook' becomes /hukum/ 'to hook something' and /hit/ 'to hit' becomes /hitim/ 'to hit someone'.

However, /baet/ 'to bite' becomes /baetim/ for some speakers and /baetem/ for others. Further, some streamlining common in the speech of young urban Pijin speakers may shorten the -Vm to /m/. Thus *ansam* 'to give an answer' instead of *ansar-em*, *kalam* 'to colour something' instead of *kalar-em*, etc.

There are more exceptions. While -*em* seems to function as the default suffix, -*im* appears more likely in neologisms such as *fotokopim* 'to photocopy something' and *faksim* 'to fax something'. Nevertheless, it appears that -*em* is always a possible realization of the transitive suffix. In this respect again, /e/ is the underspecified vowel (cf. 5.1.2.a.).

While the variation in the realization of the vowel in the transitivizing suffix is quite large, vowel harmony nevertheless determines the insertion of the vowel into the suffix whose vowel is underspecified for height or frontness.

The quality of the vowels added to the stem is determined by the stem. This applies for epenthesis, paragogue and suffixation of the transitive marker.

6.2.   Reduplication: morphophonemics

Pijin makes room for reduplication as a productive pattern in the morphology of (primarily) verbs, where it can function to modify meaning or mood. It is also present in the substrate languages of the Solomon Islands, such that it remains to be seen whether the morphophonemic rules also correspond to those of the vernaculars. Reduplication may involve either full or partial reduplication of the first syllable.

go	'to go'	*gogoo*	'after sometime'
suim	'to swim'	*susuim*	'swimming'
save	'to know'	*sasave*	'to be very knowledgeable'
dae	'to die'	*dadae*	'to pine away'
faet	'to fight'	*fafaet*	
fraet	'to be afraid'	*fafraet*	'to be very afraid'
krae/karae	'to cry'	*kakarae*	'to cry continuously'
stap	'to stay'	*sastap*	
ple	'to play'	*peple*	
siki	'to be sick'	*sisiki*	'keep being sick'
bisi	'to be busy'	*bibisi*	'to be very busy'
silip	'to sleep'	*sisilip*	'to sleep a long time'
kis	'to kiss'	*kiskis*	
presim	'to praise'	*pepresim*	
wan	'one'	*wanwan*	'one at the time'

The basic rule for verbal reduplication is to copy the first syllable of the verb and to prefix it to the root (e.g. *sasave, sisiki, kiskis*). However, contrary to what is happening in Bislama (Crowley, this volume), very rarely will speakers choose to duplicate a consonant cluster if it is in initial position. Instead, when the root starts with a cluster (a pattern predominantly found in the speech of young urbanites), speakers will copy the root's first consonant and the first vowel only (e.g. *fafraet, kakarae, sastap*). It appears that in Pijin the more optimal reduplicant is maximally of the pattern CV. The same pattern holds for one-syllable verb roots containing a diphthong, where only the first vowel of the diphthong is reduplicated (e.g. *dadae, fafaet*). Interestingly, the coda is, however, retained in some other words whose roots-initial syllable is of the CVC pattern, such as in *wanwan* and *kiskis*.

7.   Stress and intonation

In Solomons Pijin, stress follows two essential models: that of the Oceanic languages and that of English. Words derived from vernacular etyma follow the predictable stress pattern found in the Oceanic vernaculars, i.e. stress falls predominantly on the penultimate syllable as in *kokósu* 'hermit crab', *múmu* 'stone oven', *kakáme* 'swamp taro'. Pijin words derived from English etyma (the bulk of Pijin vocabulary) will have the stress fall on the first syllable as in *hóspitol* 'hospital' and *kámpani* 'company', or on the penultimate syllable as in *panikíni* 'cup', *elékson* 'election', *tráke* 'truck'. Three Pijin words are of Portuguese origin and entered Melanesian pidgins via the maritime jargon: *sáve* 'to know' and *pikiníni* 'child' follow the stress rule of Portuguese and are accentuated on the penultimate syllable, while *kalabús* 'prison' is stressed on the last syllable. These data indicate that word stress is lexically determined, and is retained on the original syllable of the etymon, regardless of what language the word is derived from, and regardless of where on the word the stress appears. (Note that section 3.3. also bears witness to the robustness of stress retention, in that case within Pijin itself.)

Intonation and sentence stress in Pijin give important cues for interpreting meaning. Intonation plays a vital role to mark sentence structure and is very distinctive. Subtle changes in intonation can dramatically change meaning and can transform an affirmative sentence into an interrogative sentence, or a sequence of clauses into relative clauses. Except for the short analysis that Jourdan (1985) provides of the importance of intonation for sentence meaning, intonation patterns in Solomons Pijin have not been described.

Perhaps increasing grammaticalization will reduce the need for intonation in conveying information and, as the language gets older and more standardized, perhaps the use of intonation will give way to grammatical markers, and the phonology will become more regular. Perhaps they will not, and individuals will continue to apply their own sets of rules to a language full of variation and possibility.

*   We wish to thank Marc Picard for the phonetic transcription that accompanies the reading passage and Kevin Tuite and Diana Apoussidou for their generous comments on earlier drafts of this article.

Exercises and study questions

1. Consider the examples in section 3.1.1. What are the distinctive features that are changed, and which ones are retained? Write out the rules for the sound changes from 'standard' Pijin to vernacular Pijin.

2. Compare the two series of Pijin regional and urban words below:

Rural	Taon	English
[sios]	[čoč]	'church'
[brata]	[braða]	'brother'
[oranis]	[orenǰ]	'orange'
[sukulu]	[skul]	'school'
[diapan]	[ǰapan]	'Japan'
[fisin]	[pɪ̌jin]	'Pijin'

a) Based on this comparison, describe the phonological differences between the rural and urban forms.

b) Whenever possible, fill in the blank in the series of words below:

Regional	Urban	English
[des]		'just'
	[čifkuk]	'chief cook'
	[tufala]	'two'
[pinis]		'finished'
		'big'
[tambu]		'taboo'
[vilis]		'village'

3. Looking at the following set of Pijin and English words, formulate the phonotactic rules that explain the form of the Pijin words. What is the preferred syllable structure of speakers who use the forms given below?

Pijin	English
sukulu	'school'
fifolo	'people'
oloketa	'altogether'
bisinisi	'business'
kolsap	'close up'
kiloko	'o'clock'

4. Consider the following verbs, and add the appropriate transitive suffix to transform them into transitive verbs. Sketch the rules of vowel harmony that are followed in order to do so.

kaekae	'eat'
finis	'finish'
tuwet	'drench'
draev	'drive'
silip	'sleep'
divaed	'divide'
put	'put'
of	'switch off'
pam	'pump'

Selected references

Please consult the General references for titles mentioned in the text but not included in the references below. For a full bibliography see the accompanying CD-ROM.

Baker, Philip
    1993   Australian influence on Melanesian Pidgin English. *Te Reo* 36: 3–67.
Beimer, Gerry
    1995   *We fo Raetem Olketa Wod Long Pijin*. Honiara: Solomon Islands Christian Association.
Bennett, Judith
    1979   Wealth of the Solomons. Ph.D. dissertation, Australian National University, Canberra.
Clark, Ross
    1979   In search of Beach-La-Mar. Towards a history of Pacific Pidgin English. *Te Reo* 22/23: 3–66.
Jourdan, Christine
    1985   Sapos iumi mitim iumi: urbanization and creolization of Solomon Islands Pijin. Ph.D. dissertation, Australian National University, Canberra.
    2002   *Pijin Dictionary*. Canberra: Pacific Linguistics.
Laracy, Hugh (ed.)
    1983   *Pacific Protest: The Maasina Rule Movement, Solomon Islands, 1944–1952*. Suva: Institute of Pacific Studies, University of the South Pacific.
Selbach, Rachel
    2000   Oketa in Solomon Islands Pijin: homophony or conceptual link between the third person plural and nominal plurality? Conference presentation at the Society of Pidgin and Creole Linguistics held under auspices of the Linguistic Society of America, Chicago, January 7, 2000.

Simons, Linda and Hugh Young
    1978   *Pijin Blong Iumi: A Guide to Solomon Islands Pijin.* Honiara: Solomon
              Islands Christian Association.
Troy, Jakelin
    1985   Australian Aboriginal contact with the English language in New South
              Wales: 1788 to 1845. B.A. Honours thesis, University of Sydney.

Tok Pisin in Papua New Guinea: phonology

Geoff P. Smith

1.   Introduction

Like various types of pidginised English around the world, the variety spoken
in the New Guinea area has been the object of interest for many years, usually
for the wrong reasons. It has in turn evinced hostility, ridicule, amusement and
more recently, serious study. Early administrators and other expatriate observers were often scathing in their contempt for what was seen merely as an im-
properly acquired and mangled form of English. It was much later that Prince
Philip characterised it as a "splendid language" but even then he failed to con-
ceal a somewhat patronising tone. It was not until the last few decades that the
language has been taken seriously on its own terms, and although even today
many negative attitudes persist, it is at last receiving some of the respect it
deserves. This variety, now so widely spoken in Papua New Guinea, is "based
on" English in the sense that most lexical items are ultimately derived from
it, but observers will soon discover that the language is not comprehensible
to English speakers without considerable instruction. It has sometimes been
referred to as "Melanesian Pidgin English", although this more accurately includes sister dialects Bislama in Vanuatu and Pijin in Solomon Islands. The
name "Neo-Melanesian" enjoyed brief currency among some academics, but
was never widely used. Most speakers refer to it simply as Tok Pisin ("talk
pidgin") or simply Pidgin. It is today Papua New Guinea's largest and fastest-
growing language and the de facto national language.

1.1.   The origins of Tok Pisin

As Crowley (this volume) points out, the early history of an English-based
contact language in the Pacific goes back to the time of early trading activities
in the newly opened-up European colonies in Australia. A New South Wales
pidgin English had already come into existence as a means of communication
between settlers and Aboriginal people, and some features of this were to appear in the early Pacific pidgin. Indeed, some elements, such as *pikinini* 'child'
and *save* 'know' based on the Portuguese *pequeño* and *sabir* respectively, may
have had a considerably longer history in maritime contact. Whaling expedi-

tions out of Sydney probably proceeded from the late 18th century, but successive interest in sandalwood and trepang (sea slug or *bêche de mer*) in the mid-19th century in the south-west and central Pacific saw a great increase in commerce and communication that favoured the formation of a stable Pacific Pidgin English. At first, ships' crews of mixed origin and shore-bound trading posts provided areas of contact, but later, large-scale population movements took place as Melanesian labourers were recruited to work on plantations in Queensland and the Pacific.

While the origins of Tok Pisin are firmly rooted in this Pacific Pidgin English, its development is somewhat different from its sister dialects. Melanesian labourers from New Britain and mainland New Guinea entered the labour trade somewhat later than those from the New Hebrides and Solomon Islands and were not involved in the Queensland plantations to the same extent, so the development of Tok Pisin proceeded along its own path. Critical in this development was the role of Germany in colonising the area. German New Guinea, or what is now the northern half of the Papua New Guinea mainland and the islands of the Bismarck Archipelago, became effectively cut off from neighbouring regions. Labourers from this area did enter the plantation economy, thus promoting conditions conducive to the stabilisation of the pidgin, but this took place mainly in Samoa in the Central Pacific. Labourers were drawn mainly from the New Guinea Islands region, although some may have been drawn from the north coast regions of the mainland as well. Since the area typically has large numbers of languages spoken by small populations, the need for a lingua franca on the plantations favoured the development of the already existing pidgin language. There may well have been some mutual influence between this variety and the Queensland "Canefield English" used by other Melanesians, but the extent of this is difficult to determine.

1.2. Early development in the New Guinea Area

At the end of the indentured labour schemes in the early years of the 20th century, labourers on the Samoan plantations were returned home. Most were initially repatriated to centres in Rabaul in East New Britain, or the Duke of York Islands, lying between New Britain and New Ireland in the Bismarck Archipelago (Mühlhäusler 1978). From there they were taken back to their home areas unless involved in local labour schemes. Further isolation from other south-west Pacific varieties led to considerable influence from the Austronesian languages of New Britain and New Ireland, especially in the lexicon, but also in grammatical structures. Features of the grammar of the early pidgin are also likely to have been reinforced if similar to structures widely present in local languages.

As noted, Papua New Guinea is an area of great linguistic diversity. A survey by the Summer Institute of Linguistics (Grimes 1992) lists over 860 languages currently spoken in a population of 4–5 million. At the beginning of the 20th century, poor communication and contact were the rule, with traditional trading activities operating along a complex though limited network of contacts. The upsurge in activities from overseas missions, traders and administrators led to an acute need for a language of wider communication, and the newly formed pidgin of the Samoan plantations, now fairly widely known, fitted ideally. In the monolingual Samoan society, however, it was no longer of any use, and soon died out there. The development of New Guinea Pidgin English thus proceeded in German-occupied New Guinea, and as it stabilised and expanded, it came under two influences not present in other varieties in Solomon Islands and New Hebrides.

The first of these was the language of the colonial power, German. A number of lexical items of German origin were adopted, especially in certain lexical fields, such as those related to education, woodworking, agriculture and so on, where German missionaries were intimately involved with the local population. Perhaps of equal significance was the fact that the English-lexicon pidgin was now effectively removed from further contact with its lexifier language.

The second influence on the stabilising pidgin on the north coast of Mainland New Guinea was a substratum of non-Austronesian or Papuan languages. The languages of the Central Pacific as well as New Hebrides and Solomon Islands are almost uniformly Austronesian, and Austronesian languages are also dominant in the islands to the north and east of mainland New Guinea (Manus, New Britain, New Ireland and Bougainville). However, in parts of these areas, and most of the New Guinea mainland, the typologically different Papuan languages are spoken beyond a number of coastal enclaves of Austronesian speakers. The early pidgins exhibited a number of features typical of Austronesian languages, which tend to be reinforced by Austronesian-speaking populations, but there was little pressure to maintain exotic syntactic distinctions in non-Austronesian speaking areas. A good example of this is the so-called predicate marker *i*, which accords with the grammars of many Austronesian languages, and is thus retained in the Tok Pisin in these areas, but is routinely ignored in many non-Austronesian-speaking areas. Reesink (1990) has shown that some substrate syntactic features such as switch reference patterns and subordination are reflected in parallel differences in the Tok Pisin spoken in the area.

1.3. Stabilisation and expansion

After the First World War, Germany ceased to be the colonial power, and a complex arrangement was put in place, whereby the former German territory came under a UN mandate, while the southern part of the mainland, formerly British New Guinea, became the Australian external territory of Papua. In practice, the two were administered as a single entity by the Australian administration. In the territory of New Guinea, Tok Pisin continued to spread and expand, while in Papua, another lingua franca based on a local Austronesian language developed into the most widely used medium of communication. This was known as Police Motu, due to its use by the police in administration, and is today known by the name of Hiri Motu. The *hiri* was a seasonal trading expedition in the Gulf of Papua, and while a simplified trade language may have been used for this, it is likely that the pidginised Motu used today is a separate development.

At independence in 1975, the language issue was tackled by giving three languages, English, Tok Pisin and Hiri Motu, the status of "national languages", a rather vague concept which fell short of conferring on any the status of an official language. Prince Charles' speech in Tok Pisin to the newly independent parliament was a notable milestone, and although his intonation and stress patterns made it clear that he was not a speaker, and even suggested that he did not really understand everything he was reading, the gesture was widely appreciated. The designation of Hiri Motu as a national language was more controversial, and the decision was undoubtedly influenced by widespread secessionist sentiment in the Papuan provinces in the time leading up to independence. Few people see Hiri Motu as a truly national language, and its role has decreased as Tok Pisin gains more currency in what was formerly Papua, now known as the Southern Region of the country. English is the language of education and much written communication in government and administration, but it is Tok Pisin which is the de facto national language, being used in an increasing number of domains and expanding its range.

1.4. The lexicon of Tok Pisin

The great majority of lexical items derives from English. However, whether this justifies the description of Tok Pisin as a "variety of English" is open to question, especially if the grammar as well as the derivation of the lexicon is taken into account. Some of the English words in use at the time they entered the emerging pidgin in the 19th century are now obsolete although they may survive in Tok Pisin. An example is *giaman* 'lie, deceit', from the informal English "gammon" in common use at that time. Other words of English origin may be similarly difficult to recognise as they have been reinterpreted in a grammatical role. Examples include the reinterpretation of the English pronoun *he* and *him* as the predicate marker *i* and transitive suffix *-im* respectively. Most words adopted from German now appear to be obsolescent, although a few, such as *beten* 'pray' and *rausim* 'take off, expel' (from German *heraus* 'get out') are still in common use.

Words have also entered Tok Pisin from a number of other languages, and internal word-formation processes of the expanding pidgin have provided additional lexical resources. There appear to be one or two survivals from languages of the Pacific such as *lotu* 'church service' from Samoan and *kanaka* 'bush person, hillbilly' from the Hawaiian word for 'person', but by far the greatest source of non-English vocabulary are the languages of the New Britain and New Ireland area to the north-east of the New Guinea mainland. As noted above, the early pidgin spoken in Samoa took root in this area, and words needed for flora and fauna or cultural items tended to be taken from languages of this area. Tracing an exact source is not always easy, as a word may have a similar form in several related languages. Much of the confusion about specific vernacular sources for Tok Pisin etyma was cleared up by Ross (1992). Typical items from languages of this area include *kurita* 'octopus', *muruk* 'cassowary', *karuka* 'pandanus', *kunai* 'sword grass', *pukpuk* 'crocodile', *umben* 'fishing net' and many locally occurring fishes and trees. Few items from the non-Austronesian languages of the New Guinea mainland have been adopted, but borrowing is continuing. More recently, speakers of Tok Pisin who also have a reasonable command of English are borrowing a large number of items from English.

1.5.   Current status

Although the name "Pidgin" is frequently used to refer to the language, Tok Pisin is spoken by an increasing number of children as a first language, i.e. as a creole. The use of a pidgin as a first language used to be considered a critical factor in the rate of change and development of a creole as it expanded to meet a full repertoire of communicative needs. However, studies on Tok Pisin such as Sankoff and Laberge (1973) have shown that creolisation has not had the dramatic effect which might have been expected, and that children merely accelerate tendencies which had already been developing in the expanded pidgin through second language use in an increasing number of situations. As with Bislama, then, the distinction between the use of Tok Pisin as a pidgin or as a creole is somewhat fuzzy and does not seem to be as critical as was once thought.

In addition, Tok Pisin is continually expanding its geographical range into more and more remote locations, and to some extent the synchronic acquisition of the language in these situations is recapitulating its historical development. The possibility of re-pidginisation also exists in this situation, although an investigation by Holm and Kepiou in the Southern Highlands (1993) found no evidence of this.

The question of standardisation of the language has arisen frequently, but there has been little inclination for government intervention, and successive administrations have been happy to adopt a laissez faire approach, and government-sponsored written communications in Tok Pisin are notorious for their variable and at times ambiguous style (Franklin 1990). A number of initiatives have been made to regularise or standardise vocabulary and syntax, even if some such as Bálint (1969) have been more an exercise in individual creativity than a reflection of the realities of a speech community. A number of academics have made some useful comments on the issue of standardisation, but the most influential practical standards have been mission-initiated. Firstly, the Bible Society's translation of the Old and New Testament has provided a lasting standard formal register, and considerable effort has gone into dealing with the linguistic complexities involved (Mundhenk 1990). Then there is the enormous contribution of the late Father Frank Mihalic of the SVD (Society of the Divine Word). His *Jacaranda Dictionary of Melanesian Pidgin*, first published in 1957 and revised in 1971, was a huge boost to the acceptance of the language. Although, as Mihalic (1990) himself realised, much in the dictionary is now looking distinctly dated, the absence of more up-to-date competitors has ensured that it remains the most widely used dictionary of Tok Pisin and the closest to a standard that exists. In addition to this, Mihalic translated the constitution of Papua New Guinea and his work also led to the standardised style sheet of the influential *Wantok Niuspepa*, a weekly publication begun in 1969. This reports overseas and local news in a formal style, as well as more creative sports reports (Romaine 1994) and items written in a more vernacular style such as letters to the editor and traditional stories (see Lomax 1983 for an analysis). In the absence of formal investigations, it is difficult to know what effects these standards have on the language of today's speakers.

The term Tok Pisin, then, refers to a complex of first and second language varieties. These are spoken with varying degree of fluency, and influenced to varying degrees by other languages used. Much remains to be known about Tok Pisin, especially with regard to regional variation in lexico-semantics and morphosyntax. One or two small-scale corpora have appeared recently (Smith 2002; Romaine 1992), to supplement earlier studies, but some large-scale research on the language in use would be desirable before major policy initiatives.

2.   Phonology of Tok Pisin

As we have seen, the term Tok Pisin covers rather a wide range of varieties, with variation along a number of dimensions, such as the speaker's first or second language status, area of residence, degree of formality and familiarity with the lexifier, English. Different speakers vary considerably not only in core phonology, but lexis and morphosyntax as well. Indeed there is so much variation that, unlike the case with non-standard regional dialects of English, it is very difficult to identify a variety which can be considered typical or standard. However, an attempt will be made to do just this so that a yardstick can be established for comparison with other varieties of Melanesian Pidgin described in the volume.

Mühlhäusler (1975) identifies four sociolects of Tok Pisin: Bush Pidgin, Rural Pidgin, Urban Pidgin and Tok Masta, and this is a useful point of departure. Bush Pidgin is described as the somewhat unstable second language variety heavily influenced by the phonology and syntax of the mother tongue. Rural Pidgin may also be influenced to varying degrees by the first language, but is the stable variety generally used for inter-ethnic communication throughout the rural areas where Tok Pisin is spoken. There may also be a gradation between Bush Pidgin and Rural Pidgin as speakers acquire greater competence in the language. Urban Pidgin is characterised as a variety heavily influenced by English and spoken mainly in urban areas. Finally, Tok Masta, which has little relevance here, refers to the unsystematic attempts by English-speaking expatriates to incorporate Tok Pisin features into their speech, possibly in the belief that Tok Pisin is little more than a garbled form of English. In the light of today's knowledge it is not really a "variety" of Tok Pisin at all.

While this classification provided a valuable insight into variation in Tok Pisin, my impression is that the rural-urban distinction is somewhat problematic. It is possible that a more valid criterion would be emerging bilingualism in Tok Pisin and English, which is not necessarily determined by urban or rural status. Many young people in the Manus and New Ireland Provinces, for example, appear to be becoming bilingual in these languages whether resident in rural or urban areas, and there is increasing influence from English phonology in their speech. The closest to a standard among the four lects above would be rural pidgin, and it is this which most closely approximates the ideal core phonology attempted here.

2.1.   Phonemic contrasts in "Standard Rural Tok Pisin"

The phoneme inventory of Tok Pisin is somewhat reduced compared with its principal lexifier, English. There are some 24 phonemes in the core phonology, with no evidence of lexical tone. The following account is based on two standard accounts of Tok Pisin phonology, Mihalic (1971) and Laycock (1985), the latter also drawing on Laycock (1970). Mihalic based his phonology and grammar on the Tok Pisin spoken around Madang in north-east New Guinea, while Laycock's Tok Pisin materials are more wide-ranging, but mainly draw on data from the Sepik and Bougainville areas. Laycock also refers to a paper by Litteral (1970) as the most comprehensive account yet of the Tok Pisin phonological system, but unfortunately this has not been published. Comments about variation as noted by these writers, and also based on some regional data from Smith (2002), will be made as appropriate. A fuller discussion of the relationship between Tok Pisin and English will follow.

2.1.1.   Consonants

The following are the basic contrasting consonantal phonemes described in Mihalic (1971):

p	t		k
b	d		g
m	n		ŋ
v			
f		s	h
	r		
	l		
	dʒ		
w		j	

Note that this is identical to the inventory provided by Crowley for Bislama (this volume) apart from the inclusion of the affricate /dʒ/. The consonants are generally close to their IPA values.

Laycock's (1985) core inventory also identifies the above phonemes, but in addition lists six pre-nasalised stop clusters: /mp, nt, ŋk, mb, nd/ and /ŋk/. Their inclusion is justified on the basis that they do not permit epenthetic vowels. However, four fricatives /f, v, ʃ, ʒ/ are included only parenthetically as of marginal use. He observes that these fricatives may be used contrastively only in heavily Anglicised speech.

The great majority of Tok Pisin lexical items are ultimately derived from English, and a number of correspondences between English sources and Tok

Pisin words can be demonstrated. A number of these correspondences are listed in Laycock (1985: 296). The phonemes /p, t, k, s, m, n, ŋ, r/ and /y/ are generally unchanged, as in the following, all shown in initial position:

	English	Tok Pisin
/p/	*pig*	*pik*
/t/	*time*	*taim*
/k/	*kill*	*kilim*
/s/	*sun*	*san*
/m/	*man*	*man*
/n/	*name*	*nem*
/t/	*tongue*	*tang*
/r/	*rope*	*rop*
/y/	*you*	*yu*

Other phonemes in the core Tok Pisin inventory also present in English may be variably represented. Voiced stops, for example, may appear as either voiced or unvoiced in Tok Pisin in initial and medial position, but always devoiced in final position:

	English	Tok Pisin
/b/-/b/	*bag*	*bek*
/d/-/d/	*die*	*(in)dai*
/d/-/t/	*done*	*tan*
/g/-/g/	*gun*	*gan*
	bugger	*baga*
/g/-/k/	*big*	*bikpela*

Laycock does not produce any examples for English /b/ equivalent to Tok Pisin /p/, and there are only one or two very low frequency variants in my corpus (Smith 2002) such as *panara* for *banara* 'bow'.

Although the phoneme /v/ is widely used in words such as *vilis* 'village', it may variably be replaced by /f/ in words such as *faif/faiv* 'five'. Similarly, /dʒ/, which appears in initial place in words such as *joinin* 'join' and *Jun* 'June', often becomes /s/ in medial and final position, for example *jasim* 'to judge' and *bris* 'bridge'.

Other English consonants not normally found in Tok Pisin may correspond as follows:

	English	Tok Pisin
/θ/ > /t/	*think*	*ting*
	something	*samting*
	thousand	*tausen*
	teeth	*tit*

but:

	English	Tok Pisin
/θ/ > /s/	*mouth*	*maus*
/ð/ > /d/	*this*	*dispela*

but:

	English	Tok Pisin
/ð/ > /t/	*brother*	*brata*
/ʃ/ > /s/	*shine*	*sain*
	shoot	*sut(im)*
	fish	*pis*
/ʒ/ > /s/	*engine*	*ensin*
	change	*senis*
/tʃ/ > /s/	*church*	*sios*
	change	*senis*
/z/ > /s/	*cheese*	*sis*
	razor	*resa*
	cousin	*kasin*

The glottal fricative /h/ is variably present on words where /h/ is present in the English etymon. In what appears to be a case of hypercorrection, /h/ may also be added where none is present (ø) in English:

	English	Tok Pisin
/h/-/h/	*house*	*haus*
/h/-ø		*aus*
ø-ø	*afternoon*	*apinun*
ø-/h/		*hapinun*

Of the six pre-nasalised stop clusters described by Laycock, all are equivalent to their English counterparts, except for the English /nʃ/ and /nʒ/, which are rendered in Tok Pisin as *-is* in final position in *winis* 'winch' and *senis* 'change'. However, the cluster is retained with the substitution of /s/ in medial position in *ensin* 'engine'.

2.1.2. Vowels

Both Mihalic and Laycock identify a five basic vowel system: /a, e, i, o, u/. As with Bislama, these appear to be fairly close to cardinal IPA values, although little research on variation has been carried out. These are treated in turn below, showing some of the English source vowels for each.

	English	Tok Pisin
TP /a/		
/æ/	*man*	*man*
/ɑː/	*start*	*statim*
/ɒ/	*hot*	*hatpela*
/ʌ/	*lucky*	*laki*
/ɜː/	*turn*	*tanim*
TP /e/		
/e/	*head*	*het*
/æ/	*fat*	*fetpela*
/eə/	*Mary*	*meri*
/eɪ/	*plate*	*plet*
TP /i/		
/ɪ/	*give*	*givim*
/iː/	*steal*	*stilim*
TP /o/		
/əʊ/	*hold*	*holim*
/ɔː/	*call*	*kolim*
/ɒ/	*belong*	*bilong*
/ɜː/	*dirty*	*doti*
TP /u/		
/ʊ/	*put*	*putim*
/uː/	*shoot*	*sutim*

It should be noted that although *doti* 'dirty' is the commonly cited form, I found that most speakers surveyed used *deti*, more similar to the English pronunciation.

In addition, a number of diphthongs may be heard in Tok Pisin. While a greater range may be heard in varieties strongly influenced by bilingualism in English, the following are generally in common use in typical rural Tok Pisin:

/aɪ/	*sign*	*sain*
/ɪə/	*beer*	*bia*
/aʊ/	*outside*	*autsait*
/ɔɪ/	*boy*	*boi*

The English /aɪə/ is also represented (*paia* 'fire'), while /auə/ is generally heard with a semivowel: /auə/ *pawa* 'power'.

There is no evidence of contrastive use of vowel length. Standard written Tok Pisin tends to approximate the phonemic values in most cases, except that <ng> covers both /ŋ/ and /ŋg/, and geminate vowels such as in *baim* 'to buy' are not indicated (Pawley 1975).

2.2.   Variations in the core phoneme inventory

Superimposed on this idealised paradigm is considerable variation. Firstly, since the majority of the lexicon is derived from English, and Tok Pisin speakers come into increasing contact with Standard English, the likelihood of influence from English phonology is great. As Laycock has pointed out (1985: 25), Tok Pisin speakers familiar with English have potentially the whole of the English phoneme inventory at their disposal. More will be said about the relationship between the two languages below.

Another source of variability among speakers of Tok Pisin as a second language is the influence of the phonologies of other languages spoken. A pioneering study by Bee (1971) showed that this influence can be considerable. She, however, was describing a situation where Tok Pisin had been fairly recently introduced and its use marginal. Influence from substrate phonology is likely to decrease as speakers become more familiar with mainstream patterns of use.

Nevertheless, Laycock (1985) has shown that there is considerable influence from phonological patterns of other Papua New Guinea languages. The picture is undoubtedly very complex, as the 800–900 languages spoken within the country vary enormously in their phonology, so a consistent pattern of influence is only likely to be felt where there are widespread regional patterns. For example, intervocalic pre-nasalisation of voiced stops is widespread in many of the languages of the Sepik and Madang areas so far described, and this feature may appear in the Tok Pisin spoken of this region. Similarly, unvoiced stops may be realised medially as fricatives in many Highlands languages, and this feature may be preserved in the Tok Pisin of some speakers in the Highlands region.

While these variations can be observed among second language speakers, the situation among first language speakers has received less attention. Romaine (1990) looks at the variation between /p/ and /f/ in initial position by young people in Morobe and Madang provinces, including first language speakers. Greater consistency in the correspondence between initial /f/ in Tok Pisin and their English equivalents is shown to be related to such factors as urban or rural status. In rural areas, such as Indagen, there was greater variation, and some interesting observations are made, including instances of hypercorrection where initial /f/ was used on words derived from English words beginning with /p/. Smith (2002) also observes that the distinction between /p/ and /f/ is often inconsistently applied, especially in Highlands speech samples, but also in other areas such as Sepik and North Solomons, with such items as *pik* 'pig' rendered as *fik*.

In another study on a single phoneme pair, Romaine (1995) discusses discrimination of the phonemes /r/ and /l/ in the same corpus of speech from Morobe and Madang Provinces used for the study of /p/ and /f/. She again relates the use of this distinction to urban and rural status, but does report that first language urban speakers are more consistent in distinguishing /r/ from /l/, even though there is considerable variation. Among the rural speakers, those in Waritsian village were most likely to confuse the phonemes, which could be due to substrate influence, as the Adzera language does not distinguish these two sounds. Smith (2002) also found some first language speakers showing quite marked variability with regard to this contrast. In the following extract from Eastern Highlands, for example, the expected forms *lized* 'lizard', *long* 'to', *stilim* 'steal' and *lapun* 'old woman' all appear with /r/ substituted for /l/, while /l/ replaces /r/ in *rere* 'ready':

(1)   *em i kam araun **ro** disa, a kam araun **ro** disa haus na **stirim** disa kiau*
       *blo **rized** na ranawe pinis. Em kukim i stap na **leli** lo(n)gen. Em **stirim***
       *na go pinis na disa **rapun** meri i kam bek.*
       'he came around **to** this house and **stole** the **lizard**'s eggs and ran
       away. He cooked them and got them **ready**. He had **stolen** them and
       taken them away when this **old woman** came back.'

Smith (2002) also found that the contrast between voiced and unvoiced stops was often inconsistently made by first language speakers, especially from the Highlands region, but also in other areas, particularly Manus and West Sepik. This leads to words such as *pik* 'pig' being heard as *fik*, *antap* 'on top' and *paitim* 'hit' as *andap* and *paidim* and *liklik* 'small' as *liglig*. In the case of velar stops, such words as *pik* 'pig' and *dok* 'dog' may thus have a pronunciation closer to the English source as *pig* or *dog*. There is also occasionally a tendency to pre-nasalise medial voiced stops, giving forms such as *gondaun* in place of *godaun* 'go down'. Also typical of some Highlands speakers is the tendency to voice /s/ to give forms such as *dizla* for *disla* 'this'. In some areas, the voiceless alveolar stop /t/ and spirant /s/ may alternate, especially in certain words such as *sapos/tapos* 'if'.

While these features serve to give particular accents to speakers of various first languages, Laycock (1985: 304) notes that there is such internal diversity in all provinces that distinct regional accents are not likely to emerge. Although such variation generally is not so marked as to make comprehensibility a problem, he notes that the lack of a distinction between /t/ and /s/, carried over into Tok Pisin from many languages in New Ireland, New Britain, the Highlands and South Bougainville is actually "disturbing to communication" Laycock (1985: 302). More generally, peculiarities of pronunciation provide the basis for many jokes at the expense of less fluent Tok Pisin speakers, for example the humorous stories featured in the "Kanage" column of *Wantok Niuspepa*. This ridiculing of strongly non-standard features is cited by Laycock (1985: 304) as another reason why distinct regional accents are unlikely to emerge.

2.3.   Prosodic features

There is little information available on prosodic features in Tok Pisin. Those studies that have been made point to variability and the need for more detailed study. Wurm (1985) is the only detailed account of Tok Pisin intonation, and here he also discusses stress as one determinant of intonation patterns. Faraclas (1989) also looks at some of the intonation patterns among first language speakers.

2.3.1. Stress

Wurm (1985) gives an account of stress patterns based on his experience of the rural pidgin spoken in the Eastern Highlands in the late 1950s and 1960s. He notes that there is considerable variability, with stress patterns more closely resembling those of English among speakers more familiar with English. In general, he notes that stress is normally on the first syllable. In some cases, there may be a non-stressed epenthetic vowel, and occasionally this may be re-interpreted by some speakers as a phonemic vowel and given stress. Some words do have stress on other than initial syllables, for example, the following stressed on the second syllable: *orait* 'all right, then', *singaut* 'shout, call out', *sekan* 'shake hands', *sanap* 'stand up' etc. Wurm notes that stress patterns are the basis for the patterns of intonation, which is discussed in the next section.

There is the possibility that different stress may disambiguate certain word pairs, although little work seems to have been done on this. Possible candidates would be the pairs *'nating* 'nothing' and *na'ting* 'I think, probably', and *'palai* 'lizard' and *pa'lai* 'fly', although I do not have definite evidence to show that this distinction is consistently made.

In the Tok Pisin of first language speakers and fluent second language speakers who use the language as a primary vehicle of communication, considerable reduction of stressed syllables can be observed (Smith 2002). Extreme samples of speech such as the following were encountered among young people:

(2)   *mi kam na was ken l'sla diwai*
       = *mi kam na was ken long dispela diwai*
       'I came and watched again at this tree'

One effect is the cliticisation of certain words such as *long* 'in; on; at' and *bilong* (possessive), especially when preceding vowels:

(3)   *ol   meikim   kastam bl'   ol (bilong ol)*
       they   make   custom-POSS   them
       'they were doing their traditional things'

(4)   *ol   salim em   go   l'aus (long haus)*
       they   send him   go   to house
       'they sent him home'

Cliticisation of aspect particles *save (sa)* 'habitual' and *laik (la)* 'about to' also appears to be in progress. Reduction can often be quite drastic, for example, the three-syllable utterance *tso l'sla taim* recorded in the Highlands represents *tasol long dispela taim* 'but at this time' (maximally of seven syllables).

2.3.2. Intonation

Wurm's (1985) account is again based on Eastern Highlands rural pidgin from 40 to 50 years ago and, as he concedes, may not be applicable to other varieties. He describes variability mainly in terms of the rural-urban dimension, with urban implying greater familiarity with English. Wurm gives no fewer than 20 distinct intonation patterns as a result of his familiarity with this variety. These include ordinary declarative statements, and extra dimensions indicating emphasis or emotion, questions, answers and commands. There are also some special cases involving words like *orait* 'all right', *tru* 'true' and formulae such as *em tasol* 'that's all'. He notes that high pitch is the major determinant of stress, and that word stress is generally retained in declarative utterances.

One interesting observation arising from Wurm's study is that first language speakers tend to use intonation patterns acquired from interaction with second language speakers. Wurm's data are valuable as very little else is available on intonation in Tok Pisin. However, although the patterns are quite definitely identified, there is no quantitative treatment, or indication of how they were recorded. It is not clear, for example, whether the copious example sentences were contrived to illustrate these patterns, or were actual examples recorded in use. Thus their applicability to other varieties is problematic.

Faraclas (1989) looks at stress patterns among Tok Pisin speakers in East Sepik, mainly concentrating on stress reduction. He takes account of variables such as sex, first language and degree of education in English, and demonstrates that females show consistently less stress reduction than males, and that the amount of English schooling has a significant influence. He supports Wurm's observations about the importance of substrate languages and shows, rather surprisingly, that substrate interference does not appear to be significantly less among first language speakers than second language speakers. Sex differences also appear to play a significant role in creolised varieties, with females tending towards English stress patterns more than males.

Smith (2002) did not look at stress or intonation in detail, but the role of intonation in discourse was commented on. For example, the use of *nau* to signal stages in a sequence was a common feature of narratives in the New Guinea Islands provinces:

(5)   *Em nau, tupla sutim nau, tupla pasim wanpla diwai nau, na tupla*
       pasim rop wantaim leg blong em nau na tupla taitim nau na tupla
       wokabaut i kam daun.
       'now the two shot it, they fastened a branch, they fastened a rope to its
       leg, the two tied it now, the two walked down'

In each case, the word *nau* is accompanied by a distinctive rising intonation showing that one stage in the sequence is finished and another is about to begin, while the final *kam daun* is accompanied by a falling intonation to indicate completion. Wurm, too, noted the role of intonation in discourse, describing the flat intonation of *orait* in similar discourse sequences.

Intonation could possibly also have a role in disambiguating certain syntactic patterns, for example, the expression *yu no laik paitim em* would generally mean 'you do not want to hit him' or 'you are not about to hit him' when spoken with a falling intonation, but a rising intonation could indicate a meaning 'you ought to have hit him' (Smith 2002: 129). Relative clauses unmarked by relative pronouns may also depend on intonation for comprehension (Wurm 1971).

2.3.3. Phonotactics

As in English, word final /h/ and word initial /ŋ/ are not permitted. There is some variation with regard to syllable structure, especially with respect to consonant clusters. In many Austronesian languages, consonant clusters are not permitted, and this general pattern may have influenced Tok Pisin in its formative period, and still affects that used by speakers of Austronesian languages today. Generally, too, it can be assumed that the more Anglicised the variety, the greater the tendency to allow clusters of two or three consonants according to English patterns. However, little research has been done on this. The best source of information is still Pawley (1975) who looked in detail at the question of epenthetic vowels in the Tok Pisin of an informant from Rabaul. His analysis is limited to this single informant, but highlights some of the problems of deciding on whether the underlying representation is phonemic or not.

A number of possibilities are presented by Pawley's (1975) data. It may be that the underlying representation is a consonant cluster, with epenthetic vowels variably inserted in certain environments. An alternative interpretation would treat the vowels as phonemic, but elided in certain circumstances. His informant, for example, inserted considerably fewer epenthetic vowels in rapid speech, so one factor is simply speed of delivery. Some of the apparent constraints governing selection of epenthetic vowels are discussed below. Pawley tends towards treating the vowels as transitional features in consonant clusters, especially as some Papua New Guinean languages show such features in "loose" consonant cluster systems. Nevertheless, it appears that some elements which are phonemic vowels in the English source lexis have been reanalysed as epenthetic in Tok Pisin. A good example is the possessive *bilong* from the English *belong* which is normally reduced in speech to *blong*, *blo* or even cliticised as *bl'* to following words as in *bl'em* (= *bilong em*) 'his, her'.

3.   Morphological processes

There is little evidence of morphophonemic processes in Tok Pisin. Unlike Bislama, the *-im* suffix appears to be unchanged with differing root vowels. However, the case of epenthetic vowels separating consonant clusters described above may be worth investigating further. Pawley (1975) noted that a number of processes could be considered as possibilities for determining the nature of epenthetic vowels. The first is simply echoing an identical form of the stressed vowel, thus producing alternations such as the following:

English	Tok Pisin	
brother	*brata*	*barata*
clean	*klin*	*kilin*
skin	*skin*	*sikin*
twist	*krukutim*	*kurukutim*, etc.

However, in other cases, this could not explain the choice of vowel, as in

stone	*ston*	*siton*
spoon	*spun*	*sipun*
ground	*graun*	*giraun*

Similarly, clusters in final position may insert epenthetic vowels which differ from than the stressed vowel:

tax	*taks*	*takis*
six	*siks*	*sikis*
dance	*dans*	*danis*

In cases such as these it appears that /i/ is inserted in certain specifically de-fined phonetic environments, for example, in final clusters where /s/ is one element, or vowels other than /a/, unless immediately followed by /i/ or /u/ (Pawley 1975: 224).

4.   Tok Pisin and English in contact

Tok Pisin and English are now in fairly intensive contact for many Papua New Guineans, especially those who are growing up speaking Tok Pisin as a first or primary language and are receiving education through the medium of English. In principal, the education system is English-medium in most government edu-cational institutions from grade one to the end of tertiary, but in practice, a fair amount of Tok Pisin may be used. Nevertheless, many young people grow up familiar with both languages.

In a situation such as this, the question is whether a post-creole continuum is likely to develop, as has happened in other societies such as Guyana and Jamaica. A number of researchers have given indications that a post-creole continuum may be developing or may already be in place, but Siegel (1997), reviewing the available evidence, shows that the current situation falls far short of an established continuum. Smith (2002) also reviews the evidence and comes to broadly the same conclusion. Nevertheless, there is a good deal of mutual influence between the two languages in Papua New Guinea today. Many young people familiar with English engage in code-switching, where discrete chunks of English are used in discourse, and code-mixing, where elements from English are mixed in. Many English verbs, for example, are incorporated into Tok Pisin and integrated by adding the transitivising marker *-im*. In some cases the phonology of the English word is retained intact, while in other cases, there is adaptation to the phonology of Tok Pisin. The future extent and direction of this contact is not known at present. Much will depend on language and education policy decisions, but there is the distinct possibility that the two phonological systems may come to have an increasingly intimate relationship.

Exercises and study questions

1. The following are not normal Tok Pisin words. If they were to be adopted into the language as regular lexical items, how do you think they would be adapted to Tok Pisin phonology?
   spleen, strike, thimble, hammer, sponge, strength

2. Which English word is the source for these Tok Pisin words (remember that an -*im* suffix may be added to a verb stem)?
   banis, kisim, pilim, giaman, spak, olsem

3. The words in the following Tok Pisin sentences are fairly close to their English etyma. Can you work out the meaning of the sentences? (note -*im* transitive suffix and -*pela* adjectival suffix)
   Mi laik kukim rais insait long haus.
   Tupela yangpela man bin go dring wara.
   Mi lukim wanpela liklik pisin ausait long haus
   Em i bin karim kago bilong mi
   Planti pis i stap insait long solwara
   Em i bin givim plaua long meri

4. Some Tok Pisin speakers add epenthetic (extra) vowels to separate consonant clusters, while others do not. What would be the alternate form of these words when epenthetic vowels are *not* inserted? Can you guess the English meaning?
   sipun
   karai
   giraun
   porok
   kilia
   palang

Selected references

Please consult the General references for titles mentioned in the text but not included in the references below. For a full bibliography see the accompanying CD-ROM.

Bálint, András
    1969   *English-Pidgin-French Phrase Book and Sports Dictionary*. Port Moresby:
              Author.
Bee, Darlene
    1971   Phonological interference between Usarufa and Pidgin English. *Kivung* 5:
              69–95.
Faraclas, Nicholas
    1989   Prosody and creolization in Tok Pisin. *Journal of Pidgin and Creole
              Languages* 4: 132–139.
Franklin, Karl J.
    1990   On the translation of official notices into Tok Pisin. In: Verhaar (ed.),
              323–344.
Grimes, Barbara (ed.)
    1992   *Ethnologue: Languages of the World*. 12th edition Dallas, TX: Summer
              Institute of Linguistics.
Holm, John A. and Christopher Kepiou
    1993   Tok Pisin i kamap pisin gen? Is Tok Pisin repidginizing? In: Francis
              Byrne and John Holm (eds.), *Atlantic Meets Pacific: A Global View of
              Pidginization and Creolization*, 341–353. Amsterdam/Philadelphia:
              Benjamins.
Laycock, Donald C.
    1970   *Materials in New Guinea Pidgin (Coastal and Lowlands)*. (Pacific
              Linguistics D5.) Canberra: Australian National University.
    1985   Phonology: substratum elements in Tok Pisin phonology. In: Stephen A.
              Wurm and Peter Mühlhäusler (eds.), *Handbook of Tok Pisin (New Guinea
              Pidgin)*, 295–307. (Pacific Linguistics C70.) Canberra: Australian National
              University.
Litteral, Robert
    1970   The phonemes of New Guinea Pidgin. Ukarumpa: Summer Institute of
              Linguistics. Unpublished manuscript.
Lomax, R. W.
    1983   Aspects of cohesion and discourse structure in Tok Pisin (Melanesian
              Pidgin). M.A. thesis, University of Leeds.
Mihalic, Frank
    1971   *The Jacaranda Dictionary and Grammar of Melanesian Pidgin*. Milton,
              QLD: Jacaranda.
    1990   Obsolescence in the Tok Pisin vocabulary. In: Verhaar (ed.), 263–273.

Mühlhäusler, Peter
  1975   Sociolects in New Guinea Pidgin. In: Kenneth A. McElhanon (ed.), *Tok Pisini go we?* Kivung special publication, number 1, 59–75. Port Moresby: Linguistic Society of Papua New Guinea.
  1978   Samoan Plantation Pidgin and the origin of New Guinea Pidgin. *Papers in Pidgin and Creole Linguistics* 1: 7–119.
  1975   Sociolects in New Guinea Pidgin. In: kenneth A. McElhanon (ed.), Tok Pisin i go we? Kivung special publication, number 1, 59–75. Port Moresby: Linguistic Society of Papia new Guinea.
Mundhenk, Norman
  1990   Linguistic decisions in the 1987 Tok Pisin bible. In: Verhaar (ed.), 345–373.
Pawley, Andrew K.
  1975   On epenthetic vowels in New Guinea Pidgin. In: Kenneth A. McElhanon (ed.), *Tok Pisin i go we?* Kivung special publication, number 1, 215–228. Port Moresby: Linguistic Society of Papua New Guinea.
Reesink, Ger P.
  1990   Mother Tongue and Tok Pisin. In: Verhaar (ed.), 289–306.
Romaine, Suzanne
  1990   Variability and Anglicization in the distinction between p/f in young children's Tok Pisin. In: Jerold A. Edmondson, Crawford Feagin and Peter Mühlhäusler (eds.), *Development and Diversity: Language Variation across Time and Space. A Festschrift for Charles-James N. Bailey*, 173–185. Arlington, TX: Summer Institute of Linguistics.
  1992   *Language, Education and Development: Urban and Rural Tok Pisin in Papua New Guinea.* Oxford: Oxford University Press.
  1994   On the creation and expansion of registers: sports reporting in Tok Pisin. In: Douglas Biber, and Edward Finegan (eds.), *Sociolinguistic Perspectives on Register*, 59–81. Oxford/New York: Oxford University Press.
  1995   "Lice he no good": On [r] and [l] in Tok Pisin. In: Werner Abraham, Talmy Givón and Sandra A. Thompson (eds.), *Discourse Grammar and Typology: Papers in Honor of John W.M. Verhaar*, 309–318. Amsterdam/ Phildelphia: Benjamins.
Ross, Malcolm
  1992   Sources of Austronesian lexical items in Tok Pisin. In: Tom E. Dutton, Malcolm Ross and Darrel T. Tryon (eds.), *The Language Game: Papers in Memory of Donald Laycock*, 361–384. (Pacific linguistics C110.) Canberra: Australian National University.
Sankoff, Gillian and Suzanne Laberge
  1973   On the acquisition of native speakers by a language. *Kivung* 6: 32–47.
Siegel, Jeff
  1997   Pidgin and English in Melanesia: is there a continuum? *World Englishes* 16: 185–204.
Smith, Geoff P.
  2002   *Growing up with Tok Pisin: Contact, Creolization and Change in Papua New Guinea's National Language.* London: Battlebridge.

Verhaar, John W.M. (ed.)
1990   *Melanesian Pidgin and Tok Pisin*. Amsterdam/Philadelphia: Benjamins.
Wurm, Stephen A.
1971   *New Guinea Highlands Pidgin: Course materials*. (Pacific Linguistics
          D3.) Canberra: Australian National University.
1985   Phonology: intonation in Tok Pisin. In: Stephen A. Wurm and Peter
          Mühlhäusler (eds.), *Handbook of Tok Pisin* (*New Guinea Pidgin*), 309–334.
          (Pacific Linguistics C70.) Canberra: Australian National University.

Hawai'i Creole: phonology

Kent Sakoda and Jeff Siegel

1. Introduction

Hawai'i Creole is spoken by an estimated 600,000 people in the US state of Hawai'i. In the linguistics literature, it is usually called Hawai'i (or Hawaiian) Creole English, but its speakers call it "Pidgin". While Hawai'i Creole uses many words from Hawaiian and other languages, the majority of its vocabulary comes from English; however, the phonology and semantics are quite different from English. Before describing the phonology of Hawai'i Creole, this chapter presents some background information on its historical development, current use, and vocabulary.

1.1. Historical and sociolinguistic background

1.1.1. Contact and immigration

The Hawaiian Islands were populated by Polynesians some time between 200 and 400 AD. The first Europeans to visit the islands were Captain Cook and his crew in 1778. At that time the native Hawaiian population numbered somewhere between 200,000 and a million. Contact with outsiders increased when Hawai'i became a stopover in the fur trade between China and the west coast of North America, and then a centre for the sandalwood trade and the whaling industry. During this time the foreign population in Hawai'i increased while the indigenous population decreased drastically because of introduced disease. In 1848 there were only approximately 88,000 Hawaiians left.

In 1835, the first sugarcane plantation was established, and the expanding sugar industry led to the importation of labourers from many countries. About 2,000 Chinese plantation labourers arrived from 1852 to 1876, and more than 37,000 from 1877 to 1897. The majority were speakers of dialects of Cantonese Yue and Hakka, spoken in southern China. Approximately 2,450 labourers from other Pacific islands were imported from 1877 to 1887 – most from Kiribati (then the Gilbert Islands) but at least 550 from Vanuatu (then the

New Hebrides), and some from Rotuma (currently part of Fiji), New Ireland and Bougainville (parts of Papua New Guinea) and Santa Cruz (Solomon Islands).

More than 10,000 Portuguese workers were brought in from 1878 to 1887 and another 13,000 from 1906 to 1913. Nearly all of these were from the Madeira and Azores islands. Indentured labourers also came from continental Europe: 615 Scandinavians (mostly from Norway) in 1881 and 1,052 Germans between 1882 and 1885.

Steady Japanese indentured migration began in 1884, and by 1924 over 200,000 Japanese had arrived in Hawai'i. Migration from the Philippines began in 1907, and by 1930 over 100,000 Filipinos had come to Hawai'i. Other significant numbers of immigrants included 5,203 from Puerto Rico (1900–1901), 7,843 from Korea (1903–1905), approximately 3,000 from Russia (1906–1912) and about 2,000 from Spain (1907–1913).

1.1.2.   The development of Hawai'i Pidgin English

Texts from the early 1800s provide evidence that a pidginized variety of English was used to some extent in Hawai'i ports, most probably brought by sailors. It was clearly not a stable pidgin, but contained some of the features found in Chinese Pidgin English and the South Seas Jargon of the time which influenced the development of Pacific Pidgin English. Some of these include the use of *by and by* meaning 'later', *no* as a preverbal negator, *plenty* used to mean 'a lot of', *one* used as an indefinite article, and *been* as a past tense marker.

Other features of existing stable pidgins were later brought to Hawai'i by the early plantation labourers: Chinese Pidgin English by the Chinese, and Pacific Pidgin English (including early forms of Melanesian Pidgin) by the Gilbertese and Melanesian labourers. Texts from this time show a still unstable pidginized form of English with some of the features of these varieties but few of the features found in later Hawai'i Creole. The more widespread pidgin that developed on the plantations of Hawai'i was Pidgin Hawaiian.

When the plantation era began, the Hawaiians were still in control of their islands, and their language was dominant. It was the language of government and of education for all non-Euroamerican children, and it naturally became the language used to run the plantations. However, it was a pidginized form of Hawaiian that was used for communication between whites, Chinese and Hawaiians on the plantations. When labourers started coming from Portugal and other countries in the 1870s, Pidgin Hawaiian stabilized and remained as the main plantation language until the 1890s. There is evidence that some

Pidgin Hawaiian was still being used early in the 20th century, especially in rural areas.

The shift in dominance from Hawaiian to English began in 1875 when the Reciprocity Treaty with the United States was signed. This allowed free trade and a greater influx of Americans. Also the number of Hawaiians continued to decline and by 1878, the number had decreased to less than 50,000. In the decade from 1878 to 1888, there was a dramatic increase in the number of English-medium schools and a decrease in the number of Hawaiian schools. At the same time, Chinese and Portuguese families began to arrive, whereas previously most of the labourers had been single men. This meant that there was an increased number of children being exposed to English in the now English-medium public schools, including substantial numbers from the first generation of locally born children of immigrants.

During this period, English also began to gradually replace Hawaiian as the language of the plantations, and an English-lexified pidgin began to develop. At this stage, Pidgin Hawaiian was still widely used as well, and this led to many Hawaiian words coming into the English pidgin. By the end of the 19th century, Hawai'i Pidgin English (HawPE) had stabilized and had become established as a new auxiliary language.

At the beginning of the 20th century, HawPE began to be used more widely for interethnic communication outside the plantations, especially in the mixed urban areas. An important factor was the emergence of large numbers of the first generation of locally born Japanese who came into the public schools and learned HawPE from their classmates. (Another important factor was that most English speaking Euroamerican children continued to go to private schools.) Children also began to acquire HawPE from their school age siblings and use it as a second language in the home. As children grew older, many of them used HawPE more than their mother tongue.

1.1.3.   *The emergence of Hawai'i Creole*

At the turn of the century, the second generation of locally born Chinese and Portuguese began to appear on the scene. By this time, most parents were bilingual in their traditional language and HawPE, and many used this pidgin as their primary language. So in many cases, parents spoke to their new-born children in the pidgin, rather than in Cantonese or Portuguese, for example. The result was that many of this second generation of immigrants acquired HawPE as their first language.

At the same time, many Hawaiians had intermarried with Chinese and other immigrants and had children. The census of 1910 gave the figures of

26,041 Hawaiians and 12,506 Part-Hawaiians. It is likely that for many of these interethnic marriages, the language of the home was HawPE, so that many of the Part-Hawaiian children also learned the pidgin as their first language.

Since HawPE was now spoken as a first language, it was technically no longer a pidgin language, but rather a creole. So it was at this time that we can say that Hawai'i Creole began to emerge. Most linguists agree that Hawai'i Creole was established as a distinct language some time between 1905 and 1920, as more and more second generation locally born Chinese and Portuguese – later joined by larger numbers of second generation locally born Japanese – acquired it as their first language. Some time between 1920 and 1930, the number of locally born children of immigrants grew to equal the number of foreign born, and it can be said that this was the time that Hawai'i Creole became fully established as the language of the majority of the population of Hawai'i (see Roberts 2000).

1.1.4. Influence of other languages

We have already mentioned that many words from Hawaiian came into Hawai'i Creole through Pidgin Hawaiian and Pidgin English. But the structure of Hawaiian has also affected the structure of Hawai'i Creole, making it different from that of English. One example is word order. In Hawaiian, there are sentences such as *Nui ka hale*. Literally this is 'Big the house', which in English would be 'The house is big'. Similarly, in Hawai'i Creole we find sentences such as *Big, da house* and *Cute, da baby*.

Another example is the type of expression from Hawaiian such as *Auwē, ka nani!* which is literally 'Oh the pretty!' meaning 'Oh, how pretty!'. Similarly, in Hawai'i Creole we find the same kind of expression – for example, *Oh, da pretty!* and *Oh, da cute!*

Other languages also appear to have influenced the structure of Hawai'i Creole more than the vocabulary. One such language is Cantonese. For example, in Cantonese one word *yáuh* is used for both possessive and existential sentences, i.e. meaning both 'have/has' and 'there is/are', as in these examples below (from Matthews and Yip 1994):

(1)   **a.** *Kéuihdeih yáuh sāam-go jái.*
         (they *yáuh* three sons)
         'They have three sons.'

b. *Yáuh go hahksāang hóu síng.*
(*yáuh* a student very bright)
'There's a student who's very bright.'

Similarly, in Hawai'i Creole one word *get* is used for both possessive and existential, as in (2):

(2)   **a.** *They **get** three sons.*
'*They have three sons.*'
b. *Get one student he very bright.*
'There's a student who's very bright.'

Portuguese appears to have affected the structure of Hawai'i Creole even more. For instance, Portuguese uses the word *para* meaning 'for' to introduce infinitival clauses, where Standard English uses *to*, as in (3):

(3)   *Carlos é homem **para** fazer isso.*
(Charles is man for do that.)
'Charles is the man to do that.'

Similarly, *for* (or *fo*) is used in Hawai'i Creole:

(4)   *Charles is da man **fo** do 'um.*
'Charles is the man to do it.'

The Portuguese copula/auxiliary *estar* (with various conjugations such as *está*) has several different functions, including copula with locations and adjectives, auxiliary for present progressive, and marker for perfective, as in the examples in (5):

(5)   **a.** *O livro **está** sobre a mesa.*
(the book *está* on the table)
'The book is on the table.'

b. *A água **está** fria.*
(the water *está* cold)
'The water is cold.'

c. *João **está** escrevendo uma carta.*
(John *está* writing one letter)
'John is writing a letter.'

d. *A casa **está** construida.*
(the house *está* constructed)
'The house is finished.'

In Hawai'i Creole, the word *stay* has the same functions:

(6)　　**a**. *Da book **stay** on top da table.*
'The book is on the table.'

　　b. *Da water **stay** cold.*
'The water is cold.'

　　c. *John **stay** writing one letter.*
'John is writing a letter.'

　　d. *Da house **stay** pau already.*
'The house is finished.'

The phonology of Hawai'i Creole also has some similarities to that of Hawaiian, Cantonese and Portuguese, especially in the vowel system and intonation in questions, but these connections have not been studied in any detail.

Thus, the ethnic groups whose languages most influenced the structure of Hawai'i Creole seem to have been the Hawaiians, Chinese and Portuguese. But the influence of the Hawaiians declined steadily as their numbers declined and the numbers of other ethnic groups increased. By 1900, there were more Portuguese and Chinese than Hawaiians and Part-Hawaiians. Even though the Japanese were by far the largest immigrant group, their language seems to have had little effect on the structure of Hawai'i Creole. One reason for this was first pointed out by the famous Hawai'i Creole scholar, John Reinecke, who wrote (1969: 93): "The first large immigration of Japanese did not occur until 1888 when the Hawaiian, Chinese and Portuguese between them had pretty well fixed the form of the 'pidgin' [English] spoken on the plantations."

Another reason is that, as we have seen, it was the locally born members of immigrant groups who first used Pidgin English as their primary language and whose mother tongues influenced the structure of the language. This structure was then passed on to their children in the development of Hawai'i Creole. When the creole first began to emerge, the locally born population was dominated by the Chinese and Portuguese. Of these two groups, the Portuguese were the more important. In 1896, they made up over half of the locally born immigrant population. For the Portuguese, the number of locally born came to equal the number of foreign born in 1900, whereas this did not happen for the Chinese until just before 1920 and for the Japanese not until later in the 1920s (see Roberts 2000).

The Portuguese were also the most significant immigrant group in the schools. They were the first group to bring their families, and their demands for education for their children in English rather than Hawaiian were partially responsible for the increase in English-medium public schools. From the critical years of 1881 until 1905, Portuguese children were the largest immigrant group in the schools, with over 20 percent from 1890 to 1905.

Another factor was that the Portuguese, being white, were given a disproportionate number of influential positions on the plantations as skilled labourers, clerks and *lunas* 'foremen' who gave orders to other labourers. In fact, the number of Portuguese *lunas* was three times larger than that of any other group.

The Portuguese community was also the first to shift from their traditional language to Hawai'i Creole. By the late 1920s, the Portuguese had the lowest level of traditional language maintenance, and the greatest dominance of English or Hawai'i Creole in the homes, followed by the Hawaiians and then the Chinese (see Siegel 2000).

But that is not to say that Japanese has had no influence on Hawai'i Creole. Many Japanese words have come into the language, and several Hawai'i Creole expressions, such as *chicken skin* 'goose bumps', are direct translations of Japanese. Also, the way many discourse particles are used, such as *yeah* and *no* at the end of a sentence, seems to be due to Japanese influence. Furthermore, the structure of narratives in Hawai'i Creole is very similar to that of Japanese (see Masuda 2000).

1.2.   Sociolinguistic situation

Since its development, Hawai'i Creole has been used mostly as the informal language of families and friends, and has been considered an important badge of local identity, i.e. the language of people born and bred in Hawai'i, especially ethnic Hawaiians and descendants of plantation labourers. Attitudes towards the language have always been ambivalent. While recognized as being important to local culture, it has at the same time been denigrated as corrupted or "broken" English, and seen as an obstacle to learning Standard English, the official language of the schools, government and big business.

In recent years, however, there has been a great deal of advocacy for Hawai'i Creole which has resulted in changing attitudes and use in wider contexts. The turning point may have been in 1987 when the state Board of Education attempted to implement a policy which allowed only Standard English in the schools. Instead of being well-received by the community, there was a strong negative reaction from parents, teachers, university faculty and other community groups. The policy was seen as discriminatory and as an unfair attack on Hawai'i Creole and on local culture in general (Sato 1989, 1991). The debate generated many letters to local newspapers and much discussion on radio and television, the majority strongly supporting Hawai'i Creole. Similar debates have erupted since then (the most recent in 1999 and 2002), as educational administrators and some members of the public seek to blame Hawai'i Creole for poor state results in national standardized tests in reading and writing.

Since 1998, a group of people, mainly from the University of Hawai'i at Mānoa, have been meeting regularly to discuss linguistic, sociolinguistic and educational issues concerning Hawai'i Creole. This group is called "Da Pidgin Coup" (all puns intended). Following the public debate in 1999, the group wrote a position paper, "Pidgin and Education", as a basis for discussions with education officials and teachers, and for public education efforts as well. The aim was to provide information, backed up by research, about the complex relationship between Hawai'i Creole and English, and about the equally complex issues surrounding the use of Hawai'i Creole in education. (The position paper can be accessed at <www.hawaii.edu/sls/pidgin.html>.)

The expanding domains of Hawai'i Creole have mainly been in the area of literature. Over the past decades, the use of the language in short stories, plays and poetry has increased dramatically. Most notable are the works of Milton Murayama, Darrell Lum, Ed Sakamoto, Eric Chock, Gary Pak, and Lee Tonouchi (e.g. 2001). The novels of Lois-Ann Yamanaka, with their use of Hawai'i Creole in both narration and dialogue, have been successful outside of Hawai'i as well. The most remarkable extension of use of the language has been in the translation of the New Testament (*Da Jesus Book*), published in 2000. Over 11,000 copies were sold in the first year it appeared.

Nevertheless, Hawai'i Creole remains primarily a spoken language. Speakers range on a continuum from what is called the "heavy Pidgin" or "full-on Pidgin" (the basilect, or variety furthest from Standard English) to a lighter form of the creole (the acrolect, closest to Standard English). The majority of speakers speak varieties in between (the mesolects) and can switch back and forth between lighter or heavier forms of the creole as required by contextual factors such as interlocutor, topic, setting and formality. A large proportion of speakers are also completely bilingual and can switch between the creole and a form of Standard English.

There is a widespread belief that this continuum is a result of "decreolization", or a gradual change taking place in Hawai'i Creole which is resulting in it becoming more and more like English. However, evidence exists that such a continuum of variation existed from the earliest days of the language. Furthermore, the desire to project a separate local identity will most likely ensure that the language remains distinct from English. Nevertheless, there is no general agreement about what really constitutes "Pidgin" in Hawai'i. For some people, it means the basilectal variety, with its grammatical rules that are very different from those of English. For others, it means using only the local accent and some local vocabulary items.

For the purpose of this chapter, we will focus on the variety that differs most from Standard English, i.e. the basilect, but we will mention significant variants in the mesolectal varieties that are closer to English. It must be kept in mind, however, that with the nature of the creole continuum, there is a great deal of intra- and inter-speaker variation. Furthermore, with the high degree of bilingualism, the Hawai'i Creole of some speakers is affected by English.

2.   Vocabulary

The vast majority of words in Hawai'i Creole are derived from English and have the same meanings as their English etyma. However, many Hawai'i Creole words have changed in meaning or have additional meanings, including the following:

alphabet	'alphabet, letter of the alphabet'
lawn mower	'lawn mower, to mow' (e.g. *lawnmower the grass*)
package	'package, sack, paper bag'
pear	'pear, avocado'
off	'off, turn off' (e.g. *off the light*)
broke	'broke, broken, break, torn, tear, tore' (e.g. *He broke my shirt.*)
shame	'shame, shy, bashful, embarrassed'

Other words and expressions are derived from English but have changed in form and in some cases in meaning as well:

cockaroach	'cockroach, to steal or sneak away with'
beif	'bathe'
brah (*bla, blala*)	'brother'
boddah	'bother'
fut	'fart'
mento	'mental, insane'
nuff	'enough'
hybolic	'using fancy (or standard-sounding) language'
garans	'guaranteed'
laters	'see you later'
whatevahs	'whatever, it doesn't matter'

There are also many compounds and expressions made up of English-derived words that are not found in English (or at least not with the same meaning):

buckaloose	'go out of control'
bulai	'to tell lies' (*bull* + *lie*)
bolohead	'bald' (*bald* + *head*)
buddha-head	'local person of Japanese ancestry'
howzit	'greeting, how are you?'
cat tongue	'unable to drink or eat hot things'
catch air	'breathe'
chicken skin	'goose bumps'
stink eye	'dirty look'
talk stink	'talk badly about someone'
talk story	'have informal conversation, tell stories'
broke da mouth	'very delicious!'

In addition, Hawai'i Creole has many words derived from other languages. The largest number of such words (over 100) come from the Hawaiian language. Many of these have come into the English spoken in Hawai'i as well. Some examples are:

akamai	'smart'
haole	'white person (Euroamerican)' (Hawaiian *haole* 'foreigner')
hapai	'carry, pregnant' (Hawaiian *hāpai*)
huhu	'angry, offended' (Hawaiian *huhū*)
imu	'earth oven'
kapakahi	'crooked, inside-out'
keiki	'child, children'
koa	'kind of native forest tree'
kokua	'help' (Hawaiian *kōkua*)
lanai	'verandah' (Hawaiian *lānai*)
lei	'flower garland'
lilikoi	'passionfruit'
lolo	'stupid, crazy' (Hawaiian *lōlō*)
mahimahi	'dolphin fish'
manini	'stingy, undersized'
ohana	'extended family'
okole	'anus, buttocks' (Hawaiian *'ōkole*)
ono	'delicious' (Hawaiian *'ono*)

opala	'trash, rubbish' (Hawaiian *ōpala*)
pau	'finish, finished'
pilau	'rotten'
pilikia	'trouble, bother'
puka	'hole'
pupu(s)	'party snacks, finger food' (Hawaiian *pūpū*)
wahine	'woman'

Japanese has also provided many words to Hawai'i Creole (approximately 40, but some of these are used primarily by people of Japanese ancestry). Some examples are:

bachi	'punishment, retribution'
bento	'Japanese style box lunch'
bocha	'bath, bathe'
chichi(s)	'breast(s)' (Japanese *chichi* 'milk')
daikon	'kind of turnip'
janken po	'paper, scissors and stone game'
mochi	'rice patty'
musubi	'rice ball' (western Japanese)
nori	'dried seaweed'
obake	'ghost'
shishi	'urine, urinate'
shoyu	'soy sauce'
tako	'octopus'
ume	'partially dried salted sour plum pickle'
zori(s)	'rubber thong(s), flip-flops'

In addition, Hawai'i Creole has words from Portuguese and other languages:

malasada	'kind of doughnut' (Portuguese)
babooz	'idiot' (Portuguese *babosa* 'stupid, simpleton')
lihing mui	'dried sour plum' (Chinese languages)
char siu	'barbequed pork' (Chinese languages)
adobo	'Filipino way of cooking' (Filipino languages)
bago-ong	'Filipino fermented fish sauce' (Tagalog)
kimchee	'Korean spicy pickled cabbage' (Korean)
lavalava	'sarong' (Samoan)
kaukau	'food' (from Chinese Pidgin English *chowchow*)

Finally, there are some compounds, blends, and expressions made up of words from English and other languages. Example include:

haolefied	'become like a white person' (Hawaiian *haole* 'foreigner')
onolicious	'delicious' (Hawaiian *'ono* 'delicious')
hanabata	'snot' (Japanese *hana* 'nose', *bata* from English *butter*)
hele on	'move on' (Hawaiian *hele* 'go, come, move')
hulihuli chicken	'chicken barbecued on a spit' (Hawaiian *huli* 'to turn')
kalua pig	'pig baked in an underground oven' (Hawaiian *kalua* 'bake in ground oven')
kukui nuts	'candlenuts' (Hawaiian *kukui* 'candlenut tree')
poi dog	'mixed breed dog' (Hawaiian *poi* 'pounded taro')
chawan cut	'haircut shaped like an inverted rice bowl' (Japanese *chawan* 'rice bowl')
daikon legs	'white, short and fat legs' (Japanese *daikon* 'a kind of turnip')
buta kaukau	'pig slop' (Japanese *buta* 'pig', Hawai'i Creole *kaukau* 'food')

3.   Phonemic contrasts and phonetic realizations

Hawai'i Creole phonology has been studied in greatest detail by Carol Odo (1975, 1977; Bickerton and Odo 1976), and some of the analyses below are based on her work.

3.1.   Vowels

3.1.1. *Basilectal Hawai'i Creole*

The typical vowels of basilectal Hawai'i Creole are given in Table 1, and those that differ from General American English are described below. The keywords used by Wells (1982) are employed here, except when a particular word is not found in basilectal Hawai'i Creole. In such cases, an alternative with the same vowel quality that is found in the language is given (with Wells' word following in brackets).

Table 1.   Typical vowels of basilectal Hawai'i Creole

FIT [KIT]	i	FACE	eɪ ~ e	SQUARE	eɑ
DRESS	æ̞ ~ ɛ	PALM	ɑ	START	ɑ
TRAP	æ̞	THOUGHT	ɔ	NORTH	ɔ
LOT	ɔ	GOAT	oʊ ~ o	FORCE	ɔ
STUFF [STRUT]	ɑ ~ ʌ	GOOSE	u	CURE	uɑ
FOOT	u	PRICE	ɑɪ	happY	i
ASK [BATH]	æ̞	CHOICE	oɪ ~ ɔɪ	lettER	ɑ
COUGH [CLOTH]	ɔ	MOUTH	ɑʊ	horsES	e
NURSE	ɝ	NEAR	iɑ	commA	ɑ
LEAVE [FLEECE]	i > ij				

FIT [KIT]
What is [ɪ] in English is usually raised and slightly tensed in basilectal Hawai'i Creole, especially in monosyllabic words and stressed syllables, so that for basilectal speakers *fit* and *feet* have the same pronunciation.

DRESS
[æ] may be raised to [ɛ] in all environments.

STUFF [STRUT]
Variation between [ɑ] and [ʌ] is context-free and unconditioned. For most basilectal speakers, *but* and *baht* (the unit of Thai currency) would be pronounced the same.

FOOT
What is [ʊ] in English is usually raised and slightly tensed, especially in monosyllabic words and stressed syllables, so that for most basilectal speakers *look* and *Luke* have the same pronunciation.

NURSE
The R-coloured vowel [ɝ] is found only in monosyllabic words or stressed syllables (see section 3.2.3. below).

LEAVE [FLEECE]
[i] is laxer than in English. Some speakers, especially those affected by English, may lengthen or diphthongize [i].

FACE
[eɪ] is usually realized as [e] word internally before a voiceless consonant, as in [mek] 'make', and word-finally, such as [de] 'day'.

GOAT
[oʊ] may be realized as [o] especially at the end of a word, such as *know* [no], or preceding [m], as in [kʰom] 'comb' and [homwɜɹk] 'homework'.

NEAR, SQUARE
What is post-vocalic ʀ in word-final position in varieties of American English is syllabified as [ɑ] after /i/ and /e/.

START
Basilectal Hawai'i Creole does not have ʀ-coloured vowels, except for [ɜɹ] (see section 3.2.3. below).

NORTH, FORCE
The difference between the vowel in these two items found in General American English is neutralized in Hawai'i Creole as [ɔ] (without the post-vocalic ʀ) in monosyllabic words and stressed syllables and as [o] in unstressed syllables (see section 3.2.3.).

CURE
Post-vocalic ʀ is syllabified as [ɑ] after [ʊ] in word-final position.

lettER
What is [ər] (= [ɚ]) in General American English is [ɑ] in basilectal Hawai'i Creole in open unstressed syllables.

horsES
What is schwa [ə] in closed syllables in most varieties of English is [e] in basilectal Hawai'i Creole.

commA
English schwa [ə] in open syllables is [ɑ] in basilectal Hawai'i Creole.

In summary, basilectal Hawai'i Creole speakers normally have a seven-vowel system:

```
   /i/                            /u/
      /e/                      /o/
         /æ/    /ɑ/    /ɔ/
```

/i/ ranges from a raised relatively tense [ɪ] to a slightly lax [i] and /u/ from a relatively raised and tense [ʊ] to a slightly lax [u]; /ɑ/ ranges from [ɑ] to [ʌ]. The following diphthongs are also present: /eɪ/, /aʊ/, /aɪ/, /ɔɪ/ and /oʊ/. Basilectal Hawai'i Creole has only one R-coloured vowel: /ɜr/, occurring only in stressed syllables.

3.1.2. Mesolectal Hawai'i Creole

In mesolectal varieties, the distinctive basilectal vowels vary with the corresponding vowels in General American English. The exceptions are that the raising and tensing of [ɪ] and [ʊ] is generally avoided (since it is a salient marker of basilectal speech). Thus, for speakers of mesolectal and acrolectal varieties, /i/, /ɪ/, /u/ and /ʊ/ are separate phonemes.

The typical mesolectal vowels are shown in Table 2, with further discussion below.

Table 2.   Typical vowels of mesolectal Hawai'i Creole

FIT [KIT]	ɪ	FACE	eɪ ~ e	SQUARE	eɑ ~ er
DRESS	ɛ ~ æ̝	PALM	ɑ	START	ɑ ~ ɑr
TRAP	æ̝ ~ æ	THOUGHT	ɔ > ɒ	NORTH	ɔ ~ or
LOT	ɔ ~ ɑ > ɒ	GOAT	oʊ ~ o	FORCE	ɔ ~ or
STUFF [STRUT]	ɑ ~ ʌ	GOOSE	u	CURE	uɑ ~ ur
FOOT	ʊ	PRICE	ɑɪ	happY	i
ASK [BATH]	æ̝ ~ æ	CHOICE	oɪ ~ ɔɪ	lettER	ɑ ~ ər = [ɚ]
COUGH [CLOTH]	ɔ > ɒ	MOUTH	aʊ	horsES	e ~ ə ~ ɪ
NURSE	ɜr	NEAR	iɑ ~ ir	commA	ɑ ~ ə
LEAVE [FLEECE]	i > ij				

Many varieties of American English are spoken in Hawai'i. For Hawai'i Creole speakers who speak varieties with the THOUGHT-LOT merger, the distinctions in the vowels in LOT, COUGH [CLOTH] and [THOUGHT] are neutralized, and the vowel is pronounced as [ɒ] which may vary with [ɔ]. Because of this factor, there is some intra- and inter-speaker variation in the pronunciation of certain lexical items ([ɑ] vs. [ɒ] or [ɔ]): for example, in *job*, *stop*, *dock*, *problem* and *model* (Odo 1977). Because of the fact that [ʌ] in STUFF [STRUT] is still pronounced as [ɑ] by some mesolectal speakers, there are some speakers who pronounce *cot* and *caught* the same [kʰɔt] or [kʰɒt] in contrast with *cut* [kʰat], and others who pronounce *cot* and *cut* the same [kʰat] in contrast with *caught* [kʰɔt].

3.2.   Consonants

The consonants of both basilectal and mesolectal Hawai'i Creole are basically the same as those of General American English. However, there are a few differences, and these are discussed below.

3.2.1. Stops

The Hawai'i Creole voiceless stops differ from those of General American English in some phonetic realizations. First, like English, voiceless stops are aspirated when they occur at the beginning of a syllable with primary stress, but unlike English they may be aspirated in other syllables as well, for example ['mak ʰet] 'market' and ['kʰat ʰen] 'carton' (see section 6.1.).

Second, voiceless stops that occur at the end of a word or at the end of a syllable followed by a consonant may be unreleased or glottalized, that is, pronounced with both oral articulation and glottal closure. In rapid speech [t] in this position may become a glottal stop, e.g. [naʔ] 'not'.

Third, /t/ and /d/ are palatalized before /r/: [tʃri] 'tree', [dʒraɪ] 'dry'.

Finally, /t/ and /d/ are often used in place of what are /θ/ and /ð/ respectively in General American English (see below).

Like General American English, /t/ and /d/ are flapped intervocalically in an unstressed syllable in normal speech, as in [miɾiŋ] 'meeting' and [baɾi] 'body'. However, some flaps occur in Hawai'i Creole where they are not found in General American English because of some of the differences in realizations described above, for example [wɪɾaut] 'without' (because of /θ/ in place of /t/) and [poɾogi] 'Portuguese' because of /ɔ/ in place of /ɔr/.

3.2.2. Fricatives

With regard to TH, General American English /θ/ occurs as [θ] and [t] or [tʰ] in free variation in basilectal Hawai'i Creole, and /ð/ as [ð] and [d], for example: [tʰɔt] 'thought', [wit] 'with' and [dæt] 'that', [ɑdɑ] 'other'. For two items, [f] has replaced [ð]: [bɜrfde] 'birthday' and [beɪf] 'bathe'. In mesolectal varieties, [θ] and [ð] are more frequent.

Some speakers lack [ʒ] in their phonemic inventory and substitute /dʒ/ as in [medʒɑ] 'measure'. /s/ is often palatalized before both /tʃ/ and /r/: [ʃtʃrit] 'street', [groʃri] 'grocery'.

/v/ may be deleted between voiced sounds: [eritiŋ] 'everything', [neɑ] 'never', [oɑ] 'over'.

3.2.3. Liquids

Post-vocalic R

/r/ as the coda of a syllable is generally not found in basilectal Hawai'i Creole. What is /ɑr/ in General American English is realized as [ɑ], for example in [hɑd] 'hard', [pɑkiŋ] 'parking'; /ɛr/ is realized as [e] when followed by another sound: [sked] 'scared'; /ɔr/ and /or/ are realized as [ɔ] in stressed syllables and [o] in unstressed syllables, e.g. ['fɔtʃen] 'fortune' vs. [pʰoˈtʃreɪ] 'portray'. (The exceptions are the grammatical morphemes [fo] and [mo] derived from *for* and *more*.)

In word-final position, what is post-vocalic R in other varieties is syllabified as [ɑ] in basilectal Hawai'i Creole after /i/, /u/, /o/, /ɑɪ/ and /e/. Consider the examples [diɑ] 'deer', [puɑ] 'poor', [stoɑ] 'store', [fɑɪɑ] 'fire', [wælfeɑ] 'welfare'.

As mentioned above, the only post-vocalic R or R-coloured vowel in Hawai'i Creole is [ɜr], and it is found only in stressed syllables: [bɜrd] 'bird', [riˈtɜrn] 'return'. In unstressed syllables, what is [ɜr] or [ər] in other varieties is realized as [e] when followed by another sound and as [ɑ] at the end of a word: ['rɑ̰ bet] 'Robert', ['reked] 'record (noun)', ['pʰepɑ] 'paper', ['fiŋgɑ] 'finger'.

L vocalization

/l/ is generally "dark" or velar [ɫ], especially in syllable codas. Syllabic /l/ in English is often replaced by [o] in the basilect, for instance in [tʃɹɑbo] 'trouble', [æpo] 'apple', [pʰipo] 'people'. Preconsonantal /l/ may become [o], [ʊ] or [u] – for example: [meok] 'milk', [hæup] 'help'. In some words, there is variation, such as [rio] ~ [riu] ~ [ril] 'real'.

3.2.4. Other consonants

Hawai'i Creole also has the flap [ɾ] as a separate phoneme, found in Japanese borrowings, such as [kɑɾate] 'karate' and [kɑɾaoke] 'karaoke'. The /ɾ/ phoneme can be shown to contrast with /l/ in two Hawai'i Creole loanwords: [kɑɾaɪ] 'spicy hot' (from Japanese) and [kɑlaɪ] 'hoeing' (from Hawaiian).

Hawai'i Creole has the additional affricate /ts/ as well, occurring in word-initial position, as in [tsunɑmi] 'tidal wave' and [tsuɾu] 'crane made from folded paper'.

Many speakers of Hawai'i Creole also use the glottal stop [ʔ] in words derived from Hawaiian, for example in [kɑmaʔɑɪnɑ] 'person born in Hawai'i or long term resident' and [niʔihɑʊ] 'Ni'ihau' (an island in the Hawaiian group).

4. Orthography

There is no standard orthography for Hawai'i Creole. In both popular literature and the New Testament translation, various etymological orthographies are used, based on the conventional spelling of English. An autonomous phonemic orthography, designed by Carol Odo (Bickerton and Odo 1976), is normally used by linguists, and on rare occasions in other contexts, such as in the printed program of the "Wat, Bada yu?" conference held in 1999 on "Hawai'i Creole, local identities and strategies for multicultural learning". (Also, Lee Tonouchi uses the Odo orthography in one short story in his book *Da Word*). The Odo orthography will also be used for the remainder of this chapter.

In the Odo orthography, the consonants are represented by their IPA equivalents except for the following:

/ŋ/	ng
/ʃ/	sh
/ʒ/	zh
/tʃ/	ch
/dʒ/	j
/j/	y
/ɾ/	D
/ʔ/	'

The simple vowels, diphthongs and the ʀ-coloured vowel are represented by the following orthographic symbols:

/i/	i
/e/	e
/æ/	æ (or ae or ɑe)
/ɑ/	a or ɑ
/u/	u

/o/	o
/ɔ/	aw
/eɪ/	ei
/aʊ/	au or ɑu
/ɑɪ/	ai or ɑi
/oɪ/	oi
/oʊ/	ou
/ɜr/	r

5.   Phonotactics

Hawai'i Creole has phonotactics similar to those of English, with the exception of final consonant clusters.

a) Where the final consonant clusters /pt/, /kt/, /ft/, /st/, /ld/ and /nd/ are found in English, the final stop (/t/ or /d/) is absent in basilectal Hawai'i Creole, for example: *raep* /ræp/ 'wrapped', *aek* /æk/ 'act', *sawf* /sɔf/ 'soft', *laes* /læs/ 'last', *kol* /kol/ 'cold', *spen* /spen/ 'spend'.

b) In the final consonant clusters /ts/, /ks/ and /dz/, the stop may be absent: *wats* /wɑts/ ~ /wɑs/ 'what's', *foks* /foks/ ~ /fos/ 'folks', *kidz* /kidz/ ~ /kiz/ 'kids'.

c) In the clusters /fr/ and /pr/, the /r/ is deleted if there is an /r/ in the onset of the next syllable: *pograem* /pogræm/ 'program', *fashchreited* /faʃchreɪted/ 'frustrated', *laibaeri* /lɑɪbæri/ 'library'.

6.   Prosodic features

6.1.   Stress

In Hawai'i Creole, morphologically simple words of two syllables derived from English usually have primary stress on the same syllable as in English. However, there are some exceptions, as illustrated by the following examples (with the stressed syllable in Hawai'i Creole and in the English equivalent both shown in bold): *beisbawl* /beɪsˈbɔl/ '**base**ball', *chapstik* /tʃɑpˈstik/ '**chop**stick', *hedeik* /hedˈeɪk/ '**head**ache', *dedlain* /dædˈlɑɪn/ '**dead**line' (Odo 1975: 16). Of words that have more than two syllables, there are many words in Hawai'i Creole which have primary stress on a different syllable from that in English. This is especially true of English words in which the first syllable is stressed, such as words ending in *-ary, -ony* or *-ory* (Bickerton and Odo 1976: 50). Take, for example, *dikshanaeri* /dikʃɑˈnæri/ 'dictionary', *inventawri* /invænˈtɔri/ 'inventory', *saeramoni* /sæɾɑˈmoni/ 'ceremony'. Other examples are: *harakein* /hɑɾɑˈkeɪn/ 'hurricane', *aelkahawl* /ælkɑˈhɔl/ 'alcohol', *shchrawbæri* /ʃtʃɾɔˈbæri/ 'strawberry', *haspitol* /hɑsˈpitol/ 'hospital', and *kaetalawg* /kætɑˈlɔg/ 'catalogue'.

Another way in which Hawai'i Creole differs from English, at least in the basilectal and mesolectal varieties, is that syllables that do not have primary stress receive slightly more stress than in English. A syllable that has tertiary stress in English may have secondary stress in Hawai'i Creole. So for example, one may hear the following pronunciations: /ˈbeɪˌbi/ 'baby', /ˈbilˌdiŋ/ 'building' (Odo 1975: 15). Also, as mentioned above, vowels in syllables without primary or secondary stress are not necessarily reduced to schwa, but rather the full vowel is used. This also leads to syllables being given secondary stress in Hawai'i Creole when they are unstressed or given tertiary stress in English. This secondary stress may also result in voiceless stops being aspirated where there is no aspiration in English, e.g. *Jæpæniz* [ˌdʒæˌpʰæˈniz] 'Japanese', *kiten* [ˈkʰiˌtʰen] 'kitten', *chikin* [ˈtʃʰiˌkʰin] 'chicken'.

6.2. Speech rhythm

The combination of full vowels rather than schwa and secondary stress in non-primary-stressed syllables means that syllables in Hawai'i Creole tend to have more equal prominence in terms of loudness and duration than syllables in English. There is also greater stress than in English on function words, such as articles, prepositions, modals, and preverbal tense and aspect markers. Therefore, Hawai'i Creole is usually classified as a syllable-timed language, rather than a stress-timed language such as English (Vanderslice and Pierson 1967).

At the same time, syllables or words may be extended or drawled for emphasis, as in (7):

(7)   a. *E, yu wen go si da gem yestade? Waz ri::l gu:::d, bra.*
           (*Eh, you wen go see da game yesterday? Was re::al goo:::d, brah!*)
           'Hey, did you go see the game yesterday? It was **really** good.'

6.3. Pitch and register

The characteristic range of pitch in Hawai'i Creole is wider than in English, especially with regard to higher pitch.

With regard to voice quality, there are two different registers that are common features of the language. Firstly, the use of raspy voice in drawled syllables or words (mentioned above) or in short periods of extended speech functions as a kind of intensifier or as a marker of "heavy" Hawai'i Creole and is used more commonly by men than women. Secondly, the use of the upper levels of the range of Hawai'i Creole pitch that some researchers have said is a marker of female speech.

6.4.   Intonation

One of the most striking differences between Hawai'i Creole and varieties of English is in the intonation of yes-no questions. In most varieties of American English, for example, the pattern is rising, starting with mid pitch and finishing with high pitch. But in Hawai'i Creole, the pattern is falling, starting with high pitch and dropping to low pitch in the last syllable and then a terminal steadying or slight rise:

(8)   *³E, yu wan laif ¹gad?¹*
        'Are you a life guard?'

Tag questions with *ye* [jæ], *e* [ʔɛ], *ha* [hɑ] and *no* are very common in Hawai'i Creole. At the end of a sentence, they usually have high pitch with terminal rise. Another tag is also used: *o wat* ('or what'). This is added to the end of a statement without pausing, and given low pitch and stress:

(9)   *²Yu laik go ³Maui ¹o wat?¹*
        'Do you want to go to Maui or what?'

7.   Current issues

The last detailed research into Hawai'i Creole phonology was carried out in the 1970s (Odo 1975; Bickerton and Odo 1976). While the findings still appear to apply to modern basilectal speakers, it is obvious that more up-to-date data collection and phonological analysis are a top priority. Such research will also throw light on some important questions concerning decreolization in the language. It is generally believed that with more widespread education and bilingualism in English, Hawai'i Creole has been changing to become more like English. This is certainly true in some grammatical constructions – for example, in the more widespread use of *is* and *was* as copulas (rather than zero copula). However, little is known about the extent to which various aspects of basilectal phonology have been changing in the direction of English.

Another area for further research is the extent of the influence of other languages on the phonology of Hawai'i Creole. Suggestions have been made that the unreleased final consonants are a result of the influence of Chinese languages, and that the vowel system of basilectal Hawai'i Creole and the sentence level intonation in questions are a result of the influence of Hawaiian or Portuguese. But the validity of these suggestions has yet to be examined.

Exercises and study questions

1. Match the Hawai'i Creole word or phrase with its meaning:

a) *keiki*	'food'
b) *tako*	'dirty look'
c) *pau*	'goose bumps'
d) *stink eye*	'child, children'
e) *babooz*	'finished'
f) *hanabata*	'delicious'
g) *kaukau*	'shy, embarrassed'
h) *wahine*	'octopus'
i) *shame*	'idiot'
j) *ono*	'rotten'
k) *chicken skin*	'snot'
l) *pilau*	'woman'

2. The following Hawai'i Creole words derived from English are written in IPA, and their meaning is given. Write them in the Odo orthography.

a) tɔk	'talk'
b) lɑɪk	'like'
c) faʊl	'foul'
d) neɪʃen	'nation'
e) fit	'feet'
f) wɜrk	'work'
g) kætʃ	'catch'
h) ʃeɪd	'shade'
i) voʊt	'vote'
j) dʒɑmp	'jump'

3. Which language may have affected the structure of each of the following sentences from Hawai'i Creole:

a) *Wi nomo mane fo bai wan TV.* 'We don't have money to buy a TV.'
b) *Get wan wahine in Hilo shi get 12 kidz.* 'There's a woman in Hilo who has 12 kids.'
c) *Smat doz gaiz.* 'Those guys are smart.'
d) *Lisa ste riding daet buk.* 'Lisa is reading that book.'
e) *O, da stupid!* 'Oh, how stupid!'

4. Although English serves as the lexifier language for Hawai'i Creole, the inventory of sounds and the phonological system of the two varieties are different from each other. As a result of these differences, English speakers often mishear what Hawai'i Creole speakers say. The list on the left below contains various meanings intended by Creole speakers when saying particular words. The list on the right contains the words that English speakers mistakenly think the Creole speakers are saying. See if you can match the misheard word on the right with the intended meaning on the left and provide a possible reason for the misunderstanding.

a) 'a young dog'	salary
b) 'the number after 2'	feet
c) 'slender, crisp. light green vegetable'	fool
d) 'opposite of expensive'	shock
e) 'opposite of empty'	poppy
g) 'the two' (as "in ___ of them")	teak
h) 'a seizure' (as in "a ___ of laughter")	robber
j) 'material that stretches and bounces'	chip
k) 'man-eating fish'	tree
l) 'opposite of thin' or 'a bug on your dog'	boat

5. Listen to the transcribed example of Hawai'i Creole. Write down at least five words that come from English but have a different pronunciation. Write each one in IPA and give its English origin.

6. How would the following words of English origin be pronounced in basilectal Hawai'i Creole? (Write your answers in IPA.)

a) ghost
b) bubble
c) park
d) father
e) drive
f) course
g) steer
h) pepper
i) think
j) tire
k) truck
l) progression

Selected references

Please consult the General references for titles mentioned in the text but not included in the references below. For a full bibliography see the accompanying CD-ROM.

Bickerton, Derek and Carol Odo
    1976   *Change and Variation in Hawaiian English. Volume 1: General Phonology and Pidgin Syntax.* Honolulu: Social Sciences and Linguistics Institute, University of Hawaii.
Masuda, Hirokuni
    2000   *The Genesis of Discourse Grammar: Universals and Substrata in Guyanese, Hawaii Creole, and Japanese.* Frankfurt/New York: Lang.
Matthews, Stephen and Virginia Yip
    1994   *Cantonese: A Comprehensive Grammar.* London/New York: Routledge.
Odo, Carol
    1975   Phonological processes in the English dialect of Hawaii. Ph.D. dissertation, University of Hawaii, Honolulu.
    1977   Phonological representations in Hawaiian English. *University of Hawaii Working Papers in Linguistics* 9: 77–85.
Reinecke, John
    1969   *Language and Dialect in Hawaii: A Sociolinguistic History to 1935.* Honolulu: University of Hawaii Press.
Roberts, Sarah J.
    2000   Nativization and genesis of Hawaiian creole. In: John H. McWhorter (ed.), *Language Change and Language Contact in Pidgins and Creoles,* 257–300. Amsterdam/Philadelphia: Benjamins.
Sato, Charlene J.
    1989   A nonstandard approach to standard English. *TESOL Quarterly* 23: 259–282.
    1991   Sociolinguistic variation and attitudes in Hawaii. In: Cheshire (ed.), 647–663.
Siegel, Jeff
    2000   Substrate influence in Hawai'i Creole English. *Language in Society* 29: 197–236.
Tonouchi, Lee
    2001   *Da Word.* Honolulu: Bamboo Ridge Press.
Vanderslice, Ralph and Laura Shun Pierson
    1967   Prosodic features of Hawaiian English. *Quarterly Journal of Speech* 53: 156–166.

Fiji English: phonology[*]

Jan Tent and France Mugler

1. Introduction

Fiji is a group of over 300 islands in the southern Pacific Ocean, straddling the International Date Line. The islands were first settled about 3,000 years ago by speakers of Austronesian languages whose ancestors had come from South-East Asia, sweeping through Melanesia to the eastern islands of Polynesia. Sporadic contact with Europeans initiated through exploration was followed by the arrival of marooned sailors and deserters. Towards the beginning of the nineteenth century came sundry beachcombers, traders in sandalwood and *bêche-de-mer* (sea-cucumber). They were followed in the 1830s by missionaries, and in the next three decades by land-hungry settlers from nearby Australia and New Zealand on whose plantations worked Pacific island labourers recruited through blackbirding (kidnapping). In 1874 a group of Fijian chiefs, through a Deed of Cession, signed over the Fiji islands to the British. The colony had to pay for itself and about 60,000 indentured labourers were brought from India between 1879 and 1916 to work on plantations, mostly of sugarcane. In 1920 all indenture contracts expired and most Indians stayed on to farm small land parcels leased from Fijian landowners, or ventured into trades or small businesses. Fiji became independent in 1970 and has since suffered two major coups d'état, in 1987 and again in 2000.

Fiji has a population of nearly 800,000, about 51% of whom are indigenous Fijians and 44% Indo-Fijians (or 'Fiji Indians'). The remainder comprise small groups of other Pacific islanders, Chinese, 'Europeans' (i.e. Caucasians or 'Whites') and 'part-Europeans' (i.e. people of mixed Fijian and European descent). In spite of its small population, Fiji has a rich mix of languages and cultures. Fijian is spoken not only by indigenous Fijians but also by many part-Europeans, Chinese, Rotumans and other Pacific islanders. The major language among Indo-Fijians is Fiji Hindi (or *Fiji Baat*), a koiné (an admixture of related dialects) which developed during the indenture period from the contact between the various dialects of Hindi spoken by most of the labourers from North India. Dravidian languages such as Tamil, Telugu and Malayalam are spoken by small and ever dwindling numbers of descendants of labourers from South India, while Gujarati and Punjabi were introduced after indenture by free migrants. There are also small groups of speakers of Rotuman, Kiribati, Tuvaluan and other Pacific languages, as well as several Chinese languages and dialects.

The first tokens of presence of English in Fiji were probably borrowings introduced into Fijian by Tongans, who had a long history of trade with Fiji and had contact with English speakers earlier. Beachcombers and traders, who often became fluent in Fijian, were another vector for borrowings, while Methodist missionaries introduced religious terms, although they evangelised in Fijian. After Cession, English became the working language of the colonial administration. Catholic schools spearheaded the use of English in education and by the 1890s it had spread to all schools, including those that Indians had to establish themselves for their children. In the 1930s the promotion of English was spurred by the colonial authorities' belief that a "neutral" lingua franca or a "link/bridging" language was needed to allow Fijians and Indo-Fijians to live together in harmony. English was seen as the appropriate, if not the only, language to fulfil that role. The local languages were considered linguistically deficient and unable to fill this need, as shown by this pronouncement about Fijian by Cyril Cato, a prominent educator at the time:

> In a country where many races and languages mingle as they do in Fiji, a common language is essential. Fijian can never become this, for its poverty of ideas and expressions is such that it cannot meet the modern demands upon such a language (cited in Geraghty 1984: 41).

During this time, Fiji's education system came under the control of the New Zealand education authorities. The influx of New Zealand teachers meant that English had to be the sole medium of instruction, as few were prepared to learn Fijian or Hindi. English is now the sole official medium of instruction after the first three years of primary school, although code switching is frequent both in the classroom and on the playground.

English is a second language for nearly all Fiji Islanders, with speakers' proficiency ranging from rudimentary to very high. Only 1% to 3% of the population speak English as their first language. Nevertheless, English has a high profile and fairly widespread use, especially in urban areas. Thanks to its colonial past, English remains an official language, along with Fijian and Hindi. While the 1997 Constitution states that the three languages "have equal status", English prevails in most official spheres. In Parliament, for instance, it is the language of debate and record, although members of both Houses occasionally speak in Fijian or Hindi. English also predominates in the media, particularly on television and now online, in print, and to a lesser extent, on the radio. English has also been the major medium of expression in literature so far. Another major role of English in Fiji is as a lingua franca, particularly between native speakers of Fijian and of Fiji Hindi, although significant numbers of both groups know each other's language or a pidginised variety thereof.

The variety of English that operates as the official reference point in Fiji is an external standard. Traditionally it was British English, which continues to be seen by many speakers as the model to aspire to, although the local varieties which approximate to standard metropolitan varieties of English have incorporated features from Australian, New Zealand and, increasingly, American English.

English in Fiji is characterised by a great deal of variation, which can be ascribed to two major factors: differences in exposure through education and the media, and the speaker's first language. Someone from a low socio-economic group or living in a rural area or an outer island will typically hear and read far less English – and have far less need to use it – than a middle-class urban professional. As for the first language of English users, the two major groups, native speakers of Fijian and of Fiji Hindi, are of nearly equal size. The influence of the first language is most noticeable in the phonology of Fiji English, particularly in what is sometimes called the "basilect" (the variety most removed from the norm), where one can arguably distinguish between "Fijian English" and "Indo-Fijian English". Differences in grammar and vocabulary are not nearly as great, and most borrowings from Fijian and Fiji Hindi are common to Fijian and Indo-Fijian speakers of English. Differences between the two groups shade off at the "acrolectal" (prestige) end of the continuum, but while the speech of many "educated"' people tends to approximate a metropolitan standard, the influence of the first language is to some extent independent of education and exposure.

Siegel (1989, 1991) recognises that 'Fiji English' constitutes a continuum, and notes that it is in the basilect that most of the distinctive features are found. Lynch and Mugler (1999) observe that within Fiji, the term tends to refer only to the basilectal end of the spectrum, perhaps because only that lect is recognised as distinctive. The following citation confirms this:

> "Their English [that of pupils at a local primary school] is perfect too. They don't speak that Fijian English urban students use: 'us gang, me ga, trues up.' I'm very proud of that," Mr X [head teacher] said. (*Fiji Times*, 9/7/1997)

Kelly (1975), who pioneered the study of Fiji English with recordings of schoolgirls, refers to this lect as "the dialect", Moag and Moag (1977) as "Colloquial Fiji English", Geraghty (1975, 1977, 1984, 1997) as "Fiji Pidgin English", and Siegel (1986, 1987, 1989, 1991) as "Basilectal Fiji English". Kelly's "dialect" is too vague, while Geraghty's "Fiji Pidgin English" is inaccurate, since the lect exhibits only a few of the lexical and grammatical features of pidgins in general or of Melanesian Pidgin English in particular. Moreover, there is no historical evidence that the lect was ever a stable pidgin (Siegel 1987: 237–238). Moag and Moag's "Colloquial Fiji English" is too general, as it could be applied to a wide range of lects within the Fiji English spectrum. Siegel's "Basilectal Fiji English" is probably the most accurate but its negative connotation is unfortunate.

Siegel (1987: 238) suggests that the lect can be classified as a "creoloid" (i.e. a language which exhibits creole-like features although it did not develop from a pidgin) akin to Colloquial or Basilectal Singapore English, since:

- it displays some creole-like grammatical features;
- it shows "substratum" influences, mostly from Fijian and Fiji Hindi;
- English (which functions as the standard, superordinate language) is one of the official languages of Fiji; and
- it is used for most (but certainly not all) communication between speakers of different native languages

Perhaps the most accurate descriptive label for the English of Fiji would be "Fiji Varieties/Variants of English". However, for the sake of simplicity, we shall continue to use the expression "Fiji English" as a cover term, in line with Siegel (1989). However, instead of his "Basilectal Fiji English", we have adopted the term "Pure Fiji English" (after Fox 2003) to refer to the variety most heavily influenced by the substratum languages, and "Modified Fiji English" for the lects which most approximate standard metropolitan English (both at the phonological and morpho-syntactic levels), while still retaining some distinctive local features.

As for variation across speakers of different first languages, the most readily identifiable and widespread varieties are "Fijian Fiji English" and "Indo-Fijian Fiji English". The Pure Fiji English spoken by part-Europeans and Fijians is essentially a single variety. This is not surprising, since part-Europeans usually identify socially, culturally and ethnically with the Fijian community. Since Independence, part-Europeans have shifted away from their historical identification with colonial European heritage and have moved towards reclaiming their Fijian roots. Part-European speakers of Modified Fiji English, however, still tend to align themselves with the European community, and linguistic features of their English reflect this social association, although many are bi-dialectal in the Pure and Modified varieties. Fiji English is also spoken by Chinese and part-Chinese, Rotumans and other small Pacific islander groups, with each variety having its distinctive features, although their Fiji English tends to be closer to the Fijian than the Indo-Fijian variety.

Certain features of Fiji English are heard in the speech of most Fiji Islanders, regardless of their first language, while others are more specifically characteristic of Fijian and Indo-Fijian Fiji English. Numerous features are also found in the colloquial varieties of English spoken in countries where it is the first language of the majority, while others also exist in other parts of the world where English is a second language, and still others are characteristic of pidgins or creoles. This last group may have developed independently, perhaps as a result of universal tendencies in a restricted language environment. They could be remnants of Melanesian Pidgin English introduced to Fiji by labourers on plantations in the nineteenth century (see Siegel 1987), or both.

Since English is a second (sometimes a third) language for nearly all Fiji Islanders, there is considerable phonological transfer from L1, at both the segmental and suprasegmental levels. The degree of transfer varies substantially, with speakers of Pure Fiji English usually exhibiting the highest degree of transfer. Detailed phonological descriptions of all varieties of Fiji English are beyond our scope, and we shall concentrate on the key characteristics of Pure Fiji English as spoken by Fijians and Indo-Fijians. Even though they share a number of phonological features, these lects are nevertheless still phonologically quite distinct at the Pure Fiji English end of the spectrum. At the Modified end, however, these differences are much less pronounced and the two varieties may at times be almost indistinguishable. Our descriptions are based on personal observation, over 80 hours of recorded interviews, written and printed pronunciation spellings (see Tent 2000), previously published analyses of Fiji English (particularly Kelly 1975), and the recordings made for this volume. Before each description, brief outlines of the phonologies of Fijian and Fiji Hindi are provided.

2.   Pure Fiji English (Fijian and part-European speakers)

In order to understand the phonology of the Fijian and part-European variety of Pure Fiji English phonology a brief overview of the phonology of Fijian needs to be considered. The phonology of Fijian has been described in detail by Geraghty (1983) and Schütz (1985). The consonant and vowel phonemes of Fijian are presented in Figures 1 and 2 respectively. Note that:

– Symbols in parentheses are found in English loanwords.
– Vowel length is phonemic.
– The diphthongs are /ai/, /ei/, /oi/, /ao/, /iu/, /eu/, /au/ and /ou/.

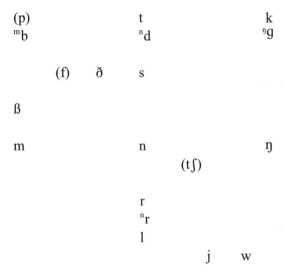

Figure 1.　The consonant phonemes of Fijian

i iː   u uː

e eː   o oː

a aː

Figure 2.　The vowel phonemes of Fijian

The following are the most common phonological features of the Pure Fiji English spoken by Fijians and part-Europeans. Many of these may be heard in the accompanying recordings on the CD-ROM.

2.1.　Consonants

Stops
1. Voiceless stops are unaspirated, e.g. *pan* > [p˭ɛn], *talk* [t˭ɔk], *corner* [k˭ɒna].
2. Stops in word final position, especially voiceless stops, are often unreleased, e.g. *like that* > [laikˀ dɛtˀ].
3. In word final position, voiced stops often are voiceless, e.g. *scared* > [sket], *rob* > [rɒp], *leg* > [lek].

4. Most speakers have /t/ in *think* > [tiŋk], *three* > [tri], *through* > [tru], *bath* > [bat], etc. and [d] in *this* > [dis], *brother* > [bradɐ], *breathe* > [brid], etc., despite Fijian having /ð/.
5. Sometimes, /d/ is palatalised before [ju], e.g. *during* > [dʲuriŋ].
6. Only in the Purest of Fiji English is /b/ is prenasalised, e.g. *bye* > [ᵐbai].

Fricatives
1. Some speakers have only one apico-dental fricative, the voiced /ð/, e.g. *this* > [ðis], *thanks* > [ðɛŋks].
2. Similarly, while some speakers have /β/ in initial and medial position for *very* > [βeri], *never* > [neβa], most have /f/ in final position for *five* > [faif], and *cave* > [keːf].
3. Fijian has only one sibilant, the voiceless post-alveolar /s/, a sound intermediate between the /s/ and /ʃ/ of Standard English. Most commonly, the /ʃ/ of Standard English is realised as /s/ as in: *sure* > [suɐ] and *insure* > [insuɐ], *pollution* > [pɒlusen], *English* > [iŋlis], *British* > [britis], *shock* > [sɒk], *parachute* > [parɐsut]. On the other hand, the grooved palato-alveolar fricative [ʃ] also often occurs, particularly in words that contain two or more voiceless sibilants, e.g. *socialising* > [ʃoʃɐlaisin], *associate* [ɛʃoʃiɛt].
4. Standard English words containing the voiced post-alveolar fricative /ʒ/, such as *measure*, *confusion* and *usual*, are often realised as [meʃɐ ~ mezɐ], [kɒnfjuʃen ~ kɒnfjuzen], [juʃuɐl ~ juzuɐl] respectively.
5. Syllable final /z/ is nearly always [s], e.g. *cruise* > [krus], *noise* > [noᵉs], including the plural and third person singular morphemes, e.g. *years* > [jis], *boys* > [boᵉs], *cleans* > [klins]. This feature, along with the devoicing of voiced stops described above (3.), suggests that Pure Fiji English may have a general devoicing rule for these consonants in final position.

Affricates
We only find [ts] in Pure Fiji English, e.g. *touch* > [tats], *much* [mats], *each* > [its], *change* > [tseːnts], *beach* > [bits], *lunch* > [lants], *future* > [fjutsɐ], *teacher* [titsɐ], etc., and occasionally [tʃ] or [dz], e.g. *large* > [latʃ], *ginger* > [dzindzɐ].

Approximants
1. Post-vocalic /l/ is always 'clear' (i.e. non-velarised), e.g. *sell* > [sel].
2. /r/ is trilled or flapped.
3. /j/ and /w/ are weakly articulated.

Consonant clusters
1. For many speakers, words which include consonant clusters in Standard
   English are often articulated in Pure Fiji English with epenthetic vowels,
   after the Fijian pattern of nativising English loanwords, e.g. *sitoa* < 'store',
   kirimu < 'cream' (both of which have become fully nativised into Fijian,
   but also occur in Pure Fiji English), as well as *Burns Philp* > [filɐp], *film*
   > [filɐm].
2. On the other hand, many words may end with a single consonant, e.g. *toast*
   > [tos], *around* > [ɐraʊn], *friend* > [fren], *don't* > [don], *Marist High*
   > [maris hai], *district* > [distrik]. However, as in other varieties of English,
   final /-ks/ does occur, particularly in the metathesis of the consonant cluster
   /-sk-/ as in *ask* > [aks].

Figure 3 shows the consonant phonemes of Pure Fijian Fiji English with their
most common phonetic realisations.

2.2.   Monophthongs and diphthongs

At the phonemic level, Pure Fijian English has a five vowel system, based on Fijian. In addition, the length and quality distinctions of standard varieties of English are neutralised. Most of the monophthongs of Pure Fiji English are tense but
short, as opposed to Standard English tense/long versus lax/short. Examples in-

p [p⁼ ~ p]	**t** [t⁼ ~ t]	**k** [k⁼ ~ k]
b [b ~ ᵐb, b ~ p]	**d**[d ~ t]	**g** [g ~ k]

f θ [t̪ ~ ð ~ θ] **s** [s ~ ʃ] ʃ [s ~ ʃ] **h**
v [v ~ β ~ f] **ð** [d ~ ð] **z** [z ~ s] **ʒ** [s ~ ʃ ~ ʒ]

tʃ [ts]
dʒ [ts ~ dz ~ tʃ]

m **n** **ŋ**

r [r ~ ɾ]
l

j w

Figure 3.   The consonant phonemes of Pure Fijian Fiji English and their common
                 phonetic realisations

clude such items as: *reach* and *rich* > [rits]; *beach* and *bitch* > [bits]; *march* and *much* > [mats]; *port* and *pot* > [pɒt], *sport* and *spot* > [spɒt], *caught/court* and *cot* > [kɒt] (e.g. *basketball court* > [basketbɒl kɒt]); *fool* and *full* > [ful]; and *cloak* and *clock* > [klɒk].

Evidence for this neutralisation of length and quality is reflected in frequent pronunciation spellings in the local tabloids:

(1)   a. *Situations wanted: Baby **seater** available [...]. (Fiji Times, 23/2/1995)*

       b. *A wife driving from a back-**sit** is comparable to a husband cooking from the dining room table. (Daily Post, 1/6/1999)*

       c. *Naitasiri North's sensational victory over giant Nadi upset the apple-**cut**. (Daily Post, 4/9/1995)*

       d. *His face was a bit swollen and he also **spotted** a black eye. (Daily Post, 8/5/1995)*

       e. *The roads of Labasa ... **portholes** are everywhere. (Fiji Times, 19/5/1999)*

       f. *She [a sex worker] told the Sun that most of her clients were top-class businessmen and police officers. "It is surprising that most of my customers are big **shorts** of our country." (Fiji Sun, 4/12/1999)*

       g. *Mr T. told prison offices to provide V. with 10 **fullscap** pages and a pen [...] (Fiji Times, 9/6/1999)*

Fijian has eight diphthongs (/ai/, /ei/, /oi/, /ao/, /iu/, /eu/, /au/, /ou/), five of which (/ai/, /ei/, /oi/, /au/ and /ou/) are similar to the diphthongs of standard metropolitan English, and are often realised in Pure Fiji English as such. Nevertheless, they are sometimes instead realised as monophthongs by many speakers, especially the FACE, CHOICE and GOAT vowels (see below). Fijian does not have any centring diphthongs like those in Standard English NEAR, SQUARE and CURE. These are realised in Pure Fiji English as monophthongs or falling diphthongs (see below).

The following are descriptions of the most common variants of the Pure Fiji English vowels as articulated by Fijians. As stated above, there is considerable variation within this lect due to the speaker's place of residence (largely rural vs. urban), competence as a speaker of Standard English, educational background and general exposure to standard metropolitan English. (Note that the lexical items in parentheses indicate those used in the accompanying recording of the lexical set. It was found that these words were more appropriate for the Fiji context.)

KIT (FIT) and FLEECE (REEF)

Phonemically the KIT and FLEECE vowels are not distinguished, however, phonetically, they are slightly different. The KIT vowel is short, retracted and lowered [i], approximating the position of [ɪ], but retaining an [i]-like quality. The FLEECE vowel tends to be a short or for some speakers a half-long [i]. Examples showing the lack of phonemic distinction between these vowels are often found in Fiji's tabloids:

(2)   a.   *[...]the roof and the air-condition* [sic] *were leaking, water **sipped** intothe rooms [...].* (*Fiji Times*, 25/4/2003)

        b.   *Her family was rudely awaken* [sic] *from its midday slumber as floodwaters **sipped** into the living room and rose to about 1.5 metres.* (*Fiji Times*, 17/3/2003)

        c.   *One year ago since you took your **leave**
To our arms of our God your life to g**ive**.
The tears we cried, we cried with **bliss**,
For Jehovah God has called His servant in **peace**.* (*Fiji Times*, 3/3/2003)

DRESS and TRAP (BACK)

Similarly, there is no phonemic distinction between the DRESS and TRAP vowels. However, the DRESS vowel is a slightly lowered and short [e], whilst the TRAP vowel tends to be a slightly raised and short [ɛ], e.g. *that* > [ðɛt], *Lami* > [lɛmi], *Nadi* > [nɛndi], *land* > [lɛn]. Nevertheless, it is difficult to phonetically distinguish between the DRESS and TRAP vowels in many speakers.

The realisation of TRAP as [ɛ] gives rise to the following common spelling pronunciations:

(3)   a.   *Eight people [...] **peddled** to safety when a boat they were in ran aground [...]* (*Fiji Times*, 26/2/1987)

        b.   *We have no injury worries and the players have slowly recovered from jet-**leg**.* (*Daily Post*, 29/3/1996)

        c.   *Residents affected by water cuts in a densely-populated area **tempered** with water mains.* (*Fiji Times*, 20/1/2003)

        d.   *Top scorer for the Veimataqali Imperial was **Elex** Konrote.* (*Fiji Times,* 20/1/2003)

The lack of phonemic distinction between these two vowels is further highlighted by the following example:

(4)   *Vidiri steps on the **paddle** and just keeps going, no slowing down.* (*Daily Post*, 10/6/1998)

LOT (POT), CLOTH (OFF), THOUGHT, NORTH and FORCE

There is no phonemic distinction between the vowels of LOT and CLOTH. Phonetically, they are nearly identical, i.e. a raised [ɒ], although LOT is usually extra short. For some speakers, LOT is realised as an extra short and lowered [ɔ]. As noted above, for many speakers of Pure Fiji English, the LOT vowel is also not phonemically distinct from NORTH and FORCE, thus giving rise to examples such as (1d), (1e), and (1f) above.

Although there is some slight phonetic variation between these three vowels, they are virtually identical, and are generally realised as a raised [ɒ] or a lowered [ɔ]. In the case of THOUGHT, the vowel also tends to be extra short and may be lengthened somewhat in FORCE [ɒ].

STRUT (CUT), BATH (GRASS), PALM and START

Phonemically these four vowels are the same and are realised as [a]. Phonetically there is some variation: both STRUT and BATH have retracted [a], with BATH tending to be extra short, and PALM and START are both realised simply as [a] or an extra short [a] (especially the PALM vowel).

FOOT and GOOSE (LOOSE)

These two vowels tend not to be phonemically distinguished, hence, *full* and *fool* are not a minimal pair (see example [1g] above). They are phonetically very similar: the FOOT vowel may be articulated with a raised [o] or lowered [u], whereas GOOSE varies between a lowered and advanced [u] and at times a slightly lengthened [u] (see also 4.3. below).

NURSE

This vowel is usually realised as [ɛ] or a retracted [ɛ], e.g. *church* > [tsɛts], *girls* > [gɛls], *turn* > [tɛn]. Under certain conditions NURSE may also be realised as [ɒ]. This seems to occur after /w/ as in *work* > [wɒk]; however, this could be a spelling pronunciation.

FACE

Although Fijian has the diphthong /ei/, it is not uncommon to find speakers of Pure Fiji English using [e], [eː] or [eⁱ] (with a weak and short second target) in FACE, e.g. *make* > [mek], *day* > [deː], *okay* > [okeⁱ]. The lengthened and diphthongised targets tend to occur in syllable final position.

GOAT
Similarly, although Fijian has /ou/, the GOAT vowel tends to be realised with a monophthong – a lowered [o], a lowered and lengthened [oː], or [oᵘ] (with a weak and short second target), e.g. *don't* > [don], *post* > [poːs].

PRICE
Speakers of Pure Fiji English usually realise the PRICE vowel as the diphthong [ai], though the second target tends to be very short.

CHOICE
As with the FACE and GOAT vowels, CHOICE is also generally realised as a monophthong or a diphthong with a weak and short second target: [o], [oː] or [oᵉ] where [o] is lowered and the second target of the diphthong does not go as far as [i].

MOUTH
MOUTH is articulated with a diphthong, resembling the Fijian /au/. The first target, [a], is always retracted and quite short, whilst the second target varies between a weakly articulated [o], or a relatively strongly articulated and raised [ʊ].

NEAR, SQUARE and CURE
The centring diphthongs found in Standard English NEAR, SQUARE and CURE all tend to be realised as monophthongs in closed syllables, but falling diphthongs in open syllables. Thus, *years* > [jis], *tears* > [tis], *scared* > [sket], Mary > [meri], *insurance* > [insurɐns], *during* > [dʲuriŋ]; *beer* > [biɐ], swear > [sweɐ], *insure* > [insuɐ]. Each diphthong's second target tends to be an extra short [ɐ]. There is a lot of variation in the articulation of the CURE vowel, especially in words like *tour*. This is seen in all other varieties of English as well. In many varieties the diphthong has coalesced into [ɔ], or is articulated as an [ɔə] glide. This extreme variation, or instability, is perhaps because the vowel of CURE is the least frequent of vocalic sounds.

*happ*Y
The final vowel of *happ*Y is an extra short, retracted and lowered [i]. The vowel still tends to carry a considerably greater degree of stress than in Standard English.

*lett*ER
The final syllable of *lett*ER also receives a considerably greater degree of stress than in Standard English, and is generally realised as [ɐ].

*hors*ES
This vowel, too, receives a considerable amount of stress, more so than in Standard English, though perhaps not as much as in the *lett*ER and *comm*A vowels. The final element of *hors*ES is commonly realised with an extra short [ɐ].

*comm*A (*VISA*)
The most usual articulation of the *comm*A vowel is a lowered and advanced [ɐ].

Table 1 summarises the most common phonetic realisations of the vowels of Pure Fiji English as articulated by Fijians.

Table 1. Phonetic realisations of Pure Fiji English vowels (Fijian speakers) – summary

Lexical set	Pure Fiji English (Fijian speakers)
KIT (FIT)	i̞
DRESS	e̞
TRAP (BACK)	ɛ̞
LOT (POT)	ɒ̆ ~ ɔ̆
STRUT (CUT)	a̱
FOOT	o̞ ~ ʉ
BATH (GRASS)	ă̱
CLOTH (OFF)	ɒ̞
NURSE	ɛ ~ ɛ̞
FLEECE (REEF)	i ~ iˑ
FACE	e ~ eː ~ eⁱ
PALM	ă ~ a
THOUGHT	ɒ̆ ~ ɔ̆
GOAT	o̞ ~ o̞ː ~ o̞ᵘ
GOOSE (LOOSE)	ʉ̟ ~ uˑ
PRICE	aĭ
CHOICE	o ~ oː ~ o̞ᵉ

Table 1. (continued) Phonetic realisations of Pure Fiji English vowels
(Fijian speakers) – summary

Lexical set	Pure Fiji English (Fijian speakers)
MOUTH	ă̞ ° ~ ă̞ ʊ̞
NEAR	i ~ iĕ
SQUARE	e ~ eĕ
START	ă ~ a
NORTH	o̞ ~ ɔ
FORCE	o̞ ~ o̞ˑ ~ ɔ
CURE	u ~ ʉɐ ~ uɐ
*happ*Y	ḭ̆
*lett*ER	ɐ ~ a̠ ~ ă̠
*hors*ES	ĕ
*comm*A (*VISA*)	ɐ̟ ~ a̠ ~ ă̠

Figure 4 shows the vowel phonemes of Pure Fijian Fiji English with their most common phonetic realisations.

i   **u** [u ~ o]

e [e ~ ɛ]   **ɔ** [ɔ ~ ɒ]

          a [a ~ ɐ]

Figure 4. The vowel phonemes of Pure Fijian Fiji English and their common phonetic realisations

2.3.   Lexical stress

The rules for stress assignment in Fijian are not entirely agreed upon (see Schütz 1999 for a summary). In many cases lexical stress is predictable in that it always falls on the penultimate mora, i.e. the penultimate syllable, if the vowel in the last syllable is short, and on the first part of the long vowel in the last syllable if the vowel is long. However, this appears to be true only for the last stress in the word, any preceding stress is unpredictable. In words with more than one stress, it is not always clear which is primary and which secondary.

Since in Standard English lexical stress is unpredictable, lexical stress patterns do not coincide with those in either Pure, or sometimes even Modified, Fiji English. Syllables which are unstressed in Standard English are often stressed in Fijian English, while Standard English stressed syllables are often realised in Fijian English with less stress or none. Examples from our data include: *cholesterol* > ['kɒleˌstrɒl], *amicable* > [ˌɛ'mikabɐl]. We found this to be especially the case with words beginning with unstressed *con-* in Standard English. This element very often receives a primary stress in Fijian English, e.g. *considerate* > ['kɒnˌsidɐret], *continue* > ['kɒnˌtinu], *convinced* ['kɒnˌvinst].

2.4.   Syntactic stress

The most conspicuous characteristic of Fijian Fiji English sentence rhythm is that each syllable tends to receive an equal amount of stress (i.e. syllable-timed), with the last syllable (or stress group) being indicated by a fall in pitch. Without having conducted empirical research on Fijian English or Fijian syntactic stress patterns, our observations seem to indicate that sentence rhythm in both languages is very similar if not the same, that is, there tends to be equal stress on each stress group, with just a fall of pitch at the end of the sentence. In addition to this, it is our impression that the main verb in unmarked sentences is often given more stress than any of the other sentence elements. Some examples from Tent's recordings include:

(5)   a.   *I **háve** one brother in Canada.*
      b.   *The next door neighbour all the time **básh** his wife when he cut [drunk].*
      c.   *I am **stáyin**g in Samabula.*
      d.   *Are you **cómin**g to the meke tonight?*
      e.   *Where **ís** the class?*

This seems to be characteristic of not only Pure Fiji English but often also Modified Fiji English. It is not uncommon to hear newsreaders on Fiji television or radio news use this syntactic stress pattern.

2.5.   Intonation

The most prominent suprasegmental property of Fijian Fiji English is the overall higher pitch patterns than in Standard English. This is especially marked in yes/no-questions, which start at a high pitch and typically end with a very rapid rise and sudden drop in pitch (which follows the intonation contour of Fijian), e.g.

(Are) you ready to go ? (Fijian Fiji English)

Are you ready to go ? (Standard English)

Pio, you like some rourou ?

3.   Pure Fiji English (Indo-Fijian speakers)

In order to understand the phonology of Pure Fiji English as spoken by Fiji's Indo-Fijians, a brief overview of the phonology of Fiji Hindi is required. While it does not vary significantly from that of Standard Hindi (Siegel 1975; Moag 1977, 1979; Arms 1998), there are a few notable differences. Siegel (1975, 1987: 8) notes that for many Fiji Hindi speakers [ʋ] and [b], [pʰ] and [f], [dʒ] and [z], and [ʃ] and [s] occur in free variation or an intermediate sound is used. Furthermore, [ɲ], [ɳ] and [ŋ] are allophones of /n/ when preceding a consonant, and [l] is often replaced by [r] (Moag 1979), e.g. Fiji Hindi *baar* for Standard Hindi *baal* 'hair'. On the other hand, Arms (1998: 2) claims that "[f] has completely replaced the primary [consonant] [pʰ]" (see also Hobbs 1985). For example, we have [fuːl] for 'flower', rather than [pʰuːl]. Arms points out that this is also the case in some dialects of Hindi in India, while in others, the two sounds are in free variation. He adds that they are "certainly not in free variation in Fiji, but [f] has in some cases given way to unaspirated [p]". He cites as examples [hapta] 'week' (rather than [hafta]) and [fuppa] 'father's sister's husband' (rather than [fuffa]) and notes that in the latter the initial [f] is retained while medially it has changed to [p]. He adds that "for some speakers the change of [f] to [p] takes place optionally in many vocabulary items." Thus /f/ has become part of the phonemic inventory of Hindi – including Fiji

Hindi – via three sources: Perso-Arabic loanwords, borrowings from English, and etymological /pʰ/. Arms also claims that [ʃ] has merged with [s] for many speakers, especially in rural areas.

The sounds which are used in Standard Hindi for the pronunciation of words of Perso-Arabic origin are not normally found in Fiji Hindi; neither are they in most colloquial varieties of Indian Hindi. For example, [z] is realised as [ʒ] in Fiji Hindi, as in Colloquial Hindi (Bhatia 1995: 16), except in some proper nouns. This is true even among Indo-Fijian Muslims, whose lexicon includes more such words and who would use such words more often. Other examples include [x], which is realised as [kʰ], as in the name *Khan*, for instance. The same is true of the voiced counterpart, which is simply pronounced as a velar, rather than uvular, [g].

As for vowels, Hindi has a set of five pairs of vowels whose phonetic relationship is reflected in the Devanagari orthography. Three are pairs of short versus long vowels: /a/ and /aː/, /i/ and /iː/, and /u/ and /uː/. The mid vowels /e/ and /o/ are long and have not short vowels, but the diphthongs /ai/ and /au/ as their counterpart.

In Fiji Hindi long and short vowels do not always contrast. Siegel (1975: 130) claims that vowel length is not differentiated (especially [i] vs. [iː] and [u] vs. [uː]), and this seems particularly true in final position. Similarly, with the exception of a few monosyllabic words, the two diphthongs do not occur in word final position. In any case, they constitute only about 1% of all vocalic occurrences (Arms 1998: 3). It is unclear whether vowel nasalisation, which occurs phonetically, is ever phonemic.

The consonant and vowel phonemes of Fiji Hindi are presented in Figures 5 and 6 respectively.

Although Standard and Fiji Hindi are phonologically similar, Pure Fiji English as spoken by Indo-Fijians differs from the "typical" Indian English of the subcontinent in a number of ways. For instance:

- Indo-Fijian English is, as a general rule, non-rhotic.
- Pure Indo-Fijian English has monophthongised diphthongs.
- The realisation of alveolars as retroflexes is much less common in Indo-Fijian English, though some speakers of Pure Fiji English do exhibit this characteristic.

It is clear that much further empirical study needs to be carried both on the phonology of Fiji Hindi, and on the English spoken by Indo-Fijians. The following are the most common phonological features of Pure Fiji English as spoken by Indo-Fijians.

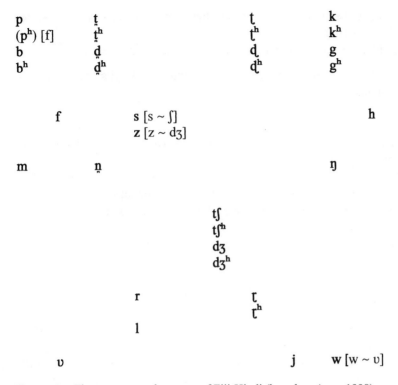

Figure 5.   The consonant phonemes of Fiji-Hindi (based on Arms 1998)

i iː   u uː

eː   ə   oː

                           aː

Figure 6.   The vowel phonemes of Fiji Hindi

3.1.   Consonants

Stops

1. Even though aspiration is present in Fiji Hindi, voiceless stops are unaspirated. Indeed, in Fiji Hindi, as in varieties of Hindi in general, aspiration is
phonemic. Phonetically, aspiration in Hindi seems to be more strongly articulated than in English (Bhatia 1995: 14). Perhaps the stops of English are

perceived as being unaspirated rather than merely more weakly aspirated than those of Hindi.

2. In word final position, voiceless stops are normally unreleased.

These two features, then, are identical in the Pure Fiji English of Fijians and of Indo-Fijians.

Fricatives

1. The dental fricatives /θ/ and /ð/ are generally realised as dental stops, with the first being aspirated [t̪ʰ].

2. Fiji Hindi does not contrast between /ʃ/ and /s/, which have merged as /s/, and many English words with /ʃ/ have been nativised into Fiji Hindi with /s/, e.g. *masīn* < 'machine', *sabal* < 'shovel', *burūs* < 'brush' (see Siegel 1991). Pure Indo-Fijian English does not contrast between /ʃ/ and /s/ either, resulting in homophonous pairs such as *self* and *shelf*. A nice example of this in print is:

(6)   *Wanted to buy: Old chicken **mess** wire.* (Advertisement from an Indo-Fijian in *Daily Post*, 5/9/1998)

3. Final /z/ is often realised as [s] or devoiced [z̥], e.g. *dolls* > [dols], *shoes* > [sus], *please* > [plis].

4. The voiced palato-alveolar fricative /ʒ/ is realised as [z], [s] or [ʃ]: *measure* > [mezə] ~ [mesə], *confusion* > [konfjuʃən].

These last two features are the same as in Fijian Fiji English.

Approximants

1. Post-vocalic /l/ is "clear", as in Fijian Fiji English.

2. The approximant /r/ generally only occurs in initial and medial positions and is normally flapped or trilled, as it is in Fijian Fiji English.

3. Initial /j/ is sometimes realised with an [i] onglide, e.g. *year* > [ijia], *you* > [iju].

Consonant clusters

1. The Pure Fiji English of Indo-Fijian speakers, like that of Fijians, allows few consonant clusters, especially in final position e.g. *last* > [las], although /ks/ does frequently occur, especially in [aks] for *ask,* also as in Fijian English.

2. Consonant clusters, both initial and final, quite commonly receive an epenthetic vowel in Pure Indo-Fijian English, e.g. *free* > [fari], *plate* > [pilet], *film* > [filam], *blouse* > [bilaus], *pliers* > [pilaias], etc. Epenthetic vowels

are particularly common in older English loans that have been fully nativised in Fiji Hindi, e.g. *farāk* < 'frock', *gilās* < 'glass', *kulubāl* < 'crowbar' (Siegel 1991); however, this tendency is not as strong nowadays.

The regular past tense morpheme {-ed} sometimes receives an [ɛd] pronunciation when in Standard English it is rendered as [d] or [t], e.g. *robbed* > [rɔbɛd], *asked* [askɛd], *learned* (verb) > [lɛnɛd]. However, this is probably due to a spelling pronunciation.

3. Word initial /s+C/ clusters typically have a syllable initial prothetic /i/, e.g. *school* > [iskul], *foolscaps* > [fuliskeps], *student* > [istudent], *sport* > [ispot], etc. This is clearly an influence of the first language since Hindi (both standard and Fiji varieties) does not allow such initial consonant clusters. Fiji Hindi has also nativised English loans with a prothetic vowel, e.g. *astabal* < 'stable', *isTimā* < 'steamer' (Siegel 1991).

The consonant phonemes of Pure Indo-Fijian Fiji English and their most common phonetic realisations are shown in Figure 7.

p [p⁼ ~ p] 　　　　　　**t** [t̪⁼ ~ t ~ t̪] 　　　　　**k** [k⁼ ~ k]
b [b] 　　　　　　　　**d** [d̪] 　　　　　　　　　**g**

　　f 　　　　**θ** [t̪ ~ t̪ʰ] 　**s** 　　　**ʃ** [s] 　　　　　**h**
　　v [v ~ w] 　**ð** [d̪ ~ d̪ʰ ~ d̪] **z** 　　**3** [z ~ s ~ ʃ]

　　　　　　　　　　　　　　　　tʃ
　　　　　　　　　　　　　　　　dʒ

m 　　　　　　　　　　**n** 　　　　　　　　　**ŋ**

　　　　　　　　　　　r [r ~ ɾ]
　　　　　　　　　　　l

　　　　　　　　　　　　　　　　　　j 　　**w** [w ~ v]

Figure 7.   The consonant phonemes of Pure Indo-Fijian Fiji English and their common phonetic realisations

3.2.   Monophthongs and diphthongs

The Pure Fiji English of Indo-Fijians is characterised by lack of distinction in vowel quality, and, for some, vowel quantity. This neutralisation is responsible for many pronunciation spellings (see below). Phonemically, Pure Fiji English as spoken by Indo-Fijians is a five vowel system, although phonetically, like Fiji Hindi, it also has a schwa.

Even though Fiji Hindi has only two diphthongs, /əi/ and /əu/, most diphthongs of English are realised as diaphones by Indo-Fijian speakers, albeit they are phonetically somewhat different from those in Standard English. Some diphthongs, however, can be realised as monophthongs by speakers of Pure Fiji English (see below).

KIT (FIT) and FLEECE (REEF)
The KIT and FLEECE vowels are not phonemically distinguished. This neutralisation often leads to misspellings such as those illustrated in (3a), (3b) and (3c) in section 2.2. above. Phonetically, the KIT vowel is retracted and slightly lowered [i], whilst FLEECE varies between a short and half-long [i].

DRESS and TRAP (BACK)
The TRAP and DRESS vowels are not phonemically distinct and tend also to be phonetically identical, i.e. a slightly raised [ɛ], leading to examples such as those in (4) above and: *than* and *then* > [dʰɛn], *sand* and *send* > [sɛnd], *gas* and *guess* > [gɛs]. Siegel (1991) has also noted that Fiji Hindi also regularly substitutes [ɛ] for [æ] in English loanwords.

LOT (POT), CLOTH (OFF), THOUGHT, NORTH and FORCE
The LOT and CLOTH vowels are commonly realised as a lowered [ɔ], and in the case of LOT, some speakers articulate it as an extra short vowel. As with Fijian speakers of Pure Fiji English, many Indo-Fijian speakers do not make a phonemic distinction between the LOT/CLOTH vowels and THOUGHT/NORTH/ FORCE vowels, giving rise to *caught* and *cot* > [kɔt], and examples such as those in (1e), (1f) and (1g) above. THOUGHT, NORTH and FORCE are phonetically very similar; they are all slight variants of [ɔ]. THOUGHT is articulated as a lowered and at times extra short [ɔ], whilst NORTH and FORCE both vary between simply a raised [ɔ] and a half-long raised [ɔ]. Note also Fiji Hindi's nativisation of the English loans *force* > *fos* [fɔs], *sauce* > *sos* [sɔs] and *torch* > *Toc* [ʈɔtʃ] (Siegel 1991).

STRUT (CUT), BATH (GRASS), PALM and START
There is no phonemic distinction in this set, and the vowels are realised as variations of [a]: STRUT as a retracted [a], often extra short; BATH as retracted [a], and sometimes half-long; PALM simply as [a] or half-long [a]; START as retracted [a], and sometimes extra short. In polysyllabic words containing the STRUT vowel, this vowel is often realised as schwa (see 3.4. below).

FOOT and GOOSE (LOOSE)
There is no phonemic distinction between these two vowels. They are articulated as advanced forms of [u], though the FOOT vowel tends to be somewhat lower than that of GOOSE, which can also have a lengthened form. The lack of phonemic distinction between these vowels often leads to neutralisations like *full* and *fool* > [ful], *pull* and *pool* > [pul], or *look* and *Luke* > [luk] for most Indo-Fijian speakers of Pure Fiji Hindi (see also 4.3. below).

NURSE
This vowel has quite a wide range of realisations. It ranges from [ɛ], [ɛː], [ɐ], [ə], [ə] to [a], however, [ɛ] or [ɛː] are the most common realisations. The latter can be seen by the way English loans containing the NURSE vowel have been nativised into Fiji Hindi, e.g. *keTin* [kɛʈin] < 'curtain', *šet* [ʃeːt] < 'shirt' (from Siegel 1991).

FACE
The FACE diphthong is most often realised by Indo-Fijian speakers as a monophthong – a lengthened [e], e.g. *day* > [deː], *occupation* > [ɔkupeːʃən]. Note also Fiji Hindi's *esTet* [əsʈeːt] < *estate*, *kek* [keːk] < *cake*, *pleT* [pleːʈ] < *plate* (Siegel 1991). For those speakers who articulate FACE as a diphthong, the second target [i] is generally only weakly articulated.

GOAT
This diphthong is also most generally realised as a monophthong, namely a half long [o], and when it does have a second target, [u], this is also weakly articulated.

PRICE
Unlike the previous two items, the vocalic target of PRICE is realised by most Indo-Fijian speakers of Pure Fiji English almost like a diphthong. However, the lingual glide from its first to second target tends to be more restricted (i.e. shorter) than what is generally heard in standard metropolitan Englishes. The first target is largely realised as a retracted and lowered [ɐ] which is fol-

lowed by a lingual glide which tends not to go much further than a slightly raised [e].

CHOICE

The vowel in this word is also articulated as a diphthong by most speakers; however, the glide between the two targets tends to be less constrained than for PRICE, and is strongly articulated. The starting point for CHOICE is a rather advanced [ɔ], followed by a glide all the way up to a quite forcefully articulated [i].

MOUTH

As with the PRICE diphthong, MOUTH also has quite a restricted glide to the second target. The starting point is usually an extra short and considerably retracted [a]. The glide up to the second target remains relatively flat, moving towards quite a strongly articulated [ɔ].

NEAR, SQUARE and CURE

The centring diphthongs found in standard metropolitan English NEAR, SQUARE and CURE are all realised as strongly articulated falling diphthongs. The second target is generally always an extra short but prominent [ɐ]. The first target of NEAR is [ɪ], that of SQUARE a retracted [ɛ], and that of CURE tends to be a [ʉ].

*happ*Y

Like for Fijian speakers of Pure Fiji English, the final vowel of *happ*Y is an extra short, retracted and lowered [i]. It also receives more stress than in Standard English.

*lett*ER

The final syllable of *lett*ER also receives more stress than in Standard English, and is most usually realised as an advanced and extra short [ɐ].

*hors*ES

For most speakers this vowel tends to be unstressed and is realised as a schwa.

*comm*A (*VIS*A)

The most usual articulation of the *comm*A vowel is a retracted and extra short [a]. Once again, the vowel is given more stress than in Standard English.

Table 2 provides a summary of the most common phonetic realisations of the vowels of Pure Fiji English as articulated by Indo-Fijians.

Table 2. Phonetic realisations of Pure Fiji English vowels (Indo-Fijian speakers) – summary

Lexical set	Pure Fiji English (Indo-Fijian speakers)
KIT (FIT)	i̯
DRESS	ɛ̆
TRAP (BACK)	ɛ̆
LOT (POT)	ɔ̆ ~ ɔ
STRUT (CUT)	ă̠ ~ a̠ ~ ə
FOOT	ʉ̞
BATH (GRASS)	ă̠ ~ a̠·
CLOTH (OFF)	ɔ
NURSE	ɛ ~ ɛː ~ ɐ ~ ɘ ~ ə ~ a
FLEECE (REEF)	i ~ i·
FACE	eː ~ eːⁱ
PALM	a ~ a·
THOUGHT	ɔ̆ ~ ɔ
GOAT	o· ~ oᵘ
GOOSE (LOOSE)	ʉ ~ ʉː
PRICE	ɐ̯ɛ̯
CHOICE	ɔ̯ɪ
MOUTH	ă̠ɔ
NEAR	ɪɐ̆
SQUARE	ɛ̠ɐ̆
START	ă̠ ~ a̠
NORTH	ɔ ~ ɔ·
FORCE	ɔ ~ ɔ·
CURE	ʉɐ̆
*happ*Y	ĭ
*lett*ER	ɐ̠̆
*hors*ES	ə
*comm*A (*VISA*)	a̠

The vowel phonemes of Pure Indo-Fijian Fiji English and their most common phonetic realisations are shown in Figure 8.

i [i ~ iː]   **u** [u ~ uː]

ɛ [ɛ]   **ɔ** [ɔ ~ ɔː]

       a [a ~ ə]

Figure 8.   The vowel phonemes of Pure Indo-Fijian Fiji English and their common phonetic realisations

3.3.   Lexical stress

The status and even the existence of stress in Hindi are controversial. Many authors claim that Hindi does not have stress, while most of those who argue that it does agree that stress is not phonemic and that it is phonetically weaker than in English. Most of these claims are based on impressions rather than empirical data, but Ohala's acoustic study (1986) shows that stress, though not phonemic, does have phonetic correlates (essentially pitch). Since lexical stress in Hindi normally seems to fall on the penultimate syllable, placement of lexical stress in English polysyllabic words is one of the most conspicuous characteristics of Indo-Fijian English (and also Indian English). Lexical stress patterns include:

1. The assignment of primary stress to the initial syllable of words such as *develop* > ['dɛvələp], *constrict* > ['kɔnˌstrik], *event* > ['iˌvɛnt], etc., is extremely common.
2. Other polysyllabic words that receive irregular stress assignment may in some cases be due to a failure to realise the variation in stress of related words, e.g. *necessary* > [nə'sɛs(ə)ri], perhaps following the stress pattern of the noun *necéssity*.
3. As seen above, the unstressed vowels of Standard English *happ*Y, *lett*ER and *comm*A are usually given more stress than in Standard English, but still less stress than the first syllable.

3.4.   Syntactic stress

Hindi is a so-called syllable-timed language unlike Standard English which is stress-timed. Hindi (including Fiji Hindi) does not have a strong syntactic stress pattern, at least not to the extent that unstressed syllables are markedly reduced or hurried as they are in English. The total duration of the utterance in Hindi is dependent more on the number of syllables it contains than on the number and position of stressed syllables, as it is in English. In Hindi, the tendency to raise pitch rather than increase loudness to indicate emphasis also contributes to this quality. Words that are normally accented in unmarked Standard English sentences are often left unaccented in the English of Indo-Fijians and vice versa.

3.5. Intonation

The intonation contours of the Pure Fiji English of Indo-Fijians are very different from those of Indian English. However, the rising terminal intonation of English 'yes/no' questions which is reserved for expressions of surprise in Hindi are carried over into Indo-Fijian English. The characteristic Indo-Fijian interrogative pattern, in which the end of a 'yes/no' question is marked by a rise followed by a fall in pitch (like that of Pure Fiji English of Fijian speakers), is quite unlike the Standard English norm. This sometimes leads to misunderstanding between speakers of Standard English and Pure Fiji English, particularly in polite requests, when the requestor gives the impression that a positive reply is expected.

4.   Some shared phonological features

Apart from the phonological similarities between the Fijian and Indo-Fijian varieties of Pure Fiji English as outlined above, there are a number of other shared phonological features. We describe the three most distinct ones here, all of which are characteristic of L2 English. Although the first two characteristics are grammatical features (see also Mugler and Tent, this volume) they seem to have phonological causes. Both involve the absence of inflectional suffixes, which appears to be the result of consonant cluster reduction, also noted above.

4.1.   Absence of {-ed}

The absence of the written and spoken {-ed} suffix, whether articulated as [t], [d] or [əd], in past tense forms and participial adjectives is very common in all varieties of Pure Fiji English. Some examples from Tent's (2000) corpus of spoken Fiji English include:

(7)   a. *Would you like some **ice** water?*
       b. *You can buy **dry** fish at the market.*
       c. *Many people in the Pacific eat **tin** fish.*
       d. *This hotel doesn't have **aircondition** rooms.*
       e. *This office is **close** for the day.*

Some examples of pronunciation spellings are given in (8). Interestingly, many involve the {-ed} suffix following a voiceless consonant which normally results in assimilation, with a realisation as [t]. The adjoining of two voiceless consonants may further make the perception of the suffix more difficult.

(8)   a. *"He is bleeding internally. Its* [sic] *most probably a case of an aggravated ulcer in its **advance** stage," he* [a doctor] *said.* (*The Daily Post*, 10/4/1996)
       b. *A few **clap** down* [i.e. 'clapped out'] *diggers barely able to move have been hired and can be seen digging away at penal rate* [sic] *working full swing during the weekends.* (*Sunday Post*, 30/11/1997)
       c. ***Experience** Signwriters to start immediately at Vanua Signs Limited. Phone 381553 for interview.* (Positions Vacant column, *The Fiji Times*, 19/7/1994)
       d. *River sand, **crush** metal and garden soil we deliver Phone 362663 Jalil* (For Sale column, *The Fiji Times*, 19/5/1994, 1/6/1994, 6/7/1994, 7/7/1994, 10/9/1994)
       e. *The case was heard behind **close** doors* (*Daily Post*, 15/10/1999)

It is worth mentioning that the addition of the {-ed} suffix to adjectives is also quite common, e.g. *I am the mother of three teenaged daughters*. It seems only to be a feature of written English, frequently seen with the adjective *mature*, often seen in positions vacant advertisements in the local tabloids:

(9)   a. *Housegirl required urgently, be **matured**, to baby sit and do housework. Have to be good with children. Phone Ferin 386348.* (Positions Vacant column, *Fiji Times*, 10/9/1994)
       b. *The police are **matured** people and we do not expect such an order against them.* (From a Fijian university student's written answer in a test, 9/8/1994)

The following example shows both the absence and addition of the {-ed} suffix in adjoining words:

(10)   *An **Experience matured** live in housegirl required.* [...] (Positions Vacant column, *The Fiji Times*, 2/12/1994).

Cases of {-ed} addition are either malapropisms or instances of hypercorrection (especially since this addition seems to manifest itself predominantly in writing or print), a common phenomenon in L2 English. Once again, more research needs to be conducted to unravel exactly what is going on here.

4.2. Absence of {-s}

The absence of the third person singular present tense verb suffix and the {-s} plural morpheme (both in writing and speech) are as ubiquitous in Fiji English as in most other L2 varieties of English. It could be argued that printed examples are merely misprints, were it not for the fact that the feature is so common in speech and so regularly seen in writing and print. Some examples include:

(11)   a. *Price of Used Equipment **depend** mainly on size, age, hours Used*
          [sic] *and actual condition of the units.* (*The Daily Post*, 10/5/1994)
       b. *The money in grog **keep** the wheels of economy* [sic] *rolling.*
          (Letters to the Editor, *The Daily Post*, 8/8/1994)

4.3. Absence of yod in non-primary stressed /Cju/ syllables

The deletion of the palatal glide or approximant [j] (commonly referred to as "yod") in primary stressed /Cju/ syllables is found in varying degrees in the "inner circle" Englishes (Kachru 1985: 12) and is generally the result of various historical processes. Most of these varieties (e.g. Cockney, Estuary, General American, Australian, New Zealand, South African English etc.) occupy positions between that of conservative Received Pronunciation, which has the least amount of yod-deletion, and East Anglian English, which deletes yod in *all* phonological environments (Wells 1982). The most common type of yod-deletion is found after alveolars and dentals, e.g. in General American English (Wells 1982) and in Cockney (Wells 1982). In these two varieties, the deletion only occurs after alveolars and dentals – not after labials or velars. Therefore, items such as *music* and *cute* are never realised as *[muzik] or *[kut]. With the exception of East Anglian English, yod-deletion in non-primary stressed syllables (no matter what the preceding consonant) is not usually found in any "inner circle" variety.

With the exception of those lexical items in which yod has been historically deleted in most varieties of English (e.g. *rude*, *blue*), another type of yod-deletion occurs in Fiji English and is probably the most prominent phonological feature across the whole spectrum of its speakers. It involves the absence of yod in non-primary stressed syllables, not only after alveolars and dentals (with no evidence of [tj] > [tʃ] or [dj] > [dʒ] coalescence), but also after labials and velars, e.g. *regular* > [ˈregula], *stimulate* > [ˈstimuleːt], *annual* > [ˈɛnuɐl], *situation* > [situˈeːʃɐn], *popular* > [ˈpɔpula], *educate* > [ˈɛdukeːt], *fabulous* > [ˈfɛbuləs], *occupation* > [ɔkuˈpeːʃɐn].

Tent (2001) conducted a detailed quantitative analysis of this phenomenon and found that although it is dynamic and complex, the absence of yod in non-primary stressed /Cju/ syllables was primarily a characteristic of L2 Fiji English. However, it had gradually evolved into a phonological shibboleth of many, if not most, L1 Fiji English speakers. The distinct clines in yodless pronunciation in terms of age, gender and level of education indicate that a change is in progress. The younger the speaker is, the more yodless is the pronunciation, while the more educated the speaker is, the more yod is used (or retained) in this particular phonological environment.

There is also a tendency for females to favour a yod pronunciation, which concurs with the findings of most other social dialect studies which report that women tend to use a more standard or prestige pronunciation. The tendency for males to favour yodless pronunciations, especially the younger ones, suggests that the phenomenon is a marker of covert prestige, maleness, and group identity (i.e. being speakers of Fiji English). The desire to identify with the local community is strong and is manifested linguistically. The reasons for the retention of yodless /Cju/ syllables, and indeed its increase among young Fiji English speakers, may well be because its speakers do not wish to alienate themselves from those within their own speech community.

Educated speakers in Tent's study also have yodless /Cju/ syllables, but to a lesser extent. This suggests that these speakers may be more linguistically sensitive and aspire to speak Modified Fiji English. More empirically based sociolinguistic research in this area is required to determine how strongly pressure to conform to the local norm is felt by the various sub-groups of Fiji English speakers, and to what degree this depends on how closely enmeshed the speaker is in the community.

On the other hand, some speakers realise *blew* as [bliu] and *flew* as [fliu]. For those speakers, *blue* and *blew*, and *flu* and *flew* are homophonous. This yod insertion may be more common among Indo-Fijians, but it is also present in the pronunciation of some Fijians. It may be an over-generalisation of the pronunciation of orthographic <-ew> in general (e.g. *few* [fju], *new* [nju]), or more specifically in the past tense of strong verbs (e.g. *knew* [nju]). Some informants seem to think that this is a teacher-induced error. These observations are, however, based on data from only about thirty informants, and confirmation would require more systematic empirical study.

5. Conclusion

The descriptions we have given of Fijian and Indo-Fijian Fiji English, including the pervasive absence of yod, illustrate the complexity and multifariousness of Fiji English phonology. Since the variety is overwhelmingly an L2 English, many of its phonological features are the result of phonological transfer from the first languages involved. Although this makes it no less interesting than any L1 variety of English, it does make it rather more difficult to analyse and characterise (at least from a phonological perspective). Unlike L1 varieties of English, L2 varieties, such as Fiji English, have the added variable of degree of competence: wide variation in competence in the language results in great differences in pronunciation.

A description and analysis of the phonology of Fiji English should not merely focus on the phonology of its L1 speakers, even though this would certainly be much more straightforward. To do so would present only a very small aspect of the complete phonological picture. What is needed are careful and detailed descriptions of each speech community's variety of Fiji English. This has been achieved by Tent (2001) for a single variable, absence of yod, but the overall task is far more complex, and the pronunciation of more phonological variables needs to be empirically investigated.

Apart from the L2 phonological features outlined above, Fiji English has several features that are also attested in English-based pidgins/creoles and basilectal/casual register native Englishes, some of which include:

- the common reduction of the {-ing} morpheme to [ɪn],
- the reduction of final consonant clusters, especially with /-Ct/ and /-Cd/ clusters,
- the metathesis of clusters such as [-sk-] as in *ask*, and
- the insertion of epenthetic vowel in final /-lC/ clusters, e.g. *Burns Philp* > [filɐp], *film* > [filam], *milk* > [milik]

We have argued that Fiji English is not a homogeneous variety but a group of co-existent systems or a series of continua. The phonological sketches we have presented above bear this out, but also show the need for a greater amount of detailed research and analysis for each system. What we have attempted to do here is lay the foundation for such studies by presenting an overview of Fiji English phonology. Future sociolinguistic studies concerning other linguistic features will also show to what extent our interpretations are well-founded.

*   We are much indebted to all our informants, in particular those who kindly agreed to be recorded, and many of the students enrolled in LL311 (Varieties of English) at the University of the South Pacific in Semester 1, 2003. We are also grateful to Maraia Lesuma and Ravi Nair for helping with the recordings, David Blair for helping with the phonetic transcriptions, and to Paul Geraghty for his valuable comments. Finally, we would like to thank Kate Burridge and Bernd Kortmann for their suggestions to improve our two papers. Errors and shortcomings are, of course, our own.

Exercises and study questions

1. Listen carefully to the samples of spoken Fiji English on the accompanying CD ROM. Try to identify examples of the following features of Pure Fiji English:
   (a) a lack of phonemic distinction between vowels that are normally distinguished in standard English varieties
   (b) intonation patterns
   (c) sentence tags
   (d) article use
   (e) pronoun use
   (f) different verbs compared with varieties of standard English
   (g) sentences that do not have a copula or auxiliary verb where varieties of standard English would normally have one
   (h) different preposition/particle use compared with varieties of standard English
   (i) tense/aspect marking
   (j) adverbs which are used in a distinctive way (e.g. as aspect markers or redundantly)

2. Based on other articles in the Handbook, outline some of the similarities and differences between Indo-Fijian English and Indian English on the one hand, and Indian South African English, on the other hand.

3. Based on other articles in the Handbook, outline some of the similarities and differences between Fiji English and English varieties spoken in former British colonies that are also multilingual, e.g. Singapore, Malaysia, and varieties spoken in the Caribbean and Africa.

4. Listen carefully to the samples of spoken Fiji English on the accompanying CD ROM. Can you identify some of the lexical borrowings (loan words) from Fijian or Hindi. Can you guess what they mean from the context?

Selected references

Please consult the General references for titles mentioned in the text but not included in the references below. For a full bibliography see the accompanying CD-ROM.

Arms, Fr. David G.
  1998   Tendencies in Fiji Hindi. In: Jan Tent and France Mugler (eds), *SICOL: Proceedings of the Second International Conference on Oceanic Linguistics, Volume I: Language Contact*, 1–10. (Pacific Linguistics C 141.) Canberra: Pacific Linguistics.

Bhatia, Tej
  1995   *Colloquial Hindi*. London/New York: Motilal Banarsidass.

Fox, Julian
  2003   English in Fiji: defining the lect: a sketch grammar of Pure Fiji English. M.A. thesis, Department of Literature and Language, University of the South Pacific, Suva.

Geraghty, Paul
  1975   Fijian and English in schools. *Outpost* 3: 20–23.
  1977   Fiji pidgin and bilingual education. *Fiji English Teachers Journal* 12: 2–8.
  1983   *The History of the Fijian Languages*. Honolulu: University of Hawai'i Press.
  1984   Language policy in Fiji and Rotuma. In: George B. Milner, David G. Arms and Paul Geraghty (eds.), *Duivosavosa: Fiji's Languages: Their Use and Their Future*, 32–84. (Fiji Museum Bulletin No. 8.) Suva: Fiji Museum.
  1997   The ethnic basis of society in Fiji. In: Brij V. Lal and Tomasi R. Vakatora (eds.), *Fiji Constitution Review Commission Research Papers, Volume 1: Fiji in Transition*, 1–23. Suva: University of the South Pacific.

Hobbs, Susan
  1985   *Fiji Hindi – English, English – Fiji Hindi Dictionary*. Fiji: Ministry of Education.

Kachru, Braj B.
  1985   Standards, codification and sociolinguistic realism in the English language in the outer circle. In: Randolf Quirk and Henry G. Widdowson (eds.), *English in the World*, 11–30. Cambridge: Cambridge University Press.

Kelly, Sr. Francis
  1975   The English spoken colloquially by a group of adolescents in Suva. *Fiji English Teachers Journal* 11: 19–43.

Moag, Rodney F.
  1977   *Fiji Hindi: A Basic Course and Reference Grammar*. Canberra: Australian National University Press.
  1979   Linguistic adaptations of the Fiji Indians. In: Vijay Mishra (ed.), *Rama's Banishment*, 112–138. Auckland: Heinemann Educational Books.

Moag, Rodney F. and Louisa B. Moag
  1977   English in Fiji, some perspectives and the need for language planning. *Fiji English Teachers Journal* 13: 2–26.
Ohala, Manjari
  1986   A search for the phonetic correlates of Hindi stress. In: Bhadriraju Krishnamurti (ed.), *South Asian Languages: Structure, Convergence and Diglossia*, 81–92. Delhi: Motilal Banarsidass.
Schütz, Albert
  1985   *The Fijian Language*. Honolulu: University of Hawai'i Press.
  1999   Fijian accent. *Oceanic Linguistics* 38: 139–151.
Siegel, Jeff
  1975   Fiji Hindustani. *University of Hawaii Working Papers in Linguistics* 7: 127–144.
  1986   Pidgin English in Fiji: a sociolinguistic history. *Pacific Studies* 9: 53–106.
  1987   *Language Contact in a Plantation Environment: A Sociolinguistic History of Fiji*. Cambridge: Cambridge University Press.
  1989   English in Fiji. *World Englishes* 8: 47–58.
  1991   Variation in Fiji English. In: Cheshire (ed.), 664–674.
Tent, Jan
  2000   The dynamics of Fiji English: a study of its use, users and features. Ph.D. dissertation, Department of Anthropology, University of Otago, Dunedin.
  2001   Yod deletion in Fiji English: phonological shibboleth or L2 English? *Language Variation and Change* 13: 161–191.

Norfolk Island-Pitcairn English: phonetics and phonology

John Ingram and Peter Mühlhäusler

1. Introduction

1.1. What is Norfuk?

The label 'Variety of English', when applied to the ways of speaking of the descendants of the Bounty mutineers and their Tahitian spouses, is somewhat problematic, and the relationship of these to other varieties featuring in this volume is complex. Earlier judgments on the linguistic nature of the language (surveyed by Mühlhäusler 1998) vary considerably and include characterisations such as dialect of English, dialect of Beach-la-Mar, mixed language, patois, cant, pidgin and creole. A similar range of labels is encountered among present-day speakers, and there is no agreement among them whether the variety spoken on Pitcairn Island and Norfolk Island are varieties of English, one separate language, or two separate languages. It appears that the wish to distinguish Pitkern from Norfuk as two separate named languages is growing and we have conformed to this wish. We have also opted to concentrate on the varieties spoken on Norfolk Island, as this is where the vast majority of present-day speakers reside (about 900 as against 50 on Pitcairn) and Norfolk is where Mühlhäusler has conducted fieldwork over several years. Sociopolitical problems make fieldwork on Pitcairn impractical at the moment.

The difficulties experienced in obtaining an adequate characterisation of Norfuk result from a number of factors.

(a) very patchy documentation
(b) Norfuk is not a focused language (see LePage and Tabouret-Keller 1985), where all community members agree on norms and standards, and what is called Norfuk ranges from forms that are mutually unintelligible with English, to others that differ only by a few stereotypical expressions.
(c) Both Pitkern and Norfuk have always been spoken side by side acrolectal varieties of English (British and Australian on Norfolk, British and American on Pitcairn). On Norfolk, standard British English until recently served as the role-model for educated islanders, and "murdering the King" was the local expression for speaking Norfuk. It is noted that some families

spoke English only, whereas in other families, Norfuk was the preferred language.

(d) Code mixing is pervasive; there are virtually no examples, even from older conservative speakers, which do not involve code-switching.

(e) Norfuk has been an esoteric language, not readily accessible to outsiders. It has also been a stigmatised language with a long history of persecution by the education system.

At present, the Norfolk Islanders are in the process of deciding on questions such as language name, lexical and grammatical norms, writing system and social role. To turn a large number of individual ways of speaking into a language in the sense of a modern standard language is a difficult technical and political process which leaves much room for conflict. It would seem very unwise for an outsider to tell people what their language is, or what it should be. We have refrained from privileging any of the suggested orthographies, word-choices, word-meanings or grammatical structures. Normalising the data at this point in the history of the language could do a great deal of damage and the reader is asked to forgive instances of inconsistency and vagueness on certain points.

1.2.   Geographical information

Pitcairn Island is situated in an isolated part of the Central South Pacific Ocean (24° 01'S x 130° 06'W), the distance from New Zealand from where it is administered being greater than that between Sweden and India. Its landmass is less than five square kilometres and its present population around 50, with a possibility that it will be abandoned.

Norfolk Island is located 1,575 kilometres east of Australia in the South Pacific Ocean (24° 05'S x 167° 59E). It occupies an area of 34.6 square kilometres and has a permanent population of about 2,600. It is visited by about 30,000 tourists per annum, with projected numbers exceeding 50,000 in the near future.

1.3.   Sociohistorical background

What has been written about the social history of the language again comprises quite a few varying accounts, with certain key factors such as the early presence of a West-Indian English speaker or the impact of the Melanesian Mission generally not being discussed (Mühlhäusler 2002). The story of the mutiny on the Bounty has been popularised by numerous novels, plays and films, and Pitcairn Island, where the Bounty mutineers settled in 1792, has come to stand as a metaphor for a South Sea Utopia. When nine British sailors, twelve Tahitian and Tubudian women and six Tahitian men arrived on Pitcairn, the island was uninhabited.

By 1800, following a period of violence, John Adams was the sole survivor with 10 women and 23 children. When he died in 1829 the island had become a model Christian community of about 80. Because of food and water shortages, Pitcairn Islanders were removed to Tahiti in 1821, but returned to the island in the same year. In 1839 the population had grown to 100, by 1850 it had reached 156. As fishstocks became scarce and the island degraded, in 1853 the inhabitants solicited the aid of the British Government to transfer them to another island which had become uninhabited, Norfolk. In 1856 all 194 Pitcairn Islanders settled on Norfolk, but a number of families returned to Pitcairn shortly afterwards.

Norfolk Island was discovered by Captain Cook in 1779 and because of its ample natural resources and isolated position was made a British Penal Colony in 1888. The first penal settlement was abandoned in 1814, but a second penal settlement was built in 1825 at a location for the "extremist punishment short of death" (Hoare 1982: 35) and "a cesspool of sodomy, massacre and exploitation" (Christian 1982: 12).

Following much criticism, the settlement was closed down in 1854. The third settlement is that by the Pitcairners who arrived in 1856 and were given title to about 1/4 of the total land area rather than the entire island as they had been led to believe. One reason for this is that the Melanesian mission, operating from Auckland, also had designs on Norfolk, and they were granted about 400 hectares of land in 1867. A boarding school catering for about two hundred students from different parts of Melanesia was set up and remained in operation until 1920.

Both islands thus provide laboratory conditions to study linguistic processes such as language contact, dialect mixing, and languages in competition. Different linguists have tended to concentrate on only one of these, as key factor, ignoring that all of them were important at some point in the history of Pitkern and Norfuk, plus other factors such as deliberate creation of language.

Ross and Moverley (1964) characterise what they called Pitcairnese as the outcome of language mixing, and provide numerous details about Tahitian lexicon and grammar, as well as details on dialect features. They provide details on the provenance and likely dialect affiliation of the mutineers (1964: 49, 137). As most men were killed in the first years of settlement, only the following are likely to have influenced the emerging language: Matthew Quintal (Cornishman), William McKoy (Scotsman), Edward Young (St. Kitts, West Indies), and John Adams (Cockney). The two principal linguistic socialisers for the first generation of children born on Pitcairn were Young and Adams. Young contributed a number of St. Kitts pronunciations and lexemes, [l] for [r] in words such as *stole* 'story', *klai* 'cry', and *morga* 'thin'. John Adams created the social conditions in which standard acrolectal English against all demographic odds could prevail as the dominant language of the community.

There is ample evidence that the Tahitians were not regarded as full human beings by the white members of the community and that racism was strong. This is reflected, for instance, in the absence of place-names remembering the non-European settlers. To date, no Tahitian woman is thus remembered by a place-name on either Pitcairn or Norfolk Island, though there now is a revaluation and appreciation of the Tahitian contribution and the word *formaadha* 'foremother' is being used in modern Norfuk.

Tahitian dress, language and eventually diet were gradually suppressed and given up, and policies put in place that were based on British and American models. Of particular importance has been the education system, which has tended to be in the hands of outsiders (Englishmen, American Seventh Day Adventist missionaries, and finally New Zealanders on Pitcairn Island; first British and then Australian teachers on Norfolk). Evidence from language use and attitudes in the Norfolk Education System suggests that from about 1900, language became a major issue and generations of teachers were actively involved in marginalising, suppressing and ridiculing the Norfuk Language. Children who spoke it were punished, and a sense of shame remains when older islanders speak the language in front of outsiders. More positive attitudes towards Norfuk date from the late 1980s, and in the late 1990s Norfuk language was formally introduced into the school as part of Norfolk Studies. There are now plans to teach Norfuk Language from Preschool to Year 10.

The ambivalent attitudes towards Norfuk are reflected in two areas of language mixing. First, it is remarkable that words of Tahitian origin tend to be predominant in marked domains of language: taboo words, negative characterisations, undesirable and unnatural phenomena and properties. Examples include: *eeyulla* 'adolescent, immature, or not dry behind the ears'; *gari* 'accumulation of dirt, dust, grime, grease, etc.'; *hoopaye* 'mucous secreted in the nose'; *howa-howa* 'to soil one's pants from a bowel movement, have diarrhoea'; *hullo* (1) 'a person of no consequence', (2) 'having nothing of any value; dirt poor'; *iti* 'any of the wasting diseases but mainly referring to tuberculosis'; *iwi* 'stunted, undersized'; *laha* (also *lu-hu*) 'dandruff'; *loosah* 'menses, menstruation'; *maioe* 'given to whimpering or crying a lot, like a child, but not necessarily a child'; *nanu* 'jealous'; *pontoo* 'unkempt, scruffy'; *po-o* 'barren or unfertile soil'; *tarpou* 'stains on the hands caused from peeling some fruits and vegetables'; *tinai* (1) 'to gaze at with envy', (2) 'an avaricious person'; *toohi* 'to curse, blaspheme, or swear'; *uuaa* 'sitting ungraciously'; *uma-oola* 'awkward, ungainly, clumsy'.

Some of these words may have originated in the nursery context rather than being indices of negative racial attitudes, but the overwhelming impression is that Tahitian words are the semantically marked forms: 98% of the forms in the 100-word standard Swadesh list are of English origin (the exception being *ak-lan* 'we' and the form *lieg* which stands for 'foot' and 'leg') and only about 5% of all words come from sources other than English (Tahitian, St. Kitts, Melanesian Pidgin English).

A second remarkable property is that words of English, Tahitian and other languages do not differ, as they do in most contact languages, in their susceptibility to morphosyntactic rules, suggesting a full integration of the two languages.

(1)   progressive marker *-en*
   a. *Yu tuhien.*
      'You are swearing'.
   b.. *Mais aanti kuken f kresmes.*
      'My aunt is cooking for Christmas'.

(2)   stages of comparison
   a. *agli – aglia – aglies*
      'ugly – uglier – ugliest'
   b. *pili – pilia – pilies*
      'sticky – stickier – stickiest'
   c. *meyameya – mayameyara – meyameyares*
      'withered – more withered – most withered'
   d. *morga – morgara – morgares*
      'thin – thinner – thinnest'

The single most important question regarding Pitkern/Norfuk remains its linguistic nature. In spite of considerable interest from dialectologists, creolists and researchers into language contact phenomena, most conclusions have been presented on the basis of very sketchy evidence and second-hand information, and the task to provide an observationally adequate account of the development and present-day use of Pitkern/Norfuk is far from completed. A particular obstacle has been the assumption that one is dealing with a single monolithic phenomenon, whereas in fact there is strong evidence for historical discontinuities, extensive idiolectal variation and a wide range of proficiencies.

For instance, the very few samples of Pitkern from the 1820s bear relatively little similarity to present-day varieties. Captain Raine (1824: 37) recorded the following observations about the low level of literacy and simplicity of lifestyle:

> In their conversation they were always anxious for information on the Scriptures, and expressed their sorrow that they did not understand all they read. One of them in talking with the Doctor showed such a knowledge of the Scriptures as is worthy of remark, particularly as it evinced their simplicity and harmlessness; the subject was a quarrelling, on which he said, 'Suppose one man strike me, I no strike again, for the Book says, suppose one strike you on one side, turn the other to him; suppose he bad man strike me I no strike him, because no good that; suppose he kill me, he can't kill the soul – he no can grasp that, that go to God, much better place than here.' At another time, pointing to all the scene around him, and to the Heavens, he said, 'God make all these, sun, moon, and stars and' he added, with surprise, 'the book say some people live who not know who made these!' This appeared to him a great sin. They all of them frequently said, 'if they no pray to God they grow wicked, and then God have nothing to do with the wicked, you know'.

Differences with present-day varieties in the areas of word order, use of relativisers and tags are evident. In common with present-day Norfuk are negation, conditional clauses and code mixing.

There probably never was a totally homogeneous speech community in the sense that every member believed they were speaking a language other than English, or in the sense of sharing the same linguistic role models, and there are still differences in lexical choice and pronunciation among different families. The language emerged in the tension between Tahitians and British, Islanders and Outsiders, Royalists and Independence Supporters. Some of the unique factors in the history of the language include:

(a) Pitcairn Island was the first English-speaking territory with compulsory literacy (from the 1820s). John Adams, towards the end of his life, invited English teachers to the island who not only ran the education system, but played a full part in many aspects of community life and were role models for community members. Proficiency in British Standard English has been held in high regard since their arrival. For speakers under the age of 30, Australian English has become the most widely accepted model.

(b) Literacy, for a significant part of its history, was strongly associated with religion, the Bible and religious texts being the predominant reading materials, and Biblical language an important model. Children were exposed to Biblical English from early childhood and it seems unlikely that any child was allowed to grow up without a thorough knowledge of this variety. Literate forms of Tahitian were not employed by the Pitcairners, and Pitkern/Norfuk was never used for religious writings or discourses.

(c) Pitkern/Norfuk is not a language in which all its speakers' needs can be expressed. It has a very limited vocabulary, about 1500 words (Eira, Magdalena and Mühlhäusler 2002), and it has not been used for public and high functions until very recently. However, since about 1990 the visibility of Norfuk has increased significantly. It features on the signage of the National Parks, the airport and departure forms, the names of businesses e.g. *Nuffka Apartments* 'Kingfisher or Norfolker', *Wetls Daun A'Taun* 'victuals down in Kingston Town' and house names *Dii el duu* 'able to do, make do', *Mais hoem* and in local songs.

(d) The extent to which Pitkern/Norfuk was socially institutionalised appears to vary with political circumstances and the desire of the population to express a separate identity. Greater use of Pitkern/Norfuk and concomitant loss of proficiency in English appear to coincide with the wish to distinguish oneself from outsiders. Laycock (1989) suggested that Pitkern/Norfuk came into being as a cant, in 1836, when the entire Pitcairn community was briefly resettled in Tahiti and found themselves at odds with the moral laxness which prevailed there at the time. However, the deliberate distancing from acrolectal English is documented even before the mutiny, when sailors mixed Tahitian expressions with English in order to taunt their unpopular captain.

The wish not to be Australian has been a strong motif in maintaining a separate form of speech on Norfolk Island, and the current conflict between Pitcairn Islanders and Britain (over a matter of police investigation) may trigger off a revival of the Pitcairn variety. Pitkern/Norfuk thus can be studied as an indicator of changing perceptions of identity. The situation on Norfolk Island today is reminiscent of Labov's observations on Martha's Vineyard (1972b), where non-standard forms have become reactivated by members of the younger generation opposed to mass tourism from the mainland. The tendency of past researchers to regard the Norfolk Island language from a purely structural perspective must be regarded as problematic, as structural properties cannot easily be separated from sociohistorical forces. If anything, it is the indexical rather than the structural and referential properties of Pitkern/Norfuk that lend this language its special character. As regards deviations from standard English, no single cause or explanation seems sufficient. Unsurprisingly, a number of features from older, eighteenth-century English are retained, though contemporary varieties of British, New Zealand, Australian and American English are influencing the language today.

The fact that the language developed on a remote island has led observers to believe that it developed in isolation. The exact opposite appears to be the case, however. Apart from a brief period before 1810, outside visitors were a very common phenomenon on Pitcairn (Pitcairn Island was one of the main ports of call in the Pacific until the arrival of modern intercontinental air traffic). Outsiders (not descended from the mutineers) form a significant part of both communities. Intermarriage is common, and both communities were actively involved in whaling, mission work and travelled for education and health purposes. Some of the generalisations about Island Creoles (Chaudenson 1998) apply to Pitkern and Norfuk as well.

The presence of a number of creole features (Harrison 1972: 223; Romaine 1988: 65) in Pitkern/Norfuk has been a source of confusion as researchers have failed to distinguish between creolisation in situ and the diffusion of creole features from St. Kitts (typologically Pitkern/Norfuk is much closer to the Atlantic Creoles than the Pacific ones, as demonstrated by Baker 1999: 315–364). Little work has been done on the influence of Pidgin English, which was widely used in the whaling industry and also by the Melanesian islanders on Norfolk. There were two possible time frames which favoured creolisation. One between about 1795 and 1815, on Pitcairn Island, and two in some of the more remote parts of Norfolk Island where a few families appear to have used predominantly Pitkern/Norfuk.

One of the crucial bits of evidence, informal speech of young children at these dates, is missing. The children that we have observed on Norfolk Island in recent years are dominant speakers of English. Flint and Harrison's data suggest that there was a change from Norfuk to English being the dominant language of the young generation in the 1950s.

2.   Norfuk speech

Reliable observational evidence on Norfuk speech and its changing characteristics are scarce. By far and away the best source of evidence – a window on Norfuk vernacular – at a time when the language was more actively used in the community, is provided by a set of 17 tape-recorded dialogues obtained by Elwyn Flint on a field trip to Norfolk Island in 1957. Elwyn Flint was a linguist at the University of Queensland from the 1950s up to the early 1970s. Flint had an abiding interest in peripheral varieties of English and language contact situations. He was a diligent collector of speech recordings from diverse communities throughout rural Queensland. Around the time when Flint was conducting his field work, Norfolk Island was coming under the influence of a second wave of massive external influence, primarily from Australian and New Zealand English. Subsequent work by Harrison and Laycock in the 1970s indicates that the stable diglossia that pertained up until Flint's investigations no longer exists. Flint himself noted its loss, which is apparent from even cursory examination of the 17 recorded dialogues.

The following sketch represents an attempt to isolate some salient phonetic and phonological characteristics of Norfuk vernacular as it was in 1957, and to document some of the changes which have taken place up to the present day. The analysis is based on a finite corpus of data (the 17 dialogues: approximately 40 minutes of continuous recorded speech), supplemented by keyword lists of seven present-day speakers of Norfuk vernacular. From this data base, it is possible to: a) convey in some detail the flavour of Norfuk phonetics, b) to lay a basis for further investigation into the evolution of Pitcairn-Norfuk Creole(s), c) to provide something of a yardstick for evaluating the current state of sociolinguistic variation on Norfolk Island today and d) to provide guidelines for those concerned with language revival as to the properties of 'authentic' Norfuk vernacular as it was spoken some two generations previous to the present time. Clearly, it is not possible on this data base to reconstruct a comprehensive picture of the phonology of Norfuk. An attempt to do so for present-day Norfuk would probably be misconceived. Norfuk today may constitute a collection of individual speech registers that are parasitic upon the variety of standard Norfolk English which is habitually used in the daily discourse of Norfolk Islanders, outside of the circumscribed contexts in which they use the Norfuk register. Norfuk, as described here, represents a prominent feature in the topography of spoken language variation in Norfolk Island, but its linguistic significance needs to be assessed within a broader sociolinguistic context, the outlines of which are described elsewhere and are the subject of on-going research.

Two sets of speech recordings form the basis of the present analysis: (i) a selection from the Flint dialogues recorded in 1957 and (ii) an elicitation of a set of citation forms based on a key word list for comparison of English dialects (Wells 1982; Foulkes and Dougherty 1999) provided by seven regular speakers of Norfuk recorded in November 2002.

2.1.   The Flint recordings

The 17 tape recorded dialogues were obtained under conditions stimulating customary Norfuk usage, i.e. two or sometimes more informants, with no interviewer present, engaged in a semi-spontaneous conversation on topics that would be expected to elicit Norfuk vernacular usage. The dialogues were partly scripted, but largely spontaneous. The conversations obtained were, for the most part, natural-sounding, expressive, and seemingly unselfconscious.

Flint produced two transcriptions of each dialogue with the assistance of the informants, directly following the recording session: an H(igh register) form, English translation, and a broad phonetic transcription of the actual speech in the Norfuk L(ow register) form. The phonetic transcription was obviously allophonic, rather than phonemic, but it was informed by Flint's extensive knowledge of Norfolk Island and Pitcairn vernaculars.

Some analysis of the material had been undertaken and reported previously (Flint 1961), and we made use of this in selecting the materials on which the present paper is based. Flint was interested in the relative impact upon intelligibility, of phonological, lexical and syntactic features of the Norfuk Vernacular for English listeners. He employed a linguist, with considerable experience transcribing English contact vernaculars, but not specifically with Pitcairn or Norfuk, to attempt an utterance-by-utterance English translation, under controlled listening conditions. In this way an intelligibility score for each of the 17 dialogues was obtained. There was considerable variation in the intelligibility scores, reflecting a complex of factors, one of which was the 'depth' of Norfuk usage sustained by the participants in a given dialogue.

For the present analysis, we selected the dialogue with the lowest intelligibility rating for detailed phonetic analysis, in order to obtain the 'broadest' or most authentic samples of Norfuk vernacular, with least contamination by code-switching or interference from the standard English or H variety. The two speakers were a 60+-year-old male and a 60+ female. The dialogue provided approximately 500 words for each speaker. The dialogue was originally recorded on a reel-to-reel tape recorder and subsequently dubbed onto a gramophone recording (LP 33rpm) by Flint. The gramophone recording was digitised for the present analysis (.wav files, 16 bit quantisation, 11.2 KHz sampling rate). The dialogue may be accessed on the accompanying CD-ROM.

2.2.   The keyword recordings

The Keyword list used for eliciting contemporary pronunciation contains a proportion of words that are attested Norfuk forms (indicated in bold on the word list). Speakers were invited to pronounce those items on the list that they recognised as words in Norfuk. This resulted in various selections by different speakers.

3.   Methodology

A combination of auditory and acoustic analysis was used to describe the phonetic characteristics of spoken Norfuk and to draw some inferences about Norfuk phonology. Some preliminary comment on the method of analysis is required.

3.1.   Phonetic transcription

Phonetic transcriptions were made generally in accordance with the conventions of the IPA, with some slight modifications to the set of vowel symbols used, as noted below. Phonetic transcriptions were guided primarily by auditory impression and secondarily by acoustic (spectrographic) observation.

Present day Norfolk Island English falls within the 'cultivated'–'broad' accent continuum of Australian English (Bernard 1989). The speech of many Norfolk Islanders when they are not using Norfuk may be indistinguishable from Australian English to most ears. Contemporary Norfolk English has probably also come under some influence from New Zealand English. These influences of contemporary regional Englishes are relevant for the ecology of language use on Norfolk Island today. However, the predominant formative influence of English on Norfuk, the traditional vernacular, would have been from the variety of 18th-century English spoken by the sailor Adams and the other Bounty mutineers, from the original generation of settlement on Pitcairn Island. Norfuk has its own highly distinctive accent and prosody, but it is frequently code-mixed with Norfolk English. Consequently, Australian English provides an appropriate phonetic frame of reference for evaluating Norfuk speech.

In deference to traditions of Australian English phonetics and to the habits of the transcriber, certain liberties have been taken with the IPA symbols for vowel quality transcription.

(a) The symbol [a] denotes a low (open) central vowel that is distinctively long [aː] or short [a] in Australian English (*card* - *cud*) with no significant difference in vowel quality. (The symbol [ʌ] is traditionally employed, inappropriately for the lax vowel in AusE *cud*. A case may be made for adopting the symbol [ɐ] for the lax low central vowel of Australian English.) Norfuk [aː] sounds identical to the long open [aː] of AusE (*hard*) in some speakers and closer to the more retracted [ɑː] of RP in others.

(b) The symbol [ɔː] represents a long rounded back mid-high vowel in AusE (*bought, caught*). It is actually closer to cardinal [o] and to the vowel quality of Australian English [ʊ] (*put, could*) than it is to the mid-low back and rounded cardinal [ɔ]. Habit is my poor excuse for preserving this transcription practice. There is a small quality difference between these two vowels in Australian English (aside from their obvious difference in length). The lips are slightly more protruded for [ʊ] than [ɔ].

3.2.   Context, coarticulation effects and undershoot in vowel transcription

Consistent with the view that vowel sounds are interpreted by the ear as contextually coherent linguistic targets, the decision was taken to represent familiar-sounding vowels and diphthongs as they were perceived/heard in whole-word citation forms. The ear always evaluates speech sounds in context and automatically compensates for coarticulation effects and articulatory undershoot, hearing the intended target, rather than the 'underachieved' peak in the attained formant trajectory.

For example, in the Norfuk vowel cluster (describable as a diphthong followed by a short vowel or as a triphthong) of the word *fire,* the second element is perceived as a high front vowel [i] or [ɪ]: [faɪa]. But if one attends only to the central region of the vowel cluster, isolated from context, this segment has the auditory quality of a low or mid-low front or central vowel [æ] - [ə]. Clearly, this is a case of articulatory undershoot of the off-glide target of the diphthong. Our speech perception mechanism automatically compensates for articulatory undershoot when listening to the vowel in whole-word context. In so doing, tacit phonetic and phonological knowledge of the listener is applied to the perception of the auditory stimulus. A more stable percept is achieved by judging vowel quality in whole word contexts, but at the possible cost of undue contamination of phonetic judgements by phonological expectations from the listener's native language.

4.   Vowels

For characterising Norfuk vernacular, the vowel sounds are far more important than the consonants, which differ minimally from those of Australian or New Zealand English. A preliminary analysis of two of the broadest Norfuk speakers from the Flint dialogues is presented (sections 4.1.–4.3.), followed by an analysis of the keyword citation forms from seven contemporary Norfuk speakers.

4.1. Single target vowels

To provide an initial characterisation of the Norfolk vowel space, and in order to reference points for inter-dialect comparisons, the single target, lax (short) vowels, ([ɪ], [a], [ɛ], [ʊ]) and long [aː], were plotted for each speaker, within the vowel space of Australian English (see Figure 1). The formant values for the Norfuk vowels represent average measurements (centroids) obtained from 5–10 tokens per speaker. The formant values were statistically normalised to take account of differences in speakers' vocal tract size and were plotted using the Bark scale frequency transformation. The Australian English reference vowels represent centroid values of the cultivated, general, and broad varieties reported by Bernard (1989). The Norfuk formant measurements were made from stressed lexical items, that occurred in discourse where no vowel reduction was evident. Nevertheless, some shrinkage of the vowel space in relation to Bernard's measurements is to be expected, because his data were obtained from citation forms spoken in isolation and not culled from connected speech.

The somewhat lower and centralised target positions for Norfuk high vowels [ɪ] and [ʊ] are likely due to articulatory undershoot in connected speech compared with the Australian English citation forms. However, the lower target position of Norfuk [ɛ] compared with its Australian English counterpart is significant. One notable instance of allophonic variation was found among these lax vowels. The short front vowel [ɛ] lowers to [æ] before /l/. Although sometimes found as a phonetic tendency among speakers of Australian English, it seems to be more strongly marked in Norfolk vernacular, falling clearly within the vowel quality domain of [æ] (see Figure 1). Flint suggests that there is no native contrast between [æ] and [a] in the Norfuk and that [æ] forms derive from the influence of Australian English through standard Norfolk English (the H variety). However, the data from our two speakers appear to suggest otherwise. Both [a] and [æ] forms are found in lexical items of English origin, but their lexical distribution is different from that of Australian English. In Table 1, bold print indicates [æ] pronunciation in Australian English.

Table 1. Distribution of [æ] ~ [a] in Norfuk (Flint dialogues)

[a]	[æ]	[æ̞]	[ɛ]
stand	matter	*as*	*catch*
that	*and*		*glad*
yam	*hat*		*bank*
than	*am*		*glad that*

Table 1. (continued)   Distribution of [æ] ~ [a] in Norfuk (Flint dialogues)

[a]	[æ]	[æ̞]	[ɛ]
dance	*saddle*		*saddle*
laugh	*catfish*		*thank*
hard	*chapel*		
start	*saddle*		
partner	*thank*		
darling	*fashioned*		
ma	*anthem*		
can't	*anniversary*		
	have		
	granny		

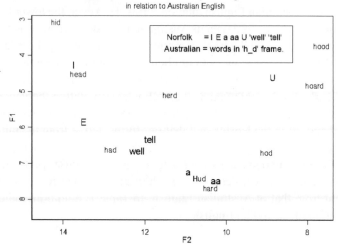

Formant plot: Norfolk monophthongal vowels
in relation to Australian English

Figure 1.   Some Norfuk monophthongs relative to Australian vowels (source: Bernard 1989). Mid vowel formant frequencies, F1 and F2, bark scaled.

If the standard account of the historical split of Middle English short /a/ is correct, these forms may provide a clue to the regional English dialect which had a dominant influence in the formation of the original Norfolk Island contact creole. The original split took place when ME /a/ lengthened (and in some dialects retracted) before voiceless anterior fricatives (*laugh, path, grass*). Subsequently, and incompletely, the change spread to nasal obstruent clusters (*dance, grant, demand*), resulting in the well-known regional and lexical variability found in these forms today. Although the data here is limited, it suggests a southern English dialect influence in the formation of Norfuk vernacular.

4.2. Back vowels

Norfuk may not possess as many phonemic contrasts as Australian English among its back vowels. Further analysis is needed. However, it is clear that, even if the number of contrasts is comparable, their distribution among cognate lexical forms is different, and there are also clear differences in phonetic implementation of the contrasts. Table 2 shows the phonetic correspondences that were found among cognate forms for the distinction between [ɒ] and [ɔː] which is found in Australian English and other non-rhotic varieties.

Table 2. Correspondences between Norfuk and Australian English [ɒ] and [ɔː]

Norfuk [ɒ] Australian Eng. [ɒ]	Norfuk [ɔː] Australian Eng. [ɒ]	Norfuk [ɔː] Australian Eng. [ɔː]
(be)cause	off	form 'person, guy'
what(s)	long	horse
got	along	thought
	on	all
	strong	Norfolk
	sorry	morn(ing)
		more

It is notable that the short counterpart of [ɔː] is much more restricted in its distribution in Norfuk than in Australian English. The Norfuk short [ɒ] was limited to a few closed-class items, leading one to suspect that at least in earlier varieties of Norfuk there was no productive phonological contrast between long and short (or tense and lax) non-high back vowels. The short vowel forms may simply represent phonetically reduced function words. This is supported by acoustic analysis of vowel quality differences between Norfuk [ɒ] and [ɔ], shown in Figure 2.

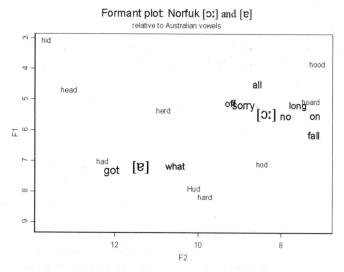

Figure 2.   Formant plots for Norfuk back vowels: long [ɔ] and short [ɒ] (plotted as [ɐ]) shown relative to Australian English monophthongs.

Norfuk [ɔ:] occupied a similar position in vowel space to its Australian English counterpart. The short vowel was quite centralised and more broadly scattered over vowel space than is indicated by the centroid plots for the multiple tokens of *what* and *got*. Phonetically this short vowel is more appropriately labelled [ɐ].

4.3.   Diphthongs

Norfuk /oʊ/ (*home*) has its vowel nucleus close to [ɔ], somewhat fronted, and usually with a perceptible schwa off-glide (see Table 3). The obvious outlier in this series (all from our male speaker) is the form *y'know*, which seems to be a borrowing from Australian or standard Norfolk English.

Table 3.   Instances of Norfuk /oʊ/

know	[nɔˤ:]
y'know	[nəʉ]
home	[hɔːᵊm]
most	[mɔˤ,ᵊst]
go	[gɔːᵊ]
road	[ɹɔˤ,ᵊd]

With the exception of the outlier (*y 'know*), the formant trajectories for the off-glide in the diphthongs have a forward movement. This diphthong is quite a distinctive marker of Norfuk accent. However, it does not appear to be phonologically contrastive with Norfuk [ɔ:].

Norfuk [aʊ] (*down, now, mouth*) showed a good deal of phonetic variability. In general, it shows evidence of incomplete lowering of the nucleus, as in other conservative regional dialects (Scots English, Canadian English, etc.). The range of phonetic variation for [aʊ] can be illustrated with the following tokens from our male speaker:

Table 4. Phonetic variation in [aʊ]

down	[dɑʊn]
out	[aʊt]
down	[dəʊn]
mouth	[məʊθ]
now	[nəʊ]
round	[ɹəʊnd]
out	[aʊt]
plough	[plaʊ]

To quantify this variation, we took formant measurements of the nucleus. The degree of lowering of the nucleus in the F1-F2 space corresponded with impressionistic transcription. Clearly, the word *plough seems to be a borrowing from Australian English.*

Norfuk [aɪ] evinces incomplete lowering of the nucleus, as also found in conservative regional English dialects. The environment for this incomplete lowering (often referred to as 'Canadian Raising' for its prevalence in Eastern Canadian English) is before voiceless obstruents in closed syllables. Our impressionistic transcriptions of [aɪ] tokens in stressed syllables showed some evidence of this rule in Norfuk.

Table 5. Phonetic variation in Norfuk /aɪ/

[aɪ]	[əɪ]	[ɛɪ]	[eɪ]
I	side	kinda	kinda
my's	ripe	like	
I	ripe	outside	
ripe	china		

Table 5. (continued)   Phonetic variation in Norfuk /aɪ/

[aɪ]	[əɪ]	[ɛɪ]	[eɪ]
china	sometime		
my's	right		
I	like		
pine	night		
mind	like		
Irish			
my			
my's			

Norfuk [eə] (which corresponds to Australian or Standard Norfolk English [eɪ]) is either a monophthong or an opening diphthong which is highly recognisable (as it is in Irish English). The range of variation illustrated in Table 6 is quite large, as the following tokens suggest. There was no obvious phonological conditioning for this variation.

Table 6.   Phonetic variation in Norfuk /eə/

[ɪe]	[e:]	[e]	[eɛ]	[eə]
gate	take	take	late	away
potato	make	take	baby	baby
anyway		make	take	plain
		take	way	
		take	make	
		anyway		
		same		

4.4.   Vowel variation in contemporary Norfuk

From the keyword list a number of comparisons were attempted, to try to ascertain vowel shifts or lexical changes in pronunciation that may have taken place in Norfuk over the period of the late 1950s to the present day. These comparisons are summarised in Table 7 below. The data sets are too small for any but the most tentative observations. However, they generate some useful hypotheses to guide subsequent inquiry.

There is no evidence of substantial change in phonetic realisation of the short lax vowels [ɪ - ɛ - a - ʊ] between the Flint samples from 1957 and the keyword sample from 2002. One might look for evidence that Norfuk [ɛ] has raised towards the Australian English equivalent ([e], *bed*). But this was apparent in only one token elicitation of *dress*, a word that is probably not part of Norfuk vocabulary. It is interesting to note that words in Norfuk which have cognate forms in standard English (e.g. *never, head*) are not only categorically distinct in length or vowel quality from the standard Australian or Norfolk English pronunciation, but are so in ways that represent alternative phoneme categories in standard English. This is what might be expected if Norfuk speakers were using standard English phonemic categories to differentiate lexical items of Norfuk from their cognates in standard English. Early Norfuk probably had no phonemic contrast between [ɛ] and [æ]. Note the wide variability in [æ ~ a] English-sourced Norfolk words from the Flint sample in Table 1 above.

Standard English		Norfuk
dress	/dɹes/	——
never	/nevə/	/næwə/
head	/hed/	/heɪd/

There is possibly a lesson here for teaching Norfuk to English speakers. In certain cases, an English word may be given 'Norfuk' colour simply by substituting one English vowel phoneme for another. A similar case of phonemic mapping between standard English and Norfuk arises in cognate forms involving the back vowels /əʊ, ɔː, ɒ/. These sounds are usually realised in Norfuk as long [ɔː], often with a centering off-glide, or as short [ɒ]. English source words containing /əʊ/ can flag their Norfuk status by phonemicising as /ɔː/ or /ɒ/.

Table 7.   Comparisons of Norfuk vowels THEN and NOW in relation to Australian English vowels

Short or lax vowels			
Norfuk 1957	**Norfuk 2002**	**AusE**	
ɪ	ɪ	ɪ	No notable differences
			dress: Not a Norfuk word?
			never [næʊwə] (2002)
ɛ	e - æ	e	head: [heɪd], [heɛd], [heːd] (2002)
a	a	a	No notable differences
			happy: [hæpɪ], [hæpɪ] (2002)
a- æ - ɛ	ɐ̞ - æ	æ	wide allophonic variation (1957)
ʊ	ʊ	ʊ	no notable differences
ɒ - ɔː	ɔː	ɒ	cloth: [kʰlɔːθ] (2002)

Table 7. (continued)   Comparisons of Norfuk vowels THEN and NOW in relation to Australian English vowels

Long vowels and diphthongs

Norfuk 1957	Norfuk 2002	AusE	
	iː - ɪi	ɪi	meat [miːtʰ], neither, free (2002)
ɪe - eː	eɛ - eː	æɪ - eɪ	fatal [feɛtɫ], face (2002)
ɔːᵊ	ɒ	əʉ	home [hɔːᵊm] (1957) throat [θɹɒtʰ], goat [gɒtʰ] (2002)
ɔː	ɔː	ɔː	daughter [dɔːta], horses [hɔːs], thought [θɔːtʰ] (2002)
əʊ - ɑʊ	ɐʉ	aʉ	*mouth* [mɐʉθ] (2002)

In this way, as in the case of /e/ words discussed above, systematic substitutions by phonetically related sounds may be employed to mark the special status of Norfuk lexical items. Whether this is what in fact happens is a matter of speculation, but should be testable through further analysis of the phonetic forms and distributions of these sounds in the Flint corpus and further elicitation of contemporary speech samples.

4.5.   Norfuk vowel phonemes

Our preliminary analysis of vowels in the speech of two broad Norfuk speakers gathered in the late 1950s reveals a wide range of phonetic variation, and the nature of the available data does not permit us to pursue a conventional phonemic analysis (eliciting minimal pairs, testing informants for contrasts and in various phonological environments etc.). However, it seems that even at the time of Flint's survey, the pronunciation of Norfuk words reflected their diverse lexical origins and grammatical status. It may be useful to adopt a notion from Lexical Phonology and to distinguish between a core stratum and a peripheral stratum of phonological contrasts. The core stratum applies to the stock of P-N historical lexical items (for which 18th-century English was the lexifier) and to the vestiges of the original creole grammatical forms (such as *se* 'copular' etc.). The peripheral stratum of phonological contrasts applies to more recent English loan words and 'code-switchings', which are parasitic upon the speakers' knowledge of standard Norfolk English.

Our tentative proposal for a set of core stratum Norfuk vowels is summarised in Figure 3.

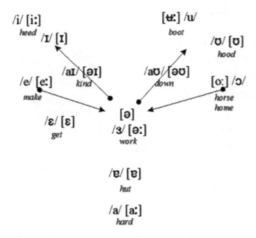

Figure 3.   Core stratum Norfuk vowels and diphthongs

4.6.   Norfuk intonation

Traditional Norfuk speech is noted for its highly distinctive and engaging intonation, a characteristic that apparently is in danger of being lost. The Flint recordings provide a valuable record of this aspect of Norfolk speech. Our formal description of Norfuk intonation is even more partial and preliminary than that of the segmental phonology. However, the basic problem is the same: separating stylistic and idiosyncratic features of individual voices from the systemic aspects of Norfuk prosody. In the case of intonation, the task is complicated by the lack of a widely accepted descriptive framework. We have adopted what might be called a 'simplified Pierrehumbert-Beckman' set of descriptive tags, aiming to annotate the major pitch and temporal features of the intonation contour.

The present system aims to represent local peaks and troughs as well as the overall shape of the fundamental frequency contour, pause breaks, and regions of slowed speech delivery. The main features of the annotation are illustrated in Table 8. Table 9 illustrates the text annotation of several utterances and Figures 4 and 5 illustrate how the tags are applied to the speech signal of selected utterances. Conversational Norfuk seems to an English ear to employ a wide pitch range with much expressive highlighting achieved by local changes of pitch and voice tempo. The use of temporally expanded vowels in accented syllables, or local reductions in speech tempo, is a distinctive feature of Norfuk prosody, illustrated in the second sentence of the text annotation (Table 9) and the speech signal (Figure 4).

Table 8.   Prosodic annotation tags

H	Major pitch peak in f_0 contour
h	Minor pitch peak in f_0 contour
L	Major pitch trough in f_0 contour
l	Minor pitch trough in f_0 contour
ds	Downstep: a step down or lowering of accentual pitch range
cre	Crescendo: a sequence of rising pitch accents
!	A prosodic boundary-marking pitch accent
'keeeep'	A temporally expanded syllable nucleus, in this case for word 'keep'
br	A junctural break or pause

Table 9.   Text annotation of intonation features (see Table 8 for symbol legend)

	LHL...L!
A01	well darling I sorry I so late as this
	Hal...h.L.ds.hl ..H........L!
B02	wha thing bin keeeep you
	LH.........................LH!..br....lhl..lhl....lhl!
A03	well when I done a work I hurry home
	LH...hl...hl!
A04	coming round our bend you know gen Ma Deil
	L..H..L...H...hl.......H.................................LH!
A05	I see dis big form staanding down gen our gate
	l....h.cre h.cre....h...H.............................lh!.....LH..........HL!
A06	he tell now you get down den or I'll go up dere baarber hold you!
	H...L
B07	oooh!

The word *keep* achieves accentual prominence by the exaggerated length of the vowel nucleus. The interrogative expression as a whole achieves illocutionary force by starting close to the top of the speaker's pitch range, with successive accented syllables down-stepped to the nuclear accent on the verb. There is substantial pre-pausal lengthening on *you, as part of the phrase-final boundary tone. But we have not annotated this feature, because it is a ubiquitous prosodic cue to phrase-final position in English and many other languages.*

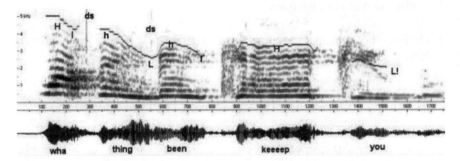

Figure 4. Prosodic annotation for dialogue utterance B03, aligned to f_0 trace

Down-stepping of accented syllables within the phrase in B03 may simply be a consequence of starting at the top of the speaker's pitch range and may have no particular pragmatic significance. However, the complementary effect on the pitch contour labelled 'crescendo' here, a succession of up-stepping accents leading to a nuclear 'hat' accent on barber hold in utterance A06, does seem to carry mimetic meaning as direct reported speech, mimicking the agitated state of speaker, (see Figure 5).

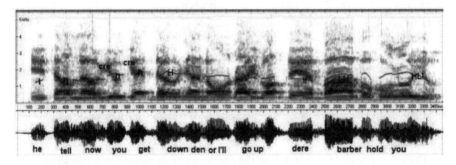

Figure 5. Prosodic annotation for A6, aligned to f_0 trace

The translation for this sentence that Flint gives is 'He said now you get down here or I'll go up there and give you a good hiding.' We guess the expression *barber hold* refers to the leather strap that barbers used to sharpen razors.

It is an open question whether mimetic features of intonation observed in reported speech dialogue should be regarded as part of Norfuk prosody or treated as 'paralinguistic' (i.e. as part of an individual speaker's capacity for expressive elaboration or embellishment of a narrative). Our analysis of Norfuk prosody is in its infancy and these kinds of questions require more data analysis.

Exercises and study questions

1. Outline the principal pronunciation differences between contemporary Norfuk and Australian English.

2. Discuss the influence of regional varieties of English in the development of Norfuk.

3. Can one distinguish between short and long vowel phonemes in Norfuk?

4. How have recent loanwords from Australian English affected Norfuk phonology?

5. How has the pronunciation of Norfuk changed between 1960 and 1990?

6. Can the standard English spelling system be adapted to cater for the Norfuk language?

Selected references

Please consult the General references for titles mentioned in the text but not included in the references below. For a full bibliography see the accompanying CD-ROM.

Baker, Philip
    1999   Investigating the origin and diffusion of shared features among the Atlantic English Creoles. In: Baker and Bruyn (eds.), 315–364.
Bernard, John R.
    1989   Quantitative aspects of the sounds of Australian English. In: Collins and Blair (eds.), 187–204.
Chaudenson, Robert
    1998   Insularité et créolité: de l'usage de quelques métaphores. *Plurilinguismes* 15: 1–26.
Christian, Glynn
    1982   *Fragile Paradise.* Boston and Toronto: Little, Brown and Co.
Eira, Christine, Melina Magdalena and Peter Mühlhäusler
    2002   *A Draft Dictionary of the Norfolk Language.* Adelaide: Discipline of Linguistics.
Flint, Elwyn
    1961   Bilingual interaction between Norfolk Island Language and English. Paper presented to the 1st Conference of the Linguistic Circle of Canberra.
Harrison, Shirley
    1972   The languages of Norfolk Island. M.A. thesis, Macquarie University, North Ryde.

Hoare, Merval
    1982   *Norfolk Island: An Outline of its History 1774–1968*. St Lucia: University of Queensland Press.
Laycock, Donald
    1989   The status of Pitcairn-Norfolk: creole dialect, or cant. In: Ulrich Ammon (ed.), *Status and Function of Languages and Language Varieties*, 608–629. Berlin: de Gruyter.
Mühlhäusler, Peter
    1998   How creoloid can you get? *Journal of Pidgin and Creole Languages* 13: 355–372.
    2002   Pidgin English and the Melanesian Mission. *Journal of Pidgin and Creole Languages* 17: 237–263.

Synopsis: phonetics and phonology of English spoken in the Pacific and Australasian region

Kate Burridge

1. Introduction

The following discussion describes the most significant phonological features of the varieties of English spoken in the Pacific and Australasian region. To simplify the discussion, we have broadly divided the brief descriptions here into those of native Englishes (Australian and New Zealand English) and of contact Englishes (Kriol, Cape York Creole, Bislama, Tok Pisin, Solomon Islands Pijin, Hawai'i Creole, Fiji English and Norfuk).

The sound system of any language will defy completely uniform and unambiguous description and it is always difficult in a short summary such as this one to do justice to the rich diversity that inevitably exists. This holds particularly for the contact languages represented here. These show enormous regional and idiolectal variation and their phonological inventories differ considerably depending upon two main factors:

- the influence of local vernacular languages (which may or may not be the first language of speakers), and
- contact with English – for certain (particularly urban) groups a growing force of influence.

Typically these languages range from varieties close to standard English in everything but accent (the *acrolect*) through to so-called heavy creoles that are not mutually intelligible with the standard (the *basilect*). In between these two extremes there exists a range of varieties (or *mesolects*). This kind of variation means that some phonological aspects of the more extreme varieties of Aboriginal English will be creole-like. Nonetheless we have decided to consider both Aboriginal English and Maori English under the umbrella of Australian and New Zealand English. For reasons provided in the Introduction, it paints a more accurate picture to separate these two varieties from the creoles and other contact varieties whose phonological repertoires pattern more closely the systems of the relevant substrate languages than that of English.

2. Significant features of New Zealand and Australian English – vowels

2.1. Short vowels

Australian and New Zealand varieties of English show an unusual pattern involving a general raising of short front vowels. Most striking is the raising of the DRESS and TRAP vowels in NZE. This is less evident in AusE, although it does occur. In some parts of Australia, particularly on the east coast (for example in Melbourne) the KIT vowel is also raised. In NZE, however, this vowel is lowered and centralized (although less centralized in Maori English than in Pakeha English). The pronunciation of the KIT vowel is an outstanding feature of this dialect and has become a shibboleth for distinguishing New Zealand and Australian speakers. As noted in the chapters by Bauer and Warren and also Gordon and Maclagan, Australians parody the New Zealand KIT vowel with their STRUT vowel; in fact, the vowel that most NZE speakers use here is a central vowel that is slightly more open than schwa.

These two major dialects of Antipodean English have in common a number of vowel mergers currently underway in prelateral environments. For example, in both varieties a sociolinguistic variable is the neutralization of DRESS and TRAP before laterals. For many younger speakers the word *shell* and *shall* and *Alan* and *Ellen* are no longer distinguishable. In NZE the neutralized vowel is typically more open and more retracted than either DRESS or TRAP, although vowels intermediate between DRESS and TRAP are also heard. AusE speakers usually merge these vowels in favour of [æ]. In Australia this merger is also reported as being regionally differentiated, occurring in both Melbourne and Brisbane, but generally absent from the other major cities.

There is a parallel phenomenon occurring with respect to the LOT and GOAT vowels: for many speakers the words *doll* and *dole* are not distinguished. The GOOSE and FOOT vowels and the FLEECE and KIT vowels are also in the process of merging in prelateral position, in this case in the direction of the short vowels. For example, *fool* is merging on *full* and *feel* is merging on *fill*. Moreover, in NZE the distinction between the vowels of KIT and FOOT is also frequently lost in this environment, so that pairs of words like *pill* and *pull* become indistinguishable. It therefore follows from the previous mergers that for some speakers of NZE the KIT and GOOSE vowels are also indistinguishable (as in *fill* and *fool* and *pill* and *pool*). Note that the prelateral lowering of vowels has also been noted as being especially marked in the Norfolk vernacular, in particular for DRESS. In NZE a merger between KIT and STRUT is sometimes heard prelaterally (as in *kilt* and *cult*).

In both NZE and AusE the FOOT vowel is a typically a mid-high back (slightly rounded) vowel [ʊ]. However, NZE is showing evidence of a change underway towards a vowel that is both centralized and unrounded.

The STRUT vowel is a low and central vowel. In both dialects it shares phonetic qualities with the START vowel. Accordingly, the vowels in pairs of words such as *cut* and *cart* are distinguished largely by length.

Speakers of Aboriginal English, especially those falling closer to the creole end of the continuum, may not distinguish between KIT and FLEECE or between DRESS and TRAP. In this variety the STRUT vowel often alternates with various front or back vowels from among the following: /ʌ ~ ɪ ~ æ ~ ɒ/. Mid back vowels are often used interchangeably or may, under influence from the creole, alternate with /o/.

2.2.   Long vowels

A striking feature of the FLEECE vowel in both AusE and NZE is the evidence of ongliding; this is most obvious among speakers at the broad end of the spectrum. In AusE the GOOSE vowel is also diphthongized and in both dialects this vowel is considerably fronted (markedly so in Maori English). As mentioned earlier, both the FLEECE and GOOSE vowels are neutralized with other vowels before laterals.

Of particular interest with respect to variation elsewhere in the English-speaking world are the regional differences in the BATH vowel class. In Australia there is striking social, stylistic and regional variation between the TRAP and PALM vowels. In NZE the variation is less apparent; most New Zealanders use the PALM vowel in words such as *example* and *dance* (the exceptions are those older South Island speakers who use the TRAP vowel in the BATH lexical set). Despite the variation that exists within these two countries, this feature is considered another shibboleth to distinguish Australian and New Zealand varieties of English.

In both dialects there are diphthong variants with central offglides of the START and THOUGHT vowels. The NURSE vowel is long mid-high central; it is fairly stable in both varieties, although fronted for some broad speakers. In Aboriginal English it is often replaced by a mid front vowel (either /ɛ/ or /e/).

2.3.   Diphthongs

The rising diphthongs in AusE and NZE are significantly different from other dialects of English. They are also important differentiators for the social variants within these two dialects. This is especially true for the FACE, PRICE and

MOUTH vowels. Compared to their RP equivalents, FACE has a more open starting point; PRICE a raised and backed first target, especially for broad speakers; the back-rising diphthong MOUTH has a fronted and first target, again most notably for the broad end of the spectrum. The other back-rising diphthong GOAT has an open and central starting position with a closing glide approximating the GOOSE vowel. CHOICE shows the least variation for these dialects.

One of the most characteristic features of falling diphthongs in Australia and New Zealand is the monophthongal [ɔ] pronunciation for the CURE vowel. This is evident in the pronunciation of lexical items such as *poor, moor, sure* and *tour*. If the CURE vowel occurs it is generally following /j/. In parts of Australia the quality of the offglide for the NEAR vowel is weak and is often realized as length; in NZE a long monophthongal variant also appears before liquids /l/ and /r/. A more striking feature of New Zealand is the variable merger that is currently taking place between the vowels of NEAR and SQUARE. For most young speakers pairs of words such as *rear* and *rare* or *cheer* and *chair* are not distinguishable. Although there has been considerable debate over the years concerning the quality of the neutralized vowel, most linguists now agree the merger is in favour of a high variant [iə].

2.4.   Weak vowels

The unstressed vowels in lettER, horsES and commA are realized with a wide range of different qualities around the vowel space of [ə], depending on the context. The unstressed vowel in happY is generally realized as [i], although broad variants can show dipthongization here. In Aboriginal English schwa is typically replaced either by the mid central vowel /ʌ/ or by a low central vowel /a/.

Widespread throughout New Zealand and Australia is the pronunciation of the past participles of the nine verbs – *grown, flown, blown, known, mown, sewn, shown, sown* and *thrown* – as disyllables (hence, for example, [grouən] and [flouən]). In New Zealand both pronunciations are regarded equally correct; in Australia the disyllabic variant still attracts widespread condemnation.

3.   Significant features of New Zealand and Australian English – consonants

3.1.   Stops

Widely used by Australians and New Zealanders is a flap or tap [ɾ] variant of /t/ in intervocalic final positions (as in *get it* and *sort of*) and medial positions (as in *better* and *beauty*). This variant also occurs commonly preceding syllabic laterals and nasals (as in *bottle* and *button*). There is also a glottalized version of /t/ that can be heard more usually in medial contexts (such as *cutlass*) and in end positions (such as *shut*), less so intervocalically (as in *get out*).

These varieties share with many other English dialects the feature of palatalization of /t, d, s, z/ preceding the GOOSE vowel [u]. There is, however, considerable variation between the pronunciations with yod and with palatals, as in *tune* [tjun] versus [tʃun]. The palatalized variants are more likely to occur when the syllable is unstressed (as in *fortune* and *educate*).

A pronunciation of /t/ that has come to be associated with AusE is affrication. It is most obvious in prepausal positions and has been linked particularly to middle class and female speech. Both AusE and NZE are also showing evidence of a complex assimilation taking place in the consonant clusters /tr/ and /str/ – the affricated realizations [tʃɹ] and [ʃtɹ] are becoming increasingly frequent in these varieties. The word *tree*, for example, is pronounced as [tʃɹi]. In younger speakers there are also signs of this affricated pronunciation extending to the /stj/ cluster of words such as *student*.

In Aboriginal English the distinction between voiced and voiceless stops is not strongly maintained. The preference is for voiceless stops, especially in word-final position. The alveolar stop /t/ is often rhotacized between vowels, as in *shut up* [ʃʌɾʌp]. Maori English shows evidence of a loss of aspiration on voiceless stops.

3.2.   Fricatives

Devoicing of voiced fricatives is a general feature of NZE, and is particularly evident in Maori English. In Aboriginal English there is a preference for stop over fricative articulation – labio-dental fricatives [f] and [v] are often replaced by stops.

One widespread feature that AusE shares with other English dialects is the substitution of /f/ and /v/ for dental fricatives /ð/ and /θ/. This is particularly evident in frequent words such as *with* and *them*. In NZE this is not a major tendency, although /f/ does occasionally substitute for /θ/. This feature is more common in casual conversation and is still very stigmatised in both dialects. In

Aboriginal English these dental fricatives are often replaced by alveolar stops /t/ and /d/ (occasionally /s/ is substituted for /θ/) and in Maori English, surprisingly, by affricates /dð/ and /tθ/.

All these varieties share with many others the deletion of [h] in initial position, especially in unstressed contexts (as in the case of the pronouns *him* and *her*). When deleted in stressed positions it attracts censure. Aboriginal English shows evidence of hypercorrection; [h] often appears initially in words where it does not occur in standard English.

In Aboriginal English, sibilants are not always distinguished and affricates are frequently realized as /ʃ/.

3.3. Glides

As in other parts of the English-speaking world the distinction between /w/ and /hw/ has virtually disappeared, so that for most speakers pairs of words such as *witch* and *which* are indistinguishable. The /hw/ cluster is preserved only for the most conservative speakers of these varieties (most notably the older speakers in the Southland in New Zealand).

Yod-dropping is variable in both New Zealand and Australia. After clusters (as in *blue*) and after /r/ (as in *rule*) /j/ has totally disappeared. It is now also rarely heard after /l/ (as in *lewd*), although it is preserved in syllables that do not carry the primary stress (as in *prelude*). Following alveolar consonants there is considerable variation. While yod is usually deleted after [θ] in words such as *enthusiasm* as well as after /s/ and /z/ (as in *assume* and *presume*), speakers vary between pronunciations with yod and those where palatalization has occurred. After /t/ and /d/ the most usual pronunciation is an affricate (cf. discussion above). Following /n/ there is the sort of lexical variation that is expected of a change in progress; for example, the yod typically disappears in *nude* but tends to be retained in *news*. As is the case elsewhere in the English-speaking world, yod is best preserved after labials (as in *beauty* and *fume*) and velars (as in *cute*).

3.4. Sonorants /r/ and /l/

Australian and New Zealand English show the different allophones of /l/ that occur in RP; namely, a slightly velarized lateral in onset positions and a considerably darker version in coda position. There is also evidence of increasing vocalization of /l/ in both dialects (thought not uniformly throughout) – the variant is a back vowel [u] that may or may not be rounded or labialized. The contexts that promote vocalized /l/ are: final cluster (as in *milk*), end position (as in *pill*) and syllabic environments (such as *buckle*).

These varieties are non-rhotic; in other words, /r/ is not pronounced in post-vocalic position. Most striking, therefore, is the variable rhoticity found in the Southern part of the South Island of New Zealand. In this variety the pronunciation of /r/ is most consistently maintained in the NURSE lexical set, and there is considerable variation in other contexts.

Australian and New Zealand English have a liaison feature known as linking R, whereby /r/ is pronounced in final position if there is a following vowel, as in phrases such as *far off*. Both varieties also show the so-called intrusive R whereby /r/ is inserted to link adjacent vowels, as in phrases such as *idea(r) of* and *law(r) and order*. There is also evidence of intrusive R in word-internal environments such as *drawing* and *however*. This liaison rule has also extended to laterals. In other words, the vocalization of /l/ has triggered a linking L (or, in some cases, a linking W) where a following word begins with a vowel, as in the phrase *feel it*.

Throughout NZ and Australia there is evidence of American English influence, particularly in the realm of vocabulary. Borrowed expressions and catch-phrases are often pronounced with a kind of pseudo-American /r/. Many popular singers also adopt an American rhotic pronunciation.

The substitution of [n] for [ŋ] in words ending in *-ing* and [ŋk] for final [ŋ] in the group of indefinite pronouns *something, anything* and *nothing* are features these Antipodean varieties share with many others, most notably those of South East England. The latter feature, however, is still stigmatized and is typically confined to the broad varieties. It continues to attract fierce criticism.

4.   Prosodic features of Australian and New Zealand English

The most striking prosodic feature of these varieties of English is the high rising contour on declarative clauses. It is especially common in narratives. The feature goes by various names, but most usually High Rising Tone/Terminal (HRT) or Australian Questioning Intonation.

Maori English shows a strong tendency to syllable-timing, under the influence of the mora-based timing of the Maori language. There are also strikingly different features within both Maori and Aboriginal English prosody, most notably with respect to voice quality and rhythm.

5.   Significant features of contact languages – vowels

As mentioned above, variation within these speech communities is considerable and surveying the phonetic and phonological features of these languages is extremely difficult on account of varying degrees of interference from local vernaculars and from the lexifier language English. These two influences have a significant effect on the extent and the nature of the vowel inventories that we find here.

As in the case of pidgins and creoles elsewhere, the contact languages in this region show vowel systems that are considerably reduced. This means that there is substantial vowel neutralization and consequently these languages permit much larger numbers of homophones (words that are pronounced the same) than do other varieties of English. Bislama, Solomon Islands Pijin, Tok Pisin (with roots in earlier Melanesian Pidgin), Fiji English and the Australian creoles, Cape York Creole and Kriol, all share a five vowel contrast: /i/, /u/, /e/, /o/, /a/. The phonetic realization of these segments is generally close to the cardinal IPA values. Hawai'i Creole has a seven vowel inventory, with additional low vowels in front and back position. With the exception of Kriol, vowel length is not phonemically distinctive.

Where vowel neutralization has occurred, these languages can show a fairly regular correspondence between the creole words and their corresponding English etyma. For example, in Bislama the English vowels START, TRAP and STRUT regularly correlate with /a/. However, the correspondences are not always predictable; the NURSE vowel in Bislama, for example, can correspond to /o/, /a/ and /e/.

Diphthongs are usually monophthongized (FACE is typically realized as [e]; GOAT as [o]). There is, however, considerable variation, especially word-finally. For example, centering diphthongs with a schwa off-glide (corresponding to post-vocalic /r/ in rhotic varieties) in words such as *more* and *where* vary between monophthongal variants /o/ and /e/ and vowel sequences of /oa/ and /ea/. Generally speaking, better-educated speakers are more likely to contrast diphthongized and monophthongal vowels and have at their disposal a greater range of diphthongs.

Some of these varieties have rules of vowel harmony, especially between affixes and stems. For example, the Melanesian Pidgin varieties and the Australian creoles have in common a transitive verb suffix -V*m* where the vowel harmonizes with the final vowel of the verb root. In Solomon Islands Pijin, vowels that are inserted within consonant clusters and word finally (see discussion below) also typically harmonize; for example *sukulu* 'school', *tarae* 'try', *bisinisi* 'business'.

6.   Significant features of contact languages – consonants

These languages show the basic consonant phonemes of English, but possess a considerably smaller inventory of sounds. There is also substantial variation relating to the substrate languages. Kriol, for example, has additional lamino-palatal and retroflexed consonants that are not found in standard English. Generally, phonetic interference from vernaculars is more obvious in the language of older, especially rural, speakers. The extent of the influence depends on whether or not these vernaculars are the first language of speakers, as well as on education (which will inevitably increase contact with English). As in the case of vowels, speakers with a better command of English usually have expanded consonant inventories. Consequently, the following are very general tendencies and readers are advised to revisit the chapters for specific details of each of these languages.

6.1.   Stops

The most heavy creole varieties typically do not show contrastive voicing for stops. They may appear voiced or unvoiced, although there is a general preference for voiceless (unaspirated) stops in all environments. Where a contrast is made between voiced and voiceless stops, the voicing distinction is typically lost word-finally; hence pairs of words such as *dog* and *dock* will be homophonous. Intervocalic flapping (or tapping) is widespread in these varieties.

Hawai'i Creole shows both voiced and voiceless stops and there is aspiration where a force of air follows the release of the voiceless stop. Aspiration is generally more in evidence than in other varieties of English because of the prevalence of syllables with secondary stress (for example, it occurs medially in words such as *carton* and *kitten*). Where they occur word-finally, however, voiceless stops are typically unreleased or glottalized. In addition, Hawai'i Creole shows affricated pronunciations of /t/ and /d/ where they occur before /r/.

A particularly striking feature of the varieties of Melanesian Pidgin is the presence of prenasalized voiced stops; in other words, /b, d, g/ are pronounced as /ᵐb, ⁿd and ᵑg/. Fiji English also shows prenasalization, but only of /b/.

6.2.   Fricatives

Fricatives are generally absent from the heaviest creole varieties, with the exception of /s/ – it is usual for stops to substitute for both fricatives and affricates. Sibilant contrasts between /s/, /z/, /ʃ/ and /ʒ/ are generally merged as /s/.

Where fricatives occur, the voicing contrast is not consistently maintained; devoicing is especially common word-finally. The contrast between /f/ and /v/ appears to be particularly unstable, with /f/ often substituting for /v/. Dental fricatives are typically substituted with stops.

Glottal fricative /h/ is variably maintained in these creoles. Examples of hypercorrection can also be found; for example Tok Pisin *hapinum ~ apinum* 'afternoon'.

6.3.   Sonorants

These varieties all show three distinct nasal phonemes. Basilectal Kriol shows an additional retroflexed and palatalized nasal. Note that Bislama has a palatal nasal word-finally for words of French origin such as *champagne*.

The rhotic /r/ is generally realized in these languages as an alveolar flap (or trill). Post-vocalic /r/ does not occur; however, Hawai'i Creole shows R-colouring of the NURSE vowel in stressed syllables.

In Hawai'i Creole L-vocalization is common in syllable codas and before consonants. In other contact varieties postvocalic /l/ is typically non-velarized.

6.4.   Phonotactics

These languages show distinct preference for an open CVCV structure. Consequently consonants are often dropped from clusters, especially word-finally; e.g. Kriol *ek* 'ax'. Speakers will also insert epenthetic vowels to avoid consonant clusters. As described earlier, these epenthetic vowels often conform to the rules of vowel harmony. However, increased contact with English can bring about the loss of these epenthetic vowels – consonant clusters are therefore more evident in speakers of urban varieties where English influence is stronger (through schooling, for example).

The open syllable target also means that some speakers will add final vowels. For example, in the Pijin of older, mostly rural speakers *sukul* becomes *sukulu* 'school' and *bisinis* becomes *bisinisi* 'business'.

7.   Prosodic features of the contact languages

The most distinctive prosodic feature of these languages is their syllabic rhythm; unlike the stress-timed quality of standard English, in these varieties syllables show more or less equal force in terms of loudness and of duration.

Exercises and study questions

The following exercises are based on the brief descriptions provided in the synopsis chapter. You might also wish to revisit relevant individual chapters (for this region and elsewhere) and the CD-ROM for more specific details.

1. New Zealand English and Australian English vowels have a number of features in common, particularly where vowel mergers are involved. Identify the most significant of these shared features. Generalize where you can.

2. There are a number of consonantal features that New Zealand and Australian English share with other major English dialects. Briefly describe these.

3. Identify some of the most noteworthy phonological characteristics of both Aboriginal English and Maori English. Focus on those features that differ most significantly from the L1 varieties of the respective regions.

4. Describe the process of yod-dropping. Give examples of the sort of variation encountered in Australia and New Zealand. Consult the other regional synopses and identify other varieties that share this feature.

5. With specific examples, give a brief account of the two liaison features described here for Australian and New Zealand English sonorants. Consult the other regional synopses and identify any other varieties that show similar liaison features.

6. Give a brief account of the most significant vocalic features of the contact varieties described in this synopsis chapter. Compare these features with those that have been described for contact varieties elsewhere in the world. Generalize where possible.

7. What is vowel harmony and, with examples, describe how this process works for some of the contact varieties of this region.

8. Identify the most striking consonantal features of the most "heavy" creole varieties of the Pacific and Australasia. Compare your findings with descriptions of creole accents elsewhere in the world. Again, generalize where possible.

9. Provide a summary of the most notable vowel and consonant features that distinguish the contact varieties from the L1 varieties of this region.

Morphology and Syntax

New Zealand English: morphosyntax

Marianne Hundt, Jennifer Hay and Elizabeth Gordon

1.   Introduction

The study of New Zealand English (NZE) has concentrated almost exclusively on phonology and vocabulary, with syntax and morphology notably absent. It is not until the late 1980s that New Zealand syntax is described in Bauer (1987, 1989a–c, 1994), Quinn (1995, 2000) and Hundt (1998). Some of the descriptions are based on personal observation and some on empirical research and elicitation experiments (e.g. Bauer 1987).

Proponents of the null hypothesis (e.g. Todd and Hancock 1986) claim that NZE grammar is (virtually) identical with British English (BrE) grammar. (The term 'British' English is used because some of the data on which this article is based come from corpora of standard written British English.) BrE, however, can no longer be the model against which varieties such as NZE are to be measured. The morphology and syntax of Standard English in New Zealand do not differ categorically from those of standard British and American English. But even if, in terms of grammar, usage in New Zealand is found to agree closely with the standards of the United States and Britain, that does not mean that it makes no sense to speak of New Zealand English morphosyntax. Differences between national standards are a question of degree. The standard in New Zealand can therefore best be described in relation to other national varieties, such as BrE, American English (AmE) and Australian English (AusE). As far as grammar is concerned, the following two types of difference between NZE and other national varieties can be expected: a) statistical tendencies, i.e. structures used more or less frequently in NZE than in other varieties, resulting in a characteristic NZE mix of pan-English features and b) genuine NZE collocations/idioms, i.e. unsystematic peculiarities at the interface of grammar and the lexicon.

One reason that early research on NZE concentrated on phonetics and phonology (see Bauer and Warren, this volume) as well as the lexicon was because it is in these aspects NZE differed most obviously from other national varieties. The New Zealand accent and vocabulary were not only perceptually more salient but also easier to describe empirically than morphosyntactic aspects of NZE. It is therefore symptomatic that the first monograph on NZE, Bell and

Holmes (1990), largely neglects the grammar. The most recent volume (Bell and Kuiper 2000) features only two articles on grammatical aspects.

The first studies that investigated NZE morphosyntax empirically (Bauer 1987, 1988, 1989a–c) were based on elicitation tests. Before the compilation of the Wellington Corpus of Written New Zealand English (WCNZE), elicitation tests such as Bauer's were the only way to approach the grammar of NZE empirically. Two book-length studies that have explored the WCNZE for the study of NZE morphology and syntax are Hundt (1998) and Sigley (1997).

This paper deals separately with patterns of standard and non-standard morphosyntax in NZE. Discussion of the former (sections 2 and 3) focusses primarily on data from written corpora, whereas discussion of the second (section 4) is focussed on data from spoken sources.

The data for the discussion of standard NZE morphosyntax come from one million-word corpora of British, American, New Zealand and Australian English (cf. the full bibliography on the CD-ROM for manuals providing background information on the individual corpora):

corpus	corpus abbreviation	variety	sampling period
Lancaster-Oslo/Bergen Corpus	LOB	BrE	1961
Freiburg-LOB Corpus of British English	FLOB	BrE	1991
Brown corpus	Brown	AmE	1961
Freiburg-Brown Corpus of American English	Frown	AmE	1992
Wellington Corpus of Written New Zealand English	WCNZE	NZE	1980s
Australian Corpus of English	ACE	AusE	1980s

Occasionally, evidence from the spoken component of the British National Corpus (BNC) and from the spoken corpus of NZE (WCSNZE) are used. Additional data comes from newspapers available on CD-ROM (the 1991 *Guardian* for BrE and the 1992 *Miami Herald* for AmE) and machine-readable versions of two New Zealand newspapers, the *Dominion* and the *Evening Post* (*DOM/EVP*).

There is very little data available on patterns of non-standard NZE morphosyntactic patterns. In section 4 we outline what is known about non-standard patterns, illustrating the phenomenon with examples extracted from the CanterburyCorpus.Thiscorpusconsistsofrecordingsmadebystudentsenrolled in the New Zealand English Course at the University of Canterbury over the last 10 years. The limited patterns of regional variation are discussed in section 5.

2.   Morphology

2.1.   Verb morphology

NZE verb morphology is interesting as far as irregular verbs are concerned. In an ongoing regularization process involving verbs such as *spoil* or *dream*, NZE can be placed relative to AmE, BrE and AusE. For *prove* and *get*, on the other hand, the irregular form persists in some varieties of English, sometimes involving functional specialisation. we will look at these two areas of verb morphology in turn.

AmE has been expected to lead world English in the long-term regularisation of irregular past tense forms. For verbs such as *spoil, leap* or *spill* AmE is said to prefer the regular *-ed* preterite and past participle forms (cf. Quirk et al. 1985: 104). Peters (1994) compares verb morphology in LOB and Brown with that in ACE (see Collins and Peters, this volume). She concludes that "[...] the Australian data is a law unto itself. It shows no consistent commitment to either British or American patterns, and does not lend support to the notion that Australian English is now heavily influenced by American" (Peters 1994: 157). Table 1 supplements Peters' results from Brown, LOB and the ACE with data obtained from searches in the FLOB and Frown corpora and the WCNZE. The search included the following verbs: *burn, dream, lean, leap, learn, smell, spell, spill* and *spoil*. Care was taken to exclude homonyms like *(to) smelt* or the noun *spelt* from the count.

Table 1.   Irregular and regular past tense

	-ed		*-t*	**Total**
Brown	265	95.3%	13	278
Frown	232	93.5%	16	248
LOB	153	65.1%	82	235
FLOB	149	68.7%	68	217
WCNZE	127	56.4%	98	225
ACE	142	56.6%	109	251

The relative frequency of regular verb forms in Brown shows that AmE, thirty years ago, had almost reached the putative endpoint of the regularisation process. This still holds for AmE in the early 1990s, despite the fact that the ratio of irregular forms is higher in Frown than in Brown. Table 1 also shows that the relative frequency of irregular and regular verb forms in NZE and AusE is very similar. BrE, on the other hand, appears to be more advanced in the regularisation of irregular past tense forms. The overall increase in regular verb forms in FLOB is sufficient to produce a marked contrast between BrE and the two Southern Hemisphere varieties which proved significant at the 1% level in a chi-square test The term *colonial lag* thus appropriately describes the relation between BrE and the two younger colonial varieties, which exhibit a greater conservatism. The older colonial variety, American English, is the most innovative.

In addition to this more or less superficial quantitative analysis, it is possible to focus on possible functional differences. The regular and the irregular form of the verbs are not necessarily functionally equivalent. Quirk et al. (1985: 106), for instance, claim that the irregular forms of *burn* and *learn* are used more frequently as past participles than as preterite forms. The past participle, in turn, may function as both a verb and an adjective. Data obtained from a corpus of newspaper language indicate that the irregular participle is predominantly used with adjectival function in AmE but more frequently as a verb in BrE and NZE, as the following figures show (for raw frequencies, see Hundt 1998: 31):

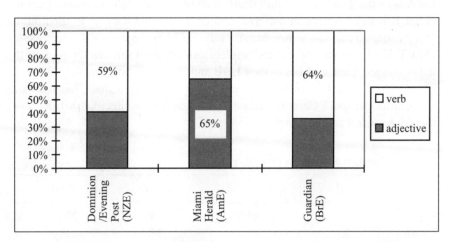

Figure 1.   Functional analysis of *burnt*

Regional differences have also been observed regarding the use of *prove*. But in this case the irregular past participle *proven* is more typical of AmE. Corpus

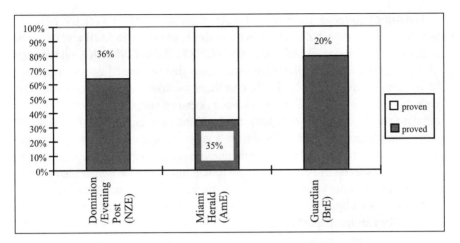

Figure 2   Proved vs. *proven*

data (Figure 2) again suggest that NZE takes an intermediate position between BrE and AmE in the use of the past participles *proved* and *proven*.

A close look at the functions of *proven* shows that it is used significantly more frequently as a verb in the *Dominion/Evening Post* (66 occurrences/59%) than in the *Guardian* (38 occurrences/34%). A comparison of the WCNZE with FLOB confirms that *proven* is relatively more frequent in NZE than in BrE: the New Zealand corpus yields 15 occurrences of *proven* and 32 of the participle *proved*; FLOB contains only 8 instances of *proven* but 50 examples of the regular participle *proved*. Data from spoken New Zealand corpora show that *proven* is not used more frequently in spoken NZE. The WCSNZE contains approximately 1 million words, too, but it yielded only 3 occurrences of *proven* and 11 occurrences of the regular participle. Similarly, the Canterbury Corpus contains approximately 900,000 words of spoken New Zealand English, with 3 examples of *proven*, and 12 examples of *proved*. The variable is thus relatively *in*frequent in spoken NZE. As far as functional differences are concerned, data from two elicitation experiments (Bauer 1987 and 1989c) indicate that there might be a cline of irregularity in NZE: active past participles are more often regular than passive participles, and that passive participles, in turn, are more often regular than participles in attributive position. In principle, this also holds for the material collected from the *Dominion* and *Evening Post*. Of the 111 instances of *proven*, 45 were examples of the attributive use, 35 were active participles and 31 passive participles. But taken together, active and passive participles outnumbered the cases in which *proven* was used attributively.

The use of *gotten* as the past participle of *get* seems to be a relatively recent innovation in spoken NZE. There is no example of *gotten* in LOB and only one each in the FLOB corpus, ACE and the WCNZE. Bauer (1987: 46), on the basis of the evidence from an elicitation test, claims that the use of *gotten* appears to be a recent innovation in NZE. He considers it a likely example of AmE influence (Bauer 1994: 418). Corpus evidence does not support the view that the irregular form is part of the (written) standard language use in New Zealand. The only example from the WCNZE is from a very colloquial dialogue passage of a novel. Of the 8 examples from the *Dominion* and *Evening Post*, 5 are quotations of the direct speech of Americans. The remaining 3 uses of *gotten* also support the view that it is not yet part of the core grammar of NZE: one (in a letter to the editor) was used by a Maori writer, the second occurred in a quotation of direct speech from an Irish speaker, and the third was used by a New Zealander – the topic was Reggae music – who had "[...] just returned from two years in London [...]" (*Dominion*, 26/1/1995: 20). Preliminary evidence that *gotten* might be more frequent in Maori than in Pakeha speech comes from the spontaneous conversations in the spoken New Zealand corpus (a Pakeha is a New Zealander of European decent): of the 8 occurrences, 7 were uttered by Maori speakers, most of them in the age-group 20–25 years. The data from this corpus also suggest that the irregular variant is not used more frequently in spoken than in written NZE. The acceptability ratings Bauer (1987a) obtained in his pilot test may have been caused by two factors: first, informants were asked to rate sentences that had allegedly been produced by non-native speakers of English, a task in which obvious Americanisms are more likely to be left uncorrected even if the respondents would not use them themselves; second, the subjects were undergraduate students at Victoria University, Wellington, and Bauer (1987: 49) himself allows for possible influence of the age factor on the results for *gotten*. Quinn (1995: 152–154) also obtained high acceptability ratings in a survey among high school students in the South Island. These high acceptability ratings may coincide with an increase in frequency of the verb form. The Canterbury Corpus, recorded more recently than the spoken New Zealand Corpus, contains 14 instances of *gotten*, none of which appear particularly marked. Examples are given below.

(1)   *and then I caught two sharks and no one else had **gotten** anything but then the big red cod was pulled in by Alan* (1994JP)

(2)   *you know we got our friendship's **gotten** stronger and stronger and stronger* (1999IK)

(3)   *one straight to Univer- ah straight to Polytech out of school and done a journalism course which had **gotten** me a job straight in the industry* (1998HC)

2.2.   Noun morphology

An interesting feature of variation between national varieties of English in the noun phrase is that between the *s*- and the *of*-genitive. Prototypical nouns, i.e. conscious, volitionally acting, animate creatures like *John* or *the dog*, are more likely to occur with the *s*-genitive than things or more abstract entities. The semantic restrictions on the use of the *s*-genitive developed only after the *of*-phrase construction started to be used as an alternative pattern. An interesting, more recent development is the weakening of the semantic restrictions, a trend in which AmE is apparently more advanced than BrE. Corpus evidence from the press sections of the corpora (Table 2) shows that the overall frequency of *s*-genitives in both the WCNZE and the ACE is considerably lower than in FLOB and Frown. This suggests that the two Southern Hemisphere variet-ies may be lagging behind in the development towards a greater use of the inflected genitive.

Table 2.   The *s*-genitive in four varieties of English – absolute (#) and relative (%) frequency

	WCNZE		LOB		FLOB	
	#	%	#	%	#	%
personal names	364	27	443	38	692	40
personal nouns	259	19	259	22	245	14
collective nouns	289	21	175	15	311	18
(higher) animals	12	1	5	0.4	9	0.5
geograph. nouns	238	18	159	14	286	16
temporal nouns	110	8	80	7	120	7
other nouns	76	6	38	3	79	4.5
Total	1348	100	1159	99.4	1742	100

	ACE		Brown		Frown	
	#	%	#	%	#	%
personal names	433	31	466	37	687	38
personal nouns	257	18	238	19	281	16
collective nouns	233	17	191	15	280	16
(higher) animals	6	0.4	6	0.5	1	0
geograph. nouns	295	21	207	16	313	17
temporal nouns	87	6	83	6.5	85	5
other nouns	78	6	74	6	145	8
Total	1389	99.4	1265	100	1792	100

That diachronic change, on the whole, is likely to be more important than re-gional differences in the use of inflected genitives can be shown in a com-parison of the press sections of LOB and Brown with their 1990s counterparts: more significant differences can be found between LOB and FLOB or Brown and Frown than between LOB and Brown or FLOB and Frown. The most strik-ing regional difference concerns the category 'other nouns'. The press section of Brown contains significantly more *s*-genitives with nouns from this cat-egory than the press section of LOB. This difference also exists between Frown and FLOB. Furthermore, a comparison of WCNZE and ACE with Frown also demonstrates that the American corpus contains significantly more inflected genitives with 'other nouns' than the corpora of the two Southern Hemisphere varieties. The obvious conclusion is that AmE is leading the change towards a greater use of inflected genitives with non-prototypical nouns. The younger colonial varieties are closer to BrE in this respect than to AmE. Future studies will probably confirm that journalistic texts take the lead in the increasing use of the *s*-genitive. Preliminary evidence for this hypothesis comes from a com-parison of the press sections with subcorpora of nonfictional writing tailored to match the press sections in size (Hundt 1997: 139). A growing use of *s*-geni-tives was also observed in the nonfictional sections, both in BrE and AmE, but the overall frequency of *s*-genitives in the 1990s nonfictional sub-corpora had not quite reached the level observed for the 1960s press sections in both BrE and AmE.

3.   Syntax

Syntactic variation in national varieties of English spans a fairly wide field, covering aspectual differences, mood, the use of auxiliaries, *do*-support in ne-gation, relativization patterns, agreement with collective nouns, noun-phrase structure and voice. We will look at these in turn.

3.1.   Aspect

Historically, the systematic distinction between past and perfect is a fairly recent development in English. It had not been grammaticalised in BrE when the first settlers arrived in America. Its scarcity in AmE has therefore been interpreted as an aspect of colonial lag. As New Zealand was settled after the grammaticalisation of the present perfect we would expect usage to resemble BrE rather than AmE. A detailed analysis of all occurrences of *have* in the corpora would be necessary to verify hypotheses on differences between national varieties. Instead, a microscopic approach was chosen: three temporal adverbials were chosen for a closer analysis (*yet*, *since* and *just*) which are said to vary as to their co-occurrence with either the simple past or the present perfect. AmE is said to favour the simple past with these adverbials. Corpus data, however, reveal that the perfective aspect is still preferred with *yet* and *since* in all national varieties of English. The use of nonperfective forms can mostly be ascribed to one of the exceptions attested in Quirk et al. (1985: 1016–1017), such as the use of *it* + *be* + a time expression or references to situations distanced in past time. Aspectual variation with *yet* and *since* therefore seems to be a case of stable (non-regional) variation rather than ongoing syntactic change. Corpus data on *just* are not conclusive as there are only between 10 and 18 instances in each corpus with possible variation of preterite or perfective verb forms. The only cases where *just* collocates with the simple past are from Frown. The New Zealand material does not provide evidence of this type of variation. The perfective appears to be the preferred aspect in formal (written) standard varieties of English with the temporal adverbials *yet*, *since* and *just*. However, *just* seems to be on the verge of becoming acceptable with the simple past or 'colloquial preterite' in the reporting style of American newspapers. AmE probably has preserved a certain amount of variation in the spoken language (colonial lag) from where it is now reintroduced into the written medium (colonial innovation). BrE, NZE and AusE can be described as being more advanced in the grammaticalization of the opposition between the simple past and the present perfect.

Bauer (1987, 1989a) claims that in NZE a reverse development can be observed, i.e. the generalisation of the present perfect to simple-past-contexts as in *I haven't talked to him last week*. There is some evidence that this change is not only happening in NZE. Trudgill (1984: 42) claims that there is an increase in the usage of such sentences as *I've seen him last year* or *He's done it two days ago* in Southern BrE. Interestingly, Bauer's examples are all from the news programme of the prestigious news station *Radio New Zealand*. Even though they were collected from spoken texts, they do not appear to be the result of spoken replannings, e.g. afterthoughts of the type *I have seen him yesterday, in fact*, as the following example illustrates (quoted from Bauer 1989a: 71):

(4)　　*Sanctions have been imposed by the UN thirteen years ago.* (Radio New Zealand news, 12/79)

This innovation does not seem to have made it into written usage: the New Zealand corpus does not give evidence of *yesterday* being used with the present perfect. Even in the spoken New Zealand corpus, *yesterday* and the present perfect co-occur only once (in a judge's summation). But the example does not illustrate a generalisation of the present perfect to past contexts:

(5)   *now the second point is that you must come please er to your er*
       verdict solely on the evidence which you have heard yesterday and
       today (MUJ009)

Bauer (1994: 401) thus rightly includes the generalisation of the present perfect to simple-past contexts among the non-standard features of NZE grammar.

Mair and Hundt (1995: 114, 121–122) have shown that in a comparison of progressive forms in LOB, FLOB, Brown and Frown, the diachronic factor is more important than the synchronic one: significant differences in the overall frequency of progressive forms were found between LOB and FLOB and Brown and Frown but not between LOB and Brown or FLOB and Frown. It is therefore not surprising that the differences between the WCNZE, LOB and Brown and between ACE, LOB and Brown also proved significant, while there were no significant differences between the number of progressives in the WCNZE and ACE. What is surprising, though, is that the differences between the WCNZE and ACE on the one hand and Frown on the other did prove significant. (The figures are based on the analysis of the press sections, only.)

Table 3.   Progressive forms – Overall frequencies

WCNZE	LOB	Brown
802	606	593
ACE	FLOB	Frown
789	716	663

The two Southern Hemisphere varieties thus appear to be more advanced in the change towards a more frequent use of progressives than AmE. BrE takes an intermediate position between the younger colonial varieties (NZE and AusE) and AmE. It is important to bear in mind that this interpretation is based on the assumption that the analysis of other relevant parameters (e.g. the finite-verb/non-finite verb ratio) would produce comparable results for all corpora. This assumption has recently been proved to hold true (Mair et al. 2002).

Both the WCNZE and ACE contain examples of stative verbs like *think, hear, feel* in the progressive, but these uses are neither new nor frequent enough to explain the difference between the Southern Hemisphere varieties and AmE. The same applies to other uses discussed in Mair and Hundt (1995). The ACE, for instance, contains a nice example of *always* followed by a progressive without a negative emotional undertone, a use which is likely to have contributed to the weakening of the restrictions on the use of progressives (see Mair and Hundt 1995: 119):

(6)   *I think that being a mother is also very sensuous. You're always being touched and cuddled. You enjoy that intimacy.* (ACE, A14 107–108)

Further studies will therefore have to show whether the difference between NZE and AusE on the one hand and AmE on the other is accidental or not.

Kuiper (1990: 31) claims that in NZE, the progressive aspect often combines with future time. Corpus data on the use of *will* + *be* *ing and *will* + verb (see Hundt 1998: 77) seem to confirm Kuiper's hypothesis as the press section of the WCNZE contains significantly more future progressives than Brown, Frown and ACE. But this is a trait which NZE appears to share with BrE. Furthermore, the more frequent use of the future progressive does not go hand in hand with a less frequent use of the 'unmarked' future. Additional evidence is needed to verify that both NZE and BrE differ from other varieties of English in their use of the future progressive.

3.2.   Mood

In subordinate clauses after expressions of demand, recommendation, intention etc., AmE is generally said to prefer the mandative subjunctive, e.g. *I propose that he talk*. This usage is considered formal in BrE, where a periphrastic construction with the modal auxiliary *should* followed by an infinitive is more common. Corpus evidence shows that AmE is leading world English in a revival of the mandative subjunctive. NZE and AusE are more advanced in their use of the subjunctive form than BrE, as the following figure shows:

With all this evidence of AmE providing the model for other varieties of World English, we should not forget that there is also a certain amount of overlap in features not found in AmE. The indicative in subordinate clauses after suasive verbs, nouns and adjectives is a case in point. This is a feature that NZE shares with BrE, as the following examples from FLOB and the WCNZE show:

(7)   *Holmfirth Police Community Forum is now writing to the Tory MP to complain at his lack of support and request he attends the next meeting of the forum* [...]. (FLOB, A30 231)

(8)   *I recommend that this meeting passes a motion tonight commissioning me to travel to Wellington* [...]. (WCNZE, K59 161)

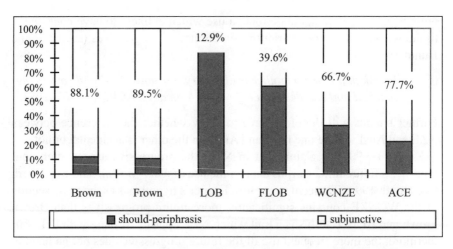

Figure 3.   Mandative subjunctive vs. *should*-periphrasis in four varieties of English

3.3.   Auxiliaries

The avoidance of *shall* is a feature which is said to distinguish NZE, AusE and AmE from BrE. But NZE allegedly resembles Scottish English (ScE) in taking the avoidance one step further: *will* is apparently used instead of *shall* with first-person pronouns in questions to express offers or suggestions as in *Will I close the window?* Table 4 summarizes the corpus data on the use of *shall* and *will* (the negated forms *shan't* and *won't* are included in the figures):

Table 4.   *Shall* and *will* (press sections only)

	WCNZE	ACE	LOB	FLOB	Brown	Frown
shall	2	5	27	20	26	8
will	680	656	625	668	681	596

Corpus data confirm the view that NZE is even more advanced in avoiding *shall* than AmE and AusE. The comparison of the press section of the WCNZE with those of LOB, FLOB and Brown produced significant results; the differences between the WCNZE, Frown and ACE, on the other hand, are not significant. That *shall* is used rather sparingly not only in NZE but also in AmE and AusE is confirmed in a comparison of the whole WCNZE with the other corpora: the New Zealand corpus contains only 143 instances of *shall*. Even though *shall* has decreased significantly from 348 in LOB to only 200 in FLOB, the difference between the WCNZE and the more recent British corpus is still significant. In the 1960s, *shall* was still fairly frequent in AmE, as the 267 instances in Brown indicate, but in the Frown corpus this figure has decreased to 150. In AusE, it is used even more sparingly (the ACE corpus yields a mere 85 instances of *shall*).

The use of *will* with first-person pronouns in questions expressing offers or suggestions is far from frequent in the WCNZE: there is only one example in an informal context (narrative dialogue): *"Babe, will I ring us a taxi and take you to the doctor?"* (K32 145). *Shall*, on the other hand, is used in 11 instances with the first person to express an offer or suggestion. The use of *will* in this context thus appears to be informal in NZE. Data from the spoken corpus of NZE, however, do not support the hypothesis that *will* is used more frequently with first-person pronouns to express offers or suggestions in informal spoken texts. The corpus does not contain a single example of this pattern. Despite this evidence, Trudgill and Hannah still list this pattern as one of the few grammatical New Zealandisms in the most recent edition of *International English* (2002: 25). Corpus data clearly show that the use of *will* with first-person subjects in questions expressing offers or suggestions is not part of standard NZE usage. It may be typical of Southland English, a regional variety strongly influenced by ScE (see section 5).

An aspect which is discussed both in the context of differences between national standards and ongoing syntactic change is the use of the modal semi-auxiliary *have to* and the modal idiom *have got to*. The data from the press sections for both modal expressions are summarized in Table 5. *Have got to* did not occur frequently enough to be treated separately. Table 5 also includes occurrences of the modal idiom where *have* is omitted.

Table 5. Have (got) to

	WCNZE	**LOB**	**FLOB**	**Brown**	**Frown**	**ACE**
Present	70	59	78	41	70	55
Past	44	29	38	25	22	38
pres.perf.	5	9	6	2	3	3
past perf.	1	–	1	–	–	–
Future	17	8	26	12	20	18
Would	10	19	12	12	15	13
Modal	3	6	8	3	7	5
inf.	2	–	3	2	–	–
Total	152	130	172	97	137	132

The increasing use of *have (got) to* is clearly an example of ongoing change in which BrE is most advanced, followed by NZE with both AmE and AusE lagging behind. That this is not a text-type specific development has been shown with additional data from nonfictional subcorpora (Hundt 1997: 144). The usage is extremely common in spontaneous speech, as evidenced by high frequency counts in the Canterbury Corpus (1310 examples of *have to*, 161 of *have got to*).

Table 5 includes instances where the auxiliary is omitted. This omission is said to be very informal or non-standard in written English. The few cases in which the auxiliary is deleted in the corpora seem to confirm this; it is only deleted in quotations of direct speech, in titles or clearly informal contexts. See also section 4.1. for discussion of *have*-drop patterns in informal speech.

The marginal modal auxiliaries *dare* and *need* have attracted comments from linguists both in terms of regional variation and diachronic change. Comments on regional differences between BrE and AmE suggest that the development from a modal auxiliary towards a full lexical verb is more advanced in transatlantic English: *dare* and *need* as auxiliaries are rarer in AmE than in BrE (cf. Trudgill and Hannah 2002: 60). Bauer (1989b: 8) observed that New Zealand informants also showed a preference for mixed constructions with *dare*. He also found that NZE resembled AmE in the preference for *do*-support (1989b: 14). The auxiliary pattern, however, did not prove to be "recessive", which in Bauer's opinion suggests that in the use of these auxiliaries NZE is closer to BrE than to AmE. Corpus data, while confirming the trend towards a greater use of the full-verb pattern, surprisingly do not reveal regional differences in the use of this variable. Table 6 is based on the analysis of all occurrences of *need* followed by an infinitive in the complete Brown, LOB, FLOB and Frown corpora and the WCNZE. Occurrences with emphatic *do* in affirmative contexts are not included. Blends of the auxiliary and full verb construction were also not included in Table 6.

Table 6.   Need

	full-verb construction			auxiliary construction		
	affirmative	**negative**	**question**	**affirmative**	**negative**	**question**
Brown	53	12	1	4	27	1
Frown	135	18	-	7	31	-
LOB	45	8	-	12	61	-
FLOB	163	16	1	7	28	5
WCNZE	171	13	-	6	24	1

The trend towards the full-verb pattern is even more pronounced in spoken data. A search for *need* in non-assertive contexts in the WCSNZE yielded 38 occurrences of the full-verb pattern (33 negative declarative sentences and five questions) but only one auxiliary pattern.

Surprisingly, the corpus data provide evidence that the auxiliary pattern is not restricted to non-assertive contexts, as Quirk et al. (1985: 138) claim. The following examples show that the modal use of *need* also occurs in genuinely affirmative contexts:

(9)   *The louder the noise, the shorter daily exposure need be before this occurs.* (WCNZE, F31 42)

The material studied also yielded a few examples of blends between the auxiliary and the full-verb construction of *need*. An example from the New Zealand newspaper *Evening Post* illustrates this pattern:

(10)   *Computer security problems can cost small businesses more proportionally than big businesses, because a small business security breach needs only be a small problem while a big business breach has to be a whopper to have the same impact.* (*Evening Post* 3/12/1994: 28)

The data on *dare* from the one-million-word corpora are too meagre to verify any hypotheses on diachronic change or regional variation, as Table 7 shows:

Table 7.   Dare

	auxiliary	blend	main verb	Total
Brown	4	9	14	27
Frown	8	8	13	29
LOB	9	14	9	32
FLOB	8	11	8	27
WCNZE	4	7	8	19

A possible conclusion based on this table would be that the auxiliary pattern is less frequent in NZE than in BrE, but this may well have to be attributed to the slightly lower overall frequency of *dare* + infinitive in the WCNZE. The data on *dare* from these corpora are therefore far from conclusive. Further evidence from larger newspaper corpora was collected for *dare*. The *Dominion* and *Evening Post* yielded only 51 occurrences of the verb *dare*. Of these, 18 were examples of the main-verb construction, 23 were pure auxiliary constructions and 10 were blends. For the comparison with BrE and AmE, samples of the same size were selected from the *Guardian* (1991) and *Miami Herald* (1992). On the basis of this evidence, NZE appears to be closer to BrE than to AmE: the sample from the *Guardian* yielded 20 occurrences of the main-verb construction, 19 auxiliary patterns and 12 blends. The *Miami Herald* sample, on the other hand, confirmed that in AmE the auxiliary pattern is used far less frequently (6 occurrences) while blends are almost as frequent as main-verb constructions (22 and 23 instances, respectively). Blends in the New Zealand sample were significantly less frequent than in the American sample. No significant differences were found in a comparison of the New Zealand with the British newspaper material. This suggests that usage patterns of *dare* in NZE are more or less the same as in BrE. AmE is the variety which is most advanced in the change towards the lexical verb pattern.

For the marginal modal *ought (to)*, corpus data confirm that there is no regional difference at all (see Hundt 1998: 66). *To*-deletion is rare but attested in affirmative contexts for both NZE and AmE, despite the fact that it is described as "unacceptable" in Quirk et al. (1985: 140). Even though examples of *to*-less constructions with affirmative *ought* are still rare, they provide some evidence of a development towards the central modal auxiliary pattern:

(11)   *And as such he ought be carrying out our will.* (*Evening Post*, 22/11/1994: 4)

(12)   *A house with a formal living room, formal dining room, casual family room and breakfast nook and small, paneled library with a fireplace and shutters ought do the trick.* (*Miami Herald*, 18/12/1992)

As with *ought (to)*, corpus evidence on *used to* in non-affirmative contexts is extremely scarce. In the WCNZE, the marginal modal occurs 129 times. The only relevant instance of negation comes from the fiction section and illustrates the main verb pattern:

(13)   *Tennis isn't all that strong on the Shore – or it didn't used to be.* (K81 174)

Data from the spoken New Zealand corpus also provide some evidence of the main verb pattern rather than the auxiliary pattern with *used to*: *do*-support is used in all four examples of non-affirmative *used to* (all examples are from the spontaneous conversations-section of the corpus). NZE does not show a preference for contracted negations of *used to*. The absence of regional variation thus probably holds even more strongly for *used to*.

3.4.   Negation

Negation patterns are not only of interest with respect to auxiliary usage but also in the context of full verb *have* and the mandative subjunctive. We look at these in turn.

The stative use of *have* meaning 'possess' varies in negations and interrogatives both diachronically and regionally. Simple *have* is the formal construction in BrE with the more common alternative *have got*. AmE is said to prefer *do*-support. In the dynamic senses of the full verb (i.e. 'receive', 'take', 'experience') both BrE and AmE normally have *do*-support. Bauer's (1989a: 80) results on the stative use of *have* suggest that in NZE, both *have got* and *do*-periphrasis are common variants of simple *have* with a slight preference for *do*-support. Corpus evidence on the stative and dynamic uses of *have* in negations and interrogatives are summarized in the following table (from Hundt 1998: 56):

Table 8.   Full verb *have* in negations and interrogatives (press sections only)

	WCNZE	ACE	LOB	FLOB	Brown	Frown
simple *have*	6	1	9	2	1	1
do-support	24	22	5	14	7	25
have got	2	1	6	4	–	2
Total	32	24	20	20	8	28

Even though the difference in the total number of lexical *have* in negations and interrogatives makes a comparison difficult, a few interesting trends can be gleaned from the corpus data. *Do*-support has become the dominant pattern in BrE. *Have got* does not appear to be a real alternative in any of the recently compiled press sections.

The relatively high frequency of simple *have* in the WCNZE can easily be explained. Two instances are quotations from the Bible, which contains formal and archaic language. Of the remaining four examples, two are contracted negations. The informal character of contractions thus seems to counteract the formal stylistic connotations associated with simple *have*:

(14)   *Those of us who haven't much faith in public education* [...]. (WCNZE, A42 82)

Furthermore, corpus data from the whole WCNZE confirm that *do*-support is clearly the favoured construction in negatives and interrogatives of the full verb *have* in NZE:

Table 9.   Full verb *have* in interrogatives and negations in the WCNZE

	press	non-fiction	fiction	Total
simple *have*	6	5	8	19 (12.2%)
do-support	24	39	43	106 (67.9%)
have got	2	4	25	31 (19.9%)
Total	32	48	76	156 (100%)

The relatively high frequency of *have got* in fictional texts suggests that *have got* is felt to be very informal. It is not surprising, therefore, that 14 instances of *have got* co-occur with contractions (either of the negation particle or *have*), and five with non-standard features such as *have*-deletion (four occurrences) and *ain't* (one example); all 25 instances of *have got* are used in fictional dialogue or interior monologue, not in descriptive passages. *Have got* thus seems to be unusual in formal written NZE. Additional evidence that it is not preferred to *do*-support in informal contexts, either, comes from the spoken New Zealand corpus. A search for negated forms of the full verb *have* in the spontaneous dialogue section of the corpus (approximately half a million words) yielded 162 occurrences with *do*-support but only 105 with *got*. The search was limited to *not*-negation and those cases where no more than two other elements intervened between the forms of *have* and *do/got*. A more refined search may produce slightly different results but is likely to confirm the general outcome, i.e. that negation of full verb *have* with *got* is not preferred to *do*-support in informal NZE.

Above, we saw that AmE provides the model for World English in the revival of the mandative subjunctive. Interestingly, other varieties of English also seem to be following AmE in terms of negation patterns in mandative sentences. AmE has preserved an old negation pattern in which the negative particle *not* simply precedes the subjunctive, as in *I suggest that he not be suspended*. This option is also available in NZE, as the following example from *The Dominion* shows:

(15)   *It is **important that** the college **not be seen** to be a party to a cover-up.*
       (*The Dominion*, 29/12/1994: 9)

This feature is one that NZE shares with BrE and with its Australian cousin. Peters (personal communication) found two cases of negated subjunctives in the ACE. Both were examples of negated passive subjunctives.

3.5.   Relativization

In a systematic comparison of the New Zealand corpora with LOB, Brown and Flob, Sigley (1997: 477) found that NZE patterned almost identically with BrE in relativizer strategies; AmE turned out to be the divergent variety in favouring relative *that* in impersonal subject relative clauses.

3.6.   Agreement

In English, collective nouns like *team* or *government* can, in principle, be used with both singular and plural concord marking on verbs or pronouns. What makes this dual concord interesting for a description of NZE syntax is the regional variation in the preference for concord types: BrE speakers are said to have a choice between singular and plural concord whereas speakers of AmE are generally believed to treat collective nouns as singular. Singular concord, overall, is more likely to occur with verbs than with pronouns. This is probably linked to the usual proximity of verbal concord and the possibility of pronominal concord to extend over sentence boundaries. The greater probability of plural pronouns with (singular) collective nouns, even in AmE, often results in mixed concord if both verb and pronoun occur: *The committee **has** not yet decided how **they** should react to the Governor's letter*. Ongoing linguistic change in BrE towards a greater use of singular concord makes the matter even more complex.

The evidence for this variable is based on sets of 100 occurrences of both verbal and pronominal concord with five nouns sampled from *The Dominion* and *Evening Post*, the *Guardian* and the *Miami Herald*. Evidence for AusE (from the 1995 *Sydney Morning Herald, SMH*) comes from a study by Levin (2001: 167). The nouns were chosen to represent three groups with different concord patterns: (a) a tendency towards singular or grammatical concord (*government* and *committee*), (b) variation between singular and plural concord in BrE (*team* and *family*) and (c) preference for plural or notional concord in BrE (*police*).

Table 10.   Verbal and pronominal concord (singular : pluial)

VERBAL	DOM/EVP		SMH		Guardian		Miami Herald	
government	100	: 0	100	: 0	100	: 0	100	: 0
committee	99	: 1	95	: 5	97	: 3	100	: 0
team	93	: 7	93	: 7	62	: 38	98	: 2
family	59	: 41	84	: 16	72	: 28	97	: 3
police	1	: 99	–		1	: 99	0	: 100

Table 10. (continued)   Verbal and pronominal concord (singular : plural)

PRONOMINAL	DOM/EVP	SMH	Guardian	Miami Herald
government	97 : 3	93 : 7	96 : 4	95 : 5
committee	94 : 6	85 : 15	92 : 8	91 : 9
team	64 : 36	60 : 40	23 : 77	65 : 35
family	29 : 71	29 : 61	26 : 74	18 : 82
police	0 : 100	–	3 : 97	1 : 99

With the exception of *police*, the figures for verbal concord confirm the view that AmE nearly always has the singular, even with nouns like *team* and *family*. In BrE, these nouns still pattern quite frequently with the plural. NZE is very similar to AmE in the use of singular verbal concord with *team*. With the noun *family*, however, speakers of NZE still use plural verbal concord frequently, a preference also found in BrE. AusE patterns closely to both NZE and BrE but has a higher proportion of singular verbal concord with *family*. When it comes to pronominal concord, however, all varieties prefer plural pronouns over singular concord with *family*.

If the general development is one from notional towards grammatical verbal concord (see Levin: 2001: 36–39 and 86–87), NZE could be seen as more advanced in this development than BrE but not quite as advanced as AmE. AusE is close to AmE in that it prefers singular verbal concord with *family*. The concord patterns for the other nouns are closer to the distribution found in BrE. A more comprehensive study based on a larger number of nouns will have to verify whether this is actually the case. Levin (2001: 159), on the basis of a larger set of nouns, found that AusE was more innovative than BrE but lagging behind AmE in the general shift towards more singular concord. The collective noun *police* shows that grammatical concord may also be of the plural-type.

The only statistically significant regional difference in pronominal concord patterns is that for *team*: this collective noun shows a clear preference for plural pronominal concord in BrE, but not in NZE or AmE. The most interesting result emerging from a comparison of verbal and pronominal concord is that AmE, while generally showing a clear tendency towards singular concord with verbs, has (with the exception of *team*) the highest figures for plural pronominal concord. It therefore does not come as a surprise that American data show the highest incidence of mixed concord (28), followed by the British (18) and New Zealand samples (7). This is especially surprising because the NZE sample, on the whole, shows a greater tendency towards singular verbal concord than BrE. The reason why mixed concord occurred less frequently in the NZE sample may be that we are dealing with edited material. It would be interesting to see whether on the basis of comparable spoken corpora New Zealanders would be found to use less or as much mixed concord as American speakers.

In sum, variable verbal concord does not seem to be deeply rooted in the grammatical system. Pronominal concord, on the other hand, is still much more variable. This is especially the case with nouns like *family* and *team*, for which singular grammatical concord has not become an almost absolute rule yet. But the fact that even singular collective nouns like *government* and *committee* occasionally occur with plural pronouns shows that pronominal concord may turn out to be a stronghold for notional concord in the long run. Future studies will have to show whether this holds even more for unedited spoken language.

3.7. Complementation

As pointed out in the introduction, differences among national varieties of English often occur at the interface of grammar and the lexicon. Bauer (1989c: 15–16), for instance, found that his New Zealand informants preferred *in the weekend* over *at* or *on the weekend*.

National varieties of English differ in their choice of preposition following *different*. Historically, *to* is the oldest one, followed by *from* and *than*. Nevertheless, *from* is the variant recommended in most usage guides; *different to* has a long tradition of being attacked by purists as 'illogical' (on the grounds that *to* is not used after the verb *to differ*). *Different than* is said to be more acceptable in AmE, where it can even be used to introduce a noun phrase rather than a clause (e.g. *My parents are very different than yours*). In BrE, it is recommended as a stylistically preferable choice to *different from that which*.

Table 11. Prepositions used after *different*

	WCNZE	ACE	LOB	Brown	FLOB	Frown	ACE
from	47	32	34	39	52	42	32
to	8	10	7	0	9	0	10
than	2	0	1	6	0	5	0

The figures confirm intuitions about regional differences in the use of prepositions after *different*. Further evidence from larger newspaper corpora (Hundt 1998: 107–108) supports the trend indicated in Table 11: *different from* is the preferred variant in all three varieties, *different than* is avoided in both BrE and NZE. Interestingly, the American variant with *than* is also avoided in spoken

NZE and BrE. In terms of language history we may therefore be witnessing a genuinely divergent development: the (almost) complete avoidance of *different than* in BrE and NZE which appears to be firmly rooted in AmE. NZE and AusE both share the variant *different to* with BrE, an option that seems to be avoided in AmE. Interestingly, the Canterbury Corpus of spoken English has slightly more tokens of *different to* (23) than *different from* (17). Some individual speakers contribute tokens to both counts, as illustrated by the following two examples, both produced by the same speaker.

(16)   *oh so man yes it's very **different to** what it is today with all the computers and a very different . style of . work* (1994JT)

(17)   *I was speaking just the other day to a man who came from . North of Auckland and he had a very marked accent and yet he's a born and bred New Zealander . and was very **different from** the way that we speak in the South Island* (1994JT)

The avoidance of *different than* is also evident in the Canterbury Corpus – with just 4 examples.

In BrE, the verbs *protest* and *appeal* both typically take prepositional objects as their complements. In AmE, both verbs can be used without the preposition. They are mentioned in the context of possible American influence on NZE grammar (cf. Gordon and Deverson 1985). Bauer (1994: 418) is careful about claims that there is direct influence from AmE; he says the innovative form in NZE often coincides with the AmE form. Evidence from standard one-million-word corpora suggests that *protest* without a preposition might be more frequent in NZE than in BrE (Hundt 1998: 110). But the figures from these corpora are too small to draw any definite conclusions. Additional data from newspapers indicate that NZE uses the variant without the preposition more often than BrE but not quite as frequently as AmE. Interestingly, most of the occurrences of *protest* without a preposition are from the *Evening Post* and only few from the *Dominion*. Together with information from the style-sheets of the two newspapers, this distribution indicates that the variable might be socially stratified in NZE: the style sheet of the *Dominion* proscribes the use of *protest* and *appeal* without a preposition, while that of the *Evening Post* does not comment on the usage of these verbs.

Corpus data for the verb *appeal* with or without *against* were even more extreme than those for the complementation patterns of *protest*. There was not a single instance of *appeal against* in the whole year of the *Miami Herald* investigated. Out of the 100 instances of *appeal* from the *Guardian*, on the other hand, only one was without *against*. Again, the data from the *Dominion* and *Evening Post* at first sight seem to suggest that NZE takes an intermediate position between BrE and AmE: of the 169 instances of the verb *appeal* followed by a noun phrase, 89 occurred with the preposition. Closer inspection revealed that the variant with *against* is preferred in the *Dominion*, whereas *appeal* without a preposition is the dominant pattern in the *Evening Post*.

If we bear in mind not only the general attitude towards American influences on NZE but also that language prescription and actual usage often diverge, the evidence from the New Zealand newspapers could be interpreted slightly differently: complementation patterns of *protest* and *appeal* in NZE, on the whole, might be closer to those in AmE than to BrE preferences. In this case, only a minority of conservative speakers would be trying to keep up the linguistic link with Britain. Future studies, based on less heavily edited material, will have to verify this hypothesis. Preliminary evidence from spoken New Zealand corpora suggests that *appeal* without a preposition is probably by now a well-established variant in NZE: in the three examples from the WCSNZE where variation is possible, and the two examples from the Canterbury Corpus, *appeal* is used consistently without a preposition.

Among lexico-grammatical features worth investigating in NZE, we find a usage which is likely to be typical of NZE but not of BrE or AmE: the use of *farewell* as a transitive verb (e.g. *They farewelled retiring members of staff*). Evidence from the WCNZE and the other one-million-word corpora suggests that this verb is indeed a Southern Hemisphere idiosyncrasy: there were 4 instances of transitive *farewell* in the WCNZE and one in the ACE, but none in any of the other corpora.

3.8. Noun-phrase structure

Bell (1982: 251, 255) claims that determiner deletion (e.g. *Prime Minister David Lange* instead of *the Prime Minister, David Lange*) in NZE is an example of the influence of AmE. Jucker (1992), on the other hand, is able to show the social stratification of this variable in BrE. The growing acceptability of determiner deletion in noun phrase name appositions that Bell discovered for NZE is probably not due to regional variation but could be triggered by social/stylistic factors instead.

3.9. The *get*-passive

Sussex (1982: 90) claims that *get*-passives are most frequently used in AmE, with AusE taking an intermediate position between BrE and AmE. He further states that "[...] they are more common now in Australian English than they were a decade ago." He attributes this change within AusE to the influence of AmE (see Collins and Peters, this volume). The comment on the internal change within AusE again suggests that this variable of possible regional variation is not a diachronically stable one. The question is whether AmE is really more advanced in this ongoing change than BrE, AusE and NZE. The question is also whether AmE is having an influence on other national varieties or whether we are dealing with a case of parallel but independent development.

Possible candidates for *get*-passives are all instances of *get* (i.e. *get, gets, got, gotten, getting*) followed by a past participle. In a qualitative analysis, the passive uses of *get* + past participle have to be distinguished from those where the participle functions as an adjective (as in *he got drunk*); some instances are ambiguous between a passive and an adjectival reading (e.g. *he got dressed*).

Table 12.   Get + participle – passives and related constructions in four varieties of English

	passive		adjectival	ambiguous	Total
Brown	31	42.5 %	30	12	73
Frown	64	45.7 %	57	19	140
LOB	35	38.5 %	29	27	91
FLOB	51	44.3 %	42	22	115
ACE	43	51.2 %	25	16	84
WCNZE	63	55.3 %	30	21	114

The data in Table 12 do not corroborate Sussex's hypothesis that AmE is the most advanced national variety in the spread of the *get*-passive. The results obtained from stylistically balanced one-million-word corpora do not provide evidence of significant regional differences in the use of *get*-passives. A look at the figures from Frown and FLOB suggests that the very slight gap in relative frequencies of the passive construction between Brown and LOB has almost levelled out over the last thirty years. Surprisingly, though, the New Zealand and Australian corpora yield higher relative frequencies of *get*-passive constructions than any of the other corpora if we calculate the relative frequency of *get*-passives against the overall number of constructions where a form of *get* is followed by a past participle. Alternatively, the relative frequency of *get*-passives could be obtained by using the overall number of *get*-construction as a basis. In this case, the relative frequencies in the four national varieties are all close to the 4 per cent mark:

Table 13.   *Get*-passives – relative frequency in relation to overall number of *get*-con-
structions

	get-constructions	*get*-passives	
Brown	1340	31	2.3 %
Frown	1646	64	3.9 %
LOB	1380	35	2.5 %
FLOB	1346	51	3.8 %
ACE	1058	43	4.0 %
WCNZE	1669	63	3.8 %

On the whole, then, the difference in the use of the *get*-passive is probably not so much regional as stylistic: most usage guides comment on the stylistic markedness of the *get*-passive, which is described as being informal or even colloquial. For a description of syntactic variation in national varieties of English it is important to distinguish genuine regional divergence from parallel diachronic developments.

4.   Non-standard patterns

In this section we will consider the use of some mainstream non-standard forms. This description is selective rather than exhaustive. Where possible, examples of forms discussed are given from the Canterbury Corpus of speakers born 1930–1980, collected by students at the University of Canterbury. All of the non-standard variants discussed are also attested in other varieties of English. Very little work has been conducted on non-standard patterns of syntax in New Zealand English, and so this section is relatively brief. This is not because there is a lack of morphosyntactic variation in NZE, but rather because there has been a lack of scholarly attention to such variation. The study of non-standard patterns presents special challenges, as speakers are prone to switch to more standard variants when being tape-recorded.

Early educationalists complained about the use of non-standard forms by school pupils. In 1882, for example, the Wellington school inspector Robert Lee complained about pronunciation and syntax: "Another boy said, 'Don't never go no further ner (sic) the top of the 'ill.' The language of the playground teams with such expressions. If all teachers were to join in the games with the express purpose of trying to make reformation in this matter, something might be done." (from the *Appendices to the Journal of the House of Representa-*

tives 1880–1930, short *AJHR*). The school inspectors' complaints were almost all about expressions such as *I seen it* and *He done it* and the use of *like* as a conjunction. Below is an example of a Wellington school inspector of 1915 complaining about 'get' and 'got':

> the misuse of the unfortunate words *get* and *got*. The examples of this failing: 'After dinner I got cleaned.' 'Charles 1 got executed.' 'I've got a shilling in my pocket.' 'I got to school late.' 'I've got to milk ten cows.' 'The children got tired of playing.' 'When we got to Auckland we got our luggage together and got off the train.' (*AJHR* E2ApCxii)

Brosnahan (1971: 24) also points to non-standard grammatical forms in New Zealand English: "Sequences such as *I seen it, youse kids, he would of gone*, are all forms which can be heard in what I may here term a sub-ENZE (educated NZE) dialect. Let me stress that these are usual and even appropriate forms in that dialect."

However, while it is clear that there are a range of non-standard forms in NZE, these have not been systematically studied. For most variants we are therefore able to state that they exist, but have much less evidence regarding the exact social conditioning involved.

4.1. Deletion of auxiliary *have*

Jacob (1990) and Holmes, Bell and Boyce (1991) investigate the omission of the auxiliary *have* in a range of syntactic environments. Both find that Maori speakers omit the auxiliary at greater rates than Pakeha speakers. Holmes', Bell's and Boyce's (1991) interview data show that working class speakers show more omission than middle class, and males more than females. Quinn's (1995) survey results also show an effect of socio-economic class. She finds large variation in acceptance of *have*-drop according to linguistic environment, with a high rate of acceptance for *you gotta*, and a relatively low rate of acceptance for *we got*, and *I been*.

Since *have*-drop is clearly marked (as evidenced by its lack of appearance in written language) and the contracted form *gotta* seems equally marked, it is not particularly surprising that Quinn (1995: 125) observes a clear preference for *have*-dropping with the marked form *gotta* and much lower acceptability rates for auxiliary omission with *got* and *been* in her study of grammatical variation among New Zealand teenagers. Several examples of *have*-drop from the Canterbury Corpus are given below.

(18)   *And so there's lots of potential for it to go wrong – yum – but **we gotta** make sure it goes right.* (2000WR)

(19) *We better* get some veges. (1994DA)

The variation in preterite and past participle form of irregular verbs was regularly commented on by school inspectors. In Durkin's (1972) study of 75 West Coast school children aged 10–12 the children were asked to fill in the gap in the following sentences:

(20) a. *Today I see the girl. Yesterday I ____ the girl.*
      b. *Today I do my work. Yesterday I ____ my work.*

Her results show a high degree of lexical variation. For the first sentence, only 7% of the sample used *seen*, but 32% used *done* in the second sentence (1972: 112). Some twenty years later, Quinn also tested the acceptability of preterite *seen* and *come* in the sentences:

(21) a. *I'm sure I **seen** her put her car in the garage.*
      b. *He **come** all the way up from London, just to see the soccer match.*

Of the 176 14–15-year-old students who responded, 52 fully accepted *seen* and 70 fully accepted *come* (Quinn 1995: 40). The Canterbury corpus includes examples with a relatively wide variety of verbs, including *done, seen, brung, run, come, drunk, rung.*

(22) *I basically **come** home from pony trek and I just had to take over. I **seen** what sort of state mum was in and I took over* (1995HB)

(23) *I lived in Aussie for – what was it – two months til I **run** out a money and **come** home and got a job back at North's again.* (1994DA)

A speaker from an earlier corpus held at the University of Canterbury, born 1930, comments on this usage explicitly:

(24) *we used to talk a little bit like the Maoris and we used to say "what do you think of that, eh" . um . I never . I never did say . "I seen this" I used to say "I saw this" e- and yet a lot of kids in in Rotorua did say "I seen this" and "I done that" um . and those were very common in Rotorua.*

4.2. *Yous*

Durkin (1972) reported that the plural form of *you* among West Coast school children was often *yous*. While it was corrected in school, it was regularly used outside school and by those who had left school. Bauer's (1987) questionnaire from 44 university linguistics students included the following sentence:

(25)   *I asked the children, are **yous** ready yet.*

Only six students did not change the *yous* to *you*, but given the make up of the subject group, such a result is not unexpected. Examples from the Canterbury Corpus are given below.

(26)   *um that team that beat **yous** by what was it five nil* (1999AR)

(27)   *so **yous** had to rent or something?* (2001GJ)

There is a possibility that this is an age-graded feature. Despite the fact that the feature has been attested at least since the early seventies (Durkin 1972), it is only amongst the younger speakers in the Canterbury Corpus (recorded some 20 years after Durkin's study) that *yous* is attested.

In a survey of high school students conducted by Quinn (1995), more than half of the 179 respondents accepted *yous*, and many of those who did not accept it offered an alternative such as *you guys*. *You guys* is more frequent than *yous* in the Canterbury Corpus. Examples are given below.

(28)   *so **you guys** gonna get another cat?* (2002SB)

(29)   *I mean how much do they pay **you guys**?* (2001MA)

4.3.   Negation

Ain't can be used by speakers of non-standard NZE, as illustrated by the examples below.

(30)   *They were like skinny little runts . they ordered one each and you're just like it was like you took it out and it was like ha ha have fun boys you **ain't** gonna be able to finish it.* (2002MJ)

(31)   *Which is what I suspect keeps a lot of people in Wellington cause it sure **ain't** the weather.* (1998HC)

Negative concord, also known as multiple negation, is not particularly common overall, although Jacob (1991) reports a fairly high rate of negative concord among Maori speakers, whereas there were none in her corpus of Pakeha speakers. Below we give one of the very few examples of negative concord in the Canterbury Corpus (which contains predominantly Pakeha speakers):

(32)   *it was good too . cos when you're everyone's off their faces in the cell and you're passing the joint along . an you just have a sing along and someone's singing the blues – got your tape deck blasting – choice . the screws come in and smell it . but most of the times **they don't do nothing*** (1994BS)

4.4. *Would/could/should of*

Quinn's (1995) survey results show a high level of acceptance of *of* instead of *have* following modal verbs. Relevant examples from the Canterbury Corpus are given below.

(33) but I **would of** had I waited another six months I **would of** been just over the correct age but. because I was so sweet they wanted me there. (1999SM)

(34) oh yeah that **would of** been fun (1994DB)

(35) I couldn't go back to school. and. well I **could of** there's no there's no excuse not to (2000BK)

4.5. Co-ordinated pronouns

There is a considerable amount of variation with pronoun case, particularly with co-ordinated pairs including first person pronouns (Quinn 1995, 2002), such as those illustrated below. See Quinn (2002) for extended discussion.

(36) that was a hard case eh cos **me and my mate** were at the hospital (1994BS)

(37) no wonder **her and I** look blurry eyed at school (1994HH)

(38) we were playing drinking games one night and **me and her** were the only ones left. so instantly clicked from there. (1994DA)

4.6. Adjectives

Hundt (1998) reports that monosyllable adjectives do not occur with *more* in standard NZE, nor is there evidence for double comparatives. However, Quinn (1995) found that acceptance of double comparatives among high school students ranges from about 24%–40% (depending on the adjective). There is certainly no shortage of examples of double comparatives in the Canterbury Corpus, as shown below:

(39) I prefer the A.O.G. because it's **more ragier** (1994BS)

(40) because. they ended up one class being **more brighter** than the other (1997DBR)

(41) well we were the **most luckiest** out of the lot (1996MK)

There are also examples of adjectives which would be formed with *-er* in the standard being modified by *more*:

(42)   *but your your work's **more close** than our work eh cos our work's bigger* (1994DA)

(43)   *what are we. Like **more naughty*** (1998OM)

4.7.   Singular BE with plural subjects

Hay and Schreier (no date) examine the historical evolution of subject-verb-concord in NZE. They investigate the usage of singular agreement with plural NP subjects (existentials and non-existentials) over the last 150 years. The results demonstrate that the NZE subject verb concord system has undergone considerable reorganization during this time. In the dialect contact phase of the creation of NZE, there was a consistent force towards standardization, with singular concord in both existential (e.g. *there's dogs*) and non-existential environments (e.g. *we was happy*) showing a steady decrease. This decrease continued until the end of the 19th century, when singular concord in non-existentials bottomed out – the feature is close to non-existent in 20th-century NZE. At this time, existentials apparently became dissociated from the non-existentials, and, liberated from the standardizing force, the use of singular concord in existentials began to increase. In modern spoken NZE, we find high rates of singular concord in existentials (highest among non-professional speakers, and men). Male non-professionals use more than 80% singular concord, and all groups use more than 50%. Results reported by Bell (2000) also demonstrate that singular concord in existentials tends to be more frequent among Maori speakers than Pakeha speakers.

5.   Regional variation

There is almost no work documenting regional variation in morphosyntax in New Zealand. However, Bartlett (1992) suggests some features which may be potentially unique to Southland, a part of New Zealand which was subject to more Scottish influence than elsewhere. These include:

– The use of the past participle following *needs* and *wants*, as in *the baby needs fed*.
– The use of *will* with first-person subjects in questions (*will I close the door*).

– Lack of contraction of not (e.g. *did you not?*).
– The deletion of prepositions in certain contexts (e.g. *he came out hospital*).

6.   Conclusion

The distinction of regional variation from language change is an important requirement for the description of an emerging NZE standard. As it turns out, however, this distinction is a very difficult, if not an impossible one to make. Two examples illustrating this problem are the use of *proven* and the mandative subjunctive, which have commonly been described as conservatisms typical of AmE. (Note how even these almost standard examples of synchronic regional differences in World English are closely related to diachronic aspects of language use.) Both 'Americanisms' have been gaining ground in other national varieties of English. Ongoing language change may thus lead to a dilution of previous regional differences. The difficulty in distinguishing between regional and diachronic variation is partly due to a general development within World English pointed out by Gordon and Deverson (1985: 53): the last fifty years have seen a convergence of regional varieties with the predominance of AmE variants leading to a levelling of differences. "We can refer to this trend as the *internationalisation* of English, as opposed to its (previous) *regionalisation*." (This applies mainly to the internationalisation of standard grammar. Different accents and lexical regionalisms are likely to remain obvious markers of national varieties of English.) Often, AmE is leading World English in a number of converging trends (see Figure 5). Ultimately, however, it will remain difficult to prove whether changes in one national variety are actually due to influence from another variety or whether the development simply coincides with the variants preferred in another national standard.

The other reason why it is ultimately impossible to make a clear distinction between regional variation and language change is the underlying Saussurean dichotomy of the synchronic vs. the diachronic approach to the study of language. The distinction is too strict: synchronic regional variation is just as much part of ongoing linguistic change as social or stylistic variation. In this light, synchronic 'snapshots' focusing on regional differences can be interpreted as stages in the (regional) diffusion of a change. Figure 4 illustrates some possible synchronic rankings of national varieties with respect to ongoing language change.

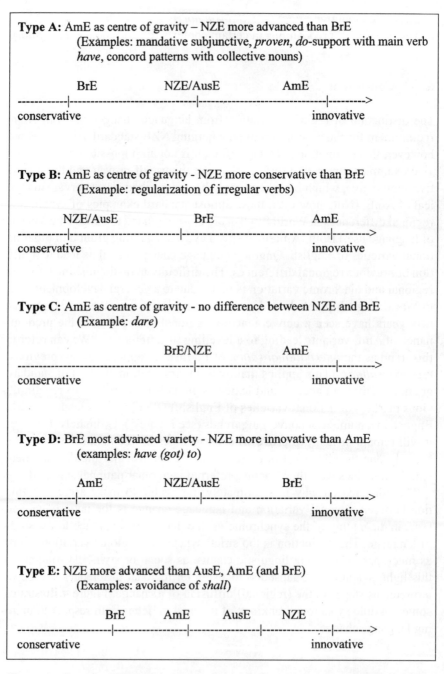

Type A: AmE as centre of gravity – NZE more advanced than BrE
(Examples: mandative subjunctive, *proven*, *do*-support with main verb *have*, concord patterns with collective nouns)

Type B: AmE as centre of gravity - NZE more conservative than BrE
(Example: regularization of irregular verbs)

Type C: AmE as centre of gravity - no difference between NZE and BrE
(Example: *dare*)

Type D: BrE most advanced variety - NZE more innovative than AmE
(examples: *have (got) to*)

Type E: NZE more advanced than AusE, AmE (and BrE)
(Examples: avoidance of *shall*)

Figure 4.   Locating NZE in relation to other varieties with respect to ongoing change

As research on morphosyntactic variation in NZE advances, we will also need to pay careful attention to the nature of the data we have available. For example, a questionnaire administered by students enrolled in a sociolinguistics course at the University of Canterbury in 2002 highlights the need to distinguish between self-report data and corpus data. Despite the fact that singular concord with existentials is the norm in the Canterbury Corpus, written sentences containing singular concord rated as low as an average of 1.35 on a small scale of 1 to 3 (where 1 = "I would never use this", and 3 = "I would use a sentence like this in both formal and informal contexts"). Despite the extremely frequent use of singular concord with *there* in spoken English, self-report data suggests that there is a certain level of stigma associated with the construction. This indicates that, for some of the other constructions discussed above, the questionnaire data reported may systematically under-estimate the actual degree of use.

Elicitation tests may provide useful supplementary data to the analysis of corpora, not least because of the possibility of targeting phenomena. A good example would be question tags after *used to*, which are extremely infrequent in natural (written) language. But natural language use may be quite different from the results obtained in a relatively artificial test situation. It is therefore not surprising that we find some inconsistencies in the comparison of elicitation and corpus data. Some examples of contradictory evidence were discussed in section 2.1. Sometimes, corpus data may also confirm elicitation task findings. The high acceptability rates of *proven* observed by Bauer (1987), for example, do not seem to have been caused by the fact that his subjects were undergraduate students and thus relatively young. Corpus evidence shows that *proven* is definitely gaining ground in standard NZE. An important point on which corpus data have confirmed Bauer's elicitation task results is that NZE, while sharing some features with both BrE and AmE, is not identical with either of them.

Exercises and study questions

1. Of the non-standard variables discussed in this article, identify one which you think is likely to be age-graded and one which is likely to be a change in progress. What kind of evidence would be required in order to demonstrate that your hypothesis is correct?

2. Some of the variables discussed are extremely rare in spontaneous speech. One way to study them without a large corpus is to construct a questionnaire. Can you think of any other approaches which might be constructive?

3. The use of *of* rather than *have* after modals (e.g. *would of, could of*) tends to be a feature of spoken NZE more than of written forms of the dialect. However, studying this variable in spoken language presents special challenges. What do you think these might be? How might one get around them?

4. For some varieties of English it has been claimed that variation with possessive (HAVE) is dependent on the type of thing possessed. Consider concrete versus abstract possessions (a bag; an idea), or inalienable versus alienable possessions (long legs; a long skirt). Is it your intuition that such factors should affect the likelihood of do-support, or the use of have-got? Are there any other factors relating to the type of thing possessed which could potentially play a role? Construct a questionnaire designed to test your hypotheses or use a corpus.

5. Identify the most striking features of NZE in the tense-aspect-mood domain. How do these features fit in with the behaviour and/or development of the relevant items in (standard and especially non-standard) varieties of British, American and Australian English?

Selected references

Please consult the General references for titles mentioned in the text but not included in the references below. For a full bibliography see the accompanying CD-ROM.

Bartlett, Christopher
    1992   Regional variation in New Zealand English: the case of Southland. *New Zealand English Newsletter* 6: 5–15.
Bauer, Laurie
    1987   New Zealand English morphology: some experimental evidence. *Te Reo: Journal of the Linguistic Society of New Zealand* 30: 37–53.
    1988   Number agreement with collective nouns in New Zealand English. *Australian Journal of Linguistics* 8: 247–259.
    1989a   The verb *have* in New Zealand English. *English World-Wide* 10: 69–83.
    1989b   Marginal modals in New Zealand English. *Te Reo: Journal of the Linguistic Society of New Zealand* 32: 3–16.
    1989c   Irregularity in past non-finite verb forms and a note on the New Zealand weekend. *New Zealand English Newsletter* 3: 13–16.
    1994   English in New Zealand. In: Burchfield (ed.), 382–429.

Bell, Allan
  1982   "This isn't the BBC": colonialism in New Zealand English. *Applied Linguistics* 3: 246–258.
  2000   Maori and Pakeha English: a case study. In: Bell and Kuiper (eds.), 221–248.
Bell, Allan and Janet Holmes (eds.)
  1990   *New Zealand Ways of Speaking English.* Clevedon: Multilingual Matters.
Brosnahan, Leonard F.
  1971   *Grammar Usage and the Teacher.* New Zealand Council for Educational Research.
Durkin, M.E.
  1972   A study of the pronunciation, oral grammar and vocabulary of West Coast schoolchildren. M.A. thesis, University of Canterbury.
Gordon, Elizabeth and Tony Deverson
  1985   *New Zealand English: An Introduction to New Zealand Speech and Usage.* Auckland: Heinemann.
Hay, Jennifer and Daniel Schreier
  2004   Reversing the trajectory of language change: subject – verb agreement with BE in New Zealand English. *Language Variation and Change* 16: 209–235.
Holmes, Janet, Allan Bell and Mary Boyce
  1991   *Variation and Change in New Zealand English. A Social Dialect Investigation.* Project report to the Social Sciences Committee of the Foundation for Research, Science and Technology. Wellington: Department of Linguistics, Victoria University.
Hundt, Marianne
  1997   Has BrE been catching up with AmE over the past thirty years? In: Magnus Ljung (ed.), *Corpus-Based Studies in English. Papers from the Seventeenth International Conference on English Language Research on Computerized Corpora (ICAME 17)*, 135–151. Amsterdam: Rodopi.
  1998   *New Zealand English Grammar – Fact or Fiction? A Corpus-Based Study in Morphosyntactic Variation.* Amsterdam/Philadelphia: Benjamins.
Jacob, Jenny
  1990   A grammatical comparison of the spoken English of Maori and Pakeha women in Levin. M.A. thesis, Victoria University, Wellington.
  1991   A grammatical comparison of the casual speech of Maori and Pakeha women in Levin. *Te Reo* 34: 53–70.
Jucker, Andreas H.
  1992   *Social Stylistics. Syntactic Variation in British Newspapers.* Berlin/New York: Mouton de Gruyter.
Kuiper, Koenraad
  1990   Some more areas for research in New Zealand English syntax. *New Zealand English Newsletter* 4: 31–34.
Levin, Magnus
  2001   *Agreement with Collective Nouns in English.* Lund: Lund Studies in English.

Mair, Christian and Marianne Hundt
  1995   Why is the progressive becoming more frequent in English? A cor-
            pus-based investigation of language change in progress. *Zeitschrift für
            Anglistik und Amerikanistik* 43: 111–122.
Mair, Christian, Marianne Hundt, Geoffrey Leech und Nicholas Smith
  2002   Short term diachronic shifts in part-of-speech frequencies: a comparison
            of the tagged LOB and F-LOB Corpora. *International Journal of Corpus
            Linguistics* 7: 245–264.
Peters, Pam
  1994   American and British influence in Australian verb morphology. In: Udo
            Fries and Edgar Schneider (eds.), *Creating and Using English Language
            Corpora. Papers from the Fourteenth International Conference on English
            Language Research on Computerized Corpora, Zürich 1993*, 149–158.
            Amsterdam: Rodopi.
Quinn, Heidi
  1995   Variation in NZE syntax and morphology: a study of the acceptance and
            use of grammatical variants among Canterbury and West Coast teenagers.
            M.A. thesis, University of Canterbury.
  2000   Variation in New Zealand English syntax and morphology. In: Bell and
            Kuiper (eds.), 173–197.
  2002   The distribution of pronoun case forms in English. Ph.D. dissertation,
            University of Canterbury.
Quirk, Randolph, Sidney Greenbaum, Geoffrey Leech and Jan Svartvik
  1985   *A Comprehensive Grammar of the English Language.* London: Longman.
Sigley, Robert
  1997   Choosing your relatives: relative clauses in New Zealand English. Ph.D.
            dissertation, Victoria University, Wellington.
Sussex, Roland
  1982   A note on the *get*-passive construction. *Australian Journal of Linguistics*
            2: 83–92.
Todd, Loreto and Ian Hancock
  1986   *International English Usage. A Comprehensive Survey of Written and
            Spoken English World-Wide.* Beckenham: Croom Helm.

Australian English: morphology and syntax

Peter Collins and Pam Peters

1. Introduction

Australian English (AusE) must be counted among the "settler" varieties of the English-speaking world, transported by convicts and immigrants, and quickly established as the official language of the under-inhabited "Great South Land". It is one of the "major" varieties, in Svartvik's (1997) overview, and may or may not be in some sense a regional standard. Görlach (1990) projected it within an Antipodean standard in his model of the world's Englishes, but AusE has continued to evolve since then, and research on various fronts (lexical, morphological and syntactic) has documented many more distinctive features than had previously been recognized. The first question is whether such features make Australian English endonormative – consolidating its own norms as an independent national standard – and then whether it constitutes some kind of regional standard in the antipodes, with or without New Zealand English (NZE).

The endonormativity of Australian English is readily argued in terms of its lexicon, now documented in indigenous dictionaries (*Macquarie Dictionary* 1981; *Australian Concise Oxford* 1991) and several usage guides (*Penguin Working Words* 1993; *Modern Australian Usage* 1993; *Cambridge Australian English Style Guide* 1995). Distinctive aspects of its lexical morphology have also been documented (Dabke 1976; Simpson, this volume). But the case has still to be argued in relation to its inflectional morphology and syntax. Much of the research conducted to date has focused on elements of the verb phrase in AusE (aspect, voice, mood, modality), but it has also extended to the interface between grammar and lexis in different ways of expressing comparison and alternative case selections. The following discussion will review the findings on these and other research frontiers, in order to examine the case for the endonormativity of AusE grammar. The focus will be on whether its morphosyntactic norms are markedly different from those of British English (BrE) and American English (AmE). Our assumption will be that there is only a weak case, if it turns out that the Australian norms are simply positioned somewhere between the British and American on the same scale. Wherever possible, comparisons will also be made between Australian and New Zealand morphosyntactic norms, in order to see whether there is any support for the notion of an antipodean standard.

2.   Sources

The research carried out on Australian and New Zealand English has been based primarily on two kinds of source material: written texts included in computer corpora and elicitation tests from smaller and larger groups of subjects.

The computer corpus most often referred to in what follows is the Australian Corpus of English (ACE) held at Macquarie University, consisting of 1 million words of published material from 1986. In structure, ACE matches the Brown (University) corpus of American English from 1961, and the LOB (Lancaster-Oslo-Bergen) corpus of British English material, also from 1961. Matching updates of these, the so-called Frown and FLOB corpora, were compiled with 1991 texts at the University of Freiburg. The Wellington corpus of New Zealand English (WC) consisting of texts from 1986, and the Indian Kohlhapur corpus, with texts from 1976, also referred to below, are structured in the same way. All these parallel corpora are heterogeneous in content, thus representing a variety of users and uses. Other corpora referred to in what follows are relatively homogeneous, e.g. archival material from a single newspaper, as indicated.

Data taken from published source material (as in corpora such as ACE) provides us with what might be called "standard" Australian usage – that which has been vetted by professional editors, and typically written by people in their middle or older years. It is thus somewhat limited in terms of the sociolinguistic spectrum, and not geared to provide evidence on usage which is primarily spoken, or more current among younger users of the language. It is nevertheless useful for the commoner morphosyntactic variables.

Other evidence to be discussed comes via elicitation, from population surveys undertaken in particular locations and settings, e.g. among tertiary students, or Australia-wide, through the magazine *Australian Style*. Data derived from these surveys help to widen the sociolinguistic base of information, and provide broader insights into usage at large (i.e. not just written). Elicited data thus complement data derived from text corpora, and helps to provide triangulation. It is also invaluable for the less frequent linguistic variants, which could only occur in sufficient numbers in a very large corpus.

Apart from these two kinds of primary source material, the research studies reviewed below make some use of secondary references such as dictionaries, usage guides and descriptive grammars, whose synthesis of particular variables adds further dimensions to the discussion.

3. The variables

3.1. Irregular verb morphology: past tense and past participle

Past tense:
The conjugational patterns of English strong verbs have been breaking up since the Norman Conquest, with continuous reductions in every paradigm. In late 20th century English, none of the original strong verbs had more than three parts (*give/gave/given*), and the tendency to reduce to two parts (*bring/brought*), or just one (*hit*), shows the direction of the tide. The reduction to two (irregular) parts consolidates among the strong verbs what has long been the pattern of weak verbs (*talk/talked*). Other once strong verbs such as *mow, sow, stride, strive*, and *thrive* are moving towards complete regularity in AmE, though the trend is slower in BrE. The extent to which AusE matches the British or American variety may therefore be an index of its relative independence as a regional norm.

In AmE, the reduction of the third part in verbs such as *shrink, sing, sink, spring, stink* is well advanced, in terms of what up-to-date reference dictionaries such as Merriam-Webster (2000) present as standard forms. They include *shrunk* for the past tense of *shrink, sunk* for *sink*, none of which is indicated as acceptable in current British English, according to the *New Oxford Dictionary of English* (1998). The *Macquarie Dictionary* (1997) admits some, suggesting that Australian usage on this set of verbs is intermediate between the American and the British.

A large survey of verb morphology involving over 1100 respondents throughout Australia was conducted in 2002 through *Australian Style*. The survey presented a series of sentences in which the past tense had to be supplied, and the results show that Australians too are engaged in reducing these verb paradigms from three to two parts, especially younger members of the population. For more than two thirds of the under 25s, *shrunk, sunk, sprung* were the normal form for the past tense, and for about half of those under 45, as shown in Table 1.

Table 1.   Results of *Australian Style* (2002) survey of irregular past tense forms

Age		10–24	25–44	45–64	65+
	n =	347	149	336	256
shrank		31%	45%	69%	79%
shrunk		69%	55%	31%	21%
		(in: *My old woolly jumper...... in the wash.*)			
sank		34%	53%	78%	87%
sunk		66%	47%	22%	13%
		(in: *Their dog ......his teeth into the visitor's leg.*)			
sprang		24%	48%	65%	76%
sprung		76%	52%	35%	24%
		(in: *In heavy seas the ship ...... a leak.*)			

The table shows well-entrenched use of the *u*-forms as common Australian usage, and a trend like that of AmE on these verbs.

Past participle:
The *Australian Style* survey also returned results on the use of some irregular past participles, including *beaten*, *gotten*, *proven*, *sawn*, *shorn*, *sown*, *stridden*, *striven*, and *woven*. Most of these were supported by the majority (though not *stridden*), but the support from the under 45s was usually less than that of those 45 and over, in some cases very much less, as for *shorn* as past participle of *shear*, and *striven* for *strive*, both of them down 27% on the average for the population overall. The most remarkable exceptions to this pattern were the cases of *proven* and *gotten* (used intransitively), shown in the Table 2.

Table 2.   Results of *Australian Style* survey of irregular past participles

Age		10–24	25–44	45–64	65+
	n =	347	149	336	256
proved		26%	27%	46%	68%
proven		74%	73%	54%	32%
		(in: *The inquiry has not ...... that they were negligent.*)			

Table 2. (continued)   Results of *Australian Style* survey of irregular past participles

Age		10–24	25–44	45–64	65+
got	(intr.)	31%	42%	65%	83%
gotten	(intr.)	69%	58%	35%	17%
	(in: *She had never ...... so angry before.*)				
got	(tr.)	87%	93%	97%	98%
gotten	(tr.)	13%	7%	3%	2%
	(in: *I haven't ...... a hotel booking yet.*)				

The results for *proved/proven* and intransitive *got/gotten* show remarkable age stratification, with a majority of younger respondents (under 45 for *gotten*, under 65 for *proven*) favoring the *-en* form. These results tally interestingly with those extracted by Peters (1993: 156–157) from corpus data (ACE, LOB, Brown), where the Australian results for *beaten, drunken, proven* stand strong beside those from the British and American data. And though *gotten* did not emerge from the corpus data as a feature of written AusE, it is certainly heard in everyday speech, and the data elicited in the *Australian Style* survey confirm this. Those antipathetic to AmE would deny its presence, but it is evidently there in the usage of younger and middle-aged persons.

The data elicited for *got/gotten* also point to the fact that AusE usage diverges from that associated with AmE, because the *Australian Style* data show that *gotten* is preferred for intransitive constructions. The overall results (all ages) for the two test sentences were quite divergent:

(1)   *She had never got* (54%)/*gotten* (46%) *so angry before.*

(2)   *I haven't got* (93%)/*gotten* (7%) *a hotel booking yet.*

The markedly different results for the transitive and intransitive constructions are quite unlike the older American pattern, in which *gotten* is used for something acquired, and *got* for something possessed; or indeed the newer pattern, in which *gotten* can be used for the acquisitive, causative and intransitive uses, but *got* is still reserved for having something in hand (Trudgill and Hannah 2002). The Australian transitive/intransitive dichotomy reconfigures the roles of *gotten/got* quite independently of AmE. The use of *gotten* may owe something to colonial lag (being also used by Scottish immigrants), as well as to more recent influence from the US. But it does suggest a difference in kind rather than degree, and therefore supports the strong case for endonormativity on this point of verb morphology. Data from spoken corpora would be needed to confirm it, but the evidence so far is drawn from a very large popular survey.

3.2.   Aspect: progressive and perfect

The progressive aspect has undergone substantial growth in Late Modern English. Hundt (1998; Hundt, Hay and Gordon, this volume) provides further evidence of its expanding use in her four-way comparisons of AusE, BrE, AmE and NZE, using standard corpora from the 1960s (Brown, LOB), 1980s (ACE, WC) and 1990s (Frown, FLOB). Her findings show that the two southern hemisphere varieties make more frequent use of the progressive than the northern hemisphere varieties. AmE turns out to be the least advanced of the set. In this respect, AusE and NZE seem to be leading the fray, and clearly not reflecting a trend already established in AmE. There were no significant differences between AusE and NZE in Hundt's data, suggesting that this development may qualify as an element of an emerging antipodean standard, and broader endonormativity within the South Pacific.

Present perfect aspect:
The generalization of the present perfect to simple past contexts as in *Then he's hit her on the head* is a relatively new development which was being reported in colloquial BrE as early as the 1970s (see for example Trudgill 1978: 13). The usage has been attested in various world Englishes, with Trudgill and Hannah (2002: 134) singling out Indian English (IndE) for special mention.
   A recent study by Engel and Ritz (2000) suggests that this use of the present perfect is more advanced in AusE than in the other varieties. Its distribution, according to Engel and Ritz, is as follows: "(1) in combination with past temporal adverbials; (2) in sequences indicating narrative progression; (3) in alternation with the simple past and the present tense to express stylistic contrast" (2000: 119). Engel and Ritz found it used extensively in narratives on Australian radio chat shows, with tokens often alternating with both the simple past tense and the "historic present":

(3)   a. *In the morning he's **stuck** an 'I love Redman' sticker on her back ...*
       b. *Everyone's **looking** at her and she's really sort of paranoid.*
       c. *She finally **got** home to her husband and kids and they've just **pissed** themselves laughing.* (Engel and Ritz 2000)

The material published so far by Engel and Ritz is symptomatic rather than quantitative, but a comprehensive comparative study is in preparation. Their survey of recent sociolinguistic literature on the use of the present perfect, and their finding of great flexibility of this usage in AusE suggests that the present perfect is "more widespread" in AusE than it is in BrE or AmE. If they are right, this development supports the strong claim for endonormativity in AusE.

3.3.   Voice: the *get*-passive

The increasing popularity of the *get*-passive in all world Englishes is noted by Mair and Hundt (1997), among others, and attributed to the greater colloquialization of the written norm. An earlier paper by Sussex (1982: 90) suggested that the preference for *get*-passives over *be*-passives was stronger in AmE than in AusE and stronger in AusE than in BrE, and that any Australian increase in the use of *get*-passives could be seen as evidence of American influence. The likelihood of this has been called in question by Collins's (1996) research, based on more than five million words of written and spoken data from four standard corpora, and two of the ICE (International Corpus of English) corpora. His findings (1996: 53–54) showed the frequency of *get*-passives to be comparable in AmE and BrE, higher in AusE than in either of those, and higher still in IndE than in AusE. Its use in IndE is a remarkable development away from the "Babu English" ("flower English") of the past, and seems to reflect increasing Indian exposure to more conversational forms of English.

Australian levels of use of the *get*-passive, in writing as well as speech, puts it at the extreme end of the scale of L1 varieties. But the use of *get*-passives in a (relatively) nearby L2 variety reduces the strength of the claim for its endonormativity in AusE.

3.4.   Mood: the mandative subjunctive

Divergent regional trends in the use of the subjunctive have been noted by a number of modern English grammarians. Use of the mandative subjunctive, i.e. after expressions of demand, recommendation, intention, etc., seems to have varied considerably. AmE is strongly inclined to use the mandative subjunctive, as in *I recommend that he talk to a specialist*, while BrE prefers the periphrastic construction with the modal auxiliary *should*, as in *I recommend that he should talk to a specialist*.

Australian use of the mandative subjunctive presently lies somewhere between that of AmE and BrE, in comparative corpus data used by Peters (1998a). Elicitation data derived from an *Australian Style* survey (1993) on the use of the subjunctive also confirmed its currency for the mandative, in counterpoint to its decline in expressing hypothetical conditions and other traditional uses. NZE occupies a similar intermediate position between AmE and BrE in the use of the mandative, according to Hundt (1998). Her comparison of data from the Wellington Corpus and ACE led her to conclude that "while there is no statistically significant difference between the two Southern Hemisphere varieties in the use of the subjunctives, the two differ in their relation to the center of gravity for this change: AusE has come closer to the pattern observed in AmE of the 1960s than NZE" (1998: 97).

Both AusE and NZE are inside the scale that stretches towards American usage, and not at the extreme end for L1 varieties. Whether this is a matter of "colonial lag" (from 19th century British influence), or 20th century American influence across the Pacific, is debatable. It may be a combination of both. Either way the mandative subjunctive provides only weak support for any claim by Australia, or the antipodes, to endonormativity.

3.5.   Modality 1: *shall/will, may/might*

shall/will:
The distinction between *shall* and *will* has been much discussed in usage handbooks and prescriptive grammars. Australian teachers from several different types of high school questioned by Watson (1978) gave *will* in *I will be twenty-one tomorrow* an acceptability rating of 94%, suggesting that Australians have little time for (or perhaps awareness of) the "rules" for *will* and *shall*.

Comparative data from a variety of Australian, British and American corpora, written and spoken (totalling 225,000 words) show that *shall* is more frequent in BrE than in AmE or AusE, and more frequent in AmE than in AusE (Collins 1991b). This suggests that "*shall* is obsolescent in Australian English and lingers on only in root meanings in formal genres" (1991b: 190). The figures in Table 3 below (based on Collins's written data, representing tokens per 10,000 words), suggest that *shall* is in fact obsolescent in all three varieties, but most notably in AusE.

Table 3.   The relative frequencies of *will* and *shall* in Australian, British and American data

	AusE	BrE	AmE
will	34.2	28.0	27.0
shall	1.2	3.5	2.7

The figures show that *shall* is more frequent in BrE than AmE, and more frequent in AmE than in AusE. By contrast the AusE figure for *will* is higher than in the other varieties, suggesting its compensatory role as the uses of *shall* decline. The conclusion has been underscored by Hundt (1998: 59), in a four-way comparison of AusE with AmE, NZE and BrE, based on newspaper reportage. Hundt noted Australian avoidance of *shall* in massive frequency differences for *shall* and *will* (6 : 656). Her figures show BrE standing apart in its tolerance of *shall*, and its decreasing popularity in AmE in the later 20th century, visible in diachronic comparisons between Brown and Frown, but less marked in FLOB/LOB. The Australian disinclination to use *shall* is thus part of a larger world-wide trend. The claim for endonormativity here must be in terms of a difference in degree rather than in kind, though the fact that the Australian norms are set at one end of the scale makes them stronger rather than weaker.

May/might:

The use of *may/might* in Australia shows two unusual applications that seem to be on the margins of standard English grammar. These are the use of *may* to express past possibility and hypothetical possibility, as a viable alternative to *might* and *could*. The earliest Australian evidence for this comes from an elicitation test (Collins 1988) in which informants (186 undergraduates) were presented with a questionnaire involving stimulus sentences containing periphrastic modal expressions such as "be possible that", "be obliged to" and "give X permission to", and instructed to "Fill the slot with a word or words you think expresses the same meaning". Two key items, and the proportional responses, were:

(4)   *He suggested that it was possible that the driver fell asleep at the*
       controls
       He suggested that the driver _____ have fallen asleep
       might 40%   *may* 31%   *could* 28%   other 1%

(5)   *It is possible that criminals would be advantaged by such a law.*
       Criminals _____ be advantaged by such a law
       could 43%   *may* 32%   *might* 18%   other 7%

The selection of *may* by almost one third of informants in both sentences may reflect a general disinclination among Australian speakers – more pronounced among some than others – to backshift in reported speech. An example discussed by Newbrook (2001: 121) is *Kim said she has a bad cold* (= Newbrook's [24]), as opposed to *Kim said she had a bad cold* (= Newbrook's [25]). He comments that:

> In the native-English-speaking world generally, (25) is preferred wherever possible; it is always used unless 'Kim' still has her cold at the time of utterance, when (24) might – but still need not – be selected instead. In contrast, Australian students often report that they prefer (24) over (25) wherever the sense permits.

Newbrook also notes the Australian use of present tense *may* in the apodoses of remote conditional constructions (as in [5]) above, with its implicit protasis), with an example from ACE:

(6)   *If we found out why these things happen, prevention **may** be possible.*

For many Australians, it would seem, *might* is not the past tense of *may* (as least as used epistemically), a tendency found in many varieties of English.

3.6.   Modality 2: non-assertive forms of *must, ought (to), have (to), need (to) and dare (to)*

must:
Epistemic *must* has been claimed to lack (or "normally" lack) a negative form (Coates 1983: 46). In Australian research based on a corpus of four kinds of written/spoken material comprising 225,000 words, Collins (1991a) found epistemic *mustn't* occurring – all tokens in conversation – with the same frequency as epistemic *can't*, with which it is semantically parallel.

(7)   *He **mustn't** have wanted the coupons because he came up and give them to me.*

ought (to):
A widespread tendency for *ought* to be avoided in questions and negatives has been noted (e.g. by Trudgill and Hannah 2002). Australian research, based on comparative corpus data as well as elicitation studies, suggests that this avoidance works strongly in favour of *should*. Table 4 below presents the data derived by Collins (1991a) from his 225,000-word written/spoken corpus. The figures for *ought* and *should* (normalized to tokens per 10,000 words) show that *ought* is not only considerably less popular than *should* in all three varieties, but also comparatively less popular in AusE than in AmE and BrE.

Table 4.   Relative frequencies of *should* and *ought*

	AusE	BrE	AmE
should	7.5	12.9	9.2
ought	0.3	1.1	0.7

Evidence of the increasing unpopularity of *ought* in AusE comes, for example, from elicitation tests conducted by Collins in the 1970s. In Collins's study (1979: 11), he noted the unpopularity of *ought* in non-assertive contexts. When asked to supply an interrogative tag for *He ought to see a psychiatrist*, 30% of his undergraduate informants supplied *shouldn't*; 35% did so for *They ought to visit us more often*; and 57% for *Mary ought to have warned us earlier*.

The decline of *ought* is also demonstrated by Hundt (1998: 66): her four-way comparison of *ought* in newspaper language reveals a dispreference that is marginally stronger in AusE than in BrE, AmE, or NZE. The case of non-assertive *ought* is thus negative evidence for endonormativity in AusE. The similar pattern in NZE would also make it an element of standard antipodean grammar.

have (to) and *need (to)*:
The use of *do*-periphrasis with *have (to)* and *need (to)* in negatives and interrogatives has variously been noted as a discriminator between American and British varieties of English. While AmE inclines strongly towards *do*-periphrasis, BrE maintains the auxiliary status of *have/need* by using them both as operators. Elicitation tests carried out by Collins (1989: 142–143) show that Australian usage leans heavily towards the American pattern for both items. When asked to supply an interrogative tag for *have to* in the sentence *They have to make a decision by Friday*, more than three quarters of Collins's undergraduate informants selected *don't they?* over *haven't they?*. Australian usage of *need* is likewise closer to the American than the British pattern. In Collins's "preference" test, 62% of informants opted for *They don't need to make an appointment* as against 38% for *They needn't make an appointment*. The behaviour of *have (to)* and *need (to)* in non-assertive contexts thus reveals a shift away from British norms; but to the extent that the patterns are as in AmE, they lend no support to the stronger case for endonormativity.

dare (to):
The trend towards *do*-periphrasis with *dare*, as for *need*, is far more advanced in AmE than it is in BrE (Hundt 1998: 65). Not uncommon with *dare* are blends of the *do* and operator constructions (e.g. *They didn't dare complain*). Hundt's data, taken from CD-ROM archives of the *Guardian*, demonstrated British support for both *do*-periphrasis and the operator construction, with blends of the two being roughly half as popular as each of these options. By contrast, the American data from archives of the *Miami Herald*, showed that blends were as popular as *do*-periphrasis, with the operator construction receiving little support. Table 5 presents the figures:

Table 5.   Non-assertive constructions with *dare* in AmE and BrE.

	Do	**Operator**	**Blends** *(+do/-to)*
AmE	23	6	22
BrE	20	19	12

Collins's elicitation tests (1989: 143) based on undergraduate respondents suggest that the trends in AusE broadly reflect those of AmE. His informants were as disinclined to use the operator variant as the users of AmE, but favoured *do*-periphrasis with the bare infinitive far more strongly, as shown by the rankings of their responses on the selection test. Presented with the three sentences *We didn't dare tell jokes*, *We didn't dare to tell jokes*, and *We dared not tell jokes*, the first was given a positive rating by 73 informants, the second by 38 and the third by 32.

On this shifting feature of the English modal system, younger Australians are probably further ahead with the *do*-periphrasis than their counterparts elsewhere. If their usage is shared with the rest of the Australian community, it constitutes further evidence of endonormativity in the grammar of AusE.

3.6.   Comparative structures: some lexicogrammatical patterns with *different from/to/ than, less/fewer* and *like/as*

The expression of comparison is subject to a good deal of lexicogrammatical variation across the national varieties. Each of the items below has been intensively discussed in the prescriptive handbooks, concerned as to the propriety or otherwise of the variants. The judgments of these handbooks vary considerably, those concerned with AmE presenting a broader spectrum of opinion than the BrE (Peters and Young 1996: 321–322). Some Australian preferences may be explained in terms of the influence of AmE, others by the less conservative nature of AusE (by comparison with, say, BrE).

different from/to/than:
Most usage guides recommend *from* as the "correct" preposition following *different(ly)*. Even though historically *to* is older than *from* and *than*, purists object to its use on the grounds that it contradicts the sense of separation or dissociation conveyed by the (etymological) prefix constituting the first syllable of *different*.

Despite the preference for *different from* over *different to* expressed in some Australian usage books (e.g. *Modern Australian Usage* 1993), Australians seem to prefer *different to* – at least in informal registers. According to Walshe (1972: 259–260): "the most popular usage is *different to*, though *different from* is by no means uncommon, and *different than* is sometimes heard". In Collins's (1979) elicitation test, the context of use emerged as a very important factor. When *different to* was the focus of attention in test sentences, undergraduate respondents viewed it with considerable distaste, but not in all contexts. The sentence *Is bicycle riding very different to motor bike riding?* was judged acceptable by the vast majority of informants in informal speech, but accepted by less than half of the informants for formal writing. Data from the ACE corpus suggests the relative unacceptability of *different to* in written texts. There *different from* outnumbers *different to* in the ratio of 6 : 1 (Peters 1995: 203–204), while the representation of *than* is smaller still, suggesting that it has yet to make inroads into standard AusE. AusE, it can be said in conclusion, is nevertheless its own remarkable blend of BrE and AmE, in its use of all three variants, with some claim to endonormativity therein.

Less/fewer:

The use of *less* rather than *fewer* with the plurals of count nouns has been censured in many usage handbooks on both BrE and AmE (Peters and Young 1996: 328–330). Elicitation studies in the UK and Australia suggest that British speakers are more conservative on this than Australians. Consider especially the acceptability of *less* + plural noun at 47% for Australian teachers (Watson 1978), and at (72%) for Australian undergraduates (Collins 1979: 43). A nationwide survey through *Australian Style* reports an overall acceptance rate of 50%, and 58% for under 25s. Hudson (1993: 149–150) notes that the use of *less* may sometimes be semantically motivated: one might distinguish between *We want less taxes* (meaning 'We want the total amount collected to be less') and *We want fewer taxes* (meaning 'There should be fewer channels of collection'). The growing acceptance of *less* with plural nouns (Peters 1995: 276) can be seen in the more informal prose in ACE, in narratives and dialogue. Though *less* in this role is less frequent than *fewer*, its very presence in edited material suggests the direction of AusE with this usage. The dearth of usage commentators in the US or the UK who accept it means that AusE is taking the lead in this regard.

like/as:

Despite the furore created in the United States in the 1960s by the advertising slogan "Winston tastes good, like a cigarette should", conjunctive *like* is widely used in AmE. It appears with no restrictive label in the major contemporary American dictionaries, as noted by Peters (1995: 447). In BrE conjunctive *like* is still held at arm's length by the warning "unacceptable in formal English" (*New Oxford English Dictionary* 1998). Current Australian practice is more like the American than British, where conjunctive *like* is rare outside colloquial contexts. Collins's Australian informants (1979: 37) were tolerant of conjunctive *like*, giving it a rating of 65%, although it was judged a good deal more acceptable in informal than formal genres. Australian high school students and teachers are even more inclined to accept it. Comparative data on AusE, AmE and BrE from the parallel corpora (e.g. Peters and Delbridge 1997: 310) show that while British tolerance of conjunctive *like* extends only to fiction, in American and Australian sources it appears both in fiction and a variety of nonfictional writing – from newspapers and magazines to *belles lettres* – in all but the most formal categories such as academic and bureaucratic prose. The AusE position is thus much like AmE.

3.7.   Case selection: after *than*; with gerunds; *who/whom*

Than + pronoun:
Enshrined in many usage manuals is a pedantic preference for nominative pronouns after *than*, designed to confirm the status of *than* as a conjunction introducing an elliptical clause, rather than operating as a preposition. Compare:

(8)   a. *He had drunk far more than I and he was at least forty years older*
           (ACE, G23)
       b. *The statue had become a boy some years older than me*
           (ACE, L13)

In Australian elicitation studies based on undergraduate subjects, the average figure for prepositional *than* is higher than in the UK. *Than me* etc. is strongly associated with informal spoken contexts, and *than I* with formal writing. This differentiation is confirmed by the dearth of prepositional *than* in nonfiction writing in ACE, and its presence in fictional and interpersonal writing.

The tendency to prefer the accusative personal pronoun over the nominative in speech is part of a more general trend towards a common case (Wales 1996: 107). She finds it in both L1 and L2 varieties of English, and so its endorsement among younger Australians is consistent with world-wide trends rather than a distinctive local feature.

Pronoun + gerund-participle:
The choice of personal pronoun to precede *-ing* forms of the verb has challenged grammarians for centuries: whether to use the genitive forms *my*, *your*,

his etc., to emphasize the nominal character of the gerund-participle, or to use the accusative forms *me, you, him* etc., which reflect its underlying verbal character. Compare:

(9)   a. *...mad as she was at his going away* (Brown, K25)
      b. *No one was allowed to climb it on account of it being rotten* (ACE, G12)

There seem to be some constraints on the second construction (the "fused participle"), most notably that the construction is largely avoided in subject position (Peters 1995: 309). Data on post-verbal use of the construction show that while AmE and BrE prefer the genitive form over the accusative, AusE goes the other way: The differences emerge in data from the parallel corpora, including all combinations of personal pronouns with the gerund-participle except those where there was no possibility of selecting the pronoun's case, as in kept it running.

Table 6. Instances of the use of genitive and accusative pronouns with gerund-particles

	Brown		LOB		ACE	
	gen	accus	gen	accus	gen	accus
Non-fiction (Categories A–J)	18	0	29	6	12	12
Fiction (Categories K+)	19	8	22	13	4	10
Totals:	37	8	51	19	16	22

The Australian data reverse the relationship between the two constructions in fiction, and show no preference for the genitive in non-fiction. This might be a reflection of the relative recency of ACE (1986) as opposed to LOB/Brown with data from 1961, except that the results seem to tally with established usage in both the UK and the US.

    The table presents a marked contrast between the results for Brown and LOB on the one hand, and those from ACE on the other. While AmE and BrE prefer the genitive construction, AusE goes the opposite way, with the accusative preferred overall and especially in fiction. This Australian use of the accusative with gerund-participles is a feature in which AusE is setting its own pace, and clearly endonormative. It is a further context in which the object pronoun takes the place of another member of the paradigm.

whom:

The decline of *whom* has been commented on since the 18th century, but the details of its continuing use still make it a point of regional divergence. Its relatively stronger use in BrE than either AmE or AusE is demonstrated by comparative frequencies from LOB, Brown and ACE. The use of *whom* in AmE and AusE is still strongly associated with its use with prepositions, especially *of*, *to*, *for* and *with*. In such cases it cannot be substituted by *which* (it lacks the feature human/animate), nor by *that* (because *that* cannot be governed by a preposition). Table 7 shows all instances of *whom* that occur following prepositions in the British, American and Australian data, as well as those which occur clause-initially as objects of a following verb. Cases of *whom* with a stranded preposition (two in Brown and one in LOB) have been excluded.

Table 7.   Occurrences of *whom* after prepositions, and clause-initially

	Brown	**LOB**	**ACE**
after prep	96	138	84
clause initial	48	67	32
total	144	205	116

The data in Table 7 shows that a higher percentage of *whom* occurs in prepositional constructions in AusE (72%) than in AmE (67%) or BrE (67%).

Closer inspection of the corpus data by category suggests that clause-initial *whom* (interrogative or relative) is stylistically marked in both AmE and AusE, but more or less standard in BrE. Table 8 presents raw and normalized figures relative to the number of words in those categories expressed as percentages.

Table 8.   Occurrences of clause-initial *whom* in fiction and nonfiction writing

	Brown	**LOB**	**ACE**
in nonfiction (corpus categories A–J)	40 (.0053)	54 (.0072)	28 (.0036)
in fiction (corpus categories K +)	9 (.0032)	14 (.0052)	5 (.0020)

Almost all of the examples of *whom* were in relative constructions: very few examples of the interrogative appeared in the data, apart from a cluster of biblical quotations in Brown, using *Whom shall ye fear?* The British use of relative *whom* is higher altogether than the American or the Australian, and strongly maintained in fiction. The Brown data evidences a distinctly lower use of clause-initial *whom* in fiction and in the ACE data its use is strongly associated with nonfiction.

In AusE, *whom* is associated more with the formal end of the scale. The frequencies from the various ACE categories line up with the results of elicitation tests carried out by Collins (1979) on undergraduates: *whom* was rejected by 75% of them in informal contexts, while up to 51% accepted *who* in formal contexts. Australians thus seem to be more generally inclined than the British to avoid clause-initial *whom*, though standard American usage advanced in this direction earlier in the 20th century. In this element of morphosyntax, the Australian position is therefore not endonormative.

4.   Conclusion: Australian endonormativity in grammar

Some of the variables discussed above provide arguments for the endonormativity of Australian grammar, such as the applications of *gotten* and *got*, the use of *less* with countable nouns, and of accusative pronouns with gerund-participles. In its dispreference for *shall* and for the operator use of *dare*, Australian grammar is at the frontiers of English world-wide. But many of the cases discussed illustrate more intensive use of what are evidently the norms of BrE or AmE. Even so they can be seen as "new configurations" in AusE (Peters and Fee 1989) of the raw material of BrE and AmE. Access to AmE, particularly in the 20th century, has provided additional variants for the users of AusE, and prompted some adjustments to the British base of grammar brought through continuous immigration from Britain, and continuous administrative, social and cultural connections. The interplay between the colonial and post-colonial inheritance has catalyzed a number of small but distinctive developments in AusE.

At various points in this discussion, comparisons have been made with NZE, raising the question as to whether AusE and NZE between them form some kind of southern hemisphere standard, distinct from that of the two supervarieties in the northern hemisphere. In some aspects of grammar, AusE and NZE show identical trends. In their increasing use of the progressive and dispreference for *oughtn't*, both seem to be in the vanguard. Yet for many of the issues discussed, comparative data from New Zealand are not yet available to show the parity of developments on both sides of the Tasman. Since NZE is usually thought of as more closely associated with BrE than is AusE (partly because of its less diverse immigration history), it seems less likely that the two varieties could constitute a common standard.

AusE grammar does seem to be evolving elements of its own, reconfiguring the patterns of alternative constructions, and recalibrating the stylistic status of elements of some, so that *fewer* and *whom* rate as more formal and *like* less informal. It has absorbed elements of AmE grammar to complement its BrE foundations, but these have effectively been "Australianized" (Peters 1998b), rather than resulting in a totally "Americanized" variety in the South Pacific. The distinctive elements of the Australian lexicon add their weight to any claim for the existence of an Australian standard. AusE seems indeed to have evolved to Stage 5 in Schneider's (2003) scale of New Englishes: one that is endonormatively stabilized, and able to support its own internal kinds of differentiation. The divergent patterns of usage found for younger and older Australians are clear evidence of this. They are also elements out of which AusE may distinguish itself further from BrE and AmE in the future.

Exercises and study questions

1. Construct a "tag-test" to elicit information about the behaviour of *have (to)*, *need (to)*, *dare (to)* and *used (to)* in negative/interrogative contexts: e.g. *Tom has to leave early*, [*hasn't he?/doesn't he?*]. Try it out on a small group of people and compare the preference for the operator and *do*-periphrastic variants. How do you explain your findings? You might also wish to include *'d better* and *'d rather* in your test.

2. Can you provide any evidence (not just grammatical, but possibly also phonological and/or lexical) to suggest that AusE is less similar to BrE than NZE is?

3. Collect examples of *shall* and identify the styles of usage with which it is associated. Do you find a tendency for it to be used more in writing or speech, more in formal or informal usage, more by older or younger speakers?

4. Is epistemic *mustn't* (e.g. *She mustn't have been feeling well*) always synonymous with epistemic *can't*? Can you construct a pair of sentences in which they are not synonymous?

5. Suggest a reason, or reasons, for the rising popularity of the present perfect in simple past contexts (e.g. *Then he's hit her on the head*) in AusE.

6. Are *get*-passives freely interchangeable with *be*-passives in (Australian) English? If not, can you think of situations where they are not? Can you think of any reasons for the rising popularity of *get*-passives?

7. Studies have indicated that there are dialectal differences in the frequency of the mandative subjunctive vis-a-vis the construction with *should*. Are there also stylistic differences?

8. Devise a small survey to determine informants' preferences in constructions where there is variable case selection: nominative or accusative pronoun after *than*; genitive or accusative pronoun with the gerund-participle; accusative *whom* or nominative *who* as object. Are your findings in accordance with statements made about these constructions in usage handbooks?

9. Devise a survey to ascertain respondents' preferences with verbs that exhibit variation in the forms of the past tense (e.g. *shrank/shrunk, stank/stunk, sank/sunk*).

Selected references

Please consult the General references for titles mentioned in the text but not included in the references below. For a full bibliography see the accompanying CD-ROM.

Coates, Jennifer
 1983   *The Semantics of the Modal Auxiliaries*. London: Croom Helm.
Collins, Peter
 1979   Elicitation experiments on acceptability. *Working Papers of the Speech and Language Research Centre, Macquarie University* 2: 1–49.
 1988   The semantics of some modals in contemporary Australian English. *Australian Journal of Linguistics* 8: 261–286.
 1989   Divided and debatable usage in Australian English. In: Collins and Blair (eds.), 138–149.
 1991a The modals of obligation and necessity in Australian English. In: Karin Aijmer, Bengt Altenberg and Jan Svartvik (eds.), *English Corpus Linguistics: Studies in Honour of Jan Svartvik*, 145–165. London: Longman.
 1991b *Will* and *shall* in Australian English. In: Stig Johansson and Anna-Brita Stenström (eds.), *English Computer Corpora*, 181–200. Berlin/New York: Mouton de Gruyter.
 1996   *Get*-passives in English. *World Englishes* 15: 43–56.
Dabke, Roswitha
 1976   *The Morphology of Australian English*. München: Fink.
Engel, Dulcie M. and Ritz, Marie-Eve A.
 2000   The use of the present perfect in Australian English. *Australian Journal of Linguistics* 20: 119–140.
Görlach, Manfred
 1990   *Studies in the History of the English Language*. Heidelberg: Winter.

Hudson, Nicholas
    1993   *Modern Australian Usage.* Melbourne: Oxford University Press.
Hundt, Marianne
    1998   *New Zealand English Grammar: Fact or Fiction? A Corpus-Based Study
              in Morphosyntactic Variation.* Amsterdam/Philadelphia: Benjamins.
Mair, Christian and Marianne Hundt
    1997   The corpus-based approach to language change in progress. In: Uwe
              Böker and Hans Sauer (eds.), *Anglistentag 1996 Dresden – Proceedings*,
              71–82. Trier: Wissenschaftlicher Verlag.
Newbrook, Mark
    2001   Syntactic features and norms in Australian English. In: Blair and Collins
              (eds.), 113–132.
Peters, Pam
    1993   American and British influence on Australian verb morphology. In: Udo
              Fries, Gunnel Tottie and Peter Schneider (eds.), *Creating and Using
              English Language Corpora*, 248–255. Amsterdam: Rodopi.
    1995   *Cambridge Australian English Style Guide.* Melbourne: Cambridge
              University Press.
    1998a   The survival of the subjunctive. Evidence of its use in Australia and else-
              where. *English World-Wide* 19: 87–103.
    1998b   Australian English. In: Philip Bell and Roger Bell (eds.), *Americanization
              and Australia*, 32–44. Sydney: University of New South Wales Press.
Peters, Pam and Arthur Delbridge
    1997   Fowler's legacy. In: Edgar Schneider (ed.), *Englishes around the World*,
              Volume 2, 301–318. Amsterdam/Philadelphia: Benjamins.
Peters, Pam and Margery Fee
    1989   New configurations: the balance of British and American English features
              in Australian and Canadian English. *Australian Journal of Linguistics* 9:
              135–147.
Peters, Pam and Wendy Young
    1996   English grammar and the lexicography of usage. *Journal of English
              Linguistics* 25: 315–331.
Schneider, Edgar W.
    2003   Evolution(s) in global Englishes. In: Pam Peters (ed.), *From Local to
              Global English*, 3–23. Sydney: Dictionary Research Centre.
Sussex, Roland
    1982   A note on the *get*-passive construction. *Australian Journal of Linguis-
              tics* 2: 83–92.
Svartvik, Jan
    1997   Varieties of English: major and minor. In: Lindquist, Estling, Klintborg
              and Levin (eds.), 15–27.
Trudgill, Peter
    1978   Introduction: sociolinguistics and sociolinguistics. In: Trudgill (ed.), 1–
              18.

Wales, Katie
   1996   *Personal Pronouns in Present-Day English.* Cambridge: Cambridge
             University Press.
Walshe, Robert D.
   1972   Guide to usage and style. In: George W. Turner (ed.), *Good Australian
             English and Good New Zealand English*, 259–260. Sydney: Reed
             Education.
Watson, Keith
   1978   Teachers' attitudes to usage. *ALAA (Applied Linguistics Association of
             Australia) Occasional Papers* 2: 32–40.

Australian Vernacular English: some grammatical characteristics*

Andrew Pawley

1. Introduction

Australian Vernacular English (AusVE) is a variety which can be heard in the informal speech of some Australians, especially working-class and country men. It is characterised by the frequent occurrence of certain phonological and grammatical features that are rare or absent in more standard varieties. Table 1 gives commonly-occurring AusVE variants of some grammatical and quasi-grammatical variables.

Table 1. AusVE variants of some grammatical variables

	Variable	AusVE value
1.	(Gender assignment) pronoun for inanimate referents	*he/she* for inanimates
2.	(*were* subject-verb agreement) *were* after *you* or plural subject	*was, 's* /wəz/, /əz/, /ɨz/
3.	(Past tense of strong verbs) (*came, did, ran, saw,* etc.)	*come, done, run, seen,* etc.
4.	(Past participle of strong verbs) *gone, lain, seen, taken, thrown,* etc.	*went, laid, saw, took, threw,* etc.
5.	(Negative concord with indeterminate) NEG + V + *a/any/ever/either*	NEG + verb + *no/none/never/neither*
6.	(Past tense negation) *did* + NEG + infinitive verb	*never* + past-tense verb
7.	(Non-standard *don't*) *doesn't*	*don't*
8.	(Present perfect) *have* + past participle	past participle
9.	(Narrative tense) past tense	historic present tense

Table 1. (continued)   AusVE variants of some grammatical variables

Variable	AusVE value
10. (Adjective/adverb merger) V + ADV (*quickly/well/proper*/etc.)	V + ADJ (*quick/good/nice*/etc.)
12. (First singular object pronoun in requests) verb of transfer/obtaining + *me*	verb of transfer/obtaining + *us*
13. (Third singular generic pronoun) *he or she*	*they*
14. (Subject relative pronoun ellipsis) subject + *that/which* + relative clause	subject + rel. clause
15. (Subject ellipsis) SUBJ.PRO + V	Vtr + NP
16. (Subject auxiliary ellipsis before transitive verb) (SUBJ.PRO + AUX + Vtr + NP)	Vtr + NP)
17. (Subject *be* ellipsis before adjective or noun) (NP + *be* + ADJ or ART + N)	ADJ or ART + N
18 (*as...as* ellipsis) SUBJ.PRO + *be* + *as* + ADJ + N + *as* + S	ADJ + *as* + S
19. (There/it *be* ellipsis before negated NP) *there/it* + *be* + NEG + NP + (LOC)	NEG + NP + (LOC)
20. (Subject verb ellipsis before preposition) SUBJ + V + PREP (+ LOC)	PREP (+ LOC)
21. (Salient definite NP) Proper NP or DET + NP	*old* + Proper.NP DET + *old* + NP
22. (*those*)	*them*
23. (NP *and the others*)	NP *and them*
24. (*this one, that one*, etc.)	*this fella, that fella*, etc.
25. (S, *though*)	S, *but*

In AusVE there is also frequent use of informal values of a wide range of lexically-specific phonological variables, e.g. *h*-dropping, *-in* instead of *-ing*, *'ey* and *'em* for *they* and *them*, *me* and *meself*/*miself*/ for *my* and *myself* or *m'self*, *be* for *by*, *a* for *an* and *thuh* rather than *thee* before a vowel, *a* for unstressed *have* or *'ve*, and such other casual pronunciations as *fella, Mondy, Tuesdy, gimme, gonna, wanna* and *dunno*. Three samples of AusVE speech follow, with features of particular interest in bold type.

(1)   (Tasmania: Harv, farmer and businessman, in his sixties)
      *and on the corner was this **ol'** mountain duck with some little **fellas**, y' know, an' you'd 've **swore** a wing was **broke**, y' know.*
      *'E – 'e – 'e **run** away across the paddock with ...this broken wing.*

(1) contains the non-standard participle forms *swore* and *broke*, the non-standard past form *run*, *fellas* for *fellows* and the adjective *old*, used before definite common nouns and personal names to refer to a salient character in the narrative.

Examples (2) and (3), and a good many later examples are from a conversation recorded in 1974 in Scottsdale, Tasmania, in which two friends, Harv (Harvey) and Chas (Charles), tell stories about local characters to one another and to Harv's wife and sister.

(2)   Harv: *e 'd **a** et – the Dagwood* [eaten the large sandwich] *if 'e'd **a** caught it, if 'e could **a** got it off the dog.*
               *He wouldn **a** seen anything wrong with that. Talk about eatin it after the dog went under the house...*
      Chas: ***Yiz** would **a took** it off 'im.*

(3)   Chas: *I thought to **meself** "Possession's nine points of the bloody law."*
      Harv: *And when 'e came up to you you **never 'AD 'er*** [the bottle of beer].
      Chas: *No, I **never 'AD 'er**.*
               *...I put **'er** down. I **'AD** to. I put **'er** down THAT BLOODY QUICK that I blew the TOP off **'er**.*

Example (2) has the non-standard second person plural pronoun *yiz*, the participle *took* for standard *taken* and the regular (five out of five) use of *a* for unstressed auxiliary *'ve*. In (3) the bottle of beer is consistently feminine (five out of five pronouns), non-standard *never* occurs for *didn't*, and *meself* occurs for *myself* or *m'self*.

Speech that shows the full range of AusVE grammatical features listed in Table 1 may be called 'basilectal', the basilect being the style most removed from the most formal prestige or 'acrolectal' style. Some Australians consistently use basilectal AusVE in conversation while others use only a part of the range of AusVE features, tending to excluding those features that are stigmatised as typical of 'uneducated' speech. AusVE may be contrasted with two other mainstream varieties of Australian English, each also covering a fairly broad zone on the stylistic scale. *Standard Australian Colloquial English* (StAusColE) is the dominant variety of many Australians, and is strongly linked to middle class upbringings, occupations and aspirations. Its grammar is closer to that of standard colloquial English in the UK and North America than to that of basilectal AusVE (but see Collins 1989; Collins and Peters, this volume). *Standard Australian Formal English* (StAusFE) is a self-conscious variety, largely restricted to formal contexts. Its grammar differs little from the formal spoken English of the UK or North America. Insofar as StAusFE departs from colloquial speech, it is a writing-based variety and is nobody's mother tongue. Of course, this three-way distinction greatly simplifies the full complexities of the situation – one can argue for a stylistic continuum – but it is a useful simplification. In our Tasmanian corpus, for instance, one can easily distinguish paradigmatic AusVE speakers from paradigmatic StAusColE speakers according to the frequencies with which they use diagnostic variants of grammatical and phonological variables.

While individuals vary in their stylistic range and flexibility most speakers of AusVE are polylectal, able to shift up and down the stylistic scale according to their linguistic purpose and the company they are in. Socially, the use of non-standard values of linguistic variables marks informality, and sometimes solidarity and intimacy. When men in the countryside or working-class men in the cities meet informally to work or to socialise, frequent use of a wide range of AusVE features is *de rigeur*. The more informal and relaxed the situation the higher the incidence of non-standard features.

In historical terms, basilectal AusVE is noteworthy in that it strongly preserves certain variants which were widely used in the English spoken in England in the 18th century and earlier, but which have now largely dropped out of use in more standard varieties. Many of the characteristics distinguishing AusVE from StAusColE and StAusFE are retained in certain other non-standard varieties of English spoken in other parts of the world, a testament to the power of peer-group transmission of speech norms.

The emergent Australian working-class vernacular had probably stabilised by the mid-19th century, some two generations after the British colonisation of Australia. The strongest input into this speech tradition appears to have come from the dialects of southeast England, especially London Cockney (Horvath 1985; Ward 1958). From 1788 to 1851 Australia served as a penal colony of Great Britain and the convicts formed a virtual slave-labour class for the small middle and upper class of military officers, merchants and large landowners. While the 168,000 convicts who arrived in this period came from all parts of Britain and

Ireland, the enterprising Londoners, described as garrulous, articulate and quick-witted, were said to dominate the lower strata of Australian society. During its first few generations the colony was characterised by sharp class antagonisms and equally sharp differences in speech between this small elite class and a large lower class made up primarily of convicts and their children (known as the 'currency lads and lasses'). The convicts and their children made up the majority of the colony's population until about 1860. Urban wage labourers, clerks and tradesmen formed a growing intermediate class, who in their speech largely followed the demographically dominant group. In the second half of the 19th century Australian working men tended to be highly mobile, seeking work in various regions, with movement peaking during periodic gold rushes, and this mobility ensured that regional differences in working-class speech remained small.

The remainder of the paper discusses a selection of the most salient grammatical features of AusVE and briefly comments on their history. There have been relatively few systematic studies of grammatical features that are socially significant in the Australian English speech community. Among the exceptions are Anna Shnukal's work on Cessnock speech (Shnukal 1978, 1982, 1989) and Edina Eisikovits' study of the speech of Inner-Sydney working-class adolescents (Eisikovits 1981, 1987, 1989a,b). The discussion will also draw quite heavily on data from Tasmania because this is the one region for which the writer has a sizeable corpus of transcripts, consisting mainly of conversations tape-recorded and transcribed by Frances Syder and myself between 1974 and 1987. The transcripts represent about 15 different speakers, almost all from northern Tasmania, and total around 80,000 words (of which about half consists mainly of AusVE speech). The sample of AusVE speakers in the AusVE material is heavily biased towards males. I also draw on analyses of several variables in this data by students in graduate courses I taught at the University Auckland in the late 1980s. Other sources include the author's notes on overheard conversations and spontaneous speech on radio and TV, a doctoral thesis on auctions (Harris 1992), the *Australian National Dictionary* (Ramson 1988), and dialogue from several regionally-based works of fiction by Australian authors: *Bonanza* and *Mo Burdekin*, novels set in the Queensland outback around 1900 (Campion 1941, 1942), stories set in southern rural Queensland in the late 19th century (Rudd 1954), and *The Sentimental Bloke*, verse tales by an author raised in South Australia in the late 19th century, told in 'robust vernacular' through the voice of a rough Melbourne city lad in the early years of the 20th century (Dennis 1950), and *They're a Weird Mob*, a novel set in Sydney in the 1950s (Culotta 1957).

Of course, fictional dialogue needs to be treated with caution as data, and none of our conclusions about contemporary patterns of usage rests primarily on evidence from this source. The chief values of the fictional material are that it (i) extends regional coverage, providing evidence that certain features recorded in natural speech from a few parts of Australia are/were also present elsewhere, (ii) extends our temporal range, giving data from 100 years ago, and (iii) indicates which features of AusVE were most salient to the authors of the fictional works.

The following is a key to abbreviations used in the transcript passages cited here:

ADJ = adjective, ADV = adverb, AUX = auxiliary verb, ART = article, CAPITALS = peak or main stress in a tone group, DET = determiner, INDEF = indefinite, LOC = locative phrase, N = noun, NEG = Negative, NP = noun phrase, PREP = preposition, PRO = pronoun, S = sentence, SUBJ = grammatical subject, V = verb, [bracketed words] = editorial comment, "," = non-final intonation juncture, "." = final intonation juncture, "/" = cutoff in mid tone group, either by the speaker or another party, "-" = pause of less than half a second in mid-construction, "–" = pause of more than half a second in mid-construction.

2.   Pronominal gender assignment to inanimates and animals

2.1.   Animating inanimate referents

A striking feature of AusVE is the frequency with which an animate pronoun, *he* or *she* (or an accusative or genitive variant), is used instead of neuter *it* to refer to inanimate things such as trees, axes, houses, roads, rain, jobs and situations, and to living creatures of unknown sex, such as birds, fish and mosquitoes. The use of a masculine or feminine pronoun for an inanimate referent will be referred to here as *animation*. Animation of specific referents only occurs some of the time in AusVE, as the following example shows:

(4)   (Tasmania: Chas is telling a story to Harv and others.)
    *... and I was leadin', pullin' this **hay** up with one o' them -- what they call a grabstacker...*
    *and Tim...he **mighta** been building the stack, I think, Tim, prob'ly with loose hay....*
    *They'd sweep **'er** in/...sweep **'er** in, and then...they 'ad a pole up in the air, and **they was** pulling **it** [the hay] over a block, y' see. Gettin' **it** up. That's how they got **it** up on top of the stack, this hay.*

Before we consider what makes a speaker choose to animate a referent it will be convenient to examine the rules for deciding when a referent will be *he* and when it will be *she*. The assignment of a particular animate gender to a referent will be termed *(animate) gender assignment*. Gender assignment in AusVE differs in at least two fundamental respects from the gender systems of languages such as Italian and German. In the latter, gender is (a) assigned to nouns and (b) the gender of particular nouns is (mostly) arbitrary, i.e. the connection is a grammatical one, not motivated by inherent features of the referent. In AusVE, by contrast, gender is (a) assigned to referents rather than nouns (this is also the case in Standard English) and (b) animate gender assignment to inanimate referents is based on logical principles, to be defined below. Different animate genders may be assigned to the same noun when it refers to a male or female being, or to different senses of a polysemous noun, or to the same noun. For example, a particular fish or a kangaroo will *he*, except when it is known that it is a female, when it is *she*. Gender assignment is never to the nouns *fish* or *kangaroo* as nouns. And any noun, or at least any concrete noun, such as *river*, *house*, *car*, or *leg*, may be used to refer to a model of the prototypical referent, as in miniature figures, or to a piece or position in a game or puzzle. Such models may be treated as portable objects (see 2.4.) , which are subject to rules of gender assignment that differ from those associated with 'real' rivers, houses, cars and legs (see 2.2. and 2.3.). In much the same way, literal and metaphorical uses of the same word can have different gender assignments. One can loosely speak of gender as being assigned to a particular noun in discourse, so long as we keep in mind that the noun represents the referent.

AusVE has two separate systems of gender assignment, which apply to mutually exclusive classes of referents. There is a class whose members may be either masculine or feminine. This class consists roughly of portable goods, specifically goods that are represented by count nouns as opposed to mass nouns. Gender assignment in this class is based on pragmatic principles. The other class has fixed gender, i.e. some members are consistently masculine, the rest are consistently feminine. This class consists of all remaining things (including animals, plants, features of the inanimate natural environment, abstract entities, non-portable inanimate objects and things that form a mass). Gender assignment is based on inherent attributes of the referent.

2.2.   Things that are consistently masculine

Referents that are consistently masculine consist chiefly of (i) plants, and (ii) animals of unknown sex. It also includes (iii) vehicle-driver combinations when the driver's gender is unknown and (iv) male private parts. Animals and plants can be unified as a natural semantic class, namely, living things.

Trees and other plants:
In (5) Mark comments on the plants as he walks around his 40 acre patch of Tasmanian bushland with his cousin Ken, visiting from Canberra. Trees, and other plants, living and dead, upright and fallen, are consistently *he* – 19 out of 19 in this extract.

(5)   *There's a **tree** up here died for no apparent REAson.*
        'E was healthy – 'n there 'e is, DEAD! ... I felled 'im [another dead
        tree]. *'E was DANgerous. That one there, **he**'s a stringybark.*
        [points] *'E's a blackwood. That one there, 'e's a wild cherry.*
        Has little cherries on 'im and they're good to eat TOO, them cherries.
        [points] *an' 'e's a peppermint. See the leaves, they're DIFFerent.*
        ...That stringybark [points], *'e's got a left-handed twist* [in the grain of
        the wood and bark] *They reckon 'e'll still split if 'e's got a left-handed
        twist, but that'd be testin 'em. See, **he** don't start twistin till 'e gets
        above that limb, does 'e? Hard as a bull's forehead, that bloody wood is.*
        *...The **snottygobble*** [parasitic creeper] *is into this one, but 'e's not goin
        to kill 'im. ... See **that log** lyin there Got a load of wood in 'im, 'asn't 'e?*

In (6) Bill, a bushman from New South Wales, is talking to another man about cutting timber for slab housing, for a film made by the Australian Parks Services:

(6)   *What we'll be looking for is **a tree** with a straight barrel on 'im. You
        can tell after you've hit 'im if 'e's sound. The tree 'll talk to you when
        'e's startin to crack.*

In (7) Rex, a Tasmanian businessman, recalls how his nephew Ken and his son Mark, as small boys, tried to pull out a large turnip:

(7)   Rex: *I was ploughing there and I'd 'ad some turnips in...
                and there was a big **turnip** there, E was like that, y' know,
                nearly as big as a kerosene tin, and you two fellas **was** down
                there tryin to get **it** out... you'd...twisted 'im, and pulled the
                thing,*
        Ken: *an' we couldn't get 'im*
        Rex: *Couldn't get 'im. ...yiz ha/ you had 'im loose and you didn't
                realize ...y' had 'im broke off at the/*
        Ken: *root.*
        Rex: *At the root. But 'e was a big turnip. Yiz'd worked on it!*

(8)   (Tasmania: Ken has called on his Uncle Bill, a man in his 80s, who
        has just started a small vegetable patch next to the lawn.)
        Ken: *What's that growing in the lawn there? Are you cultivating that?*
        Bill: *That's a **carrot**! I've been watering 'im, lookin after 'im.*

(9)   (Tasmania: Mark is talking to his wife, Jill.)
        Mark: *What are y' lookin at?*
        Jill: *I'm lookin at **that tree**.*
        Mark: *How's 'e doin?*
        Jill: *Looks sad. The grubs are not doin much for 'im.*

(10)   (Tasmania: Ken's cousin, Pauline, is describing one of her garden
        plants.)
        *I had a **Golden Snail** and **he** climbed all over the place.*

(11)   (Middle-aged man, Coff's Harbour, NSW)
        a. [Of a **pawpaw** tree] *'E's only small but 'e bears a lot of fruit*
        b. *This **passion fruit**, **he** used to scramble all over the place. But 'e
            died.*
        c. *This one here, this **avocado**, – **he** ran wild and I cut the top off 'im.*

(12)   ('The Gardening Program', ABC television: Comment by one of two
        middle-aged men, both gardeners, who are looking at a small shrubby
        flowering plant.)
        ***He**'s been cut, by the look of it.*

Animals of unknown sex:
In formal English an animal of unknown sex, e.g. a wild mammal or bird, or
a fish, snake or mosquito, usually takes a neuter animate pronoun. AusVE differs in strongly preferring use of an animate pronoun. The animate pronoun is
invariably masculine. In (13) Harv is talking about men in Tasmania poaching
sheep during the Depression years.

(13)   Harv: *But what they used to like to do about the day before they came
                back, was to get **one of Von Breddow's sheep** y' see, as close to
                home as they could there, and they'd kill 'im and hang 'im up
                in the – in the scrub you see,*

        Chas: *Yes.*

        Harv: *...sometimes they'd hang 'im up tonight y' see, and go to pick
                'im up tomorrow night, **he**'d be gone. Some of the other fellas
                seen 'im.*

(14)   (Tasmania: Mark is telling Ken about a wild goat that he shot.)
　　　Ken:　*You didn't eat 'im?*
　　　Mark:　*Well, 'e wasn't no teenager.*
　　　Ken:　*'E'd a been pretty tough.*

(15)   (Tasmania: Electrolux salesman is talking about a blocked vacuum
　　　cleaner he was asked to fix. The machine turned out to be inhabited by
　　　a colony of mice.)
　　　*I took the hose off the front... 'n there was a blimmin **mouse** sitting...*
　　　*lookin... so I stood the machine up 'n gave it a shake... so **he** couldn't*
　　　*see which way **he** was goin... 'n emptied the bag, 'n the mouse took*
　　　*off. But when I first opened the vacuum cleaner **he** looked at me...*

Vehicle + controller:
There is one category of referents that, at first appearance, seems to run counter
to a general convention (see 2.3.) that vehicles, when animated, are feminine.
This is when a vehicle (car, truck, small boat or plane) is named or indicated,
and assigned masculine gender, as in (16).

(16)   (Middle-aged woman from Tumut, a country town in NSW.)
　　　a.　*There's a **BMW** right behind you. **He's** impatient to pass.*
　　　b.　*Watch out for that big **truck** there. '**E's** all over the road.*

In such cases, however, the vehicle is a metonym standing for the controlling
agent (driver, skipper, pilot), or for a unit consisting of a vehicle and its controller, which is seen to be 'doing something'. When the driver is known to be
female the use of *he* is no longer acceptable. Thus, this use of *he* for vehicle +
driver can be regarded as another case of masculine as the unmarked gender,
when applied to living things.

2.3.　Things that are consistently feminine

Apart from portable count nouns, the rest of the biologically inanimate uni-
verse – the inanimate environment, situations, vehicles, buildings, and so on
– is feminine in animated style.
Abstract referents:
For abstract entities and events, such as a principle, a time or season, law, job,
situation, action, utterance, emotions, the neuter pronoun is generally preferred,
but when such a referent is animated, the pronoun is always feminine.

(17)   (Malcolm Johnston, jockey, *The Weekend Australian* 23, 24/10/1999)
　　　*But the **Cox Plate** is a test of endurance and character for horse and*
　　　*rider...and I'll tell you what, **she** is a deadset pressure cooker.*

(18)   (Pat Rafter, tennis player from Queensland, talking about whether his **retirement** will be decisive. *The Australian*, 21/1/2001)
She'll be clean, mate, don't worry about that.

(19)   (Tasmanian man, Noel, reporting an exchange during a closely-contested **game** of Australian Rules football, on which Wing had placed a bet.)
*"What do you think about the **game**, Wing?" 'E said, "**She**'s tight!'"*

(20)   (Tasmania: Harv is talking about a tense situation associated with the snaring of game.)
*I bet **she** was on out there, when they was snarin', them fellas… nobody could go near another bloke's snares, could they? Or they'd get shot.*

(21)   (Tasmania: Real estate agent refers first to his **job** and second to a **delicate situation** at work.)
*When **she**'s your livelihood **she**'s a bit awkward.*

(22)   (Tasmania: Ken's cousin, Nigel, is a man in his 30s who had been working at two jobs.)
Nigel: *I've given up me **morning job**.*
Ken: *Have you?*
Nigel: *Yeah, I gave '**er** away. I'm a new man.*

(23)   (Sydney: A builder is talking to friends, *They're a Weird Mob*, 81)
*But this time I'm tell' yez about we was **buildin' a garage**. **She** was an excavation job.*

(24)   (Ken is talking by phone to his cousin Mark, who is in Tasmania.)
Ken: *I thought m' **birthday** was still a long way off.*
Max: *No, **she's** just around the corner.*

(25)   (Victoria: Farmer from Lightning Ridge, referring to prospects for the end of a drought, on ABC radio, 11/11/2002)
*I'd sooner it didn't rain till March, then we'd have the bad year over and done with, and hopefully, from then on **she**'ll be good.*

Inanimate elements of the natural physical world:
   Land, mountains, rivers, soil, grass, minerals, fire, rain, sun, moon, the cold, wind, etc. are consistently feminine when animated.

(26)   (Northern Territory: John Joshua, quoted in *The Canberra Times*, 9/8/1998)
*…that **river**, **she** is dangerous with all them crocodiles.*

(27)   (Coff's Harbour, NSW: Local resident, a middle-aged man, is looking
         out to sea for a whale.)
         *She's a rough **sea** today.*

⊣ (28)   (Canberra, Australian Capital Territory. Man speaking of the **wind**.)
         She's a bit keen today. Should've brung me fur coat.

(29)   (Queensland: Farmer referring to a **storm**.)
         She made a mess of that crop.

The next two examples are from two novels by Sarah Campion, set in the
Queensland countryside around the end of the 19th century. In the following
passages the speakers are talking about drilling for **artesian water**, and a **gold-mine**, respectively.

(30)   *"Garn, y'old crow, stop croaking and look at the **water**. Howzit
         goin', mates?"..."**She's** come at last, blast **her** pretty eyes. Gawd, we
         wos long enough gittin' downta **it**. But **she's** comin' up nice, now,..."*
         (*Bonanza*, 206–207)

(31)   *"They've started stoping wi' four men on No. 2 winze, west 'o the shaft,
         in two foot o' stone. **She** ain't eggsackly bonzer, but **she's** good enough.
         Stopes between 3 and 4 winzes'll 'ave ter lie till sich time as they gits
         mullock room at No. 3." "Wot, you talkin' o the **Bull Frog** that's let
         on tribute. Cor, **she** ain't no blunny good, **she's** a bad 'un **she** is, a fair
         cow."* (*Mo Burdekin*, 246)

Constructions and their fixed parts:
Man-made elements in the landscape, such as roads, dams, bridges and houses,
and their parts, are consistently feminine.

(32)   (Tasmania: Real estate agent, showing off a hill-side **house**.)
         She's certainly got a view, this one.

(33)   (Sydney: Builders talking about a **cottage**, *They're a Weird Mob*, 90)
         *We're gunna put a new front on '**er**. ...Yeah. We're gunna wreck '**er**
         terday.*

(34)   (Tasmania: Men talking about a rural community hall.)
         Ken: *We couldn't find the ol' **Forester Hall**.*
         Noel: *No, **she's** gone.*

(35)   (Tasmania: Speaker is Harv, conversing with Chas and others.)
         *He hoed 'is boot into the **door**, and of course **she's** got a cross-piece
         in – them old-fashioned **doors**, y'know.*

(36)   (Tasmania: Harv, talking to friends)
        He...shut 'im [a sheep] *up in the* **shed***...But* **she** *was only one o' them*
        old – built out of studs and...round spars.

Body-parts:
All body-parts other than male genitals are feminine.

(37)   (Queensland man, in reply to an inquiry about his **knee**.)
        She's *a lot better than* **she** *was, I can tell you that.*

(38)   (Tasmanian man, of a wisdom tooth.)
        She *was no use to me anyway, so I 'ad* **her** *out.*

Vehicles:
Vehicles show a very high frequency of animation. Except for the special case
noted above, the animate pronoun is invariably feminine. The referents in (39)
and (40) are a truck and a bulldozer, respectively.

(39)   (Tasmania: Chas)
        Alec 'ad this old **D30 International** *and they're cartin wood* [short
        gap in recording] *and by jees* **she** *went down, this* **truck***! I'm not sure*
        they didn't unload the wood and still couldn't get **'er** *out.*

(40)   (Tasmania: Harv)
        But when 'e first bought the **bulldozer** *'e told me he took* **'er** *out in the*
        bush and he'd be taking **'er** *up all them big stringy gums... and the old*
        bulldozer's got one claw up on this 'ere, on a green root y' see, and
        she's *just skidding on* **'er***... Well, 'e don't know what to do about it,*
        Alec, 'e just opened up and left **'er** *there. Just swears at* **'er***.*

2.4.   Things that may be either masculine or feminine

Referents that can take either masculine or feminine pronouns consist roughly
of individuated portable goods, e.g. tools, small machines, and items of food,
furniture and clothes. In the next two examples each speaker is talking about
timber that has been cut.

(41)   (A bushman from country New South Wales, is talking about cutting
        timber for slab housing. The timber is masculine. Note the shift from
        he to *she* here when the topic moves from the cutting of a post to the
        removal of a wedge.) *Mostly the slab you cut in the bush, you loaded*
        'im *on to your transport and took* **'im** *home to work on* **'im** *at the*
        homestead itself... The first post you've got to make fairly even, make

*'im 10 inches or 8 inches wide. You lay 'im flat and you square 'im
half way down, you square 'im fairly even, then you turn 'im over....
Mostly you can leave 'er* [the wedge] *up on the* [timber]

(42)   (Tasmania: Harv is talking about the block of wood in a chopping
         contest and the block is feminine.)
         *... 'e was off say three or five or whatever. When they said "FIVE!"
         'e's no sooner* [unclear] *than 'e HIT 'er* [the block], *y' know, and 'e
         chopped two or three six-inch nails CLEAN off...*

What makes a speaker assign a particular animate gender in a particular case?
There has been lively debate over this matter, though the debaters agree that
speakers are using pragmatic principles of some sort. One possibility is that
feminine gender is the unmarked gender for all portable goods, as it is for features of the inanimate environment, and that it is only the choice of masculine
gender that we have to explain. Another hypothesis (Pawley 2002) is that a crucial factor in gender assignment is whether the speaker's attitude to the referent
is one of attachment or detachment. If the object is seen as something of personal value it will be *she*. Thus, someone's hat, axe, knife, pen, table or fridge
will be *she* (see [45–48] for supporting examples). By contrast, if an item is
seen merely as an 'object', something towards which the speaker feels indiffer-
ent, it will be *he* (in animated style, otherwise *it*). Using the masculine pronoun
is appropriate, for example, when a salesman is talking about the goods he is
selling or a tradesman is talking about objects he is working with. A qualifier is
in order here. The bulk of the evidence on animate gender assignment comes
from male speech. There is some evidence that certain speakers of Standard
Colloquial English, particularly middle class women, follow somewhat different conventions from paradigmatic AusVE speakers when assigning animate
gender to portable goods (Jane Simpson, personal communication).

   Wierzbicka (2002) argues, with some justification, that the attachment/de-
tachment hypothesis cannot explain all cases of gender assignment to referents
of variable gender. There are cases where *she* is used where no 'attachment' is
discernable, but there is emotional involvement, e.g. interest, satisfaction, ir-
ritation. Wierzbicka offers an additional explanation. Because animate gender
assignment is a stylistic feature that originates in men's speech (though it is im-
itated by women), she says, we cannot fully understand how it works without
reference to male attitudes to men and women in Australian society. Use of *she*
implies that the speaker is thinking of the object as like a woman, for example,
as having characteristics that fit male stereotypes of women, e.g. being beauti-
ful, pleasing, temperamental or incompetent, or as being something that a man
can do things to. Thus, Wierzbicka suggests that the shift from a masculine to

a feminine object pronoun in (43) is motivated by the reference to full force being applied to the object. Example (44) might be explained the same way.

(43)   (Tasmania: Max is talking to Ken, who is using a screwdriver to tighten a tricky screw.)
        Max: *Bloody oath! You're getting' **'im** tight! Tighten **'im**. --- OK, **'e's** tight.* [a bit later] *Give it to **'er**!*

(44)   (Sydney: A builder is explaining things to a novice. *They're a Weird Mob*, 79)
        *"Show yer how to work the **lever**. Pull **'er** out like this, then let **'er** swing down. But 'old **'er**."* [The **concrete** ran into the barrow.] *"Not a bad mix, bit boney. Then yer swing **'er** [the lever] over ter Pat again, an' 'ave a bludge while 'e's fillin' **'er** [the concrete mixer] up. Okay?"*

By contrast, when a man uses *he* to refer to a portable object, Wierzbicka suggests, it is to convey an attitude of emotional neutrality or objectivity towards it, as a man thinks of other men. This is an attitude subtly different from 'detachment' insofar as 'objectivity' signals professional competence or expertise. Thus, one might explain the bushman's use of *he* in (42) for the slabs of timber he is shaping and auctioneer's use of *he* in (51) for the electric floor polisher as cases of speakers showing a professional attitude towards the goods being made or sold.

These hypotheses offering a semantic-pragmatic explanation of variable gender assignment are difficult to test. One needs to look at a sizeable sample of cases where one or the other animate gender is assigned to portable objects and see whether statistically significant distributional patterns emerge. Thus, while the shift from *him* to *her* in (43) is consistent with Wierzbicka's 'doing something to a thing with force' explanation, this is a single example and could be due to chance. There are cases where a feminine pronoun is assigned to a portable object participant (actor or undergoer) in a context where it has no obvious 'feminine' associations.

Machines and tools:
Whatever the reason may be, the fact is that some kinds of portable goods have a more consistent association with feminine gender than other kinds. Machines and tools – radios, TVs, power saws, vacuum cleaners, hammers and axes, for instance – are more likely to be feminine when animated than, say, a pen or a cup, or a screw or a nail.

(45)   (Harv describes an incident in a wood-chopping competition in Tasmania, where an axeman damages a valuable axe he has borrowed.)

*Ol' Kit...'e 'ad the only **choppin axe** John Behan 'ad, Nobody 'ad TWO them days y' know, in the bad old days, and John 'ad a pretty good axe...they got Kit entered in this Chop y' know...and 'e fetches **'er** [the axe] and 'e looks at **'er**, y' see, ...and 'e holds **'er** round to John, and 'e's got a great big gap CLEAN through the FACE of **'er**.*

(46)   (Tasmania: Mark is looking at a **timber gun** that is his personal property.)
       *That timber gun, **she** splits the log open.*

(47)   (Sydney: A man thanks his workmates for some gifts. *They're a Weird Mob*, 120)
       *'**she**'s a good **tape measure**. Er...thanks for oilin 'er. This **trowel**. **She**'s ...er...**she**'s a good trowel.'*

(48)   (A man from Queensland is talking to another about a **computer**, over morning tea.)
       *You'll be doing this the old-fashioned way, Bill. The modern way is to take your **computer** 'nd set **'er** up in the village.*

(49)   (Farmer talking about an electric fence, in advertisement on TV.)
       *Try nature's test, piece of grass on the **fence**. Feel a tingle? **She**'s workin!*

However, an individual machine or tool that is not someone's personal possession is sometimes masculine. The following examples are consistent with either the detachment or the professional objectivity interpretations.

(50)   (Electrician, from Canberra, trying different **switches** on a switch board.)
       *Let's try **him**. No, well it must be **this fella**.*

(51)   (Melbourne auctioneer, talking about a floor polisher [Harris 1992: 235])
       *Lot 4 A once again **electric floor polisher**... quick 20 bucks for **'im** ... 2 and a half dollars who wants **'im** first up can 'ave **'im** floor polisher 2 and a half ooh not very impressive crowd today Laurie and Christmas is coming up too nobody want **'im** 2 and a half bucks quick I'll put **'im** with lot 5 Laurie. Can't say we don't try*

Implements used in games:
Implements used in games are *she* when animated, at least in cases when the referent is being used in a game. For example the ball and the stumps used in cricket are *she*, as is the pitch on which the game is played. In (52a) a cricket

commentator on Channel 9 is referring to one of the stumps as a batsman is bowled out and in (52b) the same commentator is referring to the cricket ball, which has been snicked and flies to a slip fielder.

(52)   a.   *Look at that middle stump! Back **she** goes! ...And the West Indies are one for 60.*
        b.   *He nearly dropped **'er**. That was a near thing!*

The detachment and objectivity ('like a man') hypotheses correctly predict that occasionally there will also be circumstances under which implements used in games will take a masculine pronoun, e.g. bats and balls being placed as objects for display in a shop.

Furniture, carpets:
There are examples of furniture with both masculine and feminine pronouns:

(54)   (A salesman in the town of Launceston, Tasmania, is showing carpets to two customers. He made roughly 50 pronominal references to carpets. All were masculine.)
        *That **fella** he's a poly* [polyester blend], ***he's** two fifty* [two hundred and fifty dollars] ***He's** a blend, **that bloke**. I've had **'im** for a while, it'd be nice to turn **'im** over. I'll give **'im** to you for four hundred.*

(55)   (Tasmanian woman, to a man shifting a **table** in her house.)
        *Put **'er** down here.*

Food and drink:
Items of food and drink are usually feminine but occasionally masculine.

(56)   (Tasmania: Same conversation as [2] above.)

        Harv: *...when the dog took the i-, the/ the **leg of mutton** under the house?... Bill's just coming in, I s'pose when the dog, when 'e sees 'im come out with **'er**.*
        Chas: *...Bill went in to carve the meat up and out come the bloody dog.*
        Harv: *With the meat!...*
        Chas: *"No," 'e said "**She**'ll be blamed well all right." ...a bit of blamed dirt on **it** won't 'urt you*
        Harv: *And took **'er** in and put **'er** on the plate!*
        Chas: *Yeah. Carved 'er up. Yeah.*

Massed materials:
Mass materials, e.g. hay (see [4]), water (30), gold (31), and cement are nearly always feminine, as in (57) and (58).

(57)   (Men talking on a Sydney building site. *They're a Weird Mob*, 102)

    a.   [of a **load of loam**] *"There **she** is," said Dennis.*
    b.   *"Bloody black **mortar**. **She's** a bastard."*

(58)   (Australian chef from Melbourne, ABC Television, 9/8/2002)
    *Let's have a look at the **oil*** [heating in a pan]. *Wah! **She's** hot!*

Just one example has been noted where a mass noun is masculine.

(59)   (Tasmania: Harv recalls how men illegally would shoot possums
    out of season and dry and hide the skins until the restricted season
    ended.)
    *...they used to be terrible careful where they planted **it*** [their
    collection of dried skins]... *wherever they'd secreted **their catch**,
    like ... As they built **'im** up, y'see, from week to week, and then...*
    [when the season ended] *they could bring **'im** out and take **'im** home*

2.5.   Concluding remarks about animation

Let us return to the question of when a speaker chooses to animate a particular
referent. There seems to be a number of factors that correlate with animation.

(i)   Speech style and social context:
    The higher the incidence of informal variants in the discourse the more
    likely it is the speaker will animate. The incidence of informal variants in
    turn correlates with formality of social context.

(ii)   Inherent salience:
    Inherent salience is important in the case of plants and animals. When
    referring to animals of unknown sex, animation is most frequent with rela-
    tively large animals, such as mammals, reptiles, birds and fish, and least
    frequent with small creatures such as insects and snails. Similarly, large
    plants are more likely to be animated than small ones. Large vehicles –
    cars, trucks, bulldozers, ships, planes – are very often animated and smaller
    vehicles – bicycles, carts, wheelbarrows – less often.

(iii)   Individuation:
    In his comparative studies of English dialects which use animate pronouns
    for inanimate referents Peter Siemund (2002, 2007) argues that this fea-
    ture is strongly associated with individuation of referents. Concrete nouns
    are more likely to be animated than abstract nouns and count nouns more

likely than mass nouns. There is some truth in these generalisations but they need qualifying with regard to AusVE.

(iv) Salience or topicality in the discourse:

Any referent can be made a focus of interest, a topic, and in that event, it is likely to be animated. Once a speaker has chosen to refer to a particular referent by an animate or inanimate pronoun, he or she is likely to keep to that choice in immediately following references within the same discourse unit (narrative, joke etc.), as long as it remains a prominent participant in the discourse. This is nicely illustrated in (60), where Chas tells a story about being accused of poaching timber, and Harv collaborates with him in constructing a coda to the episode.

(60) (Tasmania: same conversation as example [2] above.)

Chas: *...but Frazer an – we 'ad a bloody row over some WOOD... We* **was** *up there cuttin and Frazer come onto us y' see,... "oh well", he said, "I suppose you can 'ave* **'im** *[a tree] but we already 'AD* **'im**, *all bar a few pieces, cut up and loaded, and Frazer said "I s'pose you can 'ave* **'im**," *'e said, "Yeah, but don't touch that one over THERE". But we'd been passing* **'im** *with the AXE, and* **'e** *was only a bit of – bloody – papery -SHELL.* **'E** *wasn't/*

Harv: **'E** *wasn't WORTH it.*

Chas: *No. That's why we LEFT* **'im**. *We'd 'AD* **'im**.

Harv: *You left* **'im** *for FRAzer, wi- with PLEAsure.*

Chas: *Yes.*

Harv: *Not eNOUGH of* **'im**.

Chas: *No!* **'e** *was/*

Harv: *Too ROTTen'.*

Chas: *Yeah.* **'e** *was DRY enough but* **'e** *was on'y about an inch or an inch and a 'alf THICK...*

2.6.   Historical and comparative note

Historical and comparative data show that central features of the AusVE system of gender assignment go back some centuries in the history of English. Historical records indicate that a pattern of gender assignment quite like the AusVE system was part of middle class speech in 17th and 18th century England (Pawley 2002). The same system occurs in New Zealand Vernacular English and it appears that there are close parallels in parts of North America (Mathiot and Roberts 1978; Siemund 2002, 2007; Wagner 2005).

3.   Non-standard verb forms

3.1.   *were:* subject-verb agreement

The variable *were*: subject verb agreement refers to the alternation between *was* and *were* in three contexts: (i) when the subject of a verb is a plural pronoun or plural count noun, as in *we were talking*, (ii) when the subject is singular *you*, and (iii) after an existential *there* subject with a plural count noun in predicate position, as in *There were about 50 people there*.

Standard Formal English requires *were* in contexts (i)–(iii). In Colloquial English *were* occurs in (i) and (ii) while either *was* or *were* are acceptable in (iii). Paradigmatic AusVE speakers prefer *was* in all three contexts. And whereas some non-standard varieties of English in Britain and the USA show *was*-generalisation only in affirmative sentences, AusVE speakers also use it is negatives, as in e.g. (61j, k).

Wyld (1953) observes that *was* was commonly used by speakers of English of all classes during the 16th to the 18th centuries. Sir Thomas Seymour writes in 1544: "Such sowders and maryners as *was* shept at Harwyche". Alexander Pope (1718) writes to Lady Mary Montagu Wortley: "I shall look upon you as many years younger than you *was*." In the same century Henry Fielding, in *Love in Several Masques*, has Vermella say: "pray sir, how *was* you cured of your love?"

Context 1: Subject is a plural pronoun (*we, you, they*):

(61)   (All Tasmanian: one woman, Tamar: a, and four men: Chas: b–d, Rex: e–f, Noel: g, Harv: h–k.)
   a. *we was apparently, having an argument…when we was milking*
   b. *they 'ad a pole up in the air, and **they was** pulling it* [the hay] *over a block…*
   c. *…and **they was** taking pigs to the sale…and **they was** helping catch 'em.*
   d. ***We was** up there cuttin and Frazer come onto us y' see,…*
   e. *and **you two fellas was** down there tryin to get it out…*
   f. *I remember **us two boys was** workin in the paddock,…*
   g. ***We was** winning easily*
   h. *and they – o' course 'e drops the axe and away 'e goes, and the last Percy seen of 'im was **they was** goin over the brow o' the hill…*
   i. *…**lots of fellas** that **was** fairly close to home*
   j. ***the cows wasn't** milked.*

k. ***they*** [pieces of a skiff holding seeds for broadcasting] ***wasn't a bad apparatus.***

l. *an' here's **these possums, they was** all skinned.*

(62)   (Queensland: Drilling for artesian water. *Bonanza*, 206–207)
*Gawd, **we wos** long enough gittin' downta it. But she's comin' up nice, now,...*

(63)   (Sydney: Two builders arguing the point while drinking in a hotel. *They're a Weird Mob*, 73)
*'Course **they was**.' 'Mightna been.' 'I got two quid to say **they was**.'*

(64)   (Sydney: Builders on holiday. *They're a Weird Mob*, 73)
*Wondered wot **yez was** doin' with the guns.*

Context 2: subject is singular *you*:

(65)   (Tasmania: speakers are Harv: a–c, his brother Rex: d, Rex's wife, Tamar: e and Harv's wife, D: f.)
a. *You soon convinced him **you was** entitled to the timber that was on it?*
b. *....until they found out what sort of a fella **you was**, and whether **you was** really trying.*
c. *But **you 'us** [was] goin along pretty well, Chas.*
d. ***You was** late again.*
e. ***Was you?** mm.*
f. ***You was** too cunning for that, Chas.*

(66)   (Sydney: Builders conversing. *They're a Weird Mob*, 133)
***You was** a jackeroo once, **wasn't you** Den?*

Table 2 compares two groups of Tasmanians, one consisting of nine whose colloquial style is predominantly AusVE speakers and three who are StAusColE speakers. The total number of occurrences of *was* and *were* for each of four grammatical contexts (subject of the verb distinguished as *we, you, they* or plural NP and *there* with plural NP) appear in the columns to the left and the percentages showing overall frequency on the right.

Table 2.   *were*: subject agreement

AusVE speakers (N = 9)			
	was	*were*	% *was*
we	29	29	50
you	17	19	46
they/NP	53	86	39
there	19	3	86
	132	123	52
StAusColE speakers (N = 3)			
	was	*were*	% *was*
we	2	14	14
you	0	9	0
they/NP	0	27	0
there	4	1	80
	6	51	11

It can be seen that the *there*-context is non-diagnostic: for both groups of speakers *was* is the normal form after *there*. In each of the other contexts, however, there is a sharp difference between AusVE and StAusColE speakers: the AusVE group used *was* about 40 percent of the time in each environment while the StAusColE group varied between zero (with *we* and *you*) and 14 percent (with *they*/NP).

The distributional pattern is different for present tense forms. Non-standard *is* for standard *are* occurs about 15 percent of the time in our sample of AusVE speakers and almost as often among StAusColE speakers. All these uses of *is* are with a plural subject or predicate nominal, none with singular *you*, and most link existential *there* with a plural noun phrase. However, many examples of *is* with plural subjects were found in Australian works of fiction dating from about a century ago.

(67)   (Melbourne: *The Sentimental Bloke*)
　　a.　*when **things is** goin' crook* (*The Sentimental Bloke*, 30)
　　b.　***them words…is** singin' in me 'ead the 'ole day long.* (*The Sentimental Bloke*, 34)
　　c.　*Me **days an' nights is** full of schemes and plans* (*The Sentimental Bloke*, 32)
　　d.　***These is** 'appy days* (*The Sentimental Bloke*, 15)
　　a.　*"A boy!" she sez, "An' **bofe is** doin' well"* (*The Sentimental Bloke*, 35)

(68)   (Queensland: *On Our Selection*)
  a. *Dave, the **hens is** all off the roost. (On Our Selection, 95)*
  b. *"Well, you know," said Mother quietly, "**the boys is** men now"*
       (On Our Selection, 155)

This material suggests that *is*-generalisation may have been more common in AusVE speech 100 years ago than now.

3.2.   Non-standard past tense and participial forms of strong verbs

The past and participial forms of strong verbs have been notoriously unstable in English since at least the 12th century, because the various patterns of the inflectional paradigms provide diverse models for change by analogy. Today's standard past and participial forms were in many cases not yesterday's standard forms. Thus, the modern preterite *broke* is an innovation replacing earlier *brake*. The participle *helped* has replaced *holpen*. Lady Mary Wortley in a letter in 1513 asserts that "all the verses were *wrote* by me". In *Sense and Sensibility*, Jane Austen has Lucy Steele say "he has never *gave* me a moment's alarm".

In AusVE speech several strong verbs show non-standard past and past participle forms, with the same form being used for both. In a study of working-class adolescent speech in inner-city Sidney, Eisikovits (1987) reports merger of the simple past and past participle form in at least some instances for the following: *become, brang, come, broke, done, give, rung, seen, sung, swum,* and *took.* She also found (Eisikovits 1989a) that female speakers tend to decrease their use of non-standard forms with age while males, if anything, tend to increase their use of such forms.

(69)   (Inner-Sydney adolescents, reported in Eisikovits 1987)
  a. *Someone might 'a **took** 'em.*
  b. *I know a kid who **got bit** by a horse.*
  c. *I got a letter sent home an me mum **seen** it.*
  d. *His mate took a photo and **give** it to him.*
  e. *We were talking about when she **run** away from home.*

The data from Tasmania exhibit the same pattern of merger of past tense and past participle forms. Irregular past tense forms in the Tasmanian material include *become, brung, come, done, give, run* and *swum* and *seen.* Participle forms include *bit, broke, et, fell, give, knowed, laid, swore, took* and *went.*

(70)   (Tasmania, Noel tells his cousins about Uncle Bill's return from New Zealand.)

*'E **come** into the shop after 'e **come** back, y' see, and 'e **come** into the door ... so they went an' 'e **come** in, and 'e said "I'm BACK, y' know"*

(71)   (Tasmania:)

a.   *an' 'ere's Claude, he'd **laid** down under the pine hedge, y' see, ...I don't know how he **come** to get this name.* [Harv, reminiscing about a local character]

b.   *I should **'ve threw** the buggers over the fence there.* [Chas, referring to bottles of beer]

c.   *I couldn't **'ve went** home.* [Chas]

d.   *'You bloody well oughtn't to," 'e said, "I **give** you away tonight!"* [Chas, quoting his father-in-law, Mick, tell Mick's daughter that he had given her hand in marriage]

(71)   (Queensland: *On Our Selection*)

a.   *Dave's **got bit** by a adder.* (Joe, *On Our Selection*, 51)

b.   *I never said I **was bit**.* (Dave, *On Our Selection*, 54)

c.   *He's **bit** me.* (Joe, *On Our Selection*, 93)

(72)   (Melbourne: *The Sentimental Bloke*)

a.   *I'd **a give** a quid To 'ad it on the quite wivout this fuss* (*The Sentimental Bloke*, 26)

b.   *I dunno 'ow I **done** it in the end* (*The Sentimental Bloke*, 14)

c.   *Wot in the 'ell's 'e think I **come** there for?* (*The Sentimental Bloke*, 27)

d.   *I **seen** 'er in the markit first uv all* (*The Sentimental Bloke*, 12)

e.   *Some of the other fellas **seen** 'im* (*The Sentimental Bloke*, 27)

f.   *We **'ave trod** around Egypt's burnin's sand* (*The Sentimental Bloke*, 49)

Other Tasmanian examples appear in examples (1–2), (5), (7–8), (28) and (61) above.

In the Tasmanian corpus there is a clear distinction between the AusVE and StAusColE speakers in the treatment of these four strong verbs. Nine speakers of AusVE speakers averaged 65.4 percent for non-standard past forms of *come*, *do*, *give*, *see*. Three StAusColE speakers in Tasmania, in the same conversational corpus, averaged 6.3 percent non-standard forms. There was considerable variation among the AusVE speakers, with basilectal speakers averaging

80 to 100 percent non-standard forms and some others showing much lower percentages.

Other strong verbs occur less often with non-standard past forms but there is still a marked difference between AusVE and StAusColE speakers in the Tasmanian corpus. A count of past tense and participial forms for the 10 most frequent strong forms showed a fairly consistent pattern. The highest six scores for non-standard forms were all between 30 and 39 percent for AusVE speakers, with an average of 31 percent. This compares with only 3.3 percent for the three StAusColE speakers.

Given that many of the non-standard forms used in AusVE are found in many other non-standard varieties of English around the world, varieties that have been separate from AusVE for at least two centuries, we can conclude that AusVE has in these cases retained usages that were current in varieties of British English in 1800 or earlier.

3.3.   Non-standard *don't*

AusVE shows another usage retained from standard colloquial speech of the 18th century: *don't* for standard *doesn't*.

(73)   (Tasmanian men)
  a. Mark:*See, he **don't** start twistin till 'e gets above that limb, does 'e?*
  b. Harv: *...and Shep'-/ o' course 'e's a cunning old fella, 'e **don't** run away with it, y'see, 'e just walks off with it,...*
  c. Harv: *Well, 'e **don't** know what to do about it, Alec.*

(74)   (Sydney: Builders, *They're a Weird Mob*)
  a. *If 'e **don't** work 'e **don't** eat.' (They're a Weird Mob, 98)*
  b. *'E **don't** like dirt in 'is backyard. (They're a Weird Mob, 37)*

(75)   (Melbourne: *The Sentimental Bloke*, 48)
    *It **don't** fit in our plan*

3.4.   Merger of simple past and present perfect

Eisikovits (1989b) found evidence for some weakening of the opposition between simple past and present perfective in working-class Sydney adolescent speech. The auxiliary *have* was often omitted before past participles, as in:

(76)   a. *I only **been** there a coupla times.*
  b. *We haven't started this year but we **done** it before.*

The dropping of *have* was more frequent and more acceptable before the participle *got* than before *been*, and more common and acceptable before *been* than before other participles. Engels and Ritz (2000) present evidence that the present perfect is generally used for a wider range of functions in Australian English than in either British or American English.

4.   Negation

4.1.   Negative concord with indeterminates

Until the 18th century double negatives were the norm in English speech in constructions containing a negated verb followed by one or more NPs introduced by an indeterminate element: *a*, *any*, *anything*, *ever* or *either*. That is, a negative occurred not only before the main verb (or its auxiliary), but also on at least the first indeterminate element, a pattern known as negative concord. Negative concord is found in many contemporary non-standard English varieties, always as an optional rule which is applied more commonly to indeterminates inside the clause than outside it.

Double negatives are frequent in AusVE. All the recorded examples are limited to one indeterminate, there being no cases in the data of two indeterminates in the same negative sentence.

(77)   (Tasmanian men.)
   a.   *We wouldn't go no further* (Chas)
   b.   *Unless he's got you signed up he can't do nothing* (Harv)
   c.   *She wouldn't want no tractor* (Harv)
   d.   *I couldn't see no snake* (Harv)
   e.   *I never said nothing for a while* (Chas)
   f.   *No, definitely, he never had nothing to do with it* (Chas)
   g.   *an' I never caught nothing* (Scottie)

(78)   (Sydney: Builders. *They're a Weird Mob*)

   a.   *I didn't see nothing.*
   b.   *They don't want none of his money.*

(79)   (Melbourne: *The Sentimental Bloke*)
   a.   *It weren't no guyver neither* (*The Sentimental Bloke*, 13)
   b.   *'Ere's me, 'oo never took no 'eed 'o life* (*The Sentimental Bloke*,24)
   c.   *there ain't no certs* (*The Sentimental Bloke*, 25)
   d.   *I ain't got nothin' worth the fightin' for* (*The Sentimental Bloke*, 44)

4.2.   Non-standard *never*

In constructions where a past tense verb is negated, AusVE speakers generally use *never* for the auxiliary plus negative, i.e. *did not*, or *didn't*, is replaced by *never.* All the following cases are semantically equivalent to standard punctual *didn't* + infinitive verb, not to *never* + past tense verb.

(80)   (Tasmanian men: Chas: a–c, Harv: d–e)
   a.   *He **never** had the timber.*
   b.   *I **never** said nothing for a while.*
   c.   *He **never** done anything.*
   d.   *He **never** woke up to it then?*
   e.   *You **never** opened the bar ...*

(81)   (Melbourne: *The Sentimental Bloke*)
   a.   *'Ere's me, 'oo **never** took **no** 'eed 'o life* (*The Sentimental Bloke*, 24)
   b.   *A squarer tom, I swear, I **never** seen* (*The Sentimental Bloke*, 13)

5.   Personal pronouns

5.1.   General remarks

The personal pronoun system used in AusVE conforms to that of StAusColE, and Standard English, in most respects. However, AusVE has some optional pronominal usages that depart from Standard Formal English, some of which it shares with StAusColE. These include the use of:

(a)   first person plural accusative *us*, for first person singular *me*, when the speaker makes a request for something to be given to or obtained for him/ her, e.g. *Give us a light for me pipe, Give us him, Dig us out a pudlick* (*They're a Weird Mob*, 53, 56, 92)
(b)   first person plural accusative *us*, for nominative *we*, in NPs of form *us* (ADJ) N, e.g. *us two boys* (see [61 e])
(c)   a distinctive second person plural pronoun (*yiz, youse*)
(d)   masculine and feminine pronouns for inanimates (see section 2)
(e)   third person singular generic *they*, for standard *he*, or *he or she*

Features (a)–(b) are shared with StAusColE, although the frequency of (b) is higher in AusVE. (c) is stigmatised and its claims to a position in StAusColE are borderline. When the Prime Minister of Australia said *I love yiz all*, on a radio talkback show in 2002, it was front page news. Letters to the newspapers expressed surprise, pleasure or amusement at the unexpected informality. Feature (d) is equally common in StAusColE and some people have recently come to use it in formal spoken and written contexts. The following section elaborates on (c).

5.2.   Second person plural *yiz*

Speakers of Tasmanian Vernacular English optionally distinguish between second person singular *you* (subject and object) and second person plural, usually pronounced /jəz, jɨz/, sometimes spelt *yez, yiz* or *y's*, with an emphatic variant [yuwz], usually spelt *youse* or *you's*. These forms of the plural pronoun are paralleled in Ireland (see Filppula, British Isles volume) and are sometimes attributed to the Irish component of Australia's early colonists.

(82)   (Tasmania: Rex is talking to his nephew Ken.)
...***yiz** ha/you had 'im loose and you didn't realize*
...*y' had 'im broke off...at the root...*
But 'e was a big turnip. ***Yiz** 'd worked on it!*

(83)   (Tasmania: same conversation as [2])
Harv: *Talk about eatin it after the dog went under the house,...*
Chas: ***Yiz** woulda took it off 'im.*

(84)   (NSW: *They're a Weird Mob*; a–c are men, d is a woman.)
a.   *Wondered wot **yez** was doin' with the guns.* (*They're a Weird Mob*, 43)
b.   *But this time I'm tell' **yez** about we was buildin' a garage.* (*They're a Weird Mob*, 42)
c.   *Do **yez** want a ride down in the truck or don't **yez**?* (*They're a Weird Mob*, 41)
d.   *Where were **youse** this mornin?* (*They're a Weird Mob*, 147)

(85)   (Queensland: *On Our Selection*, 88)
*A circus!" Sal put in, "A pretty circus **you's** 'd have!"*

6.   Ellipsis

6.1.   Ellipsis of relative marker after subjects

When forming restrictive relative clauses, Standard Formal English allows a choice between the relative markers *which, that,* and no marker (zero) with one exception: ellipsis of the relative marker (zero marking) is not acceptable when the relative pronoun is the subject of the relative clause. AusVE speakers seldom use *which* as a relative marker. In a sample of four Tasmanian speakers the choices of relative clause marker had the following frequencies: *that* 48.8 percent, zero 46.5 percent, *which* 4.7 percent.

In AusVE zero-marking is also possible for subjects. In a study of Cessnock speech, a small country town in New South Wales, Shnukal (1989) found that working-class informants on average used zero 50 percent of the time for relativised subjects and middle class speakers only 17 percent. Some 'careful' middle class speakers showed no use of zero-marking. Zero marking is most common when the relativised subject is also the subject of the matrix clause. Matrix clauses that permit zero-marking typically postulate the existence of an entity (*there be* + NP, NP + *have* + NP). Examples of zero-marking of relativised subjects follow, with the position of the zero indicated by '#':

(86)   (Cessnock, NSW [Shnukal 1989: 71])
   a.   *Then I have my youngest son # lives in Cessnock.*
   b.   *I knew a girl # worked in an office down the street there.*
   c.   *Edwards was the only one v # used to be out there.*
   d.   *I think it was only one out of about ten of us # did the finals.*
   e.   *I would say that anybody #'d be earning over 12,000 dollars a year would probably be policemen...*

(87)   (Tasmanian men)

   a.   *'Ere* [There] *w's one # used to charge through a hole in the fence.* (Chas)
   b.   *There's a tree up there # died for no apparent reason.* (Mark)

Each of the examples in (88) shows a relative clause within a relative clause, with the relative marker left out in both cases. The speaker is a man from Tennant Creek, Northern Territory.

(88)   a.   *There's a bloke # works for them # goes bull-catching in the Gulf.*
   b.   *There's a fellow # came from Canberra # owns it.*

6.2.   Ellipsis of clause-initial constituents

AusVE dialogue and narrative are characterised by a wider variety of ellipses in clause-initial position than is acceptable in more standard styles. In narratives and in first-speaker or initiating position in dialogue interchanges, for example, speakers often omit a subject pronoun before a verb phrase and sometimes leave out both subject pronoun and auxiliary verb before a main verb, or subject pronoun with existential verb before a predicate nominal, or a main verb before a prepositional phrase.

Six kinds of ellipses were singled out for mention in Table 1 (variables 15–20) and five of these are shown below. The contextual conditions constraining these ellipses cannot be discussed in detail here but the examples should give a general indication. In the examples that follow the omitted material is reconstructed and added in square brackets. In some cases what is what is left out is not a particular lexical unit but a broader category of material, whose meaning is recoverable up to a point.

Subject ellipsis:
SUBJ.PRO + VP => VP

Examples (89–95) are all from Tasmania:
(89) Chas: *No, I picked him up.* [I] *Picked him up on the road.*
      Harv: *Oh.* [You] *Gave him a ride?*

(90) (Chas is describing how a bushman slipped on a piece of bark.)
      Harv: *Ha! ha!*
      Chas: [He] *Nearly bit the end off 'is PIPE.*
      Harv: *Ha! ha! ha!* [He] *Went down on the greasy bark.*

(91) Chas: *No, I got in. I was in bed.* [I] *Got in.* [I] *Got home.*

(92) Harv: *'E just opened up and left 'er there.* [He] *Just swears at 'er.*

(93) Harv: *And* [he] *took 'er* [the leg of lamb] *in and put 'er on the plate!*
      Chas: *Yeah.* [He] *Carved 'er up. Yeah.*

(95) Mark: *'E's a wild cherry.* [He] *Has little cherries on 'im and they're good to eat too, them cherries.*

Subject + auxiliary ellipsis before a transitive verb:
(SUBJ.PRO + AUX + Vtr + OBJECT) => Vtr + OBJECT

(96) a. [I will] *See yez in the mornin'.* (*They're a Weird Mob*, 75)
      b. [I would] *Sooner 'ave a beer* (*They're a Weird Mob*, 49)
      c. [Do you] *Get the idea?* (*They're a Weird Mob*, 49)
      d. [Do you] *Reckon 'e pulled 'im?* (*They're a Weird Mob*, 73)
      e. '[It would] *Take too long 'aving' a bath before tea'*, said Joe (*They're a Weird Mob*, 49)
      f. [Would you] *Care for a swig mate?* (*They're a Weird Mob*, 143)

Subject + *be* + article ellipsis before an adjectival phrase:
NP + *be*-TENSE + ART + (ADJ) + N   =>   ADJ + N

Examples (97) and (98) are from a Tasmanian conversation and a Melbourne auction call, respectively.

(97)   Chas: *By jeez,* [it was a] *hell of a bloody performance.*

(98)   Auctioneer: *ooh* [It's a] *not very impressive crowd today Laurie*

(99)   a. [He's the] *Best hoop* [jockey] *in the country, the old Darb.*
            (*They're a Weird Mob*, 72)
        b. [He's a] *Shrewd 'ead the old Cooky.* (*They're a Weird Mob*, 72)
        c. [Is he a] *Friend of yours?* (*They're a Weird Mob*, 56)
        d. [It's a] *Wonder the stewards didn't 'ave 'im up.* (*They're a Weird Mob*, 72)
        d. [You're a] *Funny bugger, aren't yer?* (*They're a Weird Mob*, 65)

There + *be* ellipsis before a negative:
There + *be* -TENSE + NEG + N + (LOC)   =>   NEG + N + (LOC)

Examples (100–102) are from Tasmania:
(100)   Chas: *I went up to the old road y' know 'nd* [there was] *no bugger home*

(101)   Harv: *'nd one of them* [the police] *charged straight through…into the parlour, y' know and –* [there was] *no one there.*

(102)   Harv: *You left* **'im** *for* FRAzer, *wi- with* PLEAsure.
        Chas: *Yes.*
        Harv: [There was] *Not eNOUGH of* **'im.**

as…as ellipsis:
SUBJ.PRO + *be*-TENSE + *as* + ADJ + N + *as* + S => (*as*) ADJ + N + *as* + S

Comparative constructions like *X is as quiet as a mouse* and *X is as straight as you'll ever get it,* can be reduced by (a) omitting the subject (always a definite NP) and the verb, or, (b) by omitting these plus the first *as*.

(103)   a. [He's as] *Good as anybody you'd get.* (Sydney: *They're a Weird Mob*, 50)
        b. [She was as] *Fast as any horse over a mile.* (Tasmania: Ken)

subject + verb ellipsis before preposition:

SUBJ + V + PP   =>   PP

A prepositional phrase is sometimes used sentence-initially without a supporting subject or verb. Although most such phrases occur as part of imperative constructions, as in (103), it we also find declaratives of this form, as in (104).

(104)   Harv: *Off with you in the bar, Rev! In the bar. Quick." I said, "In the bar!"*

(105)   Chas: *...and the old horse got a bit sick of it. Backwards and bloody forwards all the time.*

The varieties and uses of ellipses in conversational and narrative speech have not been extensively studied. Systematic use of clause-initial elisions is a characteristic of certain other spoken genres of English, such as play-by-play sporting commentaries and auction-calling (Kuiper 1996). There such elisions have a dual function, contributing to economy of speech and heightening dramatic effect.

9.   Conclusion

AusVE is arguably an endangered language. It is true that the absolute number of AusVE speakers has risen over the past century as the Australian population has increased from about 3.7 million to 20 million. However, AusVE speakers make up a diminishing proportion of the total population, as more people stay at school longer and move into white collar jobs where non-standard speech styles are marginalised. All the indications are that upwardly mobile Australians adopt StAusColE as their public, mainstream style. Will AusVE fade away completely in the next generation or two, or survive only in a few remote corners of the community?

AusVE is bound to change, bound to lose a few of its distinctive elements and to add others. But it is likely to remain strong on its home ground. This home ground is in those places where people, especially men, gather to do manual work, to play sports or to socialise with their mates. In these contexts AusVE has much covert prestige, even among men who by occupation and income rank as decidedly middle class. Even its more hackneyed clichés and formulae encompass values that are deep-rooted in Australian society, such as giving everyone 'a fair go' (roughly, an equal opportunity) and those that Wierzbicka (1991: 3, 165–182) labels "mateship", "masculine toughness", "antiverbosity" and "antisentimentality", disrespect for authority, a dislike of "whingers" (constant complainers), "bludgers" (those who sponge on mates) and "dobbers" (those who betray a mate by reporting his wrongdoing to authority) and an enjoyment of "chiacking" (rough teasing, giving cheek), "shouting" (buying rounds of drinks for friends and even for the house) and "yarning" (unhurried, relaxed conversation). And the best AusVE speech has a marvellous economy of expression, lively imagery and droll humour and an earthiness that more standard speech seldom matches.

Be that as it may, AusVE is a variety of English whose grammar and discourse conventions remain little-studied. There is room for systematic research on many individual variables that have so been only casually investigated, on how variants cluster, and on women's use of AusVE variants, and on differences between age groups and across regions.

* I am indebted to Kate Burridge for extensive and perceptive comments on a draft, to Bernd Kortmann, Pam Peters and Jane Simpson for valuable suggestions, and to my Tasmanian relatives for providing wonderful conversation on which I have drawn heavily. For preliminary analysis of several variables in this data I am indebted to students in graduate courses I taught at the University Auckland in the late 1980s: Dennis Brown, Mercedes Maroto-Camino, Britta Christiansen, Jonathan Lane and Rosalind West.

Exercises and study questions

1. Translate examples (1)–(3) into Standard Colloquial English.

2. Some of the AVE examples contain constructions that are rare or absent in Standard Formal English, e.g. left- and right-dislocation, preposition + verb + subject, Imperative: *off with* NP. See how many such constructions you can find.

3. Isolate examples of clause-initial ellipsis in the examples. Try to reconstruct the 'missing constituents'. Do you think it is justified to treat such ellipses as the result of deletion of specific lexical and grammatical constituents that are present in underlying or deep structure?

4. In formal English the feminine pronoun is commonly used for a few kinds of inanimate referents. Which are these?

5. Some people might say that 'animate gender assignment', as found in AVE, is a kind of personification, where a non-human referent is endowed with

a range of human qualities. Others would say that, although it is semantically motivated, animate gender assignment is purely a grammatical feature. Discuss the criteria that might resolve this disagreement.

6. Summarise the competing explanations that have been proposed to explain cases of variable animate gender assignment – where portable goods are sometimes *he* and sometimes *she* – in AVE. Use the full range of evidence in the chapter to evaluate these.

7. Do you think AVE should be considered a social dialect of English or just a style?

8. The author suggests (a) that AVE is an endangered language but (b) it is likely to survive in restricted contexts. Evaluate the arguments for these views.

Selected references

Please consult the General references for titles mentioned in the text but not included in the references below. For a full bibliography see the accompanying CD-ROM.

Campion, Sarah
    1941   *Mo Burdekin.* London: Peter Davies.
    1942   *Bonanza.* London: Peter Davies.
Collins, Peter
    1989   Sociolinguistics in Australia: a survey. In: Collins and Blair (eds.), 3–20.
Culotta, Nino [John O'Grady]
    1957   *They're a Weird Mob.* Birkenhead, Auckland: Reed Books. Republished by Humour Books.
Dennis, Clarence James
    1950   *Selected Poetry of C.J. Dennis.* Sydney: Angus and Robertson.
Eisikovits, Edina
    1981   Inner-Sydney English: an investigation of grammatical variation in adolescent speech. Ph.D. dissertation, University of Sydney.
    1987   Variation in the lexical verb in Inner-Sydney English. *Australian Journal of Linguistics* 7: 1–24.
    1989a   Variation in the perfective in Inner-Sydney English. *Australian Journal of Linguistics* 9: 3–20.
    1989b   Girl-talk/boy-talk: sex differences in adolescent speech. In: Collins and Blair (eds.), 35–64.
Engels, Dulcie and Eve Ritz
    2000   The use of the present perfect in Australian English. *Australian Journal of Linguistics* 20: 119–140.

Harris, Elisabeth
    1992   'Auction this day'. Ph.D. dissertation, Department of Linguistics, La
            Trobe University, Melbourne.
Horvath, Barbara
    1985   *Variation in Australian English. The Sociolects of Sydney.* Cambridge:
            Cambridge University Press.
Kuiper, Koenraad
    1996   *Smooth Talkers. The Linguistic Performance of Auctioneers and Sports-
            casters.* Mahwah, NJ: Lawrence Erlbaum.
Mathiot, Madeleine and Marjorie Roberts
    1978   Sex roles as revealed through referential gender in American English.
            In: Madeleine Mathiot (ed.), *Ethnolinguistics: Boas, Sapir and Whorf
            Revisited*, 1–47. The Hague: Mouton.
Pawley, Andrew
    2002   Using he and she for inanimate objects in English: questions of gram-
            mar and world view. In: Nick Enfield (ed.), *Ethnosyntax: Explorations in
            Language and Culture*, 110–137. Oxford: Oxford University Press.
Ramson, William S.
    1988   *Australian National Dictionary.* Melbourne: Oxford University Press.
Rudd, Steele
    1954   *On Our Selection and On Our New Selection.* Sydney: Angus and
            Robertson.
Siemund, Peter
    2002   Animate pronouns for inanimate objects: pronominal gender in English re-
            gional varieties. In: Dieter Kastovsky, Gunther Kaltenbröck and Susanne
            Reichl (eds.), *Anglistentag 2001 Wien – Proceedings*, 19–34. Trier:
            Wissenschaftlicher Verlag.
    2007   *Pronominal Gender in English: A Study of English Varieties from a Cross-
            Linguistic Perspective.* London: Routledge.
Shnukal, Anna
    1978   A sociolinguistic study of Australian English. Phonological and syntactic
            variation in Cessnock, New South Wales. Ph.D. dissertation, Georgetown
            University, Washington D.C.
    1982   You're getting' somethink for nothing: two phonological variables in Aus-
            tralian English. *Australian Journal of Linguistics* 2: 197–212.
    1989   Variable relative pronoun absence in Australian English. In: Collins and
            Blair (eds.), 70–77.
Wagner, Susanne
    2005   Gender in varieties of English pronouns: Southwest England. In: Kortmann,
            Herrmann, Pietsch and Wagner, 211–367.
Ward, Russel
    1958   *The Australian Legend.* Melbourne: Oxford University Press.

Wierzbicka, Anna
  1991   *Cross-Cultural Pragmatics. The Semantics of Human Interaction.* Berlin/
          New York: Mouton de Gruyter.
  2002   Sexism in grammar: the semantics of gender in Australian English.
          Anthropological Linguistics 44: 143–177.
Wyld, Henry C.
  1953   *A History of Modern Colloquial English.* 3rd edition. Oxford: Blackwell.

Hypocoristics in Australian English[*]

Jane Simpson

1.   Introduction

A characteristic of English is the existence of alternative forms of words or names (*mozzie, mosquito; Mountie, Mountford* [surname]), which share part of the same form, have the same denotation, but have different connotations and different levels of formality. The use of such alternative forms is widespread in Australia:

> Aren't we reaching the inane, when we Australians start accepting *beddie, cardie* (cardigan), *Chrissie pressie, ciggie, habbie* (haberdashery), *leckie* (lecture), *prossie* (prostitute), *sandie* (sandwich), *tabbie* (tablet), *weepie,* and *yewie* (U-turn)? Of course, these and other habits are not restricted to Australia, but the increase in their popularity here is phenomenal. (Gunn 1972: 60)

While Australian English does employ similar forms in babytalk, these forms are used by adults in everyday speech and writing. They are mentioned in popular works on Australian English (Keesing 1982), and many examples are to be found in word-lists of Australian English. They are also common in New Zealand.

Alternative forms of words are often given labels based on meaning such as "hypocoristic" or "diminutive", or labels according to form, such as "abbreviation", "clipping", "shortening". The latter are inadequate because alternative forms of words with similar connotations may also be created by adding endings to monosyllabic words. Thus *connie/conductor* (shortening plus suffixation) and *blockie* 'person who has a farm/orchard on a block' (suffixation), and *dieso/diesel mechanic* (shortening plus suffixation) and *birdo/bird-watcher* (suffixation) all provide an informal way of talking about a person's occupation and do not seem to differ in connotation, regardless of whether shortening or suffixation is used. Likewise *gifty/gift* (suffixation) and *prezzie/present* (shortening plus suffixation) do not differ in connotation. There also seems no difference in connotation between these methods of forming hypocoristics, and forming hypocoristics by shortening words which naturally end in a sound like one of the suffixes. *Dermo/dermatitis* (shortening plus suffix), and *gastro/gastro-enteritis* (shortening) do not differ in connotation.

In this paper I propose that shortening, shortening plus suffix, and suffixation can all be seen as deriving words by matching forms to templates. I call words derived in this way *hypocoristics* for want of a better label. The data derives from 1740 hypocoristics collected by David Nash and me from Australian speakers and written sources, other authors' works (Dabke 1976; Dermody 1980; Wierzbicka 1984; Taylor 1992; McAndrew 1992), talk-back radio, and our observations over the last sixteen years. Most of the collection is incorporated into a dictionary (Sussex forthcoming). Babytalk (Mühlhäusler 1983) and personal names (Poynton 1984; Taylor 1992) will not be discussed. I consider first the phonological and morphological properties of hypocoristic formation, and then comment briefly on the uses and meanings of hypocoristics.

2.   Templates for hypocoristic formation

To capture the similarity in meaning between the three ways of creating alternative names (shortening, shortening plus suffixation, and suffixation), we can adopt the proposal of Weeda (1992), building on work by John McCarthy and Alan Prince, that such relations are best generalised as the aligning of the original form with a "template". The meaning can then be associated with the template, thus explaining the similarity in meaning of the forms created by shortening and those created by suffixation. Thus *connie* is formed by aligning the three-syllable form *conductor* with a two-syllable template, the second syllable of which ends in /i/. *Blockie* is formed by aligning the one-syllable form *block* with the same two-syllable template.

(a) reduction to the first syllable (or part thereof) and adding an ending:

$$\begin{array}{ccc} \sigma & & \sigma \\ \Delta & & | \\ \textbf{con} \mid ductor & \textbf{i} & \rightarrow \quad connie \end{array}$$

(b) adding one of the endings to a monosyllabic word:

$$\begin{array}{ccc} \sigma & & \sigma \\ \Delta & & | \\ \textbf{block} \mid \textit{?farmer?} & \textbf{i} & \rightarrow \quad blockie \end{array}$$

If the first two syllables of a word happen to match the template, then there is shortening without suffixation (the final vowel may change form due to being stressed).

(c) keeping the first two syllables of a word whose second syllable matches one of the endings:

$$\begin{array}{cc} \sigma & \sigma \\ \Delta & | \end{array}$$

card   *i gan*   →   *cardie*
             [ə]   [i:]

There is also a monosyllabic template for shortening.

(d) reduction to the first syllable (or part thereof):

$$\begin{array}{c} \sigma \\ \Delta \end{array}$$

ump | ire   →   ump

These templates accommodate more than just alternative forms of words, they also allow derivation of new words which are not alternatives to the base. Australians may refer to an alcoholic as an *alko, alkie, wino, plonko, dipso*, or a *goomie* if they drink methylated spirits. *Alko/alkie* are formed by aligning the four-syllable source *alcoholic* with a two-syllable template, the second syllable of which ends in /i/ or /o/, and *dipso* has a similar origin from *dipsomaniac*. But there is no obvious source meaning 'alcoholic' involving the word *wine* or *plonk* (alcohol), or *goom* (methylated spirits). While *alcoholic* and *alko* share their denotation, *wino, plonko* and *goomie* do not have the same denotation as the words from which they are derived.

Thus the main strategies for forming hypocoristic words (proper names or common nouns) in Australian English involve the creation of one or two-syllable words which fit certain templates. These can be categorised into nine classes, which include seven of Taylor's (1992) eight morpho-phonological classes of alternative names for first names and surnames. (I exclude the extensions used in babytalk and lover's talk: *Suzykins, Mikeypoodles, Brendy Poos* [Mühlhäusler 1983; Poynton 1984], as well as the jocular *-aroo* in the *Soccaroos*, a soccer team). Seven of the eight classes also apply to alternative words for common nouns. I list these below in order of commonness in our data-set, adding two smaller classes. Taylor's eighth class consists of renditions of names including foreign name particles, but his examples can all be subsumed under existing templates: *Deek/(Robert) Di Castella* fits the monosyllabic template; *Hacca/(Robert) Holmes à Court*, fits the syllable plus /a/ template, via the acronym, and has the added pun; *the Von/(Norman) Von Nida* fits the "the" pattern. The forms in "the" are restricted to proper names (including place names), and are discussed in Simpson (2001). The forms in /s/ and two syllables are also mostly restricted to proper names.

Table 1.   Major templates for forming hypocoristic words in Australian English

Template		Number of forms in data	Percen- tage	Hypoco- ristic	Base form '
/i/	syllable plus /i(s)/ (Taylor's class 2)	824	47%	*coldie* *gladdie*	*a cold beer* *gladiolus*
/o/	syllable plus /o/ (Taylor's class 4)	333	19%	*prawno* *journo*	*prawn seller* *journalist*
1 syl	one syllable (Taylor's class 1)	200	11%	*pav*	*pavlova* (me- ringue pudding)
/a/*	syllable plus /(z)a/ ([ə]) (Taylor's class 3)	145	8%	*boozer* *ekka* *Mazza*	*pub* (from 'booze' alcohol) *ecstasy tablet* *Marian*
the	"the" followed by one or two syllables (Taylor's class 6)	125	7%	*The Don* *The Weal* *The Brindies*	*Donald Bradman* *Camooweal* *The Brindabella Mountains*
/as/	syllable plus /as/ ([əz]) (Taylor's class 5)	48	3%	*chocker(s)* *Tuggers*	*chock-full* *Tuggeranong* (Canberra sub- urb)
/s/	syllable plus /s/ (Taylor's class 5)	34	2%	*scrotes* *Jules*	*scrotum* *Julie, Julia*
2 syl	two syllables	17	1%	*chrysanth* *Mullum*	*chrysanthemum* *Mullumbimby*
Acr	acronyms (Taylor's class 7)	14	1%	*E* *KI*	*ecstasy tablet* *Kangaroo Island*
	SUBTOTAL	1740			

* I use /a/ to refer to the ending usually spelled <-er>, which is pronounced as a mid central vowel in Australian English, or as a syllabic /r/ in Irish or American English.

3.   Phonological and morphological properties

The major phonological problems in forming English hypocoristics are dis- cussed in Weeda (1992), and for Australian English in Simpson (2001). They arise in reanalysis of morpheme boundaries, and in determining the number and size of the syllables to be kept in polysyllabic reductions.

Obvious morpheme boundaries are usually respected so that words are broken up at the putative morpheme boundary: *towie/towtruck driver*, rather than **towtie*. Rare exceptions are *strawbs/strawberries*. Forms like *reno/renovation* contain old morpheme boundaries (compare *innovation*) as do composite names: *Lapa/La Perouse* (place in New South Wales).

Normally only one syllable of the base word is kept in a hypocoristic, although a few exceptions do exist, mostly words with short initial syllables, *anotherie*, *dilutie* ('worker with diluted skills', McAndrew 1992), *colourie* 'marble', *sophisto/sophisticated*, *dissolvo/dissolving stitches*, or Graeco-Latin prefixes ending in /o/, *physio/physiotherapist*. Others include *enduro/endurance bike track, fantazzo/fantastic*.

The first part of the template is usually the maximal initial part of the base word which can be a word-final syllable *insto/institutional share-holder*, unless the original matches both syllables of the template, *anthro/anthropologist*. /o/ forms generally take more consonants than /i/ forms: compare *aggro/aggressive* with *aggie/agricultural student* (the *agri* of *agribusiness* is a different kind of blend). However this is not always so: *cappo/capstan cigarette* rather than **capsto*.

The major modifications involve:
- The alteration of /fricativeC/ clusters in reductions of polysyllabic forms, either by deleting the /s/: *lakky band/elastic band, plakky bag/plastic bag* or by deleting the second consonant and voicing the fricative: *arvo/afternoon*, *Aussie* (pronounced [z])/*Australian, fantazzo/fantastic, mozzie/mosquito*, and even *Kazi* people/*Kastelorizo* denizens, a Greek island off Turkey;
- the substitution of liquids by /z/ on personal names (*Shazza/Shaz/Sharon*, *Ez/Ellen*). This is another solution to the longstanding English problem of how to make pet names of personal names starting (C)(C)V(V)RV (Taylor 1992). However this solution has not yet been applied to common nouns: *paro/paralytic* (drunk), *warry/war story*;
- the substitution of short vowels for long vowels or diphthongs: *Rizza/Ryan*, *Razza/Rachel, Chaz/Charles*;
- the occasional insertion of /b/: *freebie/free thing, Kimbo/Kim*.

Hypocoristics created by these templates can undergo further compounding: *ex-banky/ex-bank-worker, no-schoolie/*child that does not go to *school, non-rezzie/non-residential student, hot crossie/hot cross bun* (Dermody 1980). Another notable feature is the maintenance of plural in plural or pluralia tantum forms:

boardies/board-shorts, The Goldies/The Goldfields hotel, and the addition of plural when forms are reanalysed as pluralia tantum forms: *cozzies=bathers/ bathing-costume*.

3.1.   One syllable plus /i/

This is the most common hypocoristic form in our data. In both general and Australian English it is often associated with babytalk and adult play babytalk (*doggie* 'dog', *tummy* 'stomach'). In Australian English it has been used for derived words, and in normal adult conversation and writing, since the nineteenth century. Thus Morris (1898) has *beardie*, 'a kind of codfish', *gummy* 'shark species', *roughy* 'Victorian fish'. The alternative form was used in casual writing by the early twentieth century – a letter written by a South Australian soldier in World War I contains: "There were chrysanthemum curtains to the windows and withal real *crysies* and marigolds arranged on the tables." (Jacob 1919: 38).

Proper names often have hypocoristics in /i/, whether first names (*Mushy/ Mushtaq Abdullah*, a sportsman [*The Australian*, 5/8/2002: 29]), or surnames: (*Warnie/Shane Warne* [a well-known cricketer]). Taylor (1992) suggests that /i/ is more common as a suffix to monosyllabic surnames than on truncated surnames, but /i/ does occur on truncations: *the Woodies* (the sportsmen Mark Woodforde and Todd Woodbridge), *Mountie* (the anthropologist Charles Mountford – form recorded in private letter in 1934).

/i/ is also suffixed to brandnames: *Lykie* (*Lycoming* aeroplane engine); placenames *Palmie/Palm Beach*, religions *Prezzie/Presbyterian*, denizens of a place: *Bankie* 'inhabitant of *Bankstown*, a suburb of Sydney', and sportsteams, *the Swannies/the Sydney Swans*.

/i/ appears on a wide range of nouns (Dabke 1976; McAndrew 1992), including monosyllabic common nouns forming names of occupations: *speechie/ speech pathologist*, *kelpie/kelp-harvester*, and reductions of polysyllabic words: *pollie/politician*, *devvie/developer*. /i/ is also found on a range of other alternative words: *serries* (*serepax* tranquillisers).

While some polysyllabic adjectives have alternative shortened forms using /i/: *plakky/plastic*, *marvey/marvellous*, the effect of adding /i/ to a monosyllabic adjective is often to create a noun: an *oldie, toughy, quickie, coldie*. The denotations of the derived nouns vary widely: a *bluey* may be a blue swimmer crab, a bedroll, a blue woollen cloth (all from the *Macquarie Dictionary*), a summons, a bill, the name of several Australian lizards, a policeman, a singlet, or a blue plastic sheet put on bed for incontinence.

Some verbs have alternative forms in /i/: *spitty/to spit-polish*. As with adjectives, /i/ is occasionally added to verbs to create nouns: *clippie* 'ticket examiner', *twisty/twist* (a brand of savoury snack). But the stressed suffix *-ee* which forms verbs from nouns is probably a different suffix (*escapee, refugee, absentee*; Dabke 1976). These forms are not alternative words, and are often more than two syllables long. However, the two syllable forms are only distinguished by stress (*grantee*), and some forms have two interpretations, thus both *blockee* and *blockie* appear for 'someone farming a block of land'.

Some appear with /is/ [iz], where the /s/ may be the possessive found in business names: *Pennies* (*Penfolds* a business name), the pluralia tantum of 'works': *steelies/steelworks*, in the brandnames of babies' nappies *Huggies/hug*, and in pseudo-babytalk words for food, drink and events involving them, *drinkies, nibblies, Weeties* (cereal brandname), and in the phrase formation *I've got the munchies* (= 'I feel hungry').

3.2.   One syllable plus /o/

In many English varieties forms with /o/ are used for words of three or more syllables whose second syllable is open and spelled with an /o/: *limo/limousine, mayo/mayonnaise, porno/pornography*. The same is true in Australian English: *speedo/speedometer, geo/geologist*, including occasionally more than two syllables, *medico/medical practitioner* (cf. *medico-legal work*). /o/ is also found on brandnames in many English varieties: *creamo* (non-dairy creamer) is an American example, and the British cartoonist Giles used /o/ for invented brandnames in his cartoons: *Cracko, Brecko, Laxo* (all breakfast foods). Australian English has *Sealo/seal* (brandname of sealed silo), *Speedos/speed* (brandname of swimming costume).

Irish English has /o/ on first names and surnames (e.g. *Jayo/ Jason*), and this use is quite widespread in Australia, particularly on men's names (Dabke 1976): first names: *Davo/David*, and surnames: *Demo/Dempster*. /o/ on proper names occurs more commonly with shortenings, rather than additions of /o/ to a monosyllabic name (Taylor 1992). /o/ is also used for followers of a religion: the *Salvoes/the Salvation Army*. It is used on placenames: *Rotto/Rottnest Island* (Simpson 2001).

In Irish English /o/ is also found on some common nouns denoting occupations or types of people: *journo/journalist*. Australian English has many such forms: *misho/missionary, misso/Miscellaneous Workers' Union member, reffo/refugee*. New words for types of people are derived from adding /o/ to one syllable words: *pisso/piss* 'sewerage worker' (Dabke 1976). The punning blends *aspro* 'male prostitute' and 'associate professor' also fit this pattern.

/o/ appears on a range of other common nouns: *greaso/grease, greasy* 'fish shop', *compo/compensation, bizzo/business*. /o/ also occurs on adjectives *snazzo/snazzy* 'stylishly attractive', *obno/obnoxious, troppo/tropical* = 'mad', *techo/technical*. /o/ also occasionally occurs on participles: *recoed* ['riːkoʊd]/ *reconditioned* (engine). Occasionally a verb can be created: *gutto/* < *gutless* 'to do something cowardly', as in: "I'm supposed to have these tests, but I keep *gutto*ing out." (private e-mail to J. Simpson 1/9/1995).

3.3.   First syllable only

This strategy is common in other English varieties. In Australian English it is found on both proper names and common words. Proper names include first names (*Sophe/Sophie*), surnames (*Newk/John Newcombe*), placenames (*Oz/ Australia*), denizens of places (*the Vics*/denizens of *Victoria*), business names (*Tatts Lotto/Tattersdalls lottery*), or sports teams (*the Tiges*/the Balmain *Tigers* Rugby League team). Unusual examples taking the final syllable include several Australian Rules football team names: *the Pies/the Magpies* (Collingwood team) (compare *maggie*, the usual hypocoristic for 'magpie').

Common nouns include names for types of person (*crim/criminal*), names for things (*daff/daffodil* or *daphne*), names for attributes *(beaut/beauty)*. This strategy is sometimes used on verbs: *to veg out/to vegetate*.

3.4.   One syllable plus /a/

The hypocoristic use of /a/ was recorded in England from Oxford students' slang on placenames: *Padder/Paddington Station* (Jespersen 1942: 233). In Australian English it often appears on placenames as a result of just taking the first two syllables of the name: *Coona/Coonabarabran* (NSW). It is found on a few placenames: *Macker/Macquarie University*, and from an acronym: *the Wacka/the Western Australian Cricket Ground*.

/a/ is also found on proper names, usually with a change of liquid to /z/: *Mazza/ Marilyn; Wozza/Wally, Warren, Warwick*. This change has been extended to other consonants: *Brezza/Brett*.

It is hard to tease out the hypocoristic use of /a/ from quasi-agentive *-er* attached to nouns. The /er/ of *broomer* 'person who sweeps the shearing floor' (Dabke 1976) could be the quasi-agentive *-er*. Reductions of polysyllabic words such as *acca/acker* 'academic staff member' seem to fit the same pattern. It is possible that *gutser* etc. in *come a gutser/cropper/greaser* 'fall off' could also be quasi-agentive. However, others do not have even quasi-agentive meanings: *bummer/bum* 'bad thing' (cf. *what a bummer/whopper*), *sanger* 'sandwich', *boozer* 'pub', from *booze* 'alcohol', *rubber* 'pub' from rhyming slang *rubberdy-dub*. A prearranged parliamentary question is a *Dorothy Dix* or a *Dorothy Dixer*, suggesting that the *-er* does not have much agentive meaning. The well-known *cuppa/cup of tea or coffee* fits the same form.

There are occasional examples of adjectives: *imma/immature, para/paralytic* 'drunk'. On verbs the use of /a/ is hard to distinguish from agentive *-er*. While *killer* 'cow to be killed' and *chopper* as 'cow sold for pet food' are derived from the verbs *kill* and *chop, chopper* as 'helicopter' has several sources: onomatopoeia (the noise of the helicopter) and evocative of 'copter' as well, perhaps of the blades *chopping* the air.

3.5.   One syllable plus /as/

The ending is pronounced [əz]. It has been common in British English slang also used in Australia (*champers/champagne, Honkers/Hong Kong, starkers/stark naked, chockers/chock-full*), and Taylor (1992) suggests that they are seen as British English. However in the last twenty-five years the use of /as/ has increased in Australia, e.g. *ackers/acne, spackers/spastic* 'drunk'. It is common in Australia on proper names: surnames *Knappers/Tim Knapstein*, a well-known wine-maker (*Sydney Morning Herald Good Weekend*, 24/10/1998: 85), first names *Anders/Andrew*, and place names *Lajas/Lajamanu*. There are some ambiguous forms: *Maccas/McDonalds* fast food could be /a/+plural/possessive *-s*, or /as/.

3.6.   The *s*-ending

This ending /s/ ([s], [z], [əz]) is rarely found on common nouns in normal speech; it is mostly found on proper names, and in babytalk and lovers' pet names: *Hi sweetums/ducks/cuddles/possums. Time for dindins/milkies/beddie-byes now.* (Mühlhäusler 1983; Taylor 1992). As such it has fewer constraints on the number of syllables of the stem to which it attaches. On common nouns the same form appears in the ill-health/bad feeling constructions: *He's got/he gives me the shits/runs/irrits/creeps/heebiejeebies*, but the meaning appears to relate to other plural form diseases like measles and mumps. Whether endings such as /as/ or short forms such as *Baz* (*Barry/Bazza*) should be analysed as containing the *s*-ending is a matter for investigation.

4.   History and users of hypocoristics

Most studies of Australian English have been based on written sources and on the researchers' intuitions about spoken English. *The Macquarie Diction-*

ary and the *Australian National Dictionary* (*AND*) are the products of lexicographers working in Sydney or Canberra. While the lexicographers have
made considerable efforts to overcome their regional bias, existing claims
about Australian speech are generally based on information from a limited
set of dialects and registers, mostly from New South Wales (e.g. McAndrew
1992; Taylor 1992), and Victoria (e.g. Dabke 1976 and Dermody 1980 rely
chiefly on Victorian informants). A bigger collection of diminutives (Sussex
forthcoming) is in preparation. So far, no quantitative study has been done of
who uses which hypocoristics when, and of the history of hypocoristic use in
Australia. The area is wide open for a thorough socio-historical investigation.
In what follows, I sketch some starting-points for further work.

Morris (1898) is an early collection of new words (including some slang) and
new uses of old words found in Australia and New Zealand. He read widely,
but notes that his collection is biased toward Victorian forms. There are only a
few examples of the strategies discussed here: /i/ and /a/ predominate. Dabke
(1976) notes the competition between /i/ and /a/ as ways of deriving words for
people or things associated with what the noun base denotes. /i/ is found early:
bullocky/bullock team driver (earliest *AND* citation 1869). However, Morris
has slightly more /a/ words derived from nouns than /i/ words: *long-sleever*
'big drink', *piner* 'person cutting huon *pine*', *sundowner* 'swagman', *Waler*
'New South *Wales* horse', *scrubber* 'wild horse or bullock', *Derwenter* 'released convict from Hobart'. He also has a couple of /a~i/ variants: *slusher/
slushy* 'cook's assistant at shearing-time', *swaggie* as 'humorous variation on
swagman' comparable with *swagger* in New Zealand. Dabke adds more variants between /a/ and /i/: *surfer/surfy*, *bullocky/bullocker*, *broomey/broomer*,
and suggests that /i/ has taken over the derivational use from /a/ on nouns.

Morris also has one example of an alternative word: *Tassy* 'a pet name for
Tasmania' used by Victorian cricketers. Dabke (1976), observing the lack of /o/
final words in Morris, suggests that /o/ was not yet established in the language
(although *mado* 'shark species' is a possible example). Taylor (1992) notes that
in 1905 /a/ appears on hypocoristics of personal names in a Sydney school:
Knocker/Knox, *Jonah/Jones*, *Modger/Maurice*, and suggests that it may have
been more common than /o/. This all suggests that in the 1890s, in general
Australian writing and in Melbourne speech, /a/ and /i/ were the most common
ways of forming new words, that /i/ was in use for hypocoristics and not just in
babytalk, that /o/ and /as/ were not yet established in Melbourne speech.

The development of /o/ probably resulted from a confluence of sources
(McAndrew 1992). One is calls and street cries: *smoke oh/smoke ho!* 'work-
break' (earliest *AND* citation 1865, from a Melbourne magazine), "Milk
oh!" *milk-oh* 'milk-seller' (earliest *AND* citation 1907) and *bottle-oh* 'per-

son who sells bottles' (earliest *AND* citation 1898 from a Sydney magazine). McAndrew (1992) observes that the /o/ suffix is strongest in the former penal colonies in New South Wales, Victoria, Tasmania and Queensland, and less strong in South Australia, which was a colony of free settlers. This is in part born out by the distribution of place-names with hypocoristics ending in /o/, which is strongest in New South Wales – I have recorded 27 there compared with three in Queensland and eight in Victoria. Only two forms have been recorded in South Australia, in 2002 from teenagers, *Coro/Coromandel Valley* and *Mazzo/Maslins Beach* (more commonly *Maslins*). Neither form was recognised by older consultants. However the prevalence of "deflationary -o forms" may stem not from the "anti-authoritarian, larrikin societies of former penal settlements" as McAndrew (1992: 180) proposes, but rather from the fact that the penal colonies of New South Wales and Queensland had many people of Irish origin who may have been using the /o/ hypocoristic of Irish English. Since the Irish were, by and large, in the underclasses, their speech would have taken a while to enter into written language and thus into dictionaries. The suggestion that /o/ was used by the underclasses accords with Taylor's assertion that most of these templates "were originally – indeed still were as recently as my boyhood [in Sydney] in the 1940s – only encountered in the language of working-class Australian men" (Taylor 1992: 520).

Like Taylor, other sources also comment on the use of /o/ and /i/ forms by men (Dabke 1976: 36; McAndrew 1992), and to a lesser extent, the use of /i/ forms by women (Gunn 1972: 60). Keesing (1985) notes the comparative absence in earlier discussions of alternative forms in /i/ used by women (*cardie/cardigan*). Some authors express a distaste for these, which may reflect a greater use by women of certain /i/ hypocoristics such as *lippie/lipstick* that are more readily seen as babytalk than are /i/ hypocoristics used as names of occupations such as *shitty/sanitation cart worker*.

5.   Meaning and uses of hypocoristics

One of the difficulties assigning meanings to the templates described here is that there is no hard and fast line between new words and alternative words. At one extreme are forms like *blockie* which, as Dabke (1976: 41) notes, has no obvious full form, *smoko* and *stackie/stack* 'library officer who takes books to and from the library stacks'. At the other are forms like *lippie* which, presumably, are always seen as alternative words, and so are likely to contrast in connotation with the full form. In between, there is much speaker variation.

Some people might always use the word *wharfy* for *wharfside worker*, and so for them the word probably lacks the connotations of *lippie*. Others might alternate, and so for them *wharfy* probably has different connotations from *wharfside worker*.

Taylor (1992) argues that for proper names the difference between /i/ and /o/ is mostly morphologically determined, rather than semantically determined. However, both McAndrew (1992) and Wierzbicka (1984) find differences in the meaning and use of the /i/ hypocoristic and /o/ hypocoristic on alternative words. McAndrew (1992: 174) writes: "If the Aussie diminutives seem mostly elegant, affectionate and familiar, the contractions ending in /o/ are more coarse, vigorous, excessive [...] Far from diminutives, they are pejoratives denoting clumsiness, roughness, ugliness, contempt, laziness, carelessness and excess." Wierzbicka (1984: 128–129) suggests that the /i/ hypocoristic on common nouns is a "depreciative", which expresses informality and solidarity. She describes its meaning:

> We sent you a prezzie (we are having a barbie)
> I don't think of it as a big thing
> I assume you think of it in the same way
> talking about it I am in a good mood
> (as people are when talking about small things towards which they feel good feelings)

While McAndrews's pejorative /o/ fits with the American use of the ending *creepo/creepy person*, *weirdo/weird person* etc., Wierzbicka (1984: 129) describes the use of the /o/ hypocoristic (on examples like *journo/journalist*, *demo/demonstration*), as something which conveys "toughness, informality, good humour and anti-intellectualism". She describes its meaning:

> I don't think of it as anything special
> I am used to it
> I assume that you think of it in the same way
> talking about it I don't want to use long words
> (as people who think of it as something special do)

If the differences between the endings is purely semantic, then variation in uses of form would be expected, both between base forms and hypocoristics, and between types of hypocoristics. That is, we might expect *journalist* to appear as both *journo* and *journie* with different meanings. But they do not. *Journo* is the favoured form. Occasionally there are pairs. Sometimes one form, usually an /i/ form, is seen as babytalk: Dabke (1976) notes *goody/goodoh*, *kiddy/*

kiddo, and compare *jarmies~PJs/pyjamas*, and *kanga* (babytalk)*~roo/kangaroo*. However, sometimes different hypocoristics have different denotations, with the /o/ form more likely to denote a person: *herp* 'reptile', *herpo* 'herpetologist'; *chockie* 'chocolate', *chocko* 'chocolate soldier' (Army reserve); *sickie* 'sick leave', *sicko* 'psychologically sick person'; *plazzo* 'plastic nappy', *plakky* 'plastic' (adjective). But often there are no clear differences: *milky~milko/milkman*, *commy~commo/communist*, *weirdy~weirdo/weird person*, *garbie ~garbo/garbage collector*, *kindie~kinder/kindergarten*; *bottlie~bottlo/bottle merchant*, *sammie~sandie~sangie~sanger~sambo/sandwich*, *preggie~preggo~preggers/pregnant*, *Proddo~Proddy/Protestant*, *pro~prozzo~prostie~prozzie/prostitute*. Speakers who use more than one hypocoristic may assign to them the meanings proposed by Wierzbicka. But if a speaker uses only one of the possible hypocoristics, for them the hypocoristic may have a general meaning of informality, and not the proposed fine-grained differences. This remains to be explored.

* This paper is derived from work David Nash and I have been doing on hypocoristics in Australian English, originally inspired by Anna Wierzbicka's work, and now also in collaboration with Roland Sussex. The data is available at: http://www.arts.usyd.edu.au/departs/linguistics/research/hypocoristic/ We thank the following people for providing Australian English data: our families, Brett Baker, Linda Barwick, Jason Berends, Pauline Bryant (and the listeners to Angela Catterns' programme on 2BL 20/8/1998), Kate Burridge (and the listeners to Terry Laidler's programme on 3LO 4/11/1998), David Bradley, Peter Campbell, David Carrick, Miriam Corris, Rachel Dallas, Alan Dench, Mark Donohue, Mark Durie, Ian Green, Arlene Harvey, Andrew Ingram, Jason Johnston, Kevin Keeffe, Mary Laughren, Sarah Lee, Oliver Mayo, John and Sue McEntee, Bill McGregor, Marcia Mediati, Daphne Nash, Bill Palmer, Bruce Rigsby, Lila San Roque, Adam Schembri, Roland Sussex and participants in his online discussion group <langtalk-l@arts.uq.edu.au>, Brian Taylor, Michael Walsh, David Wilkins and Monty Wilkinson, and audiences at the Australian Linguistics Society Annual Meeting, 1986 and the Department of Linguistics Seminar, University of Sydney 1998. For Irish English data we are grateful to Maire NíChíosain. None of these people are responsible for our recording of their data or for the use we have made of it. For discussion of the theoretical description of hypocoristics over many years we thank Toni Borowsky, John McCarthy, Heather Robinson, Donca Steriade, Anna Wierzbicka. For preparation of the on-line site we thank Sarah Lee and Lila San Roque.

Exercises and study questions

1. Sandwiches are called variously: *sambo, sammo, sanger* (velar nasal), *sang-go* (velar nasal plus velar stop), *sammie*. List the strategies used to make these alternative names.

2. By the sixteenth century *Doll (y)* was used as a pet name for *Dorothy, Moll(y)* or *Poll(y)* for *Mary, Hal* for *Harry*, and *Sal(ly)* for *Sarah*. Taylor (1992: 512) says that in 1905 in Sydney a boy called Maurice was called *Modger*, and *Charles* was called *Chilla*. In 1950 in Sydney Taylor himself had "a mate named Barry whom we all called Bazza, a nextdoor neighbour known as Ecker (his mum called him Eric) and an Uncle Maurice who was always referred to as Mockie." (Taylor 1992: 512).

   Compare these alternative forms for proper names with those given in the text (especially forms such as *Barry/Bazza/Baz, Ellen/Ez*), and work out what strategies are being used to form them. List any alternative forms for the full names concerned that you use, (or have noticed) and describe the strategies involved in forming the alternative names.

3. Examine the following alternative names for place-names. What principle(s) would you propose for these?
   The Ridge/Lightning Ridge (place in New South Wales)
   The Hill/Broken Hill (place in New South Wales)
   The Crossing/Fitzroy Crossing (place in Western Australia)
   The Cross/King's Cross (place in New South Wales)
   The Bower/Fairy Bower(place in New South Wales)

   Now examine the following alternative names. Extend your principle to accommodate these.

   The Isa/Mount Isa (place in Queensland)
   The Rat/Ballarat (place in Victoria) [ˌbælˈɤræt], [bælˈɤræt]
   The Reach/Longreach (place in Queensland) [ˌlɒŋritʃ]
   The Nard/The Esplanade Hotel (hotel in Western Australia) [ˌɛsplˈʌnad]
   The Loo/Woollomooloo (place in New South Wales) [wʊlˈʌmˌʌlu]
   The Gong/Mittagong or *Wollongong* (place in New South Wales) [ˌwʊlˈʌngɒŋ]

   Now examine the following alternative names. Can your principle, together with the strategies described in this paper, accommodate these?

   The Dangi/Urandangi (place in Queensland) [jurˈʌn̪dændʒi]
   The Curry/Cloncurry (place in Queensland) [klɒn̪kʌri]

The Cutta/Tarcutta (place in New South Wales) [ṭaktʌtʌ́]
The Gabba/Woolloongabba cricket ground (place in Queensland)
[wʊlʌ́ŋgæbʌ́]

Lastly, consider *The Fern* [ˌfɐn] used by some people for *Redfern* [ˌrɛdfʌ́n]
(place in New South Wales). Can you account for this?

4. Discuss possible reasons for use of /o/ as a pejorative suffix, considering the
   following examples:

Lebbo	Lebanese (insulting)
Gippo	Egyptian (insulting)
Abo	Aboriginal (insulting)
Seppo	American (septic tank rhymes with Yank) (insulting)
Freddo	non-English-speaking foreigner (Freddo frog (brandname of chocolate frog) rhymes with 'wog', a derogatory name for a foreigner) (insulting)
herpo	herpetologist (often used as self-description)
birdo	birdwatcher (often used as self-description)
botto	amateur botanists
buggo	bug(insect)-collectors
ambo	ambulance driver (often used as self-description)
the *Missos*	the members of the Miscellaneous Workers Union (self-description)
fisho	fisherman or fish-sellers (not insulting)
milko	milkmen (not insulting)
fruito	fruit-sellers (not insulting)
prawno	prawn fishermen (not insulting)

5. Wierzbicka and McAndrew claim that the use of the /i/ and /o/ suffixes indicates national characteristics of Australians, such as anti-authoritarian-
   ism, egalitarianism, and dislike of the pretentiousness of using long words.
   Provide arguments for and against the idea that the use of suffixes could
   reveal something about national characteristics.

6. Devise a project to collect alternative names for people, things or places in
   a variety of English, and work out how you would explore the meaning and
   use of these alternative names.

Selected references

Please consult the General references for titles mentioned in the text but not included in the references below. For a full bibliography see the accompanying CD-ROM.

Dabke, Roswitha
  1976   *Morphology of Australian English*. München: Fink.
Dermody, Anthony Christopher
  1980   Word abbreviation and suffixing in Australian English. B.A. Honours thesis, La Trobe University, Melbourne.
Gunn, Jeannie S.
  1972   Change in Australian idiom. In: George W. Turner (ed.), *Good Australian English and good New Zealand English*, 47–63. Sydney: Reed Education.
Jacob, John
  1919   *Home letters of a soldier-student*. Adelaide: G Hassall and Son.
Jespersen, Otto
  1942   A Modern English Grammar on Historical Principles, Part VI: Morphology. Copenhagen: Ejnar Munksgaard.
Keesing, Nancy
  1982   *Lily on the Dustbin: Slang of Australian Women and Families*. Ringwood, VIC: Penguin Books Australia Ltd.
McAndrew, Alex
  1992   Hosties and Garbos: a look behind diminutives and pejoratives in Australian English. In: Claudia Blank (ed.), *Language and Civilization: A Concerted Profusion of Essays and Studies in Honour of Otto Hietsch*, 166–184. Frankfurt am Main: Lang.
Morris, Edward E.
  1898   *Austral English: A Dictionary of Australasian Words, Phrases and Usages*. London: Macmillan.
Mühlhäusler, Peter
  1983   Stinkiepoos, cuddles and related matters. *Australian Journal of Linguistics* 3: 75–91.
Poynton, Cate
  1984   Names as vocatives: forms and functions. *Nottingham Linguistic Circular* 13: 1–34.
Simpson, Jane
  2001   Hypocoristics of place-names in Australian English. In: Blair and Collins (eds.), 89–112.
Sussex, Roland
  forthcoming   *Dictionary of Australian Diminutives*.

Taylor, Brian A.
  1992   Otto 988 to Ocker 1988: The morphological treatment of personal names
          in Old High German and colloquial Australian English. In: Claudia Blank
          (ed.), *Language and Civilization: A Concerted Profusion of Essays and
          Studies in Honour of Otto Hietsch*, 505–536. Frankfurt am Main: Lang.
Weeda, Don
  1992   Word truncation in prosodic morphology. Ph.D. dissertation, University of
          Texas, Austin.
Wierzbicka, Anna
  1984   Diminutives and depreciatives: semantic representation for derivational
          categories. *Quaderni di Semantica* 5: 123–130.

Australian creoles and Aboriginal English: morphology and syntax

Ian G. Malcolm

1. Introduction

This chapter is concerned with the three major varieties of "restructured English" (Holm 1988–1989: 538) which are currently spoken by Aboriginal and Torres Strait Islander Australians: Kriol, Torres Strait Creole and Aboriginal English. A brief overview of the contact experience leading to the development of these varieties is provided in Malcolm (this volume) and will not be repeated here. These English-derived forms of communication constitute the home languages of the majority of Indigenous Australians, having supplanted more than half of the estimated original 250 Indigenous languages spoken in Australia in 1788 when it was claimed and occupied by the British. Kriol is spoken in an area extending from the far north of Western Australia, across the Northern Territory and into western Queensland. Torres Strait Creole is spoken in the Torres Strait Islands between Cape York and Papua New Guinea, and along the north coast of the Queensland mainland. Aboriginal English, with some regional variation, is spoken in Aboriginal and Torres Strait Islander communities throughout Australia.

The restructuring of the English superstrate which has led to the development of Australian creoles has involved, initially, the appropriation for cross-cultural communicative purposes of a basically English lexicon, often in association with the relexification of Indigenous conceptualizations, concurrent with the radical simplification of the English morphology and syntax. Under ongoing Indigenous substrate influence, as the simplified code has functioned increasingly for communication among Indigenous speakers, it has gone through a "developmental continuum" (Mühlhäusler 1997) towards a stabilized form as a new contact language. Further stabilization and elaboration, under specific sociolinguistic conditions, led, in the Northern Territory, to the development of Kriol on the basis of one pidgin foundation and, in the Torres Strait Islands, to the development of Torres Strait Creole on the basis of another pidgin foundation. Aboriginal English developed in different parts of the country from pre-existing pidgins of which one, New South Wales Pidgin, was dominant. It also underwent ongoing influence from standard and non-standard varieties of

English spoken in Australia and in some places from creoles, whether stable or going through a "restructuring continuum" (Mühlhäusler 1997) back towards the superstrate language. In Kriol and Torres Strait Creole it is possible to observe in the morphology and syntax innovative processes which are a part of the developmental continuum away from English. In Aboriginal English there are traces of these processes but also evidences of the restructuring continuum under the influence of Standard English.

2.   Morphology and syntax of Australian creoles

The morphology and syntax of Australian creoles will be traced here using, where possible, the categories developed by Holm (1988–1989) for the description of Atlantic creoles, and will thus facilitate comparison across hemispheres. Features and speech samples cited come from more detailed descriptions. For Kriol there are Hudson (1981), Sandefur (1979, 1991a,b), Sharpe and Sandefur (1976, 1977), Fraser (1977) and Steffensen (1977), and for Torres Strait Creole Crowley and Rigsby (1979), Dutton (1970) and Shnukal (1988, 1991). To avoid interrupting the flow of the text, these sources will not always be individually referenced.

2.1.   Verb phrase

2.1.1.   Subject-verb agreement

Subject-verb agreement is not normally an issue, since there is little or no inflectional morphology and words tend to be monomorphemic (Shnukal 1991: 187). Where the creole is restructuring towards English, inflected and uninflected forms of the verb may be used interchangeably without regard to subject agreement. Sandefur (1979: 138) has pointed out that, although it does not have concord between the subject and verb in terms of number, Kriol may observe concord between verb and object, in that continuative aspect in the verb co-occurs with a plural, but not a singular, object.

2.1.2.   The unmarked verb

Holm (1988–1989: 150) observes that in Atlantic creoles the unmarked verb may refer "to whatever time is in focus, which is either clear from the context or specified at the beginning of the discourse." This may also be the case with Australian creoles. Kriol verbs carry no tense inflection. In Torres Strait Creole, the verb is usually used with the simplest indicative form and the tense needs to be inferred, as in *Me go* 'I went'.

2.1.3. Tense

Although the unmarked verb may imply tense, there is also an optional pre-verbal past tense marker, *bin* (or *imin*), as in *dog i bin kambek* 'the dog has returned' or *im bin gilim me* 'he hit me'. *Bin* is derived from *been* and, under the influence of restructuring towards English, may be replaced by *been*. In Torres Strait Creole, another form of *bin* is *bi*, as in *we bi gou* 'we went'.

Future tense may be expressed in Kriol with the pre-verbal future tense marker *gona* (or *na*), with *andi*, as in *Im andi jilib jaya* 'He will sleep there', or (at least in child speech) with *gotta* (*garra*) (Fraser 1977: 154). Alternatively, the future meaning may be expressed through the adverb *tumaro*. In Torres Strait Creole, future is optionally signalled by the pre-verbal marker *go*.

2.1.4. Aspect

Perfect aspect, in Kriol, may be expressed with the adverbial *na* at the end of the clause. Continuous aspect may be expressed with the suffix *-bad* (or *-obad*), as in *im bin megimbad ginu* 'he was making a canoe'. Alternatively, with intransitive verbs, continuous aspect may be expressed through reduplication, as in *im bin gray gray* 'he was crying'. Kriol expresses progressive aspect with the marker *-in*, as in *jing-in-at* 'singing out, calling'. Durative or iterative aspect may be expressed in Kriol with *-bat*, as in *silip-in-bat-silip-in-a-bat* 'sleeping'. Habitual state may be expressed by the reduplication of adjectives (Steffensen 1977).

In Torres Strait Creole, Shnukal (1991: 189) identifies six core aspect markers: *kip* (iterative), *nomo* (cessative), *oltaim* (habitual), *pinis* (completive), *stat* (inceptive) and *stil* (continuative).

2.1.5. Negation

In Kriol, the verb may be negated by a preposed modal *gan* 'cannot' or *nomo*, as in *Yu nomo bin albim mi* 'You didn't help me'. *No* and *nomo* operate similarly in Torres Strait Creole, except that in this creole *nomo* may be placed at the end of the sentence. When using past tense, Torres Strait Creole speakers may negate the verb by preceding it with *neba*.

2.1.6. Forms of be

There are few traces of the Standard English verb *be* in Australian creoles. Equational sentences do not require the copula in the present tense in Kriol, hence *Olabat bigbala yem* 'They are big yams' (Sandefur 1979: 123), or in Torres Strait Creole, hence *Mislam i boi blo Kemuel* 'Mislam is Kemuel's son' (Shnukal 1991: 189–190). However, a copula is required where the past tense is salient, as in *Olabat bin bigbala yem* 'They were big yams'. The same principle applies to descriptive sentences, as in the following examples from Torres Strait Creole: *Kaikai i redi nau* 'The meal is ready now' (Shnukal 1991: 190) and *Ai bi fored* 'I was in the bows' (Dutton 1970: 147). Another variant current in the Kimberley is *bin bi*, as in *I bin bi nugudwan* 'He was unwell'. Existential sentences (in Kriol and in Torres Strait Creole) do not use 'be' but 'got', as in *I gad kap ya* 'There is a cup here' (Shnukal 1991: 190). 'Be' does not function as an auxiliary, except in the form of the pre-verbal past tense marker *bin*, sometimes contracted to *imin*, as in *Imin gaman* 'He came'.

2.1.7. Parataxis

In Atlantic creoles Holm (1988–1989: 183) has observed the occurrence of serial verbs, which he describes as follows: "a series of two (or more) verbs; they both have the same subject and are not joined by a conjunction ('and') or a complementizer ('to') as they would be in European languages." A similar (though not identical) feature was observed by Dutton (1970: 145) in Torres Strait Creole, where he found a tendency to place a large number of short sentences side by side without conjunctions. His transcription into "informal English" reads "me fellow go down take spear me two go fishing go that way me two go now come front point and looked that all the same thread there..." Shnukal (1988: 81–82) refers to this phenomenon as "verb chaining", as in *Da bot i kam anka ya* 'The boat came and anchored here' and *Em i ledaun de krai* 'He was lying there weeping.'

2.1.8. Passive

The passive, where it occurs (and it has been rarely recorded in the literature) is formed with *git*, as in *Olabat andi* ('will') *git kil* 'They will be/get killed' (Sandefur 1979: 137). Hudson (1981: 115) identifies *git* with an inchoative derivational affix ('become') found in most traditional Aboriginal languages.

2.1.9. Transitive

Verbs used transitively may be marked with a suffix, most commonly *-im*, as in *Im gilim geŋgarru* 'He is hitting a kangaroo' (Sharpe and Sandefur 1976) or *Im bin chak-im spia* 'He threw the spear' (Crowley and Rigsby 1979). There are a number of other variants of the suffix, including *-am*, *-em*, *-um*, *-i* and *-it* in Kriol and *-em*, *-e*, *-i* in Torres Strait Creole. In Kriol, there is vowel harmony between the final vowel of the verb stem and the vowel of the suffix, although the unstressed vowel may be neutralized (Hudson 1981: 37). When a transitive suffix is used, it is possible for the object to be deleted (Sandefur 1979: 116). Although it is normal for verbs used transitively to be marked, the suffix may be omitted where there are no other verb suffixes and the object is overtly stated (Hudson 1981: 37).

2.1.10. The adverb

The adverbial element in the verb phrase in Australian creoles is commonly expressed through suffixing. Sandefur (1979: 117–118) has identified nine adverbial suffixes in Kriol: *-an* 'on', *-ap* 'up', *-at* 'out', *-bek* 'back', *dan* 'down', *-in* 'in', *op* 'off', *-ran* 'around' and *-wei* 'away'. Shnukal (1991: 187) has referred to "four adjective and adverb suffixes, *-kain*, *-said*, *-taim* and *-wei*, which express approximation, location, time and manner, respectively." Fraser (1977) observed in Fitzroy Crossing Children's Pidgin the common use of the free adverb morphemes *epritime* 'always', *longtime* 'a long time ago' and *longway*.

2.2. Noun phrase

In Kriol, the noun phrase consists of a noun, optionally modified by adjectives and pronouns (Sandefur 1979: 77). In Torres Strait Creole, it consists of "an obligatory noun or pronoun and four optional elements. The order of these elements is: determiner, quantifier, adjective, noun/pronoun, preposition phrase" (Shnukal 1991: 188).

2.2.1. Determiners

Steffensen (1977) has observed that in Kriol the demonstrative system (*jad~dad*, *dij*) takes over part of the function performed by articles in Standard English, and that the determiner is often omitted. This corresponds to the process observed by Holm (1988–1989) with respect to Atlantic creoles. In Fitzroy Crossing Children's Pidgin /tat/ or /ta/ may occur in the place of a determiner

(Fraser 1977: 199). Another variant, /dædə/, has been observed in a post-creole context in Halls Creek. Torres Strait Creole has four articles, all of which are optional: *da* 'the' (singular, definite), *dem* 'the' (plural, definite), *wan* 'a, an' (singular, indefinite) and *ol* 'in general' (plural, generic) (Shnukal 1988: 24). The use of *wan*, derived from Standard English *one*, as an indefinite article is not peculiar to Australian creoles. It is attested, for example, in Miskito Coast Creole English by Holm (1988–1989: 192). Dutton (1970: 148) observes that Torres Strait Creole speakers may add *the* or *a* where they would not be required in Standard English, as in *the las Sunday* 'last Sunday' and *come in a two dinghi* 'came in two dinghies'. This could be seen as evidence of decreolization in process.

2.2.2. Number

Australian creoles do not inflect the noun for plural number. The only exception to this is the reduplicated plural used in *olmenolmen* 'old men' and *olgolgamen* 'old women' (Sharpe and Sandefur 1977: 54). Plural may be indicated by a collective nominal such as *mab* or *lad*, as in *dad lad men* 'those men' or a quantifier such as *bigmab*, *lada* 'much, many', *oldə* 'all the' or *sambala* 'some'. The general plural quantifier *alla* is used in Fitzroy Crossing (Fraser 1977). Torres Strait Creole employs six general quantifiers: *lelbet* 'a few', *olgeda* 'all', *plenti* 'many', *pulap* 'plenty of' and *tumas* 'too many' (Shnukal 1991: 188).

2.2.3. Gender

Australian creole nouns do not inflect for gender. In Torres Strait Creole it is possible (though not obligatory) to mark gender by the use of the adjectives *man* 'male' and *oman* 'female', as in *man ata* 'grandfather' and *oman ata* 'grandmother' (Shnukal 1991: 188).

2.2.4. Possession

Possession is not marked on the noun but is expressed by a derivative of Standard English *belong*, namely *bla* or *blanga* in Kriol, as in *Dad san bla mai sista im lib la Sydney* 'My sister's son lives in Sydney', or /bəloŋ/ in Torres Strait Creole, as in /neim bəloŋ kenu/ 'canoe's name'. Another form, common in the Kimberley, is *fo* (< *for*), as in *Tharran bla Trisa fo dedi* 'That is Teresa's father's'.

2.2.5. Pronouns

The personal pronoun morphology of Australian creoles is distinctive and incorporates a number of discriminations not common to Standard English. In addition to singular and plural, dual number is marked, and first person dual and plural pronouns have alternative forms to make explicit the inclusion or exclusion of the person spoken to. On the other hand, neither the subject/object distinction nor the third person singular gender distinction is strongly maintained (as is the case with many other creoles [Holm 1988–1989]). The recognition of the semantic categories of dual and inclusive is something Kriol and Torres Strait Creole share with many of Australia's Indigenous languages (Koch 2000: 38). In Kriol, most personal pronouns have several variants. In some cases the variation is on a regional basis (see e.g. Sandefur 1979: 89) and in other cases on a stylistic (i.e. acrolectal vs. basilectal) basis. Table 1 shows the main variant forms which have been reported on the basis of research carried out in the Northern Territory (Steffensen 1977; Sharpe and Sandefur 1976; Sandefur 1979) and Western Australia. Forms reported from Western Australia are shown in bold. In order to standardize the orthography, the conventions of Hudson (1981) are used in all cases. It should be noted that Koch (2000: 38) has provided a description of what he calls Aboriginal Pidgin, spoken in Central Australia. The forms he lists (though not shown here) are among the variants listed for Kriol in Table 1 and, in particular, those recorded from Western Australia. Koch sees Aboriginal Pidgin, on the basis of its maintenance of dual number and the inclusive/exclusive distinction, as related both to Melanesian Pidgin English and to Australian Indigenous languages.

Table 1.   Personal pronouns of Kriol

	Singular	**Dual**	**Plural**
first person inclusive		*yunmi* **minyu** **wi** (subj) **as** (obj)	*yunmalabat* *minalabat* *yunminalabat* **wi** **wilat** **wi** **as** (obj)

Table 1. (continued)   Personal pronouns of Kriol

	Singular	Dual	Plural
exclusive	*ai* (subj)	*mindupla*	*melabat*
	mi (subj or obj)	*mindapala*	*mipala*
	ai (subj)	**mindupala**	*wi*
	a (subj)	*wi*	**mela**
	mi (obj)	*as* (obj)	**mipala**
			wi
			as (obj)
second person	*yu*	*yundapala*	*yupala*
	yu	*yundupala*	*yumab*
		yunpala	*yuwalabat*
		yundupala	*yumpala*
			yu
			yupala
third person	*i*	*dupala*	*alabat*
	im	*imdupala*	*olabat*
	i (fem or masc)*	**dupala**	*olobat*
	im (masc, S or O)*		*al*
	it (fem, S or O)*		*dei* (subj)
			dem (obj)
			je
			dei (subj)
			dem (obj)
			olabat
			ol
			olap
			tat lat

*   These distinctions have been reported for Fitzroy Crossing Children's Pidgin by Fraser (1977).

Table 2.   Personal pronouns of Torres Strait Creole (Broken)

	Singular	Dual	Plural
first person			*yumi*
inclusive	*ai* (subj) *mi* (obj)	*yumi/wi* (subj or obj)	*yumpla/wi* (subj or obj)
		mitu/wi (subj or obj)	
exclusive			*mipla/wi* (subj or obj)
second person	*yu, yə*	*yutu* (subj or obj)	*yupla* (sub, obj)
third person	*em, i* ('he, she, it')	*demtu* (subj or obj)	*demplaa/ol* (subj)
			dempla/em (obj)

(Data based on Shnukal 1988, supplemented by Dutton 1970. Forms reported only by Dutton are shown in bold.)

The Torres Strait Creole personal pronoun system contrasts with the Standard English system in similar ways to the Kriol system. However, it differs from Kriol in some of its distinctive pronoun forms as well as in exhibiting less variation. As Shnukal (1991: 187) has shown, its morphology is unified by consistent use of bound personal pronoun suffixes, *-tu* (dual) and *-pla* (plural).

Both Kriol and Torres Strait Creole have distinctive possessive pronouns/ determiners. These are shown in Table 3, which reproduces data for Kriol (in bold) from Hudson (1981: 46) and for Torres Strait Creole from Shnukal (1988: 26). The Kriol examples shown here could be added too, in that "basically the personal pronouns are simply placed before a noun to indicate possession" (Sandefur 1979: 89).

Table 3. Possessive pronouns/determiners of Kriol and Torres Strait Creole (Broken)

	Singular	**Dual**	**Plural**
first person inclusive	*mai*	*yumi*	*yumpla*
exclusive	**main ~ mainwan**	*mitu*	*mipla*
second person	*yu*, **yuswan**	*yutu*	*yupla*, **yuswan**
third person	*em*, **is**	*demtu*	*dempla*, **deya**

Kriol has a reflexive pronoun *mijalb*, *mijelb* or, in the Kimberley, *jelp* which is invariant for all persons. In addition, there are in Kriol reciprocal pronouns *mijamed* 'together' and *gija* 'each other'. Torres Strait Creole has a set of reflexive pronouns formed by suffixing *-selp* to the above possessive forms, as shown in Table 4, derived from Shnukal (1988: 33).

Table 4. Reflexive personal pronouns of Torres Strait Creole (Broken)

	Singular	**Dual**	**Plural**
first person inclusive	*maiselp/miselp*	*yumiselp*	*yumplaselp*
exclusive		*mituselp*	*miplaselp*
second person	*yuselp*	*yutuselp*	*yuplaselp*
third person	*emselp*	*demtuselp*	*demplaselp*

2.2.6. *Adjectives*

As Sandefur (1979: 100) has noted, it is not always easy to distinguish adjectives from nouns in Kriol, as they frequently occur with nominalising suffixes *-bala*, *-wan* (as in *longpala* 'long one', *kukwan* 'ripe' and *nukutwan* 'bad one' [Fraser 1977]) and, occasionally, *-baga*. It is noted by Steffensen (1977) that the suffixes are used with numerals, as in *dubala boi* 'two boys', and are omitted in the prenominal position. The same author also notes that the adjective may be reduplicated to indicate plurality in the noun. Torres Strait Creole has a somewhat different pattern of suffixing and reduplication. Shnukal (1991: 187), as already noted in 2.1.10., lists four suffixes which may be used with adjectives or adverbs: *-kain* (approximation), *-said* (location), *-taim* (time) and *-wei* (manner). She also notes that reduplication may be used to intensify the meaning of the adjective, as in *kalakala* 'multi-coloured' and *spotspot* 'spotted.'

2.2.7. *Prepositions and enclitics*

With respect to Atlantic creoles, Holm (1988–1989: 207) has noted the tendency to use a generalized locative such as *na* to embrace 'in', 'at' and 'to', and the close linking of such prepositions to the verbs they accompany. These tendencies are present in Australian creoles. With respect to Kriol, Steffensen (1977) observed four prepositions: *la~langa* (locative), *bla~blanga* (possessive), *bram* (ablative) and *garrim* (associative). To these, Sharpe and Sandefur (1976, 1977) add *fo* (purposive). Shnukal (1991: 189) identifies four basic prepositions in Torres Strait Creole which may have been the only prepositions in the pidgin from which it is derived: *lo* (location, from 'along'), *go* (goal, from 'go'), *kam* (source, from 'come') and *blo* (possession, from 'belong').

There are also a number of enclitics or "second order suffixes" (Sandefur 1991a: 207), derived from English prepositions, which modify the meaning of verbs to which they are attached, as in *Im bin buldan* 'He fell down'. Other examples include *-ap* 'up', *-bek* 'back', *-ad* 'out', *-in* 'in', *-an* 'on' and *-we* 'away' (Sharpe and Sandefur 1976). A partly overlapping set of bound suffixes occurs in Torres Strait Creole, i.e., *-ap* 'up', *-aut* 'out', *-baut* 'about', *-daun* 'down', *-op* 'off', *-raun* 'around' and *-wei* 'away' (Shnukal 1991: 187).

2.3. Structure of sentences

2.3.1. Statements

As is most common in Atlantic creoles (Holm 1988–1989: 211), the basic word order in Australian creoles is SVO. The subject is always the noun phrase coming before the verb, as in *Det olgaman silip* 'The woman is asleep', and the object follows the transitive verb, as in *Det olgaman kukumbat daga* 'The woman is cooking food', although the object can be brought to the beginning for purposes of topicalization, as in *Ola daga, deibin binijimap* 'They ate all the food' (Sandefur 1991a: 208).

2.3.2. Questions

Questions may be formed in Kriol by intonation, as in *I shut-im up?* 'Will I stop it?' *I can go?* 'Can I go?', *You like-im?* 'Do you like it?' (Fraser 1977). Alternatively, they can be formed with the interrogative pronouns *hu* 'who', *blau/blanga hu/hu blanga* 'whose', *wanim* 'what', *wijan* 'which' as in *Hu bin dagat?* 'Who has eaten?', *Waijan mikibul bin binij?* 'Which young bull died?' (Sandefur 1979: 96–98), or *weya* (or its variant /wεːdət/), as in *weya dijan iya?* 'whereabouts' (Sharpe and Sandefur 1977: 60). A third option is the use of the tag question markers *ngi* or *intit*, accompanied by rising pitch (Sharpe and Sandefur 1977: 57). Torres Strait Creole also forms questions by intonation, or with the use of interrogative pronouns *hau* 'how', *haumach* 'how much, how many', *wee* 'where', *wen* 'when', *hu bla* 'whose' and *wanim* 'what' (Crowley and Rigsby 1979). The question tag *eh* also occurs regularly in Torres Strait Creole (Dutton 1970).

2.3.3. Conjunctions

In Kriol, simple sentences are coordinated with *an* 'and', though, according to Steffensen (1977), this may also express subordination. Sharpe and Sandefur (1977: 57) list seven conjunctions: *an* 'and', *bat* 'but', *buji/bunji* 'if', *anles* 'unless', *dumaji* 'because', *wen* 'when' and *weya* 'where'. Torres Strait Creole, as described by Shnukal (1988, 1991), may express coordination with *ane* or *an* or *ene* 'and', *bat* 'but', *insted* or *matha* 'instead', and *o* 'or' and may express subordination with *apta* 'after', *bipo* 'before', *sun* 'as soon as', *til* 'until', *wen* 'when, after, as', or with causal complementizers *bikos*, *daswai* and *prom*, conditional complementizers *ip* and *orels* and purpose complementizers *po and slong*.

2.3.4. Embedding

There are a number of different ways of marking relative clauses in Kriol. These include the use of prepositional phrases, as in *Main andi gadim modiga andi kaman* 'My auntie with a car is coming' or *Wanbala olmen waya imin we: k langa Elsi bin dalim me* 'A certain man who worked at Elsey Station told me' (Sandefur 1979: 107). Alternatively, it is possible simply to incorporate one clause into another, as in *Jadan olmen ai bin luk, im sikbala* 'That man I saw is sick' (Sandefur 1979: 172). Relative clauses may also be formed with *wan*, as in *Dij buk wan ai bin gibit yu im olwan* (Steffensen 1977). In Torres Strait Creole, embedded clauses may be introduced with conjunctions (see 2.3.3.) as in *Apta we kam baik prom sos, wi go greibyad* 'After we get back from church, we'll go to the cemetery' (Shnukal 1988: 77). Relative clauses may be introduced with *we*, as in *Dat stori we yu bi spik i prapa paniwan* 'That story you told was very funny', or (as in Kriol) may have no relative pronoun, as in *Ai lukraun mai klos ai bin luzim* 'I looked for my dress (that) I had lost' (Shnukal 1988: 81).

2.3.5. Verb repetition

Iterative aspect may be expressed in both Kriol and Torres Strait Creole by repeating the verb, with the number of repetitions reflecting the intended emphasis, as in *Yu ran ran go!* 'Keep running!' *Em i go go go* 'He kept on going and going and going...' (Shnukal 1988: 51); *Ay ben wed wed wed wed wed wed najing* 'I waited for ages but nothing (came)' (Sharpe and Sandefur 1977: 53).

2.3.6. Predicate marking

A pronoun, or pronoun-derived form, may be used in both Kriol and Torres Strait Creole to mark the division between the subject and predicate, as in *sambala boi de bin go* 'some boys went', *dad gel im getin fat* 'that girl is getting fat' (Steffensen 1977), and *Dog i dig-im graun fa kaikai boun* 'The dog is digging the ground to eat the bone' (Crowley and Rigsby 1979).

2.3.7. Object deletion

In Kriol, the direct object may be deleted if it is recoverable from the context, as in *Imbin kukumbat* 'She cooked (the food)' (Sandefur 1991a: 208). This is associated with the practice of transitive suffixing of the verb (see 2.1.9.).

2.3.8. Pre-sentence modification

Crowley and Rigsby (1979) have reported that a small number of words in Torres Strait Creole may operate as 'pre-sentence modifiers', being placed at the beginning of a sentence to provide aspectual and/or tense extension to the meaning of the verb, as in *Klosap me go luk yu* 'I'll see you soon'. The words which operate this way are: *klosap* (immediate future), *baimbai* (distant future), *stil* (continuative), *oredi* (completive) and *mait* (dubitive) (see also 2.1.4.).

2.3.9. Post-sentence modification

Another set of words have been identified by Crowley and Rigsby (1979) as occurring at the end of a sentence to give aspectual modification to the verb, as in *Ol kaikai wanwan* 'They ate one after the other'. These words are: *pinis* (completive), *gen* (repetitive), *trai* (attemptive), *nau* (inceptive), *wanwan* (sequentive) and *yet* (continuative) (see also 2.1.4.).

3. Morphology and syntax of Aboriginal English

Unlike the creoles, Aboriginal English is distributed across communities in all areas of Australia. In some places there is contemporary influence from creoles which may result in transfer and interlanguage features. In most places the influence from pidgin/creole is less direct. The discussion here will focus on features which would seem to be systematically a part of Aboriginal English, though their occurrence may be variable.

3.1. Verb phrase

3.1.1. Subject-verb agreement

Aboriginal English is much less regular than Standard English in marking agreement of the third person present tense verb with a singular subject. Hence, *he get wild* 'he gets/got wild'; *this go on top* 'this goes on top'; *he don't* 'he doesn't'. This is a widespread finding from all States/Territories studied, and from both rural and urban areas (Alexander 1965; Flint 1968; Eagleson 1977; Koch 1991: 98; Harkins 1994: 74; Elwell 1977; Eagleson, Kaldor and Malcolm 1982: 91; Malcolm 1995: 135). The (frequent) non-observance of subject-verb agreement leads to the regularization of the morphology of the verb *to be* for all persons in the past tense, hence *We was awake*; *me and Tommy was awake*; *they was comin to Wagin*. This, with elision of the initial consonant and vowel of the verb, leads to /aiz/ for 'I was' as in *I-z goin'* (Sharpe 1977: 47; cf. Readdy 1961: 94).

3.1.2.   The unmarked verb

The unmarked verb may often carry past tense meaning, as in *He hook him* 'He hooked him'; *one time we go there* 'went there once'. The past sense, if relevant, is retrievable from the context or from the co-text, as in *Last night me and my big brother fight*. The unmarked verb may occasionally function as an auxiliary or copula as in *I be cold* 'I am cold'.

3.1.3.   Tense

Past tense marking is (as noted in 3.1.2.) optional in Aboriginal English although it is not completely absent. Past tense verbs are more frequently marked than unmarked and if past tense meaning is salient, there are cues other than verb inflection by which the listener can infer it. In narrative, the past tense may be marked early in the narrative and assumed thereafter. Where the past tense is marked, there are several common variants apart from that which corresponds to the Standard English form. With certain verbs (such as *see, do, come* and *run*) the form which corresponds to the past participle in Standard English (*seen, done, come, run*) may be used to express simple past tense. Some verbs have past tense forms which do not exist in Standard English, such as *brang, brung*. Some verbs which require vowel change for past tense in Standard English are liable to be inflected with the regular past tense morpheme, as in *shined* 'shone'. In some cases, in both remote and urban areas, the past tense may be doubly marked, as in *camed* 'came' or *didn't stayed*. The creole past tense marker *bin*, sometimes phonetically altered to *been* in accordance with restructuring towards Standard English (as in *We never been la court* 'We did not go to court' [Eades 1996: 134]), is strongly present in most less urbanized areas, though Harkins (1994: 74) saw it as on decline in Alice Springs. The sense of *bin* is past, but not necessarily with the non-continuous sense of the simple past in Standard English

The perfect tense is rarely expressed in Aboriginal English, and, where it is, the auxiliary is not present (Readdy 1961: 100; Eagleson 1977: 537–538).

Future tense is (as in informal Standard English) often unmarked and is not shown in the modal auxiliary nearly as often as in Standard English. It is most commonly expressed with a form, or derivative, of the verb *go* or (less commonly) *get*, e.g. *going to, gonna, got to, gotta*.

3.1.4. Aspect

On the basis of data from North-West Queensland, it has been claimed that the *bin* preverbal past tense marker may signify perfective aspect, as in *You bin come from Calvert* 'You come (or, have come) from Calvert' (Flint 1971: 3). However, *bin* in other areas may co-occur with the Kriol continuous aspect marker *-bat*, as in *M...'e bin tellimbat R to go in that place E bin drown* 'M...kept telling R to go to the place where E went under' (Eagleson, Kaldor and Malcolm 1982: 91). We have observed that *bin* does not signify perfective aspect in Kriol. It may, then, be that Flint's example represents a relexification of the Standard English perfect form 'you have come' in a variety where restructuring towards Standard English is taking place.

Progressive aspect is marked in Aboriginal English by the use of the present participle, normally without the auxiliary, as in *I sitting down, he laughing, I sneakin*. The auxiliary may be added where past tense marking is relevant, as in [*they*] *was playin* (Readdy 1961: 100).

3.1.5. Negation

The auxiliary verb, where there is one, may be negated by *not* (often reduced to *n* [Sharpe 1977: 45]), e.g. *You caan eatim raw*. Otherwise, a negator (*not, never* and, in Central Australia, *nomore* [Koch 1991]) may precede the verb, as in *Nail not float* 'The nail does not float' or *I ad no shirt on and bees never sting me* 'I had no shirt on and the bees didn't sting me'. Double negatives are not uncommon, e.g. *They didn't have no shirt*.

3.1.6. Forms of be

The copula is very often absent in stative clauses, as in *That a pretty snake* 'That's a pretty snake,' though sometimes *bin* may be used where the tense is relevant, as in *I bin young fella den* (Flint 1971: 3). The copula is not required to link a subject with its adjective complement, hence *He blind* 'He's blind'. The preferred way of forming existential clauses is also to avoid *be* in favour of *got*, as in *E got some sand there* 'There is some sand'. Alternatively, such clauses may be verbless (*Some sand there*). As has been noted above, Aboriginal English does not characteristically use *be* to form progressive verb forms except in the past tense (see 3.1.4.) or to form negative statements (see 3.1.5.). The morphology of *be* is simplified, in that, in the past tense, *was* serves for all persons (see 3.1.1.; note also 3.1.8. below).

3.1.7.   Parataxis

The pattern observed in 2.1.7. is reflected to some extent in Aboriginal English, which does not make use of conjunctions as extensively as Standard English to link successive clauses. A Western Australian example is *I try to shout for D... the win' blow me, knock me over, so I fell an' laid down 'n I trieda git u' 'n win' know me over again* (Kaldor and Malcolm 1979: 414). In Queensland, Readdy (1961: 114) observed that the paratactic structure, with sentences following one another with only pauses in between, was the commonest in her data, and Flint (1968, 1971) observed the common occurrence of coordinated clauses linked only with pauses or *and*. A similar pattern was noted by Elwell (1977) in the Northern Territory: *You can get kangaroo, you bring it someone meat, I'll eat it.*

3.1.8.   Passive

The passive occurs rarely in Aboriginal English. Active voice is used in contexts where Standard English might use the passive (e.g. *A bee sting him* 'He was stung by a bee'). Where Aboriginal English speakers use the passive, they form it either without an auxiliary verb, as in *Most books made of paper* or with a form of the auxiliary verb *get*, as in *Uncle Steve, he got hit.*

3.1.9.   Transitive

Although the transitive verb suffix *-im* or *-em* is essentially a feature of creole rather than Aboriginal English, it has been reported as occurring in Aboriginal English among speakers from relatively remote areas of Queensland (Flint 1971), Central Australia (Koch 1991; Sharpe 1977) and Western Australia (Eagleson, Kaldor and Malcolm 1982: 91), as in *I bin eatim up goanna* 'I ate up the goanna' or *We seeim buffalo got big horn* 'We saw a buffalo with big horns' (Eagleson, Kaldor and Malcolm 1982: 91).

3.1.10. The adverb

In common with other non-standard varieties of English, Aboriginal English may not use the *-ly* suffix on adverbs where it is required in Standard English, hence *You can easy do it*. On the other hand, Aboriginal English, following Australian creoles, may introduce its own suffixes to mark adverbs for manner or time, as in *long-way, quick-way, north-way, wobbly-way, dark-time, all-time* and *late-time*.

3.2. Noun phrase

3.2.1. Determiners

It has been observed by Holm (1988–1989: 191) that "[e]xcept for the decreolized varieties (e.g. Jamaican Creole English *di* 'the'), the creoles appear not to have borrowed definite articles from the superstrate languages but rather to have created them anew from demonstratives and other particles." We observed this trend in Australian creoles which commonly use variants of *that* and *one* where Standard English would use the definite and indefinite articles, respectively (2.2.1.). The tendency to substitute the demonstrative for the definite article is a commonly-reported feature of Aboriginal English (Readdy 1961; Eagleson 1977: 539; Flint 1968, 1971: 2; Alexander 1965: 65, 1968), as in *Dat door bin close* 'The door closed'. The tendency to substitute *one* for the indefinite article is also often reported (Sharpe 1977; Readdy 1961: 100; Flint 1968, 1971: 2; Alexander 1965; Kaldor and Malcolm 1979: 422), as in *They seen one green snake tangled round a tree* 'They saw a green snake tangled round a tree' (Alexander 1965: 66). Articles are frequently omitted in contexts where they are required in Standard English (Flint 1968, 1971: 2), as in *We was playing game*, though they may also be apparently redundantly inserted, as in *Bloke with the long hair* (Kaldor and Malcolm 1979: 422).

3.2.2. Number

It is a widespread feature of Aboriginal English not to mark the noun consistently for plural. Often, though the plural inflection is missing, the plurality of the noun is evident by other means, as in *Some plum over there* 'There are some plums over there'; *Two man in a jeep* 'There are two men in a jeep' or *ten dollar* 'ten dollars'. An alternative pluralizer *-mob* (from Kriol, see section 2.2.2.) may be used occasionally in some areas, as in *clean water-mob* 'lots of clean water' (Sharpe 1977). Some nouns which function as mass nouns in Standard English are count nouns in Aboriginal English and may therefore be pluralized, as with *woods* 'bits of wood', *irons* 'pieces of iron', *dusts* 'clouds of dust' (Sharpe 1977: 48), *glasses* 'bits of glass', or *police* 'police officer'. Nouns with irregular plurals may still receive the regular noun plural morpheme, as in *two childrens*.

3.2.3. Gender

The gender distinctions made in Standard English do not always apply in Aboriginal English. The third person singular personal and possessive pronoun forms may be used interchangeably between male and female referents, as in *He a big girl* 'She's a big girl' and *That he dress* 'That's her dress'. In some areas *e* functions as a gender-inclusive pronoun form, hence *My mother, when e gonna talk language e talk* 'When my mother intends to talk in Aboriginal language she does so'(Kaldor and Malcolm 1979: 422).

3.2.4. Possession

Nouns tend not to be marked for possession with the *-s* suffix, especially in some areas. Hence, juxtaposition alone may enable possessive to be inferred in, for example, *That my Daddy car* or *Look at John boat*. In some areas, alternative possessive markers have been retained from creole, as in *Gun belong to Hedley* (Readdy 1961: 100; cf. Koch 1991, 2000), *Long time he was for my sister husband* 'A long time ago he was my sister's husband', or *Rachel mob-for dog bin die* 'Rachel's people's dog died' (Kaldor and Malcolm 1979: 422). As in Kriol (2.2.5.), personal pronouns may function as possessive adjectives without having possessive marking, as in *im dog* 'his dog'.

3.2.5. Kin relation marking

In Central Australian Aboriginal English, Koch (2000: 43–44) has observed the adoption of a new suffix which he calls a 'kin relation marker'. The suffix is the term *-gether* (from 'together') and it essentially creates a kin dyad with the family member with which it is used. Hence, *father-gether* means the dyad of father and child, *mother-gether*, mother and child, *brother-gether*, elder brother and younger brother or sister, *sister-gether*, elder sister and younger brother or sister, and *cousin-gether*, a pair of cross-cousins, one of whom is male. These terms all have corresponding terms in the Kaytetye language.

3.2.6. Pronouns

Aboriginal English speakers in some areas may transfer some creole personal pronoun forms into their speech. Aboriginal English as a whole, however, has a different system, as shown in Table 5. The forms shown bring together data from Queensland, the Northern Territory and Western Australia and exclude what seem likely to be unmodified transfers from creole. Certain creole-influenced forms have only been reported from Queensland and are therefore marked as such. This does not imply that the other forms do not occur in Queensland. The variation among forms may be less random than appears on the table, in that, for example, the *me* form of the subject pronoun is most likely to occur in multiple subjects (e.g. *Me and Sharon*).

Table 5.   Personal pronouns of Aboriginal English

	Singular	**Dual**	**Plural**
first person	*I ~ me* (subj) *me* (obj)		*we ~ us*
first person inclusive			*we ~ afla* (Qld) (S, O)
first person exclusive			*mifela* (Qld) (subj)
second person	*you*	*you two, you-n-him* (SE Qld)	*you, youse* *you mob* (SE Qld) *youfla* (Qld) (S, O)
third person	*(h)e ~ (h)im* (subj, masc/fem/inan) *(h)im* (obj, masc/ fem/inan) *she* (subj, fem) *it* (subj, pred, inan)	*dattufela ~ distufela* (NW Qld) (subj, obj)	*they, dey* (subj) *them, dem* (subj, obj)

Personal pronouns, as mentioned above (3.2.4.), may often function as possessive pronouns in Aboriginal English. The possessive pronouns of Aboriginal English, where they differ from the personal pronouns, are shown in Table 6.

Table 6.   Possessive pronouns of Aboriginal English

	Singular	**Plural**
first person	*my, moofla* (Qld)	*our*
second person	*your*	*your*
third person	*(h)is, (h)e's, (h)er, its*	*their, deir*

Aboriginal English reflexive pronouns in the third person tend to incorporate the possessive rather than the personal pronouns before the reflexive suffix, hence *hisself* 'himself'; *theirself, theirselves* 'themselves'. The pattern of reflexives is thus regularized in keeping with that of the first and second person reflexive pronouns.

3.2.7.   Adjectives

In Aboriginal English, adjectives may not be inflected for the comparative and superlative, though the superlative suffix *-est* may be used for emphasis, as in *biggest mob o emus* 'a very big flock of emus'. The *-est* suffix may also be used in a way that would be considered redundant in Standard English, as in *most rottenest* (Eagleson 1977: 538). Some expressions that would need to be expressed predicatively in Standard English may be expressed attributively in Aboriginal English, as in *long way country* 'a country far away' (Flint 1971: 3). One influence from creole (and also, perhaps, from Indigenous languages) is the frequent use of nominalising suffixes on adjectives, as in *black-one, hot-one, sweet-one, slippery-one, shorty-one, good-one, new-one, same-one* (Bavin and Shopen 1985: 83).

3.2.8.   Prepositions

Prepositions which are required in Standard English are often not required in Aboriginal English, as in *We was gonna go Derby* 'We were going to go to Derby' (Eagleson, Kaldor and Malcolm 1982: 100), or *We bin wait loooong time* 'We waited for a very long time' (Eades 1996: 134). The infinitive marker *to* may be omitted, as in *I bin go dere work*. The locative prepositions *in, at* and *on* may often be interchanged, omitted or, in some Kriol-influenced areas, replaced with *la* or *longa*, as in *We always go la ol' town* 'we always go to the old town' or *young guy longa book* 'the young man in the book'. Where two prepositions are required in Standard English, one may be used, i.e. *up* for 'up at', *out* for 'out at' (Alexander 1965: 66).

3.3.   Structure of sentences

3.3.1.   Statements

The basic statement form in Aboriginal English is, as in Standard English, following the SVO or S(V)C pattern. Variations from the basic word order are possible to serve the purposes of topicalization of a subject (as in *'Yungagees'-da's sort of a real way of sayin goanna* [Malcolm 1995: iii]) or the expression of an "afterthought" as in *five sheeps fat one* 'five fat sheep' (Eagleson, Kaldor and Malcolm 1985: 104; cf. Koch 1991: 98; see further 3.3.6.).

3.3.2. Questions

The inversion of subject and verb/auxiliary is much less common in Aboriginal English than in Standard English. Rather, questions may be indicated by intonation, as in *You like banana?* 'Do you like bananas?' or by the use of a final question tag. One of the most widespread tags is *-eh*, as in *He can walk, eh?* (cf. 2.3.2. above), but this may also be used with a falling intonation, in which case it functions not as a question marker but as a confirmation elicitation, as in *We bin give you a lot of shell, eh* ↓. Other tags which may be used in different areas to form questions include *you know, init, inti, ina, na* and *ana*. Questions may also be formed in Aboriginal English through the use of interrogative pronouns, though their use sometimes differs from Standard English, as in *Who your name?* 'What is your name?'.

3.3.3. Embedding

As in creole, embedded relative clauses may have no relative pronoun (Sharpe 1977; Readdy 1961: 100; Koch 1991). Where a relative pronoun is used, it may not be the same as in Standard English. In some contexts (e.g. Sydney), *what* may be used in place of the Standard English *that*, as in *I got one mate what goes to a Catholic school.* Generally, embedded clauses are not common in Aboriginal English, which (as noted in 3.1.7. above) prefers a paratactic arrangement of clauses.

3.3.4. Phrase and sentence repetition

There is some evidence of a greater amount of repetition of phrases and sentences in Aboriginal English than in Standard English. This may be illustrated in the following extract: *...when R go into hospital, mela bin get in; mela bin liar-cry. E bin cry for one doctor gonna take my toothache! E bin cry...* 'when R went to hospital we got in; we were pretending to cry. He was crying for a doctor to take away his toothache! He cried...' (Eagleson, Kaldor and Malcolm 1982: 102). Sharpe (1976: 6) has observed that Queensland Aboriginal English is particularly prone to the repetition of phrases and sentences, and she sees this as a response on the part of its speakers to the unusually high utterance rate in that area, which may adversely affect intelligibility. The tolerance of repetition in Aboriginal English may be better understood as a discourse or pragmatic rather than a grammatical feature.

3.3.5. Predicate marking

It was noted (2.3.5.) that in creoles, the predicate phrase may be signalled by a marker (usually derived from *he* or *they*). This phenomenon has been identified under many different names, including "nominal appositives" (Steffensen 1977), "concord particles" (Crowley and Rigsby 1979) and "pronominal cross-referencing". The latter term is used by Elwell (1977) in describing a pattern in Aboriginal English as spoken in the Northern Territory, which she sees as corresponding to a structure within local languages. She exemplifies it as follows: *If I find it kangaroo; We, all de kid, we going to somewhere we gonna play*. The recovery of the subject in this way is not uncommon in nonstandard Australian English, and is also widespread in Aboriginal English in all areas, e.g. *Dese um two boys dey's teasing this owl* 'Two boys were teasing an owl' (Kimberley, Western Australia); *The policeman he heard this banging* (Sydney) (Eagleson, Kaldor and Malcolm 1982: 232).

3.3.6. Post-sentence modification

Aboriginal English shares with creoles a tendency towards post-sentence modification. This sometimes occurs with the use of a completion marker, such as *finish* or *das all* when a narrative has been concluded. It also is built into the grammar by means of a constraint on the amount of information which can be expressed within one clause. There are many examples of an "afterthought" structure (as referred to in 3.3.1.) being used, where some information is appended to, rather than included in, the clause. Some examples from Kaldor and Malcolm (1979: 423) are: *This tree here close-up one; man make that fire smoky one; we bin see one bird, flying one.*

3.3.7. Successive pronoun subject deletion

It has frequently been observed (e.g. Readdy 1961: 114; Flint 1968, 1971) that subjects, once introduced, may not be repeated although there are successive verbs which relate to them. This may be particularly characteristic of narration. This is another aspect of parataxis (3.1.7.).

3.3.8. Associated motion

An unusual feature of Aboriginal English has been related by Koch (2000) to the influence of Central Australian languages. This feature involves the use of what appear to be two main verbs in the sentence, as in *Twofella bin go 'n wait for ...them bullock*; or *Nother mob go down long creek and go and drink water*. Koch (2000: 49) sees such structures as enabling the expression of associated motion which may be prior to, immediately subsequent to, or concurrent with the main activity. The indigenous language influences leading to this feature may exist, or have existed, in languages beyond Central Australia, in that similar patterns have been recorded in Western Australia, for instance in the following exchange:

A: *they go there chargin on don't they*
B: *yeah yeah go drinkin dere*

3.3.9. Embedded observation

A similar feature has been observed in both Central and Western Australian contexts, where the verb *see* is accompanied by another verb, as in *I saw him was running behind me*. This is not, in my view, embedding but rather fusion of *I saw him* and *He was running behind me*, and it relates to what, in my view, is the Indigenous Australian "cultural imperative" of reporting on one's observations. The matter observed and the act of observation are given equal prominence in the manner of reporting.

4.   Practical and research issues

The use of Holm's (1988–1989) categories for the account given in this chapter enables some comparisons to be made between Australian creoles and Atlantic creoles. The similarities, which further research could attempt to account for, include the reduced marking (by comparison with Standard English) of inflection on nouns and verbs, the use of an anterior tense marker derived from the verb *be*, the preverbal use of *no* or *neva* (but not *gan*) to mark negation, the reduced use (or non-use) of the copula in equative and adjectival constructions, the serial verb construction, the lack of a passive construction, the replacement of definite articles with demonstratives and indefinite articles with the numeral *one*, the expression of possession by juxtaposing nouns (though this is not the only way of expressing possession in Australian creoles), the use of a general locative to cover 'in', 'at' and 'on', the maintenance of SVO word order, and the marking of questions by intonation, tags or initial question markers.

On the other hand, the morphosyntax of Australian creoles is distinctive in other ways. It does not use a form based on *there* to express progressive aspect, nor a form based on *do* to express habitual or completive aspect. It does not use the complementizer *for*, though it does perform the same function with forms based on personal pronouns. It has its own system of marking transitive verbs and it has a distinctive set of enclitics derived from English prepositions. The personal pronoun systems of Australian creoles seem to be distinctive in the strength of their recognition of the inclusive/exclusive and singular/dual/plural discriminations.

As we have considered Australian creoles and Aboriginal English together in this description, it is possible also to make comparisons between the creoles and Aboriginal English. In many ways, as we would expect, the Aboriginal English forms come close to acrolectal forms in the creoles, but the similarities are greatest in areas where there is contemporary influence on Aboriginal English from the creoles. Aboriginal English as a whole does not maintain transitive verb marking, nor does it incorporate inclusive and exclusive forms in its pronoun system, though there is some evidence of a tendency to maintain ways of expressing duality. The tense of the verb, the number of the noun subject, the number and gender of the pronoun are all much less salient in Aboriginal English than in Standard English morphology. The marking of verb tense preverbally is strongly maintained with respect to the future tense and selectively maintained with respect to the past tense. While Aboriginal English does not fully maintain the systems of adjective and adverb marking (*-taim*, *-wei*) of the creoles, it does carry these systems over to some extent, as it does the system of enclitics (as seen in expressions like *learn up*), and it does commonly use *that/dat* in place of *the* and *one* in place of *a*. There is also a marked reluctance among Aboriginal English speakers to use the verb *to be* as copula or auxiliary, except to mark the past tense.

The question of the indebtedness of Aboriginal English to Indigenous languages, both those still spoken and those which formed the original substrate of the pidgins from which it developed, has been pursued by a number of scholars. Harkins (1994) and Sharpe (1976), among others, have argued that this indebtedness is considerable. It can be demonstrated not only in phonology, morphology and syntax, but, perhaps more strongly, in pragmatics and semantics.

Much of the research reported on here dates back several decades, indicating that the study of the morphology and syntax of Australian creoles and Aboriginal English have not been the focus of much contemporary attention. The emphasis of research has shifted from grammatical analysis to the analysis of discourse, genre, lexico-semantics and conceptualization, and to the more applied areas of literacy, bilingual and bidialectal education and the use of these varieties in cross-cultural communication especially in legal contexts. These areas are important in extending the understanding the dynamics of the restructuring and management of English by Aboriginal speakers, but do not come within the purview of this chapter.

Exercises and study questions

1. Australian forms of pidgin and creole English have in the past, according to Sandefur (1991b: 117, 119), been described by English-speaking Australians as "barbarous," "ridiculous," "careless," and "nothing but bastardized English." Sandefur (1991b: 120) dates attitude change (where it has occurred) from the 1970s, which saw systematic description of Kriol by linguists and its incorporation into bilingual education programmes. What linguistic and social factors are most influential in generating attitudes towards pidgin and creole and in facilitating attitude change?

2. In English, "two couples" implies four people, but in Kriol *dubala kapul* implies two people (Sandefur 1991b: 123). Can you account for this difference and relate it to the respective grammatical systems of the two languages?

3. A non-Aboriginal person became annoyed at being addressed by an Aboriginal Kriol speaker in the following terms: *Yu garra gibit me lif?* (Sandefur 1991b: 123). He assumed that the Kriol speaker was telling him he was obliged to give him a lift. Can you account for this miscommunication?

4. Consider the following classroom exchange and how the confusion between the teacher and pupil can be related to a morphophonemic difference between Aboriginal English and Standard English:

   "Benny wants Miss W. to write down for him the word 'his' which he wishes to use in a piece of writing."

Benny:	*His* (/hi:z/)
Miss W:	*His?*
Benny:	*His* (/hi:z/)
Miss W:	*He's* (She writes it)

   (Benny resumes writing and, after a short interval, shows his work to the teacher).

Benny:	*His* (/hi:z/), *Miss Winter, 'is, his* (/hi:z/)?
Miss W:	*That's he's ...*
	Is it his you wanted?
Benny:	*No, that's right. 'is breakfast.*
Miss W:	*His, is it?*

Benny: *Oh yeah, 'is, 'is. I know 'ow to write that.*

Miss W: *Wait a moment, 'cause that's not what I gave you. I thought you wanted he's.* (She writes *his*). *That's it, there. That right?*

Benny: *'Is breakfast.*
     (from Malcolm 1982: 160).

5. Account for the variable use of the verb *to be* in the following conversational fragments from Western Australian schoolchildren (Kaldor and Malcolm 1979: 414–415; Eagleson, Kaldor and Malcolm 1982: 97):

I been up there ... I been there when I was little.
We was gonna go Derby.
One of my dog he chasin little cats.
E brownish and some of them blackish (referring to bush kangaroos)
I been give her a little bit.
We been get im cook, really cook.
We bin go longway.
We bin tellim not to gib us nothing, e bin still gibim.
A: *Has anybody ever eaten a goanna?*
B: *I bin.*

6. Consider and explain the processes of English simplification or restructuring which are exhibited in the following English utterances of Aboriginal children:

a) A: *Do you want a game?*
    B: *Yeah I wanta.* ('Yes, I do')
b) *I'll take the photo, eh?* ('Shall I take the photo?')
c) *We was goin bush.* ('We were going away into the bush')
d) *Somethin getting wrong ere.* ('There's something wrong here')
e) *bury im up* ('bury him/her/it')
f) *E must ad a nest there.* ('There must have been a nest there')
g) *Reynold don't go to school.* ('Reynold doesn't go to school')
h) *We bin go long way in the Land Rover.* ('We drove a long way in the Land Rover')
i) *She be shy.* ('She's shy')
j) *E every time get drunk.* ('He/she is often drunk')

7. How have English forms been taken over to serve Aboriginal functions (Koch 2000) in the case of the following features of Aboriginal English as spoken in Central Australia?
   a) dual number in pronouns
   b) inclusion/exclusion in pronouns
   c) gender-free third person singular personal pronouns
   d) kin relation marker
   e) associated motion

8. Comment on the morphosyntax of the following extract of a Kriol text (text and translation from Sharpe and Sandefur 1977: 58–59):

   dagbala na, dagbala na. jen, jen ledi im bin dalim me,
   (It was dark then.   Then the lady   told me,)
   o olmen, olmen,   jarran bas im andi gamab abas nayn.
   ("Oh old man, old man, that bus is going to come at 9.30.")
   o wal   du led fo mi,   du co- du cul nayd daym.
   ("Oh well, too late for me, too co- too cold night time,)
   gulbala.   ay bin dog.   o yunmi wed.   maydbi yunmi
   (it'll be cool," I   said.   "Oh   wait, maybe we'll)
   bayndim muwa naja drag.
   (find   another   truck.")

Selected references

Please consult the General references for titles mentioned in the text but not included in the references below. For a full bibliography see the accompanying CD-ROM.

Alexander, Diane H.
   1965   Yarrabah Aboriginal English. B.A. Honours thesis, Department of English, University of Queensland.
   1968   Woorabinda Australian Aboriginal English. M.A. thesis, Department of English, University of Queensland, St Lucia.
Bavin, Edith and Timothy Shopen
   1985   Warlpiri and English: languages in contact. In: Michael Clyne (ed.), *Australia, Meeting Place of Languages*, 81–94. Canberra: Australian National University Press.
Crowley, Terry and Bruce Rigsby
   1979   Cape York Creole. In: Timothy Shopen (ed.), *Languages and Their Status*, 153–207. Cambridge, MA: Winthrop.

Dutton, Thomas
  1970   Informal English in the Torres Straits. In: William S. Ramson (ed.),
           English Transported: Essays on Australasian English, 137–160. Canberra:
           Australian National University Press.
Eades, Diana
  1996   Aboriginal English. In: Stephen A. Wurm, Peter Mühlhäusler and Darrell
           T. Tryon (eds.), *Atlas of Languages of Intercultural Communication in the
           Pacific, Asia and the Americas*, Volume 2.1, 133–141. Berlin: Mouton de
           Gruyter.
Eagleson, Robert
  1977   English and the urban Aboriginal. *Meanjin* 4: 535–544.
Eagleson, Robert D., Susan Kaldor and Ian G. Malcolm
  1982   *English and the Aboriginal Child.* Canberra: Curriculum Development
           Centre.
Elwell, Vanessa M. R.
  1977   Multilingualism and Lingua Francas among Australian Aborigines: a case
           study of Maningrida. B.A. Honours thesis, Australian National University,
           Canberra.
Flint, Elwyn
  1968   Aboriginal English: linguistic description as an aid to teaching. *English in
           Australia* 6: 3–22.
Flint, Elwyn H.
  1971   The Aboriginal English of informants in the 40–60+ age group in a far
           North-Western Queensland community. Paper presented to the 43rd
           ANZAAS Congress, Brisbane.
Fraser, Jill
  1977   A phonological analysis of Fitzroy Crossing Children's Pidgin. *Work
           Papers of SIL-AAB* A 1: 145–204.
Harkins, Jean
  1994   *Bridging Two Worlds: Aboriginal English and Cross-Cultural
           Understanding.* St Lucia: University of Queensland Press.
Hudson, Joyce
  1981   Grammatical and semantic aspects of Fitzroy Valley Kriol. M.A. thesis,
           Australian National University, Canberra.
Kaldor, Susan and Ian G. Malcolm
  1979   The language of the school and the language of the Western Australian
           Aboriginal schoolchild – implications for education. In: Ronald M. Berndt
           and Catherine H. Berndt (eds.), *Aborigines of the West: Their Past and
           Their Present*, 406–437. Perth: University of Western Australia Press.
Koch, Harold
  1991   Language and communication in Aboriginal land claim hearings. In:
           Suzanne Romaine (ed.), *Language in Australia*, 94–103. Cambridge:
           Cambridge University Press.
  2000   Central Australian Aboriginal English in comparison with the
           morphosyntactic categories of Kaytetye. *Asian Englishes* 3: 32–58.

Malcolm, Ian G.
  1995   *Language and Communication Enhancement for Two-Way Education.*
          Mount Lawley, Western Australia: Edith Cowan University, in collabora-
          tion with the Education Department of Western Australia.
Readdy, Coral
  1961   South Queensland Aboriginal English. B.A. Honours thesis, Department
          of English, University of Queensland, St Lucia.
Sandefur, John R.
  1979   *An Australian Creole in the Northern Territory: A Description of Ngukurr-
          Bamyili Dialects* (Part 1). Work Papers of SIL-AAB, Series B, Volume 3.
          Darwin: Summer Institute of Linguistics.
  1991a   A sketch of the structure of Kriol. In: Suzanne Romaine (ed.), *Language
          in Australia*, 204–212. Cambridge: Cambridge University Press.
  1991b   The problem of the transparency of Kriol. In: Ian G. Malcolm (ed.),
          Linguistics in the Service of Society: Essays to Honour Susan Kaldor,
          115–129. Perth: Institute of Applied Language Studies, Edith Cowan
          University.
Sharpe, Margaret C.
  1976   *The English of Alice Springs Aboriginal Children: Report to Teachers,*
          Part 1. Alice Springs: Traeger Park Primary School.
  1977   Alice Springs Aboriginal English. In: Ed Brumby and Eric Vaszolyi (eds.),
          Language Problems and Aboriginal Education, 45–50. Mount Lawley,
          Western Australia: Aboriginal Teacher Education Program, Mount Lawley
          College of Advanced Education.
Sharpe, Margaret C. and John Sandefur
  1976   The creole language of the Katherine and Roper River areas, Northern
          Territory. In: Michael Clyne (ed.), *Australia Talks: Essays on the Sociology
          of Australian Immigrant and Aboriginal Languages*, 63–77. Research
          School of Pacific Studies, Australian National University.
  1977   A brief description of Roper Creole. In: Ed Brumby and Eric Vaszolyi
          (eds.), *Language Problems and Aboriginal Education*, 51–60. Mount
          Lawley, Western Australia: Aboriginal Teacher Education Program,
          Mount Lawley College of Advanced Education.
Shnukal, Anna
  1988   *Broken: An Introduction to the Creole Language of Torres Strait.* Canberra:
          Research School of Pacific and Asian Studies, Australian National
          University.
  1991   Torres Strait Creole. In: Suzanne Romaine (ed.), *Language in Australia*,
          180–194. Cambridge: Cambridge University Press.
Steffensen, Margaret
  1977   *A Description of Bamyili Creole.* Darwin: Department of Education.

Bislama: morphology and syntax*

Terry Crowley

1.   Introduction

Bislama is a predominantly English-lexifier radically restructured contact language – also described as a pidgin or a creole – that is spoken as the consti-
tutionally declared national language of Vanuatu alongside eighty or so local
vernaculars. For more details of the historical and sociolinguistic background
of Bislama, see the accompanying chapter on Bislama phonetics and phonology (Crowley, this volume).

In keeping with pidgins and creoles in general, Bislama exhibits morphological reduction vis-à-vis English. None of the inflectional morphology of
English has survived into Bislama as productive processes. Some inflectional
suffixes have survived, though these have been reanalyzed as inseparable parts
of noun and verb roots in Bislama, e.g. *anis* 'ant' (< *ant-s*), *prestem* 'press' (<
press-ed 'em).

The inflectional categories of English nouns and verbs are either not marked
at all in Bislama, or they are marked syntactically by means of phrase-level
modifiers of some kind. The past tense suffix on English verbs is systematically lost, with the distinction between present *I float* and *I floated* being expressed by the absence versus presence of a pre-verbal auxiliary *bin* (< *been*),
i.e. *mi flot* and *mi bin flot*. The suffixed plural markers on English nouns are
again systematically lost, and plural is distinguished from singular by means
of the preposed plural marker *ol* (< *all*), e.g. *trak* 'car' and *ol trak* 'cars'. The
suffixed genitive marker on English nouns is expressed in Bislama by means
of a prepositional construction with the possessor noun introduced by *blo(ng)*
(which derives from the English verb *belong*). Thus, 'Kali's car' is expressed
as *trak blo(ng) Kali*. Further discussion of each of these constructions can be
found in the relevant sections below.

Productive patterns of derivational morphology in English have also been
lost or reduced to largely unproductive status. A nominalized verbal construction such as *my swimming saved me*, for example, is not expressed in Bislama
by means of a gerund. Rather, the only option for encoding such a meaning is
to recast this construction in terms of the underlying verb, as in (1):

(1) *Mi bin swim mo i mekem mi sef.*
 'I swam and it saved me (i.e. made me safe).'

Verb-noun pairs such as *demonstret* 'demonstrate' and *demonstresen* 'demonstration' involve processes that are less than fully predictable in English. With a much smaller proportion of the lexicon of Bislama comprizing "learned" vocabulary such as this for most the population, such patterns are arguably even less productive in Bislama.

Most of the derivational morphology that we find in Bislama represents new developments out of material that began as lexical forms in English rather than continuations of superstrate morphological patterns. Thus, the third person singular masculine object pronoun *him* has been reanalyzed in Bislama as a transitive marker on verbs which has come to acquire a causative function. Compare, therefore, the following:

(2) *Wota i boel.*
 'The water is boiling.'

(3) *Kali i boelem wota.*
 'Kali boiled the water.'

Other examples of lexical forms which have been morphologized in Bislama are discussed below. To date, there has been no publicly available comprehensive grammatical account of the language. Tryon (1987) adopts a pedagogical approach and presents some of the main patterns, though many details (and much variation) are ignored. Other substantial sources (e.g. Crowley 1990: 200–351; Meyerhoff 2000) concentrate only on selected aspects of the grammar without aiming to be comprehensive.

Given the restriction on length imposed on this chapter, the following discussion, too, cannot be exhaustive, and many interesting (and poorly described) features have necessarily been dealt with extremely briefly. The main features of the morphology and syntax of Bislama are presented in a way that allows for comparison with varieties such as Solomons Pijin and Tok Pisin, as well as other varieties of English covered in this Handbook. There are various structures in Bislama which are markedly different from those of English for which mention is made of significant similarities between Bislama and the Oceanic substrate.

2.   Nominal morphology

Nominal compounds are common in Bislama. A variety of patterns can be found, with one of the commonest being adjective + noun constructions, e.g. *smol-traosis* 'underwear' (< *smol* 'little' + *traosis* 'shorts'), *swit-blad* 'diabetes' (< *swit* 'sweet' + *blad* 'blood'). The boundary between word-level and phrase-level phenomena plagues any discussion of compounding in Bislama (as it does in many languages), especially when we consider that a single-word form such as *long-nek* 'reef heron' (< *long* 'long' + *nek* 'neck') means exactly the same as the two-word form *long-fala nek* (see section 4.2. for a discussion of the adjectival suffix *-fala*). There is a handful of compound nouns derived instead on the basis of noun + adjective order, e.g. *sik-nogud* 'venereal disease' (< *sik* 'disease' + *nogud* 'bad'). An additional small number of compounds is built up of an initial element that is a verb with a following noun, e.g. *stil-man* 'thief' (< *stil* 'steal' + *man* 'man, person').

There is a large number of compounds which involve two nouns together. Longer established compounds are typically formed on the basis of HEAD + MODIFIER order, as in *sos-pima* 'chilli sauce' (< *sos* 'sauce' + *pima* 'chilli'), *lif-kokonas* 'coconut frond' (< *lif* 'leaf' + *kokonas* 'coconut'), following the construction that is typically found in Oceanic languages. However, more recently formed compounds tend to follow the MODIFIER + HEAD order that we find in English, e.g. *turis-bot* 'cruise vessel' (< *turis* 'tourist' + *bot* 'boat'), *stori-haos* 'multi-storey building' (< *stori* 'storey' + *haos* 'house, building'). Some nouns appear with constituents in either order in free variation, e.g. *gras-nil* and *nil-gras* '*Mimosa pudica*' (< *gras* 'grass' + *nil* 'thorn, prickle').

3.   Pronouns

There is a single set of pronouns in Bislama, in contrast to the separate subject, object and possessive pronouns of English. Subject and object forms are distinguished by position vis-à-vis the verb, while possession is expressed by means of the same pronominal forms appearing after the possessive preposition *blo(ng)*. Thus:

(4)   *Mi bin salem trak blo(ng) yu.*
       'I sold your car.'

The pronoun system of Bislama marks a radically different set of contrasts to those categories that are formally marked in Standard English. The three-way gender distinction in the third person singular is lost with Bislama having the gender-neutral pronoun *hem*. The two-way number distinction of English has been expanded in Bislama into a four-way distinction between singular, dual, trial and plural. In the first person non-singular forms, there also is a systematic distinction in Bislama between inclusive and exclusive pronouns. We therefore find the paradigm set out in Table 1.1.

Table 1.1.   Bislama pronouns

	Singular		**Dual**	**Trial**	**Plural**
1	mi	Inclusive	yumitu(fala)	yumitrifala	yumi
		Exclusive	mitufala	mitrifala	mifala
2	yu		yutufala	yutrifala	yufala
3	hem		tufala	trifala	ol(geta)

The English origin of the forms of these pronouns should be obvious, i.e. *mi* < me, *hem* < him, *yumi* < you + me, *yufala* < you + fellows. The source of some of the categories that are marked, however, is clearly not English in origin. The substrate Oceanic languages involved in the initial formation of Bislama typically make exactly the same kinds of categorial distinctions that we find in Bislama, so this aspect of the pronoun paradigm is very likely to be of substrate origin.

It will be obvious from this paradigm that there are some recurring formal similarities between different pronouns. Non-singular pronouns often – though by no means always – involve the element *-fala*, obviously deriving from English *fellow(s)*. The dual and trial forms are all derived with the elements *-tu* and *-tri* respectively, which correspond in shape to the numerals *tu* 'two' and *tri* 'three' respectively in Bislama. However, these numerals have clearly been grammaticalized in this paradigm, as other numerals cannot be incorporated into pronouns in the same way. A pronoun referring to six individuals, for instance, must be expressed by means of a numeral postmodifier in conjunction with a plural pronoun, e.g. *mifala sikis* 'we (exclusive) six', and not **misikisfala*.

4.   Noun phrases

Noun phrases can consist of a nominal or pronominal head associated with a range of modifiers, as described in turn under the following headings.

4.1.   Quantifiers

Nouns can be preceded by the number marker *ol* 'plural', or any of the following quantifiers: *olgeta* 'all', *evri* 'each, every', *fulap, plande, staka* 'many', *eni* 'any', *sam* 'some', *tumas* 'a lot, too much of, too many of', *naf* 'enough'. We therefore find examples such as *ol man* 'people, men', *olgeta man* 'all the people/men', *evri man* 'each/every man', *fulap man* 'many people'. We sometimes find the pluralizer *ol* redundantly appearing in association with some of these other quantifiers, with *ol* generally appearing closest to the noun, e.g. *fulap ol man* 'many people'.

Also appearing before nouns are the numerals, e.g. *sikis woman* 'six women', as well as the interrogative *hamas* 'how much, how many', e.g. *hamas trak* 'how many cars'. These forms do not co-occur with the plural marker *ol*, i.e. **sikis ol woman*. Numerals differ from the quantifiers described in the preceding paragraph in that they can accept the adjectival suffix *-fala* (see section 4.2.), e.g. *sikis-fala trak* 'the six cars'.

Pronouns differ from nouns in that they do not accept noun phrase premodifiers. However, some of the premodifiers presented above can be used as postmodifiers in association with pronouns. This includes any of the numerals, e.g. *mifala sikis* 'six of us (exclusive)', *olgeta hamas* 'how many of them'. Some of the other nominal premodifiers also appear as pronominal postmodifiers, e.g. *yufala plande* 'many of you'. The nominal premodifier *evri* corresponds to the pronominal postmodifier *evriwan*, e.g. *yumi evriwan* 'each one of us (inclusive)'.

4.2.   Adjectives

Most adjectives precede the noun phrase head in Bislama, e.g. *stret ansa* 'correct answer', *rabis tingting* 'terrible idea', *sting mit* 'rotten meat'. There is, however, a small subset of adjectives which follow the head, e.g. *man nogud* 'bad person', *haos olbaot* 'ordinary house'. There is a preference for only a single adjective to be associated with a noun in Bislama, so a complex phrase such as *big black dog* in English is likely to be expressed in Bislama with one attribute expressed by means of an adjective and the other expressed in a relative clause, e.g. *big-fala dog we i blak* 'big dog which is black'.

There is a subset of premodifying adjectives which can accept the suffix *-fala*, which represents the morphologization of the noun *fellow* in English. One of the functions of the suffix *-fala* is to indicate that the quality expressed by the adjective is especially characteristic of the referent of the noun with which it is associated. Contrast *gud wok* 'good job' and *gud-fala wok* 'especially good job'. The same suffix can also be used to mark definiteness of a noun phrase, as in (5):

(5)   *Mi karem wan waet trak. Waetfala trak ya i stap long garaj.*
        'I have a white car. That white car is in the garage.'

Adjectives which accept this suffix are predominantly, though by no means exclusively, monosyllabic. It should be pointed out that there are also mono-syllabic adjectives which do not accept this suffix. Thus, while we encounter forms such as *sot-fala* 'short', *naes-fala* 'nice' and *swit-fala* 'sweet', we find only *hot* 'hot', *wael* 'wild' and *drae* 'dry', never **hot-fala, *wael-fala* and **drae-fala*.

Adjectives can also fairly freely accept the derivational suffix *-wan* which has arisen out of the morphologization of English *one*. This creates nouns out of adjectives, where the noun usually refers to an entity characterized by the quality expressed in the adjectival root, e.g. *smol* 'small' > *smol-wan* 'small one'. For many speakers, *-fala* and *-wan* are mutually exclusive, though younger speakers are increasingly able to add the nominalizing suffix *-wan* to an adjective carrying *-fala* where that suffix performs the characterizing function referred to above. Contrast, therefore, *sot-wan* 'short one' and *sot-fala-wan* 'especially short one'.

Adjectives often reduplicate according to the same formal patterns that are described in section 5.1. for verbs. In fact, given the lack of inflectional mor-phology in Bislama, it is often difficult in any case to draw a rigid distinction between adjectives and intransitive verbs. Adjectives are often reduplicated when they are associated with plural rather than singular nouns, e.g. *longfala plang* 'long plank', *ol long-longfala plang* 'long planks'. Another function of adjectival reduplication is to express concentration of a quality, e.g. *fas* 'stuck' > *fas-fas* 'well and truly stuck'.

4.3.   Demonstrative

Bislama has only a single demonstrative form, and it has additional functions as well. The form *ya* (< 'here') appears after a nominal head. This can simply express definiteness, e.g. *man ya* 'the man', or it can perform a general demon-strative function (making no reference to number), meaning 'this man/person' or 'that man/person' (or, with the plural phrase *ol man ya*, 'these men/people' or 'those men/people'). In order to disambiguate the multiple senses of *ya*, we sometimes find the proximate demonstrative sense being expressed as *ya nao* 'this/these' and the distant demonstrative sense as *ya lo(ng)we* 'that/those', e.g. *trak ya nao* 'this car', *ol trak ya lo(ng)we* 'those cars'.

4.4.   Complex noun phrases

Coordinate noun phrases can also be linked in the same way as clausal coordination, using the coordinator *mo*, e.g. *Kali mo Janet* 'Kali and Janet'. There are, however, other options available for the expression of noun phrase coordination. One possibility is to use the accompanitive preposition *wetem* 'with', e.g. *Kali wetem Janet*. Where a pronoun is coordinated with a noun, a rather different construction can be used in which a non-singular pronoun representing the sum of the coordinated noun phrases is preposed to the noun. Thus, the meaning *Janet and I* can be expressed in Bislama in one of three ways: *mi mo Janet, mi wetem Janet, mitufala Janet*.

Relative clauses in Bislama are introduced by the relativizer *we*, e.g. *tija we i toktok* 'the teacher who is talking'. Relativized non-subject noun phrases are marked by means of a pronominal copy at the site of the deleted co-referential noun phrase, as in (6):

(6)   *Mi harem tija we ol studen oli laekem hem.*
       'I hear the teacher who the students like.'

Bislama allows noun phrases from a wide range of structural positions to be relativized. The following, for example, illustrates the relativization of a prepositional object:

(7)   *Mi harem tija we ol studen oli givim buk lo hem.*
       'I hear the teacher who the students gave the book to.'

5.   Verb morphology

As mentioned above, there is no inflectional morphology in Bislama. The productive morphological processes involving Bislama verb morphology are all derivational in nature.

5.1.   Reduplication

Although reduplication is not a productive feature of English morphology, it is quite commonly encountered in Bislama verbal morphology. Although the substrate languages also exhibit fairly productive patterns of verbal reduplication, both the forms and functions of reduplication tend to be somewhat constrained in the world's languages, so this is perhaps an area of Bislama grammar where a search for a substrate origin is not totally convincing.

A variety of different patterns of reduplication are encountered in Bislama, both from the perspective of the forms that it takes and the functions that it expresses. Reduplication is normally partial rather than full, involving the repetition of material from the first syllable or the first two syllables of the verb root. Since there are relatively few verb roots longer than two syllables, many instances of reduplication are actually indeterminate between the two patterns, e.g. *ron* 'run' > *ron-ron*.

Partial reduplication covers a range of possibilities, including repetition of only an initial syllable, e.g. *fogivim* 'forgive' > *fo-fogivim*, *brekem* 'break' > *bre-brekem*, *faetem* 'punch' > *fae-faetem*. An additional pattern involves repetition of initial CV(V) along with a following consonant, e.g. *kilim* 'kill' > *kil-kilim*, *jenis* 'change' > *jen-jenis*, *laekem* 'like' > *laek-laekem*, *save* 'know' > *sav-save*. Reduplication occasionally also involves the repetition of material from the second syllable along with the repetition of the initial syllable, e.g. *difren* 'be different' > *difre-difren*.

A root can reduplicate on more than one of these patterns at the same time. Thus, *brok* 'break' can reduplicate as *bro-brok* or as *brok-brok*. Some roots also appear in slightly different shapes involving the optional presence of epenthetic vowels between initial consonant clusters, resulting in competing reduplicated forms such as the following: *s(i)mol* 'be small' > *smol-smol, smo-smol, si-simol, sim-simol*.

Verbal reduplication expresses a range of functions in Bislama, including the following:

- random or distributed action, e.g. *foldaon* 'fall' > *fol-foldaon* 'fall all over the place'
- habitual action, e.g. *giaman* 'tell lie' > *giam-giaman* 'tell lies all the time'
- reciprocal action, e.g. *save* 'know' > *sav-save* 'know each other'

No single pattern of reduplication is associated with any specific function, so if a verb is reduplicated according to more than one pattern (as is frequently the case), these forms may be associated with any of these functions.

5.2. Suffixation

The frequently encountered verbal suffix /-Vm/ alternates in shape in ways that were described in the chapter on Bislama phonetics and phonology (Crowley, this volume). These morphophonemic alternations represent a significant point of contrast between Bislama on the one hand and Solomons Pijin and Tok Pisin on the other, where such alternations are either less apparent, or simply non-existent.

This suffix is regularly attached to transitive verbs in Bislama. We therefore encounter intransitive-transitive pairs such as *kuk* 'cook (intr.)' > *kuk-um* 'cook (tr.)', *stil* 'steal (intr.)' > *stil-im* 'steal (tr.)', *smok* 'smoke (intr.)' > *smok-em* 'smoke (tr.), *skras* 'itch' > *skras-em* 'scratch, scrape'. Many transitive verbs ending in this suffix do not have corresponding unsuffixed intransitive forms so the verb invariably appears with this suffix, e.g. *kar-em* 'carry', *tal-em* 'tell', *sper-em* 'spear'. Sometimes, the root of a verb carrying the transitive suffix is not an intransitive verb but belongs instead to some other word class. Thus, corresponding to *melek-em* 'extract cream out of (grated coconut)' and *hama-rem* 'hammer (tr.)' we find *melek* 'coconut cream' and *hama* 'hammer (noun)' respectively.

This transitive suffix is so productive that any newly introduced transitive verb from English will automatically appear with the suffix, e.g. *imel-em* 'email (someone)'. However, there is a small subset of transitive verbs which irregularly appear without any transitive suffix, including *kakae* 'eat, bite', *dring* 'drink', *luk* 'see', *save* 'know', *tokbaot* 'discuss', *lego* 'leave', *gat* 'have'. Some of these verbs can be used both transitively and intransitively with no change in shape. There is a further subset of transitive verbs which alternate between carrying the suffix /-Vm/ and having no suffix with no change of function or meaning, e.g. *singaot(-em)* 'call (tr.)', *seraot(-em)* 'distribute'.

Bislama verb morphology also involves an additional order of derivational suffixes of the shapes *-ap*, *-daon* and *-aot*. These derive from the particles *up*, *down* and *out* which are frequently encountered in English phrasal verb constructions, though they have been reanalyzed as suffixes in Bislama. We therefore find examples such as *res-em-ap* 'raise up', *kat-em-daon* 'cut down' and *poen-em-aot* 'point out'. While many forms of this type represent straightforward morphologizations of English phrasal verb collocations, some represent genuine new creations in Bislama, e.g. *tal-em-aot* 'report on' (< *tal-em* 'tell' + *-aot* 'out'). Note that, in contrast to English, these forms are completely inseparable from the verb with which they are associated, thus only (8a), but not (8b):

(8)   a. *Bae mi left-em-ap yu.*
       b. **Bae mi left-em yu ap.*
           'I will lift you up.'

6.   Verb phrases

A verb phrase without any associated pre-verbal markers can be used in the expression of any tense if appropriate contextual clues are available. A form such
as *mi go*, for example, could be used to express present, past or future tense.
However, it is much more common for future tense to be overtly marked by
bae (see below) rather than being left unmarked. An unmarked verb for which
there are no contextual clues providing information about tense will normally
be interpreted as being realis (present or past) rather than irrealis.

Imperative verbs can also be expressed by means of unmarked verbs. With
a singular imperative, the bare verb may be used, although the singular second person pronoun may precede this, e.g. *(yu) go* 'go!'. With non-singular
referents in the imperative, it is normal to include the relevant non-singular
second person pronouns, e.g. *yufala go* 'you (all) go!'. Such imperatives are
all fairly brusque. Less impolite imperatives can be expressed by using the corresponding future constructions as imperatives, e.g. *bae yu go* 'go!', even more
polite imperatives are expressed by using the verb *traem* 'try' before the verb
in question, e.g. *(yu) traem go* 'please go!', or by using the adverbial *fastaem*
'first', e.g. *kam fastaem* 'please come!'. It is worth noting that this use of *traem*
represents a significant contrast with English for which there are widespread
parallels in the substrate languages. Prohibitives are expressed by means of the
regular negative forms, i.e. *no go* 'don't go!', *yufala no go* 'don't you all go!',
bae yu no go 'don't go!', *traem no go* 'please don't go!'.

There is a variety of pre- and post-verbal modifiers that go to make up a verb
phrase in Bislama. Those forms which appear immediately before a verb include *mas* 'must', *bin* 'past (or prior past)', *jas* 'immediate past', *save* 'abilita-
tive, permissive', *stap* 'continuous, habitual', *wandem* 'desiderative, immediate future', *traem* 'try', *finis* 'completive', *stat* 'inceptive'. Immediately before
these pre-verbal modifiers we find the negative marker *no*, which can be combined with the emphatic negative marker *nating* or *wanpis* appearing after the
verb, e.g. *yu no save kam* 'you cannot come', *mi no bin toktok nating* 'I didn't
talk at all'. When the postmodifier form *yet* 'still' appears in conjunction with
the pre-verbal negative marker it means 'not yet'. Compare, therefore: *mi go
yet* 'I am still going' and *mi no go yet* 'I haven't gone yet'.

There is also a future marker of the shape *bae* which behaves somewhat differently in that it typically appears immediately before the subject of the verb
rather than appearing between the subject and the verb. Contrast, therefore,
bae mi kam 'I will come' with *mi mas kam* 'I must come'. The corresponding
form in Tok Pisin has grammaticalized beyond its behaviour in Bislama and it

now appears also between the subject and the verb. Equivalent sentences such as **mi bae go* as an alternative to *bae mi go* are ungrammatical in Bislama.

Some of these pre-verbal modifiers in Bislama tend to undergo phonological erosion. In particular, *save* is often reduced in shape to *sae*, *stap* to *sta* and *wandem* to *wande*. The form *bae* sometimes also reduces to the proclitic *b-* when followed by a vowel-initial form. Thus, *bae oli kam* 'they will come' may sometimes be heard as *b-oli kam*.

In addition to the post-verbal modifiers *yet*, *nating* and *wanpis*, we find the perfective marker *finis*, e.g. *mi go finis* 'I have gone'. Also appearing post-verbally, there is a range of modifiers which perform a range of adverbial functions, including forms such as *gud* 'properly', *nogud* 'wrongly', *krangki* 'wrongly', *stret* 'correctly' and *strong* 'strongly, hard'. These frequently appear between the verb and a following object:

(9)   *Bae mi pulum strong rop ya.*
       'I will pull the rope hard.'

(10)   *Mi mas talemaot gud ansa.*
       'I must reveal the answer properly.'

However, adverbial modifiers can also be expressed by means of the core-layer serial verb construction described in section 8.1., as in (11):

(11)   *Bae mi pulum rop ya i strong.*

7.   Simple sentences

7.1.   "Predicate marking"

Before we can discuss sentence structure, there is one aspect of the grammar which needs to be outlined first. There is no general agreement about the most appropriate way of describing "predicate marking" in Bislama. The section heading here is presented in inverted commas to indicate the unsatisfactory nature of some aspects of the analysis, while at the same time using a term that many Melanesian Pidgin specialists will immediately recognize. The treatment in this section will be necessarily sketchy, and readers are referred to the extensive literature on the subject in Melanesian Pidgin for more detailed information (see also Smith, this volume).

Between many categories of subject and a following verb in Bislama we find the unstressed particle *i*, e.g. *hem i go* '(s)he went', *mitufala i go* 'we (exclusive) went', *tufala i go* 'the two of them went', *Janet i go* 'Janet went'. This form is systematically excluded after the subject pronouns *mi* 'I' and *yu* 'you', e.g. *mi go* 'I went', *yu go* 'you went'. The form *i* frequently appears as *oli* after a plural nominal subject, and also after the third person plural pronoun subject *olgeta* 'they', e.g. *ol woman oli go* 'the women went', *olgeta oli go* 'they went'.

Many descriptions of Melanesian Pidgin have referred to *i* and *oli* in examples such as these as "predicate markers", which implies that these forms appear between a subject and a following predicate. Others have referred to these forms as "subject referencing pronouns", drawing an analogy between the behaviour of these forms and the inflectional subject cross-reference markers that are widely encountered in Oceanic languages. Such an analysis would be consistent with the fact that in addition to *mi go* 'I went', we also find *mi mi go*, where the first instance of *mi* is treated as a subject pronoun, while the second *mi* represents the subject referencing pronoun.

7.2.   Constituent order

Bislama, like English and the majority of the substrate Oceanic languages, is an SVO language, e.g. *mi stap ronron* 'I jog', *mi laekem yu* 'I like you'. Third person singular pronominal objects are often expressed by means of zero rather than the pronoun *hem*, especially when they have inanimate rather than animate reference, which means that SV transitive constructions such as the following are frequently found: *mi laekem* 'I like it'. In the same way, third person singular subjects are often omitted, with the only signal of the subject category being the predicate marker *i* before the verb. Thus, in alternation with *hem i laekem* '(s)he likes it' we may find a transitive clause consisting of just a verb phrase, i.e. *i laekem* '(s)he likes it'.

Non-subject noun phrases can be fronted to pre-subject position to express contrast. Thus, from *mi laekem taro* 'I like taro' we can derive *taro mi laekem* 'I like taro'. Constituents that have been fronted in this way are very often followed by the focus marker *nao*, e.g. *taro nao mi laekem*. When a singular inanimate noun such as *taro* is fronted in this way, there is typically no pronominal trace left behind at the original site of the shifted noun phrase. However, with a plural noun phrase, or with a noun phrase with animate reference, there will normally be a pronominal trace. Thus, from *mi laekem ol taro ya* 'I like those taros' we can derive *ol taro ya (nao) mi laekem olgeta*, while from *mi laekem yu* 'I like you', we can derive *yu (nao) mi laekem yu*.

Although the examples just presented involve movement from the verbal object position, noun phrases can be moved from any non-subject position of the clause. Prepositional objects can therefore also be readily fronted in the same way. Thus from *mi wokbaot wetem stik ya* 'I walked with that stick' we can derive *stik ya (nao) mi wokbaot wetem*. The comment just made about zero pronominal copy with inanimate singular nouns does not apply with the prepositions *lo(ng)* and *blo(ng)*. Fronted noun phrases associated with these two prepositions must always be marked by means of a pronominal copy. In contrast to the example just presented, from *trak ya lowe blo man ya* 'that car is that man's' we can derive *man ya (nao) trak ya lowe blo hem*, but not **man ya (nao) trak ya lowe blo*.

Bislama discourse allows other focussed noun phrases to appear before the subject of a clause, again with optional marking by *nao*. It is not uncommon to find constructions such as the following:

(12)   *Mifala (nao) ol jif oli toktok tumas.*

The subject of this clause is *ol jif* 'the chiefs' and the associated predicate is *oli toktok tumas* '(they) talk too much'. The noun phrase *mifala* 'we (exclusive)' which appears at the beginning of the clause does not represent a fronted constituent. Rather, this form appears here simply to indicate that the following clause is understood with respect to 'us'. The only possible translation of such a sentence in English would therefore be:

(12)′   'With respect to us, the chiefs talk too much.'

Bislama does not have a copula corresponding to the English verb *to be*. Equational sentences are therefore expressed as non-verbal constructions with the topic and comment noun phrases juxtaposed with no intervening verb:

(13)   *Mi tija blo boe blo yu.*
        'I am your son's teacher.'

With a nominal topic, there is likely to be a "predicate marker" appearing between the two constituents:

(14)   *Tija blo skul i no man blo smok.*
        'The teacher of the school is not a smoker.'

However, it is probably more common for an equational sentence to be expressed with a nominal topic to be followed by a pronoun, which is then followed by the predicate introduced by the "predicate marker", as in (15):

(15)   *Tija blo skul hem i no man blo smok.*

A significant structural difference between Bislama and English is the absence of a passive construction in Bislama. The functional equivalent of the agentless passive in English involves the use of the plural "predicate marker" *oli* with no overt (or even implied) subject noun phrase. Thus, an English sentence such as 'My car was stolen' is expressed in Bislama as:

(16)   *Oli stil-im trak blo mi.*

If such a sentence were to include an overt third person plural subject, as in *olgeta oli stili-im trak blo mi*, this could only mean 'they (i.e. some particular individuals) stole my car'.

The functional equivalent of an English passive construction with an overtly expressed agent, e.g. 'my car was stolen by the youth', involves the fronting of the focussed object in an otherwise normal active transitive construction in Bislama. Thus, corresponding to *boe ya i stil-im trak blo mi* 'the youth stole my car' we find the following as the functional equivalent of the passive construction in English:

(17)   *Trak blo mi (nao), boe ya i stil-im.*

7.3.   Prepositional phrases

Bislama has only a fairly small set of prepositions, in common with many of the Oceanic languages which make up its substrate. The prepositions, and the range of functions that they express, are listed below.

(i) *long*: This preposition generally appears in casual speech as *lo*, which often reduces further to the proclitic *l-* when the following word begins with a vowel. Thus: *lo trak* 'in the car', *l-ofis* 'in the office'. The longer form *long* is what we generally encounter in written Bislama though it is sometimes also encountered in speech, especially before a word beginning with a vowel.

This preposition expresses a wide range of functions including location, e.g. *mi wok lo Vila* 'I work in Vila', goal, e.g. *mi go lo taon* 'I am going to town', source, e.g. *mi kambak lo taon* 'I am returning from town', and instrument, e.g. *mi katem bred lo naef* 'I am cutting bread with the knife'. This preposition also precedes a patient noun phrase that follows a formally intransitive verb, allowing it to function as a pseudo-object, e.g. *mi rato long ol lif* 'I raked the leaves'. This preposition effectively functions as a default preposition when no other preposition is specifically called for, as in examples such as the following:

(18)   *Mi fraet lo dok ya.*
       'I'm afraid of that dog.'

(19)   *Mi les l-ol man blo smok.*
       'I'm sick of smokers.'

Although Bislama has only a small set of genuine prepositions, there is a set of locational markers which can be used in conjunction with these prepositions to express a broader range of meanings. Forms such as *antap* 'above', *ananit* 'beneath', *ova* 'over', *klosap* 'nearby', *lo(ng)we* 'far off', *insaed* 'inside', *aosaed* 'outside', *afta* 'after', *bifo* 'before', *bihaen* 'behind' and so on can be used before a prepositional phrase marked by *lo(ng)*. Thus, compare *pijin i flae antap* 'the bird flew above' and *pijin i flae antap lo hil* 'the bird flew above the hill'.

(ii) *blong*: This preposition alternates in shape between *blong, blo-* and *bl-* according to the same conditions just noted for *lo(ng)*. It precedes a possessor noun or pronoun phrase in a possessive construction, e.g. *naef blong papa* 'Dad's knife', *trak blo mi* 'my car'. It also marks a benefactive noun phrase, e.g. *bae mi katem bred blo yu* 'I will cut the bread for you', as well as marking a habitual or characteristic relationship between two noun phrases, e.g. *man blo smok* 'smoker'.

(iii) *from*: This expresses a causal function, as in *mi stap kof from sigaret* 'I cough because of cigarettes', as well as expressing a purposive function:

(20)   *Hem i kam from masket blong sutum man blo smok.*
        '(S)he came for a gun to shoot the smoker.'

(iv) *wetem*: This is an accompanitive preposition, as in (21):

(21)   *Bae mi toktok wetem yu.*
        'I will speak with you.'

The same form can also be used to express the instrumental function, in alternation with *lo(ng)*:

(22)   *Mi katem bret wetem naef.*
        'I am cutting bread with the knife'.

(v) *olsem*: This expresses the similative function, as in (23):

(23)   *Mi no olsem yu.*
        'I'm not like you.'

In addition, a number of forms that began as transitive verbs are currently acquiring prepositional functions. These newly developed prepositions include the following:

(vi) *kasem*: As a transitive verb, *kasem* means 'reach, arrive at', but this form can also be used as a preposition meaning 'as far as, until', as in (24):

(24)   *Bae mi stap kasem tri klok.*
       'I will stay until three o'clock.'

(vii) *bitim*: The transitive verb *bitim* means 'defeat'. As a preposition, this form
      has come to express the meaning of 'past':

(25)   *Bae mi stap bitim tri klok.*
       'I will stay past three o'clock.'

This form is also used in comparative constructions:

(26)   *Mi longfala bitim yu.*
       'I am taller than you.'

(viii) *agensem*: The verb *agensem* means 'oppose', but when used as a preposi-
       tion this form expresses the meaning of 'against':

(27)   *Bae mi toktok agensem yu.*
       'I will speak against you.'

(ix)   *raonem*: This form can be used as a verb meaning 'surround' or 'go
       around', but as a preposition it means 'around':

(28)   *Mi pulum fanis raonem yad blo buluk.*
       'I made a fence around the cattle yard.'

(x)   *folem*: Finally, the form *folem* as a verb means 'follow', but when this is
       used as a preposition it expresses the idea of 'according to':

(29)   *Mi wokem kek folem buk blo kuk.*
       'I made a cake according to the cookbook'.

7.4.   Interrogative constructions

Polar questions are very frequently distinguished from statements by means
only of a change in intonation. Alternatively, polar questions can be marked
by means of the tag *(n)o* 'or' e.g. *bae yu kam* 'you will come' > *bae yu kam
no?* 'will you come?' Such sentences represent abbreviations of longer alternatives such as *bae yu kam no bae yu no kam?* 'will you come or will you not
come?'.

   Content questions are expressed by means of the following interrogative
forms: *wanem* 'what?', *hu(ya)* 'who?', *hamas* 'how much/many?', *we(a)*
'where?', *wataem* 'when?', *wijwan* 'which?'. Some interrogative meanings
are expressed by complex interrogatives, e.g. *olsem wanem* 'how?' (< *wanem*
'why?'). These forms typically appear in a sentence in the structural posi-

tion appropriate to a corresponding statement, i.e. as we find in English without automatic movement of the interrogative form to the head of the clause, as in (30):

(30)   *Yu wokem wanem?*
       'What did you do?'

These forms can, however, be fronted in the same way as other fronted constituents:

(31)   *Wanem (nao) yu wok em?*

In contrast to English, where questions with fronted WH-words represent the unmarked pattern, in Bislama fronting of question words represents a much more strongly expressed interrogative.

8.   Complex predicates and sentences

8.1.   Serial verbs

Representing a major typological contrast with English, we find fairly extensive patterns of verb serialization of a variety of kinds in Bislama. While some of these patterns are encountered also in Tok Pisin and Solomons Pijin, other serial verb constructions appear to be restricted to Bislama, or to be more frequently encountered in Bislama than in the other varieties of Melanesian Pidgin.

Just as in many of the Oceanic substrate languages, we also find a distinction in Bislama between what we can call nuclear-layer and core-layer serial verb constructions, with the two patterns differing in the degree of structural juncture between the verbs involved. Basically, nuclear-layer serial verb constructions involve a relatively tight and more compound-like juncture between verbs, whereas core-layer serial verbs involve a loose and more subordinate-like juncture. However, clear criteria can be recognized for distinguishing between serial verbs and compounding on the one hand and subordination on the other.

With nuclear-layer serial verb constructions, we find two verbs in sequence with no marking of subordination or coordination linking the two. There is just a single "predicate marker" applying across the verb series, and there is just a single subject preceding both verbs and a single object following both verbs. An example of this kind of pattern is:

(32)   *Kali i katem spletem wud.*
       'Kali cut the log in two.'

Here, the transitive verbs *katem* 'cut' and *spletem* 'split' are associated with a single subject and a single object.

There is a fairly restricted set of verbs which can appear as the second verb in this kind of serial verb construction in Bislama. This includes transitive verbs such as *spletem* 'split', *brekem* 'break', *klinim* 'clean', *flatem* 'completely finish', *blokem* 'block', *spolem* 'damage, ruin', *hipimap* 'pile up', *finisim* 'finish' and *fasem* 'tie'. The resultant combination expresses a resultative meaning as in the following examples:

(33)   *Sera i terem brekem pepa.*
       'Sarah tore the paper in two'

(34)   *Manu i kakae flatem raes.*
       'Manu ate all of the rice.'

(35)   *Roi i sidaon blokem rod.*
       'Roy blocked the way by sitting on the road.'

There is also a handful of intransitive verbs which can appear in the second position in the same construction, including *haed* 'hide', *raf* 'be dishonest', *raon* 'go around', *taet* 'be tight' and *redi* 'prepare'. Although these forms carry no transitive suffix, they can still be followed by an object if the initial verb is transitive. Consider (36):

(36)   *Mi kukum haed ol yam.*
       'I secretly cooked the yams.'

Intransitive verbs in a serial verb construction such as this typically express the manner in which an action is performed.

Core-layer serialization differs from nuclear-layer serial verb constructions in that there can be independent object marking associated with the initial verb, and there is also likely to be "predicate marking" between the two verbs (though there is no possibility for the second verb to independently choose its own subject). Contrast the examples just given with the following core-layer serial verb construction:

(37)   a. *Kali i sendem buk i kam.*
           'Kali send the book hither.'

This differs from the nuclear-layer serial verb construction in that the serialized verb *sendem* 'send' is associated with the object *buk* 'book', and *kam* is then serialized with this whole verb phrase. If this were a nuclear-layer serial verb construction, the pattern would be:

(37)   b. **Kali i sendem kam buk.*

It is worth commenting, however, that in Solomons Pijin, this pattern is in fact how this particular meaning is typically expressed.

While nuclear-layer serial verb constructions are occasionally used for the expression of manner, it is also possible for manner to be expressed by means of core-layer serial verb constructions, as in (38):

(38)   *Hem i holem rop i taet.*
        '(S)he held the rope tightly.'

It is far more common, however, for core-layer serial verb constructions in Bislama to be associated with the expression of the directional orientation of an event, with verbs that are physically directed either to or from the speaker being serialized with the basic motion verbs *kam* 'come' and *go* 'go', as already illustrated. However, other directional (and also posture) verbs can also appear in this kind of construction:

(39)   *Hem i putum pos i slip lo graon.*
        '(S)he lay the post on the ground.'

(40)   *Maki i bin wokbaot i stap lo bus.*
        'Maki walked in the bush.'

The multiply ambiguous preposition *long* can be disambiguated in terms of its location, goal and source senses by being associated with core-layer serial verb constructions expressing direction and position. Consider (41) to (43):

(41)   *Maki i wokbaot i go lo bus.*
        'Maki walked to the bush.'

(42)   *Maki i wokbaot i kam lo bus.*
        'Maki walked from the bush.'

(43)   *Maki i wokbaot i stap lo bus.*
        'Maki walked in the bush.'

8.2.   Coordination

The form *mo* is used to link coordinate clauses:

(44)   *Bae mi kam lo haos mo bae yu wet lo mi.*
        'I will come to the house and you will wait for me.'

The form *be* is used to express adversative coordinate clauses:

(45)   *Bae mi kam lo haos be bae yu no wet lo mi.*
        'I will come to the house but you will not wait for me.'

A disjunctive relationship is expressed by *o*, which varies freely with *no*:

(46)   *Bae yu kam (n)o bae yu stap lo haos?*
        'Will you come or will you stay at home?'

8.3.   Subordinate clauses

There is a range of different kinds of subordinate clause markers in Bislama. The possessive preposition *blo(ng)* is used to introduced a purpose clause:

(47)   *Mi kam blo harem nius.*
        'I came to hear the news.'

The general oblique preposition *lo(ng)* is used to introduce a variety of non-purposive complement clauses, as in (48):

(48)   *Mi intres lo pem trak.*
        'I am interested in buying the car.'

The form *se* is used to introduce a quotative clause in which a clause containing a verb of locution is followed by the content of the utterance:

(49)   *Mi talem lo hem se bae mi kam.*
        'I told him/her that I would come.'

(50)   *Mi singaotem hem se bae i kam.*
        'I shouted to him that he should come.'

(51)   *Hem i giaman se bae i kam.*
        'He lied that he would come.'

However, this form is also used to introduce a wide variety of complement clauses in which the initial clause expresses not just contents of locutions but also thoughts and feelings in general, as in (52) to (54):

(52)   *Mi hop se bae yu kam.*
        'I hope that you will come.'

(53)   *Mi save se yu bin pem trak.*
        'I knew that you bought the car.'

(54)   *Mi bilif se yu save helpem mi.*
        'I believe that you can help me.'

The form *we* is used to express a location clause:

(55)   *Hem i putum we mi no save faenem.*
        '(S)he put it where I can't find it.'

Another very frequently encountered construction involving the subordinator *we* in Bislama is a pattern of emphasis in which a predicate is subordinated to itself by means of *we*. Thus, contrast *graon i strong* 'the ground is hard' with *graon i strong we i strong* 'the ground is really hard'. It is common for the repeated material after the subordinator *we* to be deleted, giving constructions such as *graon i strong we* meaning the same thing.

The prepositional forms *from* and *olsem* are also used to introduce particular kinds of subordinate clauses. The causal preposition *from* is used to introduce reason clauses, while the similative preposition *olsem* introduces clauses expressing similarity. Thus:

(56)   *Mi kam from yu bin singaotem mi.*
        'I came because you called me.'

(57)   *Mi wokbaot olsem yu bin talem.*
        'I walked like you said.'

The noun *taem* 'time' is used to introduce a temporal clause:

(58)   *Mi stap lo haos taem yu bin kam.*
        'I was at home when you came.'

Other subordinators in Bislama have no independent function. One such form is *sapos* 'if':

(59)   *Bae mi kam sapos yu talem.*
        'I will come if you say.'

Nomata or *nevamaen* can also be used to mean 'although, even if':

(60)   *Bae mi kam nomata yu no talem.*
        'I will come even if you don't say.'

All of the subordinators mentioned in the preceding paragraph are frequently associated with a following *we* (which normally expresses either a place clause or it introduces a relative clause within a noun phrase) or *se* (which normally introduces a quotative clause), with no apparent change of meaning. Thus, reason clauses may be introduced by *from*, *from we* or *from se* in free variation. This tendency to make use of these complex subordinators seems to be an increasing trend particularly among younger speakers.

* John Lynch is acknowledged for helpful comments on an earlier draft of this chapter. Final responsibility for all interpretation rests, of course, with the author.

Exercises and study questions

1. The following sentences all involve words with meanings that are very close to the meanings of their English source words and they are based on grammatical constructions that have been described in this chapter. Translate each sentence into English:

   Wan dog i smelem mi insaed long haos.
   Ol hos blong Maki oli stap dring wota long reva.
   Ol man oli haedem ki blong mi.
   Oli faenem finis ki blong mi.
   Maki i bin givim wanem long yu?

2. Convert the following sentences so that they express the future tense:

   Kali i bin bonem haos blong Maki 'Kali burnt Maki's house'.
   Mi no save ridim stori ya 'I can't read that story'.
   Pikinini i mas go long skul 'The child must go to school'.
   Maki i stap ronem ol faol 'Maki is chasing the chickens'.
   Polis i raet finis lo buk blo hem 'The policeman has written in his book'.

3. Take the following pairs of sentences and make the second one into a relative clause modifying a noun phrase in the first.

   Mi luk wan boe 'I can see a youth.' *Olgeta oli singaotem wan boe* 'They called a youth.'
   Haos i bon 'The house burnt down.'. *Mi nao mi wokem haos* 'I built the house.'
   Trak i sperem wol 'The car collided with the wall.' *Mi sidaon long trak* 'I sat in the car.'
   Haos blong tija i bigwan 'The teacher's house is a big one.' *Mifala i laekem tija tumas* 'We like the teacher a lot.'
   Ol woman ol planem ol yam 'The women planted the yams'. *Ol man oli karem ol yam long haos* 'The men got the yams from the house'.

4. Choose the appropriate "predicate marker" to appear in the place marked *X* in the following sentences:

   Samuel X berem puskat we i ded 'Samuel buried the dead cat'.
   Ol mama blong mifala X wokem kakae 'Our mothers are marking food'.

Mifala X no save faenem jif 'We cannot find the chief'.
Mi X jas luk hem long moning 'I just saw him in the morning'.
Olgeta X go blong singaotem jif 'They went to call the chief'.

5. Using only the vocabulary which appears in the exercises above, construct the appropriate Bislama sentences corresponding to the English sentences below:

The teacher called his mother inside the house.
I cannot smell the dead chickens.
Their policemen will not chase the children at school.
The man who we will see has read the book.
What did the woman plant in the morning?

6. Choose an appropriate noun phrase from the nouns that you find in the preceding exercises and express these as objects to the following intransitive verbs:

Jif i singaot long nakamal 'The chief called in the meeting house'.
Polis we i sidaon long sanbij i smel 'The policeman who is sitting on the beach smells'.
Nakamal i bon long moning 'The meeting house burnt down in the morning'.
Ol woman oli stap plan long garen 'The women are planting in the garden'.
Brata blong mi i rid wetem tija 'My brother is reading with the teacher'.

Selected references

Please consult the General references for titles mentioned in the text but not included in the references below. For a full bibliography see the accompanying CD-ROM.

Crowley, Terry
    1990   *Beach-la-Mar to Bislama: The Emergence of a National Language in Vanuatu.* (Oxford Studies in Language Contact). Oxford: Clarendon Press.
Meyerhoff, Miriam
    2000   *Constraints on Null Subjects in Bislama (Vanuatu).* Canberra: Pacific Linguistics.
Tryon, Darrell
    1987   *Bislama: An Introduction to the National Language of Vanuatu.* Canberra: Pacific Linguistics.

Solomon Islands Pijin: morphology and syntax*

Christine Jourdan

1.   Introduction

Pijin is the local name of the pidgin spoken in the Solomon Islands. Even though it has no official status, Pijin is the de facto national language of the country: it is used as a secondary language in the rural areas where vernacular languages are central to local cultures, and as a main language in the urban centres. An ever growing number of urbanites have Pijin as a mother tongue and have no knowledge of the vernaculars of their parents. For further details on the socio-linguistic situation of Pijin in the Solomon Islands, please refer to the accompanying chapter on phonetics and phonology of Pijin. Pijin is an English lexified language (80 percent of the vocabulary) that has been heavily shaped by local vernaculars (Keesing 1988).

Pijin is typical of pidgin and creole languages in that it displays limited morphology and syntax. Whatever resemblances one may see with English is essentially lexical, as morphology and syntax bear no fundamental resemblances with those of English. However, one sees traces of English presence in the morphology, mainly under the form of reanalyzed tokens. For instance, some inflectional suffixes present in English (plural marking, pronouns) have been reanalyzed as parts of nouns and verb roots in Pijin.

In general, none of the inflectional systems of English has survived in Pijin. Plural marking of nouns is analytical and not morphological and is marked by the preposition of a plural marker (also the third person pronoun). Verbs are not inflected for tense, which is indicated by the use of aspect markers in initial clause position or in preverbal position. Budding auxiliaries such as *bin* (*been*) appear in the preverbal slot (in some dialects of Pijin only). So do duratives such as *stap* (*stay*). Genitive marking is realized through the use of the preposition *blo blong* (derived from English *belong*) between the possessed and the possessor.

As with Bislama (Vanuatu) and Tok Pisin (Papua New Guinea), most of the derivational morphology found in Pijin is a recent development out of lexical items. Reanalysis of English lexical items was one of the most productive derivational systems of early Pijin. It is now progressively replaced by derivation of the Pijin system. Thus whereas the English third person pronoun *him* was reanalyzed early on as a transitive marker on verbs *-em*, this derivational suffix *-em* is now also used to transform nouns, adjectives and prepositions into verbal predicates. Please consult the relevant sections below for more details.

As for syntax, we find a limited amount of multifunctional words (e.g. pronouns serving also as plural or transitive markers), a limited presence (until recently) of clause marking devices (relatives, causatives, etc.), a developed set of prepositions, a large class of stative verbs and a small class of adjectives, and the preference for aspect marking rather than time marking.

In general, one has to keep in mind that many dialects of Pijin coexist in the Solomon Islands: in addition to the more basilectal and acrolectal varieties, there exist also dialects based on differences created by geography, social class, gender and age. One of the most important contrasts is between urban and rural speech. The sketch presented here cannot do justice to the rich diversity exhibited by all these dialects and is, by necessity, incomplete.

2.   Sentences and word order

Unlike English, Pijin does not have a copula, simple equational sentences are thus often non-verbal sentences of the type *Mi nao mi sif blong ples ia* 'I am the chief of this place'. In rural areas and in the speech of older people in urban areas, the predicate marker /i/ tends to be inserted in the verb phrase after the nominal or the pronominal subject, as in (1):

(1)   *Puskat nao hem i dae finis.*
       'The cat has died.'

The predicate marker is becoming increasingly optional in urban centres. In the speech of young people, it is almost non-existent.

Pijin, like most of the local vernacular languages and English, prefers SVO word order for equational and simple sentences of the type:

(2)   *Mami blong mi siki.*
       'My mother is sick.'

However, in general, topicalization (of the subject or the object) is the preferred form for informative and more complex sentences. When the subject noun phrase is the focus, a subject pronoun is often inserted in the verb phrase:

(3) a. *Pikinin blong mi hem siki long hospitol nao.*
'My child is sick at the hospital.'

Topicalization, with or without fronting of the subject or object noun phrase can be reinforced by the optional addition of the focus marker *nao*:

(3) b. *Pikinin blong mi nao hem siki long hospitol.*

When a pronoun subject is topicalized, it must be followed by the focus marker *nao*:

(4) *Hem nao hem siki.*
'He is sick.' or 'It is he who is sick.'

As with Bislama, other focused noun phrases can be located before the subject, with optional marking by *nao*, as in (5):

(5) a. *Olketa pikinin tisa kros long olketa.*
b. *Olketa pikinin nao tisa kros long olketa.*
'The teacher is upset at the children.'

In narratives, the preferred pattern involves the repetition of the last clause or words of the preceding sentence at the beginning of the next sentence, thus giving the story a gentle lull and rhythm as in (6):

(6) *Olketa pikinin go wokabaot long bus. Wokabaot long bus, olketa lukim wanfala jaean. Jaean ia aksem samfala selen long olketa. Askem samfala selen long olketa, batawea, olketa no garem nao.*
'The children went for a walk in the forest. As they went for a walk in the bush, they saw a giant. The giant asked them for some money. He asked them for some money, but they did not have any.'

This pattern is also found in local Austronesian vernacular narratives and is rather reminiscent of some structures of ritual language in Indonesia (see Fox 1974), thus indicating that it may be an Austronesian pattern.

3. Noun phrase constituents

In Pijin, the noun phrase can be composed of determiners, pronouns, nouns, qualifiers and quantifiers.

3.1.   Determiners

Unlike English, Pijin has no definite or indefinite singular article similar to English *the* or *a*. Thus singular nouns appear alone as in (7):

(7)   *Kokorako kolsap bonem eg blong hem.*
       'The chicken is ready to lay its egg.'

However, the quantifier *wanfala* 'one' is progressively becoming reanalyzed by some speakers as an indefinite singular article that would be translated in English either by 'a' or by 'one' according to context. Plural of nouns is indicated by the anteposition of the third person pronoun plural *olketa* which also means 'all'. Only the context indicates whether a proper translation is with English 'the' or with English 'all'. The demonstrative pronoun *ia* (from English *here*) is increasingly being used also as a definite article. Again, the context reveals the meaning of *ia*. Thus the sentence *Man ia mi lukim long sip* can be understood as 'I saw this man in the ship', or 'I saw the man in the ship'.

3.2.   Quantifiers

Like English, Pijin has two types of numeral quantifiers: cardinals and ordinals. Cardinals are formed by adding the suffix *-fala* derived from English *fellow* but now semantically bleached, to any of the regular numerals (e.g. in *wanfala pikinin* 'one child', *fofala dola* 'four dollars', *tuentifala man* 'twenty men'). Under the influence of English, an ever increasing number of urban speakers are dropping the suffix *-fala* from the cardinals. When emphasis on the number is needed, the suffix *-fala* is always present. Note that plural is not morphologically marked on the nouns that follow. Ordinals are formed in two ways: first, by adding the prefix *mek-* (English *make*) before the numeral, as in *mekwan* 'first', *mekfoa* 'fourth', *meksikis* 'sixth', or:

(8)   *Mekfoa sista blong mi marit long Malaita.*
       'My fourth sister is married to someone from Malaita.'

Second, by prefixing the word *namba-* 'number' to the numeral *nambawan, nambatu, nambatri,* etc. and placing the ordinal immediately before the word that is qualified, as in (9):

(9)   *Nambatri pikinin blong mi stap siki.*
       'My third child is sick.'

Lexical quantifiers such as *olketa* 'plural, all', *samfala* 'some', *plande* 'lots of', *staka* 'many, lots of', *evri* 'each, every', *lelebet* 'a few', *naf* 'enough', *tumas* 'too much, a lot of' can also be used to modify nouns as in (10):

(10)   a. *Staka pipol long maket distaem.*
            'There is a lot of people at the market today.'
        b. *Lelebet selen long pasbuk blong mi.*
            'There is a bit of money in my account.'

Note that some of these quantifiers can be used as pronouns, without accompanying nouns, according to context as in (11):

(11)   *Staka long olketa kam long naet.*
        'Many of them came at night.'

3.3.   Qualifiers

Unlike English, Pijin has a small class of true adjectives, compared to the large class of predicate adjectives that function as statives. This is a pattern found in most of the substrate Oceanic languages (Ross 1998). Except for a small group of them, they are pre-modifiers as in *bigfala sista* 'elder sister' or *gudfala waka* 'good work', and characteristically identified by the possible presence of the suffix *fala* (even though it tends to disappear from the speech of an increasing amount of speakers). For some speakers, the suffix *-fala* is simply redundant, for others it is a way to add emphasis if the general way of constructing adjectives does not involve a regular use of the suffix. These adjectives typically include colour terms, size, relative age (young or old), and numbers.

On the other hand, there exists also a large class of predicative adjectives, but given the absence of copula, these adjectives function fundamentally like verbs as in *Pikpik blong mi gris fogud* which we can render in English only by 'My pig is very fat'. For this reason I prefer to analyze them as stative verbs and so does Keesing (1988). Others, however, analyze them as adjectives, like for example Crowley (this volume) for Bislama.

3.4.   Affixes

The main derivational affixes are suffixes: they are *fala* which signals adjectives, *wan* which transforms statives or adjectives into nouns (e.g. *siki* [stative] 'sick' vs. *sikiwan* 'sick person'), and *-em* (as well as its variants *-im* and *-um*), also commonly referred to as the transitive marker (e.g. *kaekae* 'to eat' vs. *kaekaem* 'to eat something'). Beside marking the transitivity of active verbs, the transitive marker can turn nouns, statives and prepositions into transitive verbs. The noun *ren* 'rain' becomes *renim* 'rain on':

(12)   *Disfala big ren ia renim mi tumas.*
         'This big rain storm (rained on me) drenched me.'

The stative *tuwet* 'drenched, soaked' becomes transitive in the following sentence:

(13)   *Hu nao tuwetim kaleko blong mi?*
         'Who has soaked my clothes?'

The preposition *of* 'off' becomes transitive with the adjunction of *-um* (for more details see section 4.1.):

(14)   *Ofum laet ia.*
         'Switch off the light.'

3.5.   Personal pronouns

The paradigm of Pijin personal pronouns is as follows:

	Singular		**Dual**	**Trial**	**Plural**
1	*mi*	Inclusive	*iumitufala*	*iumitrifala*	*iumi*
		Exclusive	*mitufala*	*mitrifala*	*mifala*
2	*iu*		*iutufala*	*iutrifala*	*iufala*
3	*hem*		*tufala*	*trifala*	*olketa*

The presence of the suffix *-fala* derived from English *fellow* is probably due to a reanalysis of *fellow* as a plural marker in the early day of the formation of Melanesian Pidgin. This paradigm is both simple and complex. On the one hand, it is simple, because, in contrast with English, Pijin (like Bislama) does not distinguish case or gender. The position of the pronouns in the sentence with regard to the verb allows for the distinction between subject and object. Reflexivity is indicated by the addition of the adjective *seleva* 'self', as in

(15)   *Mi seleva nao wakem.*
         'I did it by myself' or 'I did it myself.'

Reciprocity is indicated by the repetition of the same pronoun in subject and object position, as in (16):

(16)   *Sapos iumi mitim iumi moa, bae iumi stori.*
　　　'If we meet each other again, we will talk.'

Possession is indicated by the expression *blong*, for example in (17):

(17)   *Sista blong mi bonem bebi blong hem.*
　　　'My sister gave birth to her child.'

On the other hand, the system is complex because, and also in contrast with English, the pronominal paradigm of Pijin makes a rather elaborate set of distinctions between singular, dual, trial and plural. In addition, pronominal forms indicate a systematic distinction between inclusive and exclusive. These features correspond exactly to the substrate languages and are clearly not of English origin.

As with English and the substrate languages, the system makes it possible to incorporate noun subjects along with the pronouns. Thus 'We young people…' can be translated by *Mifala iangwan*. But Pijin and substrate languages make use of these constructions much more frequently than English. Particularly striking, yet pervasive, are constructions of the type illustrated in (18), where the second subject is clearly included in the pronoun, but yet singled out:

(18)   *Mitufala Resina bae go maket.*
　　　'Resina and I will go to the market.'

3.6.　Nouns

Common nouns are of such forms as *ston* 'stone', *popo* 'pawpaw' and *brata* 'brother'. The great majority of the words are derived from English etyma, and English is now the main source of neologisms such as *kompiuta* 'computer', *vidio* 'video', etc. A significant number of words are from Melanesian origin, most specifically Eastern Oceanic terms (some of them pan-Solomonic): *susu* 'breast', 'milk', *nana* 'pus', *maman* 'opening', *kokosu* 'hermit crab'.

Nouns enter into three main types of constructions involving either NOUN + NOUN, MODIFIER + NOUN and VERB + NOUN. In constructions of the type NOUN + NOUN, the model, common in the substrate languages, is HEAD + MODIFIER, as in *koprahaos* 'copra shed', *lemantri* 'lemon tree', *masolman* 'strong man', *samanfisi* 'tinned fish'. So strong is the substrate model that some well-established English compound words undergo metathesis as *sitbed* 'bed-sheet', *haostakis* 'tax house', *nelfingga* 'finger nail', or *lifti* 'tea leaf'.

More common are the compounds involving MODIFIER + NOUN, as in *redsos* 'ketchup', *raonwata* 'lake, puddle', *levolples* 'flat land', *bikmere* 'important woman' *ialotri* 'Indian mulberry', *smolkisin* 'outside kitchen', or *smol-mami* 'mother's younger sister'.

A small class of compounds involve VERB + NOUN in either order, contrary to what we see in Bislama where verbs seem to precede nouns exclusively (see Crowley, this volume). A relevant example is Pijin *manstil* (*man* 'man' + *stil* 'steal') 'thief' for Bislama *stilman*. But we also have the Bislama order as in *maritbed* 'conjugal bed, double bed' or *maritkwata* 'housing for married people'.

3.7.   Plural marking

Plural marking is not always necessary provided the context makes it clear that the noun is plural. However, when plural is marked, it is marked analytically by the preposition of the third person plural pronoun *olketa* 'they, all':

(19)   *Olketa boe bae kam long naet.*
        'The boys will come at night.'

Under the pressure of English, the official language of the country and the language of education, an increasing number of common words seem to be marking plural both morphologically and analytically. That is the case for words such as *boe* 'boy' as in *olketa boes* 'the boys' and *gel* 'girl' as in *olketa gels*. Interestingly, the plural suffix *-s* is in most cases used in conjunction with the plural marker *olketa* even though I have heard some people use the morphological plural without *olketa*. Is it a case of code switching or are we talking of the development of variation in Pijin plural marking? It is hard to say at this stage.

Plural can also be marked by the preposition of indefinite nominal modifiers such as *samfala* 'some' or plural personal pronouns such as *mifala* 'we' and *iufala* 'you' and their dual, trial, inclusive forms as in (20):

(20)   *Mifofala boe go wokabaot nao.*
        'The four of us boys are going for a walk.'

Note also that some English plural forms were reanalyzed early in Pijin as singular. For instance *ants* became *anis* as in *blakanis* 'black ant'. Thus 'one ant' would be glossed as *wanfala anis* and 'the ants' would most likely be glossed in Pijin by *olketa anis*.

4.   Verb phrases

4.1.   Verbs and verbal morphology

Pijin verbs can be divided into two main classes: stative and dynamic. Stative verbs have semantic properties that give them the attributive quality usually associated in English with adjectives. But as Pijin lacks copula, these statives are fundamentally verbal, as they are in the substrate languages (Keesing no date). Consider examples like *marit* 'be married', *lesi* 'be lazy', or *finis* 'be finished'. Some of these statives can become transitive with the adjunction of the transitive marker *-em* or one of its variants.

The dynamic verbs are divided into intransitive verbs and transitive verbs. The latter are marked by the addition of a transitive marker on the intransitive form. The choice of transitive suffix to be added (*-em*, *-im* or *-um*) varies according to a rule of vocalic harmony between the stem of the verb and the transitive suffix as in the following model:

Verb stem vowel	Suffix
-a	*-em*
-e	*-em*
-i	*-im*
-o	*-em*
-u	*-um*

This "rule" is more or less regular: *huk* 'to hook' becomes *hukum* 'to hook something', *hit* 'to hit' becomes *hitim* 'to hit someone', but *baet* 'to bite' becomes *baetim* for some speakers and *baetem* for others. A general trend in the speech of young urban Pijin speakers is the shortening of *-em* to *-m*. Thus we get *ansam* 'to answer something/someone' instead of *ansarem*, or *kalam* 'to colour something' instead of *kalarem*.

The transitive suffix is very productive as it can be used with nouns (for example, *san* 'sun' becomes *sanim* 'to put in the sun') and prepositions (*ap* 'up' becomes *apum* 'to raise'). So far, it does not seem possible to append the transitive suffix to true adjectives. A good indicator of the productivity of this suffix is that any new verbs directly borrowed from English today will automatically receive the transitive suffix: *fotokopim* 'to photocopy', *faksim* 'to fax', etc. Typically, most intransitive verbs, and a small group of statives such as *marit* 'be married', *komplit* 'be finished', *hot* 'be hot', and *fraet* 'be scared', can become transitive. Thus the stative *fraet* 'be scared' can become *fraetem* 'to scare', as in (21):

(21)   *Bikfala dogi ia fraetem mi tumas.*
        'This big dog scares me a lot.'

But a number of transitive verbs do not have intransitive equivalents, such as *duim* 'do (it)', *wakem* 'make (it)', *falom* 'follow (it)', *tekem* 'take (it)'. As with Bislama, a small category of transitive verbs can be marked with the suffix or not and yet not change meaning: *drink* or *drinkim* 'to drink', *kaekae* or *kaekaem* 'to eat', etc.

   A small subset of verbs are exclusively intransitive: *save* 'to know, to facilitate, to have the habit of', *go* 'to go', *kam* 'to come', and *stap* 'to stay, to exist'. Interestingly, these verbs also function as auxiliaries and modals, and are used in serial verb constructions. *Go* and *kam* function also as directionals: when placed after an action verb, they indicate the direction of the action towards or away from the speaker (e.g. *tekem go* 'remove from here, take away', *tekem kam* 'bring', *ring go* 'phone someone', *ring kam* 'receive a phone call'). When used in conjunction with other verbs, the verb *stap* indicates origin as in (22a), or a durative as in (22b):

(22)   a. *Iu stap kam long wea?*
          'Where are you coming from?'
       b. *Mam blong mi stap siki.*
          'My mother is sick.'

The verb *save* acts as a modal indicating habituality and ability:

(23)   a. *Hem save sevis long sande.*
          'She (usually) goes to church on Sunday.'
       b. *Pita no save draeva.*
          'Peter cannot drive.'

It can also indicate desirability:

(24)   *Waswe, mi save kaekae kek tu?*
       'Tell me, may I also eat some cake?'

One could claim that the so-called transitive marker is a form of inflection as it marks agreement with the object. However, this is true when the object is a noun or a pronoun (even when it is absent, since Pijin is a third person pro-drop language), but not when the object is a verb phrase, as will be shown in the analysis of serial verb constructions in section 4.5.

4.2.   Reduplication

Contrary to English, Pijin makes room for reduplication as a productive pattern in the morphology of verbs. It is an important element of the language that can modify meaning and/or mood. It is also present in the substrate languages of the Solomon Islands.

Reduplication is used to indicate intensity, duration, or repetition of an action. Many speakers make use of it liberally throughout their speech, for affect or precision. It is a particularly important tool for story tellers who make use of it to develop the atmosphere and the meaning of their story.

go	'go'	*gogo*	'after sometime'
suim	'swim'	*susuim*	'be swimming'
fraet	'afraid'	*fafraet*	'very afraid'
krae/karae	'cry'	*kakarae*	'cry continuously'

In some cases reduplication changes the meaning of the word slightly as with:

dae	'die'	*dadae*	'pine away'
go	'go'	*gogo*	'journey'
ting	'think'	*tingting*	'thought'
was	'wash'	*waswas*	'laundry'
sing	'sing'	*singsing*	'song'

The standard patterns seem to involve reduplication of the initial syllable of the verb stem, or reduplication of the whole verb root when the consists of one syllable. In the first case we find *save* 'to know' and *sasave* 'to be very knowledgeable', *siki* 'be sick' and *sisiki* 'keep being sick', *bisi* 'be busy' and *bibisi* 'be very busy', *silip* 'to sleep' and *sisilip* 'to sleep a long time'. In the second case we find *kis* and *kiskis*.

However, other reduplication patterns reveal that the rule is not that simple. Note that one-syllable verb roots containing a diphthong will follow the general pattern above, as in *faet* 'to fight' and *fafaet*. Note also that when the verb starts with a consonant cluster (a pattern predominantly found in the speech of young urbanites), speakers will copy the first consonant and the first vowel. Thus *stap* becomes *sastap*, *presim* becomes *pepresim*, *ple* becomes *peple*. From this we conclude that the basic rule for verbal reduplication is that speakers will copy the first consonant and the first vowel. Very rarely will speakers choose to reduplicate the consonant cluster if it is in initial position, contrary to what is happening in Bislama (see Crowley, this volume).

Reduplication is rather specific to verbal morphology and is very rarely found in other parts of speech except in a few limited nouns, with or without a change of meaning in the process: *kala* 'colour' and *kalakala* 'multicolour', *wan* 'one' and *wanwan* 'one at a time, individually', *pikpik* 'pig' and *sipsip* 'sheep', *kaekae* 'food'. In these cases the whole root of the noun is reduplicated.

Note that the noun *kaekae* 'food', derived from Eastern Oceanic *kae*, is also the verb *kaekae* 'eat'. All these words entered Pijin as lexicalized reduplicated forms.

4.3.   Compound verbs

Pijin has lexicalized a small set of English verb phrases based on verbs such as *talk* (*tok*), *make* (*mek*), *hold* (*holem*), which are usually followed by a preposition, a stative verb, or a noun. When the Pijin compound is built with a preposition, some sets of verbs, such as *tok*, will have the transitive marker affixed after the preposition, as in *tokabaotem* 'talk about', *tokwetem* 'talk with', *tokdaonem* (*tok* 'talk' + *daonem* 'lower' = 'denigrate'). When the compound is built with a stative or a noun, the verb is intransitive, as in *mekenoes* = *mek* + optional epenthetic /e/ + *noes* 'noise' = 'to be noisy', *mekelaen* = *mek* 'make'+ /e/ + *laen* 'line' = 'line up', *mekwara* = *mek* + *wara* 'water' = 'to be sterile', *mektambu* = *mek* + *tambu* 'sacred, off-limit' = 'consecrate'. A relevant example is: *Olketa dadi long laen blong mi kam for mektambu long ples ia* 'The male relatives of my lineage come to consecrate this area'.

4.4.   Prepositional verbs

Like English, Pijin can use prepositions such as *of* 'off', *ap* 'up', *daon* 'down' as the verbal nucleus of transitive verbs. English has *up the ante*, Pijin has *ofum* 'to switch off, to turn off', *apum* 'to raise', *daonem* 'to lower', *antapem* 'to be on top of', *insaetim* 'to bring inside', *atsaetim* 'to bring outside'. These prepositional verbs (as with other verbs derived with the transitive suffix) have become quite prevalent in the speech of younger urbanites. On the other hand, we find in the speech of older speakers, and also of rural speakers, a distinct prevalence of constructions involving the prepositions following dynamic verbs such as *tekem* 'take' and *wakem* 'make'. Whereas they would say *Iumi mas tekem kaleko insaet from ren* 'We have to bring the clothes inside because of the rain', a young urbanite would probably say *Iumi mas insaetim kaleko from ren*. These verbs are a good example of the productivity of the suffix *-em*.

However, these verbs are different from a second type of prepositional verbs that have the morphology of transitive verbs but are used as prepositions with an object. These are typically Melanesian and are found in many substrate languages. They include *agensem* 'against', *abaotem* 'about', *raonem* 'around', *lusim* 'away from', and *wetem* 'with someone', as in (25):

(25) *Ellen nao bae mi kam wetem.*
     'It is with Ellen that I will come.'

4.5. Serial verb constructions

Verb serializations exist in Pijin only if serial constructions consisting of auxiliary + verb are in included in that category. This construction is also common in English in phrases such as *go ask, come see*, etc. In Pijin this form is quite common and involves transitive and intransitive verbs and auxiliaries such as *go* 'go', *kam* 'come', and modals such as *save* 'know, can', *wande* 'want, wish', *laek* 'want, like'. Thus there are numerous serial constructions like *go tekem* 'go and take', *go lukim* 'go and look', *kam tekem* 'come and take', *go silip* 'go and sleep', *go suim* 'go and wash', *wande kaekae* 'want to eat', or *laek stap* 'wish to stay'. It is worth noting that the verb *wandem* becomes *wande* as a modal in serial constructions. When verbs are serialized with modals, the second verb loses its transitive marker even though it is functionally transitive. Consider (26):

(26) *Dadi wande kaekae fis, ma fis nomoa nao.*
     'Daddy wants to eat fish, but there is none left.'

Another type of serial verb constructions involves VERB + VERB, but this is a rather small group limited to resultative verbs, and is certainly not as productive as can be seen in Bislama. They all involve intransitive verbs, and it would probably be just as efficient to analyze the second verb as an adverb, even though functionally these adverbs are also stative verbs: *kilim dae* = *kilim* 'beat up' + *dae* 'die' = 'beat to death', *kilim haed* = *kilim* 'beat up' + *haed* 'hide' = 'beat in an ambush'. Contrary to what is happening in Bislama, there is no verb serialization in which the second verb is also transitive.

4.6. Aspect marking

In contrast to English, Pijin does not have a tense system. It is by the use of adverbs (*taem* 'when', *taembifoa* 'in the old days', *fastaem* 'long before', etc.), prepositions (*long naet* 'at night', *long mone* 'in the morning') and aspect markers (*finis* 'finish' indicates completion, *bae* indicates that an action may or will happen), and combinations thereof, that speakers indicate the sequence of events.

    Time adverbs can occupy two slots, the preferred slot is at the very beginning of the sentence, as in (27):

(27)   a. *Taembifoa, mifala no garem trake.*
           'In the old days we did not have cars.'
        b. *Tumoro nomoa iumi go.*
           'It is tomorrow that we will go.'

Rarely do we find *Iumi go tumoro* 'We shall go tomorrow', unless the sentence is meant to be interrogative in which case the adverb is stressed with a raising intonation.

Aspect marking can occur in three different positions, depending on the respective aspect marker. The only aspect marker that appears in clause-initial position is *bae* and its variant *babae, bambae*, thus revealing the adverbial origin of this aspect marker. The presence of *bae* in the sentence indicates that the action of the verb will take place in the future (*Bae mifala go sevis* 'We will go to church'), or may take place in the future, as a possibility, and usually as a direct consequence of another action that might or might not take place. In such cases, *bae* is an irrealis marker and often appears in association with the irrealis particle *sapos*, as in (28), or with modals such as *maet* 'maybe, perhaps' and *ating* 'maybe, probably'.

(28)   *Sapos hem hotsan, bae iumi go suim long si.*
        'If the weather is good we will go swim in the ocean.'

Beyond indicating the future or the possibility of an action in the future, *bae* also indicates causality, sequentiality, etc. (Jourdan and Selbach 2001)

The second aspect-marking slot follows the subject pronoun, more rarely the subject noun, and can be occupied by only three aspect markers: *des, bin* and *bae. Jes* (interspeaker variation [dʒes ~ des]) is derived from English 'just' and indicates that the action of the verb has just taken place:

(29)   *Mi des lukim kaen pipol olsem.*
        'I have just seen this type of people.'

Keesing (1988: 39) claims that this is the result of the calquing of Pijin on the basis of local vernacular languages. In other words, Pijin speakers use their vernaculars as a template to construct these types of sentences. The point is debatable since a similar structure exists also in English. *Bin* was attested very early on in the history of Pijin, but had not been used for a long time. It has been reintroduced over the last 20 years through sustained contact with Tok Pisin and Bislama, and is distinctively part of the urban educated dialect. The influence of English in this reintroduction is not negligible either. Thus we have *Mi bin go long Ruasuara* 'I went to Ruasuara'. *Bae* also appears in that slot as a marker of future or in conjunction with irrealis propositions. On the basis of

Sankoff and Laberge's (1973) study of *bae* in Tok Pisin, theorists have posited that as a result of nativization, *bae* had moved from sentence-initial position to preverbal position, and was thus being grammaticalized as a future marker. This is not the case in Pijin where all groups of speakers overwhelmingly place *bae* in preverbal position, and most particularly adults of rural areas who use Pijin as a second language (Jourdan 1985). In addition to marking future, *bae* can also mark sequentiality of action, destination, purpose, and causality.

The last aspectual slot is located immediately after the verb, and only a small set of aspect markers can fit in it. Besides *iet* 'yet, still', this set consists of the following three markers: *finis* indicates that the action is completed, *moa* indicates the repetition of the action and *nao* that the action is taking place. I also call *nao* a statement marker. This is a false friend for speakers of English who have to be alerted to the fact that the Pijin equivalent for English *now* is *distaem* and not *nao*. All these markers are perfective, and indicate whether the action has taken place, whether it is taking place or whether it is completed, as in (30):

(30)   *Mi wakem gaden blong mifala finis.*
        'I have completed my work in our garden.'

Note here the possible ambiguity that is resolved by the context: have I finished my work in our garden? Or have I finished all the possible work in our garden?

4.7.   Adverbs

Adverbs fall into two categories. Some are distinctly stative verbs that are used in serial constructions to modify the head verb as in *kilim dae* with *kilim* 'to beat up' + *dae* 'die', or *kilim strong* 'hit hard'. The second type are adverbs that cannot be used as stative verbs. They appear in postposition and modify the verb that precedes them like *tumas* 'very, too much' in (31):

(31)   *Hem laekem bia tumas.*
        'He likes beer very much.'

Further examples are *nating* 'for no reason, only' (32a), *wantaem* 'at the same time, together' (32b), and *olowe* 'until the end, all the way' (32c):

(32)   a. *Mi ti nating.*
            'I only had tea.'
        b. *Tufala Diake wetem Muina, tufala kam wantaem.*
            'Jack and Muina came together.'

c. *Sip ia save go olowe kasem Honiara.*
  'The ship goes all the way to Honiara.'

4.8.   Prepositional phrases

Pijin makes use of a small set of prepositions such as *blong* 'belong', *long* and its variant *lo*, and *fo* 'for' in order to build prepositional phrases. The possessive *blong*, derived from English *belong*, and commonly realized in urban centers as *blo*, is also used to indicate a relation of habituality or natural connection. This latter usage can be analyzed as a form of metaphoric extension of the possessive construction (Keesing no date). In this type of construction, the preposition is located before the verb, as in *miusik blong dae* 'funeral music', *man blong stil* 'a habitual thief', or *ples blong silip* 'sleeping quarters'. In the more urban varieties, and increasingly also in other areas, the preposition *fo* tends to replace *blong* in these types of constructions, e.g. *man fo stil* 'habitual thief', *ples fo silip* 'sleeping quarters'.

The preposition *long* is by far the most versatile and multifunctional preposition. On the one hand, it acts as the instrumental preposition 'with' in sentences such as (33):

(33)   *Pikpik olketa kilim dae long akis.*
        'The pig was killed with an axe.'

It is also, and foremost, the locative preposition that can be glossed in English by 'to' and 'at':

(34)   a. *Dadi blong mi long hospital distaem.*
          'My father is now at the hospital.'
        b. *Olketa go long Makira fo holide blong olketa.*
          'They go to Makira for their vacation.'

Pijin requires directional prepositions obligatorily as in *Krismas nao mi go long hom*.

The preposition *from* establishes a causal relationship, as in (35):

(35)   *Pikinin ia siki from malaria.*
        'This child is sick because of malaria.'

Another type of prepositional phrase is constructed with prepositional verbs, i.e. prepositional verb forms that have the morphology of a transitive verb (stem + transitive suffix) but which are used as prepositions (see section 4.4. above).

4.9. Relativization

Like English, Pijin has several ways of marking relative clauses: with the relative markers *hu* and *wea*, or without, yielding what I will call here free relatives. In addition one can embed a sentence bracketed by the deictic *ia* (see Sankoff 1980). Free relatives are the earliest and still the most important way of building relative clauses in Pijin, whether the relative clause is embedded or not, and whether the focus of the relative clause (the head noun) is a subject, a direct object or another syntactic function. In the following examples, the relative clause is given in square brackets:

(36) a. *Olketa pipol [olketa ranawe] olketa go stap long bus.*
       'The people who escaped took to the forest.'
    b. *Olketa go nomoa lukim jaeian [hemi itim man].*
       'They went looking at the giant who eats people.'

These types of sentences have a particular structure: the subject pronoun co-referential with the focused head noun signals the beginning of the relative clause and serves as its subject. This is possible only when the focused head noun is co-referential with the subject of the relative clause. It is impossible, of course, in sentences where there is a switch in reference in which the head noun is the object of the relative clause, as in (37):

(37) *Pikpik [olketa kilim finis] hem fat fogud.*
     'The pig they have killed is very fat.'

The subject pronoun of an embedded clause always introduces the relative if it is co-referential with the focus head noun. If we were to remove the subject pronoun from the embedded clause, the sentence would be ungrammatical or contextually unclear, or would become a chain-claused sentence. In the latter case, only the intonation pattern and the prosody would establish the difference between a relative sentence and a chain-claused sentence. Intonation is a very important marker of relativization. In a relative sentence the pause and intonational patterns are as follows:

> *Pikpik ia hem kilim, mifala kaekaem.*
> Pig   the he killed   we ate.
> 'We ate the pig that he killed.'

As a chain-claused sentence, the pause and intonational patterns are as follows and the meaning of the sentence is totally different:

Pikpik ia, hem kilim, mifala kaekaem.
Pig   the killed   we ate.
'The pig killed it, we ate it.'

As with Tok Pisin (Sankoff and Brown 1980), the bracketing of the embedded pronominal clause by the deictic *ia* reinforces embedding and thus relativization. The presence of *ia* is not necessary, however.

Speakers of Pijin can also build relative clauses by using the relative markers *hu* and *wea*. *Wea* can be used with either people or things, whereas *hu* is used with human nouns. The former is the earliest form, and is currently more widespread. It tends to be associated with older age groups and rural populations. *Hu* is still rather rare overall, but its usage is expanding, particularly in the speech of young urbanites. As is the case in English, both markers are optional in Pijin as can be seen in the following example:

(38)   *Disfala gele (wea) mi lukim, hemi siki.*
        'The girl (whom) I saw is sick.'

4.10.   Interrogative constructions

Interrogative sentences can be formed with or without interrogative markers. In the latter case, as with relative constructions, intonation contours play an important role in the formation of interrogative sentences: a simple change of intonation (raising at the end of the sentence) changes an affirmative clause into a question:

Bae iumi go maket.   *Bae iumi go maket?*
'We will go to market.'   'Are we going to market?'

The following interrogative markers are most commonly used: *hu?* 'who?', *hao mas?* and more commonly *hamas?* 'how much/many?', *wataem?* 'when?', *waswe?* 'how?'/'what?', *wanem?* 'what?'. All these markers can be fronted, as in (39):

(39)   *Wataem nao bae iu kam?*
        'When will you come?'

More commonly they are placed at the end of the clause or sentence, without any raising of the intonation contour, as in (40):

(40) *Bae iu kam wataem?*
      'You will come when?'

* This chapter owes much to the example set by Terry Crowley in his own chapter
  on Bislama morphosyntax, and to enlightening discussions with Kevin Tuite and
  Rachel Selbach. Shortcomings and infelicities are, of course, my own.

Exercises and study questions

1. Consider the following data from Pijin.

Pijin	English
Smolfala pikinin siki tumas	The small child is very sick
Pikinin wea hem smol hem sikiwan	The child who is small is sickly
Smofala pikinin wande kaekae tumas	The small child wants to eat a lot
Wanfala pikinin silip tumas	A child sleeps a lot
Mami silipim pikinin blong hem	The mother puts her child to sleep.
Pikinin lusim mami blong hem long benk	The child drops her mother at the bank.
Olketa pikinin no wande skul	The children do not want to go to school.

a. Identify all the bound morphemes and explain their functions.
b. How is the possessive case expressed?
c. What is the morpheme for 'to be'?
d. What is the morpheme for 'the'?
e. How would you say in Pijin 'The child wants to sleep at school'?

2. Reduplication
   Consider the following sets of pairs. Explain the reduplication principles
   that make the second one possible.

Save 'know'	*Sasave* 'be knowledgeable	
Slip 'sleep'	*Sislip* 'sleep a long time'	
Stap 'stay'	*Sastap* 'stay a long time'	
Dae 'die'	*Dadae* 'pine away'	
Faet 'fight'	*Fafaet* 'fight hard'	
Foldim 'fold'	*Fofoldim* 'fold many things'	
Waka 'work	*Wawaka* 'work hard	

3. Transform the following pairs of equative sentences into relative sentences using all three construction possible for each sentence

a) */Olketa pipol go long bus/* 'People went to the forest',
   /Olketa pipol fraet fogud/ 'People were very afraid'.
b) */Mi lukim wanfala gele/* 'I have seen a girl', */Hem siki long hospitol/*
   'She is sick at the hospital'.
c) /Sip iumi lukim hem bigwan ia/ 'The ship we are looking at is big',
   /Hem silip long haba/ 'She is laying in the harbour'

4. Using the vocabulary of some of the exercises above and of the examples given in the text, translate the following sentences from English into Pijin.

a) Jack wants to go home for his vacation.
b) My mother is sick with malaria, she is in the hospital.
c) The children are very small and want to sleep.
d) The small girl does not go to the bank.
e) A ship is coming insaed the harbour.
f) I saw a girl who is small and working hard.

Selected references

Please consult the General references for titles mentioned in the text but not included in the references below. For a full bibliography see the accompanying CD-ROM.

Fox, James
   1974   Our ancestors spoke in pairs: Rotinese views of language, dialect and code.
              In: Richard Bauman and Joel Sherzer, *Explorations in the Ethnography of
              Speaking*, 65–85. Cambridge: Cambridge University Press.
Jourdan, Christine
   1985   *Sapos iumi mitim iumi*: Urbanization and creolization of Solomon Islands
              Pijin. Ph.D. dissertation, Australian National University, Canberra.
Jourdan, Christine and Rachel Selbach
   2001   "Bae revisited": has the future marker made it into the V.P. yet? Paper
              presented at the meeting of the Society for Pidgin and Creole Languages,
              Coimbra, June 26.
Keesing, Roger
   no date   Solomon Pijin: an introductory grammar. Unpublished manuscript.
Ross, Malcolm
   1998   Proto-oceanic adjectival categories and their morpho-syntax. *Oceanic
              Linguistics* 37: 85–119.

Sankoff, Gillian
   1980   *The Social Life of Language.* Philadelphia: University of Pennsylvania
            Press.
Sankoff, Gillian and Suzanne Laberge
   1973   On the acquisition of native speakers by a language. *Kivung* 6: 32–47.
Sankoff, Gillian and Penelope Brown
   1980   The origins of syntax in discourse: a case study of Tok Pisin relatives. In:
            Gillian Sankoff (ed.), *The Social Life of Language*, 211–255. Philadelphia:
            University of Pennsylvania Press.

Tok Pisin: morphology and syntax

Geoff Smith

1. Introduction

As noted in the introduction to Tok Pisin in the companion chapter on phonology (see Smith, this volume), there is a great deal of variability in the language, depending on such factors as first or second language use, region, situation, degree of bilingualism with English and so on. As a result, it is sometimes not easy to say what is permissible in the grammar and what is not. The following account of morphology and syntax is, then, again idealised to some extent. Generally accepted patterns of use are described, but where some variants occur, this is also indicated. Examples are generally taken from the corpus of first language speakers in Smith (2002), occasionally simplified for illustrative purposes of the feature under discussion.

2. Morphology

Although derivational morphology is in evidence in a variety of word-formation processes, Tok Pisin, like many other pidgin and creole languages, has not transferred a productive inflectional morphology from the lexifier. The only affixes normally encountered are the *-im* suffix, derived from English *him* and attached to transitive verbs, and two *-pela* suffixes, derived from English *fellow*. However, with the increasing influence of English among some first language varieties, some English affixes, such as the *-s* pluralising suffix, are appearing with increasing frequency.

2.1. The transitive marker *-im*

The transitivising marker *-im* is one of the most characteristic features of Melanesian Pidgin English, and its use has been recorded from the earliest pidgins of the Pacific. It is derived from the English object pronoun *him*. This form appeared in early pidgins from Australia and may have been reinforced according to Oceanic substrate patterns in the early development of Pacific pidgins (Keesing 1988). Generally, this suffix is obligatory on transitive verbs, although there are a few exceptions. About 90 of the verbs listed in Mihalic (1971) have two forms, one transitive and one intransitive, distinguished according the presence or absence of *-im*. For example, the verb *sanap* means 'to be standing up', while *sanapim* means 'to stand something up'. Other examples include the following:

(1)   a. *dring*   *dringim*
         'to be drinking'   'to drink (something)'
      b. *giaman*   *giamanim*
         'to be lying'   'to deceive (someone)' (from obsolete
                                   English *gammon* 'to deceive')
      c. *marit*   *maritim*
         'be married'   'to marry (someone)'

Occasionally the intransitive form may be reduplicated:

(2)   a. *waswas*   *wasim*
         'wash oneself, bathe'   'to wash (something)'
      b. *tok(tok)*   *tokim*
         'to talk, converse'   'to say (something), to tell (someone)'

The suffix may be used in other ways to make semantic distinctions. For example, the transitive verb *kaikai* 'to eat' is unmarked by *-im*, while *kaikaim* is glossed as 'bite' in most accounts (e.g. Mihalic 1971). More recently, however, the use of the suffix with this particular word has been described as a way of distinguishing human from non-human agents (Smith 2002). The verbs *pispis* 'urinate' and *pekpek* 'defecate' are most often used intransitively, but still do not take the *-im* suffix when transitive use is called for. The forms *pispis blut* 'Blackwater Fever' (literally 'urinate blood') and *pekpek wara* 'diarrhoea' (literally 'defecate liquid') are used, although it could be argued that the transitivity is low in these cases. Forms of these verbs with *-im* were not thought to be permissible (Dutton 1973). However, Smith (2002) has recorded the semantically distinguished forms *pekpekim* 'to lay (eggs)' and *pispisim* as both 'piss on' and 'sting'. The common verb *gat* 'to have', also used as an existential, normally does not take a transitive suffix, even when it is clearly transitive in nature: *em i gat ol naispla nambis* 'it has nice beaches'. However, occasional instances of *gatim*, considered unacceptable in most areas, have been recorded, mainly from the Eastern Highlands.

In modern Tok Pisin, especially as spoken by first language speakers, the final *-m* of the *-im* suffix is frequently elided, leaving transitive verbs marked by *-i*. The following, for example, was recorded from a young first language speaker in the Simbu province:

(3)   *ol   suti   sla   boi   ia,   ol   puti   em   lo   kar*
       'They   shoot   this   boy   ANAPH   they   put   him   in   car'

When a verb stem ends in *-i*, for example, *redim* 'to prepare', loss of *-m* can negate the transitive/intransitive distinction.

In recent years, many English verbs have been borrowed into Tok Pisin, sometimes because of greater specificity, sometimes for stylistic reasons (Smith 1994):

(4)   a. *mi   bin   witnesim   long   ai   bilong   mi*
          I   PAST   witness   with   eye   POSS   me
          'I witnessed it with my own eyes'
       b. *husat   i   bin   othoraisim?*
          who   PRED   PAST   authorise?
          'Who authorised this?'

2.2.   The *-pela* suffix

The English word *fellow* appears to have been in frequent use in the early days of contact, and has entered all varieties of Melanesian Pidgin in reinterpreted form. While in some other dialects it appears as *-fala*, the Tok Pisin version is *-pela*, now almost universally reduced by fluent speakers to *-pla*. In Tok Pisin this has taken two distinct forms, one as a marker of monosyllabic adjectives, including numerals, the other as a plural marker on pronouns.

2.2.1.   The *-pela adjectival suffix*

The *-pela* suffix on adjectives and quantifiers is superficially similar in structure to measure words or classifiers in Chinese. Phrases such as the Cantonese *yàt go yàhn* 'one person', for example, look like an exact parallel of the Tok Pisin expression *wan-pela man*. Indeed, something analogous appeared in Chinese Pidgin English in the 19th century, for example, *wan piecee man* and some influence from that direction might reasonably be suspected. However, Baker (1987) has made a detailed study of the question and specifically ruled out influence from Chinese on Tok Pisin in this respect.

There appears to be no sign that the *-pela* adjectival suffix is becoming obsolescent, in spite of its apparent redundancy and almost total lack of substrate reinforcement. A number of points, though, are worth noting. Firstly, the category of adjective in Tok Pisin is somewhat problematic, as there is considerable overlap between what can be defined as adjectives and stative verbs. Secondly, there are a number of common monosyllabic adjectives which do not take *-pela*, and only appear after the noun, e.g. *banana mau* 'ripe banana' and *han kais* 'left hand'. Lastly, a recent study of first language speakers (Smith 2002) has shown that while the full *-pela* form was heard in some slow or deliberately pronounced words, and is retained as an etymological spelling, the reduced form *-pla* is now the canonical form of this suffix among a considerable number of speakers. There are some examples of adjectives with more than one syllable taking the suffix, particularly numerals and colours (e.g. *sevenpela*, *yelopela*). Some quantifiers and demonstratives ending in *-pela* appear to follow the same pattern, although it should be noted that some words such as *dispela* 'this' and *sampela* 'some' contain bound morphs, as there are no independently occurring forms **dis* and **sam*. Indeed the status of *-(pe)la* as a suffix here is now open to question. Among first language speakers in some areas, the *-pela* suffix may take on a semantic role, for example, in distinguishing the general form *hamas* 'how much/many' from a more emphatic form *hamaspela* 'goodness knows how many' (Smith 2002: 64).

2.2.2. -pela *in the pronoun paradigm*

At some very early stage in its development, Melanesian Pidgin English speakers apparently re-interpreted the English *fellow* as a plural marker on pronouns, but this had to compete with other means of signalling plurality, and the resulting system is now somewhat complex. Tok Pisin pronouns differ from the pronouns of the main lexifier language (English) in a number of respects, as seen in a typical paradigm shown in the following table.

Person Number	**Singular**	**Dual**	**Trial**	**Plural**
First	*mi*	(excl.) *mitupela*	*mitripela*	*mipela*
		(incl.) *yumitupela*	*yumitripela*	*yumi*
Second	*yu*	*yutupela*	*yutripela*	*yupela*
Third	*em*	*(em)tupela*	*emtripela*	*ol*

The paradigm is simpler than in English in some respects, for example in that case distinctions between subject and object, or gender distinctions between masculine, feminine and neuter are not normally made. (The variable use of *en* in place of *em* after *long* and *bilong* is the only exception; *en* is the usual unstressed form, while *em* is used for emphasis.) Thus three singular forms *mi*, *yu* and *em* are equivalent to the English forms *I, me, you* (singular), *he, she, it, her* and *him*. However, the system is more complex in other respects. There is a separate plural form of the second person pronoun, and dual and often trial numbers are distinguished in addition to plural. Moreover, first person plural (and sometimes dual and trial) pronouns have distinct inclusive and exclusive forms.

It seems that the trial form is becoming less and less common, and that the canonical third person dual form is now *tupela*, making it homophonous with the numeral two. Some reduced forms are also being used with increasing frequency; in rapid speech *mipela*, for example, may be reduce to *mipla*, *mila* or *mla*, while *mitupela* and *yutupela* are routinely reduced to *mitla* and *yutla*. Thus, as with the case of *disla* described above, *-pela* here may no longer be best thought of as a suffix at all in a synchronic analysis.

2.3.   The *-s* pluralising suffix

Nouns in Tok Pisin are usually pluralised where necessary by the use of the preceding word *ol*, homophonous with the third person plural pronoun. However, the unsystematic use of the English *-s* suffix has been in evidence for many years. A few lexical items include the unanalysed plural suffix from either English (*anis* 'ant' from English 'ants') or German (*binen* 'bee' from German *Bienen* 'bees') (Mühlhäusler 1981: 39). However, neither of these suffixes became involved in widely-used productive rules during stabilisation. Mühlhäusler (1985a: 276) notes a highly variable use of the suffix in urban Tok Pisin which he interprets as a reduction of the systematic adequacy of the language as it decreolises, agreeing with Lynch's (1979: 6) characterisation of the use of *-s* as an interference phenomenon. Romaine's (1992) study of children in the Madang and Morobe Provinces gives details of 195 lexical items to which *-s* is attached and tabulates occurrences in each of the locations investigated. She concludes that animacy does have some influence, with a larger proportion of humans than animates taking the suffix, and that count nouns take *-s* considerably more often than mass nouns (Romaine 1992: 234–235). Smith's (2002) study of first language speakers shows increasing use of obligatory marking of plurals with *-s* among some speakers, often with retention of the redundant *ol* marker as well. The use of both markers with more recent lexis such as *bois* 'boys' and *gels* 'girls' is particularly evident. A few examples of *-s* pluralisation on words of non-English origin may be heard, but they are very uncommon. The nouns most commonly taking the *-s* suffix were, in order, *boi* 'boy', *fren* 'friend', *perent* 'parent', *wik* 'week', *gel* 'girl' *stiudent* 'student' and *ticha* 'teacher' i.e. mostly recent additions to the lexis, and heard frequently in bilingual contexts. For nouns ending in sibilant consonants, the normal form would be *-is*, for example, *klesis* 'classes' or *pisis* 'pieces', occasionally voiced in anglicised varieties.

2.4.   Other word-formation processes

Although many of the derivational processes of English word formation were routinely ignored in the development of Tok Pisin, Mühlhäusler (1979) showed that the language has an extensive and sophisticated facility for producing new words through internal productive processes. These processes consist of compounding to produce new series of lexemes, multifunctionality, where a new item is derived by zero affixation from a different part of speech, and reduplication. Examples of each of the above processes are illustrated below.

2.4.1.   Compounding

A wide variety of different patterns for the formation of compound nouns can be described. Mühlhäusler (1979) listed 23 "programmes" or paradigms for producing compound expressions. For example, *wantok* from *wan* 'one' and *tok* 'talk' means 'person who speaks the same language, friend.' This provides the model for further examples such as *wanwok* 'workmate' and *wanskul* 'person in the same school.' Following a different pattern, an adjective-noun compound can be used to derive a word meaning someone who has that characteristic, for example, *bikbol* 'elephantiasis' (literally 'big testicles'). Similarly, a noun-adjective compound may indicate someone or something with certain properties, for example, *aipas*, 'blind' from *ai* 'eye' and *pas* 'fast, closed'.

21 paradigms for multifunctionality were also described by Mühlhäusler (1979), whereby new parts of speech are formed from existing lexical items, a highly productive process in the early stages of pidgin development. One example involves a noun becoming an intransitive verb meaning 'to perform the work of that noun', for example, *jas* 'judge' > *jas* 'to be a judge'. The way is thereby paved for further development of a transitive verb *jasim* 'to judge'.

2.4.2.   Reduplication

Reduplication is productive in 12 patterns identified by Mühlhäusler (1979), although in modern Tok Pisin this does not seem to be as prominent as in earlier stages. An example is the "distributive meaning" expressed by reduplication of numerals in (5):

(5)   *wanpela   wanpela   ailan   i   gat   nem   bilongen   yet*
       one   one   island PRED   have   name   POSS it   REFLEX
       'Each island has its own name'

The reduplicated form emphasises that each one has a separate identity (Mühl-häusler 1985d: 439).

Occasionally, complete or partial reduplication appears with plural nouns. Two examples from Smith (2002) are:

(6)   a. *diwai   ia   i   gat   ol   nil   nil*
          tree   FOCUS   PRED   have   PL   needle   needle
          'The tree has spines'

       b. *ol   bin   taitim   ol   **rorop**   nabaut   ia*
          they   PAST   tie   PL   rope(s)   about   EMPH
          'They tied the ropes and things'

Elsewhere, Mühlhäusler (1979) predicted that the grammatical marking of plu-rality would appear on other parts of the sentence than nouns, and this appeared to be borne out by an incipient system of verb reduplication in apparent agree-ment with plural subjects in one creolised variety in Manus (Mühlhäusler 1981: 57). However, this does not appear to have been adopted more generally.

2.4.3. Phrasal elements in verbs

Many established Tok Pisin words incorporate an element derived from an English adverb, most notably *up*, *down* and *out*, such as: *karamap* 'to cover (up)', *litimap* 'to lift (up)', *painaut* 'to find out', *singaut* 'shout, call (out)', *kamdaun* 'come down', etc.

The extent to which these elements can be regarded as distinct morphemes is debatable, and in most cases it seems that, whatever the ultimate derivation, the item is used as a single unanalysed lexeme, as in:

(7)   a. *em   harim   wanpla   dok   singaut*
          'He   heard   a   dog   barking'

       b. *wanpela   diwai   i pundaun   antap   lo   pikinini*
          'A   tree   fell   on top of   the   child'

It can be seen that some of these forms appear to have completely reanalysed such original suffixes as part of the root, as evidenced by the addition of further transitive suffixes, e.g. *karamapim* 'to cover (up)', *litimapim* 'to lift (up)'.

The words *aut* 'out', *daun* 'down' and *ap* 'up' do exist as independent items, and a good case can be made for a morphemic analysis of words such as *ka-maut* 'to come out' into component morphemes *kam* 'come' and *aut* 'out'. In-deed, it is not clear whether forms such as this and *godaun* 'go down' should be written as one word or two (Smith 2002). In the last example, there is no separate word **pun*, and *pundaun* could be regarded as a single morpheme or as a bimorphemic construction containing a bound form.

3. Syntax

The canonical word order is SVO. However, occasionally for the sake of focus or emphasis, elements other than the subject may be moved to initial position. A further discussion of this kind of variation in word order for emphasis appears in section 3.5. on focus and topicalisation.

3.1. The particle *i*

A very troublesome particle traditionally referred to as the "predicate marker" is one of the most common lexical items in Tok Pisin. Keesing's (1988) discussion of its origin also refers to a role as "resumptive pronoun" and "subject referencing pronoun". The particle does often appear before the predicate but is also frequently used before verbs in other contexts, such as the post-verbal aspect markers *stap*, *kam* and *go*, for example, *mi wokobaut i go* 'I walked away'. Traditionally (see for example Mihalic 1971), the *i* has been described as obligatory between third person subjects and predicates, but not used after first and second persons:

(8) a. *mi   kam,   yu   kam,   em   i   kam*
     'I   come,   you   come,   (s)he   pred   comes'

Recent studies, however, have shown that there is a great deal of variability, and suggestions have even been made that the marker may be in the process of dropping out of use altogether (Lynch 1979; Romaine 1993). However, geographical location is an important factor here. Smith (2002) has shown that the *i* in its traditional predicate marking role is still very common in the New Guinea Islands region, but may be omitted very frequently in the Highlands and North Coast regions of the mainland. Some extreme examples are presented below, the first from New Ireland in the New Guinea Islands region and the second from the Western Highlands. Positions where the marker could but does not occur are marked by [Ø]:

(9) a. *Madang i   bik, taun i   bikpla na planti olsem planti*
      Madang PRED big, town PRED big   and many like   many

      man   i   sae raun long   taun na i   gat
      person PRED habit go   around in town and PRED have

planti ol stua na ol ka i   wok   long ron long rot.
many PL store and PL car PRED CONT in   run on   road.

'Madang is big, the town is big and there are lots of people going around in the town and there are lots of stores and cars running on the road.'

b. *mipela [Ø] go l' aus   na   [Ø] stap nau mipela [Ø] ting osem*
we   go   to house and stay   now we   think   that

[Ø] *nogat wantla problem ba   [Ø] kamap osem na   mipela*
not   one   problem FUT   arise   so   that   we

femli   olgeta mipela [Ø] go [Ø] stap lo   aus
family   all   we   go   stay   in   house

'We went to the house and stayed there thinking that there were no problems so we stayed in the house.'

It is also evident that collocation is important in determining the retention of *i*. Most occurrences in areas where the predicate is seldom marked involve the use of *i* immediately before *no, gat, dai* or *bin*, as indicated from the following Highlands samples, where predicate marking is not the rule:

(10) a. *laki   na   wanpela kar   i   no   bin   kam*
lucky and one   car PRED NEG PAST come
'Luckily no cars came'

b. *sapos wanpela kar i   bin   kam   em [Ø] ken [Ø] krukutim*
if   one   car PRED PAST come it can   crush

mi
me

'If a car had come it could have crushed me'

c. *disa meri   i   gat   bel   ia   em [Ø] kam   daun*
this woman PRED have belly FOCUS she come   down
'The woman who was pregnant came down'

d. *mipla kukim ol   tasol ol   i   no   indai yet.*
we   burn them but   they PRED NEG die   yet
'We burned them (the sorcerers) but they hadn't died yet'

In the last example it is not clear whether the lexeme is *dai* or *i(n)dai*, as both forms are commonly encountered. The same is true of the particle *inap* meaning 'capable' and also used as a modal for ability or permission. Although the original form derived from English *enough* is usually rendered as *inap*, it appears that it is frequently reinterpreted as *i* and *nap*.

In Bislama, the plural form of the predicate marker *oli* is used. This does not generally occur in Tok Pisin, and in most areas of Papua New Guinea no examples are normally encountered. There are, however, some occurrences of *ol* followed by *i* in transcripts from the New Guinea Islands region which appear to be a repeated plural pronoun, but also suggest that a reinterpretation as a plural predicate marker could be valid. It is not clear, for example, whether the following extract of speech should be written with *oli* as a plural marker or a resumptive pronoun *ol* followed by *i*:

(11) *ol man blong Kevieng ol i/oli gutpla man*
      PL man POSS Kavieng they PRED/PL PRED good man
      'Kavieng people are good people'

3.2. The verb phrase

3.2.1. Tense, mood and aspect

In the absence of inflections to mark tense, mood and aspect (TMA), a number of particles may be placed before or after the verb.

Future is marked by the particle *bai*. This is typically placed before first and second person subjects and after third person singular: *mi bai kam* 'I will come', *em bai kam* 'he/she/it will come'; but *bai yu go* 'you will go', etc.

Historically, *bai* is derived from the adverbial *by and by* placed in clause-initial position, but Sankoff and Laberge (1973) described evidence that grammaticalisation has involved reduction to a single syllable and moving to pre-verbal position. The reduction of *bai* may lead to cliticisation, as noted by Lynch (1979) and Sankoff (1986), for example:

(12) *ol i bagarap olgeta b' ol i dai*
      they PRED spoiled all FUT they PRED die
      '(If) They are completely spoiled they will die' (Smith 2002)

This grammaticalisation path might have been expected to continue to a regular and stable future tense affix, but more recently Sankoff (1991) has re-examined the status of *bai* and shown that the situation is considerably more complex. Firstly, irrealis or conditional/hypothetical modal uses complicate the picture, and iterative-habitual and punctual aspects may also be involved. More surprisingly, she notes that the particle was sometimes associated not only with future time, but also with present and past time. Romaine (1992) also looked in detail at the role of *bai* in her examination of the Tok Pisin of young people in Morobe and Madang provinces, showing that the placement of preverbal *bai* is still very much more frequent after the third person singular pronoun than first or second. She also looks at some early written materials, and questions the sequence of grammaticalisation described by Sankoff and Laberge (1973), and raises the possibility that reduction of *baimbai* and movement to preverbal position may be independent processes. Also raised is the possibility of the reinterpretation of *baimbai* as a repeated particle separated by the third person singular pronoun: *bai em bai*.

My own corpus shows that the traditional description of *bai*'s position relative to pronouns is continuing with first language speakers. It tends to be used in preverbal position much more frequently after third person pronouns, and considerably less after first and second person persons. However, it also reveals that there is considerable variation, with the *em bai* pattern almost categorical among Highlands speakers, but much more variable in other regions. In the latter case, however, no semantic distinction was identified and it appears to be a case of free variation.

In common with other pidgin and creole languages, the unmarked form of the verb is often used to indicate past, especially for non-stative verbs. However, past tense may be unambiguously marked by a preverbal particle, *bin*, derived from the English 'been' as with many other Atlantic and Pacific creoles. Some reports have indicated that the use of *bin* is declining, but it appears that there is considerable regional variation, with much greater use in the New Guinea Islands region. It also tends to be used with considerable redundancy by many first language speakers. *Bin* is almost invariably placed immediately before the verb.

In addition to past and future time reference, a number of aspectual distinctions are made with other pre-and post-verbal particles. For example, the pre-verbal particle *laik*, often appearing in the reduced forms *lai* and *la*, has a dual role to indicate 'wanting to do something' or 'being about to do something'. In some cases it is difficult to distinguish between the two meanings, and both could equally apply. This suggests substrate influence in the re-interpretation of the semantics of the English *like*, although an internal grammaticalisation path is also quite possible. (13) is an example of an ambiguous interpretation:

(13) *em*   *i*   *laik*   *go* *long* *gaden*
      'He/she PRED likes/is about to go to the garden'

In other cases, such as *em i laik dai* 'he/she is about to die' the meaning is normally unambiguous. Otherwise the meaning would be disambiguated through context. The 'about to' meaning can also be made clear by using adverbials such as *klostu* or *klosap* 'nearly' in conjunction with *la(ik)*:

(14) biknait   nau,   klostu laik   tulait
      late night   now,   nearly ABOUT TO   dawn
      'It was late at night, just before dawn'

It appears that the reduced form is more closely associated with the aspectual function than the lexical meaning 'like', but analysis is difficult due to the fact that many examples could be interpreted in both senses. It appears that the distinction between *laik* + verb with the above meanings and *laik i* + verb as a definite future described in some accounts (e.g. Dutton 1973) is no longer widely used.

Completed action is marked post-verbally by the particle *pinis* derived from the English *finish*. It appears that in earlier forms of Melanesian Pidgin English, various forms such as *bin* and *pinis* competed for past time reference before the stabilisation of *bin* as a past tense marker and *pinis* as a completive aspect marker. Mühlhäusler (1985c: 388) notes that *bin* may still imply some idea of completion. The word *pinis* occurs as a lexical verb as well as an aspect marker. The intransitive form *pinis* and transitive *pinisim* both refer to finishing or terminating something, as in *mi pinisim skul* 'I finished school'. As an aspect marker, the post-verbal *pinis* is very commonly used, as in (15):

(15) mi   kukim   pinis
      I   cook-TRANS   COMPLETIVE
      'I have cooked it'

The fact that *pinis* indicates completion has led to a role for *pinis* in sequencing discourse, often in conjunction with the word *orait* (< English *all right*), as will be described in section 4.

Habitual action is marked by the particle *save*, very often reduced to *sa* by fluent speakers. The word *save*, generally accepted to be from the Portuguese *sabir* 'to know' is common in many pidgin and creole languages worldwide, and appears to have entered some of the earliest contact varieties. However, it is generally used as an unsuffixed transitive verb with its lexical meaning 'to know', which is also present in Tok Pisin:

(16) mi   no   save   long   tok ples   bilong   yu
      I   NEG   know   about   language   POSS   you
      'I don't know your language'

Habitual action may be marked with considerable redundancy by fluent speakers, as with this extract from a young man in Bougainville:

(17)   *mipla   sa   harim   ol   gan   i   pairap.   Nau   ol   militens*
      we   HABIT   hear   PL   gun   PRED   fire.   Now   PL   militant

      sa   kam   ol   sa   brukim   ol   sto   nambaut
      HABIT   come   they HABIT   break   PL   store   about

      'We heard the guns firing. The militants came and broke into the
      stores and things'

Again substrate influence is suspected in the initial reinterpretation of the semantics of *save* in its current dual role. Ambiguous utterances are still found, where a habitual interpretation or the meaning 'to know' would be equally valid:

(18)   *Mi   save   wokim   banara*
      'I   know   how to/habitually make   a bow'

The reduction of *save* to *sa* as a habitual aspect marker could effectively differentiate it from the *save* meaning 'to know', which is generally not reduced. Lynch's data showed exactly such a categorical distinction, and he found that both *sa* and *la* were reduced only in their aspectual role, and not in their regular verbal use (1979: 8). However, more recently, it appears that fluent first language speakers are also reducing the lexical form, although my corpus shows that the reduced form *sa* is used with overwhelmingly greater frequency in its aspectual role (Smith 2002: 85).

Continuous or durative aspect may be marked pre-verbally by the expression *wok long* or post-verbally by *(i) stap*. The latter contrasts with the pre-verbal use of *stap* in Bislama. The use of *wok long* may have connotations of being busy or actively engaged in an activity. Examples of use are *mi wok long raitim pas* 'I am (busy) writing a letter' and *ol i wokabaut i stap* 'they are walking'. Occasionally, both constructions may be used together, as in *ol i wok long stori stap* 'they were telling stories'. Use of *i go* and *i kam* after the verb can indicate directionality as in *ol i wokabaut i kam* 'they were walking (towards us)' and *ol i wokabaut i go* 'they were walking away'. However, *i go* may be used after verbs to indicate something continuing for a long time. Extreme lengths of time can be indicated by repeating a number of times: *bebi wok long krai i go i go i go* 'the baby kept on crying and crying'.

In Tok Pisin, the most common modals are *mas*, *ken* and *inap*, associated with obligation, permission and possibility. The particle *mas* from English *must* can imply not only personal obligation to do something, but also an assumption that something must be true, corresponding to a distinction which is sometimes made between deontic and epistemic modality. These are illustrated respectively by *mi mas wokim wanpela samting pastaim* 'I must do something (first)' and *em mas brata bilong mi i kam* 'it must be my brother (coming)'. There is rarely any ambiguity between the two meanings.

Both *ken* from English *can* and *inap* from English *enough* can also have a modal role, implying permission or capability. Generally, *ken* implies permission (*yu no ken kam insait* 'you can't come inside') while *inap* implies capability (*mi inap pinisim dispela kaikai* 'I can finish this food'). But occasionally *inap* is also used in the former role: *inap mi tokim yu wanpela samting?* 'can I tell you something?'.

One or two other particles, although not traditionally described in this role, appear to be undergoing grammaticalisation as aspect or modal particles. The verb *kirap*, for example (from English *get up*), is frequently used in some areas in a discourse regulating role (cf. section 4 below). The particle *bek* 'back' also appears to be undergoing grammaticalisation from an adverb to a post-verbal modal particle, indicating that something is happening again after a break, equivalent to the English *re*-prefix, for example *em i marit bek* 'she re-married'. In addition, some speakers borrow English modals such as *shud* 'should', but this is uncommon, and restricted to heavily anglicised speech.

3.2.2. *Verb serialisation*

There has been considerable interest in serial verb constructions in pidgin and creole languages, mainly focussing on Atlantic Creoles. Tok Pisin, in common with other varieties of Melanesian Pidgin, has a number of such constructions, and whatever the "naturalness" of such forms, there is also substantial substrate motivation in the languages of the area. A number of verbs such as *go*, *kam* and *stap* have already been discussed in relation to their directionality and aspectual role, but other verbs may appear serially to encode more specific meanings, as in:

(19) a. *em   kam   kamap   long   ples*
          he/she come arrive at   village
          '(S)he arrived at the village'

    b. *em   i   sindaun smail long em*
          (s)he PRED sit down smile at   him/her
          '(S)he sat down smiling at him'

    c. *em   i   brumim rausim ol   pipia*
          (s)he PRED brush   discard PL rubbish
          '(S)he swept away the rubbish'

However, although in Bislama a number of serial verb constructions involving the verbs *agensem, kasem, bitim, raonem* and *folem* have developed into prepositions (Crowley 1990), this does not appear to have occurred to any significant extent in Tok Pisin. Nonetheless, some serial constructions could be involved in ongoing grammaticalisation, as with the use of *kam* and *go* described above, and also possibly with *kirap* 'get up, initiate' and *stat* 'to begin', which appear to approach an aspectual role in the examples below:

(20) a. *nau   ol   stat   kuk   lo   kleipot*
         now   they   start cook   in   clay pot
         'They started cooking in the clay pot'
      b. *ol   kirap   pait   na   ol   pait.*
         they got up/started fight and   they fight
         'A fight started'

In the case of *kirap*, there is again ambiguity between the meanings 'get up' and 'initiate' which may have motivated a re-interpretation:

(21) *dewel ia   kirap   holim em   na   em karim go lo*
       spirit ANAPH   got up/start hold him and he carry go to

      aus   blo   em.
      house POSS   him

      'The spirit got up and held him/started to hold him, and took him to his house'

3.3.   The noun phrase

The noun phrase in Tok Pisin can consist of a pronoun or a noun, either bare or accompanied by pre- or post-modifiers, such as quantifiers, other pre-nominal modifiers and post-nominal modifiers.

Pronouns are generally invariable in form, the only exception being the alternative form *-en* of the third person singular *em*. This *-en* form is only found after *long* or *bilong*. It is normally written as an enclitic, although solid evidence that its phonological status is different from that of *em* is lacking.

(22) a. *Em i haus bilong em* or *Em i haus bilongen*
         'It is his/her house'
      b. *mi givim han long em* or *mi giving han longen*
         'I have him/her a (helping) hand'

The *-en* form is generally unstressed, whereas *em* may be used to focus attention on the pronoun.

Quantifiers include numerals and the terms *olgeta* 'all', *planti* 'many', *sampela* 'some' and *liklik* 'few, small'. Examples of other pre-nominal modifiers are *wanpela* 'one', *dispela* 'this', *narapela* 'another' and *ol* (plural). The category of post-nominal modifiers includes the demonstrative *ia*, possessive constructions with *bilong*, and restrictive relative clauses or adjectives.

Sankoff and Mazzie (1991) suggest that *wanpela* and *dispela* are prime candidates for grammaticalisation as indefinite and definite articles, but report that they were used only sporadically in this role. In my own data (Smith 2002) both *wanpela* 'one' and *sampela* 'some' did continue with a quantifying role as 'one in number' and 'some but not all' but are also frequently used in a way analogous to articles:

(23) a. *mipla wetim man bilong wanpla anti blong mi*
       we   wait man POSS one/art aunt POSS me
       'We were waiting for the husband of an auntie of mine'
    b. *yu   lukim sampla abus   o   nogat?*
       you see   some game animal or not?
       'Can you see any animals (to hunt)?'

Dispela 'this' appears to be further along the grammaticalisation route, and is undergoing considerable reduction and loss of stressed syllables, indicating possible future status as a definite marker. Typical renderings are *displa, disla* or *sla*, as in:

(24) *yu kisim sla buk*
      'Take this/the book'

Moreover, *dispela* or its reduced forms are often used in conjunction with *ol* for plural referents, as in:

(25) *ol   sla ol man meri i   stap   lo ples*
      PL DEM PL man woman PRED stay/be at village
      'These people were in the village'

This suggests the possible evolution of *sla* as a singular and *slol* as a plural definite article. So far, however, this is mere conjecture extrapolating from some existing tendencies.

3.3.1. Relativisation

There are a number of ways of signalling relative clauses in Tok Pisin. These include the absence of overt markers, often accompanied by distinctive intonation (Wurm 1971), pronominalisation with personal pronouns or the relative pronouns *wonem*, *husat* and *we*, and bracketing with *ia (ya)*. In addition, the clause-final use of *longen* is frequently involved in marking relatives in the Highlands region. Some examples of each are given below.

Relatives may lack overt marking if the meaning is clear from the context, for example in (26):

(26) ol   i   lukim dispela pasin   ankol blo   em
      they   PRED see   this   fashion/behaviour uncle POSS he

      wokim
      do/make

      'They saw this kind of thing their uncle was doing'

However, in my corpus, this is most frequently used when the word *dai* is involved, as in:

(27) tupla brata   mama   i   bin   dai   stap wantaim papa
      two   brother mother PRED PAST die   live with   father
      'The two brothers whose mother had died lived with their father'

It appears that in the early days of Tok Pisin this kind of structure was more common. However, with a demand for increasing sophistication of meaning, a number of other mechanisms developed.

The use of a personal pronoun to introduce a relative may help to make the meaning more clear. In (28), for example, the relative clause is introduced by the third person singular pronoun:

(28) em   i   gat   wanpla lapun meri   em   sa   stap
      he   PRED have one   old   woman she   HABIT stay/live

      long   hap
      at   place

      'There was an old woman who lived there'

Distinct relative pronouns *(h)usat* and *we* may also be used, but these are less typical of spoken styles and are used more in the written register, for example, in *Wantok Niuspepa* reports, especially those translated from English. However, it appears that the use of *husat* as a relative may be increasing, especially in varieties in contact with English.

(29) Em   i   painim   ol   pikinini usat ol   i   biket
      he   PRED look for PL   child   who   they PRED disobedient
      'He was looking for the children who were misbehaving'

The use of *we* is interesting in that it appears to have been generalised from the meaning 'where' to a more generic relative to refer first to human, then to non-human animate and then to inanimate referents as well. The examples in (30) illustrate this gradation:

(30)   a.   *em   wanpla   baret   we   wara   sa   ron*
            it   one   drain   which   water   HABIT   run
            'It was one drain where water flowed'

       b.   *mi   bin   lukim   wanpla   krokodail   we   em   i   traim   lo*
            I   PAST   see   one   crocodile   which   it   PRED   try   to

            atekim   mipla
            attack   us

            'I saw a crocodile which tried to attack us'

       c.   *em   papa   bl'   em   we   helpim   em*
            it   father   POSS   him   who   help   him
            'It was his father who helped him'

Sankoff drew attention to another means of relativisation arising out of discourse, bracketing by the deictic particle *ia*, derived from English *here*, which is also very common as a focal or anaphoric marker. In the following example, the relative clause is delimited by *ia*:

(31)   *stereo   ia   mitla   putim   lo   kout   ia,   em   no   lukim*
        stereo   REL   we   put   in   coat   REL   he   not   see
        'The stereo which we put in the coat he didn't see'

One sometimes gains the impression from reading secondary sources that this mechanism is neat, well-defined and regular, but in reality it is much more messy. One or other of the pair is frequently omitted, and it may be difficult to decide in some cases whether an element should be interpreted as a relative clause or whether it is merely a case of anaphoric or focal reference.

In parts of the Highlands region, especially the Western Highlands, *longen* is often involved in relative clause isolation. As noted above, *longen* is the unstressed form of *long em* 'to it':

(32)   *Mi lap longen*
        'I smiled at him'

Again this structure may have arisen out of reanalysis in discourse. A gradation of examples showing the ambiguity underlying reanalysis is shown in the following. In (33) *longen* clearly refers to a location, but appears to have a secondary clause delimiting role:

(33) | em | putim | tupla | lo | wanpla | ples | we | ol | sa | putim |
|---|---|---|---|---|---|---|---|---|---|
| he | put | two | at | one | place | where | they | HABIT | put |

man	longen
man	in it

      'He put two at one place where they kept people (prisoner)'

In other cases, however, reference to location is not so easy to demonstrate, and the clause delimiting function appears primary:

(34) | i | man | Wabag | ia | em | poisinim | em | longen | ia |
|---|---|---|---|---|---|---|---|---|
| PRED | man | Wabag | REL | he | poison | him | at it | REL |

wokobaut	kam	i	go
walk	come	PRED	go

      'It was the Wabag man who poisoned him approaching'

In (34), *ia*-bracketing as described above also contributes to the delimitation of the relative clause, although in some other examples, like (35), *ia* is not present:

(35) | em | smelim | pik | tupla | bin | kilim | longen | na | em | kam |
|---|---|---|---|---|---|---|---|---|---|
| he | smell | pig | two | PAST | kill | REL | and | he | come |

klostu
close

      'He smelled the pig which the two had killed and he approached'

3.4. Complementation

A number of words such as *long, olsem, na* and in some areas *se* are used to introduce complements in Tok Pisin. Mühlhäusler (1985b) also gives *bilong, baimbai, sapos* and *we* in creolised varieties. This list represents a variety of word types: prepositions, adverbs, conjunctions and serial verb constructions, which have presumably developed during syntactic reanalysis in discourse to adopt the role of complementiser.

The word *olsem¸* frequently reduced to *osem* and sometimes further to *sem* or *se*, is the most common of the above, in particular in conjunction with the verb *tok* to introduce direct or indirect quotations:

(36) | Em | bin | tok | olsem | "mi | les | lo | yu" |
|---|---|---|---|---|---|---|---|
| he | PAST | say | COMPL | "I | tired | of | you" |

      'He said "I'm tired of you"'

It may also be used with a variety of other verbs:

(37) | *Rabaul* | *i* | *luk* | *olsem* | *i* | *gutpla* | *ples* |
|---|---|---|---|---|---|---|
| Rabaul | PRED | look | COMPL | PRED | good | place |

'Rabaul looked like it was a good place'

As noted above, *olsem* is occasionally reduced to *se*, but *se* itself has for some time been another form which is frequently used in introducing complements, as in Bislama. However, this appears to be confined to parts of the New Guinea Islands, as in this extract recorded in East New Britain:

(38) | *meri* | *ia* | *i* | *ting* | *se* | *em* | *tewel* | *ia* | *na* |
|---|---|---|---|---|---|---|---|---|
| woman | ANAPH | PRED | think | COMPL | it | spirit | EMPH | and |

em	*i*	*pret*
she	PRED	afraid

'The woman thought that it was a spirit and she was afraid'

The use of *we* in relativisation has been noted above. Its use as a complementiser appears to be uncommon in my corpus, with only one or two tokens:

(39) | *em* | *tok* | *we* | *ol* | *no* | *givim* | *em* | *planti* | *mani* |
|---|---|---|---|---|---|---|---|---|
| he | say | COMPL | they | NEG | give | him | much | money |

'He said that they did not pay enough'

3.5. Focus and topicalisation

As mentioned previously, the canonical word order is SVO, but occasionally focussed or topicalised elements appear in initial position. Sometimes topicalisation is distinguished from focus in that the topic has a co-indexed pronoun whereas focus involves emphasis without this. A number of mechanisms for focus and topicalisation exist in Tok Pisin and were first described in detail by Sankoff (1993). An example of fronting an element for focus is (40):

(40) | *pipia* | *bilong* | *em* | *yumi* | *save* | *kaikai* |
|---|---|---|---|---|---|
| rubbish | POSS | him | we | HABIT | eat |

'His rubbish is what we eat'

Question words such as *we* 'where' and *wonem* 'which' may also be fronted for emphasis:

(41) *wonem skul yu givim em?*
'Which schooling did you give him?' (Sankoff 1993)

In addition, the third person singular pronoun *em* sometimes precedes noun phrases in constructions which appear to be similar to clefts in English, as in Sankoff's example in (42):

(42)　*nogat,*　*em*　*wantok*　*i*　　*putim*　*long*　*maunten*　*ia*
　　　 no,　　it　　friend　PRED　put　　on　　mountain　EMPH
　　　 'No, it was my friend who was wearing it on the mountainside'

In addition, there are a number of distinct focal particles in Tok Pisin. One of these is the word *yet*, which appears to have been derived from English *yet*, but has been heavily influenced by the Tolai *iat*. *Iat* has a meaning similar to 'yet' but also extra meanings, including a focus marking role. In addition to the meaning similar to English 'yet' (often in the negative), the Tok Pisin *yet* can act as a reflexive, usually in conjunction with a pronoun:

(43)　a. *em*　*bin*　　*askim*　*em*　　*yet*
　　　　 he　　PAST　ask　　him　　REFLEX
　　　　 'He asked himself'

　　　 b. *em*　*bin*　　*lukautim*　*em*　*olsem*　*pikinini*　*blong*　*em*　*yet*
　　　　 she　PAST　look after　him　like　　child　　POSS　her　REFLEX
　　　　 'She looked after him like her own child'

　　　 c. *em*　*ples*　*blo*　　*mipla*　*yet*
　　　　 it　village　POSS　us　　REFLEX
　　　　 'It's our own village'

　　　 d. *yu*　*yet*　　　　　　*yu*　*les*　*lo*　*mi*
　　　　 you　FOCUS/REFLEX　you　tired　of　me
　　　　 'It's you that's tired of me'

Yet may also be used as an intensifier of adverbs or adjectives, mainly in collocation with the words *bipo* 'before' and *mo* 'more'. Typical traditional stories, for example, begin something like:

(44)　*long*　*taim*　*bifo*　*yet*　　*i*　　*gat*　*wanpla*　*yangpla*　*meri*
　　　 at　　time　before　EMPH　PRED　exist　one　　young　　girl
　　　 'Long, long ago, there was a young girl'

4.　Discourse processes

Discourse processes appear to have been involved in the grammaticalisation of some items described above. In the present section a brief look will be taken at some discourse features of Tok Pisin. Few detailed accounts of discourse features have appeared, the most detailed apparently being Lomax (1983). Lomax follows Halliday and Hassan's (1976) model and notes some ways in which cohesion is maintained, besides looking at deixis and lexical cohesion as exemplified by letters to the editor and traditional stories to *Wantok Niuspepa*.

Smith (2002) looks at some of these processes, and notes that conjunctions such as *bikos* and *bat* have been borrowed from English to provide alternatives to the more usual *long wanem* 'because' and *tasol* 'but'.

The particle *ia* (also sometimes spelled *ya* and *hia*) has already been discussed in relation to relative clause delimitation. Its other main use is as an anaphoric marker to signify that something has already been referred to:

(45)   *em   i   lukim   wanpla   lapun   man... lapun   man   ia*
       He   PRED   see   one   old   man... old   man   ANAPH

       kirap   na   tok ...
       get up   and   say

       'he saw an old man... the old man got up and said...'

In (45), the role of *kirap* 'get up, initiate' in discourse is also worth mentioning. The meaning of *em i kirap na tok olsem* is literally 'he got up and said' that which is in fact a form which sometimes appears in Papua New Guinea English, but the effect is to indicate the initiation of a new speaker's conversational turn.

The particle *pinis* has also been mentioned above (section 3.2.1.) as a completive aspect marker. Another common use is in conjunction with the term *orait* 'all right' to signal a new stage in a narrative:

(46)   *mi   kukim   rais. Kukim   pinis,   orait   mi   lusim   haus.*
       I   cook   rice. Cook   COMPLET, then I   leave   house.
       'I cooked the rice. Having cooked it, I left the house.'

Another interesting example of apparent grammaticalisation concerns the case of *yes* 'yes' and *nogat* 'no' which appear to have been reinterpreted in a discourse role. Lomax (1983: 41) notes that *yes* is a common rhetorical feature of *Wantok* letters, and appears to be best translated as 'well then' or a similar phrase:

(47)   *Mi gat bikpela kros long ol plisman. **Yes**, ol plisman ...*
       'I am very angry with the police. **Well then**, you policemen...'

In Smith (2002), a number of puzzling cases of *nogat* 'no' were examined, and it appears among some speakers in the North Coastal region of the New Guinea mainland to be best interpreted as a conjunction meaning something like 'when all of a sudden', indicating the unexpected onset of an event:

(48) a. *mipla   plei   go   ia   nogat   ol   ringim   bel*
         we   play   go   EMPH   no   they   ring   bell
         'We were playing when all of a sudden the bell rang'

      b. *Mipla   sidaun   na   stori   stap   ia   nogat   diwai*
         we   sit down   and   story   CONTIN   EMPH   no   branch

      kam.
      come

      'We were sitting telling stories when (without warning) the branch
      broke off.'

Exercises and study questions

1. Try to get the English meaning of the following. Remember that *-im* is a
   verb suffix indicating transitivity, *bin* is a past tense marker, *bai* is a future
   marker, *pinis* is a completive marker, *long* is a general preposition, *bilong* is
   possessive and *-pela* is and adjectival marker.

   a) Wanpela man i bin lukim haus
   b) Haus bilong mi i stap antap long maunten
   c) Mama bilong tupela brata i singaut long mi
   d) Meri bilong kasen bilong mi i kukim rais pinis
   e) Husat i sanap long kona?
   f) Em bai go lukim gaden bilong em

2. The following words have meanings that you could guess from English: *tambu* –
   'taboo'; *nogut* – 'no good'; *orait* – 'all right'; *gras* – 'grass'; *dai* – 'die'; *inap* –
   'enough'. However, they all have extra meanings, usually related to the semantics of other languages of the region. Can you guess the other meanings of
   these words in the following?

   a) Mi sindaun kaikai wantaim tambu bilong mi
   b) Em i paitim mi nogut tru
   c) Painim pinis, orait putim long haus
   d) Mama i katim gras bilong pikinini
   e) Kilok i dai, nau em wanem taim?
   f) Dispela meri i no inap long yu

3. Many verbs have a form with the suffix -*im* to indicate transitivity and one without for intransitive actions. Try to choose an appropriate form in the following sentences and work out the meaning:
a) Ol i wok long _____ insait long ba (dring/dringim)
b) Tupela meri i _____ long rot (pait/paitim)
c) Mama i _____ pikinini bilong em (pait/paitim)
d) Meri bilong mi i _____ bikpela gaden (wok/wokim)
e) Man ia i _____ han bilongen (bruk/brukim)
f) Ol meri i _____ klostu long wara (sanap/sanapim)

4. Using the markers *bin* and *bai*, change past to future or future to past in the following and try to work out the meaning:
a) Ol i bin sindaun bilong harim tok
b) Wanpela man bai bihainim dispela rot
c) Ol pikinini i bin lainim planti samting long skul
d) Husat bai kisim dispela moni?
e) Meri bilongen i bin karim pikinini man
f) Wanpela pik bai brukim bainis bilong gaden (*banis* = 'fence')

Selected references

Please consult the General references for titles mentioned in the text but not included in the references below. For a full bibliography see the accompanying CD-ROM.

Baker, Philip
    1987   Historical developments in Chinese Pidgin English and the nature of the relationship between various Pidgin Englishes of the Pacific region. *Journal of Pidgin and Creole Languages* 2: 163–207.
Crowley, Terry
    1990   *From Beach-la-mar to Bislama: The emergence of a national language in Vanuatu*. (Oxford Studies in Language Contact.) Oxford: Clarendon Press.
Dutton, Thomas Edward
    1973   *Conversational New Guinea Pidgin*. (Pacific Linguistics, D12.) Canberra: Australian National University.
Halliday, Michael A.K. and Ruqaiya Hasan
    1976   *Cohesion in English*. London: Longman.
Lomax, R. W.
    1983   Aspects of cohesion and discourse structure in Tok Pisin (Melanesian Pidgin). M.A. thesis, University of Leeds.

Lynch, John
   1979   Changes in Tok Pisin morphology. Paper presented at 13th PNG Linguistic Society Congress, Port Moresby.

Mihalic, Frank
   1971   *The Jacaranda Dictionary and Grammar of Melanesian Pidgin.* Milton/ Queensland: Jacaranda.

Mühlhäusler, Peter
   1979   *Growth and Structure of the Lexicon of New Guinea Pidgin.* (Pacific Linguistics, C52.) Canberra: Australian National University.
   1981   The development of the category of number in Tok Pisin. In: Pieter Muysken (ed.), *Generative Studies on Creole Languages*, 35–84. Dordrecht: Foris.
   1985a   Good and bad pidgin: nogut yu toktok kranki. In: Wurm and Mühlhäusler (eds.), 275–291.
   1985b   Internal development of Tok Pisin. In: Wurm and Mühlhäusler (eds.), 75–166.
   1985c   Syntax of Tok Pisin. In: Wurm and Mühlhäusler (eds.), 341–421.
   1985d   The lexical system of Tok Pisin. Wurm and Mühlhäusler (eds.), 423–440.

Romaine, Suzanne
   1992   *Language, Education and Development: Urban and Rural Tok Pisin in Papua New Guinea.* Oxford: Oxford University Press.
   1993   The decline of predicate marking in Tok Pisin. In: Francis Byrne and John Holm (eds.), *Atlantic meets Pacific: A global view of pidginization and creolization*, 251–260. Amsterdam/Philadelphia: Benjamins.

Sankoff, Gillian
   1991   Using the future to explain the past. In: Francis Byrne and Thom Huebner (eds.), *Development and Structure of Creole Languages: Essays in Honor of Derek Bickerton*, 61–74. Amsterdam/Philadelphia: Benjamins.
   1993   Focus in Tok Pisin. In: Francis Byrne and Donald Winford (eds.), *Focus and Grammatical Relations in Creole Languages*, 117–140. Amsterdam/ Philadelphia: Benjamins.

Sankoff, Gillian and Suzanne Laberge
   1973   On the acquisition of native speakers by a language. *Kivung* 6: 32–47.

Sankoff, Gillian and Claudia Mazzie
   1991   Determining noun phrases in Tok Pisin. *Journal of Pidgin and Creole Linguistics* 6: 1–24.

Sankoff, Gillian (ed.)
   1986   *The Social Life of Language.* Pittsburgh: University of Pennsylvania Press.

Smith, Geoff P.
   1994   Husat i bin othoraizim? New verbs in Manus Tok Pisin. Paper presented to Seventh International Conference of the Society for Pidgin and Creole Linguistics, Georgetown, Guyana, August 1994.
   2002   *Growing up with Tok Pisin: Contact, Creolization and Change in Papua New Guinea's National Language.* London: Battlebridge.

Wurm, Stephen A.
1971   *New Guinea Highlands Pidgin: Course materials.* (Pacific Linguistics, D3.) Canberra: Australian National University.
Wurm, Stephen A. and Peter Mühlhäusler (eds.)
1985   *Handbook of Tok Pisin (New Guinea Pidgin).* (Pacific Linguistics, C70.) Canberra: Australian National University.

Hawai'i Creole: morphology and syntax

Kent Sakoda and Jeff Siegel

1. Overview

Hawai'i Creole is a creole language lexified predominantly by English but also by other languages such as Hawaiian and Japanese. It is spoken by approximately 600,000 people in the American state of Hawai'i. For details on its lexicon and origins (including an account of the influence of other languages on its morphosyntax), see section 1 of the chapter on the phonology of Hawai'i Creole (Sakoda and Siegel, this volume).

Although the lexicon of Hawai'i Creole is closely related to English, its morphology and syntax are quite distinct. In general, like other creole languages, the amount of bound morphology is less than that of the lexifier language and there are quite different morphosyntactic rules for expressing tense, aspect, modality and negation, as well as for relativization, complementation and focusing.

The situation is complicated by the fact that the majority of speakers of Hawai'i Creole also know English, and there is a continuum from "heavy" varieties furthest from Standard English (the basilect) to "light" varieties closest to Standard English (the acrolect), with a great deal of variation in between (the mesolects). The description here is based primarily on the basilect, but some of the mesolectal variants are also indicated.

In this description, particular Hawai'i Creole words and grammatical morphemes are given in the text in the phonemic Odo orthography, followed in parentheses by other, mainly etymological, spellings that may be found more commonly in written versions of the language. Longer examples are also given, from both spoken and written Hawai'i Creole. The spoken examples come from recordings or from our own experience, and are given in the Odo orthography. The written examples are taken from a few works of published literature and from the Pidgin translation of the Bible (*Da Jesus Book*). These examples are given in their original orthography (i.e., as they appear in print), followed by the source (author, year and page number for literature, page number and biblical reference for examples from *Da Jesus Book*).

2.   The verb phrase

Like other creole languages, Hawai'i Creole has little bound inflectional morphology in the verb phrase. There are no agreement markers to index the number, person or gender of the subject or object. With only one exception (the -*ing*
suffix which is used to indicate the progressive), there are no affixes to indicate distinctions in tense, aspect or modality. Rather, again like other creoles,
Hawai'i Creole uses preverbal independent morphemes for this purpose.

2.1.   Tense markers

There are three different tense markers in Hawai'i Creole: for future, past, and
past habitual. Each one occurs at the beginning of the verb phrase.

Future tense is usually marked by *gon* (*goin, going*):

(1)   a. *Ai **gon** bai wan pikap.*
           'I'm going to buy a pickup.'
       b. *She **goin** miss da prom.*
           'She'll miss the prom.' (Kearns 2000: 13)

Past tense is most often indicated by *wen* (*wen', went*) before the verb:

(2)   a. *Ai **wen** si om.*
           'I saw him.'
       b. *Dey **wen** cut down da mango tree...*
           'They cut down the mango tree...' (Tonouchi 1998: 245)

The marker *wen* is sometimes reduced to *en* or just *n* as in the following example:

(3)   *Make me feel like da bugga in da play we'**n** read lass year.*
           'He makes me feel like the guy in the play we read last year.' (Kearns
           2000: 5)

Two other preverbal morphemes are also used by some speakers to mark past
tense: *bin*, especially by speakers of heavy varieties and older speakers, and
haed (*had*), especially by speakers from the island of Kaua'i:

(4)   a. *Ai **bin** klin ap mai pleis fo da halade.*
           'I cleaned up my place for the holidays.'
       b. *De **haed** ple BYU laes wik.*
           'They played BYU last week.'

A few irregular past tense verb forms from English are also frequently used. The most common is *sed* (*said*). It is rare to hear *wen sei*. Others are *sin* (*seen*) or *saw*, *keim* (*came*), and *tol* (*told*). These occur in variation with *wen si*, *wen kam* and *wen tel*. When these forms are used, they do not normally co-occur with the preverbal tense marker. Some examples are given in (5):

(5)   a. *Shi **sed** shi wen smok om.*
           (*She **said** she wen smoke em.*)
           'She said she smoked it.'
       b. *Shi **sin** wan sigaret.*
           (*She **seen** one cigarette.*)
           'She saw a cigarette.'
       c. *Hi **tol** om, No.*
           (*He **tol** em, No.*)
           'He told him, No.'

The past habitual is indicated by *yustu* (*used to*):

(6)   a. *Ai **yustu** ple futbawl.*
           'I used to play football.'
       b. *Your mahda **use to** tink so.*
           'Your mother used to think so.' (Kearns 2000: 10)

In what follows, an outline will be given of the major differences in tense marking between Hawai'i Creole and English: in Hawai'i Creole, the future tense marker *gon* (*goin, going*) can be used to mark not only actions and events that have not occurred yet, but also future actions being talked about in the past that may have occurred already, as in (7):

(7)   a. *When I went Farrington, brah, you no can talk Pidgin, you **going** run home every day from school.*
           'When I went to Farrington [High School], brother, if you couldn't speak in Pidgin, you would [have to] run home from school everyday.' (Kearns 2000: 32)
       b. *Da gai sed hi **gon** fiks mi ap wit wan blain deit.*
           'The guy said he'd fix me up with a blind date.'

Some Hawai'i Creole speakers, however, use *waz* (*was*) to mark such past-future constructions:

(8)   *He said dat she **was going** help all us guys go heaven.* (Lum 1998b: 225)

Hawai'i Creole also differs from English in the use of past tense marking in that tense neutralization often occurs. Once the past time frame is established with an adverb or a verb marked for past tense, it is not necessary to mark the subsequent verbs:

(9)   *He **went wink** at me and tell, "Choo, choo, choo" and laugh*
       backwards, you know like he sucking air in, "Hurh, hurh, hurh".
       'He **winked** at me and **said**, "Choo, choo, choo" and **laughed**
       backwards, you know like he **was sucking** air in, "Hurh, hurh, hurh".'
       (Lum 1999: 26)

Furthermore, *wen* in Hawai'i Creole is often used only to indicate relative past, i.e. something that had occurred previously in relation to the actual time being discussed. So if an event happened before another event (that is, even further in the past) then the past tense marker is used. The following sentence, for example, comes from a narrative of past events:

(10)   *Da Man/Lady stay piss off dat I **went change** da channel.*
       'The man/lady was pissed off that I had changed the channel.' (Lum
       1999: 27)

On the other hand, perhaps because of the influence of English, some Hawai'i Creole speakers, and especially writers, use the past tense marker *wen* more frequently:

(11)   *Dat time nobody **wen** bodda da peopo dat **wen** come togedda to*
       *church all ova Judea, Galilee an Samaria. Dey **wen** trus God mo an*
       *mo, an God's Spesho Spirit **wen** kokua dem.*
       'At that time nobody bothered the people that came together for
       church all over Judea, Galilee, and Samaria. They trusted God more
       and more, and God's Special Spirit helped them.' (*Da Jesus Book,
       Jesus Guys* 9: 33)

2.2.   Modals

The modals in Hawai'i Creole are separate words which occur before the verb to indicate ability, permission, possibility, volition or obligation.

kaen (*can*) indicates ability, permission or possibility:

(12)   a. *Jo **kaen** ple.*
          'Joe can play.'

   b. *You tink you* **can** *lift dis?*
      'Do you think you can lift this?' (Lum 1999: 23)

laik (*like*) indicates volition:

(13)   a. *Ai* **laik** *go Vegas.*
         'I want to go to Las Vegas.'
       b. *You* **like** *come?*
         'Do you want to come?' (Ching 1998: 182)

Note that *laik* (*like*) can also act as a verb meaning 'like' or 'want', especially before a noun phase, as in: *Mama rili laik daet wan* 'Mama really likes that one', or before the *-ing* form of a verb, as in *Ai laik going Las Vegas* 'I like going to Las Vegas'. The other modals indicate various degrees of obligation:

gata (*gotta*) and *haeftu* (*have t*o) imply some outside pressure to do something now or in the future:

(14)   a. *Ai* **gata** *bring om maiself.*
         'I've got to bring it myself.'
       b. *Okay, but I* **gotta** *eat early.*
         'Okay, but I have to eat early.' (Tonouchi 1998: 245)

(15)   a. *Jo* **haeftu** *wrk frs bifo hi kaen ple.*
         'Joe has to work first before he can play.'
       b. All da time you **have to** try your best.
         'You always have to try your best.' (Lum 1998b: 227)

beta (*bettah, better*) indicates that it would be good to do something or else something bad might happen:

(16)   a. *You* **bettah** *quit that, or we going broke yo' head!*
         'You'd better quit that or we'll break your head!' (Pak 1998a: 117)
       b. *So, you* **betta** *do um!*
         'So, you'd better do it!' (*Da Jesus Book*, 14 [Matthew 5:33])

sapostu (*suppose to*) can imply a past obligation as well as a present or future one:

(17)   a. *Bil* **sapostu** *finish hiz homwrk yestade bat hi neva finish.*
         'Bill was supposed to finish his homework yesterday, but he didn't finish it.'
       b. *You* **suppose to** *call da teachas at UH "doctah"...*
         'You're supposed to call the teachers at UH "doctor"...' (Kearns 2000: 27)

Some tense markers can occur before the modals *kaen* (*can*), *laik* (*like*), *haeftu* (*have to*), and *sapostu* (*suppose to*); however, some of these combinations are quite infrequent:

(18) a. *Hi **bin kaen** go?*
'Was it possible for him to go?'
b. *Herod **wen like** kill him.*
'Herod wanted to kill him.' (*Da Jesus Book*, 43 [Matthew 14:5])
c. *De **gon kaen** kam o wat?*
'Will they be able to come or what?'
d. *Yu **gon haeftu** pau da wrk.*
'You're going to have to finish the work.'
e. *Shi **wen sapostu** klin da haus.*
'She was supposed to clean the house.'

In some varieties, *waz* (*was*) is used to show past tense before the modal *sapostu* (*suppose to*) as well as before the future marker *gon* (*goin*, *going*) as previously mentioned:

(19) *Last weekend I **was suppose to** go wit Vernalani folks to da Pure Heart concert.* (Kearns 2000: 29)

2.3. *Chrai (try)*

The verb *chrai* (*try*) 'try' can occur after the tense marker and/or modal and before the main verb:

(20) a. *I went **try** draw one horn of plenty.*
'I tried to draw a horn of plenty.' (Lum 1998a: 71)
b. *I like **try** explain someting to you.*
'I want to try and explain something to you.' (Kearns 2000: 13)

In imperative sentences, *chrai* (*try*) functions as a mitigator:

(21) a. ***Chrai** paes da rais.*
'Could you pass the rice.'
b. *Faye, **try** wait!*
'Faye, wait a minute!' (Kearns 2000: 28)
c. *Terry, **try** look what I found!*
'Terry, have a look at what I found!' (Pak 1998a: 101)

2.4.   Aspect markers

Hawai'i Creole has three aspect markers which occur before the main verb to mark the following: progressive, perfective, inchoative, and completive. They are *ste* (*stei, stay*), *stat* (*start*), and *pau* 'finish'. Each of these markers can also occur on its own as a main verb. As aspect markers, they occur mainly before verbs which are active in Hawai'i Creole, but can also occur before some verbs which are stative, such as *kam* (*come*) 'become' (see section 2.6.).

Progressive: The most common aspect marker is *ste* (*stei, stay*), which is used to indicate progressive (or continuous) aspect. It can occur before either the plain form of the verb, or more commonly, before the verb with the progressive suffix, -*ing*:

(22)   a.   *Wi **ste** meik da plaen.*
             'We're making the plan.'
        b.   *...my grandpa **stay** listening to his Japanese radio station.*
             '...my grandpa is listening to his Japanese radio station.' (Tonouchi 1998: 245)
        c.   *I **stay** drowning my sorrows in Faye and Shakespeare.*
             'I was drowning my sorrows in Faye and Shakespeare.' (Kearns 2000: 26)

For some speakers, *ste* + *V-ing* implies an action that is in progress just at the moment, while *ste* + *V* implies a more durative or habitual action.

Nowadays in Hawai'i Creole, the aspect marker *ste* is frequently left out, and progressive aspect may be indicated with only the -*ing* form of the verb:

(23)   a.   *He helping me.*
             'He's helping me.' (Ching 1998: 187)
        b.   *She talking to herself.*
             'She's talking to herself.' (Lum 1998b: 230)
        c.   *I t'ink Chunky playing one big joke on us.*
             'I think Chunky is playing a big joke on us.' (Pak 1998a: 116)

Perfective: The marker *ste* (*stei, stay*) can also be used for perfective aspect, indicating that a condition resulting from the action of the verb, or a particular state, has been accomplished. In this case, only the plain form of the verb can be used (i.e. without the -*ing* suffix):

(24)   a.   *Ai **ste** kuk da stu awredi.*
             'I already cooked the stew.'
        b.   *Evribadi **ste** finish.*
             'Everyone is finished.'

    c. *When I **stay** come one old man…*
       'When I've become an old man…' (Kearns 2000: 26)

Inchoative: The preverbal marker *stat* (*start*) indicates that the action of the main verb is beginning. It normally co-occurs with the *-ing* suffix on the main verb:

(25)   a. *Mai sista gon **stat** pleing saka.*
       'My sister is going to start playing soccer.'
     b. *And I wen' **start** eating the Raisinets all one time.*
       'And I started eating the Raisinets all at once.' (Yamanaka 1998a: 153)

Completive: The marker *pau* is used for completive aspect. It can also be used as a main verb meaning 'finish' or an adjective meaning 'finished'. As an aspect marker, *pau* occurs before the plain form of the main verb (i.e. without the *-ing* suffix):

(26)   a. *You supposed to burn da Daruma dolls aftah you **pau** get your wish…*
       'You're supposed to burn the Daruma dolls after you've got your wish.' (Lum 1998b: 224)
     b. *Jesus **pau** use all dis kine story to teach.* (*Da Jesus Book*, 43 [Matthew 13:53])
       'Jesus finished using this kind of story to teach with.'

As for the co-occurrence of aspect markers with tense markers and modals: the tense markers can occur with the aspect markers *stat* (*start*) (see examples [25a] and [25b] above) and *ste* (*stei*, *stay*):

(27)   a. *De **gon ste** ple da geim tumaro.*
       'They'll be playing the game tomorrow.'
     b. *Hi **wen ste** it.*
       'He was eating.'

As can be seen in (27b), the *wen* + *ste* construction is used in basilectal Hawai'i Creole to indicate past progressive. In this construction, the *V-ing* form is not permitted. But in mesolectal and acrolectal varieties, the past progressive is marked with *waz* (*was*) rather than *wen* + *ste*, and this co-occurs only with the *-ing* form of the verb:

(28)   a. *De bot **waz** duing daet.*
       'They both were doing that.'

b. *What you **was** tinking?*
'What were you thinking?' (Kearns 2000: 21)

Some of the modals can also occur before *ste* (*stei, stay*), but most often with the perfective meaning:

(29)   a. *Yu **sapostu** ste mek da rais awredi.*
'You were supposed to have finished cooking the rice.'
b. *Yu **kaen** ste mek evriting bifo ai kam?*
'Can you finish doing everything before I come?'

2.5.   Serial verbs

Two verbs, *go* and *kam* (*come*), can occur in a serial construction just before the main verb or before the auxiliary or before *chrai* (*try*). These serial verbs have several functions. Most often, they indicate movement in space corresponding to the meanings of *go* and *kam* (*come*), as in the examples in (30):

(30)   a. *We can **go** find dah treasure and take 'em.*
'We can go find the treasure and take it.' (Pak 1998a: 103)
b. *Mo bettah he **come** play handball wit us.*
'It'd be better if he came to play handball with us.' (Lum 1999: 19–20)
c. *So da worka guys wen **go** check out all da roads.*
'So the workers went to check out all the roads.' (*Da Jesus Book*, 66 [Matthew 22: 10])
d. *I going **come** sit on you.*
'I'm gonna come sit on you.' (Lum 1998b: 229)

A serial verb can be preceded by a tense marker, such as *wen* or *gon* (*goin, going*), as illustrated in (30c) and (30d) above. It can also be preceded by some modals:

(31)   a. *I **gotta** go rake.* (Lum 1998b: 71)
b. *We **can** go find dah treasure.* (Pak 1998a: 103)
c. *You **like** go see one movie wit your dad?*
'Do you want to go see a movie with your dad?' (Kearns 2000: 8)

Another related function of the serial verb *go* (but not *kam*) is that it can emphasize the intention involved in the action of the main verb (as with English *to go and do something*), implying that the person involved goes out of their way to do it:

(32)   a. *Wai yu **go** du daet?*
          'Why did you go and do that?'
      b. *Shi **go** kuk rais evri de.*
          'She goes and cooks rice every day.'
      c. *So she wen **go** hug him like that.*
          'So she went and hugged him like that.' (Labov 1990: 28)

The verb *go* before the main verb can also indicate movement in time, more exactly away from the present. So, like the tense marker *gon* (*goin, going*), it can mark a future action or event, as in (33):

(33)   *Ai **go** kam tumaro.*
      'I'll come tomorrow.'

It is in this sense of movement away, plus intention, that *go* is used in some commands to indicate an action to be done elsewhere or later:

(34)   a. ***Go** color one eye fo me.*
          'Color one eye for me.' (Lum 1998b: 229)
      b. *Try **go** read da Memoirs of the Hawaiian Revolution.*
          'You should read the Memoirs of the Hawaiian Revolution.'
          (Kearns 2000: 30)

But with *go*, as opposed to tense marker *gon* (*goin, going*), the action or event is usually one that has not been previously planned, is not immediate, and may be more hypothetical than definite; in fact, the action might be intended but never take place.

(35)   a. *Mobeta wi **go** tel hr.*
          'It would be better if we tell her.'
      b. *I wen ask Fahdah Eugene fo **go** pray fo you every day.*
          'I asked Father Eugene to pray for you every day.' (Kearns 2000: 34)
      c. *Maybe das why he got all salty. Nobody pay attention to him.*
          *Nobody talk story with him. Nobody **go** bother him.*
          'Maybe that's why he got angry. Nobody paid attention to him.
          Nobody chatted with him. Nobody would bother him.' (Pak 1998b: 321)
      d. *How you tink one guy goin **go** bus inside one big moke house...?*
          'How will a guy go and break into a strong man's house...?' (*Da Jesus Book*, 36 [Matthew 12: 29])

When *go* is used in these ways (except in the imperative), it can be preceded by the tense markers *wen*, as in example (32c), and *gon* (*goin, going*), as in (35d). Serial verbs can occur either before or after aspect markers. In the following examples, *go* occurs after *ste* (*stei*, *stay*). The sense of movement indicated by *go* and the meaning of the main verb combine to express the progressive:

(36)   a.   ***Shi ste go** bai wan baeg rais.*
              'She's going to buy a bag of rice.'
        b.   ***Ai ste go** si da gai.*
              'I keep going to see the guy.'

In imperatives, *go* may be placed before the auxiliary *ste* indicating a progressive or continuous action to be carried out elsewhere or later:

(37)   a.   ***Go ste** mek da pupus.*
              'Go be making the snacks.'
        b.   ***Go ste** du om.*
              'Go be doing it.'

Go can also occur before the auxiliary when it has the function of indicating an unplanned future or hypothetical action, as in the second part of this famous example:

(38)   *Yu **go ste** go; ai **go ste** kam.*
        (*You **go stay** go; I **go stay** come.*)
        'You go ahead [i.e. keep going]; I'll be coming.'

The serial verb *go* can also be used before or after *chrai* (*try*):

(39)   a.   *Ai **go chrai** du om fo yu.*
              'I'll try to do it for you.'
        b.   *Ai laik **chrai go kam** mek kukiz wit yu.*
              (*I like **try go come** make cookies with you.*)
              'I want to try and come to make cookies with you.'

Note that, as shown in (39b), there may be two serial verbs used in one verb phrase. Here *go* indicates an unplanned future action, and *kam* indicates motion toward the listener.

2.6.   Stative versus active verbs

Hawai'i Creole grammar distinguishes between stative and active verbs. Stative verbs include *kam* (*come*) 'become', *bi* (*be*), *ste* (*stei*, *stay*) 'copula', *luk* (*look*), *fil* (*feel*), *no* (*know*) and *haev* (*have*). The serial verbs *go* or *come* occur only before active verbs. Predicate adjectives occur only after stative verbs, as in (40):

(40) a. *And den everyting come **quiet**.*
      'And then everything became quiet.' (Lum 1999: 19)
    b. *...I goin be **awesome**.*
      '...I'm going to be awesome.' (*Da Jesus Book*, 75 [Matthew 24:30])
    c. *Make their stomach look **mo skinny**.*
      'They make their stomach look skinnier.' (Lum 1999: 19)
    d. *Dey wen feel **real good** inside.*
      'They felt really good inside.' (*Da Jesus Book*, 3 [Matthew 2:10])

2.7. Summary

In summary, the VP in sentences with the structure S → NP VP can be of two types, depending on the main verb aktionsart:

stative main verb:

VP →   (tense) (modal) (chrai) (aspect) V (stative) (AdjP) (PP)
                                                          (NP)

active main verb: (sv indicates the possible position for a serial verb):

VP → (tense) (modal) (sv) (chrai) (sv) (aspect) (sv) V (active) (NP) (PP)

These two types of VP are illustrated in the following diagram. (Note that not all combinations are possible.)

(wen) (gon) (yus-tu)	(kaen) (laik) (haeftu) (sapo-stu)	(go) (kam)	(chrai)	(go) (kam)	(ste) (stat) (pau)	(go) (kam)	stative main verb or	(AdjP)	(PP)
	(gata) (beta)						active main verb	(NP)	

The mesolectal past tense marker *waz* (*was*) is not shown in this diagram. It can also occur in the following environments: before the tense marker *gon*, before the modal *sapostu* or before the *-ing* form of an active main verb (but then without any other tense-mood-aspect markers).

2.8.   The verb phrase in subjectless sentences

Both imperative sentences and existential sentences in Hawai'i Creole have the surface structure S → VP. In such sentences, tense markers, modals, aspect markers or serial verbs are not normally used before the verb. Non-past existential sentences in Hawai'i Creole usually begin with the verb *get*:

(41)   a.   ***Get*** *wan nyu bilding ova dea.*
            'There's a new building over there.'
        b.   ***Get*** *two problems wit dat translation.*
            'There are two problems with that translation.' (Kearns 2000: 27)

Past existential sentences begin with *haed* (*had*):

(42)   a.   ***Had*** *dis old green house…*
            'There was this old green house…' (Lum 1990: 60)
        b.   ***Had*** *some Pharisee guys…*
            'There were some Pharisees…' (*Da Jesus Book*, 56
            [Matthew 19:3])

3.   Verbless sentences

3.1.   Equational sentences

The first type of verbless sentence, equational sentences, are usually formed by joining two noun phrases without a copula: S → NP NP.

(43)   a.   *Mai sista wan bas jraiva.*
            'My sister is a bus driver.'
        b.   *Nau yu da baws.*
            'Now you're the boss.'

Some speakers, however, use *iz* (*is*) or *waz* (*was*) as a copula:

(44)   a.   *Brynie is da Captain.*
            'Brynie is the Captain.' (Lum 1998b: 223)
        b.   *He was one old guy.*
            'He was an old guy.' (Lum 1999: 22)

3.2.   Sentences with an adjective phrase (AdjP)

The second type of verbless sentence is made up of an AdjP and an NP. The structures of the NP and AdjP are given in section 9. below. In such sentences the AdjP may come after the NP with the structure S → NP AdjP; no copula is required.

(45) a. *Mai sista skini.*
      'My sister is skinny.'
   b. *Da buggah brown.*
      'The bugger's brown.' (Morales 1988: 72)
   c. *Da old wine mo betta.*
      'The old wine is better.' (Matthew 1997: 174)

Furthermore, as mentioned above, the Hawai'i Creole stative verb *ste* (*stei*, *stay*) may also be used before AdjPs, functioning as a copula. But it can only be used before adjectives or AdjPs that denote a non-permanent or non-intrinsic quality, or a change in conditions:

(46) a. *hi **stey** free eswy.*
      'He's free, that's why.' (bradajo 1998a: 19)
   b. *Shi **stei** sik.*
      'She is sick.'

But the following example, is not acceptable because the adjective denotes a permanent quality:

(47) **Da wahine ste shawt.*
      'The woman is short.'

Again, speakers of mesolectal varieties of Hawai'i Creole may use *iz* (*is*) or *waz* (*was*) as a copula before the AdjP:

(48) a. *His one **is** cool.* (Tonouchi 1998: 251)
   b. *Tommy Kono **was** short.* (Lum 1999: 23)

Verbless sentences with an AdjP can also have the AdjP first, followed by the NP with the structure S → AdjP NP. In such sentences a copula is not normally used.

(49) a. *Smat da dawg.*
      'The dog is smart.'
   b. *Ono da malasadas.*
      'The malasadas [local Portuguese doughnuts] are delicious.'
   c. *Too long da words.*
      'The words are too long.' (Kearns 2000: 21)

3.3.   Locational sentences

The last type of verbless sentence is the kind that gives a location, with either an adverb or a prepositional phrase: its structure is either S → NP AdvP or S → NP PP. In sentences where the location is *here* or *there* or where there is a phrase giving the location, a copula is usually not used:

(50)   a. *Mai sista hia.*
            'My sister is here.'
        b. *Kent dem insaid da haus.*
            'Kent and the others are inside the house.'

Similarly, *wea* (*where*) questions do not need a copula:

(51)   a. *Eh, wea dis guy from?*
            'Hey, where's this guy from?' (*Da Jesus Book*, 23 [Matthew 8:27])
        b. *But where dah bridge?*
            'But where's the bridge?' (Pak 1998a: 113)

But the copula *ste* (*stei, stay*) can also be used with locations:

(52)   a. *He stay inside da coffin.*
            'He's inside the coffin.' (Lum 1999: 26)
        b. *Where he stay?*
            'Where is he?' (Ching 1998: 183)

4.   Negation

4.1.   Negative markers

Hawai'i Creole sentences are normally negated by using one of four negative markers: *nat, no, neva* and *nomo*. Each one has a particular distribution.

Nat (*not*) is used in four contexts: (i) in verbless sentences, before the predicate NP, AdjP, AdvP, or PP; (ii) in sentences with a VP, before the tense marker *gon*; (iii) before the *-ing* form of the verb when it is not preceded by the aspect marker *ste*, and (iv) before the modal *sapostu*:

(53)   a. *Mai sista **nat** wan bas jraiva.*
            'My sister isn't a bus driver.'
        b. *Da baga **nat** braun.*
            'The guy isn't brown.'
        c. *Hi **nat** goin brok om.*
            'He's not going to break it.'

    d. *Da gaiz **nat** wrking.*
       'The guys aren't working.'
    e. *Yu **nat** sapostu du daet.*
       'You're not supposed to do that.'

Nat (*not*) also occurs with the modal *beta* but the order is reversed:

(54)   *Yu beta **nat** du daet.*
       'You'd better not do that.'

No is used in six contexts, all in sentences with a VP: (a) before the unmarked verb; (b) before the tense marker *gon*; (c) before the modals *kaen*, *laik*, *gata* and *haeftu*; (d) before the copula *ste*; (e) before the aspect markers *ste*, *stat* and *pau*; and (f) before the serial verbs *go* and *kam* (*come*):

(55)   a. *Da kaet **no** it fish.*
        'The cat doesn't eat fish.'
     b. *I **no** goin tell nobody.*
        'I won't tell anybody.' (*Da Jesus Book*, 2 [Matthew 1:19])
     c. *I **no** can even do twenty [pushups] in da P.E. test in school.*
        'I can't even do twenty [pushups] in the P.E. test in school.' (Lum 1999: 22)
     d. *I **no** like flunk.*
        'I don't want to flunk.' (Kearns 2000: 11)
     e. *Kaerol **no** haeftu wrk.*
        'Carol doesn't have to work.'
     f. *Da kaet **no** ste in da haus.*
        'The cat isn't in the house.'
     g. *Hi **no** ste sik.*
        'He isn't sick.'
     h. *I like pau by tonight, even if it mean I **no** go sleep.*
        'I want to finish tonight even if it means I don't sleep.' (Kearns 2000: 26)
     i. *De **no** ste lisining.*
        'They aren't listening.'
     j. *Mai sista **no** stat pleing saka.*
        'My sister hasn't started playing soccer.'
     k. *Ai **no** pau kuk da rais yet.*
        'I haven't finished cooking the rice yet.'

Negative imperatives (prohibitives) are also formed by putting *no* before the verb:

(56)   **No** *mek fan.*
     'Don't make fun.'

Either *nat* or *no* can be used before the tense marker *gon*, but for some speakers there is a slight difference: *nat* implies a contradiction or change, for example:

(57)   a. **No** *gon rein tumaro.*
        'It's not going to rain tomorrow.'
     b. **Nat** *gon rein tumaro.*
        'It's not going to rain tomorrow [even though you think it is].'

(58)   a. *Shi* **no** *gon ple saka.*
        'She's not going to play soccer.'
     b. *Shi* **nat** *gon ple saka.*
        'She's not going to play soccer [now that she's changed her mind].'

Also, note that *nat* is quite often used before *pau*, but this is when *pau* is being used as a main verb meaning 'to finish' or an adjective meaning 'finished', rather than as an aspect marker.

(59)   *Ai* **nat** *pau yet.*
     'I'm not finished yet.'

Neva (*nevah, never*) is used before the verb or aspect marker to indicate negative and past tense simultaneously:

(60)   a. *Ai* **neva** *du om.*
        'I didn't do it.'
     b. *He* **nevah** *say nutting.*
        'He didn't say anything.' (Lum 1999: 24)
     c. *De* **neva** *ste lisen.*
        'They weren't listening.'
     d. *De* **neva** *pau tek da tes.*
        'They didn't finish taking the test.'

Neva is also used before the tense marker *yustu* (*used to*):

(61)   *She* **nevah** *used to have one big fat turkey fo Tanksgiving.*
     'She didn't use to have a big fat turkey for Thanksgiving.'
     (Lum 1998a: 74)

Note that *no wen* is not normally used for past tense negation, and that *neva* does not simply mean 'not ever' as it does in English. For example, the meaning of *I never eat beans* in Hawai'i Creole is 'I didn't eat beans', not 'I don't ever eat beans'.

Nomo (*no more*), the last negative marker, is different from the others in that it is not used before a verb, a modal or an aspect marker. Rather, it occurs before an NP in a subjectless sentence to mark negative non-past existential, meaning 'there isn't' or 'there aren't'.

(62)   ***Nomo*** *kaukau in da haus.*
       'There isn't any food in the house.'

It is also used in a negative possessive sentence to mean 'doesn't have' or 'don't have':

(63)   a.   *Nau wi **nomo** ka.*
            'Now we don't have a car.'
       b.   *How come I **no more** one real glove?*
            'How come I don't have a real glove?' (Chock 1998: 29)

Two other expressions are sometimes also used for negative possessive: *no haev* (*no have*) and *no get*.

Nomo can be used to talk about things in the past – for example:

(64)   *We **no more** their kind money.*
       'We didn't have their kind of money.' (Kono 1998: 210)

But other expressions can also be used: *no haed* (*no had*), *neva haed* (*never had*), *neva haev* (*never have*), and *neva get* (*never get*):

(65)   *Neva haed TV.*
       'There wasn't any TV.'

4.2.   Other forms of negatives

Other forms of negatives are used by some Hawai'i Creole speakers. First there is the set expression *dono* or *donno* (*dunno*) which, like its English origin, means 'don't know' or 'doesn't know':

(66)   *I **dunno** who wen' tell my madda.*
       'I don't know who told my mother.' (Yamanaka 1998b: 156)

When *waz* (*was*) is used as a tense/aspect marker or copula, the negative markers *no* or *neva* can be used with it:

(67)   a.   *Shi **no** waz going.*
            'She wasn't going.'

b. *Ai wen go fo si om yestade, but hi **neva** waz hom.*
'I went to see him yesterday, but he wasn't home.'

Forms of negatives closer to English are used by some speakers of varieties of Hawai'i Creole more toward the acrolectal end of the continuum. These include: *kaenat* (*cannot*), *don* (*don't*), *diden* (*didn't*), *izen* (*isn't*), *wazen* (*wasn't*), and *won* (*won't*).

4.3.   So-called double negatives

Like many other languages, Hawai'i Creole can use a negative marker on both the verb and the noun or noun phrase, for example:

(68)   a. *Shi **neva** bring **no** kaukau.*
'She didn't bring any food.'
b. *De **no** du **nating**.*
'They didn't do anything.'
c. ***Nomo nating** insai dea.*
'There isn't anything in there.'
d *Ai **no** kaen si **nobadi**.*
'I can't see anybody.'
e *Hi **no** go **nopleis**.*
'He doesn't go anywhere.'

5.   Relativization

Hawai'i Creole has subject relative clauses similar to those in English. The relative pronouns are *hu* (*who*) and *daet* (*dat, that*):

(69)   a. *He coach everybody **who** come in da weightroom.*
'He coached everybody who came to the weightroom.'
(Lum 1999: 22)
b. *Get one noddah girl **who** no can stay still.*
'There's another girl who can't stay still.' (Kanae 1998: 208)
c. *Dey even had da funny kine gun **dat** was fat at da end.*
'They even had the strange gun that was fat at the end.'
(Lum 1998a: 71)
d. *He not jalike da teacha guys **dat** teach God's Rules.*
'He's not like the teachers that teach God's Rules.' (*Da Jesus Book*, 20 [Matthew 7:29])

However, with regard to subject relative clauses, Hawai'i Creole differs from English in two ways. First, the relative pronoun can be omitted:

(70) a. *You dah one wen show us dah map.*
'You're the one who showed us the map.' (Pak 1998a: 116)
b. *I don't know anybody study as much as you.*
'I don't know anybody who studies as much as you.' (Cataluna 2002: 6)

Second, a regular pronoun such as *hi* (*he*), *shi* (*she*) or *de* (*dey, they*) can be used in place of a relative pronoun:

(71) a. *Aes da kain gaiz de awl tawk onli.*
'That's the kind of guys who are all talk, no action.'
b. *And get one skinny boy, he just stare at my braddah.*
'And there was a skinny boy who just stared at my brother.'
(Kanae 1998: 208)

With regard to object relative clauses, Hawai'i Creole and English are similar in allowing the absence of the relative pronoun. In Hawai'i Creole, however, the relative pronoun is normally not used in object relative clauses.

(72) a. *More betta you study dat SAT prep book Auntie K wen loan you.*
'It's better if you study that SAT prep book Auntie K loaned you.'
(Kearns 2000: 4)
b. *Dis is dah bridge we standing on right now.*
'This is the bridge we're standing on right now.' (Pak 1998a: 115)

6. Complementation

6.1. Nominal clauses

Hawai'i Creole does not have clausal subjects but it does have clausal objects, similar to those of English. They may be introduced by the complementizer *daet* (*dat, that*):

(73) a. *All I can rememba is dat Latin no get one word order.*
'All I can remember is that Latin doesn't have a word order.'
(Kearns 2000: 22)
b. *She tell me she pray dat Ah Goong stay okay.*
'She told me she prays that Ah Goong is okay.' (Lum 1998a: 73)

6.2.   Infinitival clauses

Infinitival complements that are introduced by *to* in English are most often introduced by *fo* (*for*) in Hawai'i Creole:

(74)   a.   *My father said for tell you.*
              'My father said to tell you.' (Ching 1998: 187)
        b.   *He ask me fo cheer you up.*
              'He asked me to cheer you up.' (Kearns 2000: 13)
        c.   *I neva have money for buy some mo.*
              'I didn't have money to buy more.' (Yamanaka 1998b: 155)
        d.   *He teach me how fo grip da bar.*
              'He taught me how to grip the bar.' (Lum 1999: 22)
        e.   *I too chicken fo say anyting.*
              'I was too chicken [scared] to say anything.' (Lum 1998b: 230)

Hawai'i Creole also has a type of infinitival clause not found in English. Here the clause functions as the second part of an equational sentence, describing the subject by his or her habitual actions:

(75)   a.   *Hr fo tawk enikain.*
              'She's the kind who'd say anything.'
        b.   *Dem gaiz fo dringk pleni.*
              'Those guys are heavy drinkers.'

7.   Adverbial clauses

Adverbial clauses in Hawai'i Creole are similar to those of English. Examples are given below in different categories with the relevant subordinating conjunctions.

Time: *wen* (*when*), *wail* (*while*), *bifo* (*befo, before*), *aefta* (*after*)

(76)   a.   *You neva notice someting funny **when** she talk?*
              'Didn't you notice something funny when she talked?' (Kearns 2000: 13)
        b.   *And **while** he wipe his sweat..., da spotters put on two more small weights...*
              'And while he wiped his sweat..., the spotter put on two more small weights.' (Lum 1999: 22)
        c.   *I get planny Latin vocabalery fo memorize **before** I go sleep.*
              'I have a lot of Latin vocabulary to memorize before I go to sleep.' (Kearns 2000: 26)

    d. *I goin come back alive **afta** I mahke.*
      'I'm going to come back alive after I die.' (*Da Jesus Book*, 51
      [Matthew 17:9])

Location: *wea* (*where*)

(77) *Dey live ova dea wea da dead peopo stay buried.*
      'They live over there where the dead people are buried.' (*Da Jesus
      Book*, 23 [Matthew 8:28])

Purpose: *fo* (*for*)

(78) *Everybody come **fo** see dat house.*
      'Everybody comes to see that house.' (Lum 1990: 92)

Reason: *kawz* (*coz, cause, because*)

(79) *Russo tink he hot stuff **cause** he stay in high school.*
      'Russo thinks he's hot stuff because he's in high school.' (Lum 1999:
      20)

Manner: *jalaik* (*j'like, jalike, just like*)

(80) *God wen make um come back alive, **jalike** Jesus wen say befo time.*
      'God made him come back alive, just like Jesus said earlier.' (*Da
      Jesus Book*, 93 [Matthew 28:6])

Contrast: *do* (*though*), *ivendo* (*even though*)

(81) *...he look like one of da Russians **even though** he was Portogee.*
      '...he looked like one of the Russians even though he was Portuguese.'
      (Lum 1999: 24)

Conditional: *if*

(82) *But nowadays, **if** somebody no can read, everybody feega he stupid,*
      too.
      'But nowadays if somebody can't read, everyone thinks he's stupid
      too.' (Kearns 2000: 21)

Negative conditional: *o els* (*or else*)

(83) *So you bettah behave **or else** I going come sit on you.*
      'So you'd better behave or else I'm going to come and sit on you.'
      (Lum 1998b: 229)

Negative contrast: *nomaeta* (*no matta, no matter*)

(84)   *Mo betta you live foeva,* **no matta** *you no mo hand o leg.*
        'It's better to live forever, even if you don't have hands or legs.'
        (Matthew 1997: 52)

8.   Sentences linked by adverbial connectors

In addition to subordination, sentences can be linked by adverbial connectors.

Sequence: *den* (*then*), *aen den* (*an then, and then*)

(85)   a.   *Fo' long time wuz quiet.* **Den** *she wen ax me one weird question.*
              'For a long time it was quiet. Then she asked me a weird question.'
              (Tonouchi 1998: 249)
        b.   *...you gotta stand still fo at least one second before you can let um
              go.* **And den***, dey jes drop um on da floor...*
              '...you've got to stand still for at least one second before you can
              let it go. And then they just drop it on the floor.' (Lum 1999: 21)

Consequence: *so*

(86)   *My little braddah, he not mento.* **So** *you bettah stop teasing him.*
        'My brother isn't mental. So you'd better stop teasing him.' (Kanae
        1998: 208)

Negative conditional: *bambai* (*bumbye, by 'm by*); note that *bambai* (*bumbye,
by 'm by*) also functions as an adverb meaning 'later'.

(87)   a.   *Yu beta tek yo ambrela.* **Bambai** *yu get wet.*
              'You'd better take your umbrella. Otherwise you'll get wet.'
        b.   *No get da tomatoes wet,* **bumbye** *going get spots.*
              'Don't get the tomatoes wet; otherwise they're going to get spots.'
              (Lum 1998b: 225)

Cause or result: *aeswai* (*ass why*), *daeswai* (*das why, dass why, that's why*)

This is one of the most common connectors in Hawai'i Creole, occurring at
either the beginning or the end of a sentence. When it is used in initial position,
that sentence is the result and the preceding sentence is the cause:

(88)   a.   *Ai neva stadi.* **Aeswai** *ai wen flang.*
              'I didn't study. That's why I flunked.'

b. *Kennet when he fight, he always try his best. **Das why** he win.*
'When Kennet fights, he always tries his best. That's why he wins.'
(Lum 1998b: 227)

When it is used in clause-final position, that sentence is the cause and the preceding sentence is the result.

(89)   a. *she neva lai kaam clos shistey wyle **eswy**.*
       (*Shi neva laik kam klos. Shi ste wail **aeswai**.*)
       'She didn't like to come close because she was wild.' (bradajo
       1998a: 19)
   b. *Stay ova dea till I tell you fo come back. King Herod, he goin look
       fo da boy fo kill him, **dass why**.*
       'Stay over there till I tell you to come back because King Herod
       is going to look for the boy to kill him.' (*Da Jesus Book*, 4
       [Matthew 2:13])

9.   Noun phrase structure

Plural marking on Hawai'i Creole nouns is optional, although it is now being used more and more frequently. It is most common when a word ends in a vowel, as in *mai toiz* (*my toys*), and least common when a word is preceded by another word which shows quantity, as in *tu dala* (*two dollar*). When plural marking is used, it follows the morphophonemic rules of English.

However, there are many words in Hawai'i Creole which have plural marking where it is not found in English, like for example: *junks, mails, furnitures, baggages, underwears, slangs, stuffs, peoples,* and *corns* ('corn on the cob'). The basic Hawai'i Creole noun phrase has the following structure:

    NP → (DET) (QUANT) (AdjP) N (collectivizer)

Determiners include the articles *da* (*the*), *a*, and *wan* (*one*), and the demonstratives *dis* (*this, diss*), *daet* (*that, dat*) and *doz* (*those*). Quantifiers include *meni* (*many*), *sam* (*some*), and *pleni* (*plenny*) derived from English *plenty of* but used to mean 'many' or 'much', as in *pleni pipo* (*plenny peopo*) 'many people' and *pleni rais* 'much rice'. Another quantifier unique to Hawai'i Creole is *chok* (*choke*) 'very many'. Cardinal numbers, which are also quantifiers, are basically the same as in English. Ordinal numbers may be formed by putting *namba* (*number*) before the cardinal number, as in *namba tu boi* (*number two boy*) 'second son'.

An adjective phrase is made up of an adjective which may be preceded by a degree modifier, such as *mo* (*more*), *tu* (*too*), *so*, and *ril* (*real*) as in *mo big* 'bigger', *tu gud* (*too good*), *so haepi* (*so happy*) or *ril hanggri* (*real hungry*). One difference from English is that *sam* (*some*) can also be used as a degree modifier, as in *dea haus sam smawl* (*their house some small*) 'their house is really small'.

An adjective phrase can also be made up of a group of words followed by the derivational clitic *kain* (*kine, kind*) with the meaning '_____ kind of':

(90)   a. *De wen bai enikain **no nid kain** stafs.*
            'They bought many kinds of things they don't need [i.e. unneeded stuff].'
        b. *She put her hand by her mout and make **geisha-kine** giggle, so fake.*
            'She put her hand by her mouth and made a geisha kind of giggle, so fake.' (Lum 1998b: 227)

Finally, an NP can have one of several enclitics which act as collectivizers. The first is *gaiz* (*guys*). This can function to show plural, as in *da einjol gaiz* (*da angel guys*) 'the angels' and *yo aensesta gaiz* (*your ancestor guys*) 'your ancestors', or to mean something like 'and those associated with the preceding noun and its premodifiers', for example:

(91)   *She axed me where **my mom guys** went.*
        'She asked me where my mom and those with her went.' (Tonouchi 1998: 249)

Sometimes *foks* (*folks*) is used in a similar way:

(92)   *Last weekend I was suppose to go wit **Vernalani folks** to da Pure Heart concert.* (Kearns 2000: 29)

Similarly, *dem* after a noun means 'and other associated people':

(93)   a. ***Kaerol dem** wen go shaping yestade.*
            'Carol and the others went shopping yesterday.'
        b. *Lata, **Jesus dem** wen go way from Jericho town.*
            'Later, Jesus and his disciples went away from Jericho.' (*Da Jesus Book*, 61 [Matthew 20:29])

Possessive NPs are similar to those of English, except that the possessive clitic *'s* is not always required. So, it is common to hear possessive NPs such as *Jo haus* (*Joe house*) 'Joe's house' and *da wahine ka* (*da wahine car*) 'the woman's car'.

10. Pronominal system

Like English (and unlike other creole languages), Hawai'i Creole has several sets of pronouns: subject, object, possessive and reflexive. The subject and object pronouns are given in Table 1 and the possessive pronouns in Table 2:

Table 1. Hawai'i Creole subject and object pronouns

	subject	**object**
First person singular	*Ai (A, I)*	*mi (me)*
Second person singular	*yu (you)*	*yu (you)*
Third person singular	*hi (he), shi (she) [him, hr (her)]*	*him, hr (her), om (em, um)*
First person plural	*wi (we), as gaiz (us guys) [as (us)]*	*as gaiz (us guys)*
Second person plural	*yu (you), yu gaiz (you guys)*	*yu (you), yu gaiz (you guys)*
Third person plural	*de (dey, they), dem gaiz (dem guys)*	*dem gaiz (dem guys), om (em)*

Table 2. Hawai'i Creole possessive pronouns

	prenominal	**independent**
First person singular	*ma, mai (my)*	*mainz (mines)*
Second person singular	*yoa, yo (your)*	*yawz (yours)*
Third person singular	*hiz (his), hr (her)*	*hiz (his), hrz (hers)*
First person plural	*awa (our)*	*awaz (ours)*
Second person plural	*yoa/yo (your), yu gaiz (you guys)*	*yawz (yourz), yu gaiz (you guys)*
Third person plural	*dea (their)*	*deaz (theirs)*

There are also independent possessive pronouns using *wan* (*one*): *main wan* (*mine one*), *mainz wan* (*mines one*), *yawz wan* (*yours one*), *awaz wan* (*ours one*), *yu gaiz wan* (*you guys one*), *dem gaiz wan* (*them guys one*).

As can be seen, most of the Hawai'i Creole pronouns are similar to those of English, but there are some important differences. First, Hawai'i Creole subject and object pronouns most often show plural by adding *gaiz* (*guys*). Second, *it* is rarely used, except in set expressions, like *Stop it!* Rather, other words, such as *da ting* (< *the thing*) or *da kain, da kine* (< *the kind*) are used instead. More commonly, the Hawai'i Creole pronoun *om* (*em, um*) is used instead of *it* as the object pronoun. Third, there is a difference in some of the possessive pronouns, such as *yo* or *yoa* for 'your' and *mainz* (*mines*) for 'mine'. Fourth, sometimes object pronouns appear in subject position, as in *hr sik* (*her sick*) 'she's sick' and *as go* (*us go*) 'we're going'. Also, object pronouns are consistently used in some places where English uses subject pronouns, for example: *hu him*? (*who him?*) 'who is he?' and *huz san him*? (*whose son him*) 'whose son is he?'. Finally, unlike English, Hawai'i Creole sometimes uses the pronouns *hi* (*he*) and *shi* (*she*) to refer to inanimate referents where *it* is required in English, especially as a resumptive pronoun:

(94)   a.   *Da stoa **hi** open nain oklak.*
            'The store, it opens at nine o'clock.'
       b.   *Da klaes **shi** nat daet izi.*
            'The class, it isn't that easy.'
       c.   *awl dess tym da saan **he** shynin da wayv **he** braykin...*
            (*All this time, the sun, he shining, the wave, **he** breaking...*)
            'All this time, the sun, it's shining, the wave, it's breaking.'
            (bradajo 1998b: 171)

The Hawai'i Creole reflexive pronouns are shown in Table 3.

Table 3.   Hawai'i Creole reflexive pronouns

	reflexive
First person singular	*maiself* (*myself*)
Second person singular	*yoself/yuself* (*yourself*)
Third person singular	*himself, hrself* (*herself*)
First person plural	*awaself* (*ourself*)
Second person plural	*yoself/yuself* (*yourself*)
Third person plural	*demself* (*themself*)

Alternative forms are: *yuselfs* (*yourselfs*), *as gaiz self* (*us guys self*), *yu gaiz self* (*you guys self*), *dem gaiz self* (*them guys self*).

11. Focusing

Various types of movement are quite common in Hawai'i Creole for focusing on particular constituents of a sentence. Topicalization occurs as in English for focusing on the object by moving it to the front of the sentence:

(95) a. *Onli da jangk kain, hi let yu tek.*
         'Only the junky kinds, he lets you take.'
      b. *Daet wan, ai si.*
         'That one, I see.'

Left-dislocation of the subject also occurs:

(96) a. *Mai fada, **hi** no laik go wrk.*
         'My father, he didn't like to go to work.'
      b. *...my sista, **she** the boss of the sunflower seeds.*
         '...my sister, she was the boss of the sunflower seeds.' (Yamanaka 1998a: 153)
      c. *Weightlifters, **dey** no do too much.*
         'Weightlifters, they don't do too much.' (Lum 1999: 19)

Topicalization of the object and left-dislocation of the subject can occur simultaneously:

(97) *Enikain fud dis gai **hi** it.*
      'All kinds of food, this guy eats.'

Left-dislocation of the object or a locational phrase is common as well:

(98) a. *Dis wan ai wen bai **om** Longs.*
         'This one I bought at Longs.'
      b. *Dis glove, you try bend **um**, no can.*
         'This glove, if you try to bend it, you can't.' (Chock 1998: 28)
      c. *At da Y get plenny guys living **ovah dere** in da upstairs rooms.*
         'At the Y, there are lots of guys living there in the upstairs rooms.' (Lum 1999: 25)

Right-dislocation is found in Hawai'i Creole, as in English:

(99) a. *De get pleni mani, yo faemli.*
         'They have a lot of money, your family.'
      b. *Hi wan pis awf baga, daet gai.*
         'He was a really angry bugger, that guy.'

A sentence can have both object topicalization and subject right-dislocation:

(100)   *Pleni mani de get, sam gaiz.*
        'Some guys have a lot of money.'

Hawai'i Creole differs from English, however, in that the subject may be moved to the end of the sentence, similar to right-dislocation but without the use of a pronoun in the canonical position of the moved constituent.

(101)   a. *No laik ple futbawl, diz gaiz.*
            'These guys don't like to play football.'
        b. *Geting ol, as gaiz.*
            'We're getting old.'
        c. *No laik it nating, dis gai.*
            'This guy doesn't like to eat anything.'

Finally, Hawai'i Creole has cleft constructions, but unlike English, the anticipatory *it* is not used:

(102)   *Waz as gaiz hu wen laik go.*
        'It was us who wanted to go.'

Hawai'i Creole also uses cleft constructions involving clausal subjects, but again neither anticipatory *it* nor a complementizer is used.

(103)   a. *…garans he goin give you guys clotheses.*
            '…it's guaranteed that he'll give you all clothes.' (*Da Jesus Book*, 18 [Matthew 6:30])
        b. *Mo betta I stop now.*
            'It's better if I stop now.' (Kearns 2000: 26)

Exercises and study questions

1. Change the following sentence to have the meanings below. (Use the Odo orthography.)

   Jo gaiz plei futbawl. 'Joe and his friends play football.'
   a) Joe and his friends played football.
   b) Joe and his friends will play football.
   c) Joe and his friends used to play football.
   d) Joe and his friends want to play football.
   e) Joe and his friends are playing football.
   f) Joe and his friends were playing football.

2. Translate the following sentences into English.

   a) *Mai brada da baws in da faemli.*
   b) *Get wan ol haus daun dea.*
   c) *Priti, da wahine.*
   d) *Wea da haspitol?*
   e) *Haed wan big buli in awa skul.*
   f) *Daet buk mainz.*

3. Change the following Hawai'i Creole sentences from positive to negative.

   a) *De wen go luk muvi laes nait.*
   b) *Da boi ple myuzek in wan naitklab.*
   c) *Mai fada gaiz get wan fishin bout.*
   d) *Hi mai ticha fo Ingglish.*
   e) *Maeri kaen it enikain fud.*

4. Insert two of the following words in the correct order:

   stat gon wen ste pau
   a) *Hi* ____ ____ *wrk Sande.* 'He'll be working Sunday.'
   b) *Da gaiz* ____ ____ *bil wan haus.* 'The guys were building a house.'
   c) *Ai* ____ ____ *lawnmowa da yad tumaro.* 'I'll finish mowing the yard tomorrow.'
   d) Hiz fren ____ ____ *shauting aet dem.* 'His friend started shouting at them.'
   e) *Mai mada* ____ ____ *mek da shrt awredi.* 'My mother had already finished making the shirt.'

5. Fill in the blank with an appropriate complementizer, subordinate conjunction or adverbial connector.

   a) *Shi laik aes yu* _____ *help as.* 'She wants to ask you to help us.'
   b) *Hi wen luk mi lawng taim,* _____ *hi no mi.* 'He looked at me for a long time, just like he knew me.'
   c) *No foget it yo braekfes;* _____ *yu gon kam wan wikling.* 'Don't forget to eat your breakfast; otherwise you'll become a weakling.'
   d) *Hi no laik fait with mi; hi chiken* _____. 'He doesn't want to fight with me because he's chicken.'
   e) *Doz gaiz wen go Vegas* _____ *go bai wan haus.* 'Those guys went to Vegas to buy a house.'

Selected references

Please consult the General references for titles mentioned in the text but not included in the references below. For a full bibliography see the accompanying CD-ROM.

bradajo [Joseph Hadley]
    1998a   Ma[ket]stenlei. In: Chock, Harstad, Lum and Teter (eds.), 19–26.
    1998b   Feescol ajukeshen. In: Chock, Harstad, Lum and Teter (eds.), 167–172.
Cataluna, Lee
    2002   *Super Secret Squad*. Honolulu: Kumu Kahua Theatre.
Ching, Stuart
    1998   Way back to Palolo. In: Chock, Harstad, Lum and Teter (eds.), 180–190.
Chock, Eric
    1998   Da glove. In: Chock, Harstad, Lum and Teter (eds.), 28–29.
Chock, Eric, James R. Harstad, Darrell H.Y. Lum and Bill Teter (eds.)
    1998   *Growing up Local: An Anthology of Poetry and Prose from Hawai'i*. Honolulu: Bamboo Ridge.
Da Jesus Book
    2000   *Da Jesus Book* [Hawai'i Pidgin New Testament]. Orlando: Wycliffe Bible Translators.
Kanae, Lisa Linn
    1998   Short tongue. In: Chock, Harstad, Lum and Teter (eds.), 208–209.
Kearns, Yokanaan
    2000   *Pidg Latin and How Kitty Got Her Pidgin Back*. Honolulu: Honolulu Theatre for Youth and Kumu Kahua Theatre.
Kono, Juliet S.
    1998   A scolding from my father. In: Chock, Harstad, Lum and Teter (eds.), 210–211.
Labov, William
    1990   On the adequacy of natural languages: I. The development of tense. In: Singler (ed.), 1–58.
Lum, Darrell H.Y.
    1990   *Pass On, No Pass Back!* Honolulu: Bamboo Ridge Press.
    1998a   Giving tanks. In: Chock, Harstad, Lum and Teter (eds.), 71–74.
    1998b   Orphan Annie: Coloring in the eyes. In: Chock, Harstad, Lum and Teter (eds.), 222–231.
    1999   YMCA: the weightroom. In: Rickford and Romaine (eds.), 19–27.
Morales, Rodney
    1988   *The Speed of Darkness*. Honolulu: Bamboo Ridge Press.
Matthew, Kaopio
    1997   *Hawaiian Family Legends*. Honolulu: Mutual Publishing.

Pak, Gary
  1998a   The gift. In: Chock, Harstad, Lum and Teter (eds.), 98–119.
  1998b   The valley of the dead air. In: Chock, Harstad, Lum and Teter (eds.),
            319–327.
Tonouchi, Lee A.
  1998   Where to put your hands. In: Chock, Harstad, Lum and Teter (eds.),
            245–252.
Yamanaka, Lois Ann
  1998a   Boss of the food. In: Chock, Harstad, Lum and Teter (eds.), 153–154.
  1998b   Lickens. In: Chock, Harstad, Lum and Teter (eds.), 155–156.

Fiji English: morphology and syntax

France Mugler and Jan Tent

1.   Introduction

The morpho-syntax of Fiji English, like its lexicon and phonology, is hetero-
genous, with variations both across speakers with different first languages (primarily Fijian and Fiji Hindi) as well as along a continuum which goes from a
heavily substratum-influenced variety – what we have called Pure Fiji English
– to one which exhibits maximum pressure from Standard English while still
being distinctive – Modified Fiji English (see Tent and Mugler, this volume).
We attempt here to describe features typical of Fiji English, many of which are
shared by other varieties of English and of English-based pidgins and creoles,
while pointing out those which are characteristic of Pure Fiji English and probably most distinctive.

The major source of the data cited in this chapter is Jan Tent's more than
80 hours of recordings of part-European speakers, his observations of spoken
Fiji English from Fijian, Indo-Fijian and other speakers, local television news
and advertisements, accompanied by quotes from written sources, primarily
newspapers, and the plays of Fiji's Larry Thomas, which often feature a low
or middle-income multicultural setting where the characters speak Pure Fiji
English (see Tent 2000). A few more recent examples, particularly from newspapers, have been collected by France Mugler. When no source is cited after an
example, the reference is to Tent (2000).

2.   The noun phrase

2.1.   Nouns

2.1.1.   Count and non-count nouns

One of the most striking features of Fiji English nominals is the status of count
and non-count nouns (see also 2.3.). There are a number of distinctive count
nouns, preceded by an article in the singular and with a suffixed {-s} in the
plural, a feature common to many L2 Englishes (Crystal 2003: 362). Two of
the most noticeable such nouns are *slang* 'a slang expression/word', and *swear*
'a swearword' (a count noun as well as a verb):

(1)   a. *He uses a lot of **slangs** in his writing.*
      b. *The **slangs** they always use and the words, I like it.*
      c. Jo: [...] *man you should have heard all the **swears** then she ran up
         to me and wanted to slap me.* [...] (Thomas 1991: 49)
      d. *Fuck is a very bad **swear**.*

Plural forms of these two nouns are the most common distinctive count nouns
in Tent's recorded data. Indeed, his recordings contain relatively few such
nouns, while Kelly's spoken data only includes occurrences of *slangs* (1975:
41). Most examples of distinctive count nouns come from print or writing,
where this feature seems more prevalent (Tent 2000: 353–354). Other examples of distinctive count nouns include:

(2)   a. *Fiji will draft **a legislation** [...]* (Fiji One Television news,
         22/7/1993)
      b. *If I don't give my soli* [i.e. a donation], *there will be **gossips** about
         me and my family which I wouldn't want to happen.* (*Fiji Times*,
         7/12/1994)
      c. *I was cutting **firewoods** when it happened.* (Fiji One Television
         news, 31/3/1997)
      d. *The manager of our Petrol Service Station is Mr [X] who claims
         the taxi union **staffs** are not involved in the dispute with tyre repair
         boys.* (Letters to the Editor, *Daily Post*, 8/8/1994)
      e. *We don't really have the resources to accommodate all the
         necessary training **equipments** [...]* (*Fiji Times*, 1/2/2003)
      f. *We hope police will be able to arrest the culprits because we have
         suffered a loss of more than $80,000 from our belongings and
         furnitures.* (*Fiji Times*, 17/1/2003)
      g. *Ability to work with new **softwares** required.* (Positions Vacant, *Fiji
         Times* 3/2/2003)
      h. *Please go ahead and let staff know you are collecting **feedbacks**.*
         (Email to France Mugler, 4/3/2003)

There is also the occasional distinctive non-count noun:

(3)   a. *Food included sacks of flour, sugar, tins of **biscuit**, cartons of tea
         and drums of kerosene.* (*Fiji Times*, 7/1/1993)
      b. *While we respect other **religion**, this does not give the right to
         others of other **religion** to disturb people of other denominations.*
         (Letters to the Editor, *Fiji Times*, 16/8/1994)

While the absence of an {-*s*} plural morpheme can in many cases be explained on phonological grounds, i.e. to fit the syllable structure of Fiji English (Tent and Mugler, this volume), the fact that pluralised distinctive count nouns seem less common in speech than in writing suggests that hyper-correction due to the pressure of Standard English may be involved.

2.1.2. *Pluralisation of borrowings*

Count nouns borrowed from Fijian and Fiji Hindi can be pluralised in Fiji English in two ways: with an {-*s*} or a zero suffix. The following citations include examples of both kinds of plurals in Fijian borrowings:

(4) a. *The tired tourists arrived at Lautoka at noon wearing blankets and **sulu** [i.e. a wraparound] provided by Blue Lagoon. (Fiji Times,* 26/5/1999)

b. *Leading the march were elderly men in coats, **sulus**, and sandals.* (Subramani 1988: 36)

c. *The redevelopment will have four new accommodation buildings with 160 guest rooms and 47 traditional Fijian-style **bure*** [i.e. a house]. *(Fiji Times,* 27/5/1999)

d. *Eager to test the elements, they descended upon the resort like plunderers, invading the beach, the swimming pool, and the **bures**.* (Subramani 1988: 23)

Here are a few examples of zero and {-*s*} plural suffixes with Fiji Hindi borrowings:

(5) a. *How many **choli** [i.e. a short sari blouse] does she have?*

b. *That shop has the nicest and best **cholis** in Suva.*

c. *The majority of ex-**girmitiya** [i.e. indentured labourers], however, remained in agriculture.* (Lal 1992: 39)

d. *He reminds us of the Girmit indentured system served by our forefathers. He wants us to learn from the experience of the **Girmitiyas**.* (Letters to the Editor, *Daily Post,* 10/4/1996)

e. *Bhimla prepares a parcel containing two or more **rotis** [i.e. a kind of unleavened bread] with dry curry from the previous evening meal for Hari.* (Mamak 1978: 36)

f. *They want a variety because simple **roti** with only one curry doesn't go down with them," she says as she tosses some dalo leaves into a pot. (Sunday Times,* 31/8/1997)

It is worth noting that most count nouns in both Fijian and Fiji Hindi have an invariant form unmarked for number. While one could argue that {-*s*} plural marking on borrowed count nouns indicates their full nativisation into Fiji English, it does not follow that the same nouns are somehow less nativised when they have zero plural marking instead. In other words, *sulu* and *roti* are fully a part of the Fiji English lexicon, whether they appear in the plural as *sulu* or *sulus*, *roti* or *rotis*, and there are no English-derived alternatives to these borrowings. Rather, the morpho-syntactic variation corresponds to the different lects in the continuum, with the zero marking being typical of Pure Fiji English and the {-*s*} marking of Modified Fiji English.

Some Fiji English nouns are derived from English adjectives, such as *plastic* 'a plastic supermarket bag':

(6)   *"We really need to relook seriously at the use of **plastics** which makes up a majority of litter,"* he [i.e. the Environment Minister] *said.* (*Sunday Times*, 21/9/1997)

2.2.   Pronouns

2.2.1.   Gender

Gender is not normally marked in Pure Fiji English pronouns (or in the two main substratum languages) and *he* is often used as a generic:

(7)   a.   *My mother, **he**'s a primary school teacher in Labasa.*
       b.   *That woman **he** hit his husband when he cut* [i.e. was drunk].
       c.   *Mrs [X] was called to rest [...]. Always remembered by **his** sons.* (Funeral notice, *Fiji Times*, 15/1/2003)

2.2.2.   Person and number

The pronoun system of Fijian, like that of many other Oceanic languages, is much more complex than that of English since it distinguishes between singular, dual, paucal, and plural, as well as between inclusive and exclusive for all non-singular pronouns.

In Pure Fiji English, pronouns are marked for singular, dual and plural number, and for inclusivity/exclusivity. They are calqued on the model of Fijian, with the use of the suffixes -*two*, for dual, and -*gang*, for plural. Thus we have *us-two* '1dual incl.' and *us-gang* '1pl. (more than two)', *you-gang* '2pl.' etc. Although the semantic and morpho-syntactic origin of these pronouns is Fijian, they are widely used not only by native speakers of Fijian but by all speakers of Pure Fiji English. Some examples include:

(8)   a. Q: ***Us-two***'s bread?
           A: *No,* ***you people***'s bread.
       b. *Hey, how 'bout* ***us-two*** *go watch movie tonight?*
       c. ***Us-gang*** *own this store.*
       d. *C'mon* ***you-gang****, pull on this rope!*
       e. *So* ***you-gang*** *adopt children out to relatives too.*
       f. *I feel sorry for* ***you people*** *because this is one area which is
           lacking development.* (*Fiji Times,* 26/2/2003)

The plural suffix *-gang* may also occur with demonstratives (e.g. *those-gang*
and *that-gang* 'they') and seems synonymous with *people* as in *those people*:

(9)   *Man, I don't know how* ***those-gang*** [i.e. pilots] *can do it.*

Another frequent plural pronominal form in spoken Pure Fiji English is the 2pl.
you-people('s) 'you/your (more than two)':

(10)   a. Margaret: *I just don't know* ***you people****. Look at all of you.
           Everytime you are always arguing about the same thing.* [...].
           (Thomas 1989: 31)
       b. *Everytime her friends visit her, they ask her to cook Chicken in
           Chili and Plum Sauce. She tells them: "Oilei!* [i.e. Oh!] ***You people***
           not sick of this?" (*Sunday Times,* 1/9/1997)
       c. *He said* ***you people***'s *house is one nice house-ga.*

The structure pronoun + *people* corresponds to the Fiji Hindi pattern, in which
postposed *log*, literally 'people', pluralises the singular pronouns; e.g. *ham
log* 1pl., *tum log* 2pl., *i log/u log* 3pl. (see Siegel 1992). However, the *people*
pronoun plural marker is used widely by all speakers of Pure Fiji English, regardless of their first language.

2.2.3.   Third person singular pronouns

Pure Fiji English has two distinct third person singular pronouns: *fella* for
[+human] referents (male or female) and (*the*) *thing* for [-human] referents
(i.e. *it*):

(11)   a. ***Fella*** *was drinking grog* [i.e. kava] *there, during class. But his
           teaching is set* [i.e. great, good]. *But the way fella treat us, no
           good, èh?*
       b. ***Fella*** [i.e. my mother] *wake up half-past five in the morning.*

   c. Marika: *Oh Mrs Kumar I'm sorry I forgot. When I come back from school I bring it back to you,* **the thing** *at home.* (Thomas 1991: 37)

   d. Mrs Kumar: *Well* **the thing** *take time you know.* (Thomas 1991: 46)

   e. *When we have the tournament coming up,* **thing** *already finish. The club going on now.*

   f. *When you on the alarm system you press this button. When you off* **the thing** *you press that one.*

On the use of (*the*) *thing*, Kelly (1975: 29–31) notes that it appears to be a "stronger pronoun than *it*" and "is normally used in the subject of a sentence, or where a noun would occur in [Standard English]." Our data and observations confirm this.

2.2.4. Third person plural

The third person plural object pronoun *them*, preceded by *and*, is added to a singular proper noun to indicate a group of friends or relatives – a very common feature of Fiji English:

(12)   *Jone and* **them** *coming to the party tonight, èh?*

2.2.5. Who

In Pure Fiji English, the interrogative/relative pronoun *who* sometimes is used when referring to the name of someone or something:

(13)   a. *I can't remember* **who** *his name is.*

        b. *Question of the week!* **Who** *is the dog's name in the Jetson cartoon series?* (*Sunday Post*, 1/9/2002)

This is calqued on Fijian usage, where *o cei* 'who' is used in questions such as *o cei na yacana?* literally 'who's his/her name?'

2.3.   Determiners

2.3.1.   One

Perhaps the most distinctive characteristic of the Pure Fiji English determiner system is the indefinite article *one*, a typically creoloid and L2 English feature. Note that neither Fijian nor Fiji Hindi has a separate indefinite article, although each of course has a numeral 'one' (*dua* and *ek* respectively):

(14)   a. Simi: *Man you talk like **one** philosopher!* (Thomas 1991: 25)
       b. *They should have **one** security guard up here at night sitting in **one** shed.*
       c. ***One** experience cook wanted for Indian Restaurant **one** kitchen hand also required Phone 479540* (Positions Vacant, *Fiji Times*, 10/9/1994)

However, as the next two examples show, *one* is not used consistently; *a* is also often used within the same utterance or sentence:

(15)   a. ***One** Fijian man called me and he told me if I want **a** chewing gum* [...] (*Daily Post*, 27/9/1997)
       b. *I am informed, the 14-year-old boy was apparently assaulted after **a** heated argument with **one** taxi driver.* (Letters to the Editor, *Daily Post*, 8/8/1994)

Kelly (1975: 27) argues that *one* seems to be "a more emphatic form" and is generally used in the "[nominal] group forming the subject". In most cases when *a* is used "the reference is rather general", compared to *one* where "the reference is usually to a specific person or object". However, not all examples above fit this description and a more thorough analysis based on a larger sample is needed.

2.3.2. Plenty

A common quantifier is *plenty* (+ noun) 'many, lots (of), much, plenty of':

(16)   a. Josephine: [...] *You got **plenty** money?* (Thomas 1991: 21)
       b. *Like **plenty** people think of Raiwai as a criminal place.*
       c. *He remembers someone came to the village and told everyone there was a place where they could make **plenty** money.* (*Fiji Times*, 2/10/1997)

2.3.3. Zero determiner

Zero determiner seems to be more common in written than spoken Fiji English, especially before proper nouns:

(17)   a. *I met them in **Civic Centre** one time.*
       b. *When clients buy their houses from **Housing Authority**, they enter into a contract to make regular payments for them.* (Letters to the Editor, *Daily Post*, 13/8/1994)

    c. *"It has now reached **unbearable high percentage**," he said. (Fiji Times*, 1/8/1994)

    d. *I would like to thank the Public Works Department's Complaints Section for showing **caring attitude** when houses along Tamavua Road was out of water.* (Letters to the Editor, *Fiji Times*, 8/9/1994)

The reverse is also quite common, and once again, more so in writing or print than in speech, and again in particular with proper nouns:

(18)   a. ***The Enamanu Road** has been neglected for a long time.* (Letters to the Editor, *Fiji Times*, 9/8/1994)

    b. *The methods used in eliciting data is important in any research enterprise and that brings **the credibility** to the merit of the results.* (Letters to the Editor, *Fiji Times*, 16/8/1994)

    c. *Senator [X] then said that "In the Indian community it is a shameful act if someone's wife is fondled by another person and it arouses **the anger** in any man. [...]"* (Daily Post, 17/5/1995)

2.4.   Adjectives

Adjectives derived from past participles often do not carry the {*-ed*} morpheme of Standard English, as is true of many other varieties of English. This is probably because of the syllabic structure of Fiji English, in which final consonant clusters are avoided (see Tent and Mugler, this volume). The most common examples in our data are: *aircondition room, experience driver, ice water, dry fish, tin fish*, and *sugar water*.

(19)   a. *Fully **air-condition** computer lab and lecture room.* (Advertisement, *Fiji Times*, 3/2/2003)

    b. *Urgently wanted **experience** digger operators [...]* (Positions Vacant, *Fiji Times*, 15/2/2003)

On the other hand, {*-ed*} occurs sometimes in Fiji English where it does not in Standard English, probably as a hypercorrection, especially since it seems more frequent in writing and print. Perhaps the most common example is *matured* (especially in the positions vacant columns of newspapers e.g. *matured housegirl wanted*):

(20)   a. *These are children who are exposed to this kind of acts for a period of time until the child would come out in the open "TO TELL" especially when they are socially **matured** and ready to disclose the happenings.* (Daily Post, 27/9/1997)

b.   *Two bedrooms furnished flat 2 minutes walk to city/CWM, all amenities, quiet, **secured*** (To Let, *Fiji Times*, 15/2/2003)

This hypercorrection sometimes extends to nouns, as in:

(21)   *An **experienced** of 5 years will be very helpful.* (*Fiji Times*, 14/2/2003)

2.4.1.   Comparatives and superlatives

In Fiji English *more* and *most* are often preposed to the comparative and superlative forms of adjectives respectively – an archaic pleonasm in Standard English:

(22)   a.   [...] ***most tastiest, most tastiest*** [...] (Television advertisement, 1994–1995)
       b.   *Then only can we promote **more healthier** environment to live in and make Fiji more appealing to tourists as well.* (Letters to the Editor, *Fiji Times*, 28/7/1994)
       c.   [...] *the Prime Minister believes there's **more better** players here* [...] (Fiji One Television news, 10/4/1996)

Occasionally, *less* also occurs with the comparative form of an adjective:

(23)   *I don't think referees will become **less harsher** in Wellington* [...] (*Fiji Times.* 5/2/2003)

3.   The verb phrase

3.1.   Verbs derived from nouns and particles

Fiji English has some distinctive verbs derived from English nouns or particles. Examples of verb forms derived from nouns are *schooling*, *broom* and the archaic *pain*:

(24)   a.   *Today, there are 620 girls **schooling** at Jasper Williams High School.* (*Fiji Times*, 11/7/1994)
       b.   Asha: [...] *I wanted to carry on **schooling** but my father told me that I should stay at home and help my mother in the house.* [...] (Thomas 1991: 18)
       c.   *I **broom** your room after lunch, éh?*
       d.   *I was never at work on Wednesday because my back was **paining** very much.*
       e.   *No, my throat doesn't **pain** any more.*

Other examples include:

(25) a. *Please **attention** it to Bob.*
      b. *Sometimes, even your friend, she'll try to **crook** [i.e. swindle] you.*

Another such verb is *slang*, which has also undergone a semantic shift, 'to speak in English with an unnatural, i.e. non-Pure Fiji English, accent (a rebuke)'.

(26) a. *We like the way you talk to us, you not **slang** like other palagis [i.e. Europeans] when they talk to us.*
      b. *You sound stubborn [i.e. snobby] when you **slang** like that; you just wanna be a star [i.e. a show-off].*

Fiji English also has some verbs derived from nouns from languages other than English, e.g. *choro* 'to steal', from Fiji Hindi *chor* 'a thief'. While the final {-o} is an imperative suffix in Fiji Hindi (as well as standard Hindi), in Pidgin Fiji Hindi and in borrowings into Fijian and Fiji English the form with the {-o} is the verb stem:

(27) *You see those shoes? He **choro-ed** them.*

In the next example, Fiji Hindi *tilak* 'a mark made on the forehead for ornament, or to indicate sect' is used as a verb (in its past participial/adjectival form):

(28) *Here I am then, garlanded, **tilaked**, poised like a deity.* (Subramani 1988: 131)

Examples of Fijian borrowings include *meke*, a verb and a noun both in Fijian and in Fiji English meaning 'to perform a traditional dance or action song' or 'a traditional dance', and *lovo* 'an earth oven', a noun in Fijian and Fiji English, but also a verb in Fiji English with the meaning 'to cook in an earth oven'.

(29) a. *The little girls came and **meked** for the European ladies.*
      b. *Why don't we **lovo** this stuff?*
      c. *There's nothing liked **lovo-ed** pork, is there?*

In Fiji English, *on* and *off* are verbs rather than mere post-verbal particles as in Standard English, and mean 'to switch/turn on/off':

(30) *When you **on** the alarm system you press this button. When you **off** the thing you press that one.*

Similarly, *in* can be a verb, meaning 'to insert something', as in:

(31) *Jan, can you help me **in** this key?*

3.2.   Phrasal and simple verbs

Fiji English has some phrasal verbs which correspond to simple verbs in Standard English. *Cope up*, *discuss about*, and *request for* are the most common ones:

(32)   a.   *"We find it extremely hard to* **cope up** *with repairs costs,"* Mr *[X]*
            said. (*Fiji Times*, 11/5/1994)
        b.   *In this essay, I would like to* **discuss about** *[...].*
        c.   *The staff who have* **requested for** *a gown, kindly collect them from*
            me during the following times [...].

The converse also occurs, as in the frequent *pick* (Standard English 'to pick up'):

(33)   a.   *When [X] returned to the embassy to* **pick** *the passports he*
            was arrested and charged after being interviewed. (*Fiji Times*,
            28/5/1994)
        b.   Q: *What is the role of toastmasters at the Hibiscus Festival?*
            A: *They* **pick** *the queens to and from home.* (*Fiji Times*, 28/8/1999)

Other examples include *lock* 'to lock up', *throw* 'throw out', and *give* 'give up/over':

(34)   a.   *I used to* **lock** *my three daughters and go to the fields.* (*Daily Post*,
            19/2/1994)
        b.   *What we should keep and what we should* **throw***?*
        c.   *The rebels stopped the carrier and ordered the driver to move out,*
            but he refused and told them he was ready to die but would not
            give *his carrier* [i.e. truck]. (*Daily Post*, 10/8/2000)

Finally, some phrasal verbs have a different particle in Fiji English than in Standard English:

(35)   a.   *Man, he was so gone* [i.e. drunk] *he keep on* **throwing out**
            [i.e. throwing up] *all the time.*
        b.   *Villagers from Narai showed their appreciation to the Japanese*
            embassy early this year by **putting up** *a feast.* (*Fiji Times*,
            23/6/1999)

3.3.   Deletion of copula and auxiliary *be*

Equational sentences without a copula and sentences where the auxiliary *be* does not appear, are extremely common in Pure Fiji English, as indeed in L2, colloquial L1 varieties of English, as well as in pidgins and creoles:

(36)   a.   Margaret: [...] *You worse than a woman*. (Thomas 1989: 38)
       b.   *We haven't had water for the past two weeks and **this very***
            ***disgusting** because we all need water every time*. (*Fiji Times*,
            24/1/2003)
       c.   Tom: ***Nobody making** any noise, just go back and look after your*
            baby. (Thomas 1989: 19)
       d.   Mereoni: *Ia, I just don't know what **Margaret gonna** say, she will*
            get really wild. (Thomas 1989: 20)
       e.   *Because **they still** far away*.

3.4.   Tense and aspect markers

Pure Fiji English has a number of tense and aspect markers, one of which is derived from the English past participle, while others are adverbs or adverbial phrases which have become grammaticalised to various degrees.

The pre-verbal marker *been* indicates past tense:

(37)   a.   Josephine: *Man you can really bluff. You **been** tell me you gonna*
            stop drinking grog [kava] *because your work is going very badly.*
            And just look at you! (Thomas 1991: 16)
       b.   Reserve Bank: *You gang **been** open the safe and leave it like that*
            and everybody take the money or what? How come the money
            gone? [...]
            NBF [National Bank of Fiji]: *Yeah man. Trues God, malik kasam,*
            *bulului, cross my heart and hope to die, we **been** open it. That's*
            *the open door policy the Government **been** want.* (*Fiji Times*,
            23/3/1996)

The use of *been* as a past tense marker is a typical creoloid feature, widely attested in many varieties of English and in English-based pidgins and creoles. However, *been* is far less frequent in Fiji English, where tense tends to be indicated by context rather than by verb morphology, and it seems to indicate a remote past (as does the Fijian preverbal *ā*).

Among expressions which have their origin in time adverbials, *always* and *all the time* present the clearest cases of grammaticalisation, as preverbal present habitual markers (similar to, and probably calqued on, Fijian *dau* 'always, habitually, a lot' – often used to translate the simple present tense). Example (38c) below shows full grammaticalisation of *all the time*, which follows the subject noun phrase and is preposed to the lexical verb. In (38d) however, although it also follows the subject noun phrase, *all the time* does not immediately precede the verb but rather a resumptive subject pronoun, so one can argue that it is not inside the verb phrase and is therefore less grammaticalised. The semantically similar *every time* – sometimes used redundantly with *always* – is also not fully grammaticalised, as it is preposed to the subject. As for *before*, in all likelihood calqued on Fijian *i liu* and indicating a habitual past, it stands well outside the verb phrase and is best considered a sentence adverbial.

(38)   a. *Like before, a lot of fights and that **always** happening on the road.*
       b. *English here* [in Fiji] *much more different, 'cause we **always** put much more slangs in.*
       c. *Stay away from her, she **all the time** marimari* [i.e. cadge] *from people.*
       d. *The next door neighbour **all the time** he bash his wife when he cut* [i.e. drunk].
       e. Margaret: *I just don't know you people. Look at all of you.* ***Everytime** you are **always** arguing about the same thing.* [...] (Thomas 1989: 31)
       f. Mrs Kumar: *See that is why I don't like to give my rake to people.* ***Everytime** I have to ask it back.* (Thomas 1991: 37)
       g. *He said **before**, many homes did not have burglar bars.* (*The Daily Post*, 10/4/1996)

Two other time adverbials of interest are *one time*, which indicates a punctual past:

(39)   a. *I met them in Civic Centre **one time**.*
       b. *Because **one time** he come there.*

and the related *sometimes* 'some time', which can refer to both past and present:

(40)   a. *SIR – **Sometimes** back I had written a letter to this column about the deteriorating condition of the Vatuwaqa Cemetery Building and the filthy state of the toilets.* (Letters to the Editor, *Fiji Times*, 20/1/1996)
       b. *For **sometimes** now I have observed that yaqona* [i.e. kava] *drinking has been done in some work places on the campus during official work times.*

Note that the use of the pluperfect in (40a) above, where a simple past would be used in Standard English, is particularly common in print.

3.5. Subject-verb agreement

Subject-verb agreement is variable. In Pure Fiji English, the verb is often singular regardless of the number of the subject. Agreement is also often with the immediately preceding noun phrase rather than with the grammatical subject.

(41) a. ***Bulk foods is** not new in Fiji* [...] *We have it right here at Tropikana* (Advertisement, *Daily Post*, 3/9/1994)

   b. ***Suva rugby and FRL heads** for a show-down* (Headline, *Daily Post*, 18/5/1995)

   c. *I would like to thank the Public Works Department's Complaints Section for showing caring attitude when **houses** along Tamavua Road **was** out of water.* (Letters to the Editor, *Fiji Times*, 8/9/1994)

   d. *In the old days, **Hindustani programmes** over Radio Fiji **was** educational and entertaining.* (Letters to the Editor, *Fiji Times*, 27/8/1994)

In the structure *one of* + noun phrase, the noun phrase has a zero plural marker:

(42) a. *[…] one of the knife wielding **man**, allegedly grabbed her* [...] (*Fiji Times*, 2/2/2003)

   b. *Yet when one of our most respected and longest serving **leader** wants a duty free car* [...]. (*Fiji Times*, 2/2/2003)

In Pure Fiji English a pronoun referring to a preceding noun phrase is typically singular, particularly when it is distant from the (plural) noun phrase, in a prepositional phrase or a dependent clause:

(43) a. *They* [i.e. natural disasters] *devastate the entire population in **its** path.* (*Fiji Times*, 24/1/2003)

   b. *Movement Chairman [X] said members would continue to raise funds through cultural and social programmes and send **it** to SAHARA for the affected families.* (*Fiji Times*, 29/1/2003)

4.   Discourse particles

4.1.   Intensifying adverbials

4.1.1.   Full

The archaic intensifier *full* is common, and is sometimes used adverbially:

(44)   a.   *He can't hear you. He's **full** concentrating on his play.*

   b.   *One top civil servant from Niue who was in Fiji attending a meeting funded by an international organisation was sighted in one of the local hotels early in the morning walking around **full** cut* [i.e. very drunk] *with his shirt hanging out. Reports from the hotel said the senior civil servant had been up all night partying.* (*Islands Business* 29, 1/1/2003: 11)

   c.   *Oh, I love hockey **full** speed, man.*

Full is also used (adjectivally), in the common idiom *full speed* 'a lot, whole-heartedly' seen in the title of Sheree Lipton's book *Fiji, I love you, full speed.*

4.1.2.   Ga

In Pure Fiji English, the Fijian intensifier *ga* (and its calque *just*), meaning 'only, just, nevertheless, all the same, yet, but, however, but only, except' etc., may also be used adverbially:

(45)   a.   *All you allowed in the exam is one page-**ga**.*
   b.   *She don't want to watch-**ga**.*
   c.   Tom: *Ah, we just choke* [i.e. cadge] ***ga**. (Thomas 1989: 8)

The *ga* intensifier is:

(46)   a.   *Hè, you-**ga** get away from there!*
   b.   *Fella-**ga** no good, man. Just one thief.*
   c.   *She told me and she said that she never want to, but you just force line* [i.e. intimidate] *her-**ga**.*

In addition, a redundant *just* often accompanies *ga*:

(47)   a.   Q: *What do I do with this letter then?*
            A: *You just fax-**ga**.*
   b.   *Oh, I just stay home-**ga**, play sports, go play volleyball, like that, no.*
   c.   *We just hang around-**ga**.*

4.2.   Prepositional collocations

Prepositional usage often differs from that of Standard English, although the pattern of variation is difficult to assess. Here are some examples:

(48)   a.   *The influence of kava **in** these deliberation and decision is indeed mighty.* (Letters to the Editor, *Daily Post*, 8/8/1994)
b.   *With a multi-religious country such as ours we should be well versed **about** other religions as well.* (Letters to the Editor, *Fiji Times*, 6/8/1994)
c.   *SIR – I wish to express my appreciation **about** the male staff nurses at the Colonial War Memorial Hospital.* (Letters to the Editor, *Fiji Times*, 20/8/1994)
d.   *Drop completed coupon **to** box provided in all operations.*
e.   *"The vision is that youths* [i.e. young people in general] *will spend more time to contemplate **on** their life and also sign on later to be crew members,"* he said. *(Fiji Times,* 13/5/1998)

5.   Syntactic and pragmatic features

5.1.   Pronominal copying

A frequent type of pronominal copying occurs in basic Subject-Verb-Object clauses, where an appositional pronoun functions as a focus marker for the Subject noun phrase. This structure, better known as *left-dislocation*, occurs of course in a number of other languages (e.g. Chinese, colloquial French), including English. Indeed, the following examples from Fiji English could just as easily have been taken from a number of varieties of colloquial English:

(49)   a.   *My dad **he** works for FEA* [Fiji Electricity Authority].
b.   *Some* [i.e. teachers] ***they** treat us badly.*
c.   *FM 96, **they** play plenty music.*

The following examples are more distinctive but this is because of lexical or other grammatical features rather than the pronominal copying per se:

(50)   a.   *The grass-cutter, **it** making too much noise, sorry for that.*
b.   *Sometimes, even your friend, **she**'ll try to crook you.*
c.   *One teacher, Master Timoci, **fella** punched one boy, whose name Niku, because fella was laughing.*

We think that that pronominal copying may occur more frequently in Fiji English than in other colloquial varieties of English. This may be because it is reinforced by a similar structure in Fijian, which has a pronominal subject co-referent with the subject noun phrase, not only when this noun phrase is fronted but also when the sentence follows the more common Verb-Object-Subject order:

(51)   *e*   *musuka*   *na*   *dovu*   *o*
        Tuimasi
        3sg subject 'cut' + trans. marker {-*ka*} def. art. 'sugarcane' proper art.
        'Tuimasi'
        'Tuimasi cuts the sugarcane'

Kelly's data (1975: 29) also includes pronominal copying, but she notes it is "never used before the {-*ing*} form of the verb, and is rarely used in the present tense", and adds that "[t]he vast majority of instances occur in the narration of past events, and the verb is most often in the preterite form." However, the selection of examples above shows that this is not the case. Indeed, Tent's data shows that pronominal copying occurs with most (if not all) tense/aspect combinations.

Pronominal copying also occurs in relative clauses which include a resumptive pronoun with the same referent as the relative pronoun (as in Fijian):

(53)   a. *You know the software that I left **it**...the box that I left **it** on your desk*
        b. *Jan, vinaka vakalevu* [i.e. thank you very much] *for the dalo* [i.e. taro] *which you brought **it**.*
        c. *There is another burst which we are still trying to locate **it**.* (*Fiji Times*, 7/3/2003)

5.2.   Questions

In Pure Fiji English, all questions have the same word order as declarative sentences. Yes/no questions have a rising intonation contour which, as in many other varieties of colloquial English (as well as in Fijian and Fiji Hindi), indicates the interrogative nature of the sentence.

(54)   a. James: *The mailman come today?* (Thomas 1989: 36)
        b. *You want me give him one empty* [i.e. blank] *disc?*

Here are examples of *wh*-questions:

(55)   a. Mereoni: *How I'm going to eat then?* (Thomas 1989: 9)
        b. James: *Why not allowed to get a letter?* (Thomas 1989: 36)
        c. *I ask her: "Why you not want to stay in Savusavu?"*

In Pure Fiji English *how come* is frequently used for reason questions instead of Standard English *why*. While this is also found in other colloquial varieties of English (particularly American English), it seems more common in Fiji English.

5.3. Directives

The structure of 1st and 2nd person directives in Pure Fiji English often includes a subject pronoun. As Kelly (1975: 23) notes, the hortative intention of the 1st person directive is made quite explicit from both the context and its accompanying intonation.

(56) a. Margaret: *I haven't cooked yet, that's why I want **you call** Raymond so that he can go to the shop.* (Thomas 1989: 40)
     b. Valerie: [...] *Come, come **we go** and **spy**.* (Thomas 1989: 43)
     c. ***Us-two go** now!*
     d. *Master always say like this: "**You** not **talk** in class!"*

5.4. Negation

In Pure Fiji English, *never* is an emphatic negator, and the phrase *not even* is often used as a general sentence negator:

(57) a. *"Lucky they **never** hurt anyone else in my family. We fought outside, four against one," Mr [X] said.* (*The Daily Post*, 23/4/1996)
     b. *Some of us **never** always speak English very fluently.*
     c. Maika: *After his mother died, one day his brain snap.*
         Teresa: ***Not even**. The way you say it, like his brain a string or what?* (Thomas 1991: 157)

5.5. Introducers

Expressions introducing direct quotations include *go/went/said like this* (Standard English *said*), as noted by Kelly (1975: 34) and Siegel (1991: 666). Some examples from Tent's data are:

(58) a. *Then I **say like this**: "Are you okay, or what?"*
     b. *The teacher, he **go like this**: "What you boys doing here?"*

As in other colloquial varieties of English, *like* is also used as a general sentence introducer, as well as an indicator of a topic shift:

(59)   a. ***Like***, *you a part-European, right?*
        b. ***Like***, *I have three sisters and four brothers.*

5.6.   Tags and fillers

The most common question tag in Fiji English is *èh* (calqued on Fijian), and others include *na* (calqued on Fiji Hindi), invariant *isn't it* (particularly among Fiji Hindi speakers), and *or what*:

(60)   a. *Fiji Gold, mokusiga* [i.e. is wasting time], ***èh*** – *dead all the time.*
        b. *Fella was drinking grog* [kava] *there, during class. But his teaching is set* [great, good]. *But the way fella treat us is no good,* ***èh***.
        c. *We gave him as much time as the others,* ***na***?
        d. *They don't really have to do it,* ***isn't it***?
        e. *Last week's winners were the Chand family. They won a free weekend at the Regent Fiji. Is that styling it,* ***or what***?
        f. Seini: [...] *The way Alipate came in here and gave her a hiding like this was his house* ***or what***! (Thomas 1989: 26)
        g. Sereana: *Aisake, you mad* ***or what***, *people are sleeping.* (Thomas 1991: 83)

The tag-like *like that/this* is often used as a filler:

(61)   a. *Like when you asking how much for that thing, or* ***like that***.
        b. *We just stay home-ga and play volleyball,* ***like that***, *no?*
        c. *And the bus services, like in the morning* ***like that***, *thing will come after the other.*

5.7.   Greeting and leave-taking routines

Fiji English has a number of distinctive greeting and leave-taking routines. Among the most common greetings are: *how's it?* and *how's the life?* The most distinctive is *where you going?* – often shortened to *where to?* – and is used as a greeting made in passing. This formula is probably calqued on the Fijian *o lai vei?*, but it has become common among the general population. The reply is a formulaic *this/that way* or *this/that side*, normally accompanied by an indication of direction, often with a head movement, sometimes by pointing.

Another greeting used in passing is *bye*. Although it is used by all Fiji English speakers, it is more commonly heard from Fijian native speakers as it is a calque on the Fijian *moce*, which means both 'good-bye' and a passing 'hello'.

There are two common leave-taking formulae. The first is simply *okay*, which can both signal the end of a conversation and indicate the intention to leave ('I'm going now/I have to go now'). The second is *to take the lead* and is normally used when the speaker is heading for a place where the addressee is also expected to go later. This is also calqued on a Fijian formula with the verb *liu* 'to lead; to go on ahead'. The expression (e.g. *I'll take the lead/I'm taking the lead*) is used mostly, but not exclusively, by native speakers of Fijian.

6.   Conclusion

The distribution of these and other grammatical features across the Fiji English lects and speech communities has yet to be established. It is often unclear whether a feature is common to all (or even most) speakers of Fiji English. For instance, the verbs *to on/off* are probably more common than the use of the a plural marker *gang*, but whether one can say that the latter is Pure Fiji English whilst the former is Modified Fiji English is still uncertain. Similarly, absence of definite articles and the invariant tag *isn't it?* seem more prevalent among native speakers of Fiji Hindi, while the use of *us-two* and the *èh* tag are more common among native speakers of Fijian. Yet some features which can be traced to one of the substratum languages have spread to the general population. A finer analysis would need to be based on a large-scale empirical study embracing the entire continuum. In the meantime, any conclusions would be premature.

Exercises and study questions

1. Comment on the following examples:

   (a) *Ability to work with new **softwares** required.*
   (b) Q: ***Us-two**'s bread?*
       A: *No, **you people**'s bread.*
   (c) *Jone and **them** coming to the party tonight, èh?*
   (d) *[…] the Prime Minister believes there's **more better** players here […]*
   (e) Margaret: *[…] **You worse** than a woman.*

2. Comment on the communicative function of *full* and *-ga* in the following examples:

(a) *He can't hear you. He's **full** concentrating on his play.*
(b) *She don't want to watch-**ga**.*
(c) A: *You just fax-**ga**.*

Which other varieties in Australasia do you know with a marker serving the same function as *-ga*?

3. Listen carefully to the samples of spoken Fiji English on the accompanying CD ROM. Try to identify examples of the following features of Pure Fiji English:

(a) sentence tags
(b) article use
(c) pronoun use
(d) different verbs to varieties of standard English
(e) sentences that do not have a copula or auxiliary verb where varieties of standard English would normally have one
(f) different preposition/particle use to varieties standard English
(g) tense/aspect marking
(h) adverbs which are used in a distinctive way (e.g. as aspect markers or redundantly)

4. Based on your reading of other articles in this volume, outline some of the similarities and differences between the morpho-syntactic features of Indo-Fijian speakers of Pure Fiji English and those of Indian English, and Indian South African English. Feel free to start out from the features in (1)-(3).

5. Based on your reading of other articles in this volume, outline some of the similarities and differences between the morpho-syntactic and lexical features of Pure Fiji English and those of English varieties spoken in former British colonies that are also multilingual, e.g. Singapore, Malaysia, and varieties spoken in the Caribbean and Africa.

Selected references

Please consult the General references for titles mentioned in the text but not included in the references below. For a full bibliography see the accompanying CD-ROM.

Kelly, Sr. Francis
    1975   The English spoken colloquially by a group of adolescents in Suva. *Fiji English Teachers Journal* 11: 19–43.

Lal, Brij V.
   1992   *Broken Waves: A History of the Fiji Islands in the Twentieth Century*. Honolulu: University of Hawai'i Press.

Lipton, Sheree
   1972   *Fiji, I love you, full speed*. Wellington: Seven Seas.

Mamak, Alexander
   1978   *Colour, Culture and Conflict: A Study of Pluralism in Fiji*. Sydney: Pergamon Press.

Siegel, Jeff
   1991   Variation in Fiji English. In: Cheshire (ed.), 664–674.
   1992   Language change and culture change among Fiji Indians. In: Tom Dutton (ed.), *Culture Change, Language Change: Case Studies from Melanesia*, 91–113. Canberra: Pacific Linguistics.

Subramani
   1988   *The Fantasy Eaters*. Washington, D.C.: Three Continents Press.

Tent, Jan
   2000   The dynamics of Fiji English: a study of its use, users and features. Ph.D. dissertation, Department of Anthropology, University of Otago, Dunedin.

Thomas, Larry
   1989   *Just Another Day: A Play*. Suva: University of the South Pacific.

Thomas, Larry
   1991   *3 Plays: Outcasts; Yours Dearly; Men, Women and Insanity*. Suva: University of the South Pacific.

Norfolk Island-Pitcairn English (Pitkern Norfolk): morphology and syntax

Peter Mühlhäusler

1.   Introduction

Details on the history and general nature of the languages have already been given in the chapter on phonetics and phonology (Ingram and Mühlhäusler, this volume) and the reader is referred to these. The reader is reminded again that there is considerable disagreement among the Norfolk islanders as to the spelling system of the language. I have not normalized any of the spellings of the written sources used. As a consequence, the spelling in examples may be different from that given in the text.

The reader is reminded that Norfolk Island-Pitcairn English is not a well-known variety and that the range of linguistic data from which we can make judgments has been quite narrow. Formal interviews and recitation of stories by outsiders or non-speakers have been predominant (in the studies of, for example, Flint [1961], Harrison [1972] and Buffett, who is a native speaker, from the 1980s to the present), and most data collections tend to be heavily focused on decontextualized samples and translations from English. I am in the process of obtaining more natural speech samples, but given the esoteric nature of the language and the shame still associated with it, this is not a straightforward matter, apart from the time it takes to compile a representative sample single handedly. As a consequence, representative information about a number of grammatical and discourse features is not available. The reader is also reminded that the data presented have come from the Norfolk Island variety only (known as Norfuk) as ongoing political problems on Pitcairn Island have made fieldwork there impracticable.

2.   Morphology

Norfuk shares the characteristic of many creoles, koinés and mixed languages of not having a great deal of inflectional or derivational morphology: typologically it combines a low level of synthesis with a low level of fusion. Over the years some morphological features have been borrowed from acrolectal (formal or near-Standard) English and analogical extensions of the English model are in evidence.

2.1.   Inflectional morphology

Nouns are generally not inflected for number, gender or case, as in *wan salan* 'one person', *plenti salan* 'many people'. In more acrolectal speech the English possessive *'s* and the plural *-s* are encountered though:

(1)   *All Norfolk h'yu dem two, scream a haed orf right up Peter Buffett's en breech orf a horse.*
      'All Norfolk heard those two screaming their heads off all the way up to Peter Buffett's [where they] leapt off their horses.'

The emergence of plural marking appears to follow an animacy scale. Words referring to humans frequently take the plural *-s*. I have observed the same phenomenon in Tok Pisin (Mühlhäusler 1981).

(2)   a. *strienjas*
         'strangers'
      b. *ijalas*
         'overbearing youngsters'
      c. *as eyulla lettle screppers a'wae*
         'as the young striplings awakened' (Christian 1986)
      d. *One a dem pigs bit his ear clearn off.*
         'One of the pigs bit his ear right off.' (Marrington 1981: 3)

A number of Norfuk nouns always appear as English plurals, but are usually neutral with respect to number, including *geese* 'goose, geese', *grieps* 'grape, grapes', *biens* 'bean, beans', and *mais* 'mouse, mice'.

Possessive *-s* in Norfuk can be attached to pronouns to create attributive possessive pronouns such as: singular second *yus* 'your'; singular third male *his*; dual 1+2 *himiis* 'belonging to you and me'; dual 2+2 *yutuus* 'belonging to the two of you'; dual 3+3 *demtuus* 'belonging to the two of them'; plural second *yorlis* 'belonging to you guys'; and plural third, *dems* 'belonging to them'.

The *-s* ending appears to have been formed analogically from nouns with possible reinforcement by English *he – his*; the pattern is not fully regular but exhibits some suppletion (e.g. *her* instead of *his*).

With nouns, possession is signaled in two ways; by means of the preposition *for* (see section 3.7.) and morphologically by adding an *-s* to the form or noun phrase:

(3)   a. *Tommy Snar was Snar Buffett's son.*
       b. *Dad's voice cried out.* (Buffett 1999)

A number of suffixes occur with verbs and adjectives including the *-en* continuous marker (see section 3.1. on aspect), and the affixes signalling stages of comparison:

(4)   *agli – aglia – aglies*
       'ugly, uglier, ugliest'

These can also be added to polysyllabic adjectives, including reduplicated ones:

(5)   *meyameya – meyameyara – meyameyares*
       'withered, more withered, most withered'

Predicative adjectives are followed by *-en* or *-an*, sometimes linked to the base adjectival form by an intrusive segment *-w-* or *-y-*. The conditioning factors are not fully understood and there is speaker variation.

(6)   a. *hi es piyaalian*
           'he is tiny'
       b. *a horse is roughen*
           'the horse is rough'
       c. *shi se sleprewan*
           'she is slippery, untrustworthy'

2.2.   Word formation

For new words Norfuk relies heavily on borrowing from English and its derivational (word-formation) morphology appears to be of limited productivity. The various processes employed to form new words overlap, but are not a subset of, those found in English. They include:

Derivation by zero (conversion, multifunctionality): The lexical item *morga* can mean 'thin person' (N), 'thin' (ADJ), 'to make thin' (V) and 'daintily' (ADV) (Buffett 1999: 72). The extent of and constraints on zero derivation in Norfuk remains to be explored, but my own observations suggest that this is one way of making a relatively small lexicon go a long way.

Compounding: No systematic analysis of Norfuk compounding is available. Earlier suggestions that it was uncommon (e.g. Gleißner 1997: 57) reflect the absence of a comprehensive dictionary. Eira, Magdalena and Mühlhäusler (2002) have listed many compounds that do not appear in earlier work including compounds of the endocentric type, i.e. the grammatical (sub)category of the compound is identical with that of the head word:

(7) N + ADJ
baleful
'having overeaten'

(8) N + N
a. *bacca stuff*
'wild tobacco plant'
b. *baket fish*
'type of red cod'
c. *goesbad*
'ghostbird, petrel'

(9) ADJ + N
big worta
'open sea'

Norfuk also has exocentric compounds, where no single part of the compound can be identified as the head word. Examples include:

(10) N + N
faentail
'kind of bird, fantail'

(11) ADJ + N
Big Jack
'to weep' (in memory of Jack Evans who tended to be weepy)

Whereas Norfuk has borrowed many compounds from English, when it comes to finding names for endemic life forms, compounding is usually employed (cf. Mühlhäusler 2002b). Two examples are particularly noteworthy; compounds with the lexical base 'bastard' in initial position to indicate a less useful or uncultivated variety as in:

(12) a. *bastard aienwood*
'sharkwood tree'
b. *bastard oek*
'kind of oak tree'
c. *bastard taala*
'non edible taro'

The other example worth special mention are compounds beginning with *hoem* 'home' signalling something of Pitcairn origin as in:

(13) a. *hoem naenwi*
'dreamfish'

b. *hoem oefi*
   'Pitcairn variety of the oefi fish'

Reduplication: Mühlhäusler (2003) has provided a detailed analysis of reduplicated forms in Norfuk: most of these are borrowed from Tahitian or are the result of phonological simplification. Productive reduplication is not greatly in evidence, except perhaps in cases such as:

(14)   a. *break break*
           'broken into many pieces'
        b. *boney boney*
           'full of bones'
        c. *bitey bitey*
           'kind of biting insect'

Acronyms: Being used mainly as a spoken language, Norfuk does not have acronyms other than those borrowed form English, an exception being the word *lap* for a minimalist from 'little as possible'.

3.   Syntax of the Norfolk variety of Pitkern/Norfuk

Norfuk does not have agreement between nouns and verbs, or any other morpho-syntactic agreement phenomena. The basic word order of Norfolk is SVO, just as in English and most creole languages. There are, however, many subtle differences between Norfuk and English, for instance in the placement of the indirect object. Because Norfuk has tended to be described as a dialect of English these have tended to escape earlier observers. There is a great need for detailed analysis of a greater range of texts.

3.1.   Tense, modality and aspect (TMA)

TMA has been a diagnostic feature of creole languages ever since Bickerton (1981: 58) postulated his hypothesis of a biological blueprint for human language. Formally, prototypical creoles express TMA by preverbal free morphemes.

Tense: In creoles tense is usually not developed and instead, a distinction between punctual and non-punctual and anterior and non-anterior is encountered. The conventional grammars of Norfuk postulate a tense system, but on closer inspection, there may be grounds for postulating a creole system instead. Gleißner (1997: 61–62) notes that:

Tense in Norfolk is apparently not seen with respect to the moment of utterance, but in relation to the time of the main event that is talked about. In order to express that an event took place prior or later with respect to the time frame – or will take place in the future, if the time frame refers to the moment of speaking, particles are made use of. Like all verbal markers of Norfolk tense markers precede the verb.

In any event, the indication of tense in Norfuk is optional. Past tense is indicated either by a particle *se* from English *has*, as in *hi se miekaut* 'he has managed'. A second marker of past tense is *bin* which typically refers to past continuous (non-punctual) actions, as in *hi bin aut iin a boet* 'he has been out in a boat'. With *se*, note that the infinitive verb form, rather than the past participle, is used. There is an urgent need for an in-depth analysis of tense in Norfuk.

Aspect: The suffix *-en* or *-in*, signalling continuous action, is by far the most common device but *el* (< *able*) is also used for this purpose.

(15)   *all dem Real Estate maeken dem's pretty penny* (Norfolk Islander September 2000)

(16)   *yu tuhituhien*
       'you are swearing' (Buffett 1999)

(17)   *all ell doo daan goode fe sullan*
       'they are continually doing good things for people'

Habitual action is marked by the auxiliary *yuus* which signals habitual actions in past or present.

(18)   *ai yuus a' tek a' dena d'werk*
       'I [usually] take my lunch to work' (Buffett 1999)

Completed actions are expressed by a preverbal marker *dana* (< *done*) with or without preceding /s/. This construction is found in a number of English Creoles (but not St. Kitts) and in Scottish English (cf. also Kortmann 2004: 252–253) and thus would appear to reflect the influence of the mutineer William McCoy.

(19)   *when I dana werk I hurry hom*
       'when I had finished work I hurried home'

Modality: Modality in Norfuk is expressed in various parts of grammar and the choice of the language itself can indicate modality. Traditionally (Buffett 1999: 51), modality is described as being expressed by the preverbal modal auxiliaries *mait, orta, mas,* or adverbials as *baeta, should, suuna,* or *rather*.

3.2.   The copula

The uninflected forms *se(r)*, *s'*, *es* and *is* are all used as equivalents to English forms of *be*, with *se* also overlapping with English *has*. In addition, zero is found frequently where a copula is obligatory in English. As yet no comprehensive account of this aspect of grammar is available. It would require a detailed analysis of the Tahitian substratum, St. Kitts Creole, Melanesian Pidgin English, and English dialectology to provide explanations for the complexities here. The following rough generalization can be made:

1.   equative sentences usually require the copula *es*:

(20)   *yu es ners*
        'you are a nurse'

2.   adjectives frequently are introduced by zero:

(21)   *letel salan disdietis daa semiswieh*
        'children these days are so peculiar' (Flint data)

3.   *se(r)* introduces something that results from a previous occurrence, it has perfective meaning:

(22)   *ai se fatu*
        'I am exhausted'

(23)   *dem plahn is good'un when ser ripe*
        'the bananas are delicious when they are ripe'

3.3.   Negation

The main difference between acrolectal English and Norfuk is the absence of *do*-support in general negation. Instead the negators *noe*, *nort* or *naewa* (emphatic negator) appear directly before the verb phrase, as in:

(24)   *If you no pahahait it good, it a can do.*
        'If you do not pound it well enough it just won't do.'

(25)   *Bligh en eighteen dem one nawa mutiny.*
        'Bligh and eighteen who did definitely not mutiny.' (Christian 1986)

Negative imperatives are expressed by *duu* or *dan* (both probably derived from English *don't*).

(26)   *du miek agli*
        'don't pull a face' (Buffett 1999)

Then there is a number of special negative words, including *ent* ('is/are/am not') and *kaa* or *kar* 'cannot' as in (27) and (28). The past tense *cried* in (27) illustrates code shifting to English.

(27)   *Ent me, dar youngest boy cried out.*
       'It wasn't me, the youngest boy shouted.'

(28)   *He kar dunna laugh.*
       'He couldn't help but laugh.' (Harrison 1972)

3.4.   Relativization

Norfuk does not employ relative pronouns. Restrictive relative clauses are simply inserted after the noun, as in:

(29)   *De es thing in everebohdi lew iin Australia kam fram Norfolk Island.*
       'This is something with everybody from Norfolk who lives in
       Australia.' (Norfolk Islander May 2001)

(30)   *Tell all ucklun de thing yuu bin think es 'jes hawen fun.*
       'Tell all of us [islanders] what you meant by "just having fun".'
       (Norfolk Islander May 2001)

In acrolectal varieties, English relative pronouns are sometimes used:

(31)   *to all yorlye who have been so kind*
       'To all of you who have been so kind' (Norfolk Islander June 2001)

Relative clauses dealing with time or location are typically introduced by *taim/ when* 'when', *wieh* 'where' or *said/side* 'where':

(32)   *dem use a go over Rawson Hall dana side Brooky use a play da piano*
       'they are (or were) used to going over to Rawson Hall to there where
       Brooky [habitually] plays the piano' (Norfolk Islander January 2001)

(33)   *dae es jess something me and Willie like a larn when wi grow up in
       Cascade*
       'that is just something Willie and I liked to learn when we grew up in
       Cascade' (Norfolk Islander January 2001)

(34)   *ai si said yu kat*
       'show me where you cut yourself' (literally 'may I see')

3.5.   Complex sentences

Coordination of sentences differs from English only in the strong tendency to omit the conjunction *en* 'and'. The use of the other two conjunctions *bat* 'but' and *ala* 'or' is as in English.

A common type of subordination is complementation. The equivalents in Norfuk of the English complementizer *that* are zero or *fe*, as in (35) and (36):

(35)   *Es time Ø we tek notice of dem old sullen.*
'It is time that we take notice of the old people.' (Norfolk Islander November 2002)

(36)   *seed se ready jes fe pick*
'the seeds were ready to be picked' (Buffett 1999)

There also are a large number of other complementizers to embed clauses. Most of them are used as in acrolectal English, including *anless* 'unless', *orlthoe* 'although', *wail* 'while', *bifor* 'before', *kos* 'because'. But a number of different ones are noted: *dumain* 'even if', *spoesen, ifen, siemtaim* 'at the time when', *lorng as* 'as long as', *semeswieh* 'just like'. The noun *said* 'place, side' is often used in the sense of 'because', as in (37):

(37)   *mied hi klaay iise es said dem yuus' roh'nek*
'the reason he cries easily is because they pamper him too much'
[literally: 'treat him like a rotten egg'] (Buffett 1999)

Subordination (particularly non-finite) is often not signalled by any overt markers. Consider (38):

(38)   *Bussen hii f pulloo, one day orf ar Cord, he usen his shet-knife, d pride of his life.*
'(When he was) crushing periwinkles for bait one day off the Cord, he was using his sheath-knife, the pride of his life.' (Christian 1986)

3.6.   Noun phrase structure

The basic NP is a noun without any modifiers, as in:

(39)   *surf se nehse*
'the sea is rough'

Prenominal modifiers can be added, usually in the order: Determiner, Possessive Pronoun, Number, Adjective, Noun:

(40)   *dies tuu oel giel*
'these two old women'

(41)   *mais tuu black faul*
'my two black hens'

Norfuk determiners are unstable and highly variable as an older system involving a specific-non specific distinction interacts with the English acrolectal definite-indefinite distinction. No adjectival postmodifiers occur in Norfuk, but nominal possession is signalled by means of the preposition *fe, f'* as in:

(42)   *aa kau fe mais bradhas*
'that cow of my brother'

(43)   *ar pine fer Robinsons*
'Robinson's pine' [a placename]

Note the use of the definite article *ar* in (43).

3.7.   Pronominal systems

The pronominal system of Norfuk is more complex than that of English. It has singular, plural and dual, as well as an inclusive/exclusive distinction in the first person, and a special pronoun *aklan* (*uklun, ucklan*) which expresses belonging to the Pitcairner descendant community. The possessive forms are either expressed by adding *-s* or by special forms.

The basic paradigm looks as follows:

Table 1.   Norfuk personal and possessive pronouns

Subject	Object	Possessive
Singular:		
Ai	mii	mais
Yu	yuu	yus
hi	hem	his
shi	her	her
–	et	–
Dual:		
himii	himii	himiis
miienhem	miienhem	auwas
miienher	miienher	auwas
yutuu	yutuu	yutuus
demtuu	demtuu	demtuus

Table 1. (continued)   Norfuk personal and possessive pronouns

Subject	Object	Possessive
Plural:		
wi	aklan	aklan
yorlyi	yorlyi	yorlyis
dem	dem	dems

4.   Some research interests

I am currently working on a social history of the languages of Norfolk Island in an attempt to document the interplay between acrolectal varieties of English, contact with dialects of English during the days of the Melanesian Mission (cf. also Mühlhäusler 2002a), the Mota language of the Melanesian Mission which had its headquarters on Norfolk from 1867 to 1920, the Pidgin English spoken by Melanesian students and in the whaling industry, and the role of educational policies in changing the linguistic ecology of Norfolk Island.

Both Pitcairn and Norfuk were uninhabited when the Pitcairners arrived and an important question is how the new arrivals named places, flora and fauna. I have just completed a paper on place names, drawing attention to the dual naming system on Norfolk, where a large number of Norfuk names are used side by side the official Australian ones. It is remarkable that Pitcairn place names did not travel to Norfolk but that a new system developed there. Further, many place names recall individual islanders or episodes in their lives. For instance *Ar side for Beras* was named after the famous spot of the local fisherman with the nickname "Bera", *Daarnek* refers to a sharp projection rock at a good fishing spot, *Ar side for Honey's* remembers the drowning of Honey Quintal, *Simon's Water* is a non-permanent creek on a property owned by Simon.

Spatial orientation on Norfolk Island appears to follow a system of absolute reference points with two main axes (a) away from main centre and (b) from coast upwards: *Down-A-Town* is *Kingston* and *Up-in-a-Stick* 'up in the woods' is located in *Selwyn Pine Road*, in the remote forested part of the north coast. *Kingston* would also seem to be a reference point for other names. Locations far away from *Kingston* bear names such as *Out ar Mission* 'out on the mission' and *Out ar Station* 'the remote parts on the West Coast where the cable station is located'. The location of *Out Yenna* 'out yonder' is located near *Duncombe Bay. Outa Moo-o Stone* is located in the remote North.

The natural kinds that the first settlers encountered on both islands were to a very significant extent unique, endemic species. Information on how they got named provides important evidence for the debate whether names reflect innate cognitive studies or utilitarian factors. The evidence from both islands suggests that the latter is the case, and that many species that have no cultural use remain unnamed, ignored and often mismanaged. An interesting example is the expression *rokfish* 'any fish that can be caught when fishing from a coastal rock'. Ecological management on both islands has been little short of disastrous, and the inability of the new arrivals to talk about their environment may have played a role in this environmental decline (Mühlhäusler 1996). I am in the process of collecting more ethnobotanical information.

Both Pitkern and Norfuk are endangered languages and their speakers have become concerned about declining competence among the younger generation. On Norfolk Island I have been asked to work on a long-term plan to reverse language shift. A draft proposal currently being discussed has been submitted (Mühlhäusler 2002b). Part of the revival process is a syllabus for Norfuk Language which has been designed by Suzanne Evans during 2002 as part of her graduate studies at the University of Adelaide, and it is hoped that it will be implemented from 2004. Working with small languages of necessity is action research and a considerable part of my fieldwork is given to working on matters of concern to the community.

The Pitcairn/Norfuk language has often been labelled a laboratory test case for linguists, but in comparison to its potential very little actual work has been done to date. My own long-term goal is to find an explanation for the still mysterious emergence of the Pitcairn/Norfuk language on Pitcairn Island. In order to do this, it is essential to have a thorough knowledge of the sociohistorical factors that have driven this process and to employ up-to-date linguistic methods. Past researchers have concentrated on the question of English dialect influence and on the operations of a biological blueprint of creole features (Bickerton 1981). Neither the Tahitian influence nor borrowing from St. Kitts Creole has been given much attention. A main obstacle is the patchy nature of past records and the continuing variability in the language.

Part of the process of making Norfuk a language of education is the provision of teaching materials. An exhaustive dictionary of Norfuk has been prepared at the University of Adelaide (Eira, Magdalena and Mühlhäusler 2002). An outstanding problem is the question of the orthography for the language. The community remains divided as to whether to accept Buffett's proposal (1995, 1999), Nobbs Palmer's orthography (1992), or to develop another system. Because of the potential for conflict, I have judged it as opportune not to get involved in the discussions. Orthographic systems are usually determined by a large number of sociopolitical factors rather than linguistic considerations.

5.   Conclusions

Reducing an unfocussed unwritten language such as Norfuk to a linguistic grammar is not an easy task and potentially a very dangerous one for the small community that speaks it. Language written down can exercise normative pressure and restrict the healthy heterogeneity of language and use of language on Norfolk Island. Once standardized the language will be of far less interest to the linguistic profession and to its speakers. As things stand there is still a great deal of work, not just in the description of this language but also in comparing it to other English Polynesian contact varieties such as Palmerston English, Bonin English or Hawaiian Pidgin.

Exercises and study questions

1. What do words of Tahitian origin indicate about the relationship between different racial groups on Pitcairn Island?

2. Why would the spatial deixis of English be supplemented with an absolute reference system on Pitcairn and Norfolk?

3. Do varieties of English that develop on small islands share properties not encountered in other varieties?

4. What are the arguments for and against developing a standard variety of Norfuk?

5. What grammatical properties are shared by Norfuk and West Indian creoles?

6. How easy is it to trace features of Norfuk to British dialects of English?

7. The central question to decide is what relationship does Norfolk bear to contemporary English. Is it just another regional dialect of English?
   To help answer this question we need to make a number of critical observations or comparisons of the vocabulary and the grammar of the respective languages or dialects.

8. Where do the differences between Norfuk and English lie, predominantly in the syntax (grammar) or the vocabulary? On the basis of what you know about creoles, is this what you would expect to be the case for Norfuk?

9. Find the Norfuk equivalents for the following English words and in the remaining space make any observations you can about the origins of the Norfuk form (consulting a historical dictionary like the *Oxford English Dictionary* may help):

– *old timer*	– *premasticate (chew up)*
– *banana*	– *apparition*
– *octupus*	– *tonight*

10. Find Norfuk equivalents for the following expressions:

– *wait a minute*	– *came over me*
– *its no good*	– *my hair stood up*
– *for the reason that (that's why)*	– *go (off) to*
– *stuck fast*	

Selected references

Please consult the General references for titles mentioned in the text but not included in the references below. For a full bibliography see the accompanying CD-ROM.

Buffett, Alice I.
    1995   The writing of Norfolk. In: Tom Dutton, Malcolm Ross and Darrell Tryon (eds.), *The Language Game*, 75–80 [Series C–110]. Canberra: Pacific Linguistics, Australian National University.
    1999   *Speak Norfolk Today. An Encyclopedia of the Norfolk Island Language.* Norfolk Island: Himii Publishing Company.
Christian, Ena Ette
    1986   *From Myse Randa.* Norfolk Island: Photopress International.
Eira, Christine, Melina Magdalena and Peter Mühlhäusler
    2002   *A Draft Dictionary of the Norfolk Language.* Adelaide: Discipline of Linguistics.
Flint, Elwyn
    1961   Bilingual interaction between Norfolk Island Language and English. Paper presented to the first conference of the Linguistic Circle of Canberra.
Gleißner, Andrea
    1997   The dialect of Norfolk Island. M.A. thesis, Department of English and American Studies, University of Regensburg.

Harrison, Shirley
  1972   The languages of Norfolk Island. M.A. thesis, Macquarie University, North Ryde.
Kortmann, Bernd
  2004   *Do* as a tense and aspect marker in varieties of English. In: Kortmann (ed.), 245–275.
Marrington, Pauline
  1981   *In the Sweet Bye and Bye.* Sydney: Reed.
Mühlhäusler, Peter
  1981   The development of the category of number in Tok Pisin. In: Pieter Muysken (ed.), *Generative Studies on Creole Languages*, 35–84. Dordrecht: Foris.
  1996   Linguistic adaptation to changed environmental conditions: some lessons from the past. In: Alwin Fill (ed.), *Sprachökologie und Ökolinguistik*, 105–130. Tübingen: Stauffenburg.
  2002a   Pidgin English and the Melanesian Mission. *Journal of Pidgin and Creole Languages* 17: 237–263.
  2002b   A language plan for Norfolk Island. In: David Bradley and Maya Bradley (eds.), *Language Endangerment and Language Maintenance*, 167–181. London: RoutledgeCurzon.
  2003   A note on reduplication in Pitkern-Norfolk. In: Silvia Kouwenberg (ed.), *Twice as Meaningful: Morphological Reduplication in Contact Languages*, 239–243. London: Battlebridge.
Palmer, Beryl Nobbs
  1992[2]   *A Dictionary of Norfolk Words and Usages.* Norfolk Island: Photopress International.

Synopsis: morphological and syntactic variation in the Pacific and Australasia

Kate Burridge

To write a grammar of a language in one chapter is like attempting to carry away the sea in a bucket. It is an impossible task [Loreto Todd 1984: 208]

1. Introduction

If Loreto Todd is correct – writing a grammar of a language is something like trying to secure the sea in a bucket – then what we are attempting in this brief synopsis chapter must be akin to capturing numerous seas in one very small teacup. And yet, to follow on from Todd's analogy, the contents of either buckets or teacups will actually reveal quite a lot about sea-water. Of course, we cannot convey anywhere near the grammatical richness of these languages, but what we expose here are those morphosyntactic features that are most striking for this part of the world. Accordingly, we have divided the discussion into two sections. The first includes native Englishes (Australian and New Zealand English), the second contact Englishes (Kriol, Torres Strait Creole, Bislama, Tok Pisin, Solomon Islands Pijin, Hawai'i Creole, Fiji English and Norfuk), even though the grouping of individual of these varieties is subject to debate (e.g. Aboriginal English as a native variety or Norfuk as a contact variety).

The following brief descriptions highlight the constant problem of identifying shared grammatical features that are the result of contact influences and those that represent parallel but independent developments. For example, Fiji English speakers employ *one* as an indefinite article. The grammaticalisation of numerals into articles is commonplace and not surprisingly a widespread feature among creoles. Furthermore, both Fijian and Hindi (the mother tongues of many Fiji English speakers) use the numeral 'one' in this way; so the chance of contact-induced change is also high. The seeds for the change might even have been sown earlier on. Fiji English has historical links with the other Pacific creoles and these links are still evident in lexical and grammatical relics left by Melanesian Pidgin. Perhaps all we can say in such cases is that contact accelerates changes that are, in a sense, in-grained.

2.   The grammatical features of Australian and New Zealand English

This section focuses on those features that are genuinely Antipodean English and also those that are used either more or less frequently in these as opposed to other varieties, especially the two Northern Hemisphere standards. Also included here are some of the non-standard features of the vernaculars of this region. Note, that in the case of Aboriginal English, creole influence can be strong and accordingly this variety has many features typical of the contact varieties we go on to describe in more detail in section 2. Throughout the following sections the number code of those morphosyntactic features will be given in square brackets which are part of the 76-features catalogue investigated in the Global Synopsis (Kortmann and Szmrecsanyi, 2004).

2.1   Pronouns

2.1.1   Gender and number

The vernacular varieties of Antipodean English have the usual second person plural pronoun forms [3] that have become ubiquitous in the English-speaking world; namely, *yous* and *you guys*, as in *Yous'd worked on it*. But the indigenous populations of New Zealand and Australia have contributed significantly to diversity here. Some Maori speakers, for example, show a three-way distinction in second person forms: *you* (singular), *yous* (dual) and *yous fullas* (plural). Aboriginal English has gone even further in the transfer of creole pronominal features into their speech. These include distinct forms for dual (second person *you two, you-n-him*; third person *dattufela ~ distufela*); inclusive and exclusive forms for first person plural (*we ~ afla* versus *mifela*) and 2nd person plural forms (including *youse, you mob, youfla*). In addition, Aboriginal English does not always maintain the gender distinctions of the standard. The pronoun *(h)e* tends to be used as a general third person singular [8], as in *That he dress* 'That's her dress', *this old woman he started packing up.*

A striking characteristic of Australian Vernacular English (most notably that spoken in Tasmania) is the appearance of gender marking for both animate and inanimate nouns. Items of food and drink, for instance, are always feminine [7]: *I put 'er* [= the bottle of beer] *down that bloody quick that I blew the top off 'er. And* [he] *took 'er* [= leg of lamb] *in and put 'er on the plate!*

2.1.2   Case selection

As in other places, all varieties here show the declining use of *whom* in favour of *who*. *Whom* is now virtually confined to relative clauses, and in positions following prepositions. It is stylistically highly marked and considered very formal usage. Also not surprising is the preference for the oblique case over the nominative for pronouns following *than* [13] (as in *He's bigger than me*). Both these features illustrate the general trend in English towards case selection dictated by position rather than function – the nominative is largely confined to clause-initial preverbal position; accusative appears elsewhere. Preference for the accusative also extends to pronouns preceding the gerund participle, as in *He was angry at me scoring a goal.*

The features just described are commonplace for standard speakers of NZE and AusE. In addition to these, there are the non-standard pronominal forms typical of the vernacular varieties in these two countries. Once again, features like those below reveal the general preference for accusative personal pronouns:

– *them* in place of demonstrative *those*, as in *one of them things* [1]
– *me* in place of possessive *my*, as in *He's me youngest* [2]
– object forms in reflexive pronouns, as in *I thought to meself* [5]
– object forms in coordinated pronouns, as in *Me and Fred / Fred and me are coming too*; *Me and her were the last to go* [10]

Variation is rife within the last mentioned feature, the coordinated pronouns. There are at least two other patterns in evidence: (1) the 'standard', where function dictates the form of the coordinated pronoun (*Fred and I were the last ones left*; *He gave it to Fred and me*); (2) the so-called 'hypercorrect' pattern with extended uses of the nominative (*He gave it to Fred and I*). There are also hybrid structures such as *Her and I are coming too.*

Another feature of vernacular AusE (AusVE) is the use of the 1st person plural accusative pronoun *us* in place of the 1st person singular accusative pronoun *me* [11], especially after verbs of giving and receiving; for example, *Give us a light for me pipe.*

Aboriginal English shows a mixture of standard possessive pronouns and very distinctive forms such as *moofla* 'my'. In addition, oblique personal pronouns can function generally as possessive pronouns; for example *im dog* 'his dog'. Interestingly, as is typical for non-standard L1 varieties in all parts of the English-speaking world, reflexives typically generalise possessive rather than object pronoun forms, as in *hisself* and *theirself / theirselves*.

2.2   Nouns and noun phrases

2.2.1   *Nominal morphology*

Descriptions provided by the authors in this volume suggest that the Antipodean varieties are lagging behind in the general trend towards greater use of the inflected genitive. Aboriginal English stands out by not marking possession at all on the noun – juxtaposition is sufficient (*That my Daddy car*). Moreover, speakers of 'heavy' varieties have incorporated creole possessive markers such as *belong* and *for* (see section 3.2.1).

Aboriginal English tends not to mark the noun consistently for number. The plural inflection is often absent when plurality is obvious [14], either from context or via some other means; for example, *Two man in a jeep* 'There are two men in a jeep'. Where plural does occur, it is not uncommon for irregular nouns to be doubly marked, as in *childrens*. Occasionally the creole plural marker *-mob* is used; for example, *clean water-mob* 'lots of clean water'.

English dialects do not necessarily see eye to eye as to whether nouns are individuated entities or groups of unindividuated entities. In short, what is a count noun in one variety may be a mass noun in another and vice versa; for example, Aboriginal English *woods* 'bits of wood', *dusts* 'clouds of dust', *glasses* 'bits of glass'.

2.2.2   *Articles*

Aboriginal English commonly shows articles missing where they are required in the standard [17], as in *We was playing game*. Also widespread is the tendency (attested in creoles) to substitute demonstratives for definite articles (*That door bin close* 'The door closed') and the numeral *one* for the indefinite article (*They seen one green snake tangled round a tree* 'They saw a green snake tangled round a tree').

A feature of AusVE is the use of the adjective *old ~ ol'* before definite common nouns and personal names to refer to characters that are particularly salient in a narrative. For example, *And on the corner was this ol' mountain duck with some little fellas, y'know'*.

2.2.3   *Adjectives*

Doubly marked comparatives and superlatives [19] are commonplace in the vernacular varieties of this region; for example, *most rottenest*. In Aboriginal English adjectives may also go unmarked for degree. Note that when the superlative is used in this variety, it is typically for the purpose of emphasis, as in *biggest mob o emus* 'a very bit flock of emus'.

2.3   Verbs and verb phrases

2.3.1   *Tense, aspect, mood*

Both AusE and NZE are showing the extended uses of the progressive [21] that have been reported for other varieties (for example, in combination with stative verbs such as *hear* and *think*). However, corpus evidence also suggests that the use of the progressive may well be more frequent here than elsewhere.

Both varieties share with many others the generalisation of the present perfect to simple past contexts of use [25], AusE more markedly so. For example, both show the present perfect used with past time adverbials (*Then she's broken her leg*). In AusVE and NZE the perfect auxiliary *have* is frequently dropped [58]; for example, *We haven't started this year but we done it before.* In Aboriginal English auxiliary deletion is more widespread and includes *be*-deletion [57] in the progressive construction, as in *I sitting down*. Note that this variety can also omit copula *be* (e.g. *That a pretty snake* or *He blind*). If past time is relevant, *bin* can be used, as in *I bin young fella den* 'I was a young chap then'.

The use of the subjunctive after expressions of recommendation, demand, and intention (the so-called 'mandative subjunctive' as in *I insist that he be on time*) is enjoying the same revival that is evident in AmE and BrE usage. Papers in this Handbook suggest that Antipodean usage is not yet as advanced as in AmE and falls somewhere between the Northern Hemisphere varieties.

2.3.2   *Modals*

AusE and NZE show an increasing use of *of* in place of *have* after (preterite) modal verb forms *could, should* and *would*, as in *I would of waited*. Undoubtedly this is due to the equivalent pronunciation of the reduced forms of both *of* and *have* (*-ve*), perhaps also reinforced by hedging phrases such as *kind of* and *sort of*, which also convey unreality.

Shall/Will

In Antipodean usage the modal *shall* is very much in decline. Only vestiges of *shall* usage remain as more and more modal *will* encroaches on its territory. This includes first person interrogatives, such as *Will I sit in the back?*.

May/Might

NZE and AusE follow the world-wide trend for *may* and *might* to be unmarked for tense. Both appear in similar contexts to indicate past possibility and hypothetical possibility, although for some speakers *might* is marginally more tentative; for example, they report less certainty in *I think he might come* than *I think he may come*. Tentativeness is also apparent in contexts of permission. A polite request like *Might I have another piece of cake* is very indirect. However, both *may* and *might* in the permitting sense is extremely formal and is now rare in these varieties.

Must

Both NZE and AusE show an increasing use of epistemic *mustn't* [35], as in *he mustn't have arrived yet* meaning 'he can't have arrived yet'.

Have (to), Need (to), Dare (to), Ought (to)

Both varieties mirror trends reported elsewhere for these marginal (or quasi-) modals. They share with American usage a preference for *do*-support for the first three verbs (rather than the auxiliary variant without *do*); for example *He doesn't need to get a haircut* over *He needn't get a haircut* (where *need* lacks the 3rd person present singular ending and has a following infinitive without *to*). Blended constructions based on both the auxiliary and full verb pattern also exist, especially for *dare*; for example, *I didn't dare eat a peach* (showing *do*-support and *to*-deletion). Both varieties show the same declining use of *ought* in favour of *should* that occurs in other varieties.

Better/Gotta

The tendency for vernacular varieties to omit the auxiliary *have* has meant that both *better* and *gotta* are now showing modal-like behaviour, as in *we better go* and *you gotta do it*. This usage is considered very colloquial and is rarely encountered in the written language.

2.3.3   Voice

Trends in both varieties strongly suggest a growing use of the *get*-passive in writing and in speech. It is still considered to be more informal than the *be* version. In Aboriginal English the passive is rare, but when it does occur it is typically with the *get* auxiliary (*Uncle Steve, he got hit*) or without any auxiliary verb altogether (*Most books made of paper*).

2.3.4 Morphology

AusE and NZE speakers are continuing the on-going regularisation process that has been affecting strong verbs since Old English times. This levelling is particularly evident in the shift of strong verbs over to the weak [36]; for example, *show-showed-showed*. Also clearly in evidence is the collapse of the preterite and past participle forms within the diminishing class of strong verbs; in particular, the past forms such as *came, did* and *saw* are being replaced by participle forms *come, done* and *seen* [39]. For example, *Me Mum seen it*. There are also examples of verbs where the past form replaces the participle form; for example, *He's bit me* and *Someone might 'a took 'em* [38].

Vernacular varieties of NZE and AusE show invariant past tense forms for the verb *be*. *Was* is used for all persons and for both singular and plural subjects, as in *You was late again, We was winning* and *'Course they was*. The use of invariant *is* (*Things is going crook*) appears to be in decline. Singular marking in existentials with plural subjects [55] is also widespread. It now appears in writing, especially in the contracted form *there's*; for example, *There's fairies at the bottom of my garden*. In Aboriginal English existential constructions are either verbless (as in *Some sand there*) or *got* is used in construction with *e* (*E got some sand there* 'There is some sand').

This regularisation of verb morphology is generally more extensive in Aboriginal English, both urban and rural. The unmarked verb is frequently used for copula and auxiliary *be*, as in *I be cold* 'I am cold'. Zero marking for third person is also usual for verbs in the present tense [53]; for example *he get wild* 'he gets/got wild'. As this gloss illustrates, the verb can also be unmarked for past tense [40], especially if past time is clear from the context; for example *he hook him* 'he hooked him'. In narratives past tense is often indicated early and the verbs that follow are then unmarked.

Where past tense marking does occur, Aboriginal English shows the same levelling of preterite and past participle verb forms for strong verbs [36] (for example, *seen, done, come, run* to express past tense). There are also some irregular strong verb forms such as *brang* and *brung*. In English generally these monosyllabic strong verbs ending in nasals more successfully resist regularisation. They also acquire new members. Frequent in rural Australia, for instance, is the past tense form *skun* in the context of skinning a rabbit. Occasionally doubly marked past tense forms occur; for example, *camed* and *didn't stayed*. There is also evidence of the creole past tense marker *bin*, sometimes *been* [29] (see section 3.3.2). Note, that varieties of Aboriginal English spoken in remote communities also demonstrate use of the transitive verb suffix *-em* or *-im*. This is essentially a creole feature and we go on to discuss it below (section 3.3.1).

Both AusE and NZE show an increasing use of *gotten*, especially in spoken language. The resurgence of this form in these Southern Hemisphere varieties is often attributed to American English influence. But since there have always been pockets of dialectal *gotten* users downunder (Scottish immigrants, for example), its expansion may well be due to colonial lag, accelerated by AmE influence. This is also suggested by the different patterns of use. In AusE, for example, the *gotten* form is preferred for intransitive constructions and *got* for transitive constructions; for example *She's gotten really angry* versus *She's got a new car.* Moreover, the American pattern where the *got-gotten* distinction indicates something possessed versus something acquired is not apparent in these varieties.

2.4   Adverbs

It is commonplace for speakers to use adverbs (including intensifiers) without the *-ly* suffix [42] that is required of the standard language. For example, *You can easy do it.* Some varieties of Aboriginal English also have an array of adverb-forming suffixes that do not appear elsewhere; for example, *long-way, quick-way, dark-time, late-time.*

2.5   Prepositions

Vernaculars in this part of the world occasionally omit prepositions where they are required in the standard, as in (Southland, New Zealand) *He came out hospital.* This feature is most striking in Aboriginal English; for example, *Afela going Back Beach* 'We're going to Back Beach'. Extreme varieties that lie close to the creole end of the continuum may replace locative prepositions with *la* or *longa*, as in *We always go la ol' town* 'We always go to the old town'.

2.6   Negation

Well attested in vernacular speech is *don't* [48] in place of standard *doesn't* ('*E don't run away with it, y'see*), as well as the all-purpose negative auxiliary *aint* for the verb forms of *be* [45] and *have* [46]. Double negation [44] is also commonplace. Usually this involves indeterminates inside the clause; for example, *I never said nothing for a while.* Widespread, too, is the use of *never* [49] as a general negator in place of auxiliary plus *not* (for example, *You never opened it* [= 'You didn't open it']). Aboriginal English has additional possibilities; for example, *not* and *no more*, as in *Nail not float* 'The nail doesn't float'.

An additional feature that has been reported from Southland, New Zealand (probably originating in the distinctive Scottish English of that area) is a stranded *not* in questions, as in *Did you not say that?*.

2.7 Interrogatives

In these varieties, as elsewhere, it is possible to pose a *yes-no* question simply by rising intonation [74]. The following example has the structure of an ordinary declarative and is distinguished only by intonation: *So, you want to become a benthic geologist?* Increasingly in evidence is also the invariant negative tag *isn't it* [52], as in *You're going home soon, isn't it?*. Both these examples come from speakers of Standard AusE. Aboriginal English has an even more elaborate array of simplified tags, including *init, ini, ana* and *na*. These take the place of standard tags like *weren't they, didn't he*. A type of tag that Aboriginal English shares with many vernaculars is *eh*, as in *He can walk, eh?*

2.8 Composite sentences

In Aboriginal English discourse, long loosely connected structures are the norm and there is little in the way of subordination. This is the characteristically paratactic structure of spoken discourse, although it appears to be more extensive in this variety. Clause markers are often absent, as in *I bin go dere work* (with a missing complementiser). This variety also has a type of verb chaining construction where two main verbs are linked (with or without a conjunction) to express both an activity and a motion that is closely associated with that activity, as in *they go there chargin on don't they* and *Nother mob go down long creek and go and drink water.*

Relative clauses with zero marking for subjects [66] is widespread in the different vernacular varieties of this region. For example, *I knew a girl worked in an office down the street.* If relative markers are used in Aboriginal English, the relative particle *what* [61] often substitutes for *that*, as in *I got one mate what goes to a Catholic school.* In AusVE non-standard possessive relative pronouns such as *that its, thats* and *what's* [65] occasionally appear in place of standard *whose* (especially when the antecedent is inanimate).

Also widespread are the 'linking' relative clauses typical of spoken English elsewhere. These differ from standard relatives by having no antecedent (they elaborate on a stretch of discourse, often reiterating earlier information) and no missing argument in the relative clause (*which* has no grammatical function and can be replaced by a coordinating conjunction such as *and*). The following example comes from spoken AusE: *[...] unless you get 88 which some universities are not going to give those marks.*

The Southland variety of NZE is reported to have an unusual feature for this region; namely, past participles following the verbs *need* and *want*, as in *that shirt wants washed.* It is likely that this has originated from the Scottish English of the settlers in that area.

2.9   Word order

Commonly reported for Aboriginal English is expressive word order. Particularly striking is the repetition of phrases and sentences, as well as highly topic-oriented structures such as left-dislocation (*The policeman he heard this banging*) and right-dislocation (*E got lots of trucks an cars, toy one*). While these constructions are typical of spontaneous spoken language generally, it is the relative frequency and the special combination of these features that make this variety different from others.

2.10   Hypocoristics

A distinguishing characteristic of Antipodean English, especially AusE, is the rich system of nominal derivation that produces forms like *breaky* (< *breakfast*) and *rellie* or *rello* (< *relative*) and *arvo* (< *afternoon*), or what are called *hypocoristics*. Speakers shorten words and add a suffix, either -*i* or -*o*. These endings are far more extensive than the diminutive endings on pet names like *Robbo* and *Susy*. They also have very different functions.

3.   The grammatical features of the contact varieties

The following represents the most significant morphosyntactic features of the contact varieties of this region: Bislama, Pijin, Tok Pisin (varieties of Melanesian Pidgin), Hawai'i Creole, Fiji English (creole-like, but not technically a creole), Norfolk Island/Pitcairn English (typologically closer to Atlantic creoles), and the two Australian creoles Kriol and Torres Strait Creole. These languages show remarkable regional and idiolectal diversity, much of which derives from the fact they are not developing in isolation. Not only are there varying degrees of contact with local languages, many speakers know English and switch regularly between this and their creole. Readers are also reminded of the existence of the creole continuum. Languages range from the so-called 'light' varieties closest to Standard English (the 'acrolects') to the 'heavy' varieties (the 'basilects') furthest from English. We will focus the discussion on the basilectal end of the continuum, since this is where the most distinctive grammatical features are to be found.

3.1 Pronouns

The pronominal paradigms of these creoles are at the same time more simple and more complex than that of the standard. While forms are not generally distinguished for case or for gender (for example, Bislama 3rd person singular *hem* is gender neutral), the systems allow for a much more elaborate set of distinctions involving, for example, dual and perhaps even trial. Hence the two-way number system of English may expand into a four-way system – singular, dual, trial and plural. 1st person non-singular forms also distinguish between inclusive and exclusive, such as Australian creole forms *yumi* ('1st dual, including you'), *yumpla* (1st plural, including you) versus exclusive *mitu* (1st dual, excluding you), *mipla* (1st plural, excluding you). These categorial distinctions have clearly arisen from the substrate languages.

Fiji English shares many of its pronouns with the standard, but shows some of the features just mentioned. For example, the basilectal variety often lacks a gender distinction for 3rd person singular, although it can distinguish human referents (*fella*) from non-human referents (*thing*). Moreover, it has a 1st person dual inclusive pronoun *us-two*, as well as a 1st person plural (more than two) exclusive pronoun *us-gang* (*gang* is on its way to becoming a general plural marker for pronouns). Hawai'i Creole also indicates plural by adding *gaiz*. Like the standard, it has distinct subject and object forms, but there are some interesting differences, most notably, object pronouns can appear in subject position [13] (*her sik* 'she's sick').

3.2 Nouns and noun phrases

3.2.1 *Morphology*

Contact situations are generally calamitous for inflectional morphology – we need only look at English to see this. Contact with French and Norse speakers had the effect of bringing about a speedier end to inflections already undermined by normal phonological processes. Not surprisingly, then, all these contact varieties display limited morphology for both nouns and verbs.

Number tends to be implicit in the context and if it is indicated at all, it is generally not on the noun but via some kind of freestanding quantifier, such as Melanesian Pidgin *olgeta ~ ol* 'all'.

Possessive constructions generally show the possessor following the thing possessed, connected with a freestanding marker such as *blong/blo* or *fe*. For example, Australian creole *Dog blong / blo maan* 'the man's dog' and Norfuk *aa kau fe mais bradhas* 'that cow of my brother'. These speakers also use constructions that are closer to standard English. In the case of Australian creoles, examples like the following are typical of more formal social situations: *Maan dog* and *Maanz dog*.

3.2.2   Determiners

Standard English nouns are either definite or indefinite (*the emu* versus *an emu*). This is not the case for many creoles, however. For example, in Australian creoles *iymu* can mean 'the emu', 'an emu' (and also 'the emus' or 'some emus'). However, if speakers want to include this information they can draw from elsewhere, such as the system of demonstratives and numerals: *dem iymu* 'the emus', *wan iymu* 'an emu', *plenti iymu* 'some emus'. This is an area of rapid change in these varieties and many of the forms are well on their way to grammaticalising into determiners. In Pijin, for example, the quantifier *wan-fala* 'one' is currently being reanalysed as an indefinite singular article and the demonstrative pronoun *ia* (from English *here*) as a definite article.

3.2.3   Adjectives

In these varieties the class of true adjectives is small. Indeed, given the overall paucity of inflectional morphology and the fact that adjectives often reduplicate according to the same patterns as verbs (see section 3.3.1), it is sometimes difficult to make a clear distinction between these two word classes. (Note, reduplication in adjectives usually has some kind of intensifying quality, as in Bislama *fas* 'stuck' versus *fasfas* 'well and truly stuck'.)

Generally adjectives will appear before the noun and often with a derivational suffix such as Tok Pisin *-pela* (or *-pla)* and Pijin *-fala* (from English *fellow*); for example *dispela tupela naispela liklik pik* 'these two nice little pigs'. A handful of (usually intensifying) adjectives follow, as in *tok nogut* 'bad language'. Nominal modifiers also typically follow, as in *bikpela sospen ain* 'a big iron saucepan'. Australian creoles, especially those in rural areas of Western Australia, show an interesting feature with respect to the positioning of adjectival modifiers. If there are several, one usually precedes the noun. The others follow and a pronoun form *one* may be added, as in *we get five sheeps fat one*.

3.3 Verbs and verb phrases

3.3.1 Verb morphology

The creoles are creating new inflectional morphology all the time. Rather than representing the continuation of superstrate morphological patterns, however, these developments usually involve the reanalysis of what were originally English lexical forms. For example, many of the creoles in this area add some kind of suffix (-V*m*) to the end of (most) transitive verbs, as in Pijin *huk* 'to hook' versus *hukum* 'to hook something'. This represents the reanalysis of the third person singular masculine object pronoun *him*. It has become an extremely productive suffix in these languages and will appear on any new verb borrowed from English; for example, *faksim* 'to fax' and *imelim* 'email (someone)'.

Creole verbs are typically unmarked for tense. Depending on the context, Torres Strait Creole *Mi baiim kaikai* can mean 'I buy some food', 'I bought some food' or 'I will buy some food'. If required, speakers can add extra auxiliary verbs or sentence modifiers such as *bin* or *go* to indicate either past or future time: *Mi bin baiim kaikai* 'I bought some food' and *Mi go baiim kaikai* 'I will buy some food'.

Reduplication is widespread and a productive feature of verb morphology that is markedly different from other varieties of English. In these creoles it is usually partial reduplication, involving the repetition of the first syllable or first two syllables of the verb root (or material from these syllables). The pattern generally indicates intensity, duration or repetition of an action: Pijin *karae* 'cry' versus *kakarae* 'cry continuously'. There may be other meanings as well, such as reciprocal action: Bislama *save* 'know' versus *savsave* 'know each other'.

3.3.2 Tense, aspect, modality

Temporal, aspectual and modality distinctions are indicated by (usually preverbal) freestanding forms. Tok Pisin, for example, has a number of grammatical markers that it shares with other creoles of this region. These include temporal particles *bai* 'future', *laik* 'proximal future' and *bin* 'past' [29], aspectual particles *klosap* 'inceptive', *pinis* 'perfect', *save* 'habitual' [24] and *stap* 'continuous' and also modality markers *inap* 'ability', *ken* 'permission' and *mas* 'necessity'. It is interesting to note that *bin* as a past tense marker [29] occurs across the board for all the contact varieties described here.

3.3.3   Predicate marking

The various off-springs of Melanesian Pidgin have in common what can be thought of a type of verb phrase marker, namely *i*. It is generally accepted that *i* has its origin in a (third person) resumptive pronoun as part of a left dislocation structure (*That fellow, he's a fool*) and elements of this earlier construction are still apparent. For one, *i* is systematically excluded after first and second person subjects, as evident in Tok Pisin *mi kam, yu kam* 'I come, you come' versus *e i kam* 's/he comes'. However, the grammaticalisation process has already taken it a long way from its original focus construction. This is a hotly debated grammatical feature of these languages and readers are advised to check the details given in the individual chapters of this volume.

3.3.4   Serial verbs

A striking characteristic of all the contact varieties described here is the serial verb construction [72]. Typically this involves a series of verbs with no marker conjoining them. There is a single subject preceding both verbs and a single object following. Moreover, where there is a predicate marker *i*, it only appears once and has scope over the entire verb series. The following is an example from Tok Pisin: *Em i brunim rausim ol pipia* 'S/he swept away the rubbish'. There are other construction types where the verb sequences are less tight, as in this Bislama example: *Kali i sendem buk i kam* 'Kali sent the book hither'. Note, that the Standard English *come see* and *go see* constructions come nowhere near the extensive patterns of verb serialisation that are found in these varieties. This represents a significant typological divergence from English and gains its motivation primarily from the substrate languages. It is also an extremely complex and varied construction and readers are advised to check the individual chapters for precise details, especially with respect to Bislama where it features more extensively.

3.4   Prepositions

The Melanesian Pidgin varieties have a small set of prepositions, as is typical of their Oceanic substrate languages. The forms have a high functional load; for example, Bislama *long/lo* can indicate location (*lo taun* 'to town', *lo Vila* 'in Vila'), source (*lo taun* 'from town'), instrument (*lo naif* 'with (the) knife'). It can also precede patient noun phrases in construction with formally intransitive verbs.

3.5 Negation

These varieties have a range of negators, including *no* [50], *nomo*, *neba* [49]. Overwhelmingly they appear in front of the verb and any tense markers (without *do*-support); for example Torres Strait Creole *Mi no bin baiim kaikai.* 'I didn't buy any food'. Many also have a number of special negative verbs. For instance, Norfuk has *duu* or *dan* to express negative imperatives and also *ent* 'am/is/are not'. Double negation [44] is reported as occurring in Hawai'i Creole, as in *Nomo nating insai dea* 'There isn't anything in there'.

3.6 Interrogatives

These varieties all use rising intonation to form a *yes-no* question [74]. There is also a range of invariant tags, such as *e* or *o(wat)* [52]. For example (Torres Strait Creole): *Yu bin pikimup manggo?* and *Yu bin pikimup manggo, e?* 'Did you pick up the mangoes?'. Open interrogatives also lack inverted word order [73]. Moreover, the forms that correspond to the English '*wh*-words' (for example Melanesian Pidgin *wanem* 'what') do not necessarily move to the front of the sentence, but remain in the structural position of the corresponding declarative. The following example (from Bislama) has the same structure as the Standard English echo question that speakers use when they find a piece of news astonishing: *Yu wokem wanem?* 'You did what?'.

3.7 Composite sentences

The contact varieties discussed here share a characteristically paratactic structure; in other words, clauses are strung together, either without any linking item or joined by some sort of coordinating element (see also section 2.8). When subordinate clauses do occur they are indicated by a range of markers that have grammaticalised from prepositions, such as *for/fo*, *blong/blo* and *long/lo*. For example, in Hawai'i Creole what are *to* infinitives in English are introduced by *for*, as in *I too chicken fo say anyting* 'I was too scared to say anything'. An interesting development is the current reanalysis of the Melanesian Pidgin form *se* [68]. This was originally used to introduce quotative clauses, but is in the process of extending its contexts to include a range of complement clauses beyond locutions, as in the Bislama *mi hop se bai yu kam* 'I hope that you will come'.

The creoles have various ways of forming relative clauses. One is by simple embedding with no overt marking; Tok Pisin *tupla brata mama i bin dai stap wantaim papa* 'the two brothers whose mother had died lived with their father'.

They have also developed a number of optional relative markers (usually from pronouns) such as *husat* and *we*, as in Tok Pisin *em papa bl' em we helpim em* 'It was his father who helped him'. Non-subject noun phrases often leave a pronoun copy that appears in place of the deleted co-referential noun phrase [67]; Tok Pisin *Em putim tupla lo wanpla ples we ol sa putim man longen* 'He put them in a place where they kept people (in it)'.

3.8   Word order

The constituent order of these creoles is basically SVO. Pronominal objects (especially those with inanimate reference) are often omitted, as in Bislama *mi laikem* 'I like (it)'. Similarly, third person singular subjects can also be un-expressed, the only signal being the predicate marker *i*; hence, *em i laikem ~ i laikem* '(S/he) likes (it)'.

The contact varieties of this region typically do not have a passive construc-tion. Speakers can manipulate word order to exploit different sequences of noun phrases for highlighting and contrasting salient information. Speech ex-changes are typically full of highly topic-oriented structures, such as fronting (with or without special focus markers), left- and right-dislocation.

These varieties generally lack a copula corresponding to English *be* [57]. Equational sentences are therefore non-verbal constructions involving the sim-ple juxtaposition of the topic and comment noun or adjective phrase, as in Kri-ol *Olabat bigbala yem* 'They (are) big yams'. Where the topic constituent is a noun phrase there might be an intervening predicate marker, as in Torres Strait Creole *Mislam i boi blo Kemuel* 'Mislam (is) Kemuel's son'. In Hawai'i Creole and Norfuk the presence or absence of a copula-like verb can convey different meanings. For example, the following Hawai'i Creole sentence has no copula before the predicate adjective phrase because it involves a permanent quality: *Da wahine shawt* 'the woman (is) short'. In contrast, the stative verb *stei*, as in *Shi stei sik* 'She is sick', indicates that the quality is short-term.

3.9   Summary

It is not only between the creoles of Melanesian Pidgin origin that grammatical similarities exist. English-based creoles in the Pacific and Australasian regions generally, indeed world-wide, share striking resemblances. Examples of these shared features include the following. (Note, many of them also occur in non-standard varieties of English around the world; for details see the Global Syn-opsis by Kortmann and Szmrecsanyi, 2004).

- fixed basic word order, usually subject-verb
- little in the way of grammatical morphology: plural and possessive noun suffixes typically omitted; no concord between subject and verb in the present tense; past tense expressed with the base form of the verb [40]
- particles often used to indicate plurality
- possession expressed by the juxtaposition of the possessor and possessed noun phrases, or by some particle
- no case distinctions for pronouns
- prepositions frequently omitted
- *he/'e* often used as a general third person singular [8]
- elaborate pronoun systems, distinguishing, for example, dual/plural number and inclusive/exclusive (first person)
- particles used to signal tense and aspect; for example, *been/bin* for past [29], *gon(na)* or *gotta* for future
- serial verb constructions common [72]
- systematic use of reduplication (especially on verbs)
- invariant tag questions like *isn't it, init, ini, ana* and *na* [52]
- main and auxiliary verb *be* often omitted [57]
- frequent use of repetition for rhetorical effect.

When creoles are written down it is tempting to think of them as simplified forms of English. But they are very different varieties with their own distinctive grammars, and when spoken by fluent speakers they are not mutually intelligible with Standard English. Symbolically, too, it is important to emphasize their linguistic distinctiveness. In Australia, for example, the widespread destruction of indigenous languages has meant that varieties like Kriol are now an important part of these speakers' Aboriginality. As languages in their own right, these creoles have become an important means of signalling their speakers' cultural and social identity.

Exercises and study questions

The following exercises are based on the brief descriptions provided in the synopsis chapter. You might also wish to revisit relevant individual chapters (for this region and elsewhere) for more specific details, as well as the other synopses.

1. One far-reaching change that has been happening in English over many years is that position, not function, has been dictating case selection for pronouns. Give at least three examples from both Australian and New Zealand English that illustrate this trend.

2. Identify the most noteworthy grammatical characteristics of Aboriginal English. Focus on those features that could be described as creole-like.

3. The account of verbs and verb phrases given in this synopsis includes a number of shared features between the L1 and contact varieties of this region. Using specific examples, describe these similarities.

4. The term grammaticalization refers basically to the creation of grammar. Linguists studying this process examine the lexical sources that give rise to new grammatical forms and constructions, as well as the events that take place as the items turn into grammar. The varieties described in this synopsis provide clear illustrations of this process. Give at least two examples from both an L1 and contact variety.

5. At the end of the synopsis there is a summary of grammatical similarities between the English-based creoles of this region. Give specific examples of each of the features described here. Which of these have been described for contact varieties elsewhere in the world?

6. The synopsis chapter highlights the difficulty of identifying where shared grammatical features are the result of contact and where they are the result of independent but parallel developments. Drawing from both L1 and contact varieties, describe as many grammatical features as you can that illustrate this difficulty.

7. Describe the features of word order and composite sentences that are characteristic of the contact varieties of this region. In what way are they reminiscent of spontaneous spoken English?

8. Outline some of the features that have been identified in non-standard Englishes elsewhere in the world. Some of these are strongly suggestive of general tendencies, or "drifts", in the grammar of English. One of these has already been described in question (1). What additional drifts can you discover on the basis of these shared features?

Reference

Todd, Loreto
 1984   *Modern Englishes: Pidgins and Creoles.* Oxford: Basil Blackwell.

Index of subjects

A

accent (for specific accents see also *Index of varieties and languages*) 2–3, 24–25, 31, 52, 64–65, 68, 71, 78, 109, 175, 201, 218, 277, 283, 288–289, 292, 302, 305, 326, 335, 555
accommodation 548
acoustic 42, 45, 50, 79, 82, 90–93, 97, 105, 108, 161, 258, 277, 281
acquisition 156, 193
acrolect 3, 31, 138, 217, 224, 236, 267, 270, 273, 292, 364, 421, 438, 468, 514, 521, 532, 568–569, 574–578
acronym 400–401, 405, 572
adjective 214, 259–260, 308, 315, 328, 333–334, 363–364, 367, 403–406, 410, 417, 419–420, 424, 429, 432, 434, 438, 446–449, 468, 471–472, 475, 490, 503, 508, 521, 525–527, 530, 538, 549, 553–554, 570, 574, 576, 586, 594, 598
  adjective-adverb merger 363
  comparative (see *comparison*)
  demonstrative (see also *demonstrative* and *pronoun, demonstrative*)
  superlative (see *comparison*)
adolescent speech (see *youth language*)
adposition
  postposition 481
  preposition 176, 229, 264, 325, 327, 335, 352, 354, 356, 363, 393–394, 419, 424, 434, 438, 446, 450, 456–459, 462–464, 467–468, 472, 474–475, 478–479, 482, 502, 506, 510, 566, 569, 577, 585, 590, 596–597, 599
adverb 264, 363, 367, 417, 419, 424, 430, 438, 479–481, 494, 501, 506, 508, 517, 528, 536, 557, 566, 590

adverbial clause (see *subordination*)
adverbials 313, 346, 499, 557–560, 573, 587
affix 131, 299, 418, 471, 488, 497, 515, 570,
  prefix 111, 146, 183, 352, 402, 470, 501
  suffix 131, 159, 162, 182–183, 186, 192, 204, 206, 259–261, 273, 299, 308, 342, 398–399, 403–404, 408, 412–413, 417, 419, 423–424, 426, 430, 432–434, 444–452, 461, 467–472, 474–478, 482, 488–492, 494, 499, 510–511, 515, 520–521, 546, 548–550, 555, 570, 573, 586, 589–590, 592, 594–595, 599
affixation 493
affricate 45, 57, 70, 74, 81, 129–130, 134, 152, 170–171, 173, 181, 195, 227, 240, 297, 300
affrication 27, 32, 53, 73–74, 81, 296
agreement 5, 312, 323, 334, 381, 383, 416, 427, 476, 494, 515, 559, 572
  agreement marker 515
  invariant form(s) 154, 549
  subject-verb agreement 362, 381, 416, 427, 559
ain't (see *negation*)
aktionsart [situation type] 525
  durative 417, 476, 500, 520
  dynamic (see *verb*)
  stative (see *verb*)
  subordinating (see *subordination*)
allophone 45, 47, 55–56, 59
alveolar 40, 45, 53, 73, 78, 81, 129, 134, 152, 156, 170–171, 173, 200, 296–297, 301
  post- 45

animate 34, 311, 356, 367–368, 370, 374–376, 379–380, 394–395, 455, 505, 584
animation (see *pronouns, gendered*)
anterior (see *tense*)
aphesis 131, 136
apical 106, 181
apocope 131, 136, 177
apposition 327
approximant 45, 252, 261
article 229, 264, 392, 419–420, 431, 470, 503, 537, 546, 583, 586, 594
  definite 147, 431, 437, 470, 503, 565, 577, 586, 594
  indefinite 211, 420, 431, 437, 551, 583, 586
aspect 5, 202, 229, 264, 312–313, 346, 417, 427, 429, 467–479, 480–481, 495, 497–499, 500–502, 514–515, 520–521, 524–531, 557, 562, 566, 570, 572–573, 587, 595, 599
  completive 417, 427, 437, 453, 499, 509–510, 520–521
    done 330–331, 385–386, 428, 573, 587, 589
    pinis 173, 200, 417, 427, 499, 509–510, 595
  continuous (see *aspect, progressive*)
  habitual 202, 417, 437, 451, 453, 458, 482, 499–500, 515–516, 520, 534, 558, 573, 595
  invariant *be* 428, 589
  iterative 417, 426, 497
  perfective 214, 313, 429, 454, 481, 520, 522, 574
  present perfect (see *present perfect*)
  progressive [continuous] 214, 271, 314–315, 346, 357, 416–417, 429, 437, 453, 500, 515, 520–521, 524, 570, 573, 587
aspiration 53, 77, 81, 229, 251, 296, 300
assimilation 54, 59, 158, 260, 296
auxiliary 214, 264, 315, 318–321, 330, 347, 351, 363–364, 367, 386–391, 418, 428–430, 435, 438, 444, 479, 522, 524, 557, 566, 573, 587–590, 595, 599
  absence 444, 574, 598
  contraction 136, 321–322, 335
  deletion 322, 330, 557, 587, 428–429
  modal (see *modal verb*)
  semi-auxiliary 317

B

back vowel (see *vowel*)
backing 4, 179–180
basilect 31, 217–218, 226, 236, 292, 364, 514
BATH 33, 41, 49, 51–52, 67, 80, 85, 94, 111, 128, 132, 222, 224, 244, 246, 255, 257, 294
be
  invariant (see *aspect*)
been/bin
  anterior (see *tense*)
bidialectal 438
bilabial (see also *labial*) 45, 53, 129, 134
bilingualism 29, 33, 194, 198, 218, 230, 488
borrowing 27, 144, 167, 192, 282–283, 570, 579
burr 24, 66

C

Case
  accusative 354–355, 357, 359, 367, 388, 585
  genitive (see *case, possessive*)
  nominative 354, 359, 388, 585
  oblique 463, 585
  possessive 202, 204, 311–312, 354–355, 359, 367, 423, 431–433, 444, 446, 458, 467, 485, 583, 539, 569, 577–578, 585–586, 591, 594
  case selection 341, 354, 359, 585, 599
  subjective (see *case, nominative*)
centering diphthong (see *diphthong*)
central vowel (see *vowel*)

centralization 114, 117–118
CHOICE 41, 51, 92, 95, 97, 128, 132, 222, 224, 242, 245–246, 256–257, 265
clause 103, 184, 214, 298, 315, 325, 354, 356, 363, 387, 390, 417, 426, 429–430, 435–436, 455–456, 460–464, 467–469, 483–484, 505–506, 533–534, 559, 561, 576, 590–591, 597
  adverbial (see *subordination*)
  conditional (see *subordination*)
  embedded (see *subordination*)
  main [matrix] 390
  relative (see *subordination*)
  subordinate 360, 363–364, 597
clear /l/ (see /l/)
cleft 508, 542
clipping 398
cliticization 202, 424, 438, 497, 502, 538
closing (see *diphthong*)
CLOTH 91, 93–94, 116–117, 128, 132, 222, 224, 242, 245–246, 254, 257
coda 42–44, 48, 55, 87, 106–107, 183, 226, 297, 380
  cluster 106–107
colloquial variety (see *variety*)
colonial innovation 313
colonial lag 308, 312, 345, 348, 590
commA 44, 47, 61, 93, 128, 132, 222–224, 246–247, 256–258, 295
comparison 271, 352
  comparative (construction) 352, 392, 459, 554, 586
  double comparative 333
  superlative 434, 554, 586
competition 269, 407
complement clause (see *subordination*)
complementizer (see *subordination, complement clause*)
completive (see *aspect*)
completive done (see *aspect*)
compound 147, 402, 446, 460, 473, 478, 493, 570–571
concord 323–325, 332, 334, 337, 387, 416, 436, 599
  negative (see *negation, multiple*)

conditional clause (see *subordination, adverbial clause*)
conditioning 107, 118, 284, 330, 570
consonant
  cluster 130–131, 136, 158–159, 174–177, 183, 203–206, 241, 252–253, 259, 296, 299, 301, 451, 477
  deletion/reduction/simplification/dissolution etc. 110, 158, 176–178, 259, 263 (see also *coda cluster*)
  devoicing (see *devoicing*)
  final 117, 178, 228, 231, 263, 553
  substitution 100, 102, 134–135, 172, 174, 197, 296, 298, 402
constraints 3–4, 6, 117, 177–178, 204, 355, 406, 570
constriction 82
  deconstriction 121
contact
  between dialects 334
  contact language 28–31, 35, 40, 77, 142, 145, 188, 271, 292, 299–301, 415, 444, 582
  contact clause (see *subordination, zero relative*)
continuous (see *aspect, progressive*)
continuum 3, 31, 69, 91, 97, 99, 102, 132, 137, 205, 217, 236, 277, 294, 365, 415, 514, 532, 546, 549, 565, 590, 593
  post-creole 124, 137, 205
contraction 136, 143, 321–322, 335, 409
coordination 425, 450, 460, 462, 576
  coordinating conjunction 591
copula 214, 230, 264, 418, 428–429, 437–438, 456, 468, 475, 524–531, 557, 566, 574, 587, 589, 598
  copula deletion 557, 587
  copula absence 471, 475
corpus [corpora] 4, 27, 69, 72–74, 97, 193, 196, 200, 259, 275, 286, 305–333, 337–338, 342, 345,–350, 353–356, 365–366, 385–386, 488–500, 504, 507, 587

covert prestige (see *prestige*)
creole (see *variety*)
creolization (see also *decreolization*) 126, 192, 274
CURE 93, 95, 97, 116–117, 121, 128, 295

D

dark /l/ (see /l/)
declarative 103, 202, 298, 319, 562, 591, 597
decreolization (see also *creolization*) 127, 217, 230, 420
degree modifier 538
deletion 101–102, 177–178, 181, 261, 297, 327, 330, 335, 394, 426, 436, 557
  consonant (see *consonant*)
  /h/, 100–102, 130, 134–136, 156, 363
  jod/yod, 56–57, 60, 230, 261–263, 296–297, 302
  of auxiliary 330, 587
demonstrative (see also *pronoun, demonstrative*) 419, 431, 437, 449, 470, 491, 503, 537, 550, 585–586, 594
dental 40, 45, 54–55, 78, 81, 129, 134, 181, 252, 296, 301
  inter- 54, 130, 134
  labio- 45, 134, 296
  post- 54
deontic [root] (see *modality*)
determiner 327, 367, 419, 423, 431, 469–470, 537, 551–552, 576–577, 594
devoicing
  consonant, 53–56, 81, 87, 240, 296, 301
  vowel, 80
diagnostic 67, 365, 572
dialect 1, 3, 8, 24, 31, 66, 89–90, 96, 100–103, 106, 108, 124, 131–133, 151, 178, 188–189, 194, 210, 234, 236, 249, 262, 267, 269, 275, 280, 283, 293–297, 302, 330, 334, 338, 365, 379, 395,

407, 467–468, 480, 490, 572, 578–580, 586
  contact (see *contact*)
  social 21, 76, 89–90, 103, 262, 339, 395
dialectology 574
diffusion (geolinguistic) 4, 32, 113, 274, 335
diminutive 398, 407, 409, 592
diphthong 4, 40, 44, 49–52, 55, 59, 62, 70–75, 78–85, 91–99, 121–122, 128, 132–133, 150–151, 158–160, 170, 180, 183, 198, 224, 227, 238, 241–245, 250, 254–256, 278, 282–287, 294–295, 299, 402, 477
  centering 285, 299
  closing 70–73, 92, 295
  shift 51
diphthongization 44, 50, 91, 114
directives 563
dislocation
  left 541, 561, 592, 596
  right 394, 541–542, 592, 598
distribution 4–5, 52, 60, 82, 97–106, 109–113, 116, 120, 129, 133, 156, 171, 279–281, 324, 326, 346, 408, 528, 565
disyllabic 50–52, 55, 73, 78, 117, 149, 295
divergence 329, 356, 596
don't
  invariant (see *negation*)
done
  completive (see *aspect*)
double comparative (see *comparison*)
DRESS 41–43, 46–48, 52, 70–73, 80, 84, 91, 94–95, 115, 118, 121–123, 128, 132, 222, 224, 243, 246, 254, 257, 293–294
dropping 230, 387, 470, 495
  /h/ (see *deletion, /h/*)
  /j/ (see *deletion, jod/yod*)
  initial /w/ 67, 70, 72, 136, 174, 297
dual (see *pronoun* and *number*)
durative (see *aktionsart*)

E

ecology 277, 578
elicitation 28, 275, 285–286, 305–306,
  309–310, 337, 342, 347–354, 357, 435
  tests, 28, 306, 310, 337, 342, 349, 350–
  353, 357
elision 177, 427
ellipsis 363, 389–394
embedded clause (see *subordination*)
enclitic (see *cliticization*)
endonormativity 34, 341–353, 357
epenthesis 131, 136, 158, 174–177, 183
epistemic (see *modality*)
ethnicity 25–26, 44, 78
ethnolect 126–127
etymon, 152, 184, 197
existentials [presentationals] 213–214,
  334, 337, 381, 383, 391, 418, 429, 489,
  526, 531, 589

F

FACE 41, 51, 60, 62, 70, 72, 85, 90,
  92, 94–97, 99, 105, 114, 119–120, 128,
  132, 222–224, 242–246, 255, 257, 294–
  295, 299, 377
fall(ing) (see *intonation*)
feature,
  diagnostic 67, 572
  distinctive 34, 67, 78, 82, 143, 171–172,
    185, 236–237, 287, 341
  grammatical 25, 31, 34, 237, 259, 327,
    362–366, 395, 435, 561, 565, 583–
    584, 592–593, 596, 600
  interlanguage 131, 427
  morphosyntactic 434, 583–584, 592
  phonetic 137
  phonological 33, 67, 99, 127, 138, 176,
    238–239, 250, 259–263, 299
  prosodic 5, 32, 61, 82, 86, 160, 201,
    228, 233, 298, 301
  segmental 130, 238, 287
  suprasegmental 4, 130, 135, 238, 248
fieldwork 267, 568, 579

filler 564
first language (see *L1*)
flap(ping) 27, 74, 100, 152, 156, 171, 226,
  296, 300–301
FLEECE 41–49, 52, 80, 85, 90–91, 94–
  96, 99, 116, 128, 132, 222, 224, 244,
  246, 255, 257, 293–294
FOOT 41–50, 60, 80, 91, 94, 105, 116,
  128, 132, 222, 224, 244, 246, 255, 257,
  293–294
FORCE 41, 46, 50, 52, 80, 128, 132, 222–
  224, 244, 247, 254, 257
frequency 4, 57, 71, 102, 118–120, 176,
  196, 279–280, 287, 308–314, 318–322,
  328, 347–350, 356–359, 365, 367, 374,
  382, 388, 390, 488, 492, 500
  relative 308, 328–329, 592
fricative (see also *glottal fricative*) 45, 55,
  112, 129–130, 134, 137–138, 156, 171,
  173, 181, 240, 252, 296, 402
front vowel raising (see *raising*)
fronted 70, 80, 91, 94–97, 105–106, 152,
  282, 294–295, 455–456, 460, 484, 507,
  562
fronting (see also */th/-fronting*) 4, 81, 92,
  114, 179, 457, 460, 469, 507, 598
function 61–62, 68, 77, 103, 107, 125–
  126, 130–131, 135–136, 144–145, 159,
  176, 178, 182–183, 214–215, 229–230,
  237, 273, 281, 308–309, 328, 387, 393,
  418–419, 428, 431–435, 438, 441, 445,
  448–454, 457–458, 464, 471, 476, 485,
  499, 506, 519, 522, 524, 534, 536, 538,
  561, 565–566, 585, 592, 599
  grammatical 591
  syntactic 483
future (see *tense*)

G

gapping (see *subordination, zero relative*)
geminates 199
gender 27, 34, 44, 99, 116–117, 262, 362,
  368, 371, 375–376, 380, 394–395, 420–

421, 431, 438, 446, 468, 472, 491, 515, 549, 569, 584, 593
  agreement (see *agreement*)
  pronominal (see *pronoun, gendered*)
  system 368
General American 221–226, 261
genitive (see *case, possessive*)
gerund 354–355, 444, 585
  gerund-participle 354–359
get passive (see *passive*)
glide/gliding (see also *diphthong*) 56–57, 92, 106, 116–117, 121, 158, 245, 255–256, 261, 295, 297
  in- 91
  off- 91–93, 97, 99, 115–118, 121, 150–151, 278, 282–285, 295, 299
glottal 45, 53, 62, 86–87, 130, 134, 156, 197, 225, 227, 301
  fricative 130, 134, 156, 197, 301
  reinforcement 53
  stop 86, 225, 227
  word-initial 44, 56, 59, 156, 159, 227
glottalization 62, 86–87, 100–101
GOAL 128, 132
GOAT 41, 43, 48–51, 60, 70–72, 85, 87, 90, 92, 94, 97, 99, 105, 114, 116, 121, 128, 132, 222–224, 242, 245–246, 255, 257, 293, 295, 299
GOOSE 41–43, 46, 49–52, 60, 80–81, 85, 90, 92–96, 101, 105, 114–116, 121, 128, 132, 222, 224, 244, 246, 255, 257, 293–296
grammaticalization 178, 184, 312, 497–498, 501–503, 508–509, 557, 583, 596, 600
greeting 48, 219, 564
growen 73

H

/h/ deletion (see *deletion*)
habitual (see *aspect*)
happY 44, 47, 93, 132, 222, 224, 245, 247, 256–258, 295

hiatus 56
High Rising Terminal (HRT) 61, 83, 87, 103, 298
historical present 346, 362
homophony 44, 47
horsES 44, 47, 61, 93, 128, 132, 222–224, 246–247, 256–257, 295
hypocoristics 34, 398–403, 406–410, 592
hypotheticality 349, 397, 523–524, 588

I

identity 2, 25–26, 71, 77, 79, 145, 166, 216–217, 227, 262, 273, 494, 599
idiom 305, 317, 560
imperative 393–394, 437, 453, 519, 523–526, 529, 555, 574, 597
imperfective (see *aspect*)
implicational 137
  scale 137
inanimate 34, 367–368, 371–372, 375, 379–380, 388, 394, 396, 455–456, 505, 540, 584, 591, 598
indicative (see *mood*)
individuation 379
infinitive 315, 318–319, 352, 362, 388, 434, 573, 588, 597
ingliding (see *gliding*)
innovation 310, 313, 384, 402
intensifier, 230, 508, 560, 590
interdental (see *dental*)
interference 176, 203, 276, 299–300, 492
interrogative 1, 5–6, 31, 33, 50, 62, 71, 75, 87, 108, 121, 130, 138, 162, 184–185, 191, 193, 202–206, 215, 230–231, 259, 264, 268, 271, 288–290, 302, 305, 316–322, 328, 334, 337, 341, 347, 350–351, 356–358, 379, 394, 405, 411, 425, 435, 437–439, 448, 453, 459–460, 465, 480, 484–485, 490–491, 498, 507, 510, 528, 536, 542, 551, 562–565, 578–580, 587, 591, 597–600
  tag (see *tag*)
  yes/no question, 249, 562

intonation 5, 61–62, 66, 83, 103, 130, 135, 139, 160–161, 184, 191, 201–203, 215, 230–231, 248–249, 259, 264, 287–289, 298, 367, 425, 435, 437, 459, 480, 483–484, 503, 563, 591
falling 203, 435
rising 203, 562, 591, 597
invariant form 154, 549
inversion 435
subject-verb [subject-auxiliary] 362, 381, 416, 427, 559, 599
IPA, 149, 152, 195, 198, 227, 231–232, 277, 299
invariant (see *tag*)

J

jod/yod 56, 60, 261–263, 296–297
dropping (see *deletion, jod/yod*)

K

kin relation marking 432, 441
KIT 41–44, 46–47, 49, 70–73, 80, 84, 91, 94–95, 105, 116–118, 121–122, 128, 132, 222, 224, 243, 246, 254, 257, 293–294
koiné 234

L

/l/
clear/palatal/light 86
coda 43–44, 48, 87, 106–107
dark/velarised 71, 73
linking 55–56
postvocalic 115, 118, 301
vocalization (see also *coda /l/*) 32, 49, 55–56, 73, 86, 90, 100, 106–109, 118, 121–122, 226, 297–298
L1 238, 262–263, 302, 347–348, 354, 557, 585, 600
L2 259, 261–263, 347, 354, 546, 551, 557
labial 107, 118, 170

labiodental (see *dental*)
language
change 103, 108, 335
contact 269, 271, 274, 466, 511
endangered 393, 395, 579
maintenance 216
national 144, 167, 188, 191, 444, 467
shift 579
youth (see *youth*)
lateral (see also */l/ vocalization*) 45, 55, 73, 81, 114–115, 122, 129–130, 170, 297
prelateral 115–117, 121, 293
lax 93, 95, 97, 116–117, 170, 224, 241, 277, 279, 281, 284–285
left dislocation (see *dislocation*)
lengthening 93, 127, 135, 177, 288
lettER 68, 93, 128, 132, 222–224, 245–247, 256–258, 295
levelling 335, 589
lexical set 4–5, 41–43, 67, 75, 88, 139, 155, 242, 246–247, 257, 294, 298
lexicon 27–28, 34, 101, 108, 119, 139, 142, 144, 146–147, 159, 161, 167, 175, 189, 191, 199, 250, 269, 305, 325, 341, 358, 415, 445, 514, 546, 549, 570
lexifier 168, 178, 190, 194–195, 232, 286, 299, 488, 491, 514
liaison 136, 298, 302
light /l/ (see /l/)
lingua franca 29, 125–126, 143, 164–166, 189, 191, 235–236
linking 55–56, 298, 424, 460, 591, 597
liquid 81, 152, 154, 405, 489
loan word 58, 79, 264, 286
long
half- 243, 254–255
stressed syllable 53, 56, 60, 228
vowel 40–41, 47–49, 61, 78, 80, 85, 90–92, 106–107, 177, 247, 250, 286, 290, 294, 402
LOT 41, 43, 46, 48, 60, 80, 82, 93–94, 105, 128, 132, 222, 224, 244, 246, 254, 257, 293

low back merger (see *merger, LOT/ CLOTH/THOUGHT*)
lowering 179–180, 283, 288, 293

M

markedness 329
merger
   LOT/CLOTH/THOUGHT 224
   NEAR/SQUARE 32, 42–43, 49, 52, 59, 72, 75, 85, 87, 295
   NURSE/GOOSE 56
   TRAP/DRESS 84, 115, 122, 293
   FLEECE/KIT,116
   GOOSE/FOOT 116
   CURE/FOOT 116
mesolect 33, 138, 152, 218, 224–225, 229, 514, 521, 525, 527
metathesis 131, 241, 263, 473
minimal pair 43, 47, 73, 244, 286
modal (verb) 229, 315, 317–320, 333, 338, 341, 347–352, 417, 428, 476, 479, 497–501, 517–522, 529, 572–573, 587–588, 595
   epistemic *mustn't* 350, 358, 588
modality 5, 341, 348, 350, 501, 514–515, 572–573, 595
   deontic [root] 348, 501
   epistemic 350, 358, 501, 588
monophthongization 4, 117, 128
mood 183, 312, 315, 341, 347, 409, 477, 497, 587
   indicative 32–33, 315, 417
   irrealis 453, 480, 497
   realis 453
   subjunctive 27, 315, 321–322, 335, 347–348, 359, 587
mora 41, 78, 247
morphology 3–6, 32, 34–35, 159, 182–183, 303–307, 311, 341, 343, 345, 415–416, 421, 423, 427, 429, 438, 444–446, 449–452, 467, 475–478, 482, 488, 514–515, 546, 557, 568–570, 586, 589, 593–595, 599

   derivational 444–445, 467, 488, 568
   inflectional 35, 416, 444, 449–450, 455, 467, 488, 515, 568–569, 593–595
motion verb (see *verb*)
MOUTH 90, 92, 95-97, 99, 105, 128, 295

N

nasal 45, 111–113, 129–130, 134–138, 170–171, 281, 296, 301, 411, 589
nasalization 82, 199, 250
   pre-nasalized 155–156, 171, 195, 197, 300
national language (see *language*)
nativization 254, 481, 549
naturalness 501
NEAR 32, 41–43, 49–53, 59, 69–72, 75, 81, 85, 87, 92, 95, 99, 116–117, 121–122, 128, 132, 222–224, 242, 245, 247, 256–257, 295
negation 5, 272, 312, 320–322, 332, 362, 387, 417, 429, 437, 514, 528, 530, 563, 574, 590, 597
   ain't 322, 332, 373, 387
   double (see also *negation, multiple*) 387, 429, 532, 590, 597
   invariant *don't* 369, 386, 427, 560, 566
   multiple [negative concord] 332, 362, 387
   preverbal *no* 211, 437
negative attraction (see *negation*)
negative concord (see *negation, multiple*)
neutralization 42–43, 47–52, 80, 156, 242, 254–255, 293, 299, 517
non-reduction (see *vowels, unreduced/ nonreduced*)
NORTH 41, 50, 128, 132, 222–224, 244, 247, 254, 257
noun
   count 353, 368, 371, 379, 381, 431, 492, 546–549, 586
   mass 368, 379, 380, 431, 492, 586

noun phrase 5, 146, 311, 325, 327, 367, 383, 419, 425, 431, 447–450, 455–458, 464–469, 502, 508, 526, 532, 537, 546, 558–562, 569, 576, 586, 593, 596–599
nucleus 61, 106–107, 282–283, 288, 478
number
  distinction 447
  dual (marking) 35, 323, 393, 421–423, 433, 438, 441, 447, 472–474, 491–492, 549, 569, 577, 584, 593, 599
  plural 174, 176, 178, 444, 448, 467, 472, 474, 490–491, 497, 537, 549–550, 565, 569, 586, 593
    plural concord 323–324
    plural form 331, 406, 474, 492, 497, 547, 584
    plural pronoun 178, 323–325, 364, 381, 388–389, 421, 447, 455, 474, 492, 497, 584
    plural noun 353, 383, 455, 494, 559
    plural, third person 178, 186, 455–457, 474, 492, 539–540, 551
NURSE 24, 91, 94–95, 105, 128, 294, 298, 299, 301

O

object 34, 178, 355–356, 359, 363, 368, 389, 416, 419–426, 445–446, 454–457, 460–461, 466, 468–469, 472, 476, 478, 483, 488, 491, 515, 533, 539, 541, 551–552, 577–578, 585, 593, 595–596, 598
  direct 426, 483
  indirect 572
  prepositional 326, 450, 455
obstruent 42, 111–113, 281, 283
offglide (see *glide/gliding*)
onset (see also *glottal onset*) 49, 55, 72, 85, 94, 106–107, 114, 228, 297, 509
  cluster
oral 225

orthography 50, 56-59, 126, 128–130, 137, 139, 157, 227, 231, 250, 421, 514, 579

P

palatal 45, 56, 101, 129, 138, 152, 170–173, 261, 301
  /l/ (see /l/)
  lamino- 128–130, 134, 300
palatalization 100–101, 296–297
PALM 41, 49–52, 111–114, 119–121, 128, 132, 222, 224, 244, 246, 255, 257, 294
paragogue 131, 136, 175, 177, 183
participle 73, 308–309, 328, 344–345, 355, 364, 384, 387, 405, 585, 589
  gerund-participle 354–359
  past 73, 295, 307–310, 328, 331, 334, 343–344, 362, 384, 386, 428, 553, 557, 573, 589, 592
  present 429
particle 202, 216, 264, 322, 355, 400, 431, 436, 452, 454, 480, 495, 497–501, 505, 508–509, 554–556, 560, 566, 573, 595, 599
passive 309, 322, 328, 418, 430, 437, 456–457, 588, 598
  get passive 327–329, 347, 588
past tense (see *tense*)
-*pela* 206, 488, 490–492, 510, 594
perfect
  past [pluperfect] 559
  present (see *present perfect*)
perfective (see *aspect*)
pharyngeal(ization) 82
phoneme 5, 41–43, 51–52, 71, 127, 129, 152, 156, 168, 171–175, 181, 195–196, 199–200, 224, 226, 238–241, 247, 250, 253, 258, 285–286, 290, 300–301
phonotactic 5, 131, 136, 158–160, 163, 177, 185, 203, 228, 301
pidgin (see *variety*)

pitch 61–62, 66, 83, 130, 135, 202, 229–230, 248, 258–259, 287–289, 377, 425
plosive 45, 53, 55, 100
plural (see *number*)
polysyllabic 61, 117, 255, 258, 402–405, 570
possessive (see *case*)
post-creole 124, 137, 205, 420
postposition (see *adposition*)
postvocalic 24, 67, 71–75, 115, 118, 120–121, 151, 223, 226, 240, 252, 299–301
pragmatics 438
prefix (see *affix*)
prelateral (see *lateral*)
preposition (see *adposition*)
present perfect 312–314, 346, 358, 362, 386–387, 417, 428–429, 587, 595
presentationals (see *existentials*)
prestige 2, 25, 78, 89, 115, 117, 236, 364
  covert 262, 393
  overt 78–79
preverbal marker 521, 573
PRICE 90, 92, 95, 97, 99, 105, 128, 294
pro-drop 476
progressive (see *aspect*)
pronominal system (see *pronoun*)
pronoun
  copying (see *subordination, relative clause*)
  demonstrative (see also *demonstrative*) 470, 594
  dual [dual marking] 35, 323, 393, 421–423, 433, 438, 441, 447, 472–474, 491–492, 549, 569, 577, 584, 593, 599
  gendered 367
  generic 363, 388, 549
  indefinite 298
  interrogative 425, 435
  personal 354–355, 388, 421–423, 432–433, 438, 441, 472, 474, 504, 585
  possessive 423, 431, 433, 446, 539–540, 569, 576–578, 585

pronominal gender (see *pronoun, gendered*)
pronominal system 5, 539, 577
reflexive 423, 433, 508, 539–540, 585
relative (see *subordination, relative clause*)
resumptive [shadow] 495, 497, 540, 558, 562, 596
second person plural 364, 388–389, 539–540, 584
prosody 33, 277, 287, 289, 298, 483
prothesis 131, 136
purpose clause (see *subordination, adverbial clause*)

Q

quantifier 419–420, 448, 469, 471, 490–491, 502–503, 537, 552, 593–594
quantitative studies 81
question
  tag question (see *tag*)
question (see *interrogative*)
questionnaire 331, 337–338, 349
quotative 463–464, 597

R

/r/ (see also *rhoticity*)
  intrusive 55–56, 298, 570
  linking 55–56, 298
  postvocalic 24, 67, 71, 298
raising 118, 179, 224, 293
  Canadian Raising 283
Received Pronunciation [RP] 2, 44, 46, 48, 50–51, 55–56, 58–62, 65, 69, 82, 91, 108, 116, 261, 277, 295, 297
redundancy 490, 498–500
reduplication 182–183, 417, 424, 449–451, 476–477, 485, 493–494, 572, 594–595, 599
referent 367–368, 371, 374–375, 377, 379–380, 394, 432, 448, 453, 503, 550, 562, 593

inanimate 362, 367–368, 379, 394, 505, 540

regularization 176, 307–308, 427, 589

relative clause (see *subordination, relative clause*)

relative particle (see *subordination, relative clause*)

relativizer (see *subordination, relative clause*)

relexification 415, 429

restructuring 415–417, 428–429, 439–440

resultative 461, 479

retraction 91

retroflex 138, 152, 156

rhotic(ity) 32, 54, 67–68, 71, 116, 129–130, 151, 298–301

non-, 41, 54–55, 67, 120, 250, 281, 298

semi-, 24, 66

rhythm 5, 33, 41, 61, 78, 82, 84, 86, 229, 248, 298, 301, 469

right dislocation (see dislocation)

rising (see *intonation*)

rounding 114

rural

rural area 67, 172, 194, 200, 212, 236, 250, 467, 468, 481, 594

rural speaker (see speaker)

rural vs urban 25, 33, 120, 185, 194, 202, 242, 427, 589

rural pidgin 194, 201–202

S

schwa 72, 121, 150–151, 223, 229, 254–256, 282, 293, 295, 299

second language (see *L2*)

segmental features (see features)

selection 204, 341, 354, 359, 585, 599

sentence

affirmative 184, 381, 484

complex 468, 576

composite 591, 597, 600

descriptive 418

equational 418, 456, 468, 526, 534, 557, 598

existential 213, 418, 429, 526

interrogative 184, 484

negative 387

verbless 429, 526–528, 589

shortening 176, 398–400, 475

simple past (see *tense, past*)

simplicity 237, 272

simplification 4, 158–159, 365, 415, 440, 572

situation type (see *aktionsart*)

slang 27, 405–407, 546, 555

sociolect 99, 113, 120

sonorant 181

sonority 177

speaker

adolescent (see *youth language*)

educated 84, 149, 157, 262, 267, 299

female 42, 83–84, 384

male 80, 83, 282–283

rural 25, 67, 175–176, 200, 301, 478

urban 71, 176, 200, 470

speech

casual 73–74, 118, 339, 467

connected 279

direct 310, 318

indirect [reported] 289, 349

formal 74

informal 119, 274, 318, 353, 362

rapid 204, 225, 492

slow 47, 50

speech community 25–26, 30, 33, 35, 100–101, 120, 124, 155, 193, 262–263, 272, 279, 299, 306, 565

spontaneous 318, 337, 366

spelling pronunciation 61, 82, 85, 157, 243–244, 253

split

TRAP 48, 280

standard (see *variety*)

standardization 193, 334

START 41, 46–52, 56, 68, 80, 85, 91, 128, 132, 222–224, 244, 247, 255–257, 294, 299 stop (see *plosive, glottal stop*)

stress 5, 27, 41, 44, 47, 52–53, 55–56, 58, 60–61, 69, 82, 87–88, 101, 117, 130, 135–136, 149, 160–161, 175–177, 184, 191, 201–205, 222–230, 245–248, 256, 258, 261–262, 279, 283, 295–297, 300–301, 330, 363–364, 367, 399, 404, 419, 454, 480, 491, 502–505

STRUT 41, 42–46, 48–49, 60, 80, 87, 91, 94, 128, 132, 222, 224, 244, 246, 255, 257, 293–294, 299

subject (see also *case, nominative*) 323, 332, 334, 337, 342, 352, 354, 355, 362–363, 367–368, 381–383, 389,–394, 416, 418, 421, 425–427, 429, 433–436, 438, 446, 453–457, 460–461, 468–469, 472–473, 480, 483, 491, 494–495, 497, 515, 532–534, 539, 541–542, 551–552, 558–559, 561–563, 577–578, 583, 589, 591, 593, 596, 598–599

-verb concord (see *agreement*)

subjunctive (see *mood*)

subordination 5, 190, 425, 460, 536, 576, 591

  adverbial clause 536, 543

    for to as a complementizer 214

    of cause and reason [causal clause], 425, 458, 535–537

    of condition 272, 350, 425, 535–536

    of purpose 425, 463, 535

    of time 464

  complement clause 5, 325–327, 463, 506, 514, 533, 576, 597

      complementizer 418, 425, 438, 506–507, 533, 542–543, 576, 591

  embedded clause 426, 435, 437, 483–484, 597

  relative clause 184, 203, 312, 323, 363, 389–390, 426, 435, 448, 450, 464–465, 483–484, 503–509, 514, 532–533, 562, 575, 585, 591, 597

    pronoun copying 561–562

relative particle 591

relative pronoun 203, 323, 363, 390, 426, 435, 450, 504, 532–533, 551, 562, 575, 591

  relativization 5, 312, 323, 450, 483–484, 514, 532, 575

  relativizer 323, 425

  restrictive 389, 503, 575

  that 323, 389–390, 532

  what 435, 591

  zero relative 203, 363, 389–390, 426, 435, 483, 503, 533, 575, 591

subordinating conjunction 534

substrate 2, 80, 125, 156, 160, 168, 182–183, 190, 199–200, 203, 237, 292, 300, 415, 438, 445, 447, 450, 453, 455, 457, 460, 471, 473, 475, 477, 478, 488, 490, 498–501, 549, 565, 574, 593, 596

suffix (see *affix*)

superlative (see *comparison*)

superstrate 2–3, 125, 182, 415, 431, 445, 595

suprasegmental (see *feature, suprasegmental*)

syllabic 67, 100, 106–107, 118, 226, 296–297, 301, 401, 553

  /l/, 100, 107, 118

  /r/, 67, 401

syllable structure 40, 78, 159, 170, 175, 177–178, 185, 203, 548

syllable timing 135

syncope 131, 136

T

tag 147, 153, 230, 425, 459, 565, 591

  interrogative 351

  invariant 565, 597, 599

  tag question 230, 337, 425, 435, 564

tap 40, 53, 78, 81, 86, 100, 153, 170, 296

tense 5, 47, 93, 95, 116, 136, 157, 170, 224, 229, 241, 264, 281, 343, 346, 362, 372, 384, 388, 416–418, 427–429, 438, 453, 467, 479, 497, 514–519, 521–526,

528,–531, 557, 562, 566, 572–573, 587–589, 595–599

anterior 437

   anterior *been/bin* 417–419, 428–429, 444–445, 453, 467, 480, 496, 498–499, 510, 515, 519, 573, 587, 589, 595, 599

   future 315, 317, 417, 427–428, 438, 453, 465, 480–481, 497, 499, 510, 515–519, 523–524, 595, 599

   past 211, 253, 259, 262, 307–308, 313, 343–344, 346, 350, 358–359, 362, 384, 386, 388, 417–418, 427–429, 438, 444, 498–499, 510, 515–519, 525, 530, 557, 559, 573, 575, 587, 589, 595, 599

   present 261, 346, 350, 383, 418, 427, 558, 562, 589, 599

   historical present 346, 362

   tense marker 136, 417–418, 428, 515–516, 519, 521–523, 525–526, 528–530, 573, 589, 597

tensing 224

THOUGHT 41, 43–44, 49–51, 60, 68, 80, 128, 132, 222, 224, 244, 246, 254, 257, 294

time reference 498–499

tone 62, 103, 188, 288, 298, 367

   lexical 195

topicalization 425, 434, 468–469, 495, 507, 541

transitivity (see *verb*)

TRAP 41, 43, 46–49, 52, 60, 67, 70, 72–73, 80, 84, 93–94, 105, 111–115, 118–123, 128, 132, 222, 224, 243, 246, 254, 257, 293–294, 299

trill 301

triphthong 121, 278

U

unaspirated (see *aspiration*)

universals, 32

   of New Englishes 358

unreleased 225, 231, 239, 252, 300

uptalk (see *High Rising Terminal*)

urban

   area 144, 194, 212, 235, 427–428, 468

   feature (see *feature*)

   speaker (see *speaker*)

urbanization 166, 172, 176, 428

uvular 250

V

variability 5, 74, 91, 93, 101, 109, 132, 171, 199–202, 281, 283, 285, 488, 495, 579

variable 4, 32, 42, 53–57, 59–62, 68, 70, 81, 86–87, 90, 102–105, 111, 113–116, 118, 132, 139, 150, 171–172, 193, 203, 263, 295, 297–298, 309, 318, 323, 325–328, 337–338, 342–343, 357, 359, 363–366, 375–376, 381, 391, 394–395, 427, 440, 491–492, 498, 559, 577

   grammatical 362–363

   morphosyntactic 342

   non-standard 337

   phonological 103, 263, 363, 365

   sociolinguistic 43, 175, 293

variant 4, 47–48, 50, 52–54, 57, 59, 66, 73, 75, 79, 81, 84, 90–93, 95, 97, 99–103, 106, 108, 133, 135, 138–139, 152, 156, 171, 196, 218, 237, 242, 254, 294–299, 310, 321, 325–330, 335, 342, 352–353, 357–358, 362–363, 365, 367, 379, 389, 394, 407, 418–421, 425, 428, 431, 471, 475, 480, 482, 488, 514, 588

variation 2, 4, 6–7, 24–25, 30, 32–35, 40, 55, 57, 59–60, 65–69, 80–81, 89–90, 94–95, 97, 99, 105, 111–112, 114–116, 119, 133, 137–139, 145, 149, 151–152, 154–156, 159, 168, 171, 174–176, 178, 181–182, 184, 193–195, 198–203, 217–218, 222, 224, 226, 236–237, 242, 244–245, 249, 255, 258, 263, 271, 275–276, 279, 283–286, 292, 294–300, 302,

307, 311, 313, 318–320, 323, 327–331,
333–335, 338, 352, 359, 385, 407–409,
415, 421, 423, 432, 434, 445, 474, 480,
495, 498, 514, 516, 546, 549, 561, 570,
585
cross-dialectal 4
cross-linguistic 4
free 53, 156, 225, 249, 446, 464, 498
language 275
morphological 583,
morphosyntactic 3, 32, 312, 329, 337,
549, 583
patterns of 119, 307, 561
syntactic 312, 329, 583
unconditioned 222
variety (see also *Index of varieties and
languages*)
colloquial 35, 238, 250, 557, 561, 563–
564
contact variety 2–3, 23, 26, 28, 30,
32–35, 124–125, 292, 301–302, 499,
580, 583–584, 592–593, 595–600
creole 28, 30–35, 124, 126–131, 133,
135, 137–139, 145, 159, 176, 178,
192, 210–232, 267, 274–275, 280,
286, 292, 294, 299–302, 415–439,
444, 467, 488, 498–499, 501, 514–
517, 520–521, 524, 526–528, 531–
543, 572, 574, 579, 583–584, 586,
589–590, 592–598
continuum 30, 218, 592
English-based 2, 28–29, 263, 546,
557, 598, 600
L1 263
L2 347
non-standard (see also *vernacular*) 2,
25, 35, 139, 365, 381, 386, 415, 430,
598
pidgin 28–29, 299, 596
regional 25, 66, 114, 122, 124, 290,
317, 335
standard 2, 137, 168, 241, 313, 362,
365, 580

vernacular (see also *non-standard*) 25,
584–586, 588–589, 591
velar 45, 53, 118, 129, 134, 170, 200, 226,
250, 411
velarization (see also */l/ velarized*)
verb (see also *aktionsart*)
dynamic 475, 478
intransitive 417, 449, 452, 457, 461,
466, 475, 479, 493, 596
irregular 25, 307, 331, 343
modal (see *modal verb*)
motion 462
serial verb 418, 437, 454, 460–462, 476,
479, 501–502, 506, 522, 524–526,
529, 596, 599
stative 314, 468, 471, 475, 478–479,
481, 490, 524, 527, 587, 598
transitive 131, 162, 182, 186, 299, 327,
363, 391, 425, 430, 438, 452, 458–
459, 461, 472, 475–476, 478, 482,
488–489, 493, 499, 589, 595
verb form 61, 308, 310, 313, 381, 429,
482, 516, 554, 573, 589–590
verb phrase 341, 390, 416, 419, 427, 453,
455, 461, 468, 475–476, 478–497, 515,
524, 526, 554, 558, 574, 587, 595–596,
600
vocalization (see also */l/, /r/*) 32, 49,
55–56, 73, 86, 90, 100, 106–109, 118,
121–122, 226, 297–298
voicing 53, 134, 155, 157–158, 171, 300–
301, 402
voiced 40, 53, 55, 78, 81, 100, 129, 134,
138, 152, 155, 171–173, 181, 196,
199–200, 226, 239–240, 250, 252,
296, 300, 492
voiceless 40, 42, 45, 53, 55, 59, 62, 68,
77–78, 81, 87, 129, 134, 138, 152,
155–156, 171, 181, 200, 223, 225,
229, 239–240, 251–252, 260, 281,
283, 296, 300
vowel
back 56, 80, 87, 91–93, 106–107, 116,
133, 179, 281–282, 285, 294, 297

central 48, 50, 91–92, 94, 96, 114, 132–133, 149–150, 179, 277–278, 293–295, 401

devoiced [devoicing] 53, 55–56, 73, 80–81, 87, 172, 196, 240, 252, 296, 301

epenthetic 158, 172, 174–176, 195, 201, 204–206, 241, 252, 263, 301, 451

front 46, 62, 70, 72–73, 91–92, 107, 121, 132, 158–159, 278–279, 293–294

harmony 131, 174–175, 182, 186, 299, 301–302, 419

length 47, 49, 52, 57, 128, 130, 170, 178, 199, 238, 250, 299

reduction 59, 279

selection 204

underspecified 182

weak 82, 86, 295

W

word order 5, 213, 272, 425, 434, 437, 455, 468, 495, 507, 533, 562, 572, 592, 597–600

word-final 45, 53, 56, 151, 156–159, 175, 223, 226, 296, 402

word-initial 44, 56, 59, 156, 159, 227

Y

yod (see *jod*)

youth 120, 457, 465
culture 25, 78, 167, 216
language 384, 386

Z

zero relative (see *subordination, relative clause*)

Index of varieties and languages

A

Aboriginal English [AbE] 26, 30–31, 33–34, 124–139, 292, 294–298, 302, 415–443, 583–592, 600

Aboriginal languages 26, 29, 127–128, 130, 133, 135, 138, 418

Aboriginal Pidgin [AbP] 146, 421

American English [AmE] 27, 34, 61, 223–225, 230, 236, 261, 273, 298, 305–308, 310–312, 314–316, 318, 320–328, 335, 337, 341–348, 350–353, 355–358, 387, 401, 563, 587, 590

Anglo-Indian (see *Indian English*)

Anglo-Welsh (see *Welsh English*)

Antipodean English 27, 293, 584, 592

Atlantic Creole 274, 501

Australian Creole [AusC] 124–139, 415–443

Australian English [AusE] 25–27, 30–34, 48, 62, 69, 72, 75, 89–109, 111–122, 127, 131, 133–136, 147, 272, 277, 279, 281–283, 285–286, 290, 293–294, 296, 302, 305–308, 313–316, 318, 323–324, 326–327, 338, 341–361, 365–366, 387–398, 400–414, 436, 585, 587–592

Australian Vernacular English [AusVE] 34–35, 362–397, 584–587, 591

B

Barbadian Creole (see *Bajan*)

Bislama 30–34, 142–164, 167, 183, 188, 192, 195, 198, 204, 292, 299, 301, 444–469, 471–472, 474, 476–477, 479–480, 485, 497, 500, 502, 507, 583, 592–598

British English [BrE] 2, 30, 34, 102, 111–112, 236, 267, 305–309, 311–316, 318–319, 321–327, 337, 341–343, 346–348, 350–353, 355–358, 386, 406, 587

C

Canadian English [CanE] 283

Cantonese 210, 212–213, 215, 490

Celtic 8

Chinese 124, 210–213, 215–216, 220, 231, 234, 237, 490, 561

Chinese Pidgin English [ChnP] 211, 220, 490

Cockney 108, 261, 269, 365

Creole (see also *Pidgin and Creole*) 30, 33, 124, 126–127, 129–131, 138, 210, 213, 215–218, 221, 226–232, 275, 292, 299–300, 415–418, 420, 423, 425, 514–517, 520, 526, 533, 539, 543, 595, 598

Cultivated Australian English 89

D

Dravidian languages 234

Dutch 39 125

E

Early Modern English [EModE] 108

East Anglia [East Anglia(n) English] 261

Emai 547

F

Fiji English 234–266, 546–567

Fiji Hindi 33, 234, 236–238, 249–255, 258, 546, 548–551, 555, 562, 564–565

Fijian 33, 35, 234–242, 244–248, 252, 254, 256, 259–260, 263–264, 546, 548–549, 551–552, 555, 557–558, 560, 562, 564–565, 583

First Language [L1] variety 263

French, 30, 60, 143–147, 149–150, 152–154, 157–158, 160–162, 301, 561, 593

G

Ga 560
General American 221, 22–226, 261
German 30, 56, 119, 143, 189–192, 368, 492
Germanic 31
Greek 25, 402
Gujarati 234

H

Hawai'i Creole [HawC, Hawai'i Pidgin] 30, 31, 35, 210–233, 292, 299–301, 514–545, 583, 592–593, 597–598
Hawai'i English 33
Hindi 33, 234–235, 236, 249–253, 258–259, 264, 555, 564, 583

I

Indian English [AngloIndian, IndE] 346–347
Indian South African English [InSAfE] 264, 566
Irish [Irish Galeic] 64–66, 284, 310, 389, 401, 404, 408, 410
Irish English [IrE] 284, 404, 408, 410
Island Creole(s) [IslC] 274
Italian 25, 119, 368

J

Jamaican Creole [JamC] (see also *Patwa*) 431
Japanese 30, 211–213, 215–216, 219–221, 226, 229, 514, 520, 556

K

Kamtok (see *Cameroon Pidgin*)
Kriol 30–31, 33–34, 124, 126–131, 135–139, 292, 299–301, 415–426, 429, 431–432, 439, 441, 583, 592, 598–599

L

L1 variety (see *First Language variety*)
L2 variety (see *Second Language variety*)
Latin 533–534

M

Malay (see also *Bahasa Malaysia, Bazaar Malay*) 28, 125, 146
Malayalam 234
Maori 26, 29, 31–32, 39–40, 54, 57–59, 61, 64, 72, 77–87, 292–294, 296–298, 302, 310, 330, 332, 334, 584
Maori English [MaoE] 26, 31–32, 61, 77–86, 292–294, 296–298, 302
Maori Vernacular English [MVE] 78
Melanesian Pidgin 30, 32, 35, 143, 161, 188, 193–194, 211, 237–238, 271, 299–300, 421, 454–455, 460, 472, 488, 490–491, 499, 501, 574, 583, 592–593, 596–598
Middle English [ME] 280
Miskito Coast Creole (see also *Belizean Creole, Central American Creoles, Limónese Creole*) 420

N

Neo-Melanesian (see *Tok Pisin*)
New Guinea Pidgin (see *Tok Pisin*)
New South Wales Pidgin 415
New Zealand English [NZE] 8, 24, 26–27, 31–32, 34, 39–62, 64–76, 77–88, 108–109, 112, 117, 121–122, 274, 277–278, 292–298, 302, 305–342, 346–349, 351, 357–358, 583–585, 587–590, 592, 599
Norfolk English [Norfuk] 34–35, 267–292, 568–582, 583, 594, 597–598
Norman 343, 400
Northern English dialect (see *English English*)
Nova Scotian (see *African Nova Scotian English*)

O

Oceanic 160, 184, 445–447, 455, 457, 460, 471, 473, 478, 488, 549, 596
Old English [OE] 589

P

Pacific Pidgin (English) 30, 126, 189, 211
Pidgin (see also *Pidgin and Creole*) 28–30, 125–127, 129–130, 164–165, 188, 192, 194, 210–213, 215, 217, 236, 274, 419, 421–422, 454, 514, 516, 555, 578, 580
Pitcairn English [Pitkern] 267, 269, 271–274, 568, 572, 579, 592
Portuguese 125, 146, 184, 188, 211–216, 220, 225, 231, 499, 527, 535
Pure Fiji English 33, 237–242, 244–250, 252, 254–257, 259, 264, 546, 549, 550–551, 557, 559–560, 562–563, 565–566

R

Received Pronunciation [RP] (see *Index of subjects*)

S

Scots 24, 283
Scottish English [ScE, Scots] 24, 53, 61, 283, 316–317, 573, 591–592
Sea Island Creole (see *Gullah*)
Second Language [L2] variety 347
Solomon Islands Pidgin [SolP, Solomon Islands Pijin, Pijin] 30–34, 143–144, 161, 164–188, 292, 299, 301, 445, 451, 460, 462, 467–487, 583, 592, 594–595

South African English [SAfE] 261
South Seas Jargon 29–30, 142, 146, 211
Southeastern English dialect (see *English English*)
Southern English dialect (see *English English*)
Southwestern English dialect (see *English English*)
Spanish 125
St. Kitts Creole 574, 579
Standard Australian Colloquial English [StAusCE] 365
Standard Australian Formal English [StAusFE] 365
Standard English [StE] 2, 30, 128–133, 135–139, 199, 214, 216–218, 240–242, 245–246, 248, 253–254, 256, 258–259, 272, 285, 305, 368, 388, 416, 418–421, 423, 427–431, 434–435, 437–439, 446, 514, 546, 548, 551, 553–556, 559, 561, 563, 592, 594, 596–597, 599
non-standard English 387, 600

T

Tahitian 30, 146, 267, 269, 270–273, 572, 574, 579, 580
Tamil 234
Telugu 234
Tok Pisin [TP, Neomelanesian, New Guinea Pidgin] 30–33, 35, 143, 161, 164–165, 167, 188–206, 292, 299, 301, 445, 451, 453, 460, 467, 480, 484, 488–513, 569, 583, 592, 594–597
Torres Strait Creole 31, 34, 127–131, 139, 415–427, 583, 592, 595, 597–598